ISBN 978-0-265-33968-8
PIBN 10425784

THE LIFE AND TIMES

OF

THOMAS WAKLEY

FOUNDER AND FIRST EDITOR OF THE "LANCET,"
MEMBER OF PARLIAMENT FOR FINSBURY,
AND CORONER FOR WEST MIDDLESEX.

BY

S. SQUIRE SPRIGGE,

M.B. CANTAB., ETC.

"But Wakley is right sometimes," the doctor added,
judicially; "I could mention one or two points in
which Wakley is right."—*Middlemarch*, Book ii., c. 16.

WITH TWO PORTRAITS

LONGMANS, GREEN AND CO.
39 PATERNOSTER ROW, LONDON
NEW YORK AND BOMBAY
1897

Printed by BALLANTYNE, HANSON & Co.
At the Ballantyne Press

PREFATORY NOTE BY THE EDITORS
OF THE "LANCET"

THE occurrence in 1895 of the centenary of the birth of the founder of the "Lancet" seemed to us to afford a suitable opportunity of giving in the columns of the journal which he originated an extended record of his life and work. We placed the materials, some of which were easily accessible, whilst some were obtainable only from senior members of our profession and others (to all of whom we wish to tender our sincere thanks), in the hands of our friend and colleague, Dr. S. Squire Sprigge, who is responsible for the biography, both in its serial and in its present form. For the great interest and pains which he has taken in the work we may express our gratitude to him. To venture any opinion on the quality of that work is not, we think, under the circumstances, within our province—the unprejudiced reader can judge for himself. We, the eldest son and grandson respectively of Thomas Wakley, cannot, in the ordinary course of human nature, be looked upon as free from bias. Indeed such a thing would be impossible, for the senior of us was his constant companion until his death, and was associated with him in his struggles and his work during the greater part of his public career. We have been anxious in two respects—firstly, that the services rendered to the cause of medical reform (and may we say to humanity?) by the subject of this biography should not, owing to the lapse of years, be lost sight of ; and secondly, that the story of his life and work should be told by a biographer who would not view them through the imperfect lens of family affection.

One word more. This biography of a man, most of whose work was done more than fifty years ago, may be considered belated, but whoever had written the life of Thomas Wakley much sooner would have incurred the chance of causing pain to many people.

THOMAS H. WAKLEY,
THOMAS WAKLEY, Jun.,
Joint Editors of the " Lancet."

THE " LANCET " OFFICES,
April, 1897.

AUTHOR'S PREFACE

THE plan of this book has been adopted with the object of preserving continuity in the narrative. There was a period in Wakley's life when he was at the same time journalist, politician, and coroner ; but to have described these three phases of his career concurrently would have entailed constant and confusing changes of scene. Each phase is therefore told separately, while the dates indicate where the events overlap. No dates are affixed to the heads of the last eight chapters, which consist chiefly of descriptions of Wakley's general attitude towards such questions as quackery, Poor-law administration, and the adulteration of food. Instead, the dates are given of any examples chosen to illustrate this attitude.

S. SQUIRE SPRIGGE.

UNITED UNIVERSITY CLUB,
April, 1897.

CONTENTS

CHAPTER XV

[1823–1834]

CHAPTER XVI

[1823–1834]

CHAPTER XVII

[1823–1834]

CHAPTER XVIII

[1823–1834]

CHAPTER XIX

[1823–1834]

CHAPTER XX

[1823–1834]

CHAPTER XXI

[1823–1834]

CHAPTER XXII

[1823–1834]

CHAPTER XXIII

[1823–1834]

CHAPTER XXIV

[1823–1834]

CHAPTER XXX

[1835]

CHAPTER XXXI

[1836]

CHAPTER XXXII

[1836]

CHAPTER XXXIII

[1836–1837]

CHAPTER XXXIV

[1837–1841]

CHAPTER XXXV

[1841–1845]

CHAPTER XXXVI

[1846–1852]

CHAPTER XXXVII

[1827–1831]

CHAPTER XXXVIII

[1831–1839]

CHAPTER XXXIX

[1839]

CHAPTER XL

[1840-1846]

CHAPTER XLI

[1846]

CHAPTER XLII

[1846-1861]

CHAPTER XLIX

CHAPTER L

THE LIFE AND TIMES

OF

THOMAS ·WAKLEY

CHAPTER I

[1795–1815]

*The Wakleys of Membury—The Birthday of Thomas Wakley—
The Farmer's Son of the Period—Middle-class Education at the
Beginning of the Century—A Taste for the Sea—The Entry to a
Medical Career—The Influence of the Family Circle.*

THOMAS WAKLEY, the founder of the "Lancet," and the successful originator of reforms in medical politics to which are largely due the present high standard of medical education in Great Britain and the general stability of medicine as a career, had no hereditary connexion whatever with the pursuits of his lifetime. He was the descendant of a long line of landowners, who gave their Saxon name to more than one north-country village, or adopted for distinctive purposes the appellation of their dwelling-place as a name—for both proceedings were common in primitive times.

Henry Wakley, the father of the subject of this biography, was born in 1750, and acquired by will a family property in the parish of Membury, on the Devonshire side of the border between that county and Dorsetshire, and a little south of the Somersetshire dividing line. He belonged to a class now largely extinct, but one which a hundred and fifty or even fifty years ago was still very powerful in the

A

land. He was a large farmer, farming personally a holding which belonged to himself and hiring surrounding land generally on long leases, and treating it exactly as if it were his own property, subject only to an annual charge. The position of farming in England during the late Georgian and early Victorian ages made of such men a highly important class. Their private property, sometimes large, but more generally constituting but a small part of their holding, gave them an impregnable and dignified position. Their calling was a substantial and lucrative one. Many of them belonged to the oldest families in the neighbourhood, the homestead having been the headquarters of the family for generations—and this was the case with the Wakleys—while their pedigrees showed intermarriages with their greater neighbours whose rise in the social scale from yeomanry, through squirearchy, into the peerage was a theme of humorous respect among them. For the gulf between yeomanry and squirearchy was not a broad one, and was frequently bridged by a lucky marriage, a little commercial success, or some extra keen attention to agriculture on the part of a shrewd occupier. It was in this class that Mr. Henry Wakley was born, and in it he died at the great age of ninety-two, having established for himself a more than local reputation for his knowledge of agricultural affairs. He was one of the most respected authorities on things agricultural in his county and the two adjoining counties of Dorsetshire and Somersetshire, a very frequent arbitrator in disputes, and a universally trusted counsellor in times of need. He was a Government Commissioner on more than one occasion for the Enclosure of Waste Lands, and at one time was among the most extensive occupiers of land in Devonshire.

Mr. Henry Wakley had eleven children, eight sons and three daughters, and of the sons Thomas Wakley was the youngest. The exact date of his birth can only be arrived at by means of a little calculation, for his baptismal certificate, which is dated january 27th, 1802, has a footnote upon it stating that at the time of the performance of the rite the child was six years, twenty-eight weeks, and two days old. The date of his birth would therefore be july 13th, 1795, supposing that the clergyman who issued the certificate had made an accurate calculation. On the other hand, the register at Membury has a note of the birth upon July 11th, and the inference is that the clergyman who issued the certificate was wrong in his figures, and meant by a year 365 days, while he calculated the year 1800 as a leap-year, a mistake often made. If both these errors have crept into the baptismal certificate, the discrepancy is explained and the correct date is july 11th.

Mr. Henry Wakley was a just but severe parent, the very type of man to rule a large family. He gave his orders and exacted obedience of them from all ; and as his position of master was unquestioned his family had no feelings towards him that were other than respectfully affectionate. In those days the sons of the practical farmer were employed on the farm. They oversaw the hands, and if necessary did an ordinary day's labour on the farm exactly as one of those hands. In time they went about their business or professions, but while they were at home they made themselves useful. It was in this old-fashioned patriarchal mode of life that Thomas Wakley spent his boyhood, and to the frugality, self-denial, and open-air exercise that it enjoined upon him he owed, no doubt, his great bodily strength, as he certainly owed the taste for country sports that he manifested later in his life. For they were a great sporting family, renowned through the country side for their skill with the gun and their judgment of horseflesh. The three elder brothers were remarkably good shots, and the eldest of all carried on a successful business in horse-breeding on the farm. Mr. Henry Wakley, the father, was an ardent hunter. He rode regularly to hounds and with a pack of harriers, and not long before his death issued a challenge to all comers of his own age to ride a steeplechase over a fair hunting country, mounted on a horse as old as his own. At that time he was over ninety years of age and his favourite horse was thirty-three, so that it is not surprising that the gauntlet was never taken up, but the publication of the challenge shows him to have been an old man of extraordinary physique.

In such a household it is not surprising that young Wakley grew up an active boy. He would be abroad at sunrise, and, if necessary, ride the horses to the plough. And though, doubtless, the task was not one of direct compulsion, yet if he had done this under his father's orders because no other plough-boy was employed, he would have been doing what the sons of scores of other landowners were doing daily in Devonshire, and also in more advanced parts of England, more directly under the scope of urban influence and more aware that the school-master was abroad.

Although brought up in this simple and hardy manner Thomas Wakley's education was not neglected. He was sent to the best grammar schools in the neighbourhood— namely, that of Chard in Somersetshire, an endowed and ancient school, and that of Honiton in Devonshire. Chard lies about six miles north-east of Membury, and Honiton about ten miles west. To go to a boarding-school was, at the end of the last century or the beginning of this century, almost a thing unknown to the middle classes. The Royal Colleges of Eton and Winchester and six or seven other of the great public schools had reputations other than local, and so had become the great boarding institutions that they are now ; but the usual middle-class lad was educated at the nearest grammar school. As a consequence his education was prone to suffer much from the weather. A valley blocked with snow or a swollen stream would cut the young scholar off from his school for a week. Now the neigh-bourhood of Membury abounds in rich valleys, and these, with their fertile loam soil and its subsoil of gravel, while forming an ideal foundation for pasture, easily became difficult of transit for a boy on foot or on a pony. So that whether young Wakley sought instruction from the north-east at Chard, or the west at Honiton, he was always liable to be compelled to play truant by the inclement condition of the country over which he had to travel. Lighting also was expensive ninety years ago, and midnight study was not encouraged; nor would a lad, the youngest in a household devoted to country pursuits, and rising in the early grey of the morning, feel very disposed to prolong his studies far into the night. And, to add to these hindrances to study, there was nothing of the bookworm about the boy. That he made good use of his opportunities is undoubted, because no mind could have been so receptive, no wit so adaptable as his proved to be in later years, if their owner had not been trained to learn and taught to listen. But in mere book-learning Thomas Wakley did not excel. His education was sound in that it fitted him to go on learning when he found himself face to face with the problems of life. As a boy he laid a solid foundation upon which to build a more elaborate education. His writing and public speaking alike bear testimony in this direction.

When quite young he more than once expressed a desire to go to sea. He knew nothing of seafaring life. It is true that Membury is but eight miles from the channel coast, and that from the castle heights the bay of Lyme Regis can be seen spread out before the eye. But Membury is a purely agricultural place, with a purely agricultural population, and young Wakley's desire, which was real and not a mere idle expression of a passing fancy, must have been spontaneous in origin, and not inspired by any of his immediate surroundings or companions. It was an early example of his independence of thought. He obtained his desire, for when still quite young he took a voyage to Calcutta in an East Indiaman with his father's reluctant permission. It was not intended that this should be his entry into the career of a sailor, for he travelled under the care of the captain, who was a personal friend of his father. Whether, his curiosity assuaged, he would have abandoned the sea as a profession is only a subject of speculation, but it is difficult to conceive a boy with his restless, arguing, inquisitive temperament settling down to life in the merchant service, with its great demands upon patience, and its necessarily unquestioning obedience and resignation. Anyhow, circumstances worked against this voyage being a prelude to a sailor's life, for on the journey back his friend the captain died, and there was no longer any inducement to the boy to remain with the ship. He came home and returned to school, and no one heard anything from that time of his experiences on the voyage. In answer to an inquiry why he had not brought his chest back, he said that he had had quite enough to do to take care of himself, and nothing more was ever got out of him. Life in those days was rough on board a merchant ship, as rough as, or rougher than, it was on board a man-of-war, and what that means is more than hinted at in several passages of Marryat's novels, and is recorded in the biographies of our naval heroes.

His new school was at Wiveliscombe in Somersetshire, and there he remained until his choice of a future was made. It fell upon medicine. So at fifteen years of age he was duly apprenticed to a Mr. Incledon, an apothecary at Taunton, that being the very usual method in those days of commencing professional studies. For it must be remembered that before 1815, which was the date of the passing of the Apothecaries Act, the curriculum of the medical student was very vague. Previously to the passing of the Act it was not illegal for any unqualified person to practise medicine, and as a consequence there were very many people working in the medical profession who were believed by their patients to be duly qualified medical men, but who had undergone no training and been subjected to no tests. Their education had consisted either of apprenticeship to a licensed apothecary, or of a few months' discharge of the duties of dispenser to an unqualified practitioner. As it was not always possible to forecast the future of a lad, it was usual to send him to an apothecary first as an apprentice. If he did not show any remarkable aptitude or desire for any further education, that might suffice, and he could continue on the lines of his master. If, however, he desired to fly at higher game, or his parents desired it for him, he could afterwards be sent to London, Edinburgh, Glasgow, or Dublin, to walk the hospitals for a diploma. Both Thomas

Wakley and his parents wished that he should become a regularly qualified practitioner, so he was not allowed to complete his time with the Taunton apothecary, but was transferred to his brother-in-law, Mr. Phelps, a surgeon of Beaminster, as a pupil. From Mr. Phelps he went to Mr. Coulson, a member of a well-known medical family at Henley-on-Thames, as assistant, and eventually, in 1815, went to London as a student of the United Schools of St. Thomas's and Guy's, known as the Borough Hospitals.

With his start in London as a medical student his real life-work began. Hitherto he had been under the supervision of parents, elder brothers and sisters, schoolmasters and other masters, and what he did, and the way in which he did it, were not left to his choice. But in London he was alone, free to work or play, free to behave or misbehave, free to rise if he would, and equally free to fall. The real life of Thomas Wakley dates from the moment when his individuality for the first time received play, but the circumstances of his younger days exercised an influence upon his future which was often, as will be seen, easily traceable. To his country bringing-up, he owed the simplicity and bluff directness that stood him in such good stead in controversy, and to it must be attributed the wonderful physical strength and keen vitality that enabled him to work at enormous pressure for hours together with no diminution of zeal or interest. To it also he owed his hatred of all shams. His youth had been spent among a simple folk, to whom truth was everything, and in whose eyes the pretender was a particularly obnoxious person. His position in his family must also be remembered. They were a fine and jovial set of sporting men and handsome women—his brothers and sisters—and his life in contact with a large and unprejudiced group of his seniors gave him from the first a certain assurance ; but he was junior among them, and the fact would temper the assurance, for there are no keener critics of manners, and no stricter disciplinarians than the elder sister and the big brother. The boy was especially under the influence of his second sister, the wife of the rector of the parish, Mrs. Newbury by name, to whom he was devoted. In the controversial circumstances of his later life—and these were controversial, indeed—whatever his pen might have written his personal manner towards his opponents was blameless. This combination of firmness and simplicity with good-tempered courtesy he had learned in his country home ; his environment there had taught him that it was good policy, and his sister had taught him that it was the right way to behave.

So that when Thomas Wakley came to London he was well equipped for success. His physical condition was admirable—it was that of an athletic country lad, of book-learning he had a sufficiency, while his moral character had received the very training best calculated to enable him to deserve and attain a prominent position among his fellows.

CHAPTER II

[1815–1817]

The Profession at the Beginning of the Century—The Privileged Classes and the Rank and File—The Royal College of Physicians of London, the Royal College of Surgeons of England, and the Society of Apothecaries of London—The Staff of the United Hospitals—The Brothers Grainger—The Private Medical Schools —The Medical Student of the Period.

THE profession at the time that Thomas Wakley joined it, namely 1815, was divided sharply into two classes : those who were going to be leaders, and those who were going to remain in the rank and file. Now and again a man whose original conditions ought to have limited his aspirations would break through his trammels and become a leader, when in the ordinary course of events he should have remained a private ; but this occurred infrequently. The almost invariable rule was that those who were specially picked out by circumstances quite independent of merit for promotion, received that promotion, less fortunate individuals remaining in the shadow of obscurity, whatever their claims to success.

Of the men who were predestined to become leaders there were two divisions in London, corresponding to the two great divisions in the profession of healing—the physicians and the surgeons. The predestined rulers in pure medicine were the men who had acquired a recognised university degree and subsequently to graduating had been elected to the Fellowship of the Royal College of Physicians of London. The Charter of this body was granted by Henry VIII. for the advancement of medical science and for the protection of the public "against the temerity of wicked men and the practice of the ignorant"; but time had embellished its simplicity by importing into it restrictions and disabilities never dreamt of by the Royal grantor. The College had now two divisions : a smaller, the Fellows, and a larger, the Licentiates. The Licentiates paid fees, but obtained nothing in return, not even protection; for although the chief reason for paying fees was to obtain a licence to practise within seven miles of the metropolis, the College had no power to maintain for its Licentiates the monopoly thus sold to them. The Fellows, chosen from among the Licentiates under a system of favouritism, filled all the offices, and passed regulations for keeping their body select which were stupid and unjust. For example, no physician could claim admission as a Fellow unless he had graduated at Oxford or Cambridge, or had been admitted to a degree *ad eundem* at one or other of the ancient universities. This restriction carried another with it, for the graduates of Oxford and Cambridge were obliged at that time to be members of the Established Church of England, whence it followed that no Dissenter could be a Fellow of the College of Physicians. The leaders in pure surgery started in a less dignified, if more facile, manner on the saunter to a successful future. They became apprenticed, after payment of large fees, to the eminent surgeons holding posts at the different hospitals, hoping to succeed, and very generally succeeding, to the appointments of their masters. This is a somewhat crude way of stating the methods of procedure, but in the main it is true. The fees might be waived because the young man was a relative or the son of a friend of the great surgeon, but from a stranger they were exacted, and the consideration received in return was not only the ordinary instruction due from master to pupil, but a very definite promise of the reversion of some of the senior's emoluments. The understanding that the pupil should succeed his master in any hospital appoint-ments the latter might hold was generally a tacit one, though occasionally some sort of documentary evidence of the contract, something in the nature of a bond, is known to have been in existence. The eminent surgeons could not absolutely give away the hospital appointments, which were then, as they are now, in the gift of the lay governors of the hospital, but they could, and did, bring influence to bear upon the governors, and with wrong motives, or under circumstances that had the colour of wrong motives. Each man would naturally desire the election of the candidate from whom he had received an actual pecuniary consideration, for the sums thus paid were large, not infrequently amounting to £500; and the claims of merit would give way to those of expediency. The lay governors were canvassed, and it was not the best man who won, but the man whose backer most clearly acknowledged the claim upon him, and so most urgently advocated his junior's candidature among the persons possessing votes.

Hospital appointments, with all their advantages, direct and indirect, honourable and pecuniary, were given to certain Fellows of the Royal College of Physicians of London, personal influence counting for much in the matter; examinerships and lectureships at the Royal College of Surgeons of England were given to certain hospital surgeons who were elected to the desirable appointments which qualified them for their professorial duties largely in consequence of their ability to pay big fees for their introductions to big men. The man who could not pay these fees or afford a university education was fated to remain in the rank and file of his profession. There were of course exceptions, and the names of one or two will readily occur to all, but the medical corporations were slow to discover merit unless it was brought to their notice by approaching them along the usual avenues. Now and then the public would force upon their attention one who otherwise had no claim upon it, but these cases were rare, though not so very rare as they are now; and it was just as well then that they were rare as it is well now that they are nigh impossible of occurrence, for great fame won first from the laity is but seldom the proportionate reward of merit, and the knowledge that it can be readily obtained must ever seduce many from the highest aims. It is undoubted that at the beginning of the century members of the profession appealed more directly to the public for an appreciation of their scientific talents than would be deemed seemly in these days, and that, to the shame of the medical world, it was occasionally left to the public to point out to the profession who were their greatest men.

The rank and file of the profession consisted either of the general body of the two Royal corporations—*i.e.*, of those Members of the College of Surgeons and of those Licentiates of the College of Physicians who for this reason or that were debarred from rising to posts of office and responsibility—or of the Licentiates of the Society of the Apothecaries of London. The Society of Apothecaries had secured considerable power by the recent Act of 1815. This piece of legislation had for its laudable object the stopping of prescribing and dispensing by unqualified persons. It really set up an inferior order of general practitioners. For who was to limit the scope of the apothecary? Who was to say to the man who dispensed that he must not also diagnose and recommend treatment, when he had undergone examinations in chemistry, anatomy, and medicine and served an apprenticeship with a medical man? Clearly such boundaries to his duties could not be defined, and the apothecaries were recognised everywhere save in London and a few provincial centres as the family practitioners.* And as the fees of the Society of Apothecaries were low, while

---

* " Early in the Regency of George the Magnificent there lived in a small town in the West of England, called Clavering, a gentleman whose name was Pendennis. There were those alive who remembered having seen his name painted on a board which was surmounted by a gilt pestle and mortar over the door of a very humble little shop in the city of Bath, where Mr. Pendennis exercised the profession of Apothecary and Surgeon, and where he not only attended gentlemen in their sick-rooms, and ladies at the most interesting periods of their lives, but would condescend to sell a brown paper plaster to a farmer's wife across the counter, or to vend tooth-brushes, hair powder, and London perfumery."—" Pendennis," chap. ii., opening words.

those of the corporations were high ; and as the apothe-caries claimed a monopoly in dispensing and protected their Licentiates in this matter, while the corporations totally neglected the interests of their commonalties, it is not to be wondered at that large numbers of the profession made no attempt to gain any other diploma than that of L.S.A.

Thomas Wakley did not belong to the privileged classes, but yet had no idea of becoming an apothecary simply. He came to London to make his own way for himself, with no university course behind him and no friends within the ring-fence of hospital administration. A brother of his brother-in-law, Mr. Phelps, to whom he had been apprenticed, consented to look after him and to be the channel through which his modest allowance could be supplied to him, but Mr. Phelps could not assist him in the prosecution of his studies, and was possessed of no influence in the medical circles of London. That Wakley was greatly trusted by his family—trusted to an extent that no boy of his age save one who had shown himself capable of meeting considerable responsibilities would have been—is proved by the fact that he was left virtually to himself from the beginning of his London life, as far as his professional career was concerned. The United Hospitals of Guy's and St. Thomas's were recommended to him as the best institutions to "walk," as the phrase then went, by the gentlemen to whom he had been apprenticed, but nothing was definitely settled for him, and that he had a power of veto is proved by the fact that before entering any school he went round to listen to the various lecturers that he might have some personal experience to guide him in his choice. At that time it was usual for the medical student to take out a course of lectures here with one man and there with another. The United Hospitals, St. Bartholomew's, and London were the only institutions at the time that had a medical school attached to them, though certain lectures were delivered by the staff at Middlesex Hospital to their pupils. At the other hospitals students received the privilege of walking the wards and attending the practice of the charity, but their scientific education had to be obtained elsewhere. And what good they reaped from belonging to their hospitals was rendered nugatory by vexatious restrictions. At Westminster Hospital for instance, the students were only allowed in the wards from ten to twelve in the morning; at St. George's the hours were from ten till two, but no one could enter the wards without the member of the staff whose day of attendance it might be, and the staff were terribly unpunctual; at Middlesex Hospital the students were only allowed admission three times a week, and as all the surgeons made their rounds on the same day at the same time no student could see the practice of more than one of his so-called teachers. Young Wakley abided by the selection of his advisers to this extent, that he joined the school of the United Hospitals, one of the three places where he could have obtained a complete curriculum under one jurisdiction, but he decided to supplement his hospital course by attending the private school of the Graingers. He chose the hospitals because of his admiration of Sir Astley Cooper as a teacher, while the choice of a private school was one of convenience, the famous anatomical academy of the Graingers being in Webb Street, Borough, hard by.

The United Hospitals were at that time at their zenith. The story of their union is simple. The students of Guy's Hospital had by courtesy been allowed to attend the operations at St. Thomas's Hospital, and St. Thomas's had made a similar concession to Guy's. But in 1768 it was formally resolved that the pupils of each hospital should have the liberty of attending not only the operations but the surgical practice of both institutions, and the money received in fees was to be divided in certain proportions between the six surgeons of the hospitals and the two apothecaries who did their behests. From which it will be seen that the amalgamation of the two schools did not extend beyond their surgical practice. The staff of the Hospitals at the time when Thomas Wakley entered as a student was a decidedly good one, though on the surgical side it formed a remarkable example of the part that nepotism and purchased favour played in the securing of appointments. Sir Astley Cooper, or Mr. Astley Cooper, to be accurate, for he did not receive his baronetcy until six years later, ruled supreme in 1815. He had been the apprentice of the elder Henry Cline, a surgeon of almost equal celebrity in his day, and lecturer on anatomy and surgery to St. Thomas's Hospital. In 1800 Cooper became his master's colleague as lecturer, and was appointed surgeon to Guy's Hospital. In 1812 the elder Cline resigned, and his son, Henry Cline, junior, became surgeon to St. Thomas's Hospital and followed his father as joint lecturer with Sir Astley Cooper. Sharply on this came the election of three of Sir Astley Cooper's nephews—C. Aston Key, Bransby Cooper, and Frederick Tyrrell—to different posts, while the next surgical vacancies were filled by his apprentice, Benjamin Travers, and J. H. Green, Henry Cline's cousin, respectively. The aggregate ability of this group of surgeons is certain, and their individual skill was only once called into serious doubt ; but they owed their elections to other claims than their merits.

Thomas Wakley attended the joint anatomy classes of Henry Cline, senior, and Sir Astley Cooper during the autumn session of 1815 and the spring and autumn courses of 1816. These were delivered at St. Thomas's Hospital, and his signature in witness of his attendance at them is in the books of the hospital, and is a flowing and very exact facsimile of the signature of his maturer years. At Guy's Hospital he attended Sir Astley Cooper's lectures on the Practice of Surgery, where he also did his surgical dressing and ward work. In those days students dissected and acted as dressers at the same time, an arrangement that might be calculated to impress the knowledge of pathological anatomy upon them, but could not fail to have been attended with some risk to the patients. His dissecting was chiefly done at the school of the brothers Edward and Richard Grainger, which was situated in Webb Street, Borough, under the very walls of St. Thomas's Hospital. Edward Grainger was a thoroughly good anatomist, so good that he was feared by all the recognised lecturers at the metropolitan hospitals, who did everything in their power to detach his pupils from him. His laborious life and early death precluded him from literary achievement, but his memory was green in the profession for a generation after his death, and, in medicine at any rate, that comes very close to fame. He was essentially a teacher on broad lines, recognising what so many teachers fail to recognise, that it is badly spent time to instruct a student how to keep in the middle of the road or where to avoid a pitfall unless the road itself has been previously pointed out.

Richard Grainger was younger than Edward, and started in life as a Woolwich cadet, but relinquished the idea of a military career to join his brother at the Webb Street School. The sad death of Edward Grainger, when only twenty-six years of age, left Richard at the head of the school when little more than a lad, but he proved himself equal to the situation, and became, like his brother, a very efficient rival to the regular lecturers at Guy's and St. Thomas's, being popular with the students, an untiring worker and moderate in his fees. Twenty-five years after the date at which we have now arrived—i.e., in 1842—the Webb Street School was formally taken over by St. Thomas's Hospital, and Richard Grainger was appointed lecturer in anatomy and physiology in the medical school. His attainments at once became widely recognised, and the Royal Society, as an acknowledgment of the value of his researches into the anatomy of the spinal cord, made him a Fellow of their body. His ancient enemy, the College of Surgeons, appointed him Hunterian Lecturer, and he was employed by Government as an expert on several occasions where the work was of a sanitary or humanitarian nature. He died in 1861.

These private schools played a regular part in the medical education of the London student of the day and for some time to come, and, although coincident with the institution and development of schools in direct connection with all the great general hospitals of the metropolis, they became

superfluous and disappeared, they were at the time responsible for a condition of manners among the students, of
morals, of ill, and of good, that lingered for a quarter of a
century after their dissolution. The history of these schools
—Carpue's School in Dean Street, Soho ; the Gerard Street
or Dermott's School, with which was associated the Windmill Street School in Tottenham Court Road ; the Great
Windmill Street School not to be confounded with the
institution just mentioned, where the pupils were chiefly
drawn from St. George's Hospital, while the lecturers were
Sir Charles Bell, Sir Everard Home, and Mr., afterwards Sir
Benjamin Brodie ; Lane's School in Pimlico ; the Webb
Street or Graingers' School ; the Aldersgate School of Tyrrell
and Lawrence ; Brookes's School in Blenheim Street, Great
Marlborough Street, where Joshua Brookes, F.R.S., proved
himself the best practical anatomist in England ; and others
—will now never be written, for no succinct record of them
has been handed down by any one with personal knowledge
of them. Yet such a history, if the proper person were
alive to write it, would form a most interesting chapter in a
study of the rise of medical education in England ; in fact,
it would form the first chapter in such a study.

Each of these schools was conducted generally in connexion with a hospital, although they were strictly private
enterprises. The Royal College of Surgeons and the Society
of Apothecaries accepted work done at them and attendances registered at them as evidence of medical study to a
certain extent, during Wakley's career as a student ; but the
former institution never approved of the private enterprises,
and a few years later attempted to break them up altogether.
There were in these days no formal signatures required to
testify that a man had duly heard a certain number of
lectures or had been in the wards a certain length of time.
There were no precautions taken against personation at the
examinations, a thing which occurred frequently, and little
attempt was made to gauge a candidate's knowledge before
turning him loose upon the public with a licence. Testimony
to certain apprenticeship and to payment of fees for certain

B

lectures and for the privilege of attending the practice of a
hospital had to be forthcoming, and the rest was plain sailing.
It was to meet the wants of a happy-go-lucky curriculum of
this sort that the private schools existed, and the looseness
of the requirements of the examiners reacted upon the
schools, so that they became hot-beds of a Bohemianism
that was as undoubted in cold fact as it is, and ever will be,
celebrated in comic fiction.   There was nothing comparable
to the life of the medical student in London, as fostered by
the conditions under which he lived and studied at the
beginning of the century save, perhaps, the life of the
Parisian art student at that time and later.   And what the
studio of the professor, as depicted by Thackeray, Stevenson,
and Du Maurier, was to the artist, the dissecting-room was
to the medical students—a centre where all met on common
ground, the ground of professional interest, and all vied
with each other in the narration of episodes illustrative of
their ingenuity under the stress of poverty, their coolness
under the threat of the law, their personal courage, and their
physical attractiveness.   And all this inter-communication
taking place in the dissecting-room bred a familiarity with
repulsive objects which effectually did away with a proper
regard for the decencies of life, and led to the interlarding of
conversation with similes drawn from the mortuary table or
suggested by the details of anatomical research.   The result
was the establishment among the mass of the London
students of a regular and accepted tone of low shiftlessness,
which tone it became almost necessary for each man to
assume if he had it not, and an act of *esprit de corps* to
transmit to his juniors.   Bob Sawyer and Joe Muff were not
gross caricatures ; they moved in the dissecting-rooms of
the private schools, lived in the bars of Fleet Street, and had
their being in the supper-rooms of Covent Garden—not,
perhaps, as individuals, but most certainly as well-pronounced
types.   Their creators did not evolve them wholly from
inner consciousness ; they but dotted the i's and crossed the
t's of a human document not over-hard to read before such
artistic amendment.   When the medical students of much

popular fiction are accepted at the present day, as they are occasionally by a public slow to mark the signs of the times, as a fair presentment of the modern aspirant to a medical career, all who know feel bound to rise up and protest angrily; but Bob Sawyer, Joe Muff, and the egregious Tom Delorme and their friends were drawn in a spirit of caricature and exaggeration, yet with no wild disregard of facts. The London medical students of 1815, when Thomas Wakley threw in his lot with them, were very much as Dickens drew them in Mr. Pickwick's time, and the conditions under which student life was passed were responsible for much of the wildness and irregularity. The uselessness, in most cases, of aspiring to any great position in their profession, and the low standard of proficiency required of them by the examiners, were not calculated either to urge them to consistent work or to inspire them with much professional ardour. The herding together of great numbers of students at the private schools—sometimes a popular school would have as many as three hundred nominal pupils in a session —did away with any attempts to provide individual attention, while the lecturers at these institutions were not, as a rule, in a position to insist upon the presence of their pupils, to enforce order when they were present, or to check insubordination. Those who cared to work might work, and those who did not want to work need not. All medical students were not dissipated rowdies—it is not desired to convey that impression—but a large proportion led lives that might well have ended in their becoming such.

CHAPTER III

[1815-1817]

Life as a Medical Student—An Innate Puritan—The Curriculum of the Royal College of Surgeons of England in 1817—Enthusiasm for Anatomical Study—Great Dearth of Subjects for Dissection—Body-snatching and the Medical Profession.

THOMAS WAKLEY was placed by Mr. Phelps in lodgings in a small street running off Tooley Street in the Borough. In this district it was the almost invariable custom for the students of the United Hospitals to lodge, because in those days there were not the facilities that now exist of getting from one metropolitan area to another, so that it was necessary for a man to live near his work. The exact street is not known by name to his surviving relatives, and is not traceable in any documents; but this much is certain, that it is pulled down, and that, like the ancient buildings of St. Thomas's Hospital, it stood upon ground now covered by the London Bridge Railway Station. There were some twelve small streets demolished in 1862 to make way for the necessary buildings of the railway company, and among them the street in which Thomas Wakley and a friend lodged. His fellow-lodger's name was Wiltshire, and at that time there was no relationship between the two lads, but Wiltshire (who subsequently discontinued the pursuit of medicine and became an architect) afterwards married the sister of Wakley's wife.

The young student worked hard. He had sufficient self-restraint to live a laborious life at a time when it was not only unusual for a "medico," as the comic press delighted to term him, to work very hard, but unnecessary, having regard to the perfunctory nature of the tests by examination. It is easy to understand that for the country-bred lad, with home influence strong upon him, the grave licentiousness rife among the medical students of the metropolis would have no attraction. To him the coarse riots of the dissecting-room were only revolting; the orgy of porter, the Fleet Street amour, and the cutty of black tobacco, which played so large a part in the lighter side of student life, were not able to seduce him from his studies, for he cordially disliked each form of indulgence. He was abstemious by nature and cleanly by temperament, and to the end of his days cherished an unaffected and hearty dislike for the habit of smoking. His descriptions of his student days, as well as the testimony of one or two of his contemporaries, all go to show that he lived as a lad the life that he lived as a man—a life of self-respecting, sturdily independent labour. The affectionate husband of five years later was no transmuted rake; and the man who for thirty-five years of his life regularly worked fifteen hours a day did not learn the self-denial and strength under perpetual strain necessary for such a career in the vagaries of a mis-spent youth. It was his affectionate habit to attribute to the influence of his favourite sister, Mrs. Newbury, the fact that the gins into which so many of his fellow-students blundered had no teeth wherein to catch him; but, in truth, all his after-life showed such an unequivocal contempt for sensual allurements that it must be believed that he was something of the innate Puritan. It must not be supposed, however, that he was in any sort of way a milksop or a prig. He was, on the contrary, a very muscular, energetic, and hearty young man, popular with his fellow-students, and renowned among them for his physical strength and powers of endurance. He was a good and enthusiastic cricketer, a far better billiard-player than most lads of his age, and an adept at the old-fashioned game of quoits. Above all he was a brilliant boxer, and in those days the science of the gloves was more widely diffused than it is now, and it was possible for a man to get as much fighting as he desired—it was colloquially termed a ".bellyful of fighting"—without going to the expense of subscribing to an elaborate gymnasium or taking out a course of instruction with a courteous *maître d'armes*. Many a public-house had attached to it in a half-loafing, half-business capacity a pugilist who, when not occupied in keeping order for his employer, the landlord, would oblige that employer's customers by putting on the gloves with them. The Game Chicken, the public character who was "to be heerd on at the bar of the Little Helephant," was a very real person at the date of Thomas Wakley's student life—more so, in fact, than many years later, when Toots retained him—and it was with such men that the young countryman would measure his strength, and from the instructions of such men that he derived his exceptional skill. His devotion to athletic exercise sufficiently redeems him from any charge of priggishness. He had to go for his fun where his fellow-students went for theirs—to public-houses and similar resorts, for not only did boxing and billiards take him into these places, but cricket and quoits necessitated sojourns at the same social centres. But his ideas of amusement, wherever he might find himself and in whatever company, were always hardy and innocent. In particular he loved the fierce give-and-take of fighting, and rejoiced, as any natural young man will always rejoice, in his prowess ; and, if for no other reason than that he might always be in training for his chosen sport, he strictly abjured drink and tobacco.

In 1815 young Wakley was receiving an allowance of £80 a year from home, and the buying powers of £80 were considerably larger at that time than they are to-day. This was due to wants being fewer and simpler rather than to any item in the daily expenditure being cheaper. The cost of living—the bare cost of food—in London was not appreciably different then to what it is now, and the difference that existed compensated itself, one item being dearer while another was cheaper. Tea, sugar, and bread were, for instance, all considerably more costly, while beer, beef, and butter were proportionately moderate. It was in the simplicity of their wants that the poor men at the beginning of this century found salvation. The medical student did not expect to have more than rough, scanty fare. He moved in a stratum of society where to be exceedingly poor was to be like everybody else, and where to be eccentrically shabby and unconventional in dress was to emulate the manners of the choicer spirits. Consequently no money had to be spent on keeping up appearances. A roof was wanted to sleep under, but there existed no necessity for the student to have more than one room; and a public cult of the beautiful was then a thing so far unknown that people vastly more rich and fastidious than medical students were accustomed to look mainly for durability in their furniture. Also, it must be remembered that much of the student's work of those days was done in the hospitals and the lecture-rooms of the private medical schools, for the curriculum of the College of Surgeons and that of the Apothecaries' Hall were such that much evening study could not be necessary. To share one room with a friend at a weekly rental of 8s. was the usual proceeding with the student of the United Hospitals, and the domestic arrangements of Wakley and Wiltshire, who had a bedroom each and a sitting-room to boot, must have savoured of lavishness in the Borough. Their meals they obtained out of doors at ordinaries, taverns, and cook-shops, and in this respect there was not much difference between what they paid and what the clerk in London upon 30s. a week now pays. They would have found it difficult to spend less than 2s. a day; and, as a matter of fact, that sum exactly accounts for the expenditure of the whole of young Wakley's income, although we have it from himself that when he was a student he never knew what it was to want a sovereign. And he never once asked a penny from his father above his allowance, either to satisfy a creditor or gratify a taste, and if he had done so he would have taken nothing by the move, for Mr. Henry Wakley, being the arbitrary man that he was, in allowing his son

£80 a year expected him to live upon it, and said so.   Fees
would not have been less than £20 per annum ; his clothes
would have cost him £10, for he was never unconventional
in his attire, and even as a boy showed germs of the dandyism
that later distinguished him ; and the cost of his board and
lodging swallowed the rest.   Travelling was not a cause of
expenditure at the beginning of the century upon which
any watchful eye had to be kept, for the facilities for rapid
locomotion were so small that all temptation to run backwards and forwards from town to country and from work
to play was absent.   There was also but one holiday in
the medical year, and Thomas Wakley showed his sturdy
muscularity, and perhaps the fact that he found the quietest
living in the metropolis a strain on his exiguous resources,
by walking all the way from London to Membury on these
occasions.   He was once accompanied on his walk by an
elder brother, Michael, who was an accomplished pedestrian,
but on another occasion he covered the whole distance in
solitude.

The curriculum which was required of the student by the
Royal College of Surgeons of England at that day and previously to 1823 looked vastly well on paper.   The student
was required to do five years' medical study, a fact that may
come as a surprise to many who have been in the habit of
regarding the extension of the curriculum in 1892 as a
remarkably revolutionary and progressive step.   During
those five years the student was required to attend two
courses of lectures and demonstrations upon anatomy at
London, Dublin, Edinburgh, or Glasgow, and to take out
two courses of practical dissection at a recognised anatomical
school.   To this was added a year's practice to be seen in
the wards of a general hospital in one of the four cities.   The
candidate's lowest age was fixed at twenty-two.   Thomas
Wakley counted his five years dating from 1812, when he
went as apprentice to his brother-in-law.   He remained
there nearly two years, going thence to Mr. Coulson, whom
he assisted for more than one year.   He qualified in 1817.
From this distribution of his time will be seen the great

importance that was placed at that day upon apprenticeship to a general practitioner. Out of a compulsory curriculum of five years it was open to the student to spend as much time as he liked as an apprentice, working under a qualified master. True, he was compelled to see one year's practice at a hospital, to attend certain lectures, and do a certain amount of dissecting, but inasmuch as he could attend the lectures and the courses of human anatomy at the same time, while he was also seeing the practice of his hospital, his curriculum really meant one year's academic work to be added to four years' experience as assistant in a general practice. Thomas Wakley, coming to London in 1815, and attending at the United Hospitals and the Graingers' School until 1817, gave a year's more time to the scientific side of his profession than could have been exacted from him and than was usual among those students who, having no possible chance of hospital appointment, were looking to the public only for future advancement. But he spent over three years as an apprentice in the country. This is interesting to record, because it shows that the man, the key-note of whose medical policy was the maintenance of the rights of the general practitioner, had obtained a practical insight into their wrongs by considerable experience of their lives and work.

He was exceedingly fond of dissecting, and is reported to have been a sound anatomist. It is only possible to speak upon report, for his years in practice were few, and no actual cases have been handed down in the treatment or diagnosis of which he betrayed any very special knowledge of the science, while the fact that he belonged to the rank and file of the profession and was not a fee-in-hand apprentice of a hospital surgeon precluded him from all opportunity, either in ward or lecture-room, of proving that he possessed exceptional knowledge. That he considered an intimate acquaintance with the machinery of the human body an absolute essential to all medical study is revealed over and over again in his life, and he spent an amount of time in the pursuit of anatomy which was not required of him by the schedule of the College of Surgeons. For he took out three courses at St. Thomas's Hospital and also a course at the Graingers' private school (though he could but ill have spared the money necessary to buy " the parts," the expense of which was no slight consideration) when the minimum amount of dissecting required by the curriculum of the College was two courses.

The science of anatomy was in those days not so easy of acquisition as it is now. Its professors were under considerable and unsavoury suspicion among the public, and there was every temptation to be-little the study of the actual body. The dearth of bodies was one of the most serious drawbacks to a medical education. Subjects for dissection could only be obtained from two sources. The first, the legitimate source, was the gallows, the corpses of murderers being handed over to the dissecting-rooms after the criminals had suffered capital punishment. The second, the illegitimate source, was the resurrection man. The inefficiency of the first source could be shown by figures. The number of persons executed in the whole of England and Wales from 1805 to 1820, inclusive, amounted to 1150. It was known that not all these bodies were used for dissecting purposes, while the average number of students yearly entering upon their studies at the different London schools alone was estimated at nearly a thousand. And other legitimate sources—purchase, for instance—were not available. The law, by only allowing the bodies of the worst malefactors known to it to be used for anatomical purposes, stamped an obloquy upon the dissector and also upon the dissected, so that it became an awkward task to acquire a corpse from its nearest surviving relatives, while it betokened a certain absence of delicacy in the relatives to allow themselves to be tempted by money to hand over the body. As a consequence the second, or illegitimate, mode of obtaining bodies was resorted to by the professors of anatomy at the different hospitals and the proprietors of the different private schools.

Body-snatching, in fact, was practised largely and regarded

by the medical profession not so much as an infringement of the law, and an outrage upon all decency, as a necessity, painful perhaps, but with its humorous side.*   It is narrated of a distinguished surgeon, the hero of many body-snatching stories, that on one occasion he went some way out of London to bring back a body that had been procured for him from a country churchyard where the watch against this form of desecration was not so alert as it was in London, and that on his return journey he propped up the body alongside of him in his gig, having clothed it in decent out-door garb, as the readiest method of getting it into his house

---

* The closing stanzas of one of Hood's well-known comic poems, "Mary's Ghost, a Pathetic Ballad," shows that the association of ideas was present to the public mind.   Here the ghost explains that her grave has been rifled and the contents distributed among the anatomical teachers of London in the following words :—

The arm that used to take your arm
  Is took to Dr. Vyse.[1]
And both my legs are gone to walk
  The Hospital at Guy's.

I vowed that you should have my hand,
  But Fate gives us denial;
You'll find it there at Mr. Bell's[2]
  In spirits in a phial.

As for my feet, the little feet
  You used to call so pretty,
There's one I know in Bedford Row,[3]
  The t'other's in the City. [4]

I can't tell where my head has gone,
  But Dr. Carpue can;[5]
As for my trunk it's all packed up
  To go by Pickford's van.

I wish you'd go to Mr. P.[6]
  And save me such a ride.
I don't half like the outside place
  They've took for my inside.

The cock it crows, I must be gone,
  My William we must part:
And I'll be yours in death although
  Sir Astley[7] has my heart.

---

[1] Dr. Vyse cannot be traced.
[2] Sir Charles Bell, demonstrator of anatomy at the Middlesex Hospital.
[3] Abernethy lived for many years at 14, Bedford Row.
[4] The Aldersgate City School of Anatomy.
[5] Joseph Constantine Carpue, the head of a great private school of anatomy.
[6] Mr. Richard Partridge, demonstrator of anatomy at King's College Hospital.
[7] Sir Astley Cooper.

without attracting any attention. Having stopped outside a suburban public-house for refreshment, the potman who brought out the liquor naturally inquired if the other gentleman wouldn't have anything. "Damn him, no," said the great surgeon coolly, recognising that he must account at once for the silence and immobility of his companion, "damn him, he's sulky." This is only one out of hundreds of stories for which very general credence is asked in proof of the fact that before the notorious murders by Burke and Hare and Bishop and Williams body-snatching was winked at in the medical profession. And it is not to be denied that this was the case. It would have been wonderful otherwise. A knowledge of anatomy was a necessity; this knowledge could only be properly obtained by dissecting, and previously to the passing of the Anatomy Act there were no bodies to dissect. The public at large looked upon body-snatching as contrary to all the established prejudices of humanity and did not care whether anatomy was studied or not, overlooking its paramount importance to the medical man. The profession, on the other hand, had a conscientious desire to know all about the body they were going to treat, which desire could easily be strained into an intention to obtain the knowledge in spite of the public. These two attitudes were utterly irreconcilable, and, as is the case when people see things from different standpoints, a good deal of bitter feeling was occasioned. The students were compelled to depend for their acquisition of essential knowledge, in the dearth of proper subjects for dissection, upon expensive illustrated text-books and papier-mâché models made for the most part in France. Sir Charles Bell's celebrated plates were published in 1798, and were the students' main support in Thomas Wakley's time, as Lizars's plates, probably the best thing of the sort ever produced, were a decade later. The papier-mâché models of the human figure were made in Paris and to some extent in Vienna, and were like a child's picture puzzles in the use to which they were put. The student learned his topographical anatomy with them by fitting the parts in among each other in accordance with coloured diagrams and wax models. All this was felt to be, by those who knew, a very poor substitute for actual dissection of the body, and the profession were sorely troubled by the inability to obtain due facilities for learning. The apathy of the authorities did not allow of the utilising of the bodies of the unclaimed dead, and few persons were sufficiently free from prejudice to leave their bodies of their own free will to the anatomy schools. So that nothing was open to the anatomists save to get the bodies by force or fraud.

In the end this lamentable state of affairs led to crime, but for years before the notorious Burke and Hare trial the pilfering of bodies from the churchyards was known to be undertaken at the instance of members of the profession, and for the offence many persons were convicted and heavily punished. Upon this it followed that the fees to be paid to the resurrection men grew heavier in proportion as the risk grew greater and the trade developed into skilled labour. A body was worth £10 to a professor of anatomy at a hospital, and even more to the owner of a private school, inasmuch as the hospital schools obtained such bodies as were at the disposal of the Government. A student had to pay in ready money as much as £2 or £2 10s. for "a part," and the lucrative trade of body-snatching became almost a fine art, so necessary was it that the perpetrators of the sacrilege should avoid detection. The amount of empty coffins that have been discovered in the operations of sextons and in the course of the reclamation of graveyards proves beyond a doubt the prevalence of body-snatching; while the fact that the medical profession was the only class of the community benefiting by the felonies suggests the probability that the teacher of anatomy stood in the position of instigator.

CHAPTER IV

[1817–1820]

The Influences of Youth and Training—The Goodchilds—Gerard's Hall—Courtship and Marriage—The Start in Practice—Prospects in Argyll Street—Fire and Attempted Murder.

IN October, 1817, Wakley passed his examination for the Membership of the Royal College of Surgeons of England, and walked home to Membury to announce the news. It will not be amiss here to point out how much the circumstances of his home-life dictated his adult career. Brought up in the country among a simple and patriarchal folk, he positively detested shams of all sorts. A pretender was to him the biggest rogue the world could know. As a member of a large family he was endowed with a deep sense of what was fair. He obtained his own share of whatever of material enjoyment or comfort was going by favour, for he was the youngest, and could not have exacted it from his elders ; but he obtained it because it was freely recognised in Mr. Henry Wakley's house that share and share alike in common goods was the only fair plan. So that there was early implanted in his breast a keen sense of rudimentary justice—that crude kind of socialism so often seen in children—only developed to an extraordinarily high degree. He desired that every one should have his due, and in his student days this desire had developed to such a degree that towards all who belonged to classes whose manners or methods he found oppressive he could scarcely bring himself to be impartial. He had been brought up in an atmosphere of obedience as well as of equity, so that the privileges he obtained at home were the return of allegiance given. From a domestic environment

of this sort he went to a London hospital, and found a condition of things that was directly at variance with all his
primitive and deeply implanted ideas of fair-play. He found
that although he was allowed to do his part—to pay his fees
and attend his classes—the authorities were not prepared
to do their part by him. The lectures advertised were not
delivered by the eminent people who received the fees, but
by their demonstrators ; the one great practical help to the
acquisition of a sound knowledge of pathology, presence
at post-mortem examinations, could only be secured by the
clandestine feeing of the post-mortem-room porters ; the
honorary staff from whose lips he was to learn the science of
healing were capricious in their visits and were generally
dumb upon the occasions when they put in an appearance ;
the list of operations was not published to the students, and
only the favoured pupils of the staff knew what was going to
be done by the great men and when. And, to cap all these
injustices, he found that he was relegated to a class in his
profession marked out from the beginning to constitute the
rank and file, not in the least through want of personal merit,
but because he had not paid exorbitant fees to apprentice
himself to a great man. He had no objection to being a
general practitioner ; on the contrary, he desired to be. He
had lived for three years in the house of two hard-worked
members of this class. He had shared their labours and
known their trials. He could estimate the amount of good
that they did and the amount of influence for good that they
were able to exercise over the community. He saw these
men, who did their duties for the most part rigidly according
to their lights, always set on one side and looked down upon
by their privileged brethren, who had themselves obtained
their places in the medical hierarchy by purchase and not by
merit, and who, being in posts of office, took the emoluments
and omitted to do the work. These things he saw. His
sense of justice revolted at them, and none the less because
he personally suffered from their effects, and they will
sufficiently account for the attitude towards hospital officials
that he was soon to reveal, for his readiness to find them

wanting in skill, and his pertinacity in convicting them of unfairness and nepotism. His championship of the cause of the general practitioner was as obvious in its origin as it was outspoken in its activity.

It was in this mood that Wakley arrived home in the character of a qualified man. His primary intentions were to practise in the country, and he stayed for some months at Membury after being qualified, during which time he was in search of an opening. He made many friends in the neighbourhood during this his first real vacation, and that he impressed them favourably is well shown by the generous response that Devonshire and Somersetshire people were wont to make for many years to his appeals in the columns of the "Lancet," and this in cases where it could only have been the personality of the editor, and not at all the urgency of the appeal, that swayed them. But he did not find any chance of making a practice that seemed to him to offer a probability of quick success. And he did not wish to wait.

His wish to get speedily into practice was caused by the fact that he desired to become the husband of a young lady whom he had known during the last year of his student life, although he could not be said to be strictly and formally engaged to her. He had, however, obtained from her father a sort of qualified approval of his suit, accompanied with some very clear words as to the responsibilities that he would be expected to assume upon marriage. For Mr. Goodchild, the father of the girl, though a wealthy man, stated that he had no intention of supporting a son-in-law, but that his daughter's husband must maintain himself and his wife by his own labour.

Mr. Goodchild was a merchant. His warehouses and offices were in Tooley Street, and his home was at Hendon, then an absolutely rural district, being considerably less accessible to the true Londoner than Guildford, Windsor, and even Hertford are now. He was a lead merchant, and a man of wealth and large business connexions. Young Wakley made the acquaintance of the family by accident. The men in the Tooley Street works were very constantly in

need of the services of the adjoining hospitals. Mr. Goodchild was a governor of St. Thomas's Hospital and a regular
annual subscriber, but not to the extent that his income
would have warranted the hospital authorities in expecting,
or to the extent that was proportionate to the labour that
was expended upon the care of his numerous workmen by
the medical officers of the charities. He employed at that
time a very large number of hands—two or three hundred—
some of whom were daily in receipt of surgical assistance.
The treasurer of St. Thomas's Hospital, to whose attention
this was brought, sent Wakley and his friend Wiltshire to
call at Hendon, commissioning them to ask Mr. Goodchild
whether he felt disposed to support in a special manner an
appeal that was being made on behalf of the hospital, having
regard to the fact that his workmen were so largely benefited
by their proximity to the building. Mr. Goodchild not only
made a generous response to the lads' appeal—he gave them
£100—but invited them to luncheon and later to a party
at his house. The acquaintance thus made ripened into
friendship between the two students and the Goodchild
family, and the friendship between the youngest daughter
and Wakley soon became subject to a natural transformation
into love. It says a great deal for the influence that Wakley
had over those whom he desired to move, that he should
have obtained Mr. Goodchild's consent to an early, if con-
ditional, engagement ; for although he was not accepted as a
suitor for Miss Goodchild's hand while still a student, yet he
was accepted almost immediately upon becoming qualified,
and when he had no remarkably good chances of prosperity
and no expectations from home. He was one, and the
youngest, of eleven children. To the eldest son the land
would infallibly go. If he shared equally with the other
nine it was all that he could expect. Probably he would be
considered to have received his patrimony when his
indentures and his London course of study were paid for.
From a worldly point of view, therefore, he could not be
considered a good match. He had his youth and his profession, and that was all. But Mr. Goodchild was a judge

c

of men, and he saw in his daughter's suitor the stuff of which success is made, though he did not guess the direction whence that success would come, and for a time at least cordially disapproved of those very departures that made his son-in-law a man whose biography has to be written, instead of a family practitioner of medicine. It was probably with some idea of asserting his independence that Wakley thought of setting up in practice in his own part of the world. There the esteem in which his father and family were held would have been some sort of counterpoise to the wealth of the prospective father-in-law. Be that as it may, the idea came to nothing, for in 1818 he returned to London, and went into private practice in the City.

He lived at this time in Gerard's Hall, an old residential inn, and before the Fire of London the palace of the Lord Mayors of London. It possessed a remarkably fine crypt, used as a cellar, and stood in Basing Lane on a site that was afterwards cleared in the construction of Queen Victoria Street. Thither he returned and proceeded to look about him for patients and a practice, occupying himself in the meantime in completing the gaps which he felt to exist in his education. The testimony of Mr. Ivatts, the proprietor of the Hall, to his behaviour while he was that gentleman's tenant shows that, so far from feeling that because he was no longer a student he had earned the right to cease from work and consider himself completely informed—a very common attitude with the newly-fledged medical man—he doubled his energies. He was an ambitious, able, enthusiastic young lover, and intended to leave no stone unturned in his struggle to deserve his wife and support her. Mr. Ivatts had occasion under distressing circumstances that will soon be narrated to make a statement upon oath as to the manner of life pursued by Wakley at this time, and he then said that he was particularly regular in his mode of living, temperate, keeping much to himself, and exceedingly studious, rising sometimes as early as four o'clock in the morning, even in the winter, to read and write. It was often a matter of wonder in later times, to his enemies and friends alike, where he had got his great store of information, and how he came from his earliest start on a journalistic career to control so adept as well as so virile a pen. It was to the rigid self-denial of his life in Gerard's Hall that he owed both. For hours each day—hours snatched from the sleep that was due to his labours—he steadily worked, reading copiously, and writing assiduously, and it was thus that he acquired the solid information and literary skill which enabled him to become a power in journalism from the moment that he entered the lists.

During the following year an end was put to his period of probation, and he was assisted by Mr. Goodchild, now satisfied that his daughter had chosen a man capable of taking care of her, to acquire a West-end practice. The practice lay at the top of Regent Street, and its owner, Mr. Samuel Malleson, in disposing of it did not desire to dispose of his house also. Mr. Goodchild arranged that Wakley should take a house in Argyll Street, No. 5, which was hard by Mr. Malleson's house, and should purchase that gentleman's drugs and the furniture of the surgery and transport them thither. The sum of £400 was paid for the goodwill of the practice, and a similar sum as premium on the lease of the house in Argyll Street, then a fashionable and important street, and more money was paid both in Argyll Street for the fixtures and to Mr. Malleson for his stock and sundry furniture, so that £1000 would probably not have covered the immediate outlay. Mr. Goodchild was, however, a business man, and cannot be said to have made a bad investment, having satisfied himself that his future son-in-law was a trustworthy and competent man, for, of course, everything turned upon that. The practice that was obtained for £400 cash had brought in Mr. Malleson £690 during 1818, and by the autumn of 1819, when it was purchased, £560 had already been earned.

Argyll Street was then a street of reputable private residences. The town house of the Earl of Aberdeen shed an aristocratic flavour over the eastern side, and most of the inhabitants were persons of consideration if not wealth.

No. 5 was a house of fifteen rooms, including the back study, which was used as a surgery, and was of the type and date of the houses now standing in the older parts of Maddox Street. It had a double dining-room and a double drawing-room and half-a-dozen bedrooms. This house its new possessor set to work to furnish handsomely, and those of us in this generation who are sufficiently modern to have begun to appreciate again the beauty, as well as the solidity, of the effects with which our grandparents delighted to surround themselves, know that the style of upholstery in the twenties was not an economical one. Wakley would not have equipped his rooms so lavishly had he not been preparing for the almost immediate reception of a wife ; but imposing externals were every whit as valuable then as they are now in forming a good connexion, and Mr. Goodchild's sure commercial instinct would have certainly gone in support of a somewhat lavish expenditure. From the first the venture was a successful one. The young practitioner retained the old patients who had been transferred to him, and new ones called him in, both in the neighbourhood and in the City, and when in February, 1820, he brought his wife home he did so with every prospect before him of a successful career in general practice. He was married on Saturday, February 5th, 1820, at St. james's Church, Piccadilly, and the announcement of his wedding as it appears in the "News" of February 6th, takes us back a stride in history, for the same issue informed the world of the death of King George III.

But the old contrast between present security and sad trouble in the immediate future was never more dramatically exemplified than in the case of Wakley's early married life. In February he brought his young wife to her new home. His marriage was one of affection, but also one of material advantage to him, while his prospects in his professional career were exceptionally bright. Young, talented, good-looking, healthy, a married lover, and a successful man, he was beloved by his friends and respected by all with whom his profession brought him into relation. In six months his home was broken up, his house burnt to the ground, his health temporarily injured, his practice well-nigh destroyed, and last, but most serious of all, his reputation was gravely impugned, the slanders that were rife about him being as widespread as they were malignant.

On the evening of August 26th, 1820, No. 5, Argyll Street, was burnt to the ground, while a murderous attack was made upon the hapless owner. The extraordinary events that occurred on that night will have to be dealt with at some length, and to place them with perfect clearness before the reader, a digression must be made, and circumstances in the Cato Street conspiracy and the execution of the infamous Thistlewood must be detailed at the risk of appearing to give information upon matters of historical notoriety. The following is the account of the occurrences which appeared in the "Morning Chronicle" of Monday, August 28th, 1820. The information was obviously obtained in large part from Wakley himself.

ATROCIOUS ATTEMPT TO MURDER, SUPPOSED ROBBERY, AND SETTING A HOUSE ON FIRE.

Yesterday morning, about half-past one o'clock, a man called at the house of Mr. Wakley, surgeon, of No. 5, Argyll Street, Oxford Street, and knocked at the door. All the servants were in bed, and Mr. W., who was indisposed, was in his apartment putting some leeches to his temples. He placed a bandage round his head and proceeded to open the door, on doing which, a man, who appeared to be flurried, said that he had come from Mr. Ibbetson, of the Bath Hotel, Basing Lane, an old patient of Mr. Wakley's, who was dangerously ill, and required his immediate attendance. The fellow requesting a glass of cyder, as he said he was fatigued by a long journey, Mr. Wakley complied, and went downstairs to the cellar to procure him a glass. During the time it is supposed that the villain admitted some accomplices. On the Doctor's return to the passage he observed something rush towards him, and at the moment he received a tremendous blow on the head which knocked him down. It was with some instrument, and at the same time the destructive weapon of the assassin was aimed at his breast, on which he received a stab; he then thrust the instrument a second time, which passed through the collar of the Doctor's coat, waistcoat, and neckcloth, and penetrated the skin; he received other injuries, and while he lay in the passage he received violent blows and kicks from some person or persons; his abdomen was severely bruised. In this deplorable state he laid for three-quarters of an hour without the least assistance, when he was roused from his stupor by the flames in immense bodies rushing down the stairs and a dense smoke. He with difficulty arose and crawled out the back way, and climbed through the skylight leading to the house of Mr. Thompson, next door, in whose parlour he was afterwards found weltering in his blood and apparently in a dying state. He was immediately carried to the house of Mr. Parker, of Argyll Street, where Drs. Luke and Cates attended and dressed his wounds. On Mr. Wakley being supported to the above house a daring villain unfeelingly snatched at his watch and got it from his fob. He had the presence of mind to seize the villain by the collar; the property was recovered, and he was taken in custody to the watch-house. Mr. W., after being dressed, was put to bed, and yesterday morning he bled himself; and fearful that his wife, to whom he was lately married, should be alarmed by the too speedy intelligence of the atrocious deed, although in so dreadful a condition, proceeded to his country residence yesterday morning. Three-quarters of an hour elapsed before the fire was discovered by Mr. W., who, as well as he was able, gave an alarm: the servants immediately arose and made their escape. A lamplighter broke the windows of the parlour, on which the flames burst forth in a great body and the neighbourhood was in a moment illumined. The utmost confusion prevailed, and the inmates of the adjacent houses were seen, in almost a condition of nudity, taking refuge in other houses.

In a short time several engines arrived, and, having plenty of water, played with great activity on the element which seemed to threaten destruction to all around it, and persons employed in saving the furniture. In a few hours the house of Mr. Wakley was gutted, and what property there was in the house—if not stolen—was destroyed. Property consisting of guineas to an immense amount were in one of the upper apartments, and the firemen will be employed to search in order to ascertain if any robbery was committed, or if the above transaction proceeded from malice.

The mysterious affair has caused many suspicions. A short time ago Mr. Wakley received several threatening letters, signed "Jealousy is the cause, but it is from a friend." The man who called is unknown to Mr. Wakley, and the case is involved in great mystery. During the course of the day various persons of distinction about the neighbourhood made inquiry after the state of Mr. Wakley, and the answer was, " Although severely injured there are hopes of his recovery."

Fortunately the adjoining houses of Messrs. Thompson and Hodgson are not injured, save a slight scorching. So great an interest was excited by the quick circulation of the above horrid transaction that crowds of persons assembled, and Mr. Tarrant the magistrate in the course of the day attended by Mr. Dyer, took the examination at the house of Mr. Parker of the servants belonging to Mr. W. and other persons, but he himself was in such a debilitated condition that he was unable to give his deposition.

The surgeons who examined the wounds on the body of Mr. Wakley did not think that they were of so serious a nature as to affect his life, the fortunate circumstance of his having put the bandage about his head prior to opening the door prevented the violent blow he received having a serious effect. The blow was given with some heavy instrument, and must have been given with deadly intention.

No clue whatever can be found as to the parties concerned in this atrocious affair. Information was speedily given at the police establishment, and likewise to the Secretary of State's office, for the purpose of causing bills to be circulated for the apprehension of the party.

Officers have received the necessary instrument, and we trust that in a short time the persons capable of such horrible transactions may be brought to justice.

This story, as told by the "Morning Chronicle," aroused the curiosity and interest of all London. Nothing was wanting to its dramatic side. The crimes were terrible, the criminals were unknown, and the circumstances and plight of the victim gave additional sensationalism to the case.

CHAPTER V

[1820]

*The Cato Street Conspiracy—The Execution of the Ringleaders—
A Wicked Accusation—A Threatening Letter—The Origin of the
Outrages in Argyll Street—Tom Parker and the Execution of
Thistlewood and his Followers.*

ON the evening of February 23rd, 1820, there were arrested
in a loft in Cato Street, now named Horace Street, Edgware
Road, certain members of a desperate band who had
leagued themselves together to assassinate the King's
Ministers. The real origin of the plot and the real purpose
of the conspirators were never made very clear. Want
counted for something, for not a penny was found upon any
of those arrested. A form of general discontent euphoni-
ously termed " political," that bitter, vague disaffection bred
of bad circumstances and nurtured by inflammatory speeches,
counted for more. As far as Thistlewood, the leader of the
gang, went, vanity counted for most.

King George III. died on January 29th, 1820, and was succeeded by a son who, whatever his claims to good breeding
and his evidences of good nature, could not be called a good
man or be expected to make a good king. The death of the
aged monarch was a signal to the conspirators to strike their
blow. Doubtless they hoped that the inevitable muddle in
public affairs due to the devolution of the crown upon the
Regent would assist in the wide-spread panic that they
intended to create by the assassination of certain of the
virtual rulers of the country, and this hope determined the
date of their action. They had long been making their
preparations ; muskets, pistols, cutlasses, and pikes had been

secreted in a loft over a range of stables and coach-houses in
Cato Street. Here, on the evening of February 23rd, 1820,
they assembled to the number of thirty, with the deliberate
intention of making a murderous attack upon certain
members of the Cabinet who were engaged to dine with
Lord Harrowby, the Lord Privy Seal, in Grosvenor Square.
The members of the Cabinet who were Lord Harrowby's
proposed guests that night were : Lord Liverpool, the
Premier ; Lord Eldon, the Lord Chancellor ; Lord Castlereagh, the Secretary of State for Foreign Affairs ; and Mr.
Vansittart, Lord Sidmouth, Sir Robert Peel, and George
Canning ; but of these it was Lord Castlereagh whose life
was especially aimed at. Thirty conspirators in a vile cause
and in desperately poor circumstances could hardly be
expected to keep good faith with each other, and the scheme
was revealed to the Bow Street authorities. A raid was made
on the loft at the hour of rendezvous, and the misguided
wretches were caught in the act of arming themselves.
After a furious *mêlée*, in which one Bow Street officer was
shot dead, certain of the ringleaders were captured. Arthur
Thistlewood, a commissioned officer in the militia and the
only man of education who was involved in the plot—he is
said to have served his time as an apothecary—escaped ; but
the price of £1000 was put on his head and he was captured
the next day.

At the trial a man named Monument, a shoemaker, turned
King's evidence, with the result that Thistlewood, Davidson,
a negro whose seditious speeches had counted every whit as
much in the organisation of the plot as the former's social
position and superior learning, Ings a butcher, Tidd a
shoemaker, and a man named Brunt were condemned to
be hanged, drawn, and quartered, while five of their
colleagues were sentenced to penal servitude for life. The
condemned men were publicly executed at Newgate in the
presence of an enormous crowd on May Day, 1820. The
bodies were allowed to hang for half-an-hour, when they
were taken down, and in formal accordance with the words
of the sentence a masked man stepped on to the scaffold

and decapitated them, handing each severed head to an assistant, who held it up and proclaimed it to the crowd by the name of the late owner. The performer of this un-savoury task was clothed in a rough seaman's guernsey, but so deftly and speedily did he perform the decapitations that he roused in the minds of those who saw him a suspicion that he was a member of the medical profession. The crowd deeply resented the mutilation of the dead, all the more that the political glamour which had been thrown over their crime hid its foolish ugliness, and they yelled execrations mingled with groans and hisses at the man in the mask; and the feeling of disgust thus crudely expressed by the mob was echoed by many more responsible people, and was centred upon the unknown operator. It is easy, therefore, to imagine that to be under suspicion of having served his country in so bestial and degrading a fashion would be a terrible position for a young surgeon. And this is what happened to Thomas Wakley.

How did the suspicion arise? Who started it? Had it any causal connection with the terrible events in Argyll Street on the night of August 26th? These questions cannot be answered with any certainty, but the facts which guided Wakley and his legal advisers to their several opinions can be given. The belief that the decapitation of the con-spirators had been undertaken by Wakley, wherever it first originated, obtained such support as it received on account of a newspaper article which stated that the masked operator was "a young surgeon of Argyll Street," he being the only surgeon occupying a house in that small street at the time. It was found impossible to trace the originator of the phrase, which appears to have been printed without any personal feeling or any appreciation that it was tantamount to giving a name to the masked man whose anonymity was so much a subject of debate. The sentence may have been written by accident, or it may have been inspired by malice, and if the latter was the case the malice may have had a particu-larly mischievous and successful outcome. For the Cato Street conspirators were thirty in number; and as but ten of them suffered for their crimes, some of the remaining desperadoes may have planned the murderous and ruinous attack upon the man whom they believed upon public hearsay to have assisted the law in its last horrid offices upon Arthur Thistlewood and his co-conspirators. All this is purposely couched in the language of pure supposition, for no light has ever been thrown upon the real origin of the fire. To complicate matters in the search for an incendiary, Wakley had received, both before and after his marriage, anonymous letters, obviously inspired by jealousy. One of these letters, which was received in March, 1820, contained a distinct threat that his house should be burned down and himself murdered. In consequence of this threatening letter Wakley consulted his solicitors as to the advisability of increasing his insurance. The contents of the house had been originally insured for £600, but the policy dated from before his marriage. After his marriage many things were obtained—such as furniture, plate, and china, while the dresses and jewellery of Mrs. Wakley and her numerous wedding presents had also to be added to his effects. In fact, he found himself, with a distinct threat that his house would be burned down, in the unpleasant position of being secured against loss to the extent of one-half or perhaps a third of the value of his goods. His solicitors urged him to insure his effects to their proper amount and also to put the threatening letter out of his mind; but the first he delayed to do and the second he was unable to do. At last he insured for a further sum of £600, and this increase of insurance was made so short a time before the fire, with all its extraordinary circumstances, that it is hardly to be wondered at that the insurance company withheld payment, not actually alleging that the luckless owner of the house had burnt himself out, but leaving the impression by their action that such was their belief. The complete refutation of this insinuation on the part of the Hope Fire Assurance Company followed almost immediately; but during the time necessary to prepare the proper legal procedure for his vindication Wakley suffered mentally under the belief that the suspicion was wide-spread.

The actual culprits were never discovered. The question whether one of the Thistlewood gang set fire to No. 5, Argyll Street, and attempted the murder of the owner was never solved. If the writer of the anonymous letter, who had made categorical threats to do these two things, carried out his threats, he did so with impunity, for no clue to his identity was ever obtained. Wakley's lawyers seem rather to have leant to the theory that the assault and arson were the execution of the written threats. Wakley himself implicitly believed that he had been attacked by some of Thistlewood's gang, or by persons, at any rate, who sympathised with Thistlewood to this extent, that they were prepared to take vengeance upon the man whom they were informed had played the part of amateur headsman upon his person. It required a man mad with jealousy to write the anonymous letters, and it only required him to be a little madder to carry out the threats contained in them. So far the lawyers' view is tenable. But, as will be seen, Wakley was robbed as well as assaulted, and though jealousy might have dictated the burning of the house and the savage attacks upon the owner, they would not have instigated an unsuccessful rival to the meaner felony. That members of the Thistlewood gang were concerned in the matter seemed at the time probable, for men's minds were then full of the daring and vile enormity that these ruffians had planned to perpetrate against some of the more distinguished persons in the land, and no act would have seemed too stupid, causeless, and criminal to be attributed with reason to the residue of the band. It is, of course, possible that Wakley was right in his view. But in the beginning we are confronted with a coincidence that asks for much faith if any of the Thistlewood gang are to be held responsible for the Argyll Street outrage. We must believe that the exact threats made by one person in February for one reason were carried out by different persons in August, and for a different reason. Or we must believe that the jealous man seized the opportunity of the known though unreasonable fury of the coarsest socialistic party against Wakley to instigate some disciples of Thistlewood to the crimes. It is not very probable that any miscreant, however enthusiastic a follower of Thistlewood, or however nearly tied by blood or sentiment to any of that man's misguided followers, would, soon after the breaking up of the Cato Street gang, have dared to outrage the law in so public and flagrant a manner. Those of the actual band who were still at large had prices put upon their heads for high treason, and an example before their eyes warning them that capture meant subjection to the utmost rigour of the law. Their relatives and friends would for the same reasons be chary of drawing upon themselves the attention of the authorities. The supposition that the outrages were the result of an ordinary robbery with violence, planned against a man known to be recently married and in possession of much portable property, is the one that demands the least exercise of imagination, but does not fit in with all the circumstances.

Such were the theories as to the cause of the Argyll Street outrages which broke up Wakley's home, injured his health, and ruined his practice, reducing him in a few moments from a position that had been truly enviable to one that was as truly deplorable. The grave effect that the sudden and terrible check to his material prosperity and domestic happiness had upon him at the time and afterwards—it possibly determined his career, and certainly influenced his life— would warrant the lengthy treatment of the whole episode, if no other reason were present; but the action of the Hope Fire Assurance Company in withholding payment of the sums assured brought the matter before a judge, when sworn testimony to the events was supplied by eyewitnesses. In a court of law it became at once clear that the slanders attributing the burning of his house to his own hand, and the anonymous messages and murderous attack to his own imagination, were monstrous as well as foolish.

The identity of the man in the mask who assisted at the execution of Thistlewood and his followers is fairly certain.

He was in all probability a certain Tom Parker, at the date of the executions an assistant to Edward Grainger in the Webb Street anatomy school, and later dissecting-room porter at St. Thomas's Hospital, under Richard Grainger. It seems idle to repudiate for Wakley any share in the matter, but inasmuch as he himself took pains to refute the revolting and ridiculous calumny, and inasmuch as there were certainly persons at the time who believed it and others who spread it abroad, whether they believed it or not, it is best to put on record the following correspondence, which had the effect of silencing the slander entirely :—

Letter from THOMAS WAKLEY *to* J. W. PARKINS, Esq., *Sheriff of London and Middlesex.*

KENTISH TOWN, *September 21st, 1820.*

SIR,—From the period of my late catastrophe in Argyle Street, to add to my anxiety, I have been currently charged by a multitude of malignant slanderers as being the person who decapitated Thistlewood and his deluded companions in May last. Your official contradiction of this disgusting falsehood, as Sheriff of London, will confer a lasting favour on, Sir,

Your obliged servant,

(Signed)   THOMAS WAKLEY.

J. W. PARKINS, Esq.,
Sheriff of London and Middlesex.

Letter from Mr. PARKINS *to* THOMAS WAKLEY.

No. 10, NEW BRIDGE STREET, *September 25th, 1820.*

SIR,—In answer to your letter of the 21st instant I feel myself bound to comply with its contents to the utmost of my power ; but I am sorry to inform you that the whole of the disgusting business to which it relates was conducted with so much privacy and pertinacious conceal. ment from me that I was not even made acquainted with the order for the execution until the day after (Sunday, when I went to Newgate accompanied by a clergyman) it had been determined upon, and orders given for erecting the scaffold, &c., by the Lord Mayor, Bridges, and my colleague, Mr. Rothwell, who, accompanied by his deputy, had, I understood, been at the Secretary of State's office arranging the same. As to the man who decapitated the unfortunate Thistlewood and his companions, he was procured for that purpose by the prison surgeon, and his terms, £20, agreed for by Mr. Turner, Mr. Rothwell's deputy, and which wages Mr. Turner told me were repaid to him by the Home Department, as also £5 he paid to the man who held up the heads.

I did not see the man who performed the duty until he appeared on the scaffold masked, and dressed as a sailor. By the notice I then took of him (which was very particular) I perceived him to be in height about five feet five or six inches; and in answer to my inquiry the other day (in consequence of your note) who the fellow was, Mr. Turner informed me that he was a resurrection man who obtained bodies for the hospitals, and that when he asked him if he could perform the task of cutting off the heads, he replied, oh, yes, that he could do it very well, as he was in the habit of cutting off *nobs* (heads) for the purpose of obtaining *nackers* (teeth). I am glad for the honour of our country's humanity that it was no person of respectability, but a most illiterate and degraded being, as was also the wretched individual who held up the heads of the unfortunate men.

In addition to the above, I am credibly informed that the individual who decapitated Thistlewood and his companions was engaged by the under-sheriffs from Yorkshire to go there for a similar purpose, but in the performance of which sanguinary work, thank Providence, he has been disappointed.

I cannot conclude this letter without bearing testimony to the humane disposition of your heart towards the depraved young man who robbed you of your watch on the fatal night when crossing the road, and bleeding from the wounds inflicted by the assassins and incendiaries who had set fire to your house in Argyll Street.

I hope this assurance will convince every one, even the most malignant of your enemies, that it was totally impossible any one could mistake a gentleman of your appearance and height (which I conceive to be about five feet ten inches) for the person (five feet five or six inches) who performed the sanguinary duty on Thistlewood and the others in May last.

I am, Sir,
Your most obedient servant,
J. W. PARKINS, *Sheriff.*

Thomas Wakley, Esq.

Further Letter from Mr. Parkins *to* Thomas Wakley.

November, 1820.

Sir,—I hope you have not been liable to any further annoyance from the erroneous and wicked opinion which prevailed that you were the person who decapitated Thistlewood and his associates. I am inclined to think that my letter of the 25th of September has been of service to remove that impression, as a few days ago a stout woman called upon me and asked if the letter which you published was one from me, and on being informed that it was so she expressed her surprise, and said that if the man who did it could be found he would be served out or made away with. It did not occur to my recollection at the time or I would have endeavoured to trace out who those were who set your house on fire. I cannot conclude without noticing the cool indifference of Mr. Box, who could scarcely be induced to tell me who the man was that he hired for the purpose, Mr. B. stating as a reason that if the police officers knew him they would take him into custody for robbing the churchyards, and Mr. Deputy-Sheriff Turner said that it was not necessary to be more particular than merely to state on my authority that you were not the person. However, I now feel much satisfied that I gave you the letter that I did. With best wishes for your prosperity, believe me,

Yours truly,

J. W. PARKINS, Ex-Sheriff.

To Mr. T. WAKLEY,
Surgeon, Albemarle Street.

From these letters of the worthy sheriff it is clear that the Home Office employed a dissecting-room porter and a resurrectionist to assist in carrying out the sentence upon the Thistlewood gang. Mr. William Adams, F.R.C.S., has supplied information which, taken in conjunction with that afforded by the replies of Mr. Parkins to Wakley's letter of September 21st, 1820, confirms the rumour, prevalent at the time, that the Government's *aide de camp* on the gruesome occasion was " Tom Parker of Graingers'." Mr. Adams says that suspicion fell not only upon Wakley but upon his late instructor in anatomy, Edward Grainger, who was compelled to make a public denial.

" The man," Mr. Adams writes, " who really did cut off the heads I have no doubt was a man well known as ' Tom Parker,' Grainger's head dissecting-room porter. This man was a celebrated ' resurrectionist.' He told me he once took fourteen bodies out of Old St. Pancras churchyard in the night.

" That he possessed the requisite skill is proved by what I myself saw. In the year 1842 I was appointed Curator of the Museum and Demonstrator of Morbid Anatomy at St. Thomas's Hospital, and in that year we bought Grainger's School, appointed Grainger lecturer in physiology, and made other important changes. With Grainger we took several other well-known characters of the old school, and Tom Parker became my chief dead-house assistant. In 1843 I found that the museum was very short of separated bones of the skull, and I asked Tom to look out for any favourable opportunities. A young woman about eighteen years of age threw herself over Waterloo Bridge and died at the hospital. Tom said her head was just the thing I wanted, and, when we were alone after the post-mortem, he said: ' Now I should like to show you the secret of cutting off a head.' The knife, he said, would never do it, but there was a dodge in wrenching through the ligaments by twisting the head violently first to the right and then to the left after all the soft parts had been cut through. This he demonstrated on the spot by putting the girl on the floor, then raising the trunk and firmly grasping it between his knees, when he made the cut in front, sloping the knife towards the occipital articulation, and then the cut behind with the same slope of the knife. Then the violent wrench and the head came off. Tom was generally accused of being the man on the scaffold, and never denied it, but he never confessed it even to myself, next to Grainger his best friend.

" The sequel to Tom Parker's case of decapitation was remarkable. The coroner's jury returned a verdict of *felo-de-se*, and the woman was buried in unconsecrated ground close to the churchyard of St. Thomas's Hospital. The beadle of the parish and a few others were at the grave, and the beadle said his duty was to see that the body was in the coffin. This, of course, Tom Parker resisted, and a few others that were at the grave ; but the beadle got his pickaxe and forced open the coffin, when it was found that there was no head. Then the people adjourned to the public-house close by and Tom ran off to the hospital, put the head in his pocket-handkerchief, and went back to the grave and put the head on with a little sawdust over the neck. Tom Parker then went down to the public-house and faced the mob. Tom made a speech and said : ' Now this 'eer beadle says the woman was brought from St. Thomas's Hospital without her head. Now I mean to say that the beadle is drunk, and I insist that all the people here come to the grave and see for themselves.' Away the crowd went, and the woman, sure enough, had a head on, and he turned the tables upon the beadle."

It is not really of much consequence who was the actual assistant at the Thistlewood executions, but, as a matter of historical probability, the exploit rests with Tom Parker. It had evidently got abroad somehow that the Graingers' School was represented on the scaffold, some gossip from the dissecting-room having oozed out. Grainger himself was accused

D

and Wakley, an enthusiastic student, as we have already seen, of the Webb Street School, shared the same ill-fortune. The Government probably applied to Edward Grainger for assistance in a practical difficulty. The authorities could not find a man capable of performing the decapitations with dexterity, and Grainger nominated his dissecting-room porter. Is it a very wild fancy to imagine Tom Parker first waxing wise and important when rumour was busy with the name of the masked man, and allowing that, an' he would he could a tale unfold, and then shirking the confession he half desired to make and thrusting what would have seemed fame in his eyes upon his employers?

CHAPTER VI

[1820–1821]

The Effects of the Assault—The Attitude of the Hope Fire Assurance Company—Mr. William Gardiner's Pamphlet—Sworn Testimony of Eye-witnesses.

WAKLEY'S bodily condition would seem to have been pessimistically described by the "Morning Chronicle," as he was able on the morning following the injury to go to Kensington, where his wife was staying with certain members of her family.   This he did that he should be the first person to inform her that her husband was out of danger, while breaking to her the news that their home was destroyed.   His comparatively light escape was due to no want of will on the part of his assailant or assailants, but to the fortunate accident of his having placed a bandage round his head and receiving upon that protective material the blow that was so deadly in intent.   That he was stunned by the blow was also fortunate, as it prevented further injuries to his person from being inflicted with the vigour that would have inspired them had they been dealt out to a struggling man capable of resistance and of calling for help.   Then it would have been necessary for the assailants to silence him at all risks ; but as he lay inanimate and to all appearance dead the stabs and kicks were not given with whole-hearted fervour.   It requires more than ordinary callous determination to finish off an unresisting foe, and the further attacks of the ruffians, after the first stunning blow, seem to have been perfunctory.   But if his bodily ills were not as severe as first appeared, the shock that he had received . mentally

was unmistakable. Of nothing are we more assured concerning Wakley than that his personal courage was great.
Strong, hardy, healthy, and athletic, he was by physique
and temperament the very type of the man to whom
nervous terror should never come. Yet it came now, and
came in exacerbated form. He seems to have been thrown
off his balance by the horror of the attack, by the malignity
that had dictated it, and by the dread lest his foes should
even now not be satisfied, but should be following him up
with intent to carry out their extreme threats. His behaviour when beneath the roof of his opposite neighbour,
Mr. Samuel Parker, whose account of the night's work has
been preserved in the form of an affidavit, had every distinguishing mark of real and very present fear. He was
wild, excited, and stupid by turns. Home gone, practice
gone, property gone, and all in a few brief moments ; while
he had still to dread for himself and perhaps for his young
wife that the blind savagery that had instigated the attack
on his life might repeat itself at any moment. He was for a
short time at the very limits of his self-control, which is a
more terrible plight for a strong, usually calm, and reticent
man than for pliable and hysterical subjects. Undoubtedly
at this period he wanted cool and keen-sighted friends
badly, for without dispassionate advice his grief, anger, and
fear might have prompted him to actions that later he would
have regretted. Such friends he found in his solicitors,
Messrs. Pownall and Fairthorne, and in Mr. Matthew Lofty,
who was then assisting in the firm, and shortly afterwards
became a partner.*

The first step to be taken was clearly to give notice to
the fire assurance company of the loss that had been sustained. This having been done the Hope Fire Assurance

* Seventy-five years ago Thomas Wakley applied to this firm for
legal assistance, one of the then partners being his cousin. They
advised him then, and their descendants continued to advise him,
through a career in which lawyers' help was often necessary ; and the
same firm (now Messrs. Potter, Sandford, and Kilvington) to this day
remain the legal advisers of the " Lancet."

Company refused to pay, and intimated their intention of resisting the claim. Messrs. Pownall and Fairthorne at once took the matter up and advised Wakley to enforce the whole claim, and not to hear of compromise, for they saw that in such a course lay his only chance of public rehabilitation. Nothing definite was alleged against him, but the action of the company could have but one interpretation : it was intended to intimate that he was responsible for his own misfortunes. So a writ was issued against the directors with a claim for the total amount insured. Unfortunately for the plaintiff their reluctance to pay leaked out, and forthwith rumour stalked through the city in true Virgilian style. Some said that Wakley had burned down his own house. These ridiculed the idea that he was the victim of a plot on the part of the Thistlewood gang to assassinate him. Others spread the story that he had been the masked man on the scaffold at the execution of Thistlewood and his co-conspirators, furnishing by their imaginings an excellent motive for the incendiary attack that other gossips found never to have taken place. Wakley's name was in all men's mouths associated with one lie or the other. Undoubtedly he had enemies, for the persistent manner in which he was maligned will allow of no other interpretation, but their motives and their persons remain equally unknown. At this juncture a certain Mr. William Gardiner came to his aid. Gardiner was a journalist, a teacher of elocution, and a queer enthusiast with a passion for justice and a sentimental desire to see it done quickly to all his fellow-citizens. Hearing the rumours that were busy against Wakley, and concluding that they were wholly and cruelly untrue, he wrote to offer his assistance in the preparation for public circulation of a statement of all the events connected with the assault and the fire. He had a relative in the publishing trade, which made it easier for him to ensure the prompt issue of such a work. The offer was gratefully accepted by Wakley, who saw in it a very fortunate supplementing of the legal proceedings that had been instituted. For although no unnecessary delay was to take place in the prosecution of the recalcitrant company, some lapse of time there was bound to be before a jury's verdict would silence his slanderers, and during that time the uncontradicted rumours grew daily in virulence and wildness. Gardiner was a prompt man. Immediately upon receiving Wakley's letter approving of the idea he set to work, and the result was the publication at the end of September, 1820, of a pamphlet entitled " Facts relative to the Late Fire and Attempt to Murder Mr. Wakley in Argyll Street, by William Gardiner, author of Wortley, A New System of Shorthand, Poems, &c., London : T. Gardiner and Son, Princes Street, Cavendish Square ; Sherwood, Neeley, and jones, Paternoster Row ; and sold by all other booksellers. 1820. Price 1s." The pamphlet had an astonishing fore-word from the author's pen moulded on the style of the reforming divines. " That unglutted fiend," he said in respect of scandal, " whose appetite unsatiated with the destruction of a man's property must riot on his peace, and rifle the flower reputation from his brow." And again : " The viper Slander, whose venomed shape is matured in human distress, has lifted her hideous head, and, flattered by the misery of its victim, charges him with being the incendiary in order to compleat the sacrifice of his ruin." He concluded as follows : " The author, who well knows the purity of the sufferer's heart, contrary to his own wishes, for he, proudly feeling the *mens conscia recti* like the eagle on the rock, smiles at the malice of the storm, has, with the consent of his other friends, collected all the known facts of this horrible but mysterious transaction. He has principally sought the testimony of gentlemen whose rank in life lifts them above the suspicion of partiality. The task is completed without exaggeration or extortion, it is delivered fairly as received, and the public have only to peruse the same to rectify the delusion caused by the rapid and foul propagation of slander."

Following upon his enthusiastic preface Gardiner printed sworn statements as to the events of the night from Wakley himself and from all the eye-witnesses whose evidence he could obtain. He received affidavits from Mr. George Thompson, the proprietor of Wakley's house, No. 5, Argyll Street, and occupier of No. 6, Argyll Street, which stood between Lord Aberdeen's house and Wakley's; from Mr. Samuel Parker and Mr. Robert Campbell, the occupants respectively of 35 and 36, Argyll Street, the houses directly opposite Wakley's; from Mr. Campbell's butler; from Wakley's own servants; from the servants at No. 9, Argyll Street; from the medical men who attended Wakley for his wounds; and from Mr. Fairthorne and Mr. Matthew Lofty, referred to before. Wakley's deposition is given below in full. It is a history of the night's occurrences written out by himself at the time, and is nearly identical in many respects with the account given in the "Morning Chronicle."

DEPOSITION OF MR. WAKLEY RESPECTING THE MUR-DEROUS ATTACK MADE UPON HIM ON THE NIGHT OF THE 26TH OF AUGUST LAST.

(Printed in Gardiner's Pamphlet.)

Having applied two leeches to my temples in consequence of dimness of sight, and the leeches not readily taking, I was kept up till the late period of half-after 12 o'clock. About this time, when preparing for bed, I heard a knocking at the front door, upon which I lighted the candle in my bed candle-stick, placed it on the seat in the passage, and at the same time took out of it the key of the door, which I then unlocked and unbolted, demanding "Who is there?" A person answered, "I am come, sir, from Mr. Ivatts of Gerard's Hall, who is very ill, and wishes you to go immediately to see him." Having attended to Mr. Ivatts repeatedly for the last five* years I had no apprehension of danger, consequently took off the door-chain and let the man into the passage. I replied to him that "I was very sorry I could not go to see Mr. Ivatts then, being myself very unwell, but would endeavour to do so in the morning." Upon this the person said, "If your servants are not gone to bed, sir, I should be glad with a glass of something to drink, having walked very fast to your house." I told him "My servants are gone to bed, but I will get you something

---

* It was not unusual in those days for an unqualified man to have regular patients. Wakley had no surgical diploma in 1815, but he had been for three years apprenticed to medical men, and had also resided with an apothecary.

myself," asking him which he preferred, beer or cider? Choosing the latter, I took the candle from the seat in the passage (the place being sufficiently lighted for the man's accommodation by the candles in the parlour, as the door was open) and went into the dining-room to the cupboard for the key of the cider. I then went down to the kitchen to get a jug; but, not finding one, returned to the footman's pantry, where, having obtained it, I proceeded to the cellar in the back court or area and drew the cider. On my return into the passage, between the clock and the court door, and near to the foot of the stairs, I was knocked down by a blow from behind upon the upper part of the right side of my head. Whilst on the ground I received several kicks on different parts of my body, and believe that I heard voices near me, but to this I cannot swear, being at the time in such a stupefied state. When on the ground I also had inflicted on my chest two slight stabs. I cannot say how long I remained in a state of insensibility, but at length got sufficiently recovered to find that I was enveloped in flames and a suffocating smoke. I attempted to stand, but was prevented from weakness. I then crawled from the horrible danger that surrounded me into the back kitchen, where I again relapsed into a state of torpor, but presently awoke, and perceived with horror through the skylight flames issuing from all the back windows of the house. I advanced a few steps, but found in the back court a great quantity of burning pieces of wood, so by this way I had no hope of escape. The heat was intense and the smoke insufferable. My situation cannot be described; it was the very climax of horror. In my delirium I ran to the pump in order to prevent the lead which was above me from melting, as I feared it would do so, and fall in a fluid state upon my head; but finding myself nearly suffocated I miraculously hit upon the expedient of getting on a fire-screen, by which means I was enabled to get hold of a beam under the skylight. I then broke the glass and got through, passed over the leads and fence-wall between Mr. Thompson's house and mine, and went from thence into Mr. T.'s residence. About five weeks subsequent to my marriage I received an anonymous letter stating that my house would be burnt within a month, and that jealousy was the cause. About three months after the first a second letter was conveyed to me. It said, " You are not yet forgotten; your house will yet be burnt and you assassinated." The person who called was a dark-complexioned man about 5 feet 8 inches in height, with black hair growing low upon his forehead, and habited in a black coat and waist-coat, with a coloured neck handkerchief tied high over his chin, as if he had a sore throat.

(Signed)   THOMAS WAKLEY.

N.B.—From what has transpired since the fire I have every reason to suppose from the deposition of Mr. Green's servants that this attack

was made on me by some abandoned wretches who imagined I had
beheaded the traitors, and that the party had no connexion with the
writer of the anonymous letters.

Of the remaining depositions save in two cases only the
gist need be given, for the writers are a little voluminous, and
the excellent Gardiner—not a judge summing-up but an
advocate pleading—has evidently not exercised any supervision over them. The various persons deposed to what
they thought important, and he has reproduced their statements exactly as they swore to them, which was by far the
safest and most honest procedure. Mr. George Thompson,
Wakley's neighbour and landlord, confirmed his tenant's
statements in every detail where the facts had come under
his observation.

DEPOSITION OF GEORGE THOMPSON, ESQ., FREEHOLDER AND PROPRIETOR OF MR. WAKLEY'S HOUSE, NO. 6, ARGYLL STREET, AND LIVING AT NO. 5, SAME STREET.

(Printed in Gardiner's Pamphlet.)

I, George Thompson, being alarmed by the watchman's knocking at
the door between one and two o'clock on Sunday morning, the 27th
August last, drest myself with precipitation and ran into the street,
when I perceived Mr. Wakley's house, the premises adjoining mine, to
be on fire and the front door open. When I immediately returned to
my own house to endeavour to preserve my property, and exclaimed
to Mrs. Thompson, " I am afraid poor Mr. and Mrs. Wakley cannot
escape." About three-quarters of an hour after this period I perceived
Mr. Wakley at my parlour door in the passage in a state of exhaustion,
covered with blood and dirt, whom I led into the room and gave some
wine and water, which seemed a little to recover him, for he appeared
as one lost in misery and distraction. Mr. Parker, of 35 in the same
street, being with me to assist in the removal of my furniture, I exclaimed, " For God's sake, Mr. Parker, take care of Mr. Wakley and
never mind my house." They both then got over to Mr. Parker's
house, where Mr. Wakley was put to bed. The deponent then called
on Dr. Luke, requesting him to go to Mr. Parker's house and see what
assistance he could render Mr. Wakley. About four o'clock in the
morning, when the roof of Mr. Wakley's house had fallen in and I was
convinced my premises were safe, I went over to Mr. Parker's to

inquire after Mr. Wakley, who then informed me that he had been knocked down at the bottom of his own kitchen-stairs by some person or persons unknown, and when recovered from the effects of the blow, and finding himself surrounded by flames, he crawled into the back kitchen and made his escape through the skylight to the yard, and climbed over the fence-wall that divided our premises and entered into my house about the time I found him. On my return from Mr. Parker's I examined the skylight on Mr. Wakley's premises and found it broken exactly as he had described it, and, further, the marks of his feet and knees were visible on the side of the fence-wall, where he had crawled down on my premises.

(Signed)   GEORGE THOMPSON,

No. 6, Argyll Street.

(Witness) MARY HART,
September 23rd, 1820.

The deposition of Mr. Samuel Parker, Wakley's opposite neighbour, speaks to the pitiable plight in which Wakley appeared to be, both mentally and physically, when he was brought to No. 35, Argyll Street. He details the curious incident of the robbery from Wakley of his watch as he was being helped across the road, this being the occurrence to which Sheriff Parkins referred in his letter to Wakley concerning the Thistlewood executions.

DEPOSITION OF SAMUEL PARKER, ESQ.,

35, ARGYLL STREET.

(Printed in Gardiner's Pamphlet.)

About half-past one o'clock on the Sunday morning, the 27th August last, I was awakened by the springing of the watchman's rattle, a loud knocking at my door, and the cry of fire. On looking out of my window the chimneys of Mr. Wakley's house were smoking. Before I had dressed the flames gushed out of the two parlour windows, and shortly after at the street-door. I went immediately over to Mr. Thompson's, next door to Mr. Wakley's, to assist him in securing the valuable part of his property; when this was nearly effected I was informed that Mr. Wakley had not been seen, and had most probably perished. I accompanied Mr. Thompson, jun., to the top of his house. We called out there at all the windows and the upper back-leads in hopes of Mr. Wakley hearing us. When we descended I parted from Mr. Thompson, jun., in the back passage of his father's house, and I found

Mr. Wakley, I believe, supported by Mr. Thompson, sen. Mr. T. requested me to take care of him and pay no further regard to his property. Mr. Wakley was in a most dreadful state; his senses were obviously deranged, and the horror and dread he exhibited, imagining all around him to be the murderers, were excessive. He had shiver-ings, or rather tremblings, apparently the effect of mental horror, as they were accompanied with gestures and clenching of his hands which caused me to hold him firmly, lest I should suffer violence; a profuse perspiration covered his face and he showed symptoms of great agony. His hands, face, shirt, and cravat were much covered with blood and dirt, and the blood gushed from his left ear and trickled down his neck. One of Mr. Thompson's servants brought some water, which he drank greedily, and with great difficulty I restrained him from drinking of it too copiously. I then washed his face and hands, when he became more composed. On repeated questions as to the cause of his present state his only answer was, " It is murder, sir," and, in great horror and mental suffering, added, " I will tell you all soon." He continually asked, " Am I safe; where am I ? " Mr. Wakley now became more calm, but being greatly annoyed by persons passing and repassing I determined to take him over to my house; after going down the street, just at my door we were surrounded by a gang of pickpockets, one of whom Mr. Wakley saw pull his watch from his pocket, who, enraged at this act of villainy, collared the thief, who offered no resistance, and the officers coming up they took him from his grasp. I did not believe Mr. Wakley had lost anything and supposed his expressions had pro-ceeded from a return of his insanity; but upon my servant finding the watch upon the ground, which the thief had dropped, my fears were happily removed. This last effort quite overcame him, and he fell down exhausted on my hall seat; I gave him some more water and loosened his neckcloth, when a medical gentleman came to my relief and requested him to be put to bed; on the stairs he was seized with violent vomitings, and with great difficulty we got him to a chamber, where we put him to bed. Mr. Wakley's body was covered with numerous bruises or kicks, and I discovered two stabs, one on his chest and the other on his side; he recollected nothing of these, but expressed great horror at the remembrance of the kicks on his body and stomach. His sickness again returned, and was perhaps increased by the unfortunate circumstance of my servant, by mistake, having given him a cup of lamp oil instead of water, which Mr. Wakley drank off, and a little after complained the water was oily. Dr. Luke, who shortly after visited him, sent him a bottle of cider, which together with some medicine administered by Dr. Cates greatly relieved him. Both these gentlemen requested no person should be admitted into his chamber; but Mr. W.'s man-servant, who had heard his master was at Parker's, did go in, when his expressions of joy and gratitude for his master's safety were for some time too powerful for Mr. Wakley's feelings. It was about nine in the morning before Mr. W. seemed inclined to sleep, when I told him I should leave the room in hopes he could compose himself, but unknown to him I remained, judging it not right to leave him in such a state; he fell asleep, but it was agitated and broken, and he frequently exclaimed, in great agony of mind, "Save me from them, save me from them." Dr. Luke promised in the morning to take Mr. W., if he were able to go, in his carriage to Kensington, to Mrs. W., as Mr. Wakley was fearful what the consequences might be if she heard the dismal intelligence except from his own lips; myself and Dr. Luke accompanied him thither in the afternoon.

(Signed) SAMUEL PARKER.

(Witness) CHARLES PARKER.
Dated the 23rd September, 1820.

To the other depositions contained in Mr. Gardiner's pamphlet only the briefest reference need be made. Wakley's servants deposed to the fact that being awakened by the noise of the watchman giving the alarm they called out to their master and obtained no response. The housekeeper said that she found the front door unfastened, bearing out Wakley's statement that he had unlocked and unbolted it to admit the unknown bearer of the lying message—for there proved to be nothing whatever the matter with Mr. Ivatts of Gerard's Hall, who had sent no message to Wakley. Mr. Campbell, who lived opposite, and his butler, both of whom were aroused by the noise without, saw a man with a bundle under his arm run down the street into Argyll Place. The butler, who was earlier on the scene, was able to see that the man had emerged from No. 5, while he also noticed a hackney coach waiting in the street, the driver being apparently unperturbed at the conflagration which had by that time taken hold of the premises. These depositions almost established the theory of a planned robbery. The servants at No. 9, Argyll Street deposed to having heard from their area steps a group of three men, who were, like themselves, watching the fire, break out into frequent expletives signifying joy at the sight of the flames and hatred of Wakley. Their exact and ferocious expressions were deposed to on oath, and, if they did not proceed from the mouths of the guilty ruffians, still served to corroborate the undoubted fact that Wakley was a bitterly hated man by a certain set of un-principled fellows. The medical evidence was also in support of Wakley's statement. Dr. Luke referred Mr. Gardiner to the account in the " Morning Chronicle " (which has been quoted above and which, with some trifling discre-pancies, tallies entirely with Wakley's deposition) " for all facts that came to his knowledge." Mr. Cates testified to the violence of the assault that had been made. Mr. Fairthorne and Mr. Lofty deposed to the facts that Wakley had received anonymous letters threatening to burn down his house, and that they advised him to increase the insurance upon the premises and contents, which with reluctance he consented to do.

CHAPTER VII

[1821–1823]

The Action against the Hope Fire Assurance Company : Statement of Wakley's Claim—Clothes and Furniture in the Twenties—Payment in Full of Wakley's Demands—Effects on his Future of the Outrages in Argyll Street—An Unsettled Period—The Friendship of William Cobbett—The Inception of the " Lancet."

ON June 21st, 1821, the trial of the action of Wakley *v.* Barron and others, being an action to enforce payment of a claim for loss by fire upon a policy underwritten by the defendants in their capacity of directors of the Hope Fire Assurance Company, was commenced in the Court of King's Bench before Lord Chief Justice Abbott, afterwards Lord Tenterden. Wakley's claim in detail was set out under the following heads : Household goods, linen, wearing apparel, wines and liquors, printed books, and plate in his dwelling-house, £990 ; fixtures, £60 ; china and glass, £150—a total sum of £1200. Mr. Denman (afterwards Lord Chief Justice Denman), Mr. Curwood, and Mr. Adolphus were counsel for the plaintiff, while Mr. Marryat, Mr. Gurney, and Mr. F. Pollock (afterwards Chief Baron Pollock) were entrusted with the defence. Mr. Denman opened the case on the lines indicated by the depositions contained in Gardiner's pamphlet. He pointed out that the plaintiff was a young and successful man, the son of one wealthy man and the son-in-law of another, so that he could not be reasonably supposed to be in urgent want of ready money. Yet no other motive could have been present, supposing him to have burned down his own house, for with his house and surgery went not only his practice but goods to the extent of £400 in excess of the sum for which he was insured—the smallest estimate of Wakley's loss being £1600, while the terms of his policy only allowed him to claim £1200. Counsel explained the doubling of the sum insured—which until May, 1820, had been only £600—at so short a period before the fire by pointing out that the increase was due to his client's marriage. Just before that event Wakley had purchased furniture, plate, and china, and largely increased his wardrobe, while his wife had brought with her a great quantity of household linen, clothes, and other personal effects. Mr. Denman then read Wakley's affidavit as to what had occurred on the evening of the fire, which was practically identical with his deposition in Gardiner's pamphlet. He concluded his opening speech, which was recognised in legal circles at the time as a convincing piece of pleading, by saying that this affidavit, extraordinary as many of its details must appear, could not have been invented by the plaintiff for any motive ; therefore the jury should receive it as a statement of the facts. The defendants, as trustees for others, must not be "discommended" for resisting the plaintiff's claim until the transaction was fairly and candidly sifted to the bottom. As, however, he was able to prove every word of his opening statement he anticipated with confidence a verdict in his client's favour.

Mr. George Thompson, Mr. Samuel Parker, and Wakley's two servants were then called. Their evidence was practically in accord with their depositions in Gardiner's pamphlet, and remained unshaken upon cross-examination. It should be remembered that the plaintiff himself in the year 1821 was not able to go into the witness-box on his own behalf, otherwise this elaborate support of Wakley's affidavit would not perhaps have been needed.

Three very important witnesses were then called. Mr. Joseph Ashelford, an upholsterer, swore that the value of the furniture in 5, Argyll Street, a house, by the way, with a rental of £140, was £735. This does not seem a disproportionate sum when it is remembered that a rental of £140 in those days would be equivalent to one of £300 now, that the house was by no means small, and that much of its furniture had been purchased with the view of fitting it out for the reception of a bride—a period when some lavishness of expenditure is the universal rule. Mr. Samuel Malleson, from whom Wakley purchased the practice in Argyll Street and certain furniture, testified to the fact that the practice, when he was obliged through ill-health to sell it, was worth about £700 per annum. He had actually received £690 during the year 1818, his last year in full work and when he was already failing in health, this sum being exclusive of book debts. During the first seven months of 1819, the seven months preceding the transfer of the practice to Wakley, £560 had been received. Archdeacon Woollaston, the previous tenant of 5, Argyll Street, testified. that he had sold certain furniture in Argyll Street for £300 to the plaintiff. Mr. Goodchild, the plaintiff's father-in-law, proved that he had given his daughter a trousseau of the value of £300 on her marriage. Certain patients were called to prove that Wakley had a good practice, as good as, or better than, his predecessor's connexion, and could have been in no want of ready money as they actually were his debtors for attendances the accounts for which had not been rendered to them. A few of his personal friends and acquaintances testified to the fact that the house was handsomely furnished, and that marked additions to its contents were made at the time of the marriage. There was, in fact, general evidence that the young couple had started housekeeping with a profusion of plate, glass, and linen in a comfortable, and even luxurious, home.

A statement was then made showing that the plaintiff had lost over £1600 in goods, vouchers for £1050 being forthcoming. The prices of some of the goods, as valued for Wakley by his solicitors, make curious reading nowadays, and certain of the articles of attire take us straight back to the heroes and heroines of " Emma " or " Pride and Prejudice." A handsome 6ft. by 7ft. bedstead with mahogany carved and panelled feet, pillars, and brass castors ; handsome chintz furniture with French draperies, lined with pink

silk fringe, &c., new (£47 2s. 11d.), give an old-world flavour
to the catalogue; and this sumptuous couch had further
attached to it a straw palliasse (£2 10s.), a brocaded wool
mattress in a brown holland case, ticked border (£6 6s.),
and a prime goose-feather bed in a bordered tick and bolster
and two pillows (£16 16s.). Seventy pounds in all for the bed
in the front bedroom! Ten imitation rosewood cane-seat
chairs with brass ornaments (£12 10s.) and ten horsehair
cushions the same (£4 10s.), make us shudder a little for the
prevalent taste in drawing-room upholstery; but a handsome
polished steel fender and fire-irons (£12 12s.) remind us
that if our ancestors paid heavily for the equipment of their
fire-places they obtained in return beautiful and lasting
metal-work. A dozen forks and spoons priced at 28 guineas
serve to remind us that silver was of account in those days,
but four silver candlesticks at £17 16s. might be a bargain at
the price at the present moment, so beautiful was some of
the more elaborate Georgian plate. The list of books that
were burnt is interesting, as showing the bent of their
owners' minds and also the fashion of the day with regard
to gift-books. To Mrs. Wakley must be attributed a distinct
taste for verse, for it was assuredly she who sustained the
loss of Bloomfield's, Campbell's, Parnell's, Akenside's, Rowe's,
Montgomery's, Shenstone's, Collins's, and "A Lady's" poems.
The poems of Shakespeare, Burns, Milton, and Keats were
probably her husband's, as certainly were "The Automaton
Chess Games," "The Chess-player," "The Letters of junius,"
Count Volney's "Ruins," the works of Cicero, and "The
Castle of Otranto." Wakley's medical library was a large
one for the time, for in 1820 there were not special mono-
graphs by numerous authors on every subject. He seems to
have possessed many of the standard medical works of the
day, and the total value of books destroyed by the fire was
a little over £100. The wardrobe of the young couple was
extensive. Wakley, who was all his life from youth upward
a remarkably well-dressed man, had twenty pairs of trousers
of various sorts, including nankeens and Russian ducks;
and among other quaint articles of attire whose loss he

E

laments are six pairs of black silk gloves, eight purple silk handkerchiefs and seven green silk ! Mrs. Wakley's clothes were on a still more lavish scale. We find enumerated thirty-three dresses, *lingerie* in profusion, and quantities of lace, ribbons, shawls, and kerchiefs. A long embroidered white scarf is the identical article of attire without which the young woman in the steel frontispiece to the gift-books of the day was never depicted, but what a pair of purple morocco boots were like imagination fails to tell. Nor can we now clearly understand why the fantastic foot-gear should be only 12s. and the reasonable wrap £7 10s. The value of Wakley's clothes is set down in the statement of claim as £144 7s. 6d. and that of his wife's at £346 17s. The £1600, which the plaintiff claimed to have lost, was made up in the following way :—Furniture £735 8s. 11d.; plate, £168 10s. 6d.; linen, £101 11s.; books, £104 3s. 6d.; china, and glass, £163 14s. 2d.; Wakley's wardrobe, £144 7s. 6d.; and Mrs. Wakley's wardrobe, £346 17s.; making in all a total of £1764 12s. 7d. From this £100 was deducted as the estimated value of the salvage. None of the plaintiff's witnesses were seriously cross-examined, and hardly an attempt was made to shake the jury's confidence in either their good faith or veracity.

The line of the defence was that the claim was a fraud, and that goods to the value specified had not been lost ; but the suggestion that the house had been fired by any of its inhabitants was not hinted at. As a matter of fact this silly rumour had been so overwhelmingly refuted by Gardiner's pamphlet that the Hope Fire Assurance Company did not dare to put it forward in court, though they had used it as an argument wherewith to intimidate Wakley. The first witness for the defendant was a watchman, who stated that he was at the door of the house when the servants came out, and that he heard the bolt being withdrawn before the door was opened. This evidence was meant to contradict Wakley's story that he had opened the door to a false messenger from Gerard's Hall, and that being struck down at once he lay unconscious and could not have closed it again. It would also to a certain extent have disproved the theory that some of the property described by Wakley as having been in the house had been removed by a robber or robbers. The tendency of this evidence, so directly at variance with Wakley's statement and the sworn testimony of four of his witnesses—namely, his two servants and Mr. Thompson and Mr. Parker—was to incriminate the servants, a side issue which, in view of the fact that they bore excellent characters and were still in Wakley's service, was pursued no further. The result of the evidence was to convict the watchman of not having watched. A Bow Street officer deposed to having taken down from Wakley's mouth a statement of the events of the night, and to having since received the blood-stained clothes that the plaintiff was wearing at the time of his escape from the burning house. The witness's examination was conducted with the assistance of a dummy attired in Wakley's clothes, the intent being to show that the cuts in the shirt, coat, and waistcoat did not tally with the cuts in the skin; but the evidence broke down under cross-examination. The only part of the Bow Street officer's testimony that really remained unrebutted was a repetition of Wakley's sworn statement, a more remarkable case of a witness being called to curse and remaining to bless not being often seen. The head fireman of the Hope Fire Assurance Company and one of the appraisers testified that they were unable to find traces of certain properties which were alleged in the plaintiff's statement of claim to have been present in the house at the time of the fire and which were from their nature more or less imperishable, and insinuated that some of the articles found had been overcharged against the company. Dr. Luke, who saw Wakley after he had been conveyed across Argyll Street, deposed that the wounds could not have bled much, and would not have accounted for all the discoloration on his shirt. Some evidence as to the value of Mr. Samuel Malleson's furniture was also given by the owner of a house in Mill Street, where Malleson had resided while in practice, and whence certain of his furniture was transferred to Argyll Street when Wakley bought the practice. It appeared that a man had rented the house after Malleson had left, and that he, too, in his turn had gone, but had omitted to pay the rent. The owner of the house had therefore distrained, and the broker through whom the distraint was made swore that he could only find £20 worth of furniture in the house. As it turned out, however, on cross-examination that the distraint was made after Wakley had removed some or all of the goods that he had bought into his new house, the evidence went for less than nothing.

Mr. Parker was then recalled, and proved that the plaintiff's hands were severely cut when he was brought into the house, and that the hæmorrhage from these cuts might easily have caused the excessive staining of the shirt that puzzled Dr. Luke ; in making which point he incidentally confirmed Wakley's story that he had been compelled to break his way out of the burning building through a skylight.

The Lord Chief Justice summed up entirely in Wakley's favour, and the jury, after a delay of under half-an-hour, found for the plaintiff, damages £1200, or the full amount that he was able to claim under the terms of his policy. He also obtained his costs, which amounted to a sum of £281 10s., and further costs not covered by that sum were defrayed by public subscription, to which one, at least, of the jurymen subscribed, as well as the son of one of the auditors of the Hope Fire Assurance Company.*

Such was the satisfactory termination of a trial upon the issue of which hung the reputation and fortune of Thomas

---

* The " Record " in this action, consisting of many skins of parch-ment, on the back of the last of which was endorsed the " Postea," signed by the proper officer of the court, and constituting the official statement of the result of the trial, has been placed at the author's disposal by Messrs. Potter, Sandford and Kilvington. Mr. Serjeant Ballantyne, in " Some Experiences of a Barrister's Life," states that Wakley's damages were not paid, and that his action was against the County Fire Office. Each statement is completely inaccurate.

Wakley. He was paid in full, his name was cleared of the aspersions that had been showered upon it, while the public subscription to meet such of his costs as would otherwise have fallen upon himself constituted a public apology for the wrong that had been done him by rumour. But if the actual proceedings were now stayed, if his pecuniary loss was reduced to a small sum and his good repute before all men restored to him, the effects of the terrible experiences of the past ten months yet remained. And not only did they remain, but they changed the tenour of his life, forming the sharp stimulus that pricked him from the regular routine of the life of a general practitioner into a course of more free and individual assertion. He had been personally attacked, he had won, and a spirit of combat had been roused. During his time of trial he had found his friends staunch and his professional brethren ready to repudiate for him the hard and evil things that were said of him. But when the strife of battle was over it left him an unsettled man, and though there was nothing shiftless about his hesitation to embark again in private practice, surely there was nothing hard to comprehend. He had prepared all things to live the life of a general practitioner of medicine. He had chosen his locality, and furnished his house to that end. Through no fault of his own the house had been destroyed, while ten months' neglect of his practice had severed his connexion with his patients. It was necessary for him to start entirely afresh, and his reluctance was only natural. What had been done a few months ago with the ardent solicitude of a young husband had now to be done over again by a disappointed man, who, though successful in obtaining his rights in a law court, had none the less been treated with physical and moral savagery, and had lain under undeserved stigma at the moment when he was most in need of sympathy. He was some months in settling down, during which time his letters were dated from such different parts of London as Kentish Town, Hatton Garden, and Little Chelsea, which was a colloquial name for the southern part of Brompton. He was at this time a poor man. He had little or no income. It is true he had £1200, but it was necessary that he should reserve that sum, or as much of it as he was able, with a view to purchase a new practice and furnish another home. And in taking these steps he had more than ordinary reasons to be cautious. His father-in-law was a generous man and had stood by Wakley in his troubles well, but he was none the less a business man, and he resented the disappearance of the Argyll Street practice. He was just enough not to actually blame his son-in-law for the results of pure misfortune, but an able-bodied man out of employ was a sight that jarred on all his commercial instincts. Relations became strained between them, for which reason Wakley felt that it was necessary that his next start should lead straight to success. Failure would not be condoned a second time. And this feeling of responsibility led to the months of hesitation.

It was during this uncomfortable period of his life that Wakley made the acquaintance of, and matured a friendship with a man who was shortly to assist him in starting the work which afterwards became the chief business of his life —the work of medical reform. The link that bound William Cobbett and Thomas Wakley together originally was a quaint one. The Cato Street Conspiracy was a subject upon which all the papers in London wrote, and wrote persistently, and Wakley's name occurred more than once in the character of a victim to the blind brutality of Thistlewood's followers. Now it happened that William Cobbett, editor of the "Weekly Political Register" and the "Evening Post," and accepted Parliamentary candidate for Coventry, firmly believed that he, too, had been destined to be a victim to this gang. He may himself have felt conscious of what many even among his admirers knew, that his Radicalism was more fervent in expression than thorough-going in policy, and he may have, therefore, suspected that his academic declamations of socialism would be more likely to irritate the mere ruffianly mob than would the declared opposition of a Tory. But for this reason or that Cobbett believed that the Cato Street conspirators had designs upon his life, and his belief, upon which he founded several articles in his evening paper, led him to make himself known to Wakley, a man in the same plight. Cobbett was exactly the man to make an impression upon Wakley, who, though not likely to be a blind follower of any leader, was receptive and ever willing to learn. He was thirty years Wakley's senior, and had a life of chequered experiences behind him, having been gardener, private soldier, tutor in France and the United States, political pamphleteer and refugee, bookseller, and Radical journalist. He was an eloquent propagandist and a practical man in spite of the violent character of some of his political writing. In Cobbett's company Wakley met other journalists and men of the reforming type, and he saw how instinctively these men turned to pen and ink for the redress of any wrong. The acquaintanceship thus made ripened into a friendship which never waned, and there can be no doubt that Cobbett's friendship and example counted for much in Wakley's resolution, so soon now to be taken, that he would set the medical profession aright by publishing wherein it was wrong. What the reform of the political electorate was to Cobbett's pen, the reform of the profession of medicine was to be to the younger man's pen.

Two uneventful years had to go by, however, before any vague ideas that might already be in his head took definite shape. During these two years he practised his profession. After desultory work here and there in the localities already mentioned, he at last settled in practice at the north-east corner of Norfolk Street, Strand, where a good opportunity seemed to him to exist for making a lucrative livelihood. The practice was an old-established one, and the income good, but the class of patients was not the same as it had been in Argyll Street, nor was the neighbourhood so pleasant a one for residence. To Wakley these things did not matter so much as they did to his wife. He was satisfied to be doing good work, irrespectively of the class among whom it was done, and to be receiving enough money

through his labours to sustain his household.   But his wife
did not like Norfolk Street or the fact that her husband was
keeping a dispensary, and she urged him to leave, and even
to discontinue his profession if it were necessary for him to
pursue it under such disagreeable surroundings.   So in 1823
everything was ripe for the "Lancet."   Wakley had gone
through the fire of severe trials and had measured himself
with big men.   As a result he felt that there had grown up
within him the capacity to do bigger work than that upon
which he was employed.   His wife's desires for a change
ran side by side with his own inclinations.   The abuses that
Cobbett and his school were quick to spy out in the body
political, but not always quick to persuade other people to see,
were in the case of the medical profession bare to the casual
eye.   Nepotism was there rampant, ignorance was too often
exalted, and pecuniary traffic determined success.   The soul
of the reformer had always been in Wakley, and to set aright
these things he determined to take the field with a weekly
newspaper devoted to the interests of the medical profession.

CHAPTER VIII

[1823]

The " Lancet "—Its Purposes and Principles as revealed in the Original Preface—Contents of the First Number—The Promises of the Preface Fulfilled.

THE first number of the " Lancet " was issued on October 5th, 1823, which was a Sunday. It bore the imprint " Printed and published by G. L. Hutchinson, at the " Lancet " Office, 210, Strand, London, where all communications for the editor are requested to be addressed (post paid). This work is published at an early hour every Saturday morning, and sold by Knight and Lacey, Paternoster Row, and by all booksellers in the United Kingdom." It is a fact significant of the stormy career upon which the new paper at once embarked that the names of the printers and publishers were omitted from the imprints after the second number. The names reappear on the title-page to the second volume, and the connexion of the same agents with the paper is proved to be existent in 1825 by the unpleasant circumstance for them that they were made defendants in a case shortly to be mentioned and of the gravest importance not only to Wakley but to the literary world—the case of Abernethy *v.* Hutchinson, Knight and Lacey ; but the future defendants obviously did not seek from week to week any share in the notoriety that the " Lancet " rapidly began to enjoy. The editorial office at 210, Strand was a room in the printing establishment of Messrs. Hutchinson and Co., whose premises stood on the south side of the thoroughfare nearly opposite St. Clement Danes' Church, and consequently about fifty yards only from Wakley's private residence in Norfolk Street. From this it will be gathered that the true editorial office was Wakley's house, the address at 210, Strand, being only given to preserve for the editor some measure of anonymity.

The preface in which Wakley defines with boldness and some ingenuity his intentions in coming before the medical world with a new journal is given below. His boldness is shown in a manner which in these days it is hard to appreciate, for the vested interests upon which his prefatory words declared war have so long disappeared from the history of the profession that we can hardly realise that they ever had their monstrous being. .That the great hospitals of the metropolis were managed in the interests of a few rather than of the community at large seems to us now · incredible. Yet so it was. A few persons through interest or purchase obtained the appointments and became at once pledged to dispose of these appointments by similar methods when the time should arrive. The medical profession as a body were wronged by their leaders. They paid for general education and special instruction which they did not obtain ; they were examined under conditions which did not sift the grain from the chaff, so that the general intellectual status was perforce low ; and they had no voice in the election of the rulers who thus mismanaged their affairs and misappropriated their fees. The sinners, however, sat in high places and it required some boldness in an unknown young man to challenge their time-honoured methods. Wakley's ingenuity is shown by the temperate manner in which the war is declared and the large scope of the policy indicated. Not a word is said in abuse of persons flourishing under a corrupt system. Their words as theorists and their acts as clinicians are to be made public ; if they object it must be for interested reasons. But it is assumed that, being the men of distinguished light and leading that they should be, they can have no motive for desiring the shelter of the bushel ; while the publicity promised for them is not to satisfy any narrow curiosity, but to benefit the medical profession, and therefore the world at large, by furnishing an opportunity to the rank and file of that profession of remaining in intellectual touch with their leaders.

PREFACE TO NO. 1, VOLUME I., OF THE "LANCET."

(Reprinted in the second edition, but not in subsequent editions.)

" It has long been a subject of surprise and regret that in this extensive and intelligent community there has not hitherto existed a work which would convey to the Public, and to distant Practitioners as well as to Students in Medicine and Surgery, reports of the Metropolitan Hospital Lectures.

" Having for a considerable time past observed the great and increasing inquiries for such information, in a department of science so pre-eminently useful, we have been induced to offer to public notice a work calculated, as we conceive, to supply in the most ample manner whatever is valuable in these important branches of knowledge ; and as the Lectures of Sir Astley Cooper, on the theory and practice of Surgery, are probably the best of the kind delivered in Europe, we have commenced our undertaking with the introductory address of that distinguished professor given in the theatre at St. Thomas's Hospital on Wednesday evening last. The Course will be rendered complete in subsequent numbers.

' " In addition to Lectures, we propose giving under the head, Medical and Surgical Intelligence, a correct description of all the important Cases that may occur, whether in England or on any part of the civilised Continent.

" Although it is not intended to give graphic representations with each Number, yet we have made such arrangements with the most experienced draughtsmen as will enable us occasionally to do so, and in a manner, we trust, calculated to give universal satisfaction.

" The great advantage derivable from information of this description will, we hope, be sufficiently obvious to every one in the least degree conversant with medical knowledge ; any arguments therefore to prove these are unnecessary and we content ourselves by merely showing in what directions their utility will prove most active.—To the Medical and Surgical Practitioners of this City whose avocations prevent their personal attendance at the Hospitals—to Country Practitioners whose remoteness from the head-quarters, as it were, of scientific knowledge leaves them almost without the means of ascertaining its progress—to the numerous classes of Students whether here or in distant Universities—to Colonial Practitioners—and, finally, by adding to the stock of useful knowledge of every individual in these realms. In this attempt we are well aware that we shall be assailed by much *interested* opposition; but we will fearlessly discharge our duties, We hope the age of 'Mental Delusion' has passed and that mystery and concealment will no longer be encouraged. Indeed we trust that mystery and ignorance will shortly be considered synonymous. Ceremonies and signs have now lost their charms, hieroglyphics and gilded serpents their power to deceive. But for these it would be impossible to imagine how it happened that medical and dietetical knowledge, of all other the most calculated to benefit Man, should have been by him the most neglected. He studies with the greatest attention and assiduity the constitutions of his horses and dogs and learns all their peculiarities; whilst of the nature of his own he is totally uninformed and equally unskilled as regards his infant offspring. Yet a little reflection and application would enable him to avert from himself and family half the constitu-tional disorders which affect society; and in addition to these advan-tages, his acquirements in medical learning would furnish him with a test whereby he could detect and expose the impositions of ignorant practitioners."

The last paragraph of this preface conveys the real pur-pose of the new paper. The "Lancet" was devised to dis-seminate medical information primarily, and incidentally to make war upon the family intrigues and foolish nepotism that swayed the elections to lucrative posts in the metro-politan hospitals and medical corporations. A flooding light of publicity was to be let in upon hole-and-corner mischief in either class of institution. The spread of scien-tific knowledge was the first object of Wakley's paper, and he never lost sight of it; but the task of fighting the op-ponents of progress was so much more sensational in its developments that it necessarily attracted wider attention than his beneficent schemes for post-graduate education of the profession and for the amelioration of the educational condition of the student. Indeed, while he remained con-stant to his original design of supplying medical informa-tion, almost every passage in his life for the next ten years goes to prove that he considered himself to be under a mandate from the profession at large not only to keep them well posted in the scientific side of their work, but to see that the rights of the general body of practitioners were not infringed by a particular set of persons. This attitude it was that prompted him to violent attacks upon individuals; this it was that made him so intolerant to the contemporary medical press, which was written to please the eminent few rather than the profession at large ; and this it was that was responsible for all the good that arose, directly or in-directly, from the founding of the "Lancet," as it was responsible for certain errors of taste and judgment which marked the early career of the paper. An eloquent man of passionate convictions is not always prudent in balancing his phrases ; a young editor with a good cause and no one to supervise his manuscript is not always mincing in his epithets. There were things written in the early numbers of the "Lancet" that would not have appeared had the editor been a man of wider experience ; but the harm that they did was small and recoiled chiefly upon Wakley, who was never afraid to meet his liabilities, while the value of his fearlessness and ardour to the cause of reform was in-calculable.

The contents of the first number of the "Lancet" show how far the editor proposed to carry out the promises of his preface. A surgical lecture by Sir Astley Cooper, Sergeant-Surgeon to the King, occupied the place of honour. This lecture was preceded by a paragraph which gives us some idea of the position held by the eminent and eloquent surgeon at that time :—

' At half-past seven the Theatre (the theatre of St. Thomas's Hospi-tal) was crowded in every part by upwards of four hundred Students of the most respectable description ; in fact we never before witnessed so genteel a Surgical class: the sight was most pleasing, for they all appeared gentlemen of cultivated manners and good education."

A class of four hundred ! When it is remembered that all these students had paid fees of three guineas and upwards, and that the greater part of the money so collected belonged to the lecturer, it will be seen that a successful hospital lecturer occupied in those days a fine pecuniary position. And this fact explains both the eagerness of the senior men to be succeeded by their friends and their relations, and the righteousness of Wakley's contention that only the best men should hold such posts. The amiable reference to the demeanour of the audience emanated from a certain editorial prudence. The new journal was partly addressed to the students, and it was the design of its founder to make the grievances of this class a prominent feature in his arguments for medical reform, therefore it would be but ordinarily civil to put them in good conceit with themselves. The next article is headed " Politics," and its alternative title is " Enlightened Liverymen." It has no medical interest at all, but is a short display of Wakley's vehement and occasionally truculent literary style when dealing with those opposed to him in thought. Of the younger Pitt he speaks as follows :—

" His admirers, in rapture, called him a ' boy-statesman ' in his twenty-third year ; and in his forty-seventh year he was still the same ; still the official coxcomb, running after wild impracticable schemes, regardless of everything but the gratification of his own senseless, remorseless, and petty ambition."

This is hardly an accurate or temperate account of a patriotic statesman and a great fiscal politician, who guided our country autocratically, perhaps, but unselfishly and splendidly in times of her severest need. It may be taken for granted that William Cobbett inspired the sentiments ; though Pitt, the creator of peers, was not likely to be a grateful personality to the editor of a journal directed against the abuse of oligarchical privileges.

Then follows a paragraph headed " Dr. Collyer," containing an innuendo against that gentleman's character which gained double force from the fact that the subject was a well-known dissenting minister. Next we have three columns entitled " The Drama," in which Elliston's acting in the " Rivals " at Drury Lane and Kemble's in " Much Ado About Nothing " at Covent Garden come in for favourable notice. Then we come to an important department, entitled " Medical and Surgical Intelligence." It contained reports of three cases from a clinical point of view—namely, a Case of Anasarca, a Case of Hydrocephalus, and a Case of Hydatids of the Liver ; a long reply from Mr. Henry Earle, assistant surgeon to St. Bartholomew's Hospital, to Sir

Astley Cooper, who had, a little hastily, attempted to controvert his junior's views on the union of Fractured Femur; and two editorial articles, one entitled Obstruction of Blood in the Lung, and the other the Fatal Effect of Fear. In this department Wakley borrowed largely from his contemporaries. The first clinical case was communicated to his columns specially, but the second came from the " London Medical Repository" and the third from the "Edinburgh Medical and Surgical Journal." Mr. Henry Earle's letter was a judicious reply to a ridiculous accusation from Sir Astley Cooper. The great Guy's champion said that the surgeon from St. Bartholomew's took a favourable view of the chances of union of a fracture of the cervix femoris so as to exalt the practice of St. Bartholomew's Hospital, where the prognosis in this injury was good, at the expense of Guy's where it was bad. The letter was addressed to the editor of the " London Medical Repository." Of the two editorial articles only the second is original. It is an interesting little account of a case where a patient at the London Hospital died suddenly while an operation—of course, without the production of anæsthesia—was being commenced upon him for the ligature of a femoral aneurysm. Next we find a column headed " Medical Extracts." These are short, practical remarks on treatment and pathology derived from the lips or written works of Abernethy, Wilson, and Hamilton. The germ of a great idea lay hid in the next article, entitled " The Composition of Quack Medicines." In this we have the results of an analysis of Dalby's Carminative, Daffy's Elixir, and Spelbury's Antiscorbutic Drops. A batch of newspaper extracts follow, whose force and point are not very obvious to modern readers ; and the number closes with a reprint of an open letter from Charles Lamb to Robert Southey, Poet-laureate, which appeared in the " London Magazine." The number had thirty-six pages in all, and no wrapper.

As will be seen, the promise of the preface was very fairly carried out in the first number. An excellent clinical lecture followed by records of interesting cases in surgery and medicine gave the scientific information, the spread of which

Wakley put in the front of his intentions; while a free-spoken communication from a distinguished hospital official about another still more distinguished colleague gave sufficient evidence that no amount of prestige was to protect a man from criticism in the columns of the "Lancet." The analysis of certain quack remedies was the protoplasm whence the "Lancet" Special Analytical Commissions were to be evolved; and the editorial note upon a sudden death occurring at one of the metropolitan hospitals was inserted as a proof that the doings within those fastnesses of prejudice and secrecy were open to the editorial gaze.

It was characteristic of the young journalist that he should never have considered whether he had a legal right to publish Sir Astley Cooper's lectures. His intentions were good, and he expressed them somewhat in this way in sundry editorial communications :—I will publish to the medical profession the lectures of the hospital surgeons and physicians to their different classes; if they are good so much the better for the profession at large who will read them in my pages and for the students who have paid to listen to them; if they are bad their publication will let the profession see that the students are being taught by men unfit to hold the posts from which they draw large salaries, and to which they have been corruptly elected. It was a good example of fairness on Wakley's part that he should have selected Sir Astley Cooper as the first lecturer to be introduced to the medical public. Sir Astley Cooper was then at the zenith of his fame. He was a splendid lecturer, with enormous experience to draw upon and lucid methods of presenting his facts, so that the issue of his lectures was a real boon to the profession. Had Wakley desired he could have selected as a specimen lecturer some inept bungler and have reported him and criticised him simultaneously. But he desired to *in*form as much as to *re*form, and whatever his legal position might have been in the matter, consideration of which will form the subject of the next chapter, the great value that the publication of such lectures was to the medical world is beyond all doubt.

CHAPTER IX

[1823–1834]

*The First Ten Years of the " Lancet "—Their Stormy Character
—The Question of Copyright in Lectures—Sir Astley Cooper—His
Opinion on the Publication of his Lectures—His Detection of the
Unknown Editor—An Amicable Compromise.*

FOR the first ten years of its existence the " Lancet " was a
duelling ground for a series of fierce encounters between
the editor and the members of the privileged classes in
medicine. The lectures of certain of the great hospital
surgeons and physicians were reported in its pages to the
exasperation of the lecturers, and the delight of the profession
at large and the students. The great men feared that their
fees as teachers in the metropolitan schools would diminish
if the cream of their teaching could be bought for sixpence
a week instead of for £5 a session ; while every medical man
or student, unable by circumstances to attend the classes of
his leaders, rejoiced in the chance offered to him of acquiring
familiarity with their methods and theories through the
medium of print. The meetings of the medical societies,
again, were reported at the length that their importance
warranted—a proceeding which the officials of the societies
objected to as an infringement of copyright. They considered that the editor of the Transactions of the Society, a
person appointed by themselves, enjoyed the copyright as a
matter of common sense as well as common law. Briefly,
from the beginning the hospital surgeons and physicians were
ranged in unbroken phalanx in opposition to the new and,
as they considered it, mischievous print. The officials of
the medical societies followed suit ; and the office-bearers of

F

the medical corporations, the practices in two of which were scathingly reviewed in early issues of the " Lancet," were not slow to scent their foe. Every one who had anything to gain by the peaceful reign of existent methods in school, hospital, or corporation—a definition which included most of the influential members of the profession—looked with un-easiness at the growing power and popularity of the new journal.

Wakley, for his part, was quick to discover his enemies, and their tactics dictated his. For the first few weeks the " Lancet " attracted no particular attention, and such notice as it received was complimentary. Then a few of the privileged classes became frightened, and in return sought to frighten Wakley. They denounced him as a literary pirate and a disseminator of moral garbage. His replies were chiefly in the nature of reflection on the complete and fretful ineptitude of his denunciators. He pointed to his growing circulation, scattered with doubtful taste but cruel point a few nicknames, and hinted at astonishing revelations of abuses arising out of the fact that publicity had hitherto been avoided by hospital officials. As a natural pendant to his assertion that the elections to the staffs of the various metropolitan hospitals were made at the instigation of pure nepotism, accounts were given of mal-administration in the schools and malpraxis in the wards. And upon these came action and cross-action. Certain of the criticised were compelled to proceed legally against their critic, while their defence outside the law-courts, too keenly and bitterly undertaken by friends or rival journals, on more than one occasion laid the defenders open to counter-charges of misrepresentation. In the first ten years of the existence of the " Lancet " the editor was en-gaged in no less than ten actions, his opponents being eight separate persons. The proceedings in these actions con-stitute a most interesting phase in the history of medical reform. Six of these actions were actions for libel, the aggregate sum of £8000 being claimed for damages, and the aggregate sum of £155 0s. 0¼d. being awarded, while the editor's costs were largely defrayed by public subscription.

Wakley's first contest with the law was the longest and most expensive suit that he was ever engaged in, and the real question at issue was a much more important one than was stated in the pleadings or than is represented by the precedents which Lord Eldon's judgments have since formed. It was the question of the legality of the publication of certain lectures addressed to medical students by Abernethy, at that time the senior surgeon at St. Bartholomew's Hospital, and the person of professional eminence selected by Wakley to succeed Sir Astley Cooper as the chief attraction in his columns. The publication of Sir Astley Cooper's lectures in the place of honour of the new paper had proved a fine stroke of journalism—of that there could be no doubt. The lectures possessed all the qualifications that an editor would desire for his most important articles. They were excellent in material, wise, practical, and easy to follow. A large class of readers might be expected to constantly buy a paper which contained such contributions. To those seeking instruction in the broad roads of surgery as much as to those desirous of revising their knowledge of the obscurer by-paths the light shed upon their course from the clearest surgical intellect of the day was equally valuable; and Wakley could confidently count upon a respectable number of subscribers desirous of obtaining such help and such only from the paper and quite indifferent to questions of medical policy or medical reform. In short these lectures attracted and held readers. Hardly less important from a business point of view was the prestige that their publication conferred at once upon the " Lancet." For they had what first-class and useful work does not always have—that is, a widely known and distinguished signature. Sir Astley Cooper's was at the time a name to conjure with. He was at the highest point of his professional fame, his unrivalled surgical reputation being enhanced by his wealth, his handsome person, his popularity with his pupils, his recent title, and his acknowledged position in the social world.   It was impossible for the public or the profession, for rival journals or for the frightened owners of vested interests, to cry down the "Lancet" as a worthless gutter production while Wakley was issuing in its pages week by week the work of such a man, and doing so without formal protest from the lecturer. The note of scientific importance once struck by the editor gave the key to his journal.

That Sir Astley Cooper himself did not resent the publication of his lectures in the "Lancet" is certain.   We have his own opinion on the matter, as stated to his faithful surgical class, who were prepared to uphold his view and would certainly be prejudiced towards a policy of remonstrance, as such a policy would have been in support of privileges of their own for which they had paid.   The following is the first allusion made by Sir Astley Cooper to the publication of his lectures in the "Lancet," and it contains no protest against Wakley's proceedings :—

" In detailing to you the errors into which surgeons have fallen I execute a very unpleasant task—a task much more disagreeable now, from the publicity which my lectures receive, than at any former period ; but, as your pilot, it is my imperative obligation to warn you against those shoals and rocks which have foundered but too many of your predecessors.   He who publishes the lectures, however, cannot be too particular in his discretion with regard to publishing names when those names are blended, as they sometimes are, with unfortunate cases.

" When I found, week after week, that my lectures were published, and that consequently I was daily paragraphed in the newspaper, I called upon the editor of the "Lancet" and told him that I was about · · · · · to move for an injunction.   He replied, ' That will not be of any use.' Well, gentlemen, in the end I told him that if he omitted my name I should take no further steps in the matter.   He promised to do so, and as far as I have seen he has fulfilled his promise ; and, of course, I have fulfilled mine.   Indeed, the lawyer's instructions to counsel have been this very day destroyed.

" Now, gentlemen, though I did not regard the publication of my lectures I felt myself disgraced and degraded by my name forever appearing in the diurnal press.   Not a paper could I see but my name flourished in it in some form or other.   This looked so much like quackery, so much like puffing, that I am unable to describe to you how much it annoyed me. Although the publication of my lectures exposes me to the critical ordeal of my professional brethren, yet I fear it not; I care not who may be made acquainted with the doctrines I advance, the instructions I give, the principles I inculcate, while in this theatre. Therefore I am perfectly indifferent as to who publishes them, and equally indifferent as to who may be made acquainted with them."

This cannot be regarded as unqualified disapproval of a dedication to the public of property hitherto considered private. Sir Astley Cooper's attitude may be called professional but friendly. He had the foresight to know that wide dissemination of correct surgical teaching must be for the benefit of the profession of which he was the head. He had the acumen to see that to set up a claim to exclusive property in spoken words would be attended with legal and moral difficulty. His personal appreciation of his own position was not over modest at any time, and he must have felt that *his* surgical classes would always remain well attended though the heavens should fall. Therefore, for liberal reasons he would be inclined to approve of the publication of his lectures while for private reasons he would be indifferent. But for professional reasons he would at that time be bound to object. The hebdomadal appearance of his name in capital letters in a print which frankly contained some non-medical matter, though its circulation was chiefly among medical men, came as a recurring shock to his ideas of professional decency, and on this point, and the further one that his weekly lectures in the "Lancet" were daily quoted in the lay press, he based his objection. And not quite his only objection, for, as will be seen by the concluding words of the speech to his class of which we have already quoted the opening sentences, and in which he is dealing with the propriety of the publication by the "Lancet" of reports of operations at the metropolitan hospitals, he was uncertain whether his extemporary addresses, naturally couched in familiar style, would have a literary merit commensurate

with their scientific importance. With these small reserva-
tions Sir Astley Cooper may be said to have approved of
Wakley's revolutionary departure. He did not, as the smaller
fry did, scream out "robber" and "thief" :—

"Having said thus much respecting the lectures," he continued, "I
now deem it prudent, while I am on the subject, to state my opinion to
you with regard to the publication of operations; this practice, I candidly confess, appears to me to be fraught with great danger, and will,
I suspect, prove destructive to the reputation of the rising generation
of surgeons. Suppose a very young surgeon had performed the operation lately executed by myself in the other hospital, and that it had
terminated in death; suppose a young surgeon to be unfortunate for
five or six operations in succession; would not the public, with one
accord, exclaim, 'Good God! what a butcher that man is'? Such I
fear would be the general feeling, and the ruin, the absolute ruin, of the
operator, the unavoidable consequence. We must, I believe, hold a
meeting of the surgeons for the purpose of adopting some measure by
which, if possible, the system may be prevented. It is a practice to
which I am opposed, and I will put it to the candour of any man, and
ask if it be not calculated to produce much mischief? Believing this
myself, it is a practice to which I much object. With regard to my
lectures the case is different: I have a duty to perform in this theatre,
and I have no objection for the whole world to be made acquainted
with the manner in which it is discharged. I will here remark, however, that, in consequence of the colloquial style in which my lectures
are delivered, they are not in that respect calculated for publication."

The arrangement under which Sir Astley Cooper withdrew
objection to the publication of his lectures if Wakley would,
on his side, guarantee to suppress the author's name came
into force in the tenth number of the "Lancet" under somewhat droll circumstances, and was loyally kept on either side.
The name of the editor of the "Lancet" was not at first
known. "Secrecy of design when combined with rapidity of
execution," wrote that eccentric divine, the Rev. Charles Caleb
Cotton, "like the column that guided Israel in the desert, becomes the guardian pillar of light and fire to our friends and
a cloud of overwhelming and impenetrable darkness to our
enemies." The secrecy with which the "Lancet" had been

,planned and the suddenness with which it was placed before the public no doubt disconcerted the persons who would naturally be its foes. They had no time to organise either a counter-attack or a defence, nor did they know against whom to proceed. But a secret that was necessarily in the keeping of many persons did not long merit the description of impenetrable darkness, and within a few weeks it was circumstantially stated that Wakley was the enterprising editor. Other epithets were added according to the views of the speakers and their positions in the profession, but the quality of enterprise was never denied. At length it reached Sir Astley Cooper's ears that it was his old pupil at the school of the United Hospitals, Thomas Wakley, who was responsible for the unauthorised publication of the surgical lectures to the students at St. Thomas's Hospital, and the great man went personally to Norfolk Street to confer with the young editor. As has been already said, Wakley used his private house for his editorial purposes, the office a few yards away in the Strand being merely a place where communications were received and whence the business of publication took place. Sir Astley Cooper obtained admission in the character of a patient, and caught Wakley, who at the time believed his secret to be inviolate, in the act of correcting a proof of one of the lectures in question. Never did a small check serve a man to better purpose than did Sir Astley Cooper's little "score"—there is no other word—serve Wakley. The great baronet was so pleased at the success of the rather transparent ruse that had gained him entrance and at the sight of Wakley's obvious discomfiture when he found his anonymity gone that any wrath he might have been cherishing was dissolved in hearty laughter. Friendly relations had previously existed between pupil and teacher and they were at once resumed. With complete amicability the lecturer stated his views and the editor stated his. These latter could not have been otherwise than flattering to Sir Astley Cooper's pride, for Wakley's chief argument was that the publication of the lectures must be for the undoubted good of mankind.   A compromise was speedily made to the effect already stated by Sir Astley Cooper.   If Wakley would suppress the author's name no formal objection would be taken to the publication of the lectures.   The agreement was loyally kept.   In accordance with it the fifteenth and ensuing lectures of Sir Astley Cooper were issued without the author's name ; and when proceedings were afterwards instituted by Abernethy, supported by other lecturers in a similar plight, to obtain an injunction against the publisher and printers of the " Lancet," on the plea that the author's copyright in his lectures was infringed by their publication, Sir Astley Cooper took no part in the quarrel.

CHAPTER X

[1823–1834]

Abernethy v. *Hutchinson, Knight and Lacey—The Law of Copyright in Lectures—Abernethy's Position as Lecturer and Surgeon—His First Application against the " Lancet "—The Arguments Employed and their Ill-success—The Fomentation of Bad Feeling—A Second and Successful Application for an Injunction—Wakley's Further Motion—The Importance of the Case.*

ON Friday, December 10th, 1824, Mr. Abernethy, the senior surgeon of St. Bartholomew's Hospital and a great figure in the scientific world, applied to the Court of Chancery for an injunction to restrain the publishers and printers of the " Lancet " from issuing his lectures.

The law of copyright in lectures is not very clear or definite. Lectures are peculiar in their character and differ from books, inasmuch as, though they are made public by delivery, they have not necessarily a visible form capable of being copied. Nevertheless, it has been thought right by the legislature to afford them the protection of copyright. The situation of the law with respect to the protection of lectures is exactly the same now as it was in 1823. The author of any literary composition has the right at common law to prevent its publication until he has himself made it public. He does not necessarily forfeit this right by delivering his composition as a lecture. His right after delivery will be decided by 5 and 6 William IV. c. 65 :— " An Act for Preventing the Publication of Lectures without Consent." By this Act the author of any lecture or his assignee may reserve to himself the sole right of publishing the lecture by giving two days' notice of the intended delivery to two justices of the peace living within five miles from the place of delivery, unless the lecture is delivered in any university, public school, or college, or in any public foundation, or upon gift or endowment—such lectures being free. Whatever may be the origin of this provision it is little known and probably never, or very seldom, acted upon, so that statutory copyright in lectures is very seldom acquired. If the lecture has not been printed—when it falls under the head of a book—and has not been duly copyrighted according to the above proceeding, what constitutes dedication to the public ? This is what the publication of Abernethy's lectures has decided, and Lord Eldon's judgment in the case forms a much-quoted precedent.

The fact that Abernethy objected to the publication of his lectures was perfectly well known to Wakley, for his disapproving words had been actually reported as he expressed them to his class ; while certain members of that class, in obvious deference to what they knew to be their lecturer's wish, had on two occasions put out the lamp in the theatre, designing by that means to baffle the unknown shorthand reporter. In the "Lancet" of December 11th, however, the tenth lecture of the course was reported in full, with no reference to previous threats or to the commencement of legal proceedings. The subject of this lecture was Irritative Inflammation, Erysipelas, and Furunculus, and the reporter was a little cruel to the lecturer in his faithful reproduction of the colloquial peculiarities employed by Abernethy in delivery; otherwise nothing in that issue of the "Lancet" tends to show that Wakley was aware of the legal exception that had been taken to his proceedings.

"If I am wrong I shall be very happy to have my errors pointed out and corrected. *I'll be hanged* if erysipelas is not always a result of a disordered state of the digestive organs. . . . . *Egad*, it is a travelling disease, and, as I say, the parts are disposed to swell. . . . . If it be seated in an unimportant part *in the name of G*—— let it go on there. . . . . O, said the dresser, it is a case of erysipelas and he only came in last week. *Good G*——! said I, is it possible ? . . . . Ho! he had *his jawing-tacks on board*, as a sailor would say."

These are among the specimens of Abernethy's manner-
isms which were set down in the " Lancet's " unchastened
report. It can be readily understood that the speaker found
it a little embarrassing to read his expletives in cold print,
though he may have felt certain that they had added force
to his style and point to his meaning as they fell hot from
his lips, and had given a fillip to the interest of his hearers,
as apt, probably, then as now to consider attendance at
lectures a great bore. The feeling that he was occasionally
made to look foolish by the fidelity of the reporter may have
been his determining reason in making his application, but
it was well understood that as much in the initial proceedings as in the later he was only constituting himself the
mouthpiece of his order—the order of lecturers attached to
medical schools, whose equanimity was much shaken by
Wakley's irresponsible behaviour. Abernethy was second
only to Sir Astley Cooper in the surgical hierarchy of
London, and was regarded by his juniors with peculiar
reverence because in him they saw the great exponent of the
great john Hunter's teaching. Failing Sir Astley Cooper,
who was bound by his word not to object to the publication
of his own lectures, and therefore as an honourable man
was bound to refuse to assist others in questioning Wakley's
legal position in the matter, Abernethy was the strongest
man to pit against Wakley to dispute his legal status in
the affair ; just as, failing Sir Astley Cooper, Abernethy
was the best-known surgical lecturer likely to attract
readers to the paper. That Abernethy was put up to fight
the battles of his colleagues is undoubted, for he was quite
a shrewd, astute man, and would not have had any motion
made on his own behalf unless he had felt that in so doing
he was conforming to the general wish of others in his
position.

When the subject of the motion was mentioned to the
Lord Chancellor, Lord Eldon, his lordship put a case to
himself and concluded by saying, " I shall make short work
of it " ; and if his assumption of the questions that would be
before him had been completely correct he would have been

justified in doing as he promised, but, as will be seen, the
great lawyer took a narrow view. The following is the
rather extraordinary dialogue which took place between
the Lord Chancellor, the Solicitor-General (Sir Charles
Wetherell), who represented Abernethy, and Mr. Horne,
who was retained by Wakley in the interests of the defendants, Mr. Gilbert Linney Hutchinson, the publisher, and
Messrs. Knight and Lacey, the printers.

Lord ELDON: The case is to decide whether a party attending
lectures in any branch of philosophy or learning for his own information
is at liberty to publish the lectures for his own advantage. I shall
make short work of it.

Mr. HORNE: The case is not of the nature your lordship sup-
poses.

The SOLICITOR-GENERAL: Your lordship's mind has caught the
whole point in the case, and, in fact, there is nothing more to be
decided.

Mr. HORNE: His lordship cannot decide a case he has never
heard.

With this view the Lord Chancellor concurred, and being
unable to hear the case fully on the day of the application
for the injunction, in spite of an appeal of urgency on the
part of the Solicitor-General, postponed further hearing to
the date suggested by Mr. Horne—namely, December 18th.
His Lordship said that no articles were to be made use of in
the interim, with the exception of the number then in the
press and to be published the following morning. " Let us
have no more bleeding until I have examined the patient
myself and decided upon his case," was his jocular pro-
nouncement of his interdiction. He evidently felt that his
expression of opinion was ill-timed, and Sir Charles
Wetherell's commendation of his attitude, meant to confirm
him therein, caused him to veer. His premature remark
did not, however, escape the notice of the press, although
he had consented to a postponement of the trial, for the
" Morning Chronicle" of December 11th, 1824, contained the
following satirical stanzas of an uncomplimentary sort upon

his abuse of his position in thus prejudging and dismissing an unheard application :—

> " A wonder happened t'other day ;
>   I scarce know how to word it :
> THE CHANCELLOR, who loves delay,
> A case at once decided—nay,
>   Before he even heard it.

> " Horne and Wetherell well might stare
>   To find he never falter'd,
> If known next session I know where
> Some persons may their speeches spare,
>   If Eld-n be so alter'd.

> " Who knows to see this change in him
>   But it may lead to others :—
> Befriend the Catholics for a whim ;
> C-nn-ng will cease to sneak and trim,
>   And Plunket call them Brothers."

On the second day of the hearing of the motion, December 18th, 1824, an affidavit was put in by Abernethy which at great length cited the circumstances of the delivery of the lectures and gave an account of his calling forth the " hireling of the ' Lancet ' " from the ranks of his students without response. He bitterly inveighed against the appropriation of his copyright, but at the same time protested that he would never withhold from mankind any words of his the publication of which was for the true good of the public. The affidavit of the defendant Hutchinson contended that the publication was made exactly for the good of the public, and, such being the case, free publication ought to be permitted without legal restriction. He further tried to show that there was no precedent for the recognition of copyright vested in verbal utterances. Long and technical speeches from counsel on both sides followed. Sir Charles Wetherell attempted to set up a claim for exclusive copyright .in that the lectures were delivered in a private capacity to private pupils. Mr. Horne, on the other hand, maintained that it was Abernethy's public duty to deliver himself of surgical teaching in a public place for the public good ; he held that the colloquial style of the lectures sufficiently proved absence of all intention to set up a claim for literary copyright in the way such a claim should be advanced—viz., by issuing the lectures as a book; and, lastly, he alleged that Abernethy's lectures, being merely a replica of John Hunter's teaching, contained no matter in which Abernethy had any peculiar property. The Lord Chancellor on the third day decided that he had heard quite enough and, contrary to his suggested opinion of the previous week, refused to grant an application and withdrew the interim order of injunction. Thus it was temporarily decided that words used in lectures for the public benefit had no copyright vested in them and were liable to be published without reserve for the good of humanity. But Lord Eldon several times in the course of his judgment said that he would hear an argument upon the point whether there had been a breach of trust or of implied contract.

The "Lancet" of December 18th, 1824, did not contain a continuation of the report of Abernethy's course of lectures, because until the evening of that day the interim order of injunction was in force. The issue of Christmas Day also contained no lecture, being virtually a supplement devoted to an exhaustive *résumé* of the proceedings in Chancery during the preceding week; but the issue of January 1st, 1825, contained Lectures XI. and XII., being in direct continuation of Lecture X. published on December 11th, 1824, and showing that Wakley's agent had not omitted to take the notes necessary for the subsequent transcription of Abernethy's words, although the Lord Chancellor's decision in the matter was still in abeyance. This resolute and unflinching determination to have his way in the matter, as far as the law and his own ideas of right and wrong would allow him, was characteristic of the man. He was pugnacious, and to be slapped in the face did not suit his pugnacity; but there was more behind the methodical manner, in which he was careful to leave no word in the course of Abernethy's lectures unreported and no argument, legal or sentimental, of Abernethy's supporters unrefuted, than a love of fighting for a good liberal cause. He was also exceedingly proud of his journal, and at that time an interdiction of the publication of medical lectures might have made a serious difference to the circulation of the "Lancet" and the position of its editor. Many readers would have been lost ; the editor would have had much laborious prospecting to undertake before he could hope to strike an adequate substitute for the scientific wealth contained in the soil of the hospital lecture rooms ; and he would have been convicted of having done wrong. Nor do these things wholly explain his resolution in the matter of the reporting of lectures and the importance that he attached to a continuance of the practice. As there was more than pugnacity behind his attitude so there was more than self-interest. And the third factor, which dominated the other two entirely, was the reformer's spirit. To report the lectures of the surgical teachers at the big schools was to make a bold and novel attack upon the privileges of a çlass of men whom individually he might and often did admire as great in the profession that he loved, but whom collectively he considered to be corrupt, selfish, and feeble. Wakley knew that in reporting Abernethy's lectures he was defying and not a little frightening the hospital lecturers, and that amused him. He knew that terror of the verbatim reporter would compel many of them, not usually so circumspect, to be punctual in their attendance, thoughtful of what they had to say, and careful of how they said it, and this result he considered a worthy one for the paper to accomplish. And, lastly, he counted upon issuing to all medical men who required it the assistance that first-class teaching must always be. It was not Abernethy against whom he was measuring himself, for we have his own words repudiating the suggestion at the very time when the interim interdiction was in force, but all who stood between him and the carrying out of his prefatory promises to the profession that they should read these lectures in his columns and be improved by them.

"Had Mr. Abernethy," he writes in a leading article on December 18th, 1824, "consulted his own. judgment and inclination rather than the support of that corrupt and rotten system of which he is unfortunately a part, we are very certain that he would not have appeared in Chancery for the disgraceful purpose of throwing new obstacles in the path of medical science. The object of those with whom Mr. Abernethy is in concert is not so much to prevent the weekly publication of his lectures as to effect the destruction of this publication. The 'Lancet' is not suited to their taste or interest. . . . ."

Wakley's action in the matter was all a part of his reforming spirit. He did not intend to give way to the pleasure of the class whose privileges it had been his intention from the beginning to dispute, and he was resolved not to forfeit his word to the rank and file, whose moral and pecuniary support he had demanded on the specific ground that he would publish these lectures for their instruction.

Having so far won the day and successfully resisted Abernethy's attempt to obtain an injunction he would, we cannot help seeing, have been better advised to let the matter drop. It would have been more graceful and more politic to continue upon the course he had originally shaped for himself without further reference to the defeated arguments of his adversary, but further polemics were in a manner forced upon him by the acerbity with which Abernethy and his supporters received their check. Abernethy, the essence of whose complaint was that Wakley had reported him too faithfully, so that the value of the copyright in his lectures was gone, they having been brought verbatim and at a moderate price to the attention of the only public they could hope to enjoy, now said in one of his lectures :—

" If the editor of the 'Lancet' should still publish my lectures I only know, from what I have seen of those parts of them which have appeared in the newspapers, that they represent me as one of the most pert, balderdash fellows in existence. Any person would say on reading those paragraphs : 'Well, I always thought Mr. Abernethy a well-informed man, and somewhat of a scientific man, too, in the practice of his profession, but I really think he must be a very weak man.' "

Wakley was not the man to allow this aspersion of the accuracy of his journal to go unnoticed. Again, while the "Times" and the "Morning Chronicle" were to a certain

extent of opinion that Wakley was right in publishing professional lectures to the profession, one of the contemporary
medical journals, the "London Medical Repository," edited
at the time by Copland the lexicographer, expressed disapprobation in terms of unbounded indecency :—

> "As to the honesty of the transaction," ran the offensive passage,
> "it cannot require consideration. A man may just as well go to dine
> at a *restaurateur's* and, after satiating his own appetite with that portion
> of the *bonne chère* for which he paid on his own account, carry off the
> remainder of the landlord's provisions to be sold for a penny a pound
> to all who might choose to buy ; or, perhaps, we may liken the trans-
> action to that of insuring one's house, then setting it on fire, to obtain
> the large amount for which a very trifling premium was paid."

Wakley could not sit quietly down under such an insult
as was put upon him by his monthly contemporary. On
january 9th, 1825, there appeared in the "Lancet" a long
article practically daring Abernethy to attempt to interfere
again with the publication of his lectures ; for it had got
abroad that a second application was to be made to the
Lord Chancellor upon the ground, suggested by Lord
Eldon as an argument to which he would gladly listen, that
Abernethy lectured to the students under the protection of
an implied contract limiting their use in what they heard to
aural instruction. A week later, no move in this direction
having been taken by Abernethy, Wakley proceeded to
demolish the two arguments which had already been put
forward by Sir Charles Wetherell in favour of the injunction ; an unnecessary proceeding, because on these very
arguments the plaintiff lecturer had failed to obtain what he
wanted. The first argument was that Abernethy had
suffered probable pecuniary loss by the fact that no
publisher would consider favourably the issue of his lectures
in book form after they had been disseminated in sixpenny
instalments among the profession. The second was that
Abernethy had suffered certain pecuniary loss by the
abstention of students from his classes who preferred to
pay sixpence a week rather than ten pounds a year for the

privilege of learning his views. The first argument Wakley did not demolish in a very workmanlike manner. He dealt some hasty blows right and left, but he hardly made his point. He replied that Abernethy's were poor lectures and that action at law had been taken because the lecturer felt that he had been placed at the bar of public criticism as a hospital teacher, and out of regard for present and posthumous fame was anxious to prevent an exposure of his ignorance. All that was good in Abernethy's lectures was, said Wakley, to be found in Hunter's works upon whom immense plagiarism had been practised, and it was impossible to imagine Abernethy enjoying a copyright in his lectures under such circumstances and ridiculous to suppose that a publisher would be found willing to issue them in a collected form. This was not a very good rejoinder on Wakley's part, because it convicted him of bad catering for his public. To the second argument his reply was crushing, for he demonstrated that the students could not abstain from attending Abernethy's lectures if they wished, because of a by-law of the Royal College of Surgeons, recently framed by the Court of Examiners, of which Abernethy himself was at the time a member. On March 19th, 1824, the Court of Examiners resolved that certificates of attendance at lectures on the theory and practice of surgery should not be received by the Court save from the professors of surgery in certain universities, or from the teachers in certain medical schools formally attached to recognised metropolitan hospitals, or from members of the honorary staffs of such hospitals. This by-law, remarkable enough on the face of it, practically compelled all the medical students in London to attend the lectures of some five persons, of whom Abernethy was one; for at that time there was no University of London, and but six hospitals— namely, St. Bartholomew's, St. George's, the United Hospitals, the London, and the Middlesex—had acknowledged schools. Westminster Hospital, though of very ancient foundation, was but a dispensary in James Street until 1834; Charing Cross Hospital was instituted in 1818, but the present building was not erected until 1831, and prior to that date the institution only enjoyed the position of a large ambulance station, having for its particular object the care of the numerous accident cases occurring in the neighbouring streets; University College Hospital and King's College Hospital were founded respectively in 1833 'and 1839; and St. Mary's Hospital dates only from 1845. So that when it was pleaded for Abernethy that the publication of his lectures was likely to lead to the diminution of his surgical classes Wakley was, if unnecessarily forcible, certainly unanswerable in saying: " In the name of God, do not let us hear any more of such loathsome trash."

january, February, March, and April of 1825 were allowed by Abernethy to elapse before he made his second application to the Lord Chancellor for an injunction on the ground that his lectures were delivered to persons under an implied contract not to publish them, but at the end of May the application was made and the hearing was commenced on june 10th. Abernethy renewed his application obviously rather in the interest of other lecturers than in his own, for at the time his lectures were not being printed in the " Lancet," having been discontinued at the completion of the course some two months previously.

" He may possibly have vanity enough to suppose that we shall reprint his lectures," wrote Wakley. " On this point his mind may be perfectly at ease; our pages have been already obscured with his hypothetical nonsense during six tedious months, and when we read the proof of the last paragraph we felt relieved of a most intolerable incubus."

The result of the second application was that Abernethy was successful. The Lord Chancellor in his judgment to a certain extent went back on himself. He held that the lectures could not be published for profit, that if any pupil who had paid only to hear them afterwards sold them to the publisher he infringed the law, and that the publishers in so publishing them enacted "what this Court would call a fraud in a third party." He dwelt upon the practical difficulty that existed in bringing home this fraud to any one where no manuscript was in existence, but did not otherwise allow that there was any difference as far as the author's rights were concerned whether the lecture was delivered from a manuscript or as an extemporary effort. This is the judgment which forms the precedent upon which cases of infringement of copyright in lectures are decided, and in text-books upon the subject it is the case that is always quoted.

Upon November 28th, 1825, Mr. Horne applied to the Lord Chancellor to dissolve the injunction, granted against Wakley at the previous session, restraining him from continuing to publish or sell Abernethy's lectures in the " Lancet." The motion was unopposed, and Lord Eldon dissolved the injunction. This judgment did not, and does not affect the value of his previous judgment with regard to the legality of the publication of lectures, for the dissolution was granted upon new facts which were brought to the knowledge of the Court. Wakley had all along contended that it was monstrous that Abernethy should by one act confer upon himself as a member of the Court of Examiners of the Royal College of Surgeons the exclusive right of lecturing in the character of a public functionary, and by another claim the protection due to private lecturers on the ground of the injury which his reputation or pecuniary interests might sustain from the issue of his lectures in cheap form. After the injunction Abernethy had delivered an address to the students on the occasion of the opening of the session at St. Bartholomew's Hospital and this address had appeared in full in the " Lancet," precisely as if no injunction existed, on the ground that it had been delivered by Abernethy in a public capacity. No retaliatory steps were taken by Abernethy. Shortly after this, a few days only before Wakley's application for a dissolution of the injunction, Abernethy tendered his resignation as a surgeon to the governors of St. Bartholomew's Hospital whilst desiring to remain a lecturer to the institution. The governors refused to accept his resignation as a surgeon unless he also tendered his resignation as a lecturer. This recognition of an inseparable tie between the two posts of surgeon and lecturer reached Wakley's ears and supplied him with the very point in his argument for a dissolution of the injunction that he required. "Of course Abernethy's lectures are public property," he said; "they are delivered in his public capacity as surgeon to a public charity and the students of the metropolis must attend them, or lectures from some five or six other functionaries similarly situated, whether they like or no." The facts of Abernethy's offer of resignation to the governors of St. Bartholomew's Hospital were set out in the form of an affidavit, and, no one appearing to represent Abernethy in opposition to a motion for dissolution of the injunction, Lord Eldon removed the restriction.

The determined manner in which the case of Abernethy v. Hutchinson, Knight and Lacey was fought had a great effect on the prestige of the "Lancet." It showed the editor to be a resolute man willing to do battle for his opinions, and it revealed the new paper as one with a large circulation and a substantial pecuniary foundation. That both combatants did not shine to advantage in their every utterance did neither of them any personal harm, for all who watched the quarrel saw in their excited and occasionally illogical remarks only evidence of collision between two self-willed persons determined to look upon a matter from opposite views. Abernethy fought for his order and Wakley fought for his readers. That each of these eminently clear-headed men should by force of circumstances have been driven to contradict themselves out loud shows how very angry they became at different stages of the dispute. Wakley was led to pooh-pooh Abernethy's admirable qualities as a lecturer, having previously extolled them; while Abernethy, the whole gist of whose claim upon the "Lancet" for infringement of copyright was that the reports were accurate, was ill-advised enough to insinuate that they were very far from being so. Each, on the other hand, showed remarkable ingenuity in advancing his own opinions, and each won a victory that gained him credit without hurting his foe.

CHAPTER XI

[1823–1834]

The " Lancet" becomes a Rigorously Medical Paper—Wakley as a Chess-player—The Hospital Reports, or " Mirror of Hospital Practice"—Reproof to Students—The Preface to the Second Volume of the " Lancet "—Some Criticism of Hospital Procedure—Attack on Nepotism—Expulsion of Wakley from St. Thomas's Hospital.

By the end of 1825 the " Lancet " was a recognised publication of more than two years' standing, with a regular circulation of upwards of 4000 and a well-defined policy and range. Wakley kept his promises of the original preface during the first two years, but as the paper grew in authority and increased in circulation two alterations in its contents became noticeable. The first was that all attempts to interest the reader in matters outside the science, practice, and politics of medicine and the allied sciences were given up. The second was that the position of Wakley and the hospital officials towards each other had crystallised into unmistakable hostility.

The disappearance from the paper of the weekly columns entitled respectively " The Chess-table," and " The Dramatic Lancet," and " Table Talk," meant more to the editor than the importance of the articles would seem to warrant. It was a sacrifice of his own hobbies to the pressure of what he conceived to be his wholly absorbing duty. All writers who use their pens to promote certain definite serious results, political, social, financial, or what not, know how pleasant it is to have an opportunity of lightening the important labours of the day by a little desultory writing

·upon some topic in which they take a less absorbing or a more light-hearted interest. Wakley was a great chess-player, and an enthusiastic play-goer. His chess he had learned when quite a boy. It formed his chief recreation during his period of hard study in Gerard's Hall, and throughout his life he was a votary of the most absorbing and scientific of domestic games. He was one of the very few players who contested successfully with the original and celebrated automaton player ; and it was his habit, when engaged in editing his paper, to have a chess-board by his side, upon which, during the intervals of dictating and proof-reading, he would set himself problems. It is a curious fact that the " Lancet," which became after its first few numbers so rigidly a medical paper, should have been the actual journal to inaugurate the practice of publishing chess-problems and accounts of games of chess ; but Wakley, as will be seen from his own words, believed that the study of chess would form a recreation peculiarly fitted to the mind of the properly trained medical man, and so might almost form a factor in the ideal medical education.

" This is," he wrote on November 1823, "perhaps the only game to which the medical student may profitably devote any portion of his time and attention. It is liable to none of the objections which apply to games of chance, it holds out no encouragement to cupidity, and while it affords an agreeable relaxation from more serious pursuits it strengthens the intellectual faculties by the unremitting attention which it demands, and may even have some influence on our moral habits by the lessons of foresight, patience, and perseverance which it inculcates. To avoid errors on the one hand by foresight and circumspection, and to endeavour to retrieve such as are committed on the other by patient industry and perseverance,—these are matters applicable to all pro-fessions and situations in life, and which, as the American philosopher, Dr. Franklin, has observed, are constantly illustrated on the chess-board. The study of chess has, we believe, been recommended to medical students by the distinguished Professor whose lectures stand at the head of this publication (Sir Astley Cooper), and who unites to his great professional and general knowledge a very considerable degree of excellence in that scientific game. The recommendation was founded, not only on the superiority of this amusement to all others in an intellectual point of view, but upon a more benevolent motive ; for

circumstances might possibly occur in which the surgeon's acquaintance with chess might relieve the mind as much as his professional
skill could mitigate the bodily sufferings of his patient."

From this it will be understood that Wakley did not
allow his chess articles to be crowded out without a pang
nor without some little doubt that he was sacrificing to
utilitarianism a subject that had its utilitarian side.

The " Dramatic Lancet " came to an end even sooner than
the contributions to the literature of chess, and it also was
not allowed to disappear without regret. Wakley had an
extreme love of the stage. He was well read in dramatic
literature and a constant attendant at the play, a fact upon
which his future oratorical successes were largely dependent.
Many of his similes and illustrations and many of the
nicknames distributed freely by the writers in the early
numbers of his paper had their origin in the editor's histrionic
proclivities.   In omitting the notice of the drama, moreover,
Wakley was not only narrowing his range by excluding the
discussion of a subject very palatable to his own taste, but he
was taking work away from some of his press friends who,
when the " Lancet " was a small paper, and not quite limited
either in programme or performance to things medical, gave
him their assistance.

The exclusion from the columns of the " Lancet " of all but
strictly medical matter was not an important event.   It had
relation to certain idiosyncrasies of the editor, and so notice
of it finds due place in a biography ; but, as a matter of fact,
the lay matter was so small in quantity and unimportant in
quality compared with the medical that its formal omission
made no difference to the position or value of the paper.
But the second alteration, the alteration in tone towards the
hospital officials, was a very important departure.   If Wakley
had not quarrelled with the hospital surgeons as a class
many regrettable passages—regretted more by himself than
by anyone else—would never have been written.   On the
other hand, his intuition and foresight told him, and his
love of fighting supported him in the view, that unless he

declared absolute and unrelenting war upon those who were attempting to restrict his operations for reform he would fail utterly and hopelessly. And he was right. All the good that Wakley did was due to the fact that when he came to the little stream separating the province of medical journalism, as then understood, from the kingdom of the monopolist, he boldly crossed the Rubicon and declared war, recognising that fighting was his only alternative to utter ineffectiveness.

The war began in the department of the paper that is now known as "A Mirror of Hospital Practice." The reports of proceedings in hospital practice were first started regularly in the "Lancet" of November 9th, 1823—that is, in the sixth number that was issued. From this period they have been continued for seventy-three years without intermission—for the first twenty-six years under the original title of "Hospital Reports," and since then under the title of "A Mirror of Hospital Practice." Guy's Hospital and St. Thomas's Hospital came in for the most lengthy notice, the reason of this being simply that the operative surgery of Sir Astley Cooper overshadowed that of every other surgeon in the kingdom, and the most trivial procedure in surgery under his hands became a matter of professional interest. . Proceedings at St. Bartholomew's Hospital, where Abernethy was the great but infrequent operator, had allotted to them also considerable space, while the cases of Charles Bell at Middlesex and Benjamin Brodie at St. George's Hospital were usually detailed at some length. Throughout the first volume the reports were, on the whole, eulogistic. Every now and then the lack of some little convenience in ward or operating theatre was made the subject of uncomplimentary comment, but no word derogatory to the operator ever appeared. Not that there was any slurring over of the real issue of the cases out of deference to the feelings of the surgeon, for as early as November 16th, 1823, we have the fatal sequel of a case narrated in uncompromising terms. A man had died after being operated upon for stone by Sir Astley Cooper, and the death was attributed to hæmorrhage

from the artery of the bulb in a perfectly matter-of-fact way,
showing that the reporter was more concerned in giving a
truthful record of hospital surgery than of being pleasing to
eminent persons. A caustic remark on an operation undertaken for stone where the patient "was carried back to the
ward without receiving much assistance from chirurgical
skill, as no stone was extracted," was the only really
unfriendly comment on hospital surgery that Wakley allowed
himself during the first volume. On the other hand, the
journal which professedly catered largely for the medical
students did not scruple to speak severely to them of their
behaviour at lectures and to urge upon them the necessity of
paying due attention and respect to their appointed teachers.
For Wakley was no friend to rowdiness. The man who
hated that element of student life when a student looked
with no more favourable eye upon it now, and all his
counsels to his student readers were good and sober. This
must be put on record because one of the wild accusations
against him was that he stirred up the students against their
masters—his foes, the hospital surgeons. His conduct was
absolutely the reverse, and until the hospital surgeons saw
in the faithfulness of the reporting and the freedom of the
speaking in the "Lancet" menaces to their interests the
accusation was not brought forward.

But the preface to the second volume of the "Lancet" stirred
apprehensions in the hospitals. Hitherto a little wondering
among a few whether they would be subjected to what they
termed the "piracy" of their lectures had been the measure
of their objection to Wakley, but the following words had
an import serious to the surgical staffs of all the hospitals :—

" The next distinguishing feature of the "Lancet" is the publication
of Hospital Reports. It has long been a matter of astonishment that
from the different hospitals in this great metropolis no reports of cases
have been sent forth to the world. This deficiency we shall endeavour
to supply, and our reports will have this advantage over any that
might be published by the surgeons of the different institutions—that
while they would have an interest in concealing many circumstances
which might reflect discredit on themselves and the institutions to which

they belong, we cannot be influenced by any such considerations, and as the only argument that can be adduced against our reports is that they are not sufficiently authenticated we have only to observe that, by giving the cases as they occur in the hospitals, a sufficient number of checks is afforded by which our claims to the confidence of the profession may at all times be readily investigated."

Here we have the first loud sounding of the reformer's cry. This is the first time that Wakley said of the hospital surgeons—his brother practitioners—that *they* might conceal things awkward to themselves or their hospitals, in which case it would be *his* duty to reveal them. These words may be taken as the beginning of war. But no increased asperity was employed in the reporting of hospital cases. The records remained strictly fair and accurate, and Wakley was shown to have had no impending revelations in his mind when he wrote of his future intentions. His wish was to submit the deeds of the medical officers to the test of publicity, exactly as he was already submitting their words by publishing their lectures to the students. Certain hospital abuses were found fault with, the blame being secondarily apportioned to the medical staff, who were credited with ignorance of the matters detailed. Here is an example :—

" We understand that persons were allowed to vend porter in the wards of St. Thomas's Hospital, and to hawk oranges, tarts, &c. through those of Guy's. We cannot suppose that the medical officers of these institutions are aware of these facts, and on that account we refrain for the present from making any remarks on them. The abuse is too glaring to be allowed to exist by any one concerned in the treatment of the sick and who has it in his power to effect its redress."

This little paragraph, revealing as pages of writing could not do the exceeding lack of proper administration in the wards of the metropolitan hospitals seventy years ago, is the only passage that could have given offence to the most susceptible sensibility or the most uneasy official conscience. A case of lithotomy was mentioned in which Messrs. Travers, Green, Morgan, and Tyrrell diagnosed a non-existent stone, but the fact was mentioned as one of surgical interest, and no unfavourable comments were made. At length, however, a point arose upon which the "Lancet" required more light. A case of compound fracture of both bones of the leg was admitted to the wards of St. Thomas's Hospital. The patient remained eight days with only allevi- ating treatment, but finally when the parts were threatened with gangrene Mr. Travers consented to operate. The femur was amputated about three inches above the knee, and the operation was performed with very little loss of blood. Nevertheless the patient, who was in a desperate plight when surgical interference was at last resorted to, died three days afterwards. The reporter of the case to the "Lancet" put certain questions to Mr. Travers concerning the cause of the delay in operating. This may be taken as the first assertion on the part of Wakley of a right to criticise events occurring in the hospitals as good as his right to narrate them. He received no answer, but he did not make any reflection on this as an omission on Mr. Travers's part. On the contrary; in the next week's issue the reporter gave at some length an account of a case where Mr. Travers was pressed to operate upon a patient for stone, but declined to do so, as his colleagues, Mr. Key and Sir Astley Cooper, could not detect the presence of a calculus. This patient died, and a post-mortem examina- tion showed that opening of the bladder—at any rate with a view of removing a stone—would have been useless as no stone was present, and Mr. Travers was congratulated upon his discrimination. As yet the amenities were preserved.

It was Sir Astley Cooper's lectures, or rather their too faithful reporting in the "Lancet," which fired the train already laid. Sir Astley Cooper had a very intelligible and rational contempt for the routine treatment with mercury of certain complaints and expressed himself as follows to the students of the Borough Hospitals in May, 1824 :—

" To compel an unfortunate patient to undergo a course of mercury for a disease which does not require it is a proceeding which reflects disgrace and dishonour on the character of a medical institution. No consideration shall induce me to repress my feelings on this subject;

no authority shall restrain me from giving full expression to these feelings. As long as I continue a surgeon of Guy's Hospital I will endeavour to do my duty ; but I care not whether I continue a surgeon of that hospital another day.   I do say that the present treatment of patients . . . . in these hospitals, by putting them unnecessarily under a course of mercury for five or six weeks, is infamous and disgraceful. The health of a patient is, perhaps, irremediably destroyed by this treatment ; and after all not the slightest effect is produced by it on the disease."

Immediately after the publication in the " Lancet " of this vigorous indictment of his colleagues by the omnipotent prince of surgery, meeting after meeting of the surgeons of the Borough Hospitals took place, and one week later Sir Astley Cooper stated that new and improved regulations concerning these cases had been agreed upon. Wakley was not a little jubilant at this public announcement, for it enabled him to point to an undoubted instance where the publication of lectures had been of good. Sir Astley Cooper had fulminated against the abuse of the mercurial treatment at the Borough Hospitals on previous occasions to the students, but no practical reformation had ever resulted therefrom. No sooner, however, were his words made public in the " Lancet " to the whole profession than reform, drastic and salutary, followed. Wakley's little self-congratulatory crow was natural and inoffensive, but it happened that Sir Astley Cooper in making public the designs for better administration in the faulty wards made an ingenuous disclaimer of having been actuated in his previous plain-speaking by any desire to ignore the feelings of the surgeons of the Borough Hospitals. " Who are the men, gentlemen," he said, " against whom it has been supposed that these observations were directed ? Are they men whom I could possibly feel disposed to injure ? Mr. Travers was my apprentice, Mr. Green is my godson, Mr. Tyrrell is my nephew, Mr. Key is my nephew, Mr. Morgan was my apprentice." Wakley rallied Sir Astley Cooper on the nepotism thus naïvely revealed, professing himself to be convinced that it was impossible that Sir Astley Cooper should be actuated by other than friendly feelings towards such a family party—"a party united to each other, not only by the amiable ties of consanguinity, but by the no less delightful *vinculum* of a common participation in £3600 which they annually extract from the students." That same day, May 22nd, 1824, Wakley was excluded from attendance at St. Thomas's Hospital by order of the surgeons to the institution, and from that day for upwards of ten years the relations between the "Lancet" and the metropolitan hospital officials, already strained, became those of overt and uncompromising hostility. The attitude of the officials was reasonable from their point of view. They looked upon the hospitals as theirs, not the public's. As a simple chronicler of events the medical journalist would be tolerated about their paths, a certain sort of publicity having its value to them; but if he began with criticism to spy out all their ways, to reflect upon the wisdom of their operations, the language of their lectures, their ties of consanguinity, and the substantial nature of their emoluments, he must be expelled. Wakley's attitude was equally reasonable. These men, he said, fear publicity, because they habitually betray their trusts. They discharge public duties inefficiently and fear lest the public should find them out. Therefore they drive out the truth-teller from among them.

Spurred on by a sense of duty, and not made more suave in his language by a rankling sense of the insult that had been put upon him, Wakley continued his Hospital Reports; and while he defied the surgeons of St. Thomas's Hospital to prevent him from obtaining whatever information he desired, he spared no pains to prove to his readers that the "Lancet" was feared because the surgeons knew. that an ignominious exposure of their unworthiness was inevitable.

CHAPTER XII

[1823–1834]

" Hole-and-corner " Surgery—The Interference of Dr. James Johnson—The Real Simon Pure—A Powerful and Libellous Indictment—Tyrrell v. Wakley : Damages laid at Two Thousand Pounds.

IN accordance with the words of his defiance to the surgeons of St. Thomas's Hospital, Wakley continued to print weekly reports of proceedings at that institution with regularity, and to personally visit its wards and operating theatre whenever his inclination moved him, while he occasionally alluded to the action of the surgeons who had attempted to avoid publicity in scathing articles having for their common title, " Hole-and-corner " Surgery. These articles were written in a tone that precluded any idea of an amiable compromise between the offended hospital surgeons and the offended journalist. Messrs. Travers, Tyrrell, and Green, the three gentlemen under whose written authority Wakley's expulsion from the building of St. Thomas's Hospital had been designed, were contemptuously called " The Three Ninny-hammers," a nickname hallowed by Sterne, Swift, Arbuthnot, and, indirectly, Shakespeare ; and their action was criticised as a good example of the forcible-feeble behaviour to be expected from persons so designated. Mr. Travers was especially blamed for having said in an address to the students of St. Thomas's Hospital that if any student should be discovered furnishing an account of hospital cases to a newspaper he would be immediately expelled, for the hospital surgeons had not the powers necessary to carry out the threat.

The articles upon " Hole-and-corner " Surgery were not,

however, directed solely against Messrs. Travers, Tyrrell, and Green, but were partly written in reply to the article of Dr. James Johnson which appeared in the " Medico-Chirurgical Review," then being issued under his editorship. Dr. James Johnson's interference was unfortunate. To begin with, Wakley was not the man to brook interference of any sort. He could understand the opposition of the persons interested in fighting with him, and had a sympathetic feeling for a firm foe. But for any meddlesome patronage or gratuitous advice he never had anything but very uncompromising language. We have seen that an article in the " London Medical Repository," which compared the publication of Abernethy's lectures to two especially mean acts unlike in their felonious importance but alike in their meanness, formed the probable stimulus to the continuation of the legal processes before Lord Eldon that they were designed to squash. Similarly the strictures of the " Medico-Chirurgical Review" stirred into a blaze the ardour of a quarrel that if left to the parties concerned might have smouldered down and eventually gone out. Again, if the interference of the " Medico-Chirurgical Review" in favour of the action of the surgeons of St. Thomas's Hospital was unfortunate in itself, the particular line of defence adopted by Dr. johnson was doubly so when placed in opposition to a man like Wakley, who was always on the side of the public or the rank and file—a true friend of the weaker.

" No man," said the ' Medico-Chirurgical Review,' " can command success in surgical operations; and if a surgeon fail from want of dexterity he suffers mortification enough, heaven knows! in the operating-room, without being put to the cruel and demoniacal torture of seeing the failure blazoned forth to the public ! "

This argument was made the subject of utter ridicule by Wakley. He begged his readers to imagine a case in which some simple operation in surgery had been performed in a bungling and disgraceful manner, so that the patient's life was endangered by, or actually sacrificed to, the operator's want of dexterity. If such a case as this had occurred in private practice Wakley could conceive that it might be desirable to suppress the cause of failure out of tenderness to the feelings of the relatives and friends of the deceased. But the expediency of suppressing all public notice of the malpraxis of a surgeon must be defended only on an amiable, if injudicious, regard for the feelings of the friends, not out of tenderness to the ignorant operator.

"This latter," said Wakley, " is so monstrous a proposition that, prepared as we were for the imbecilities of the Hole-and-corner champions, we were somewhat staggered at the impudent absurdity with which it is advanced. . . . . Not a scintilla of compassion does the Hole-and-corner advocate suffer to escape him for the victim of the surgeon's want of dexterity ; all his sympathy is reserved for the ignorant operator."

The remarks of the "Medico-Chirurgical Review" furnished Wakley with exactly the kind of object he most relished attacking—a narrow view held by monopolists or their advocates. He combated it with a savage relish of the task, laughing at it and rending it alternately. From only one standpoint would he allow it any sort of consideration, there being only one standpoint from which regard for the feelings of the operator could be seen to affect the patient's interests. It was just possible that if cases of failure were published medical officers of public institutions would not risk their characters by performing operations necessarily attended with but doubtful chances of success. While conceding this point, Wakley held that, as no surgeon ought to operate without a hope of success, if a hospital surgeon should be deterred from discharging his duty by a dread of the press he could not be fit to hold his situation.

The preface to the volume of the "Lancet" published on October 9th, 1824 contained a very serious reflection upon Mr. Tyrrell. Sir Astley Cooper's lectures had come to a conclusion in the previous year, and the editor, in congratulating himself upon having been the medium of bringing them before the notice of the profession, made a reference to the fact that twelve of these lectures had just been

H

published by Mr. Tyrrell at the price of half-a-guinea, with illustrative cases from his own hospital practice appended. Wakley rejoiced over the fact as the invaluable principles contained in the lectures could not be too extensively diffused, but he objected to Mr. Tyrrell's action in the matter because it was marked by an act of literary dishonesty. In Wakley's opinion, the part of Mr. Tyrrell's volume, which really consisted of Sir Astley Cooper's last course of lectures, was copied paragraph for paragraph and phrase for phrase from the " Lancet," a proceeding that was inevitable if Sir Astley Cooper's lectures were to be reproduced at all, as the transcript for the " Lancet " was the only manuscript in existence. What Wakley particularly objected to was the fact that Mr. Tyrrell had concealed the source from which he had obtained his material for the book.

"He would have remained silent," he said, " if Mr. Tyrrell had not had the singular effrontery not only to conceal the source from which his fragment of the lectures is derived, but actually to represent himself in his preface as the veritable Simon Pure and to declare that his is the only correct and authentic copy. Now this is too much; it is too ludicrous to see Mr. Tyrrell alternately figuring as a Hole-and-corner Surgeon and as a humble transcriber of the pages of the ' Lancet '; at one time striving by all the contemptible artifices which we have so frequently exposed, to put down the ' Lancet '; and at another meekly sitting with our volume before him, coolly appropriating our labours, even servilely adopting our phraseology, where it differs from that of Sir Astley Cooper; and finally, with unexampled intrepidity, declaring that his is the only correct copy, for the sake of adding a little to the enormous profits which he already extracts from the pockets of the students."

A footnote to this passage said that Mr. Tyrrell had fallen into the pitfall so fatal to the plagiarist, and had transcribed passages which Sir Astley Cooper had never uttered, but which had been incorporated in the " Lancet " reports by error. This was the warning of a coming storm, but not until November 20th, 1824, was any further notice taken of Mr. Tyrrell's book. Upon that date, however, an article appeared the style and tone of which must have been adopted out of deliberate attempt to force matters to a legal contest.

The article was entitled "The Real Simon Pure,"* and accused Mr. Tyrrell in unmeasured terms of literary and professional incompetency and dishonesty, asserting that the text of Sir Astley Cooper's lectures had been bodily stolen from the "Lancet" and that the illustrative cases were badly chosen and unimportant as a whole, and that one in particular had been seriously garbled, being recorded as a success in spite of the fact that it had a fatal termination.

Terribly relentless and almost savage as this article was, as an indictment it was a masterly piece of work, and it is impossible to read it now without feeling that the pen that wrote it was moving in obedience to a mind not stirred by petty malice, but fiercely swayed by passionate conviction. That Wakley had a personal grievance against Mr. Tyrrell is not denied, and it is probable that being a very human man he was not sorry to catch him tripping; but it was not Mr. Tyrrell alone whom he had in his mind when he poured out the vials of his scornful wrath, but Tyrrell's uncle and patron, his colleagues at St. Thomas's Hospital, and all who throve by nepotism and secrecy at the institutions that should have been the purest fountains of charity and the most unprejudiced sanctuaries of science. The article commenced by taking a passage from every tenth page of Mr. Tyrrell's book, commencing at a certain place, and comparing it with the corresponding paragraph as it appeared in the "Lancet." Six such parallel passages were given and shown to be practically identical. The illustrative cases were then very roughly criticised, and here the crowning offence urged

---

* Simon Pure was a character in an early eighteenth century play entitled "A Bold Stroke for a Wife," and written by Mrs. Centlivre. The story turns upon the impersonation of a young Quaker hero by an adventurer named Feignwell, and the hero is known as the Real Simon Pure to distinguish him from his counterfeit. The nickname does not appear very well applied in the connexion that it was used by Wakley, who evidently meant by it the True Culprit, but the word "Pure" attracted him. All the tyranny of the Council of the College of Surgeons was, as will be seen later, adopted towards the commonalty to mark the difference between "Pure" Surgeons or Hospital Surgeons and mere general practitioners.

against Mr. Tyrrell was reached, for among these cases was one quoted by the author as a success, the subject of the operation having died before the issue of the work.

" This," wrote Wakley, " we consider the climax. We have toiled through a jumble of commonplace remarks, stale truisms and long-spun cases. . . . . These, it is true, we might have overlooked in benevolent compassion for the imbecility of the head that could think of adding to the value of Sir Astley Cooper's lectures by such paltry trash. . . . . He might have been content with palming upon the public *our pages* for *his own* production . . . . without having the unblushing effrontery to publish false facts. . . . . The world will hardly credit that a hospital surgeon could *publish, as a successful case, one* that we had already given the *post-mortem examination of;* such, however, is the fact, as may be proved by a reference to our own pages."

The case in question was that of a certain Thomas Denman, occasionally alluded to as Timothy Desman, who was admitted into St. Thomas's Hospital on the last day of August with a depressed compound fracture of the vertex of the skull. Mr. Tyrrell's account of the treatment of the case was as follows :—" I removed the whole of the fractured bone, which was comminuted ; one small portion had penetrated the dura mater. He has been treated just as the former patient was and has not had a bad symptom since." The case was immediately recognised as one that had been reported in the " Lancet " of the previous quarter as having a fatal termination through abscess of the left frontal lobe of the brain, and Wakley appended the account of the post-mortem examination, which he had printed at the time, as a note to Tyrrell's account of the case.

Upon this undoubtedly libellous article an action was brought against the editor of the " Lancet " and damages of £2000 were claimed.

CHAPTER XIII

[1823–1834]

Tyrrell v. *Wakley: The Case for the Plaintiff—The Case for the Defendant—The Judge's Charge—Fifty Pounds Damages Awarded —Contumacious Behaviour—The Effects of the Trial.*

THE case of Tyrrell *v.* Wakley came on for hearing on February 25th, 1825, before Lord Chief Justice Best (afterwards Lord Wynford) and a special jury. Mr. Serjeant Vaughan and Mr. Serjeant Adams appeared for the plaintiff, and Mr. Brougham (afterwards Lord Brougham) and Mr. FitzRoy Kelly (afterwards Chief Baron Kelly) for the defendant. Mr. Serjeant Vaughan, in his opening speech, referred to the deplorable state of friction between Wakley and certain of the hospital surgeons, and attempted to show that the publication of the libel was the direct and malicious outcome of Wakley's exclusion from St. Thomas's Hospital by Mr. Tyrrell and his colleagues. He justified that exclusion by saying that Wakley had made ill use of the privilege enjoyed by old students at St. Thomas's Hospital of being free of the wards and lecture-rooms of the institution after they had completed their medical curriculum ; that false statements had been made by him in his paper ; and that it had therefore been thought proper by the authorities to exclude him from the hospital. Mr. Tyrrell was one of those who put his name to the paper by which Wakley was expelled from the hospital in May, 1824 ; and from that date a series of libels on Mr. Tyrrell could be traced to the " Lancet," ending with the one now specifically complained of, which made a most direct and bitter attack on his character. The damages were laid at £2000, which counsel did not consider excessive having an eye to the scurrilous nature of the article and the wide circulation of the paper in which it appeared. Mr. Tyrrell was held up to the public in a paper with a known circulation of more than four thousand as a man who had been in the habit of publishing false statements to the world, and of attempting to raise a spurious reputation on the supposed success of his practice by publishing his unsuccessful cases without adding to his accounts their luckless terminations. The imputations were not merely of a want of talent—not merely of errors of the head—but of the worst vices of the heart. Mr. Tyrrell was practically called in the article in question a thief of another's labours and a mendacious boaster.

. One part of Mr. Serjeant Vaughan's speech certainly carried weight, and that was where he dealt with Wakley's property in the lectures. Mr. Tyrrell could not be said to have stolen from Wakley what Wakley had never legally owned—and the question of Wakley's right in these lectures was very doubtful. Some sort of right in them had been given him by Sir Astley Cooper, but how much was an open question. Moreover, as the Abernethy case was at this very time being considered in another court under the rather notorious circumstances already detailed, every one felt that the question of copyright in lectures was in an unsettled condition and that an accusation of gross literary dishonesty founded upon any assumed settlement of that question did not at the time come very well from Wakley. When Mr. Serjeant Vaughan said that the lectures were undoubtedly Sir Astley Cooper's, · and that he must be allowed to do whatever he liked with them and that he therefore was within his right in employing his nephew, Mr. Tyrrell, to publish certain of them in a book with a view to correct the inaccuracies present in the reports which had appeared in the "Lancet" he made a point and it was the only one he really did make. With regard to the imputation that Mr. Tyrrell had wilfully suppressed the fatal termination of the case of Thomas Denman, counsel contended that it was a gross libel. The account of the case in the book, of which the libel was in some sort a review, expressly dealt with the condition of the patient up to a certain date only, and when the man died later the fact was noted in a slip pasted into all the copies.

Mr. Serjeant Vaughan called witnesses, who proved Wakley's responsibility for whatever appeared in the "Lancet." The printer of the book testified to the fact that a correction was ordered to be pasted into each copy of the book at the earliest possible opportunity, though he could not swear that every copy of the book that went out from his establishment was so treated. No evidence whatever was adduced that the alleged errors in the "Lancet" reports, owing to which Mr. Tyrrell had been invited to publish a corrected edition of the lectures, ever existed. Not a single slip or flaw in them was ever alluded to by any witness, though the statement that Mr. Tyrrell's assistance in the publication of the volume had been invoked as a corrective to Wakley's inaccuracies had been much insisted upon in counsel's opening speech.

Brougham's defence of Wakley in this case was one of his finest forensic efforts. He categorically traversed each statement and implied argument that had fallen from Serjeant Vaughan's lips, and while using every sort of legal weapon in his client's behalf, comported himself with an easy gaiety that betokened a good conscience bred of a good case. He absolutely denied that Wakley was animated by any malicious feeling towards Mr. Tyrrell. Censure had been administered by a critic to a work submitted to the public's judgment—that was all. The author's character was not attacked. There was not in Wakley's article one word that constituted a perversion from liberal, free, and unfettered criticism into malignant slander. Next Mr. Brougham pointed out, not without sophistication, but with great ingenuity and eloquence, that Wakley had never been so stupid or ill-advised as to claim any copyright in Sir Astley Cooper's lectures so as to be able to preclude any one other than himself from publishing them. Wakley only claimed property in his own report, for the transcript and printing of which he had paid. He was not calling Mr.

Tyrrell a thief because Mr. Tyrrell had published ten of Sir Astley Cooper's lectures, but because he had used the "Lancet" reports of the same without acknowledgment, which reports had appeared with the tacit if not with the express sanction of their eminent author. Upon Mr. Tyrrell's plea, which was really beside the point, that the new and authorised publication had taken place because of the numerous inaccuracies which had crept into the "Lancet" reports, Brougham could afford to pour ridicule. For, first, the plagiarism that had taken place from the "Lancet" for the production of Mr. Tyrrell's book was undeniable, and to transcribe passages from a report must appear a droll way of correcting that report; while, secondly, the statement that the "Lancet" reports were incorrect was unsupported by any evidence and was manifestly an after-thought. Brougham's humour was a little unsparing, and while he was dealing with the accusation of plagiary his words were spoken to a running accompaniment of laughter.

"Here again is the incorrect account of the 'Lancet'!" he said, reading out one of the selected parallel passages. "'Certainly the formation of matter will be attended with a slight fever, but not of the hectic kind; the tongue will be clean, the pulse very little affected, and the person very slightly deranged; but after an opening is made into the part constitutional irritation sometimes comes on and life is then endangered.' A most inaccurate representation of that worthy, learned, and skilful man, Sir Astley Cooper, which he (Sir Astley Cooper) could not bear to read—which haunted him every time he heard the name of the 'Lancet'—he was punctured every time he heard it. 'So,' says he, 'I will send to Mr. Tyrrell; he is an *accurate* man; he will not publish such trash; I will send for good Mr. Tyrrell, my 'squire in medical knight-errantry, and he will publish what I really did say.' So he sends for Mr. Tyrrell, and he says, 'Mr. Tyrrell, there is sixpence for you, Mr. Tyrrell; go and lay it out in a way that is most calculated to correct the errors of the 'Lancet.' And then with this sixpence he (Mr. Tyrrell) goes and purchases a number of the 'Lancet' and tries the remedy of giving a correct account of what Sir Astley Cooper said; and, in order to do that, he gives you the following correct account: 'Certainly the formation of matter will be attended with a slight fever, but not of the hectic kind; the tongue will be clean, the pulse very little affected, and the person very slightly deranged;

but after an opening is made into the part constitutional irritation comes on, and life is then endangered.' As much alike as ever two peas were ! Indeed, no two peas were so much alike."

The pervading element of Brougham's speech was its genial banter. In this way he went through several parallel passages, reading first the "Lancet" reports, then imagining Sir Astley Cooper condemning the "Lancet" for mis-statements and sending for Mr. Tyrrell and asking him, sixpence in hand, to make the necessary correction. This Mr. Tyrrell was supposed to have done, and the resulting corrected passage was read to the jury. It was always, for practical purposes, unaltered from the form in which the "Lancet" had given it, and which the Court had just heard.

With the more serious accusation of wilful suppression of the termination of Thomas Denman's case Brougham also dealt in humorous style—a style which he considered very apt to the situation, for he asked how it was possible for the "Lancet" to state the ridiculous circumstances to their readers without rallying Mr. Tyrrell on them.

" A man is sent to the hospital," he said, " with a compound fracture of the skull. . . . . A battle begins, and then comes the skilful and powerful hand of our great champion, Mr. Tyrrell ; and he, by the skill of his movements, by his extraordinary perseverance and able tactics, soon brought the thing to a successful issue. He thought he had watched his enemy like a good and skilful commander, and fairly beaten him out of the field. So he thought and said on the 20th of September ; but unfortunately death in the end out-generalled him, and obtained the victory two days after the hasty proclamation of the good doctor's triumph. The fact was that while the plaintiff was gazetting his own promotion, while he was indulging in the fond aspirations of his own conquest, while he was making bonfires and letting off gunpowder—in the midst of rejoicings in came Death upon his patient, by a sort of lateral movement, opened his trenches, and, notwithstanding the formidable array of hospital weapons, bore away the palm of victory; horse, foot, and dragoons ; and left the poor doctors in dismay and discomfiture."

Brougham concluded by repeating that there was nothing in the "Lancet" criticism of Mr. Tyrrell's book transgressing the legitimate bounds of criticism. The author had come before the public for notice and had been noticed. His private character, his behaviour as a parent or husband, for instance, had not been attacked, but his reputation as an author had been dealt with—and that everyone who affixes his name to a book must expect.

Lord Chief justice Best summed up in an impartial manner, but the most definite words in his somewhat colourless address directed the jury to find for the plaintiff. The Lord Chief Justice considered that the phraseology adopted in the libel did convey the very imputation upon Mr. Tyrrell's private character that the defendant disclaimed for it, "otherwise he did not know what the language could mean," and it was this expression that gave Mr. Tyrrell his verdict. With regard to the case of Thomas Denman—and this was the topic upon which the strongest language was used in the libel complained of—the Lord Chief justice did not consider that Mr. Tyrrell had been treated very badly. He cavilled a little at the word " imposition," which was Wakley's term for the narration of the case to the public as a success when it was really a failure, and wished that he had had evidence before him that the *erratum* had not been seen by the author of the review. But he considered that strong observations upon the impropriety of narrating such a case to the world as a successful case were warranted and constituted fair criticism ; and if that had been all that was to be discovered in the defendant's conduct he should have directed the jury to find a verdict in his favour. But he did not consider the article in question fair criticism as a whole and could not discuss one part of the alleged libel away from the context. He pointed out, however, that the case never should have been published as an illustrative case at all—unless as a warning—by a man who knew of its fatal termination, and he held that an *erratum* did not alter the fact that it was no longer an illustrative case. To put it briefly, Lord Chief justice Best thought that Mr. Tyrrell had been libelled not so much by the things that had been said of him as by the way in which they had been said. He did not allude to the fact that certain of the copies might have

been distributed to the public without the correcting slip
until he was reminded of his omission by Wakley's counsel ;
and he accepted as accurate Serjeant Vaughan's uncorrobo-
rated and utterly untrue statement that the "Lancet" reports
of Sir Astley Cooper's lectures, being faulty, were corrected
by Mr. Tyrrell. He also informed the jury that Sir Astley
Cooper objected to the publication of his lectures in the
"Lancet," which was not only beside the question at issue;
but irreconcilable with Sir Astley Cooper's own words on
the subject.

The jury consulted for a quarter of an hour and then
returned their verdict for the plaintiff, assessing the damages
at £50.

Immediately after the trial Wakley, with characteristic
decision, or obstinacy, or audacity—for different people
would view the action in different ways—published his
opinion of the proceedings and took occasion to recapitulate
every word he had uttered previously and for using which
he had just been fined. He eulogised Brougham and was
complimentary also to Serjeant Vaughan, holding his treatment of the case to have been fair and honourable. He
took it for granted that the accusation of inaccuracy
against the "Lancet" was incorporated in the learned gentleman's brief, but thought that he must have felt ashamed at
being expected to make it, knowing that no witnesses were
to be called to support his opening words. He also rallied
Serjeant Vaughan upon his statement that the publication
of medical lectures was especially profitable. "How did he
know there was such a profit ?" asked Wakley. "If he (the
learned Serjeant) would commence the publication of the
next course of gratuitous lectures delivered by his renowned
client, Mr. Frederick Tyrrell, we will venture to assert that
by doing so for the next seven years he will not obtain sufficient profit to purchase powder for his wig."

In commenting on the summing up of the Lord Chief
justice Wakley's words became graver and his language
more forcible. He virtually charged his lordship with
taking up the cudgels in Mr. Tyrrell's behalf against the

" Lancet," accusing him, while shielded by his office, of throwing into the scale of the plaintiff's case the preponderating influence of his authority. He found the Lord Chief Justice's words to the jury wrong in two respects. First, it was not pointed out to them that no attempt was made to disprove the defendant's principal charge against the plaintiff —viz., plagiarism. " Did the plaintiff," asked Wakley, " attempt to falsify that charge ? Did he place before the jury one tittle of evidence for the purpose of negativing that assertion ? No, he did not." Yet this tacit admission of guilt was not pointed out to the jury. Secondly, Wakley held it disgraceful that the assertions that the " Lancet " reports were inaccurate and that Sir Astley Cooper was dissatisfied with them should have been made from the bench when no evidence supported either of these assertions, while words in actual contradiction of them had been put on record in the " Lancet " from Sir Astley Cooper's own lips.

Wakley protested that even if the " Lancet " had strayed from the paths of criticism in the matter of attributing to Mr. Tyrrell motives other than proper (which he still denied) the judge in the case had gone much further beyond the boundaries of his judicial duty by characterising those responsible for the production of the " Lancet " as thieves upon the unsupported statement of counsel briefed in the interests of the enemies of the " Lancet." Wakley then stated definitely that the copy of Mr. Tyrrell's work purchased by the editor of the " Lancet " from Mr. Highley on October 5th had no *erratum* slip concerning Denman's case. Further, he added that after the action was instituted he went to Mr. Highley's shop and found there several more copies similarly deficient. He concluded the article by tearing Mr. Tyrrell's additions to his eminent uncle's lectures to tatters in a manner that showed the restraining influences of a judge's ill-opinion and a fifty-pound fine to be but small, and reviewed the celebrated *erratum* for the first time by pointing out that it was written in shocking grammar—as it was.

The termination of the case of Tyrrell *v.* Wakley marked

an epoch in the career of the defendant and his journal. It was at this time that Wakley the Reformer, with the "Lancet" as his weapon, became recognised as a power. Hitherto the bitterness and violent language of some of the articles in the "Lancet," and the astounding liberality of some of the editorial views, had brought to the paper considerable measure of attention, but not of a wholly respectful sort. Some men read it, some men laughed at it, and some men wondered at it, but nobody much marked it, for its views were not sufficiently condensed and its objects not definitely concentrated. But the result of this second law-suit, taken in connexion with the case of Abernethy v. Hutchinson, revealed Wakley as the exponent of a sound, settled, and far-reaching policy for medical reform, and from the close of 1825 onwards he had as his intelligent supporters all who could benefit by such reform, and as his antagonists all who would lose by the same. For the case of Abernethy v. Hutchinson dovetailed well into the case of Tyrrell v. Wakley. The one was an entirely impersonal affair. What Wakley and Abernethy thought of one another had no bearing upon the legal question of what measure of exclusive copyright, if any, a man might have in his spoken words as a lecturer. The other was a very personal matter indeed, for Wakley made no secret that his review of Mr. Tyrrell's book was intended to hold up that gentleman to the public as a dunce and a plagiarist. Yet on each occasion Wakley had the same inspiration—the quiddity of each attitude was the desire to curtail the privileges of the hospital surgeons and enlarge those of the rank and file of the profession. In the first case he exhibited the lecturer in his public capacity as a lecturer, and said that the profession at large had a right to read his words that they might judge of the propriety with which he filled a position the emoluments of which came— and came of necessity, not of choice—out of the pockets of the London students. In the second case he exhibited a hospital surgeon as a scientific author and a prominent member of an honourable profession which is fenced about with much traditional etiquette. These posts at the various hospitals and recognised schools attached to them are valuable, said Wakley, because of the fees which they bring and because of the position which they give to their occupants. Let us take this gentleman, then, as a specimen, and see how he discharges his duties towards the profession at large, let us estimate his scientific work, and let us inquire into his views of professional right and wrong. That was the true meaning of the libellous article out of which the lawsuit of Tyrrell *v.* Wakley arose ; and the result of that suit was to reveal what had previously seemed to be aimless fault-finding as a deliberate policy ; and Wakley's subsequent actions in the cause of reform of the Royal College of Surgeons of England and within certain of the metropolitan hospitals were but developments of that policy.

CHAPTER XIV

[1823–1834]

Wakley's Crusades against Hospital Administration and the Government of the Royal College of Surgeons of England—Their Personal or Impersonal Nature — The Procuring of Hospital Reports—Specimens of this Department in Early Numbers of the " Lancet"—The Scope of these Reports.

WAKLEY now found himself with two avowed objects of attack—the administration of the metropolitan hospitals and the constitution of the Royal College of Surgeons of England—and against each he waged a relentless war. He poured scorn upon the educational system by which the students were compelled to pay large fees to support hospital surgeons who were unwilling or unable to teach them ; and he held up to ridicule the corporation which withheld from its members all the benefits it had been created to bestow.

In the Abernethy case, where Abernethy was acting as the representative of his colleagues, the holders of staff appointments at the hospitals, Wakley had fought on a purely legal question, and in the end had won the day ; while during his brief period of defeat he had continued to do the thing against which the aid of the Court had been asked. In the Tyrrell case he had subjected one of this same order to scathing criticism as a professional man and a scientific writer, and had escaped with a fine of but one-fortieth the magnitude at which the damage that he had done had been estimated, and had celebrated his escape by deliberately repeating his offence and adding to its enormity. The staffs of the various metropolitan hospitals were in a state of

expectation. On every staff in London there were men who
owed their positions to other qualifications than their
surgical attainments, and they fell a-wondering whose turn
it would be next. The authorities of the Royal College of
Surgeons of England were involved in his denunciations.
The by-law of the College, by which Abernethy and a few
others were made the only teachers whose certificates of
due attendance by the students at the London hospitals the
College would receive, had come in for unfavourable notice,
and it did not require much foresight to presage Wakley's
speedy return to the subject.

The personal or impersonal character of Wakley's attacks
must be recognised because it was identical in either crusade.
It would seem, on the one hand, that the College, being a
corporation, was open to censure that was not personal,
and that no grave want of taste could be discovered in the
designation of its constitution and behaviour as corrupt,
inept, and impertinent. The officers of the College had a
charter whereby they were guided in the administration of
its affairs, and while they conformed to their charter the
hardest things that were said about the institution reflected
in no way upon them personally. It would seem, on the
other hand, that attacks upon hospital administration were
compelled to be of a highly personal nature, inasmuch as
they were bound to resolve themselves into reflections upon
the surgical skill or intellectual grasp and verbal felicity of
the gentlemen who operated or lectured as members of the
various staffs. Wakley desired to treat both sets of abuses
in the same way, clearly perceiving that they had a common
origin in the want of unity and general apathy of the body
of the medical profession. This body he desired to arouse
to the two facts that their teachers failed in duty towards
them, and that the College of which the majority of them
were members mulcted them in fees but withheld from
them all their rightful privileges. No one glancing over the
columns of the "Lancet" during its first decade will have a
moment's hesitation in deciding that Wakley, having to
frame a method of indictment suitable to both sets of

abuses, deliberately, even wantonly, chose the personal one always. Such an opinion would be wrong. His writings teemed with personalities, his speeches derived much of their point from the same element, but he tried in every way to preserve a middle course in his indictments of the Royal College of Surgeons and of hospital officials. Into his criticism of the corporation he certainly introduced much that almost amounted to personal abuse of individuals, while it would have been possible for him to deal with the legitimate complaints of the members of the College in a more abstract manner. But his reflections upon hospital administration were directed against systems whenever feasible, and although names were introduced, and although personal remarks formed the basis of much of his fault-finding, yet it was the administration rather than the administrators that he designed to attack. He only directed his reflections upon the College against the authorities by name when he saw that to animadvert against the constitution of the College would not appeal to the minds of his audience sufficiently. Abuse of men was readily understood, but reproachful criticisms of a legal instrument were not so easy to follow. If his uncomplimentary speeches had only been aimed at the Charter of the College no widespread agitation against the existent state of affairs would ever have sprung from them. This personal turn was not necessarily given to his reflections upon the administration of the metropolitan hospitals, for his readers could thoroughly appreciate what constituted good hospital management, and no point and piquancy were given to his strictures by the unnecessary introduction of names.

It will be understood that Wakley's two separate attacks, that on hospital administration and that on the College of Surgeons, were conducted simultaneously. For the purposes of this narrative his criticism of the metropolitan hospitals will be considered first, while his struggles after reform in the College of Surgeons will be described later, but it should be remembered that he was engaged in a double war all the time; for the feeling that he had foes on either side accounted for the fierceness of some of his onslaughts, and his perpetual air of watchfulness.

The Hospital Reports which it was announced would give a true and unbiassed record from week to week of the practice within the walls of the various metropolitan institutions were watched with apprehension by all concerned in the administration of the institutions. Repeatedly denying that there could be any other reason for desiring to preclude him from reporting the cases that came under treatment in the hospitals save fear—fear lest malpraxis should be exposed or mismanagement and nepotism be revealed—he persevered steadily in his announced intention. Week after week there appeared in the " Lancet" elaborate accounts of operations, abstracts of clinical lectures, and outspoken reflections upon administrative details, every hospital in the metropolis receiving these unsolicited attentions, each being treated in exactly the same spirit— unceremoniously. Hospitals, said Wakley, are public places, supported by the piety and wealth of members of the public for the cure of their poorer brethren. And as public places they shall have publicity.

Wakley, having resolved to totally disregard all orders of expulsion, was himself a regular attendant at the Borough Hospitals and the author of many of the early reports of operative procedures at their theatres, but he was careful to make his survey of London hospital practice from week to week a comprehensive one, so that he had to employ reporters to work for him. His difficulty in doing this was twofold. It was necessary that the man who reported for him should be thoroughly competent, and privileged to go in and out of the wards at will. It was necessary also that he should be able to keep his identity unrevealed, in view of the great opposition that had been manifested by many of the hospital surgeons to the publicity threatened for their work. Travers, for instance, frankly told the students of the Borough Hospitals that he would urge the expulsion from all classes of any student detected in supplying the " Lancet "

with reports of lectures or of operative proceedings, while
Abernethy had expressed the sentiments of himself and his
colleagues at St. Bartholomew's Hospital by terming the
paid reporter of the "Lancet" "a hireling," and bidding him
stand forth to receive back his fees, which the medical
school declined to keep having regard to their tainted
source.   But as against these facts the students recognised in
the "Lancet" a strong friend to their cause, so that Wakley
obtained many offers of assistance and had from the beginning many would-be contributors to choose from.   It
was his practice to employ and pay highly a senior student
at each hospital to make regular reports for him, while he
himself or some trusted member of his staff would make a
round of the various operating theatres, dropping in now
on this and now on that institution that he might judge for
himself of the accuracy of his reporters' work.

All who possess or have access to the back numbers of the
"Lancet" can read for themselves the way in which these
reports were done ; and if they can subdue the innate
savagery of man so far as to pass over the scathing accounts
of some luckless surgeon's error to peruse the approving
records of successful operations and of well-directed innovations for the good of patient or student, they will certainly
agree that the work was fairly done.   It was also a remarkable
journalistic feat.   Short-hand had not reached its present
pitch of excellence ; telegraphy was unknown ; London
possessed no remarkable facilities for progression from place
to place ; no papers, medical or lay, gave information in the
form of a diary, from which could be learned the day and
hour at which in the interests of science a reporter ought to
be in a given place—but in spite of all these drawbacks, and
with the additional disability upon him that if his agents were
discovered all obstacles would be officially placed in their way,
Wakley produced week by week a record of doings within
the jealously guarded walls of the metropolitan hospitals.

A few extracts from these reports up to the year 1828 will
enable an estimate of their value to be arrived at ; for it will
then be possible to appreciate the amount of good that such

a system of regular criticism must have worked, and the amount of indignation and vexation that such a violation of their privacy must have aroused in the officials of the different hospitals.

In March, 1825, a man was admitted into St. George's Hospital suffering from pneumonia. He was bled in the arm by the dresser and during the little operation the brachial artery was wounded. The man was placed under one of the surgeons, who, on consultation with the physician, considered that the pulmonary trouble was too severe to warrant him in disturbing the patient by tying the brachial artery—obviously the only safe course to pursue under the unfortunate circumstances. A tight bandage was applied to the arm above the wound instead of a ligature being placed upon the vessel. The bandage remained three days untouched, when, the circulation having been occluded, mortification set in and the patient died. A coroner's jury brought in a verdict that the man died from the accidental opening of an artery in the arm and from the want of proper attention. Four months later a still worse case of malpraxis occurred at the same hospital. A man was admitted to the accident ward whose right knee was cut with a broken bottle. The house-surgeon thought that an artery was severed and applied a tight bandage. This patient was under the care of the same surgeon, who did not, as it afterwards transpired, examine the knee himself, but left the bandages undisturbed, despite the fact that the leg was much swollen above the bandage. The bandage was not removed for five days, and when it was the limb was in a terrible condition. The man died and an inquest was held at which it was elicited that the surgeon had trusted entirely to his house-surgeon, and that the younger gentleman's statements were not to be relied upon. A juror, in spite of the warnings of the coroner that he might be proceeded against for libel, persisted that there had been gross neglect in the treatment of the unfortunate man. The coroner pressed for a verdict without comment, but ultimately the jury returned their decision that "the deceased received a cut on the knee by accident and from the effects of improper surgical treatment and neglect his death was produced."

Upon these cases the "Lancet" made exceedingly severe comments and used freely the names of all concerned, holding their owners up to the contempt of the profession. Almost at the same time a man died in the Middlesex Hospital after an operation for strangulated hernia, and the writer of the "Lancet" report of the case definitely accused the senior surgeon of the hospital of having, as a first count, neglected the case, so that the unfortunate man's plight was hopeless when the operation was undertaken ; and having, as a second count, performed the operation in an exceedingly unskilful manner. The writer of the report finished by leaving discussion of the particular instance to say of the operative proceedings at the Middlesex Hospital generally that it was the regular practice at that place for the surgeon to wait before operating until all chance of recovery was gone, and that not more than one patient had recovered from an operation to relieve a strangulated hernia in the hospital for two years !

Several examples of malpraxis at Guy's Hospital and St. Thomas's Hospital were detailed at length. Two similar cases of compound fracture of the bones of the leg were admitted, one to the wards of Guy's Hospital and the other to the wards of St. Thomas's Hospital, in April, 1826, the treatment of the last of which came in for the strongest reprobation. In the former the surgeon was stated to have delayed operating until too late and then to have amputated in a clumsy manner. In the latter he was taken to task roundly for having omitted to notice that the patient was going downhill fast owing to an extensive abscess having formed, unsuspected by everybody, on the back of his thigh. All the names were given in full, and the editorial freedom of opinion was marked.

The comments showed the personal way in which Wakley dared to deal with these matters, but the times were out of joint and his treatment of hospital administration was under the circumstances judicious.

" Nothing is more easy," he wrote at this time, "than to show that our hospital system is fundamentally wrong, from the surgeon to the surgery man and from the physician to the apothecary's apprentice. The manner in which the appointments are managed is the most nefarious and in utter violation of every principle of justice and common sense. For example, an advertisement announces the resignation of a medical officer of some hospital (which, by-the-bye, too seldom happens), and how do the rival candidates arm themselves for the contest ? Not by trying to outvie each other at a public disputation, nor even at an examination in a committee-room, but by beating up the quarters of their brewers, their bakers, their tailors, and their other tradesmen, and in proportion as the candidates or their friends have influence with this class of persons, or, in other words, have a good city connexion, so are they according to the usual doctrine of chances secure of the vacant post. Now, then, men who can know nothing of the real qualifications of the candidates are the real electors of physicians and surgeons to public hospitals ; and what is the consequence ? What we too often see—that ignorant pretenders exclude men of sound talent, to the great injury of science and the great sacrifice of human life."

All of this Wakley set himself to demonstrate. The fact that the wrong men were chosen as medical officers to the hospitals could only be proved to demonstration by reporting examples of their failures. But such exposures only formed part, and not the larger part, of the work that he designed to carry out by the publication of the Hospital Reports. The general failings of the institutions as educational and administrative establishments also received uncomplimentary attention. That surgeons' pupils were idle and abused the privileges that they had purchased ; that dressers, having no proper supervision, very usually neglected their duties ; that the house-surgeons being chosen from these gentlemen were frequently ignorant ; that the nursing was often bad, and that no proper attention was paid to the diet of the patients ; that the buildings of the hospitals were sometimes uncleanly and insanitary—these and other unpleasant facts he brought to light by his elaborate system of reporting, and treated with proper out-speaking. Can it be wondered at that within the walls of the hospitals, by all save the students for whom he fought, his name was a synonym for mischief-maker and agitator ?

CHAPTER XV

[1823–1834]

*The Terrible Accusation of Malpraxis against Mr. Bransby Cooper
—The Style and Matter of the Libel—Wakley Defends himself personally—A Legal Point decided in his Favour—The Evidence for
the Defence.*

IN 1826 the printing and publishing of the "Lancet" were
transferred from 210, Strand, to Bolt Court, Fleet Street.
The new printers and publishers were Messrs. Mills,
Jowett* & Mills, a well known and highly respected firm,
so that the exchange was in every way an advance for the
paper. It was made at the instance of William Cobbett,
whose "Register" was printed by Messrs. Mills, jowett &
Mills, but with the full concurrence of Mr. G. L. Hutchinson
the original printer and publisher, who desired to escape
from the legal liabilities that seemed to him must be incurred
by business relations with Wakley. His forebodings were
justified about a year later. On March 29, 1828, there
appeared in the Hospital Reports the report of a case
which led to the most sensational lawsuit that Wakley was
ever engaged in, not excepting his suit against the Hope
Fire Assurance Company. This was the case of Bransby
Cooper *v.* Wakley. The report out of which the case arose
was the most outspoken denunciation of a piece of hospital
malpraxis possible to conceive. It was written in so
malignant a style that the terrible mischievousness of
sensational journalism was as remarkably illustrated by it
as was the power for good of a strong vindication of the

* It may be mentioned as a matter of interest that Dr. Jowett, the
celebrated Master of Balliol, was the son of Mr. Jowett in this firm.

rights and usefulness of publicity. It was at once the very best and the very worst that such a report could be. To the public it did the greatest good. To the medical profession it did both good and evil. It inflicted a serious blow upon the prestige of the hospital surgeons. But the widespread repudiation by the rank and file of the profession of the systems that could sanction such treatment as was alleged to have been meted out to Mr. Bransby Cooper's patient did public honour to the feelings of medical men. On the whole the good may be said to have outweighed the evil. To the individuals concerned no half measures were possible. The plaintiff, Mr. Bransby Cooper was inferentially called a murderer, and the defendant to justify his attitude followed the report by a leading article saying that he cared nothing for the result, but maintained the accuracy of his words, and not only his right but his duty to publish them.

The operation in question took place at Guy's Hospital, and was a lithotomy performed by Mr. Bransby Cooper, then a surgeon to the institution of three years' standing. The patient was a strong, middle-aged countryman, for whom the procedure of cutting for stone should not under ordinary circumstances have had any particularly grave risk. A definite rate of mortality occurred in such cases, and that should have been the measure of the risk. The operation, however, took a very long time and resulted fatally. Was this time consumed in honest attempt to combat extraordinary difficulties—in which case the unlucky surgeon would have commanded the sympathies of the medical profession and the public alike? Or was it frittered away in unsurgical bungling? The article in the "Lancet" left no doubt in the reader's mind what was the conclusion of the writer.

The report was headed :—

THE OPERATION OF LITHOTOMY BY MR. BRANSBY COOPER WHICH LASTED NEARLY ONE HOUR!

A footnote to the title was as follows : "The following passage occurs in John Bell's great work on surgery : 'Long and murderous operations, where the surgeon labours for an hour in extracting the stone, to the inevitable destruction of the patient' "; while the opening passages of the report show well the spirit in which it was conceived and written.

"We should," it ran, "be guilty of injustice towards this singularly gifted operator, as well as to our numerous readers, if we were to omit a full, true, and particular account of this case. It will doubtless be useful to the country 'draff' to learn how things are managed by one . of the privileged order—a hospital surgeon—nephew and surgeon, and surgeon because he is 'nephew.' The performance of this tragedy was nearly as follows :—"

The account which followed was short but horrible, and its horror was accentuated by the dramatic brevity of the recital. The word dramatic is used advisedly, for the report was cast in dramatic form. It was divided into Act I. and Act II., while the result of an examination of the body after the death of the patient was added as an epilogue. The first Act set out the preliminary steps of the operation, which took twenty minutes, and clearly insinuated that the original incision having been wrongly made the operator lost his proper appreciation of the anatomical geography of the region and attempted violently to effect a passage with his forceps where no incision had cleared the way—that, in fact, in his attempts to reach the bladder he made a false passage. The second Act, stated to have lasted half an hour, accused the operator of having hopelessly lost his head. It described him as calling for all forms of instruments, notably for one, the scoop, that must have been useless until the foreign body was actually located ; as asking for the assistance of his colleagues and even his dresser ; as complaining in front of the patient, of course unnarcotised, of his utter inability to understand the cause of his own terrible failure to extract the stone ; and, finally, when at last the operation was over, of attempting to explain the difficulties to the appalled assembly of surgeons and students while the conscious and dying patient still lay bound upon the operating table. No more terrible picture of incompetency, of want of skill, want of nerve, and want of heart could be imagined than the

picture that was drawn. The epilogue to this terrible
tragedy was in keeping. A brief description of the parts
concerned in the operation was followed by the most unmistakable insinuation that the reason why Mr. Bransby
Cooper had failed to extract the stone from the patient's
bladder was because his forceps had not at first been in the
bladder at all. In another part of the paper was the follow-
. ing savage little epigram :—

> " When Cooper's ' Nevey ' cut for stone,
>   His toils were long and heavy;
> The patient quicker parts has shewn,
>   He soon cut Cooper's ' Nevey.' "

Although this report was brief it contained a terrible
indictment of Mr. Bransby Cooper and also of Guy's
Hospital, at that time possessing the first reputation in the
kingdom for surgical practice. Stripped of all verbiage and
raising every insinuation to the dignity of a statement—
which no one could have read the article without doing—
the gist of the " Lancet " report was as follows : That the
authorities of Guy's Hospital had elected Mr. Bransby
Cooper upon their staff because he was Sir Astley Cooper's
nephew ; that he was an unskilful surgeon, and had consequently killed a patient by his gross mistakes during the
performance of an operation ; that he was so concerned at
the public exhibition of ignorance which he felt himself to
be making that he behaved with brutal callousness to the
unfortunate sufferer. (It must not be forgotten that we are
writing of the days when anæsthetics were unknown and
when, therefore, a premium was set upon rapidity of operation ; while anything like a consultation in front of a
conscious patient was held to be unprofessional and a grave
confession of weakness.) Nepotism on the part of the
management, malpraxis on the part of the officer—these
had been Wakley's outspoken and repeated accusations
against those responsible for the management of the London
hospitals. Time after time he had said that these two
factors were working secretly for ill, and equally often he

had promised that any mischief so produced should be dragged into the light of day. This was a unique occasion for keeping his word. *One* set of circumstances proved him right in *both* of his recurrent accusations. He printed those circumstances in a shape which could have left no doubt that he believed in the righteousness of his action, and he referred to them subsequently in articles even severer than the original report, and designed to open the eyes of the country " draff," as the metropolitan magnates of those days contemptuously designated their provincial brethren.

Mr. Bransby Cooper had no alternative but to bring an action against Wakley. If he had desired to do otherwise it is certain that those responsible for the medical and administrative management of Guy's Hospital would not have permitted him ; but he never had any doubt as to his course. He felt that his back was against the wall and that if he could not beat off the foe he was a ruined man, for the article in the " Lancet " was widely copied into the lay press, and a storm of popular comment was blowing round the names of Wakley, Bransby Cooper, Sir Astley Cooper, the " Lancet," and Guy's Hospital. The case originally stood to be heard in the Court of King's Bench on October 29th, 1828, but was postponed at Mr. Brougham's request, made on Wakley's behalf, until December 12th, when Wakley announced his intention of defending himself in person.

At half-past nine o'clock on the morning of Friday, December 12th, 1828, the case of Bransby Cooper *v.* Wakley came on for hearing in the Court of Queen's Bench before Lord Tenterden and a special jury. The case excited the most intense interest in the public mind. " Long before the sitting of the court at half-past nine o'clock," says the " Times, " " the different avenues leading to the court were so crowded that there was scarcely any possibility of forcing a passage. It was with the utmost difficulty, with the most active assistance of the constables and officers of the court that the counsel, jury, and witnesses could obtain an entrance." On the second day the approaches were still more thronged. At an exceedingly early hour persons were standing without the door anxious to obtain admission into the court. The officers, however, adopting a different course from that of Friday, kept the crowd at the outer door until the counsel, jury, and witnesses were admitted ; those who had assembled merely out of curiosity were not allowed to force their entrance. Several contemporary journals, the "Lancet" itself, the "Times," the "Sun," and the "Weekly Dispatch" narrate a curious little incident that happened in the crowd without Westminster Hall. A gentleman who was carrying a sword-stick had the case of it crushed by the excessive pressure of the crowd. The point of the sword came out through the bulging rent in the sheath, and was forced into a bystander's thigh. The tension of waiting and the general imagination of the fevered crowd, which was certainly set upon the consideration of horrors, gave to this small accident a serious importance, and all sorts of stories of attempts at assassination were buzzed about, the excitement not subsiding until at last the court was opened to the public.

The defendant appeared in person punctually, being assisted by Mr. Brougham and Mr. FitzRoy Kelly ; while Sir James Scarlett (afterwards Lord Abinger), Mr. F. Pollock (afterwards Chief Baron Pollock), and Mr. Scarlett represented the plaintiff. Wakley brought with him into court the cast of a child representing the position in which a patient is tied when undergoing the operation of lithotomy, the bones of a full-sized pelvis, and specimens of all the instruments alleged in the libellous report to have been used by Mr. Bransby Cooper in the fatal operation. These were placed upon a table in the well of the court.

Mr. Scarlett opened the pleadings by reading the libel, which consisted of the report of the case and the leading article upon it that had appeared in the next issue of the "Lancet." The leading article added nothing to the facts in the report, but was a most damning commentary upon the circumstances, setting out the details and calling attention to them with interjections, *nota benes*, and all sorts of verbal pilcrows. The writer, who was Wakley himself, did certainly make a disclaimer of being actuated by any malicious feeling towards Mr. Bransby Cooper, whom he was willing to believe a kind-hearted man justly popular among his pupils ; but this concession was followed by a bitter summing-up of the case against him. It could not be denied, wrote Wakley, that Mr. Bransby Cooper had taken nearly an hour to perform an operation whose average duration in the hands of skilful surgeons was six minutes. And it could not be questioned that he was indebted for his appointment to the staff of Guy's Hospital to his relationship to Sir Astley Cooper and not to his own skill.

Immediately upon the libel being read an extraordinary discussion followed. Sir james Scarlett rose to open the case, when Wakley insisted that as he had charged the plaintiff with unskilfulness and intended to prove the truth of his pleas he ought to proceed with his case before the plaintiff's case was gone into. Wakley's argument was ingenious and successful. While admitting that in general a plaintiff has the right to open his case and by consequence to have the general reply,

> " For courts of justice understand
> The plaintiff to be eldest hand,"

he submitted that there were exceptions to this rule and that his attitude of pleading justification only, and not innocence, placed his case in their category. The cases he relied on as precedents were three. The first was one of trespass, where the defendant admitted his entrance on to the plaintiff's property but pleaded right of way. Here the affirmation of the issue being thrown upon the defendant, Mr. Justice Bayley, a great jurist, and later a Baron of the Exchequer, held that the defendant had the right to begin. The other two were cases of assault and battery, where the defendant pleaded justification without adding "Not Guilty." In each of these cases Chief Justice Best and Mr. justice Bayley on consultation with brother judges had severally allowed the plea. It was Brougham who supplied Wakley with the legal information necessary to make his representation to Lord Tenterden, but it can be imagined that to hear so technical a point raised by a layman created no little sensation in the court, where the general feeling was one of sympathy for Wakley in his foolhardy attempt to conduct his own case against one of the most powerful advocates at the Bar. Sir James Scarlett strenuously opposed Wakley's application. Lord Tenterden, after a few minutes' consultation with two of his learned brothers in the adjoining courts, decided in Wakley's favour, who immediately rose to address the jury, having secured by his successful application the right to a general reply, which, with such an opponent as the Attorney-General to deal with, meant an enormous stride towards victory. Although Wakley obtained his point by relying upon precedents, he himself established a precedent while so doing, for the principle that had been allowed to prevail in cases of trespass and assault had never before been quoted as holding good in a case of libel.

Wakley's opening speech was a vindication of the view that it was of the utmost importance to the public that the management of hospitals should be efficient and that only men possessed of the highest professional skill should be elected honorary medical officers to these noble charities. Solely to maintain a high standard in the management of hospitals and in the skill and knowledge of those empowered to treat the sick and teach the students within their walls, he had published the addresses of hospital lecturers and the reports of clinical and operative procedure at the different theatres. In the ordinary course, and with no special malice whatever, he had received a report of an operation which had taken place at Guy's Hospital on a certain day. The report told so extraordinary a story that he had abstained from printing it until he had personally been assured by the contributor that it was true word for word. He then considered that he had no other course to pursue in his public character than to print the report and take the consequences. He then called his first and, as it turned out, most valuable witness, a Mr. Partridge of Colchester.

Mr. Partridge was a voluntary witness, unknown personally to Wakley. He was asked to give evidence the very day of the trial. In Brougham's brief, a document made interesting by the fact that it has upon it the pencil notes of the eminent lawyer and his exceedingly bad sketches of the anatomical distribution of the parts concerned in the operation of lithotomy, Mr. Partridge's name does not occur, while the names of all the other witnesses are given. Mr. Partridge said that he had practised surgery for fourteen years and was a prominent citizen in Colchester and an alderman of the borough. He had witnessed numerous lithotomies and had performed the operation eighteen times himself. He considered the report of the operation in the " Lancet " correct ; and he had been sitting immediately behind Mr. Bransby Cooper all the time. The operation lasted nearly an hour. Mr. Cooper appeared perplexed and hurried ; he varied his instruments perpetually and irrationally ; he expressed his wonder at the delay of extraction in front of the conscious and writhing patient. If the operator had known what he was about, said Mr. Partridge, he would have extracted the stone immediately.

Cross-examination, though severe, quite failed to shake this witness. His professional position was unimpeachable, and his motive for giving evidence could only be a desire to assist what he believed to be the cause of justice, for he was not a member of the staff of the " Lancet " and did not know Wakley by sight and scarcely by name until the morning of the trial. Wakley's other witnesses did not turn out so well. They testified to what they saw, and this in each case amounted to a confirmation of the report, but their answers under cross-examination to credit were not satisfactory. The first of these gentlemen, though a Licentiate of the Society of Apothecaries, was found to have put in false certificates in respect of his age, that he might obtain the diploma earlier than the regulations allowed. The second gentleman had succeeded Wakley as assistant to his (Wakley's) brother-in-law, Mr. Phelps of Beaminster, and was obviously interested in the issue of the case for reasons other than a desire to see abstract justice done. The third gentleman was found to be intimately acquainted with Mr. James Lambert, who wrote the report. It was felt by everybody that had it not been for Mr. Partridge, Wakley's selection of eye-witnesses out of a crowd of over two hundred persons would have been very unfortunate.

Mr. Lambert, the author of the report, came next. He maintained that the report was true and rather an under-statement than an over-statement of facts. He had attended the post-mortem examination and had there observed appearances which he considered bore out the accuracy of his report, inasmuch as they went to show that Mr. Bransby Cooper's first attempts at extraction were wrongly directed —that, in fact, he had hopelessly mistaken the anatomy of the region. Mr. Lambert did not emerge well from cross-examination. He was made to confess that he had had a personal quarrel with Mr. Cooper, and that the tone of pre-vious reports from his pen had caused his exclusion from the wards of the Middlesex and St. Thomas's Hospitals. He was also revealed as the cousin of the previous witness, who had obtained the Licentiateship of the Society of Apothe-caries by making a false statement on oath. As a whole he maintained the accuracy of his report. Sir james Scarlett was not able to shake him in his account of what happened, but he was able to prejudice his evidence in the eyes of the judge, and he did so.

Lambert was followed, fortunately for Wakley's case, by two rather better witnesses, in that their purity of motive was indubitable. Both testified to the length of time occupied by the operation and to the pitiable condition of hurry and perplexity to which Mr. Bransby Cooper was reduced by his ill-success at first. Wakley's last witness was the treasurer of St. Thomas's Hospital, a Mr. Benjamin Harrison. He was a very unwilling witness who appeared on subpœna, and in cross-examination gave Mr. Bransby

Cooper an excellent character as a surgeon. While, however, he swore that relationship to Sir Astley Cooper had had nothing to do with Mr. Bransby Cooper's election to the staff of Guy's Hospital, he would not swear that the gentleman who had been passed over, who was no relation to Sir Astley Cooper, but senior to Mr. Bransby Cooper, was not a better surgeon than the plaintiff, who had been preferred to him. Wakley then closed his case, and the court adjourned until the following day, Sir James Scarlett submitting that he would rather address a fresh jury than a jaded one.

K

CHAPTER XVI

[1823-1834]

Bransby Cooper v. Wakley—Sir James Scarlett for the Plaintiff—
The Witnesses for the Plaintiff—Wakley's Reply—The Verdict—
The Results of the Trial—The Solid Opposition to Wakley and his
Solid Following—The Attitude of the Public and the Profession—
Wakley's Expenses in the Trial Defrayed by Public Subscription.

ON the morning of Saturday, December 13th, 1828, before
an immense and very excited audience, Sir James Scarlett
rose to address the jury in behalf of the plaintiff, Mr.
Bransby Cooper. His opening words betrayed his irritation at the position in which Lord Tenterden's decision of
the previous day had placed him. He complained acri-
moniously that his client, a gentleman seeking redress for
one of the most injurious attacks upon fame and fortune
that had ever been brought to the cognisance of a court of
justice, had been placed during an entire day upon his
defence as though he were the defendant and the indictment
a criminal charge. " I have no doubt," he said, turning to
the jury, " that you are now sitting in judgment, not upon
what reparation shall be made to an injured man for one
of the basest calumnies any man could complain of, but
whether Mr. Cooper is not a party unworthy of his situation, who has contributed to shorten a man's life." He
then briefly sketched Mr. Bransby Cooper's honourable and
successful career. This started with pupilage at the
Norwich Hospital—a not irrelevant fact, for the ancient
city was famous in those days for its skilled lithotomists,
vesical calculus being a common malady with the dwellers
on the chalky soil of Norfolk. From Norwich Bransby

Cooper came to Guy's Hospital, and on completion of his time there accepted a commission in the Royal Artillery and saw service on the Continent and in Canada for three years with credit to himself.   In 1816, at the termination of the dispute with America, he left the army and after a short sojourn in Edinburgh returned to Guy's Hospital as apprentice to his uncle, Sir Astley Cooper.   His apprenticeship expired in 1823, when he was made demonstrator of anatomy.   In 1825 he was elected assistant surgeon to the hospital.   From that time forward until the publication of the libel not a word had been said against him, and counsel ridiculed the idea that Sir Astley Cooper would ever have employed a man as his assistant or his deputy in the most important surgical practice in the world without being fully assured, nephew or no nephew, that he was a highly competent operator.   He attributed Wakley's accusations of nepotism to an unbalanced sense of the importance of the "Lancet," which had arrogated to itself the position of censor of professional manners and morals.   Sir James Scarlett then explained the operation of lithotomy, very lucidly considering that he was only able to employ lay terms, and dwelt on the difficulties that might arise in its course.   Coming to the particular operation the performance of which formed the subject of the libel, he traversed most of the statements and all the insinuations contained in the alleged libel.   So far from the patient being a healthy countryman he was, said Sir james Scarlett, a stout man with a hectic complexion and disordered kidneys upon whom the operation was not performed until the agony that he suffered precluded any other course.   The delay and the employment of the various instruments were due not to any error on Mr. Bransby Cooper's part but to the peculiar difficulties of the case and the awkward position of the calculus.   The appearances in the cadaver were, he maintained, all of them in agreement with this view, save one rent in certain soft, easily lacerated tissues.   This rent, it had been insinuated by the "Lancet" reporter, had been made by Mr. Bransby Cooper's ill-directed attempts to reach the bladder with various instruments. It was, as a matter of fact to be proved by the oaths of persons who had examined the parts before the agent of the "Lancet" had handled them, made by that agent himself after death. Sir James Scarlett then denounced Mr. Lambert as a hireling, instigated by malice to write untruths, ignorant, and absolutely wanting in all decent feeling, as shown by the dramatic form into which he had cast his false report, and he wound up a vigorous piece of advocacy by asking the jury to mark their sense of indignation at the treatment that the plaintiff had received by awarding him exemplary damages. He then called Mr. Callaway, who had assisted Mr. Bransby Cooper in the performance of the operation.

Mr. Callaway testified to two things of importance: the first was that Mr. Bransby Cooper's original incision was rightly directed; the second was that the situation and shape of the stone were such as to make the extraction necessarily tedious and difficult. He confirmed the "Lancet" report in many details, such as that numerous different instruments were used, that a second incision into the bladder had to be made, and that the operator during the operation did say that he could not explain the cause of the delay; and he admitted in cross-examination that in his opinion Mr. Bransby Cooper had no knowledge of the situation of the stone. Mr. Callaway was the only medical witness called by Sir James Scarlett who actually saw the operation upon which the alleged libel was founded. The other medical witnesses were called to testify to the general difficulty of the operation and to the high character of Mr. Bransby Cooper, whilst they added for the benefit of the court their expert opinion of what had happened founded upon Mr. Callaway's evidence.

Mr. C. Aston Key, senior surgeon to Guy's Hospital and Mr. Bransby Cooper's brother-in-law, came first; then Mr. Laundy, a general practitioner, who stated that he was present once at the same operation when it was performed by that celebrated surgeon and anatomist the elder Cline, on which occasion the proceedings lasted an hour and forty minutes. Mr. Brodie (afterwards Sir Benjamin Brodie) of St. George's Hospital, President of the Royal College of Surgeons of England and of the Royal Society; Mr. Benjamin Travers, surgeon to St. Thomas's Hospital, Mr. Joseph Henry Green, surgeon to the same institution, and Mr. Dalrymple, surgeon to the Norwich Hospital, considered that Mr. Callaway's evidence showed that the skill of the operator could not be impeached.

Dr. Hodgkin, lecturer on morbid anatomy at Guy's Hospital, gave important evidence. He thought that in the unfortunate patient there had been present an anatomical conformation of the parts as revealed by post-mortem examination that would have rendered the operation a difficult one. He swore that Mr. Lambert came to him and asked permission to see the parts, and was allowed to do so in his (Dr. Hodgkin's) absence, and that on his return Mr. Lambert showed him a certain rent, the rent which it was insinuated in the report had been caused by Mr. Bransby Cooper's bungling. He at once taxed Mr. Lambert with having made the rent, it being his firm conviction that it had been made after death.

Last came Sir Astley Cooper. He confirmed the statements as to his nephew's honourable and successful career, and said that no one save the man actually operating could judge fairly of the difficulties of an operation. He gave as an explanation of the cause of the delay in the operation the fact that the bladder was empty, and narrated a case in point where contraction of an empty bladder over a calculus had caused a skilful surgeon "now present in the court" to take an hour to effect the extraction.

This completed the plaintiff's case, and Wakley rose immediately to reply. He said it was most remarkable that out of two hundred persons present the plaintiff had thought proper to call only one—a solitary one—to give evidence to his skill on the occasion out of which the libel arose, whilst a host of persons who knew nothing at all of that operation were called to speak to his professional ability. This he characterised as an attempt to practise an

imposition on the jury and on the public, but he hoped
that the jury would not be persuaded by the general opinion
of men not present at the operation that the specific facts
spoken to by the "Lancet" report did not occur. He pointed
out that Sir James Scarlett had devoted a considerable part
of his speech to miscalling Mr. Lambert, the "Lancet" reporter. Of course Mr. Lambert was a hireling, said Wakley.
He was paid for his contributions to the "Lancet" just as Sir
James Scarlett was paid for his advocacy of Mr. Bransby
Cooper. Wakley then cautioned the jury against the
evidence of "a gang of hospital surgeons" only one of
whom had seen with his own eyes the things to testify to
the accuracy of which or otherwise they had been called.
They stuck to Mr. Bransby Cooper because they knew that
his case might some day be theirs. They had come there
to bear down the weight of honest testimony by their
names and influence. The question, he contended, was not
the abstract one whether lithotomy was or was not a
difficult operation, but the particular one, whether Mr.
Bransby Cooper had performed a certain operation with
due skill. He begged the jury to ask themselves whether
they would be willing to employ the plaintiff as a surgeon if
it were necessary for them to undergo this operation. And
if they would not, he maintained that they must give a
verdict which would prevent the plaintiff from returning to
Guy's Hospital. He wound up an eloquent rather than a
closely-reasoned speech by an impassioned appeal to the
jury to consider the case of the poor in giving their verdict
—the poor who were at the mercy of the hospital surgeon.
For himself, he said, he cared nothing. He was willing to
go to prison, and willing to give up the "Lancet" if that were
found to be the course that justice dictated, but unless the
jury considered that Mr. Bransby Cooper had performed this
operation properly the plaintiff must be denied a verdict.

At the conclusion of his speech, which elicited loud
applause in court, Wakley was so overcome with excitement,
fatigue, and heat that he had to be supported into an adjoining room.

Lord Tenterden then proceeded to sum up the case. He recapitulated the evidence for the jury and spoke severely of the manner in which the report had been drawn up for the "Lancet." If the jury thought that the defendant had proved the unskilfulness of the plaintiff they were bound to give him their verdict, but they must remember that unimpeachable evidence had been given by Mr. Bransby Cooper's witnesses to the facts that numerous instruments were sometimes required in the performance of a lithotomy, and that the operation had failed many times when undertaken by most skilful surgeons. He did not agree with the plaintiff's counsel that the damages awarded, if any, should register feelings of indignation ; on the contrary, a verdict should mark cool and deliberate consideration of facts.

The jury were absent for two hours, and on their return to court delivered a verdict for the plaintiff, damages £100.

The results of the trial were not at first apparent. The verdict constituted a victory for both sides or neither. Wakley had to pay £100 in damages and nearly three times that amount in costs for having published a malicious libel. But Mr. Bransby Cooper's was a much worse plight. The sum awarded to him bore no sort of proportion, however distant, to the evil that had been said of him. Damages £100 for such an accusation ! The verdict told its own tale. Most certainly the jury believed Wakley's main statement— that the plaintiff had been guilty of malpraxis. On no other ground whatever could they have let him off so cheaply, having regard to the things that he had printed. He had accused Mr. Bransby Cooper by inference of manslaughter, making no secret of his belief that the death of the patient was the direct outcome of the ignorance of the surgeon. Mr. Bransby Cooper was a man of thirty-five years of age, enjoying a good private practice and an honourable public position. The things that had been said of him were calculated to utterly ruin him. If proved true, his scientific prestige together with his large and increasing income were both lost to him. Grave as the consequences would have been to Mr. Bransby Cooper if Wakley had obtained a verdict, heavy in due proportion should have been the damages when a verdict was given the other way. Yet of the £2000 demanded—a by no means exorbitant demand· when the nature of the libel is considered—only £100 were awarded. The jury paltered. They wished to do their duty. They felt that Mr. Bransby Cooper did not shine as an operator and that the defendant had made out his justification ; but they did not consider the libel a decent account of what had happened. So they marked a general disapproval by awarding to the plaintiff a barren victory.

The enormous interest taken in this case by the public as well as the profession made of it a landmark between the times when all sorts of abuses were rife and the times when the profession as a whole set itself, under Wakley's energetic direction, to work out its own salvation. As has already been said, when Wakley announced his intention of supplementing his reports of the lectures of hospital surgeons by accounts of the operative proceedings at different institutions he crossed the Rubicon and declared war on the heads of the profession. They looked upon his action as one of intolerable aggression to be resisted in all conceivable ways. Skirmishes had since occurred in which the victory had lain now with one side and now with the other. Here and there Wakley's reporters had been turned out of the hospitals, while on several occasions Wakley had been able to print details of hospital management or treatment the reverse of creditable to those responsible for them, and to distribute nicknames, ridiculous and adherent. But these were but skirmishes, while the case of Bransby Cooper v. Wakley was a pitched battle. Everything that it was possible to say fairly against Wakley's methods in issuing the "Lancet" could be said in reference to this case. The evidences of personal ill-feeling against a certain group of distinguished men was not wanting in it, and its publication was bound to hold the profession up to the contempt of laymen. A solid feeling of anger among the hospital officials, medical and lay, was created by Wakley's line of defence, and the damages exacted from him were not sufficiently high to cause any compensating satisfaction. At no time in his career had the editor of the " Lancet " such bitter and organised opposition to meet as immediately after this sensational trial. His reporters were expelled from the learned societies, he himself was excluded from the walls of three or four of the largest metropolitan hospitals, and, lastly, the other medical papers of the day, such as they were, were supported by all Wakley's foes, the facilities denied to the " Lancet " being given to its rivals. The partiality of this proceeding touched Wakley nearly; the rest concerned him not a whit, for the offers to assist him with information were numerous almost to the point of constituting a nuisance. But the difference made between the " Lancet," the pioneer of reform, and its imitators galled him. He had the pride of a parent in his paper, and he did not like to see the bantlings of others favoured at the expense of his sturdy offspring, however natural the preference might be in those who showed it. Wakley had been called, and was still called, a thief for reporting hospital lectures, and a malicious slanderer or a panderer to morbid tastes for publishing hospital reports. In spite of all that had been said he had persevered in his ill-doing, believing it to be exceeding well-doing. But when the leaders of the profession saw that a measure of publicity was to be their fate, while not abating their animosity to the " Lancet " they permitted the editors of other journals to do what they found in Wakley to be hideous crimes. This injustice he felt, and the feeling found vent in savage criticism of his contemporaries. They in their turn wrote in unspeakable terms of him, and the recriminatory passages, certain of which will have to be quoted in connexion with Wakley's actions against Dr. Macleod, the editor of the " Medical and Physical Journal," and Dr. James Johnson, the editor of the " Medico-Chirurgical Review," form amazing reading for these politer days.

But if Wakley had by this time created a solid opposition he had behind him a solid following. The case, which had given common cause for terror and affront to hospital

officials, had justified the policy of the " Lancet " and came
as a verification of the most burning of its editor's words
to the profession at large and also to the public. Never
had Wakley said anything in his declamations against the
evils of nepotism and the ineptitude of hospital officials
that approached in severity the words that *should* have
been used concerning the operative procedures at Guy's
Hospital supposing Mr. Bransby Cooper had bungled as
Wakley alleged. And that he had so bungled Wakley continued to declare, asserting that the " Lancet " had been cast
in damages simply because of the bad impression created by
the form of Mr. Lambert's report. The profession at large
and the public believed Wakley, and the solid opposition of
the authorities converted him in their eyes into an ill-used
man. A numerously attended public meeting was held at
the Freemasons' Tavern on the Tuesday following the verdict,
at which the following resolutions were proposed :

1. That the best interests of the medical profession and of
the public are identified with the cause of medical reform,
and that Mr. Wakley, as editor of the " Lancet," having given
the first impulse to that cause, and having subsequently
advocated it with undeviating firmness and fidelity, is entitled
to the cordial thanks and support of this meeting.

2. That the purposes for which the hospitals and infirmaries of the metropolis were founded, and that the views
of the humane contributors to their funds are materially
promoted by the weekly publication of reports detailing the
medical and surgical treatment of the unfortunate patients,
and that Mr. Wakley, having originated the practice of
publishing hospital reports, has conferred important benefits
on medical science and on the cause of humanity.

3. That the independent and imperial principles on
which the " Lancet " was first established have been preserved by Mr. Wakley at all risks ; and that a subscription
be opened for the purpose of defraying the expenses of the
late action.

4. That in accordance with the feelings that this meeting
has expressed, Mr. Wakley be invited to attend a public

dinner, and that a committee be nominated to arrange the same.

The first and third of these resolutions were carried by a very large majority—five dissentients only among three hundred persons ; the second and fourth were agreed to unanimously. In accordance with the third resolution a public subscription was opened, Wakley asking for £407 7s. 9d., being £295 10s., Mr. Bransby Cooper's costs, £100 his damages, and £12 17s. 9d., the sheriff's poundage. The sum was immediately subscribed, and the books were closed when the required total was reached, while two or three belated subscriptions which the donors did not wish to have returned to them were forwarded to the widow of Mr. Bransby Cooper's late patient.

There is one very pleasant thing to relate as an appendix to this sad and even terrible passage in Wakley's life. In after years a formal reconciliation took place between him and Mr. Bransby Cooper.

CHAPTER XVII

[1823–1834]

The Contemporary Medical Press—Its Attitude towards the "Lancet"—The "Medical and Physical Journal"—Macleod v. Wakley—Dr. James Johnson—The "Medico-Chirurgical Review" Wakley v. Johnson—The "London Medical Repository"—The "Medical Gazette."

IT has been previously noticed that the interference of other medical journals had an exceedingly irritating effect upon Wakley. The virulent articles in the " London Medical Repository" had impelled him into continued litigation with Abernethy, and the narrow protests of the " Medico-Chirurgical Review " led to the strictures upon "hole-and-corner" surgeons which resulted in the two lawsuits, Tyrrell *v.* Wakley and Bransby Cooper *v.* Wakley. It would seem at first sight that this susceptibility to criticism at the hands of the press betokened some weakness and inconsistency, as a man who gives hard blows himself ought to take punishment quietly. But this would not be quite a just estimate of the position. Wakley was a pugnacious man, and the advice of journalistic rivals for whose methods he had no respect only made him more resolute to go his own way. He did not wince under stricture, but he writhed under well-meaning advice. In the very early days of the " Lancet" his inimical attitude towards the medical press had its only explanation in this proud and pronounced restiveness, but later the position became more serious. Wakley was set up by his brother editors as a bogey-man and a terrible example. Astounding lapses of truth and decency were attributed to him, and dark hints as to his past were scattered broadcast. A paper was specially subsidised by his opponents to run counter to the " Lancet," and it, like its older contemporaries, showered personal abuse upon Wakley. Language in those days was some-what unmeasured, and Wakley's retorts were very strong, full-flavoured, and effective. The survival of the " Lancet " while all its rivals have long since succumbed keeps Wakley's language on modern record, while that of his adversaries is lost to memory. The early numbers of the " Lancet " in which this wordy warfare was waged—not, as will be seen, that the warfare always stopped at words—have often been reprinted, and many libraries possess them. All interested in the history of medicine constantly consult them, and in so doing must happen upon some of the many contentious articles. It would be difficult for such readers to acquit Wakley of scurrility, but for the right understanding of him it is necessary to know something of those against whom he was fighting and to appreciate a little the measure of offence that he received. Also the license of the time must be insisted upon, for in the twenties and thirties what now seem the necessary courtesies would have been regarded as mealy-mouthed hypocrisies.

There were three contemporary medical journals of some consequence published in London at the time that Wakley founded the " Lancet." These were the " Medical and Physical journal," the " Medico-Chirurgical Review," and the " London Medical Repository." The " Medical Gazette " followed almost immediately.

The " London Medical and Physical journal " was founded in 1799 as the " Medical and Physical journal." The original editors were Messrs. Bradley and Willick, of whom fame has nothing to relate ; but a new series was started early in the century under the editorship of Dr. Roderick Macleod. It was a decent monthly magazine of some ninety pages, with no particular reason for its existence. Its editor followed an easy conservative policy, and the bulk of its articles were translations from the foreign medical journals, with critical remarks appended, while long excerpts from scientific books were inserted as reviews. When the " Lancet " was first started

the "Medical and Physical journal" ignored its existence—
which looked like dignity. But in three years' time this
policy became laughable, because all the profession were
speaking of the revolutionary weekly paper of which the
"Medical and Physical Journal," addressed monthly to that
profession, had no cognisance. This was very well at first.
But later the "Medical and Physical journal" became frankly
imitative. Its circulation had waned, many of its subscribers
having been seduced from it by the more spirited management
of the "Lancet," and Dr. Roderick Macleod invited to his
columns contributions from hospital officials. He proposed,
in fact, to publish hospital reports as the "Lancet" was doing.
These reports, and, indeed, the whole of the journal, were subjected to bitter criticism in the "Lancet." This was natural,
and not due, it should be added, to any excess of journalistic
rivalry. It was all in the way of fair rejoinder, for Dr.
Roderick Macleod, when he found himself compelled to
notice the "Lancet" if he desired at all to register public
thought, had been severe upon it and very high with
Wakley. He had found fault with his taste in publishing
hospital reports and the lectures of hospital surgeons. Then
Dr. Roderick Macleod took to the same ill habit himself. It
is true that Wakley published independent accounts of the
medical and surgical proceedings of the day without asking
permission from anyone, and that Dr. Roderick Macleod
only published accounts sent to him by the different
operators, but this was not a distinction with so much
meaning as it would appear to have. The various hospital
surgeons had found Wakley's action in publishing these
reports to be wrong, not because their leave was not asked,
but because they considered the publicity thus afforded to
the doings within the walls of hospitals would militate
against the interests of the profession. And Dr. Roderick
Macleod's journal had approved of their view. In no uncertain terms Dr. Roderick Macleod had declared the publication of lectures and hospital reports to be a monstrous
breach of professional etiquette. Therefore, it was incon-
sistent of him to desire to publish these reports and to

consent to be the medium through which they should reach the world, and it was this inconsistency that gave Wakley his opportunity of retaliation. He took it, and unsparingly. The "Medical and Physical journal" had a yellow cover, and was termed a "Yellow Fungus," while Dr. Roderick Macleod's sonorous baptismal name was eternally introduced into the columns of the "Lancet," and always in some ridiculous connexion. Either as Roderick the Goth, or as the Editor of the Gothic Absurdity, or as plain Roderick, he was made the perpetual object of a ferocious sort of joking. Dr. Roderick Macleod answered back, but he had neither the force of his adversary nor the same popular cause. Wakley was working for the profession at large, and his methods, right or wrong, were consistent. Dr. Roderick Macleod, a member of the honorary staff of St. George's Hospital, represented his own order only, and stood convicted of tergiversation. At last the strained relations brought the rival editors into a law-court. The dispute was an entirely trivial one, but so clearly was it inevitable that a judge would sooner or later be asked to decide between them that it was well for the reputation of both and for the after chances of peace that the quarrel had no serious origin. It arose out of a difference of opinion as to the merits of what is now known as "Wardrop's method" of distal ligature for the cure of aneurysm. Dr. Macleod appears to have thought lightly of the method, and published an account of "the dissection of one of the cases of aneurysm in which the artery was *supposed* to have been tied beyond the tumour," the object of the publication being to show that Wardrop's operation had failed in this instance. Wakley then published the alleged libel, which had been intended as a rebutting statement in Mr. Wardrop's behalf, who was a highly valued member of Wakley's literary staff. He pointed out that the patient on whom the post-mortem examination had been made had died from other causes entirely than aneurysm, so that it was unfair to speak of it as a case where Mr. Wardrop's treatment had failed, and went on to say that while Dr. Macleod was ready enough to publish what he thought was a failure he had omitted to publish a successful case which had occurred some months back. The accusation was that in his character as editor Dr. Macleod had been guilty of improper partiality. As a matter of fact Dr. Macleod *had* published the successful case and Wakley had overlooked it. The defence was that the comments had been made in fair rivalry and that an oversight had occurred. Mr. Brougham, who looked after Wakley's interests, was not instructed to offer any apology. The libellous paragraph alluded to was offensively worded, and this, coupled with the absence of all apology, caused the jury to award to Dr. Macleod £5 damages out of the £100 that he claimed. Dr. Macleod resigned his position as editor shortly after this case and became editor of the "Medical Gazette" in 1827. The "London Medical and Physical journal" ceased to exist in 1833.

The "Medico-Chirurgical Review" was edited by Dr. james johnson, another of Wakley's contemporaries whose enmity to him was undoubted. Dr. james Johnson, an Irishman, was, like Wakley, the son of a farmer. He was born in 1778, and apprenticed at the age of fifteen to a medical man in Antrim. At the age of twenty he was appointed surgeon's mate in the navy, and later he served as full surgeon in the Egyptian campaign. It is worthy of note that at this time he possessed no diploma. In 1800 and 1801, being on leave, he studied at the Windmill Street School where he was a very assiduous worker. He was appointed to another ship and cruised in the Northern seas, Greenland, and Hudson's Bay. On his return he again studied in London, as he did on his return from a second cruise, spending his prize-money in walking the hospitals. In 1806 he attended the lectures of Sir Astley Cooper with assiduity, and, possibly through that great man's boundless interest, was appointed to the *Impregnable*, Captain the Duke of Clarence, afterwards William IV. This was the turning point of his career. He became surgeon to the Duke, and at the peace in 1814, when Bonaparte was believed to have been safely relegated to Elba, settled down to practice at Portsmouth, where he was very popular with the naval authorities. In 1816 he started the " Medico-Chirurgical Review." This was at first called the " Medico-Chirurgical journal," and was published monthly in collaboration with two medical friends, but in 1818 he took over the whole liability and became the sole proprietor. He then changed the title of the periodical and transformed it at the same time into a quarterly. He wrote the greater part of his Review himself. This he was competent to do, for though largely self-taught he was a widely-read, able, and industrious man. In 1821 he took the degree of M.D. St. Andrews, at that time obtainable by decidedly lax methods.

This brief sketch of Dr. James johnson, or johnstone, as he later called himself, reverting to his correct patronymic, is necessary to the comprehension of some of the personal allusions to him. The " Medico-Chirurgical Review " at the time of the issue of the " Lancet " enjoyed a large circulation and a good reputation. In the last number of 1823 Dr. james Johnson acknowledged the receipt of the early numbers of the " Lancet " in terms which seem to have been amiably meant ; but Wakley objected to their patronising ring.

" We hold it to be a breach of etiquette for one periodical publication to animadvert on the conduct of another unless attacked or interfered with itself," said the " Medico-Chirurgical Review." " We mean, of course, medical journals, for political publications use no ceremony with each other. In offering a word or two of advice to our young friend the ' Lancet,' and through him several others of our juvenile contemporaries, we trust they will not impute to us any unworthy motives, and that on mature reflection they will acknowledge the propriety of the advice we give. . . . .

" We are convinced, then, that no medical periodical publication can succeed unless conducted on *unexceptionable* principles—we mean such principles as cannot be reasonably objected to by the members of the profession. We think that the unauthorised publication of a man's lectures as they are delivered from day to day cannot be defended on principles of morality, equity, or medical ethics, and therefore we advise our junior contemporaries not to take advantages of, or rely upon, a practice which can at best but afford a temporary interest. Secondly, we would dissuade them, if in our power, from mixing up politics, theatrical criticisms, and other heterogeneous matters with medical science or literature. It is an unnatural union which cannot long hold together, and has invariably failed hitherto in every instance where it was attempted. The above exceptions made, we wish every success to the 'Lancet' and all other candidates for public favour; nor will we ever refuse to give whatever publicity they require through the medium of this journal."

The qualified proffer of friendship was rejected roughly by Wakley, who did not think that a quarterly *résumé* of things in the medical world, written in the interests of a few leading men, could be of any practical use to his revolutionary weekly print. The unceremonious manner in which Dr. James Johnson was told to care for his own business and try to obtain something readable for his own paper galled that hot-headed sailor, who seems at once to have made up his mind to demonstrate the good he might have done by the harm he could do. The following number contained an article headed " Property and Privileges of Lecturers, Hospitals, and Medical Societies Considered." It formed nearly six pages of forcibly written censure on the practice of publishing lectures, the writer challenging Wakley to produce a "single respectable testimony in favour of the practice," and saying " that the baleful influence of a private spy and public informer" will with "vampyre presence chill the current of communication between the preceptor and the pupil." This article defined the relations that were to exist between the rival editors, and for the next two years the " Lancet" and Wakley were made the subject of the most unfavourable comments by Dr. james Johnson, while Wakley answered back in like vein. Each hit very hard. Dr. James Johnson was the elder—a man with an unblemished record, the friend of the heads of the profession, accepted by them as an exponent of medical thought, an officer of the two most important scientific societies then meeting in London, and a friend of Royalty; so he may be said to have carried heavy guns. On the other hand, his acquaintance with the leaders of the medical world hampered him by taking away from him his powers of free criticism, while his quarterly form of publication precluded him from any reply to attacks made

·upon him until, perhaps, three months had elapsed. Wakley's position was not in those early days so influential as that of Dr. James Johnson, but he got thirteen shots to one, and his ease in manœuvring gave him immense advantages over his adversary.

In the third year of the issue of the "Lancet"came the action-at-law that had been expected by every one since the disputes began. Each side had been so profoundly abusive of the other that no one could guess who would be plaintiff and who defendant, but that legal. proceedings were inevitable all could see.

On june 21st, 1826, the libel action of Wakley *v.* johnson occupied the attention of the Chief Justice of the Court of Common Pleas and a special jury. The plaintiff was represented by Mr. Denman and Mr. FitzRoy Kelly ; while the defendant retained two of the most noted members of Serjeants' Inn—viz., Serjeants Vaughan and Wilde. In the libel complained of Dr. James johnson alluded to Wakley as an "outcast of medical society," who had been "accused of arson, convicted of libel, and cast in damages in a Court of Equity." These remarks alone would have been sufficient material ·upon which to base an action ; but Dr. James Johnson, who had two long years of adverse criticism to answer, went further and elaborated his unpardonable phrase, "accused of arson." In the following sentence the cruel calumny 'of Argyll Street was raked up :

" The threatened expulsion of Lucifer from the presence of the Gods on high Olympus," he wrote, "spread terror among the inhabitants of the lower regions; but happily they were spared a visit from this *firebrand*, or rather *fire factor*, as he is now generally denominated, who willingly, for once, made his exit from the postern gate."

This passage, which ·purported to describe a wholly imaginary movement on the part of certain infuriated members of the Royal College of Surgeons to expel Wakley from the gallery of the council chamber while he was speaking therefrom, was supplemented in a footnote by the following disgraceful explanation of the term—" Lucifer " :—

"The common derivation of this word is wrong," runs the footnote; "it is not from *lux* and *fero*, but from *ignis* and *facio*. (*Vide* 'Secret Memoirs of the House of Argyll.')"

Mr. Denman made the most of the cruelty of these allusions, and of another in the same article in which the public were invited to consider "a new mode of lighting the streets without lamps, and of extinguishing debts by means of fire-engines." He showed that the wicked rumours concerning the fire in Argyll Street, which had been aroused by the withholding on the part of the company of the sum insured, had been definitely disproved, that in a court of law no evidence whatever had been brought forward by the Hope Fire Assurance Company in support of the absurd suspicion, and that the company had paid Wakley's claims in full.

The defence chiefly rested on Serjeant Vaughan's attempt to demonstrate to the court the known libellous proclivities of the plaintiff. Chief justice Best paid no attention to this *tu quoque* argument (if argument it could be called), and in his summing-up said that there could be no doubt at all that the matter complained of was libellous. He instructed the jury, however, to take into account in assessing damages the aggravation and provocation which the defendant had received before he overstepped the bounds of legitimate controversy. The jury, after two minutes' consultation, found a verdict for the plaintiff for £100 and costs.

A second action brought by Wakley on the same day against the printer of the "Medico-Chirurgical Review" was settled by a compromise, Wakley being reimbursed all costs. After this action the war in words was continued for some time in both papers, but not with the spirit of bitterness with which it had opened. Eventually the quarrel died out. The "Medico-Chirurgical Review" had a longer life than the "Medical and Physical Journal," for it did not cease to appear until about 1862, and the "Lancet" interfered but little with its success from a business point of view. When it was apparent that no profit could come out of quarrelling both editors decided to bury the hatchet.

The "London Medical Repository" was another quarterly medical journal, and was edited by Dr. James Copland, F.R.S., the author of the Medical Dictionary and a man of great scientific attainments. Dr. james Copland, who had himself with some success played the part of medical reformer, ranged his forces on the side of Wakley's foes, though he is said to have come into line with his fellow editors in opposing Wakley, not through conviction but through the inadvertency of a sub-editor. As a consequence, however, of some words in slight of the "Lancet" that appeared in the "London Medical Repository" that paper was nicknamed the "Mausoleum" by Wakley, and the dulness of its erudition and the staleness of its contents were weekly held up to ridicule. Dr. james Copland was a physician and a man of science, but no journalist. Nor did he want to quarrel. The quarrels were ready-made when he blundered into them, and the abuse that he got was not directed personally at him, but at the causes that he was conceived to have espoused. His paper soon perished under the attacks of his foe, and the successful rivalry of his friends, and he betook himself to the more congenial labour of writing his well-known dictionary.

Yet one more paper must be mentioned, as its life was longer than any of those to which allusion has been made, and its opposition to Wakley more distinct, more thorough, and more effective. This was the "Medical Gazette." It first made its appearance in December, 1827, and in its address to the public avowed hatred of, and strenuous opposition to, the policy of the "Lancet." The paper was started by Brodie, Abernethy, and other hospital surgeons, who bore a bitter and very intelligible grudge against Wakley, and Dr. Roderick Macleod left the "Medical and Physical Journal" to become its editor. Wakley declared that the only object of the paper was obviously to oppose, and if possible to ruin, the "Lancet" because the "Lancet" had so ruthlessly interrupted the even tenour of the lives of the great men of the profession. The following passage from its preface denotes the

attitude of the new paper towards the question of the
publication of lectures and was accepted at once by Wakley
as a formal declaration of war :—

> " A few years ago a set of literary plunderers broke in on the peace
> and quiet of our profession. Lecturers who had spent their lives in
> collecting knowledge, arranging it for communication, and acquiring
> the difficult art of oral instruction, saw the produce of their lives
> suddenly snatched from them and published for the profit of others,
> with the additional mortification of finding what they had taken so
> much pains with disfigured by bad English and ridiculous and mis-
> chievous blunders."

The " Lancet " was not behindhand. The outward resemblance of the new newspaper to the " Lancet " was very great,
while all the editorial inspiration had been borrowed from
Wakley. " Some despicable imitations of us have arisen,"
said Wakley, " and *stunk*, and become extinguished . . . .
one or two are still *emitting a little fœtor*." In the very first
year of its existence the " Medical Gazette " published thirty
more or less bitter attacks not only on the " Lancet " but on
Wakley, while for three years a steady fight was maintained
between the rival papers. The " Medical Gazette's " method
of attacking the " Lancet " was fairly effective and very safe.
Every week the " Lancet " was searched for grammatical errors,
solecisms, or failures in taste, and any treasure-trove was
quoted as " wit," " veracity," " refinement," " good English,"
and the like. The " Medical Gazette " had a longer and more
successful career than any of the other journals that have
been mentioned. It was at first offensive but timid. Later
it amalgamated with the " Medical Times," a journal which was
started in 1839, and which came into violent contact with
Wakley under circumstances that will be narrated.

CHAPTER XVIII

[1823–1834]

The Constitution of the Royal College of Surgeons of England—A Sketch of its later History—Wakley's Attitude towards the College —The Reason for it—An Outspoken Letter—A Few Words about James Wardrop.

THE record of the first ten years of the "Lancet" has so far been stormy. Its publication was, in fact, attended with sufficient turbulence to satisfy even its editor, whose early management had a good deal of the tread-on-the-tail-of-my-coat spirit about it.

Of the innumerable small quarrels that arose and were threshed out in its columns during this decade it will serve no purpose to speak. They would not be illustrative of anything in Wakley's character left uncovered by the Irish phrase just quoted, nor would they give the reader any particularly correct view of the medical profession of the day. They were but episodes in a contentious career, the border warfare incidental to Wakley's invasion of the privileges of the leaders of the profession. In contradistinction, his fight for the right to print the lectures of hospital surgeons and his determined attacks upon hospital practice when wrongly carried on must be looked upon as organised campaigns. These formed one half of his policy of aggression as a reformer; the other half was formed by his crusade against the Royal College of Surgeons of England.

The easiest way of making Wakley's attitude towards the Royal College of Surgeons of England perfectly clear, and, for that matter, of showing him to have been right in his main contentions, would be to narrate the constitutional history of the College from the beginning ; for everything that he asked for had an excellent historical reason for being granted, and everything that he clamoured against was an abuse of the ancient rights of the general body of the craft of surgery. But it would not be correct to claim for Wakley that at the time that he commenced his crusade against the corporation of which he was a member—and so young a member—he knew the sound archæological ground on which he was standing. So far from knowing it, he never inquired into it, and had he been told that all his words and actions were justified by history he would not have considered his basis of operations solidified thereby. He was essentially the practical man, hot-blooded and rash in procedure, maybe, but eminently sensible in his demands. He saw that certain abuses flourished and he desired to cut them down. If history had been on the other side and his opponents had been able to claim for themselves a proud position of antiquarian rectitude he would not have been impressed thereby. He would only have said that times had changed and that it was imperative that the Royal College of Surgeons of England should change with them, putting it, frank Radical that he was, in phraseology that would have been unnecessarily irritating to the reactionary mind. He never would have modified his opinion.

An inquiry into the constitution of the College is hardly within the scope of this biography. All interested, whether for practical or dilettante reasons, can find scattered up and down the pages of the medical press articles and letters upon every conceivable point in the history and working of the corporation, while the late Mr. j. Flint South's work "Memorials of the Craft of Surgery in England," issued after his death under the competent editorship of Mr. D'Arcy Power, is a mine of information upon the subject. Yet a brief recapitulation of certain facts in that constitution must be given in order that the reality of the abuses against which Wakley took the field may be properly comprehended. To do this it will not be necessary to go further back than the dissolution of the old Company of Surgeons.

By the Act of 1745 it was enacted that the Master and at least one of the governors should be present at every Court, with one or two Assistants, in order to constitute a quorum. It happened at the meeting held on july 7th, 1796, that in consequence of the death of one governor and the serious illness of the other no legal Court was possible. Notwithstanding this, the Master and some Assistants determined on proceeding to business. This action proved fatal to the corporation. The opinion of counsel was taken, and it was evident that the corporation was destroyed by the illegal construction of the last Court. In the following year a Bill was brought before Parliament, at the instigation of the Court of Assistants, to indemnify the Court and to legalise its acts, as well as to procure the re-establishment of the corporation under the name of a College. This Bill had passed through the House of Commons and had been twice read in the House of Lords before the members of the corporation became aware of its purport. A petition in opposition to the Bill was at once prepared and presented to the House of Lords. This petition set forth that the Bill had been drawn up without the knowledge or sanction of the members of the late Company, who had not been convened to consider it. It further declared that the Master, Wardens, and Assistants, without the knowledge or consent of the Company, had alienated the property of the Company, had made purchases beyond the extent allowed by law, and had been guilty of gross mal-administration ; that they had not taken one material step for the public good or the advancement of the science of surgery ; that a certain number of the Court of Assistants had, as examiners, received for their private use a large share of the revenue of the Company ; that if the Bill were to become law those persons who had been guilty of this mal-administration would acquire absolute supervisal and control over the members and their affairs ; that the ancient privileges of members would be annihilated, and their right of meeting in a General Court would be taken away ; and that the Court of Assistants would be able to oblige members to swear to the observance of such laws as the Court might make, although the members themselves would have no voice in the making of these laws, and no choice in the appointment of those who should make them.   Lord Thurlow, who took up the cause of the members, argued that the petitioners against the Bill had great reason to complain.   Their privileges had been violated, and even their property invaded.   He considered that however grating it might be to the ears of some people, meaning the Court of Assistants, the members had the strongest title in the world to have their complaints heard with patience and attention.   The result of Lord Thurlow's powerful intervention was that the Bill was thrown out in the last stage.   But, in spite of the rejection of the Bill by the House of Lords, the discredited Court of Assistants of the defunct and dissolved corporation did not despair ; they continued to admit to their commonalty persons under letters testimonial, and though low in reputation and in funds, agreed on December 13th, 1799, by a unanimous vote, to accept the charge of Hunter's Museum, for which Parliament had six months before voted a sum of £15,000.   The next step followed as a matter of course : the Court of Assistants had now no difficulty, by the aid of courtly intrigue, in satisfying George III. that it was impossible to discharge its new and important trust without some method of replenishing its finances.   What Parliament had refused the King was easily prevailed upon to grant, and thus in the month of March, 1800, the College of Surgeons was established by a Royal Charter, which sanctioned most of the obnoxious provisions contained in the Bill rejected by the House of Lords.   The fact therefore stood out conspicuously in the negotiations which preceded and led up to the establishment of the College, that Parliament refused to pass a Bill which excluded members of the College from a share in its government.   Consequently, though it was, and is, true that members have no legal right to the franchise by the Charter of 1800, they had, and have, at least a moral claim.

Such is the history of the Royal College of Surgeons of England, and it must be remembered that when the "Lancet" was founded the most scandalous passage was comparatively modern history, and that the abuses had not had time to lose their distinctness of outline under any decent veil of antiquity. They were new and not hallowed by custom and years of acquiescence.

Wakley first fell foul of the Royal College of Surgeons of England because of a by-law which was passed in March, 1824, to make it compulsory for medical students to attend the lectures of certain hospital officials. The innovation appealed to him in two ways. He was publishing these lectures in the "Lancet" and the contemporary medical press was excessively disturbed in its sense of what was right thereby, and freely called him a robber. But if the lectures were compulsory for the students before they could take their diplomas the private character claimed for them by Abernethy and others was destroyed. A newspaper would have an undoubted right to report them, because it was to the public benefit to know whether instruction which the London medical man *must* receive was worth receiving. Lecturers chosen in this manner by the Council of the College were constituted public officials in their capacity as lecturers, and in addition to the importance and substantial fees thus ensured to them, could not claim all the privileges enjoyed by private individuals. In a second less direct way he was concerned in the working of this by-law. Some of the hospital surgeons appointed as the only persons whose lectures would be considered official by the Royal College of Surgeons of England charged their classes very large fees for attendance. Wakley had not been an affluent student, and had known many men poorer than himself. He was always jealous of the rights of the poor man, and he inveighed against the extraction from the pockets of students of large fees for attendance upon the classes of certain men —not, as he asserted, the best men.

When he had got as far as this—as far, that is, as the statement that the best men were not selected to deliver these compulsory lectures—all the arguments which he had used against nepotism when attacking the domestic management of the large metropolitan hospitals came into service. He declared that the authorities of the College, by playing into the hands of the hospital surgeons, made of themselves a ring, so that the corporation, which ought to have existed for the good of its members at large, really only existed for its small class of governors and the officials appointed by them. The official ring was thus arranged. The hospital surgeons appointed the lecturers to the medical schools— that is, they appointed themselves, their relations, and the gentlemen who had paid them large fees to become their apprentices. The hospital surgeons were also the authorities at the College of Surgeons, that is, they were the men who decided that the lectures of certain gentlemen should be compulsory for all medical students in London. The compulsory lectures were delivered by themselves, their relatives, or their apprentices. It was this corrupt arrangement against which Wakley worked. It moved him, as the nepotism that was prevalent at the Borough Hospitals moved him, to wrath and scorn, and his first attacks on the College had no historical foundation at all. They were consecutive to his attacks on the hospital lecturers who, though paid as public officials, desired to exclude the medical public from any participation in the benefits to accrue from hearing their words ; and they were a rider to his proposition that the hospital surgeons who did not desire to see hospital reports in print were unskilful and aware of their own limitations. But when the attack had been inaugurated on these lines the constitution of the College was ruthlessly entreated, its anatomy laid bare, and the disclosures to the members of the unfair manner in which they were being treated by their rulers led to sensational developments. These will be narrated in the chapters which follow, but it will not be out of place first to quote an open letter which appeared in the "Lancet" as early as 1825, purporting to be addressed to the Court of Examiners of the College, but really designed to catch the attention of the members. The letter, as will be seen, summarises the more obvious grievances of the members, and was written by one of the ablest members of

Wakley's staff, and one of the greatest surgeons of the day, james Wardrop.

An Open Letter addressed to the COURT OF EXAMINERS OF THE ROYAL COLLEGE OF SURGEONS.

"SIRS,—If the members of the Court of Examiners and assistants of the Royal College of Surgeons are not too much employed in collating the Hunterian MSS. or at home listening to the chirping of cock sparrows,* or writing an oration on the splendid anatomical discovery of ordinary putrefaction they, may perhaps find time to read this letter. We know that old men can recollect remote events better than those of later date. They can tell you what was done in such and such a year and will amplify all the circumstances; but they forget what happened in the last year. In other words, they can tell you what took place in their age of pleasure or in that of their ambition; they forget what they do in their age of avarice. It shall be my business to be their historian. I will endeavour to save their public actions from oblivion to receive the contempt and detestation of men of science in future ages. The court will well remember the following facts:—

"In the year 1797 the master, wardens, and assistants of the Corporation of Surgeons, without the knowledge or consent of the commonalty, presented a Bill to Parliament to elect the said corporation into a College. It was, in fact, to obtain a Bill of indemnity for squandering the property of the commonalty and trampling on their rights and privileges. Lord Thurlow, who had risen by his merit to the highest rank of his profession, saw immediately through the paltry artifices of this petty corporation. His lordship described their Bill as 'a miserable and wretched performance, in which the arrogance of the provisions maintained an equal contest with their absurdity.' The whole number of the Members at that period, exclusive of the Court, amounted only to 500. The Bill had passed the House of Commons and had been twice read in the House of Lords before it was known to the commonalty. A meeting was called by a few spirited individuals and the number soon increased to 127. They petitioned the house against the further monopoly of this avaricious corporation, and at the third reading the Bill was rejected. The commentaries upon it, with the speeches of counsel, may be found in Woodfall's Parliamentary debates.

"Some curious facts were at that time elicited. The corporation were compelled to produce their accounts, and although, as I have said before, the number of the commonalty did not exceed 500, it was

---

* Mr. Earle, a surgeon on the staff of St. Bartholomew's Hospital, was nicknamed "The Cock Sparrow."

stated that since the passing of the 18th of George II., in the year 1744, the corporation had received in fees and quarterages and by other means the sum of £80,000! and that during the said period they had put £16,000 into their own pockets!!! What they could not get by Act of Parliament they have since obtained by charters. They are become a College and style themselves President, Vice-president, and Council; but the commonalty, who of course were not consulted about the charters, are still called Members. For my own part I would as soon be called a Member as a Fellow of such a College. They take our money, give us *ex post facto* laws, lock up our property, insult us with mock orations, live at our expense, and refuse to call us by our proper names!

"For the information of my professional brethren and fellow-sufferers I communicate this piece of intelligence: 'Every member from the moment he is admitted and has paid the fee of £22 to the court and the 5s. demanded by the beadle is as unequivocally entitled to the museum and the property of the College as any member of the court.'

"I need hardly remind you, Sir, that the magnificent collection of John Hunter was purchased by Government and that a loan of a large sum of money was supplied from the same source to erect a suitable building for its reception. Do you think the motive for such liberality was that twenty-one persons should have power to lock up the museum for eight months in the year? When their Bill was before the House of Lords it was said that they had a theatre without lectures and a library without books. It is true we have now some lectures on comparative anatomy and surgery; but the man best qualified to give the lectures on the former subject is doomed to fill the servile office of conservator of the museum. They have also books, and some years ago Sir William Blizard promised that the library should soon be opened. We are still outside the door, however, and a part of the bust of Sir William, like the molten calf of the Israelites, may go down our throats (by the adulteration of bread or in the drinking of soda-water) before we shall see a book, especially the Hunterian MSS.

"The Museum is opened twice a week during four months in the year. The hours of admittance are from twelve to four o'clock. This does not extend to the whole collection, for the gallery is only accessible from twelve to two o'clock. Should the extensive and varied information and indefatigable kindness of the conservator of the museum, Mr. Clift, tempt an unfortunate individual to remain a minute after the clock has struck the hour his crime is announced by the loud and angry sound of the beadle's bell. This noisy warning is very quickly repeated, and lest he should not understand it the beadle calls out in a most autocratic tone, 'This way, sir.' The College member descends the steps muttering perhaps, as I have done, 'Any way but this way, sir.'

" If a knowledge of these facts will not rouse in the profession that spirit of opposition to the arbitrary power of the College which it is the object of these letters to excite I shall have the satisfaction to reflect that I have done my duty in making the attempt.

" BRUTUS.

" *August 27th, 1825.*"

Wardrop continued to write regularly for the " Lancet " for ten years from this date, his particular theme being the fact that promotion in the medical profession went by favour and not by merit. He spoke with conviction, because he always considered himself an unjustly slighted man by his professional brethren, who acknowledged his scientific talents, but disliked and distrusted him. Outside professional ranks, on the other hand, he enjoyed the greatest popularity. George IV., whose official attendant he was, offered him a baronetcy and omitted to pay his fees, while many of the most influential people in the land counted him as a personal friend. From his witty, unscrupulous pen came numerous anonymous attacks upon Sir Henry Halford and Sir Benjamin Brodie, and he was undoubtedly Wakley's most influential assistant during his connexion with the journal.

CHAPTER XIX

[1823–1834]

The Offensive By-law—Its Effect on the Private Schools—More Letters of " Brutus "—The Sorest Point with the Members—Dr. John Armstrong's Pamphlet—A General Meeting of the Profession suggested.

THE wording of the by-law regulating the attendance of English students upon anatomy lectures was as follows :—

" That certificates of attendance at lectures on anatomy, physiology, the theory and practice of surgery, and of the performance of dissections be not received by the Court except from the appointed professors of anatomy and surgery in the University of Dublin, Edinburgh, Glasgow, or Aberdeen, or from persons teaching in a·school acknowledged by the medical establishment of one of the recognised hospitals, or from persons being physicians or surgeons to any of these hospitals."

It will be seen that it conferred on the metropolitan hospital surgeons and lecturers an increased authority. It virtually gave them a complete monopoly in the surgical education of the London student, and this at a time when Wakley was attempting to show in the columns of the " Lancet " that these very people were selected upon corrupt principles, and that no one therefore need be surprised if they should be found unable to discharge their duties properly either towards the sick, the student, or the public. From discussing the by-law such a disputant as Wakley was bound to pass almost immediately to more general considerations. We find him at once discussing the *personnel* of the Court of Examiners and the methods which had dictated their election until, by swift retrogression, he reaches the constitution of the College.

The Court of Examiners who had issued the by-law was constituted as follows :—Sir Astley Cooper, Mr. Abernethy, Sir Everard Home, Sir William Blizard, Mr. Cline, Sir David Dundas, Mr. Forster, Sir Ludford Harvey, Mr. Lynn and Mr. Norris ; and every one of these gentlemen was a past or present lecturer at a hospital school, and directly or indirectly a pecuniary beneficiare under the working of the new law. The real purpose of the objectionable by-law was, in fact, to aggrandise the hospital surgeon. It was not only that it placed the exceedingly lucrative post of lecturer at his disposal, but it gave him a monopoly. He was not compelled to compete with the outside lecturers. Here Wakley's personal feelings no doubt dictated his view. He was himself, as we have already said, largely educated at one of these private schools, the Webb Street School. Most of the students at this school were young men who were walking the wards of Guy's Hospital or St. Thomas's Hospital, but they were not compelled to take out their anatomy course with the Graingers, who conducted the Webb Street School ; on the contrary, at Guy's Hospital Mr. Aston Key and Mr. Bransby Cooper were lecturing in anatomy ; while at St. Thomas's Hospital Mr. Joseph Henry Green and Mr. Flint South were prepared to instruct the student in the same subject ; and, as an additional facility to the student of the Borough Hospitals, if he had paid his fee as a perpetual student at the school of either hospital he could attend whichever anatomical course he chose. In spite of the embarrassment of riches that is suggested by a choice of four authorised demonstrators at the regular schools, it was a fact that the majority of the Borough students joined the Webb Street School, as Wakley had done, for the brothers Edward and Richard Grainger—exceedingly able anatomists —had a reputation as instructors that entirely put in the shade that of the four members of the combined staff of the Borough Hospitals. Consequently many fees found their way to Webb Street that should have gone to the Borough

M

Hospitals.   Now the by-law would prevent this.   It would make the brothers Grainger mere coaches, whose certificates of attendance had no real value.   Similarly, joshua Brookes, of the Theatre of Anatomy in Blenheim Street, and Carpue, whose headquarters were at Dean Street, also in Soho, were deprived of their status as official lecturers.

Now, these men, like the Graingers, were among the finest anatomists in England, and instructed the majority of the students at St. George's and Middlesex Hospitals and many from other less adjacent schools ; while of the four hospital lecturers Mr. Green alone could be considered a first-class anatomist.   Curiously enough Mr. Green's class suffered most under the system of free trade, for the com-petition of the Graingers, who had more to offer and at a lower figure, had told so severely upon the St. Thomas's School that, according to Wakley, who was in the habit, it must be remembered, of constantly attending the lecture-rooms of all the schools, public and proprietary, Mr. Green's post was becoming a sinecure.   This struck Wakley as in no way regrettable, and merely an example of the process now termed the survival of the fittest.   Therefore he saw in the by-law an unfair attempt to bolster up the incompetent hospital official and give him a monopoly in a lucrative business which he had not had enough wits to keep by his own exertion in fair competition.   Furthermore, Wakley considered that the authorities of the Royal College of Surgeons of England had betrayed their position by thus sanctioning a piece of legislation so wholly in the private favour of hospital surgeons and so inimical to the interests both of their commonalty and of the students by whom their coffers were replenished.   For it must be remembered that not only were the outside schools cheaper to attend, but they were open all the year round, while the anatomical lectures at the hospitals were only delivered during the winter season.   The evils arising from a measure condemn-ing the students to attend the lectures of the hospital officials only were therefore twofold—unnecessary delay and increased expense.   Wakley did not consider it reasonable that every student should be put to heavy expense in order to pour money into the pockets of the gentlemen from whom the Court of Examiners were chosen—viz., the hospital lecturers—and whose by-law in their own interests the College was asked to ratify. He expressed his opinion both with voice and pen that the profession as a whole should petition Parliament to abrogate the existing Charter and grant a new one, in which it should be a fundamental principle that any person to whom the power was given of making by-laws should be elected by the whole body of members and not by each other, as was the case with the Court of Examiners. These sentiments led him to inquire into the constitution of the College, to print its Charter, and to promise to spare no pains to make clear to the medical profession that he considered the existing authorities of the College to have abused their position. These are the stages by which he passed from a habit of criticising the College as the stronghold of his declared foes, the hospital surgeons, into a deliberate intent to show it as a constitutionally rotten concern, badly behaved, and of evil pedigree.

During the year 1825 letters from " Brutus " were inserted several times and always showed the intimate knowledge of the constitutional history of the Royal College of Surgeons of England that the communication from the same pen which has already been quoted so obviously displayed. The College, " Brutus " maintained, had virtually formed itself out of the old Company without any consultation with the members, and the spirit of exclusiveness thus immorally and even illegally shown had been imported into the management of the new corporation. The Court of Assistants and Examiners of the Royal College of Surgeons of England, who were placed by the Charter in the position of trustees for the members of the corporation in general, were found to have abused their trust in every direction. Presented by Government with Hunter's splendid anatomical collection, the Museum had been at once rendered inaccessible to the members by stupid restrictive regulations for eight months in the year, while no attempt to make it more useful to students by supplying a descriptive catalogue had been entered upon. The great john Hunter's work had been accepted by the Court because it was worth a large sum of money; they at once proceeded to render it valueless by withdrawing it as far as possible from all chances of intelligent notice. The Library, which it was often promised should be thrown open to the members, had been kept for the sole use of the Court of Assistants. The pecuniary status of the College, which was concealed from the members whose fees were taken and nothing rendered them in return, was laid bare by "Brutus." Since the year 1797 the receipts of the College upon a moderate calculation must have exceeded £150,000, and of this sum £32,000 must have been appropriated to the private use of the examiners, so that the concealment of the auditors' accounts had obvious reason. The members who really supported the College entirely by their fees were excluded from all voice in their own affairs; they were obliged to obtain certificates before being examined from certain persons especially chosen by the College for reasons other than their merits; and, lastly, they could only enter their own building by the back door at stated hours.

The publication of these letters aroused great excitement in the profession, and many communications were written to the "Lancet" and privately to Wakley in a similar strain, some enlarging on one grievance and some on another, but all persistently dwelling upon the last two in the category extracted from "Brutus's" bitter epistles. In particular the pettiest grievance of all, the fact that the front door of the building in Lincoln's Inn Fields was closed to them, rankled in the breasts of the members. From all parts of England the general practitioners wrote to Wakley to complain of this impertinent distinction between themselves and men whose only claim to superiority was in many instances to be found in their relationship to some inept hospital surgeon or the longer purses of the parents who provided them with education. Some of them thought that the history of the

Charter was discreditable, and many of them grumbled at the large fees that were exacted from them, but all who put pen to paper on the subject of their College—and it was a large number—based their support of a reforming movement chiefly upon their intention to obtain the right to go into their own College by the front door.

In the meantime Wakley and his correspondents in the "Lancet" were not the only critics of the action of the College in issuing the by-law concerning certificates for students. A pamphlet had been published by a Dr. john Armstrong dealing very roughly with the innovation. Dr. john Armstrong was lecturer on the principles and practice of physic at the Webb Street School, where the brothers Grainger were the proprietors and chief lecturers, so that his opinions could not be considered unbiassed. To those who believed that the motives of the Court of Examiners in framing such a by-law were wholly corrupt the Graingers must have seemed to be the particular individuals most hardly used ; therefore their colleague's opinions were necessarily received with caution. Another intimate friend of Dr. Armstrong, a Mr. Bennett, was also a well-known lecturer whose certificates were rendered valueless by the new regulations, and his case is quoted in the pamphlet as one of particular hardship. Dr. Armstrong's work was, therefore, regarded by the College as the outcome of mere partisanship. Wakley said that he saw no reason whatever to doubt the purity of motive ; his only criticism of his ally was that the view taken up by Dr. Armstrong was too narrow. Dr. Armstrong in his pamphlet contented himself with insisting upon the hard measure that had been dealt out to a number of worthy persons, whose income was largely derived from students' fees, by making their lectures practically useless as part of the surgical education of the future members of the College of Surgeons ; while Wakley looked upon this as only a minor point, the larger question being present to him by this time—viz., how the constitutional reform of the College from top to bottom, from hall porter to President, could be best effected. But Dr. Armstrong's pamphlet had its outcome. It placed the *pros* and *cons* of one point, if a small one, before a large number of persons, and prepared their minds for the developments now imminent.

Week after week the necessity for reform was urged in the " Lancet." The language might differ, but the sentiments were always the same. The result of these repeated and categorical accusations, as well as of the letters of " Brutus " and Dr. Armstrong's pamphlet, was to bring to Wakley an enormous mass of letters, showing that the dissatisfaction of the commonalty of the College with their rulers was very real and very widespread. As soon as this evidence reached him that the time was ripe for organised resistance he placed himself in the van. Hitherto, his opposition to the junto at the head of the College business had been largely a part of his general crusade against the management of the metropolitan hospitals, but when he saw that a large number of his readers were deeply stirred by the wrongs they had received at the hands of the Royal College of Surgeons of England his treatment of the subject became much more comprehensive. Instead of seeing in the abuses at the College a mere confirmation of the fact that self-elected rulers—whether presiding at lecture-room, operating-table, or examining board—were under strong temptations not to do their duties, he became aware that the profession at large was deeply moved at the way in which they were treated. Consequently he pledged himself to a definite course—namely, to the procural of measures of redress. In January, 1826, he took the first step by proposing that a meeting of the profession should be held to determine on a plan of campaign, the suggested plan being to petition the Crown to grant a new Charter or to appoint a Royal Commission to inquire into the working of the Charter granted by the late King.

CHAPTER XX

[1823-1834]

The First Public Meeting of Members of the Royal College of Surgeons of England—Mr. Lawrence's Speech from the Chair— The Condemnatory Resolutions—Wakley's Amendment—Successful Oratory.

ON Saturday, February 18th, 1826, the first public meeting of members of the Royal College of Surgeons of England was held at the Freemasons' Tavern. During twenty years following the granting of the Charter there had been open dissatisfaction amongst the members, who, be it remembered, comprised the pick of the general practitioners of England. Until 1815 it was not necessary for a medical man to hold any qualifications whatever. No Government licence, no diploma from a State-supported or State-recognised body was necessary, and, *a fortiori*, no university degree. Therefore a large proportion of the medical men in the country were what nowadays would be termed " unqualified." They possessed qualifications to practise, certainly—for example, they had generally served several years of apprenticeship to men grown grey in the pursuit of the healing art, and they were mostly sound obstetricians, expert prescribers, and accurate dispensers; but of all standing derived from the successful endurance of the tests of examination they were guiltless. This was the plight of many of the English practitioners before 1815; and even after that date, inasmuch as the Apothecaries Act was not a retrospective one, there were as many unqualified as qualified practitioners in the country. But those who were qualified had generally received their diploma from the Royal College of Surgeons of England and represented the flower of their order—the men who had gone through a recognised training at a general hospital and had satisfied independent examiners that they had made good use of their time while walking the wards.

These men were in many cases actually the same individuals who had prevented the old corporation from obtaining re-establishment at the hands of Parliament by their well-timed request to Lord Thurlow to come to their assistance. It was the outcome of their decided and united action that the House of Lords had been put upon its guard against the schemes of a few interested members of the Court of Assistants and had in 1797 refused to pass a Bill sanctioning the re-constitution of the old Barber-Surgeon Company as long as all the abuses that had crept into it during its centuries of somewhat precarious and ill-established existence made an integral part and an important parcel of its programme for a new life. These members had observed with pleasure the dissection by the great Lord Thurlow of the plans of their would-be masters and the consequent rejection of the scheme by the country. When, therefore, the Court of Assistants received three years later from King George III. a Royal Charter giving them in addition to a dignified position all the unwarrantable rights for themselves that they had previously unsuccessfully demanded from Parliament, the wronged members knew all the arguments against the granting of the Charter by heart. Yet although they were disaffected, and rightly, they made no common cause. Their leaders, who were their opponents, had received royal recognition and the fight seemed over. If there had been an outspoken and liberal medical paper in 1800 the Council and officers of the new Royal College would not have enjoyed the peaceful time that they did, but the help that could have been lent to the cause of justice by a strong editor was not then forthcoming. The only medical paper existent at the time speaking with any sort of authority was Dr. Roderick Macleod's decent but somewhat inept monthly publication, the " Medical and Physical journal," and the proclivities of this journal were aristocratic. So that Saturday, February 18th, 1826, was an important day for the reforming spirits of the College, for it was on that day that the first organised step was taken by the members against their leaders.

Mr. William Lawrence, afterwards Sir William Lawrence and President of the College, was in the chair on the occasion and was supported by Mr. Tyrrell of St. Thomas's Hospital, whose close relationship with Sir Astley Cooper and very recent law-suit against Wakley did not prevent him from realising on which side right lay. There were 1200 persons present, but a certain proportion, probably a quarter, of these were not members of the College. The general public attended, being interested in a quarrel the merits of which had been widely discussed in non-professional circles owing to Wakley's direct and uncompromising methods of comment.

Mr. Lawrence, in an eloquent opening speech, constituted himself the mouthpiece of the aggrieved members. All the points that had been insisted upon by Wakley and Wardrop were introduced into his speech. He dwelt upon the cruel and ridiculous disabilities of the members in almost the words that were used in the " Lancet" and picked to pieces in the most laughable manner the by-law precluding all but a few teachers in London, Dublin, and three Scotch towns from giving certificates of attendance upon scientific lectures. Its obvious grammatical frailty came in for notice no less than its cruelty to the students and its evidences of greed. Lawrence said it would seem that sound knowledge was the sort acquired in the winter, when the hospital lecturers were delivering their courses, while unsound knowledge was liable to be imparted in the summer, when only the excommunicated schools of the Graingers and Brookes were able to give the student the assistance and facilities for practical work that he required. After a detailed comparison of the merits of the hospital surgeons with those of the men who were now prevented from officially teaching, in the course of which he incidentally mentioned that under the College's present restrictive edict the famous school of William Hunter could not have existed, Lawrence went on to point out that the privilege of recognition must have been conceded to Scotland in some mockery, for it was well known that the schools of Aberdeen and Glasgow possessed no facilities for obtaining subjects, so that they could not give the instruction that the College had licensed them to impart. Edinburgh was different (gruesome forecast of the Burke and Hare trage-dies !), but of Aberdeen and Glasgow he said :—" We know, gentlemen, that at least anatomy cannot be studied in those places with any hope of success. We are all, I believe, aware, and no one is more ready than myself to acknow-ledge the great talents and acquirements of the gentlemen at the head of the anatomical schools in those places, but we are also aware that they are destitute of subjects, and with-out subjects, without the necessary means, no talent in the teacher, no acquisition of which he can boast, no peculiar fitness for the office of instruction in the past will avail the student in his study of anatomy." From this Lawrence diverged to touch upon a point of which telling use was afterwards made in the " Lancet," that the by-law excluded the great provincial teachers from giving recognised certifi-cates. " Need I mention," said the speaker, " Hey of Leeds, Hodgson of Birmingham, Martineau, Dalrymple, and Crosse of Norwich, and Barnes of Exeter, names that will amply warrant me in stating my conviction that the surgeons of provincial hospitals are as fully competent in the instruction of students as the favoured body who are attached to the London hospitals ? "

Mr. Tyrrell then rose, and supplemented Lawrence's re-marks by relating the history of the College and so making it clear that the ill-treatment of the members by the Council of the royal chartered organisation was a perpetuation of the abuses enacted under a corrupt corporation. He then pro-posed the following resolution :—" That the public and the members of the surgical profession very justly complain that the science of surgery has not been advanced nor its practitioners benefited either by the late Corporation or the present Royal College of Surgeons in London." Mr. Wardrop seconded the resolution, which was carried unanimously.

A second resolution was put to the effect that the new by-laws contained provisions of the most oppressive character, injurious to the rights and property of individuals, and calculated to increase the expense and difficulty of acquiring surgical knowledge and to serve the private interests of the ten examiners by whom these regulations were made. This also was carried unanimously. Next followed two resolutions condemning the exclusion by these by-laws of eminent anatomists, English, foreign, metropolitan, and provincial, from the pecuniary and honorary benefits belonging to the position of a recognised teacher of anatomy or surgery. These were carried unanimously.

A Mr. Lloyd then brought forward a resolution con-demnatory of the inaction of the College with regard to the library and the museum. The former he declared to be use-less because of its incompleteness and because such valuable books as it did contain were not accessible to the members, who had paid for them with their fees. The latter, he said, was not only closed to the members at all seasons when it would be of any practical use to them, but Hunter's splendid collection still remained uncatalogued twenty-four years after Government had presented it to the College for the promotion of medical science. Not the least contentious part of Mr. Lloyd's speech was a reference to the fact that the catalogue would now be exceedingly difficult to construct owing to an individual having destroyed John Hunter's inestimable manuscripts. The meeting cried *Hear, hear! Name! Shame!* and *Sir Everard Home!* * and the resolution was passed unanimously.

---

* It may be necessary to recall the significance of this interruption. Sir Everard Home, the first President of the Royal College of Surgeons who used that title, was John Hunter's pupil, brother-in-law, and literary executor. In discharge of his executorship he destroyed Hunter's manuscripts about three years before the date of this meeting.

The complaint with regard to the compulsory entrance of members by the back door was also put in the form of a resolution and carried unanimously.

A resolution was then brought forward by a Mr. Wigan that a committee should be appointed to present to the Council of the College a remonstrance grounded on the foregoing resolutions and requesting that the grievances therein complained of should be remedied.

So far the meeting had been remarkably at one in sentiment and language, but this resolution led to an animated discussion. It brought Wakley to the front, who, while owning that he had been the author of the advertisements summoning those interested in the reform of the College to meet at the Freemasons' Tavern, said that he did not find the results as drastic as he had hoped. Condemnatory resolutions forwarded to the College would certainly constitute a serious remonstrance to that body, but he did not believe that any remonstrance would be of avail. He wished to petition Parliament to recommend His Majesty to grant a new Charter, and one which allowed each member to have a voice in the election of those persons who were to regulate the proceedings of the College in the prosperity of which he must feel a personal as well as a national interest.

His lengthy speech was listened to with mixed feelings by his audience. He was prepared to go much further than most of them, and many of his expressions of contempt for the present rulers of the College did not meet with response. The general feeling was, in fact, favourable to civil remonstrance at the time that Wakley rose to speak on the other side. But, said Wakley, one might as well remonstrate with the Devil as with this constitutionally rotten concern—(his own words). Nothing would come of such a measure, and he urged the meeting to petition Parliament at once to abrogate the Charter. He carried the bolder spirits with him, although he frightened many who were anxious in the

He was, and is, generally believed to have made use of the papers in scientific writings to which he appended his own name, and to have burnt them for fear of detection.

cause of reform but who did not believe that such root-and-branch remedy was necessary. His speech was an eloquent effort—outspoken, combative, and closely reasoned. He set the meeting right on the legal procedure necessary to obtain an abrogation of the Charter, and summed up, with striking additions, those grievances endured by the members, which had already been made the subject of unanimous resolutions. Gradually he carried his hearers with him. Dissentient cries grew less frequent and applause waxed more unrestrained. As he felt that he was winning he in his turn made concessions to the meeting, dropping his more contentious tone and appealing to their practical sense. He concluded by proposing a long amendment to Mr. Wigan's motion to the effect that a petition founded on the resolutions already adopted, should be immediately prepared and presented to the House of Commons, praying for the appointment of a committee to inquire into the abuses thus revealed, with a view to obtaining from the King a new Charter.

Lawrence, in putting the amendment to the meeting, said a few words in favour of the original motion, but Wakley had taken the sense of the assembly by storm and his views were endorsed by a large majority.

A committee of twenty persons was then appointed to prepare the petition to the House of Commons, and the meeting adjourned.

CHAPTER XXI

[1823–1834]

The Adjourned First Meeting of the Members—Its Action—A Metrical Squib—The Refutation by the College of the Charges brought against it—The Complete Insufficiency of the Refutation.

THE members of the Royal College of Surgeons of England re-assembled on March 4th, 1826, when Mr. William Lawrence again took the chair.

The business of the meeting was to receive a report from the committee which had been appointed at the previous meeting to prepare the petition to the House of Commons. Mr. Tyrrell, the chairman of that committee, said that, although they had received no instructions to that effect from the members, they had approached the Council of the College asking them to join in the application to Parliament. These gentlemen having contemptuously refused, he proposed that the opinion of counsel should be taken as to the best mode of applying to the Legislature.

Wakley again made a forcible speech, in which he pleaded for action, the necessity for drastic reform being urgent. He read a long amendment to Tyrrell's motion, but that gentleman was ready to accept Wakley's suggestions, and with the leave of the meeting altered his original resolution so that it read as follows :—

" That the committee be at liberty generally to take such steps as they think fit to remedy the abuses now existing in the Royal College of Surgeons ; and that they shall call a general meeting of the members whenever they shall think it advisable."

Wakley seconded the resolution, which was carried

unanimously. A subscription was then opened to defray the expenses of any step the committee might desire to take.

This, the first general meeting of the College, was to lead to important developments, and the importance of Wakley's share in the movement cannot be over-estimated. He summoned the first general meeting by advertisements which he inserted upon his own initiative. He persuaded Lawrence, a member of the staff of the "Lancet" as well as a hospital-surgeon, to take the chair at the meeting, knowing that in this way he would arouse the proper spirit of instructed reform and not merely turbulent clamour for nothing in particular. It was Wakley's speaking at the meeting which led to definite steps being taken. Had it not been for his vigorous words of contempt at the passing of mere condemnatory resolutions, the meeting would have been content with effecting that much; but the members followed in his lead, and found themselves promptly committed to an appeal to the Government for redress.

Abernethy, who was the mouthpiece of the Council in their very natural refusal to join the members who were agitating for a new Charter, was made the subject of several humorous attacks in the "Lancet"; otherwise Wakley used his paper impartially. He printed the opinions of the reformers whom he represented, and whom he really led, but he gave equal space to any reply that came from the College. Abernethy was not put forward for the College because the great surgeon was the most reactionary Tory on the Council. He was nothing of the kind, and often his written or spoken words showed that he sympathised with many of the complaints that were made by the general body of the corporation against the existing management of the College. But Abernethy was a masterful man and an intellectual aristocrat. He did not approve of any opposition to a system of government for which he was partly responsible, while he belonged to a picked body of surgeons and sincerely believed that persons not so selectly situated possessed a lower order of intelligence and could not, consequently, expect to be entrusted with the conduct of their own affairs. His colleagues chose him as their spokesman because of his great public reputation and his pronounced taste for fighting. Popular with the students and the best surgeon at the great hospital of St. Bartholomew, he had an enormous public fame for honesty and bluff wit and a great scientific reputation as the person upon whom the mantle of john Hunter had seemed to fall. The following verses from Wakley's pen on Abernethy's share in the now celebrated by-law, did not constitute a fair attack as they misinterpret Abernethy's attitude, but they are worth printing as a display of metrical skill. Doggrel they are, but they say what they mean :—

JOHN ABERNETHY, LOQUITUR.

"Ye stupid fools and blundering churls, who want our leave to practice,
  Behold, I take the pains to tell what our new-fangled act is.

"We have decreed that there shall be in England but one station
  At which young men shall 'grind to pass' and have our approbation.

' With Scotland 'tis a different thing, you all know I am Scotch, sirs,
  And for my clan I do not mind to shuffle, cheat, and botch, sirs.

"In Scotland then raw lads may find three schools to one elsewhere,
  sirs,
  And those who deem this law unjust may scout it if they dare, sirs,

    *   *   *   *   *

"Moreover, 'tis our royal will, our most imperial pleasure,
  As well to fill our classes out, as swell our bags with treasure,

"That knowledge henceforth be unsound, to reason quite contrary,
  Unless obtained sometime about the month of January;

"No one shall dare to think or say that any man can truly
  Acquire the art of lopping limbs within three months of July.

"So fare ye well, confound ye all—may every ill infest ye,
  If ye shall dare to make a stir or say we have oppress'd ye."

The verses, which are extracted from a long "poem," are unfair, but it must not be supposed that their injustice to their subject had the significance of a deliberate libel.   No one believed in the accuracy of that sort of attack ; the quality of exact truth was not expected.   The metrical squib was a survival of eighteenth-century habit.   If you were taking a side in a row you wrote verses lampooning your opponent.   He replied with a pamphlet.   You hit back with an open letter.   Possibly a duel ensued.   More often some-one of the school of Gillray interposed and limned you both ridiculously, the net result being that the audience laughed and the champions laughed.

The occasion of these verses was Abernethy's presentation to the members of the College of the Council's refutation of the charges brought against the authorities.   This document is long, but it is the categorical answer of the governing body to all the charges of gross mismanagement and it would be unjust to alter it by a syllable.

' ROYAL COLLEGE OF SURGEONS, IN LONDON.

" OBSERVATIONS IN REFUTATION OF CHARGES, PUBLICLY MADE BY CERTAIN MEMBERS OF THE COLLEGE, AGAINST ITS LEGALLY CONSTITUTED AUTHORITIES.

" It is asserted that the College has not performed those duties for which it was incorporated.

" That this assertion is unfounded, will be acknowledged by all reflecting and unprejudiced persons, who compare the present state of surgery throughout the country, with that, which existed when the College received its charter in 1800; for it appears that the increased respectability of the profession may be principally attributed to the acts and regulations of the College.   This advancement may be mainly ascribed to the more extended education which has been progressively required of the candidates for its diploma ; to the zeal and talents of its professors, in displaying and communicating by public lectures, a scientific knowledge of the subjects connected with the healing art ; and to the labour and time devoted to the explanation of the contents of its Museum ; by which a strong desire for increase of knowledge has been excited.

" The inquiry into the professional education and attainments of candidates, has been rendered more strict in proportion to the general increase of knowledge.

" During one period of the late war, when the applicants for examination were unexpectedly and unprecedently numerous, in consequence of the demands of the public service, many candidates were necessarily examined at the same court, but since the peace, not more candidates have been admitted to examination at any court, than could be examined in an ample and satisfactory manner; and for some time past, each candidate for the diploma has been separately examined in the presence and hearing of the whole court; which is now the established practice.

" The examiners have so frequently referred candidates to a continuance of their studies, as to induce students in general to think seriously of their examination, and to prepare themselves for it by a proportionate degree of diligence.

" Had inquiry been made, it would have appeared that the examiners have not any pecuniary interest in the admission of candidates as members; and it cannot be improper to mention, that the remuneration received by the examiners is a very inadequate recompense for the time and labour bestowed upon the execution of their arduous and important duties.

" There is no profession into which dishonest and dishonourable persons have not at times gained admission; but the council are not aware of a single instance of an empiric having been admitted as a member; and not until lately, has it been understood, that the College possesses the power of removing any member who has been guilty of disgraceful conduct.

" It has been made a subject of complaint, that certificates of summer courses of lectures are not received by the court of examiners. That certificates are not indiscriminately received from every anatomical teacher, and that certificates of attendance on provincial hospitals are not admitted by the court; and such regulations have been censured as unjust bye-laws of the College.

" The council have in the first instance, to correct this error. There are no bye-laws on these subjects; these are regulations of the court of examiners. The council have been assured by the court of examiners, that so many certificates of attendance on lectures had been presented to them, purporting to be signed by teachers wholly unknown to them, as to render it imperative to define the certificates which in their judgment, it would be proper with a view to the public good, and respectability of the profession, to acknowledge and to receive.

" The council believe, that not any persons except the court of examiners are able to judge correctly on this subject; and while they wish to correct the erroneous supposition of the regulations in question being bye-laws of the College, they cannot but give credit to the court of examiners for the most pure and conscientious motives; and for an earnest desire to promote the dignity of the profession; and necessarily the welfare of the community; in the legitimate exercise of their discretion on these subjects.

" The court of examiners, anxious that students should attend in-structions capable of giving them enlarged and scientific views of their profession, knew not how they could obtain from distant places, any evidence of the teacher having, himself, received a liberal professional education, but by the means which they have adopted; yet, notwith-standing such regulations, it cannot be doubted that any member of the College, possessing in an eminent degree the requisite qualifications for becoming a teacher of anatomy, physiology, and pathology, which are united in the recognized schools, would so distinguish himself, as to justify the admission of his certificates. The regulations of the College must always change with the circumstances of the times.

" The subject of attendance on provincial hospitals, had repeatedly engaged the consideration of the court of examiners; but with every respect for, and the highest opinion of, the medical officers belonging to most of these excellent establishments, the council would witness with regret the indiscriminate admission of such certificates.

" The court of examiners, have under certain conditions, recognized attendance on the practice of some of those hospitals; and the council are of opinion, that it would injure the cause of chirurgical science, were the court of examiners to be controlled in the exercise of their discretion on this subject.

" In reference to the complaint of the Museum not being more freely and frequently opened to the public, and of the want of a catalogue; answers to such accusations are contained in the triennial reports from the Board of Curators to the council, in the last of which is the follow-ing summary of proceedings, with respect to the catalogue.

" ' The following recital of facts will show the council how solicitous the curators have always been that the collection should be properly explained.

' When the Hunterian Collection was received by this College, it was accompanied by two catalogues; one, explanatory of the prepara-tions in the gallery; the other, of the morbid preparations. These had been compiled by Mr. C. Clift, under the direction of Sir Everard Home, from old catalogues, formed under the superintendance of Mr. Hunter; as is proved by his hand-writing in many parts of them. The transcript must have appeared to the curators, and must be allowed, by every one, to contain a very excellent and perfect account of Mr. Hunter's views and opinions in the formation of his collection; though it must also appear very deficient in the explanation of the individual preparations.

' No one, however, supposed, until within a short time, that Mr. Hunter left any other writings of importance explanatory of his Collec-tion, than the before mentioned two catalogues.

' On the completion of the Museum, and the admission of visitors, the want of a descriptive catalogue was soon felt and expressed; and the Board of Curators, in the year 1813, prepared a printed syllabus to gratify scientific inquirers.

'The Curators also consulted Dr. Shaw, who, at the instance of the Board, prepared a third catalogue of objects in the department of natural history.

'A descriptive catalogue of the preparations, which was earnestly desired by the Trustees, has ever been a desideratum of great interest and consideration to the Board of Curators, as may be seen by its minutes.

'The Board regarded Sir Everard Home, as executor of Mr. Hunter, to be the person most proper, and best qualified to undertake the task of preparing the catalogue, which he repeatedly engaged to do.

'At length, in 1816, it was proposed, that all the Curators should become joint labourers in this great work, when Sir Everard Home declared, that it was his special duty, and that he would admit of no participation in its performance. The result of his labours was the production of a synopsis, which, doubtless, the members of the Council have perused.

'When in 1817 Sir Everard Home became a Trustee, he resigned the office of Curator ; and the Board, anxious for the completion of a descriptive catalogue of the contents of the Museum, resolved to engage the Conservator in preparing one under their own superintendance.

'In order to allow him more time for this undertaking, the Board appointed his son to be assistant in his ordinary duties. They directed that the specimens of monstrosity should be removed from the closet in which they were arranged, that it might be appropriated, during the necessary time, to the receipt of books, papers, and other things subservient to the preparation of the catalogue.

'The Board decided, that the contents of the galleries should be arranged in two divisions, each containing sub-divisions, which subdivisions should also contain series and sub-series.

'The Board further appointed Sir William Blizard, Mr. Cline, and Mr. Abernethy, to be a sub-committee for the special purpose of superintending the formation of the catalogue ; to report to the Board from time to time the progress made in it, with such observations relating thereto, as they should consider proper ; which sub-committee has presented to the Board the description of the first sub-division of the gallery, comprehending seventeen series, containing 261 preparations, which was approved by the Board, and also by the Trustees.

'When, however, the Conservator began his task of preparing the catalogue, he expressed the wish to obtain some of Mr. Hunter's manuscripts, and thus did the Board of Curators learn for the first time the extent and nature of the manuscripts left by Mr. Hunter, with relation to his collection.

'The Curators, on applying to Sir Everard Home, were informed by him, that he had burned all Mr. Hunter's manuscripts, in consequence of a promise made to Mr. Hunter to that effect.

'Amongst these manuscripts were ten volumes in folio, viz., nine on the anatomy of animals, and one on vegetables. That Mr. Hunter considered these books to be valuable, and not otherwise than creditable to himself, may be inferred by three of them being placed on the table beside him, when his portrait was painted by Sir Joshua Reynolds.

'It is said, that Sir Everard Home has even burned Mr. Hunter's manuscript lectures, which he read to his class. But the Curators cannot believe that Mr. Hunter could intend that these works should be burned as unimportant manuscripts. It must, therefore, always remain a subject of deep regret, that Sir Everard Home should have felt himself bound by his promise to Mr. Hunter, to have carried destruction to the extent to which he is said to have done; yet Sir Everard Home has not felt the same obligation to destroy all the writings on morbid anatomy; for the Curators have obtained, through the interposition of the Trustees, two folio volumes, and two solanders of cases and dissections explanatory of a considerable number of the morbid preparations.

'These books contain a careful record of the symptoms and effects of disease during life, and the alterations of structure produced, as ascertained by examination after death. They are highly creditable to Mr. Hunter, as expressing that thirst for knowledge, which led him constantly to seek it by means which we know to be the most certain, but also the most tedious, laborious, disgusting, and unostentatious.'

"The want of a catalogue, as explained in that report, is, in the opinion of the Council, a most satisfactory reason why the Museum has not hitherto been more freely opened to the profession, and why it cannot be for some time, admitting the completion of that catalogue, to be of such paramount importance as the Council deem it to be.

" It may be further observed, that the study of comparative anatomy had been formerly so little prosecuted in this country, that, though many persons were consulted, none could aid in giving a description of the individual preparations in the Hunterian Collection. The Conservator has, however, for a considerable time, been engaged in such researches and inquiries, as have enabled him, not only to give an exact account of each preparation, but also to explain Mr. Hunter's intentions in the formation of his Collection; and the more the time of the Conservator shall be occupied in explaining the contents of the Museum to visitors, the longer necessarily must the completion of the catalogue be retarded.

"With respect to the Library, its formation has been the act of the College, and is intended to aid the professional inquiries of its members, for which purpose it will, when in a proper state, be opened.

"It may be added, that of the numerous applications made by members, for permission to refer to publications therein, every one has been most readily complied with; and the same may be observed of applications to examine and to make drawings from preparations in the Museum.

"With regard to the supposed indignity offered to the members at large, by their being admitted to the theatre by a door at the back of the building, the Council, aware that any want of respect to its members would be a failure of respect to the institution itself, did not imagine that umbrage would be taken by such an arrangement; at the same time they regret that the present construction of the building precludes the practicability of an alteration.

"It is proper to observe, that no official complaint or remonstrance on this subject has ever been made to the Council. Some years since, indeed, it was mentioned to the board of curators; upon which the members, during one course of lectures, were admitted to their seats from Lincoln's-Inn Fields, through the Museum; the dust occasioned thereby, was found to be injurious to the collection, in consequence of which, the present arrangement was adopted, certainly with a view to the comfort and convenience of the members, and for the preservation of the preparations. When the theatre was built, the great influx of persons into the profession, which has since taken place could not have been anticipated; and it was then thought that the building would be more than adequate to the accommodation of all who would attend.

"It is represented, that the constitution of the College has been the cause of the alleged injuries and grievances.

"The evident object of this representation, is the subversion of the present government of the College, and the substitution of elections to offices of control and responsibility, by members, who for the most part exercise the professions of apothecaries and accoucheurs. There can be little doubt, that in the event of such an innovation, the Institution would soon cease to be a College of Surgeons or of Surgery, and a system of continual intrigue and cabal amongst the profession in general would be introduced.

"The constituted authorities of the College are conscious that they have uniformly exerted themselves to increase the scientific knowledge and respectability of the profession; and that they have never been influenced by the unworthy motives imputed to them; had any of the members of the College expressed dissatisfaction at their proceedings, they would have willingly explained the reasons of their conduct, as well as their future intentions, and have altered whatever could have been shown to be wrong; but when meetings have been convened to subvert the Charter of the College, ' under the sanction of which,' it is said, 'injustice and tyranny have been perpetrated '—when, at these meetings, the most dishonourable motives have been attributed to the members of the Council, they feel it due to themselves to offer this brief, and they trust satisfactory, explanation of their conduct.

" By Order of the Council.

" (Signed)   EDMUND BELFOUR, Secretary.

" LINCOLN-INN FIELDS,
" 26th day of April, 1826."

The Council could not have expected to check criticism on their doings by the issue of this lengthy rigmarole which contained confessions of guilt in every line. All teachers save a few were ignored because the Council could not judge between proper and improper teaching. The clinical instruction of all country hospitals was set aside because the Council "would witness with regret the indiscriminate admission of certificates " from medical men in the provinces. It did not occur to the Council that to be unable to devise a plan for deciding what certificates were good and what were bad formed an admission of complete incompetency. The Museum was closed because it was useless without a catalogue to the Hunterian collection. There was no catalogue because a member of the Council had burned the documents necessary for its construction. The Library remained shut because it was not " in a proper state to be opened." The members must enter by the back door, because the Council could not command the architectural ingenuity necessary for the provision of any other entrance.

CHAPTER XXII

[1823—1834]

The Revolt of the Members of the Royal College of Surgeons of England—Wakley's Consistent Attitude—The Members' Petition—The Navy and the Diplomas of the College—Personal Attacks upon Abernethy and Sir William Blizard—Mr. Warburton presents the Petition in the House of Commons—Sir Robert Peel for the Defence—The Decision of the House.

IT would serve no purpose to trace all the steps of the duel that now took place between the reformers and the College authorities. The part that was played in it by Wakley was throughout consistent and vigorous. The official refutation was treated by him with complete ridicule, inasmuch as it refuted nothing, but only added fresh insults to those which had already been accepted by the members for years and were now for the first time being resented. In particular, the last paragraph but one of the unfortunate document came in for scorn. The statements that the subversion of the Charter would lead to the election to offices of control and responsibility of persons "who for the most part exercised the professions of apothecaries and accoucheurs," in which case the institution would soon cease to be a College of Surgeons or Surgery, while " a system of continual intrigue and cabal amongst the profession in general would be introduced," furnished Wakley with an admirable text upon which to address the profession at large, and one of which he was not slow to avail himself. Such words he held to constitute a direct insult to the general practitioners of England as well as a distinct attempt to exercise an illegal power. While declaring in uncompromising terms that the general practitioners were much more capable of conducting the affairs of their corporation than were many of the twenty-one Councillors elected for life, and frequently displaying evidences of senility while occupying their offices, he pointed out that the Charter—the infamous Charter under which this oligarchical and irresponsible little body claimed the right to control the affairs of the members—contained no provision for the limitations which the refutation of the College attempted to lay down. There was not a word in the Charter implying any disability on the part of an apothecary or an accoucheur to occupy a seat either on the Council, the Court of Examiners, or even the Presidential bench, and he accused the existent Council of attempting to read into the Charter, already upholding no interests but their own, unwritten clauses still further securing to themselves all the benefits, honorary or pecuniary, in the power of the College to bestow. This formed an admirable rallying cry for the members and it was recognised by them as such, the "Lancet" receiving at the time an enormous access of regular readers and subscribers among the general practitioners of England, who recognised in Wakley the guardian of their interests, the man who was not only prepared to see that they received some substantial return for their fees, but also that they were treated with the respect due to them as the persons who paid.

It was not until the last day of 1826 that the petition to the House of Commons for the abrogation of the Charter reached its final stage, so that signatures could be invited for it. Spontaneous as had been the revolt of the members against their rulers, and unanimous as had been their strongly-worded resolutions of remonstrance at the general meetings, the movement would have ceased at the mere passing of these resolutions had it not been for Wakley's energy, desire for justice, and, it must be admitted, personal implacability. Lawrence was satisfied with the commotion that had been caused in the comfortable breasts of the Council and from personal reasons was desirous of peace. Many of the leaders in the agitation were also ready to lay down their arms on the promise of some slight concession. But not so Wakley. He held the meeting to their pledged course, declaimed against the perpetual delay in the preparation of the petition, and was finally able to announce that the means of redress had at last been brought within reach of the members, for the document was lying ready for signature at Freemasons' Tavern.

The petition was straightforward and comprehensive, but bore no trace of labour or research, so that it is difficult to understand why it should not have been ready for signature until the end of the year. The resolutions of remonstrance adopted at the general meetings at the Freemasons' Tavern in the spring sufficiently indicate the lines upon which it was drawn, as it was designed to meet those specific grievances. The declared object for which the Charter of 1800 was granted was " the due promotion and encouragement of the study and practice of the art and science of surgery." The principal means by which these objects were to be brought about should be the conduct of examinations into the qualifications and education of candidates for admission into the College or into the medical departments of the Navy and Army, the inference being that the certificates of the College would enable the public to distinguish between the expert and the pretender. The petition stated that the Navy had refused to accept the diploma of the College as sufficient to warrant the advance of those holding it from Assistant-Surgeon to Full-Surgeon ; while there were numerous examples of advertising quacks on the official lists of the College. The petition then pointed out that the Charter had consigned the whole management of the College to twenty-one persons, who, being elected for life themselves, had the privilege of electing whomsoever they liked, also for life, to fill any death vacancies ; that these twenty-one persons appointed ten of their own body to form a Court of Examiners and were not accountable to the members for the appropriation of the funds, nor for any other of their proceedings which were conducted in private. The petition next showed that the twenty-one governors of the College had a direct interest in keeping all the emoluments to themselves and that they did so by preventing other persons than the Court of Examiners and personal friends of that Court from delivering official lectures to the students, upon which followed naturally a representation of the grievances concerning the new by-laws as to the sources of official certificates of attendance at lectures. The framing of the petition was largely left to Wakley. He knew what the wording and arguments were going to be, and therefore constantly alluded in his articles to the action of the Navy when that department refused to accept under certain circumstances the diplomas of the College as proofs of scientific efficiency. In public speeches he urged that one of the main reasons for the existence of the College, one of the specified objects that George III. had before him in granting to the discredited corporation a Royal Charter whereon to begin a new life, was that the College should accept the responsibility of supplying the military and naval services with efficient surgeons. In this the College must be held to have failed. Wakley's second great contention was that the grant of the Royal Charter had been made to safeguard the public against quacks, the duty devolving on the College to discriminate between the charlatan and the true man of learning. Hence his object in perpetually giving prominence to the fact that there were notorious quacks, persons dealing in secret and disgraceful remedies, whose names were on the official list of the College. It was not mere mud-throwing. It was done to show that in another direction the College had been found wanting to the implied contract between its original governors and the King.

Not all Wakley's work in connexion with the framing of the petition was so restrained as his articles dealing with the shortcomings of the College from a collegiate aspect. His strictures on the personality of the Council and, in particular, on that of the Court of Examiners were abusive indeed. Sir Astley Cooper was rallied without cease on his nepotism. Sir William Blizard, who was born in 1748, was constantly reproached for his senility.

The following passage from an essay by Bernard de Mandeville on "Charity and Charity Schools" was boldly applied to Abernethy :—

"That a man with *small skill in Physic,* and *hardly any learning,* should, by vile arts, get into practice, and lay up great wealth is no mighty wonder; but that he should so deeply work himself into the good opinion of the world as to gain the general esteem of a nation, and establish a reputation beyond all his contemporaries, with no other qualities but a perfect knowledge of mankind and a capacity of making the most of it, is something extraordinary. If a man, arrived to such a height of glory, should be almost distracted with pride, sometimes give his attendance on a servant, or any mean person, for nothing, and at the same time neglect a nobleman that gives exorbitant fees, at other times refuse to leave his bottle for his business, without any regard to the quality of the persons that sent for him or the danger they are in : if he should be *surly and morose, affect to be an humourist,* treat his patients like dogs, though people of distinction, and value no man but what would deify him, and never call in question the certainty of his oracles: if he should insult all the world, *affront the first nobility,* and *extend his insolence even to the Royal Family :* if to maintain as well as to increase the fame of his sufficiency, he should scorn to consult with his betters on what emergency soever, look down with contempt on the most deserving of his profession, and never confer with any other physician but what will pay homage to his superior genius, creep to his humour, and never approach him but with all the slavish obsequiousness a court flatterer can treat a prince with: if a man in his lifetime should discover on the one hand such manifest symptoms of superlative pride, and an *insatiable greediness after wealth* at the same time, and on the other no regard to religion, or affection to his kindred, no compassion to the poor, and hardly any humanity to his fellow creatures : if he gave no proofs that he loved his country, had a public spirit, or was a lover of arts, of books, or of literature, what must we judge of his motive, the principle he acted from ? "

Sir William Blizard was thus gracefully accused of an atrabilious temperament under a paragraph simulating a pathological note and headed :

"MALFORMATION.

" The following case of misplaced viscera is particularly curious. We believe, however, that several examples of a similar kind are to be found among the members of the Court of Examiners at the College in Lincoln's-Inn Fields—we anticipate, for example, that when a post-mortem examination of Sir William Blizard shall be instituted, that the liver of this bitter knight will be found in his cranium, for during the whole of Sir William's life, his mouth has been performing the office of *a ductus communis choledochus*."

In writing in this strain it is difficult to guess whether Wakley furthered or hindered his objects. There would have been no petition at all had it not been for his energy, while his ridicule of, and apparent contempt for, the leaders of the profession certainly secured the adherence to the movement of many who would otherwise have stood aloof out of deference to great names. But his bellicose methods had their drawback. They deprived the reform party of the support of people who were at one with the members in their struggle for justice but unwilling to countenance anything with the appearance of direct malice towards the great leaders of medicine.

It was probably some such feeling as this that led to the refusal of Sir Robert Peel to present the petition to Parliament. He had almost promised to do so, but at the last moment declined, writing the following letter to the gentleman through whom the negotiations were being conducted :—

"WHITEHALL, *March 12th 1827.*

" SIR,—I beg leave to return the accompanying petition to the House of Commons praying for an appointment of a committee of enquiry into the conduct of the College of Surgeons, and I request that you will acquaint those by whom you have been deputed to address me, that I cannot undertake to present it to the House of Commons.

" I understood some days since that this petition was placed in the hands of another member of Parliament, and that he was to present it to the House of Commons.

" A copy of the petition was at the same time sent to me, and having made full enquiry into the whole subject, and finding a ready disposition on the part of those who have the management of the affairs of the College of Surgeons, to attend to any suggestions which are calculated to promote the real interests of the profession, I cannot concur in the prayer of this petition, and I, therefore, beg leave, with all due respect, to decline its presentation. I do not class with such suggestions the proposal that there should be an annual election of the Council by all the Members of the College. I have the honour to be, Sir,

" Your most obedient humble servant,

" JAMES PATY, Esq."   " ROBERT PEEL.

Peel was Home Secretary, and undoubtedly his support would have given a substantiality to the wrongs of the members of the College of Surgeons in parliamentary eyes.' But he could not, as a personal friend of Sir Astley Cooper and Abernethy, associate himself with violent attacks upon them. The reformers, failing Peel, secured an excellent man to present their petition in Mr. Henry Warburton, the member for Bridport.

Mr. Warburton was a merchant, and a calm, business-like, sensible man. He afterwards made his mark in six consecutive Parliaments as a prominent free-trader and an enthusiast in the cause of medical reform, his speeches being deliberate, effective, and unpretentious. To present this petition was his first opportunity of showing his merit in the House, and he used it in a characteristic manner.

On june 20th, 1827, Mr. Warburton rose to point out that in 1797, when the former Corporation of Surgeons were attempting to obtain from Parliament a re-establishment—the parent corporation having ceased to exist in consequence of some irregularities in its procedure—Lord Thurlow had persuaded the Lords to scout the Bill because it contained certain clauses inimical to the interests of the members. These same clauses were now, he said, in active operation under a Royal Charter against the members, who therefore prayed for relief in the full trust of obtaining it. Warburton then recapitulated almost in the words of the petition the various tribulations of the members as exemplified by the six strong resolutions of remonstrance passed at the general meeting, and concluded by moving for a return from the Royal College of Surgeons of England of all public money lent or granted to the College from 1799 to the present time. He specified the grants he required to have information upon as being those made for the purchase, building, and repairing of the College, and for the purchase of the Hunterian Museum. He also desired that the regulations under which the members of the College and the medical students were admitted to the Hunterian Museum and to the library of the College should be laid on the table, as well as the numbers of persons who had been examined by the College since 1800. He required also an account of all moneys received by the College from its members, and a detailed statement of the appropriation and expenditure of these sums and of the sums granted by the State. After a few words from a Mr. Smyth, who said that the petition was the work of interested persons and was based upon no better foundation than feelings of personal pique, Peel rose to speak in behalf of the College. He was very sympathetic to the cause of the members and the line of defence adopted was practically a confession of guilt. Peel was a trustee of the Hunterian Museum, and said that he had discussed with the Council of the College every subject of complaint preferred in the petition, and that many of the causes no longer existed, and that every one of them that appeared reasonable would be in time removed. The back-door entrance was done away with, the catalogue of the museum was being prepared, and a quarterly statement of the financial affairs of the College would for the future be made public. Mr. Peel did not consider " that there was the slightest ground of accusation against the College," but he was willing to support Warburton's motion, after the explanation the House had heard of his vote, because he considered Parliament had a right to be informed of the proceedings of an institution which had received large grants of public money.

Peel's speech was a very illogical performance. Certain complaints were made concerning the action of the Council; therefore a petition was presented to Parliament begging for an alteration in the Charter which sanctioned the abuses. Mr. Peel rose and admitted that the complaints were being attended to and would receive further attention, and yet said that the petition was presented on no proper grounds of accusation !

The House acceded to Warburton's motion and the College was called upon to render an account of its stewardship. A temporary victory was thus gained by the members.

CHAPTER XXIII

[1823–1834]

A Barren Victory—The Secession of Sir William Lawrence—His Demeanour towards Wakley—Wakley Continues to " Peg Away " —The Insult to the Medical Officers of the Navy—The Members Pass Resolutions in the Theatre of the College—Wakley Treated by the Authorities as a Broiler and Rioter—A Disgraceful Scene.

THE victory of the members of the College of Surgeons over their autocratic Council was but a barren one. In obedience to the order of the House of Commons a return was made showing that the College had received from Government £15,000 in june, 1797, for the purchase of the Hunterian Museum (this sum was not granted directly to the College, but to the executors of John Hunter, who, however, in return for it handed over the Hunterian collection to the College) ; £15,000 in July, 1806, to erect a suit- able building to contain the Hunterian Museum ; and £12,500 in April, 1810, for building purposes in connexion with the edifice in Lincoln's-Inn, a suitable home for the Museum again being mentioned as the chief object of appropriation. The return also showed that £30,000 in addition had been spent by the College in building, the money having been obtained as fees. Passing swiftly over the regulations concerning admission to the museum and certification for examinations, the return next dealt with the source of the income of the College. The years 1825 and 1826 were chosen as types, and the figures furnished showed the income for the years to have been in the gross £7261 16s. and £7704 9s. respectively. There the return ended, no details of expenditure being given. The document was laid upon the table and no debate ensued. No member of the House was sufficiently interested or sufficiently well-informed to consider it to be his duty to carry the matter further in teeth of the substantial opposition to practical reform that such men as Sir Astley Cooper, Mr. Abernethy, and Sir William Blizard had been able to secure. The wealth of the College was exposed and its meanness to its commonalty was made no less manifest; but the only people who cared for these things—viz., a reforming section of that commonalty—knew it all before, so that the victory must be considered a barren one. It was a slap in the face for the authorities, but it was not only no rout of them, it did not form even a temporary check to their course.

The committee who had organised the petition and who had hoped such great things from it were sorely disheartened, and almost immediately afterwards they received a great blow by the desertion of William Lawrence. Lawrence was a most powerful friend, and could if he chose be a most powerful foe. His mere presence at the assemblies of the reformers, being himself a hospital surgeon, and one of the class who had most to hope from the prolongation of old abuses, had been of the utmost service; while his ready pen, his eloquence, and his clear brain had served them well, both in the columns of the "Lancet" and from the chair at the general meetings. Now the prestige thrown over the movement by his participation in their counsels was gone, while the weight of his talents was thrown into the other scale, for he accepted an invitation from the Council of the College to become one of them. Wakley felt Lawrence's secession deeply, but the blow was not entirely unexpected. It will be remembered that from the first Lawrence had proposed milder counsels than suited the more thoroughgoing of the reformers, but had been always defeated by the general vote. Wakley recognised this, and when the shrill cry of "Traitor" or "Judas" was raised at the news that Lawrence had agreed to sit on the Council he did not join in it. He deplored Lawrence's action, but his language was much more measured than that of most of his followers and much milder than was expected by them. Lawrence was equally studious to preserve an outwardly amicable attitude towards Wakley, the terms of their curious truce having been arranged between them. In fact, they could not fight even if they had wished. Lawrence had been behind the scenes at the office of the "Lancet" almost from the beginning and knew things that could not be made public without immensely injuring many besides Wakley. All journals have their secrets, and sufficient has been said about the early career of the "Lancet" to show that many men must have assisted Wakley in private by giving information, while in public they considered themselves at liberty to stand aloof from the cause of reform. It must be remembered that at most hospitals if a man connected with the institution whether as a student only or as one in authority had been convicted of being on the staff of the "Lancet" his conduct would have been regarded by the surgeons as a distinct breach of trust, and he would have lost all chance of promotion at once. So that anonymity was the rule. In a perfect state of affairs this necessity for concealment could not have existed, and honourable men need not have been ashamed to hold enlightened opinions ; but in the condition of medical politics at that time it was not possible to be over-nice. Wakley had nothing to fear on his own account from any indiscretion of Lawrence, but he always made his contributors' cause his own cause ; and when Lawrence deserted the "Lancet" and the programme of the reformers Wakley felt that the future of many who had helped him was now in the hands of an adversary, one of the detested Council. But Lawrence, on the other hand, had his lips sealed by self-interest as much as by honour, though, be it said, Wakley, in common with most thoughtful persons, credited him with the finer motive. Lawrence had himself written in extraordinarily bitter terms of the leaders of the profession, and had it been known that some of the wittiest and most personal of the strictures that had been passed upon these worthies had been from his pen many among them would not have welcomed him back to the fold. They could not have exhibited even a semblance of friendship towards him. So, as has been said, a curious truce was concluded between Wakley and his late partner in the cause of reform. Lawrence was understood to esteem Wakley, and to hold his views up to a point, but not to be prepared to follow him to the extreme length that Wakley desired to go. Wakley was content to believe that Lawrence would still serve the cause of the commonalty even after he had thrown in his lot with the oligarchs, and his references to him were generally civil and always regretful.

In spite, however, of the defection of friends, the inaction of Parliament, the turbulence of some would-be reformers and the apathy of others, Wakley kept "pegging away," to use the phrase in which he himself promised that he would never desert the cause of medical reform. Every volume of the "Lancet" was prefaced by an editorial statement in which he breathed threats against the Charter of the College. Almost every issue contained some article reflecting upon the government of the College. Now and then he had some little triumph to record, as when the hated back-door entrance was done away with in 1827, or when the pressure brought by some popular teacher upon the Council to have his certificates officially recognised proved successful to its end. But generally the articles recapitulated the complaints that had so often been made, and reading them now we wonder that they did not become wearisome in the ears of those to whom they were addressed, though it is impossible to withhold admiration from their writer's marvellous perseverance. Now it was the senility of certain members of the Council, and now the dirty condition of the library, and now the hauteur of the secretary, Mr. Belfour; but, week in week out, the Council of the College were reminded that they had in Wakley a critic who was frankly inimical to the existent constitution and ever watchful for an opportunity to bring it into discredit.

The Council of the College at length redeemed the situation from a monotony of dreary bickering by furnishing

Wakley with a legitimate and sensational reason for impugn-ing their methods and manners. On February 12th, 1831, there appeared in the "Lancet" a letter stating that the surgeons of His Majesty's Navy had been notified by circular that they were not to attend the King's levées. The reason for this extraordinary order was not given or even guessed at —and we may anticipate matters by saying that it was issued by the Lords Commissioners of the Admiralty under a grievous official mistake and was almost immediately rescinded. The writer only begged the profession to rally round their insulted brethren and insist upon a proper recognition by the Court of their position as officers and gentlemen. Wakley at once responded. He stigmatised the circular as a deliberate and cold-blooded insult which the profession as a whole was bound to resent, and he urged in the "Lancet" that the following Monday at the Royal College of Surgeons, the occasion being the delivery of the Hunterian Oration, would be a good time and place for a public demon-stration of sympathy as well as for a public decision upon the steps to be taken towards the annulling of the offensive order. In consequence of this notice a large number of members attended at the College, ostensibly to hear the Hunterian Oration on Hernia, delivered by Mr. Anthony White, but with the real object of publicly protesting against the insult inflicted on the naval surgeons by the Admiralty in forbidding them to attend the King's levées. It must be understood that their assembly for such a purpose was an entire and radical innovation, amounting to an assertion that the commonalty and not the Council could decide on the business of the day.

Wakley on entering the theatre of the College was received with loud cheers and almost immediately rose to protest against the treatment to which "ships'-doctors" had been subjected. Only the members were present, the Council having not yet emerged from the shelter of the library. In the course of a humorous speech Wakley pointed out that the surgeons of the navy had as much right to be considered officers as those of the army, and moved a resolution that they ought to enjoy the same privileges. Mr. Garland, a well-known metropolitan practitioner and a keen reformer in spirit, seconded the resolution, when Wakley observed that their doings might be considered irregular as they had no chairman ; he therefore took upon himself the task of putting the resolution. It was carried with enthusiasm. The second resolution, calling upon the Council of the College to vindicate the rights and dignity of its members, was moved by Mr. T. King, and having been duly seconded was also carried with acclamation. Mr. King was a popular lecturer on surgery at the General Dispensary in Aldersgate Street, and a man of considerable scientific standing.

Just as these resolutions had been passed the officers of the College entered the theatre. Mr. Robert Keate, surgeon to St. George's Hospital, was acting as President for Mr. Headington on the occasion, and Mr. King rose and presented the resolutions to him. The discussion of these was postponed until Mr. White had delivered his oration, the acting-President having very distinctly promised that after the oration the Council would listen to what their members had to say. So poor Mr. White had to read his address to a very impatient audience, who treated his official remarks with scant ceremony, thereby evidently discomposing him. When he had finished, the acting-President, having conducted certain visitors out, divested himself of his gown, and returning said that, as a member of the Council, he was now ready to hear Mr. King. Wakley said that an agreement to postpone the hearing of their complaints had been made with the acting-President and not with his gown. Sir Astley Cooper tried to cast oil on the waters, spoke highly of the naval surgeons, and characterised the action of the Admiralty as improper. He suggested that the purpose of the members would be better served by their deputing six of their number to confer with the Council. Mr. Keate, supported by Mr. Thomas, a member of the Council, persisted that he would lay the resolutions before the Council and personally could hear no more on the subject as he was not present in an official position. The meeting terminated by Wakley's remark that the members had done *their* duty and it only remained for the President and Council to do *theirs*.

The resolutions were duly laid before the Council by Mr. Keate, but were considered "irregular," and the Council "found it impossible" to act upon them. This decision was come to by a majority of 15 to 3, the three more liberally minded men being without any comparison the three most important men on the Council—namely, Sir Astley Cooper, Lawrence, and Benjamin Brodie. Wakley considered this a gross breach of confidence. The members had heard the oration with patience on the distinct understanding that the President and Council would listen to them afterwards. At the close of the oration the acting-President found himself unable to do more than convey a message to the Council, having hung up his official position in the ante-room with his gown—a piece of quibbling that had been received by the meeting with hearty disapprobation. Consequently, in the following week Wakley again begged the profession to attend at the College and decide what course should be taken to compel the Council to espouse the cause of the oppressed naval officers. The members were enjoined to assemble at the College at three o'clock, at which hour the doors of the theatre would be open in preparation for the next Hunterian Oration at four.

Immediately upon this invitation being given by Wakley the Council issued a notice in the morning papers that the doors of the College would not be opened until a quarter to four P.M., and that no public discussions would be allowed in the theatre of the College either upon that or any other occasion. Circular notices to this effect were also posted to some of the metropolitan members. The members, however, either being ignorant of the Council's action or believing it to be a ruse, arrived in great force to the number of three or four hundred. The porter did his duty and refused to admit anybody until a quarter to four, in spite of the very inclement weather. At about twenty minutes to four Wakley arrived and demanded admission, but the porter stuck to his instructions, only exceeding them by making a special attempt to exclude the editor of the "Lancet." At twelve minutes to four the doors were thrown open, and no sooner had the theatre been filled in every part, which occupied but a minute or two, than Wakley was called for on every side. He rose to speak in a scene of confusion and uproar amounting nearly to riot. The majority of the meeting was with him, but a small opposition was noisy and demonstrative. Wakley declared that nothing need now be done until the President's arrival, when the officers of the College must be asked by the assembled members who was responsible for the advertisement and circular forbidding them to assemble in their own College.

At four o'clock the President, Council, and a *posse* of Bow Street officers entered the theatre. Wakley rose holding the circular in his hand, and tried to ask whether it was an official document issued by the Council. The President, Dr. Morson, and Mr. King, as well as Mr. Guthrie (a member of the Council), tried to make themselves heard without avail. The disorder seemed wildest in the immediate neighbourhood of Wakley, who remained on his feet without speaking, the centre of a circle of applauding supporters. A Bow Street officer was sent to order him out. The surrounding members would have rallied to his aid, but Wakley forbade them, saying that the Council had not the least power to remove him. He informed the officer of this fact, who returned to the Council saying, " Mr. Wakley knows perfectly well what he's about." The Council were exasperated, and one gentleman went so far as to suggest the use of the constables' staves. The uproar still continued and at last the President rose and left the theatre, being followed by the Council and visitors. Wakley then addressed the meeting, imploring them to preserve quiet behaviour. ·He proposed that they should put themselves in order by electing a chairman, and suggested Mr. George Walker, a surgeon at Sheerness, and a very senior member of the College. Mr. Walker was unanimously elected and Wakley at once continued his speech. He observed that they "had not listened to a lecture on *hernia*, but that *rupture* was a very appropriate subject on such an occasion." He asked the members whether they did not consider that he, had been right in inquiring of the Council whether the precious document he held in his hand had emanated from them officially ; he described it as one of the most extraordinary pieces of composition he had ever seen, and suggested that it must be the work of Mr. Belfour's cook. He said he would not move a vote of censure on the Council for the indignities to which he and his brother members had been subjected because he really thought that vote had already been as good as passed. He described for the meeting the gross insult put upon the naval surgeons by the Admiralty, and finally moved a resolution that the members deeply regretted the unsympathetic attitude of the Council as shown by the fact that they had refused to notice the resolutions of the members passed for their consideration at the previous meeting. "This refusal," said Wakley, " is another added to the already innumerable existing proofs that the President and.Council are alike indifferent to the honour, happiness, and respectability of the commonalty of this chartered College." The resolution was seconded by a Mr. Complin and carried with only two dissentients.

A few moments later Mr. Belfour, the secretary of the College, and the person whose name had been appended to the offending circular, entered the theatre and handed to Wakley a paper bearing the following words : " Mr. Wakley, you are required by the President and Council to quit the theatre." Wakley refused point-blank, when a similar order to the members, written large and pinned to a board, was held up over the lecturer's desk. No one moved. Suddenly a number of Bow Street officers rushed into the theatre and making for Wakley seized him by the collar, arms, and legs, and proceeded to expel him by force from the building. The surrounding members ran to his assistance and a tug of war ensued. While he was thus stretched out a Bow Street officer aimed a blow at his head with a truncheon. This providentially missed his head and fell upon his shoulder. His struggles were so fierce as to throw himself and half a dozen persons down several benches to the floor of the theatre. The fighting might have been prolonged in spite of the nature of the odds, for Wakley was a man of great strength and large frame and an expert boxer and wrestler, but it was not his desire to continue the brawl. He consented to leave the building, and urged his friends to forego further resistance. On getting outside the officers released their grip, when Wakley at once ordered them to take the officer into custody who had aimed the cowardly blow at him. This they refused to do, but at last two Bow Street officers to whom the previous occurrences were unknown were fetched who complied. A procession was now made to Bow Street, consisting of the Bow Street officers, the arrested man and his custodian, Wakley with his clothes hanging on him in rags, and a body of sympathetic followers. On its way through Covent Garden it collected a large and uproarious crowd, and at seven in the evening Wakley charged his assailant before the chief magistrate, Sir Richard Birnie.

In the meanwhile the members who had remained in the theatre proceeded with the business for which Wakley had convoked them. They passed a resolution that three of their number should form a deputation to the Lord Chamberlain (the Duke of Devonshire) to point out to his Grace the invidiousness of the position in which the naval medical officers had been placed by their exclusion from the levées of the Sailor-King, and they selected to represent them Messrs. Wakley, Walker, and King.

CHAPTER XXIV

[1823–1834]

Proceedings at Bow Street—Wakley continues to fight—The College institute Criminal Proceedings—The London College of Medicine—Its Prospectus—Its Failure—Wakley determines to enter Parliament.

IN 1831 the stipendiaries of the metropolis did not hold the position that they do now. They were not lawyers and they possessed the same qualifications to act as magistrates that the provincial mayors possessed, and no more. They had not the education of the country justice of the peace. Sir Richard Birnie, who was a saddler, and his fellow magistrates, who were drawn from the same class, after deliberation decided that they could not grant Wakley a warrant against Ledbitter, the Bow Street officer who had assaulted him. The reasons for this were not made very clear in words by the worthy knight, who frankly confessed his partial feelings in the matter. He seems to have considered, first, that Wakley was debating in the building of the College affairs that were not collegiate, and that, therefore, the President of the College had a right to have him removed. To this Wakley said that the wrongs of the naval surgeons, whose diplomas and certificates were very generally granted to them by the College, were exactly matters of the highest collegiate as well as professional interest, and that even had they been otherwise the man Ledbitter had struck out at him with his truncheon in a murderous way. Sir Richard Birnie then said that Ledbitter was wrongly arrested, inasmuch as the Bow Street officer who had taken him in custody was not an actual eye-witness of the alleged assault;

and it was a general instruction to the Bow Street officers that they should only arrest a man for a wrong-doing of which they had personal ken. To this argument, which was unfavourably criticised from the bench by another magistrate, Wakley responded by exhibiting his ruined clothes to the court and asking if there could be any reasonable doubt that he had been savagely assaulted. The Bow Street officers themselves, moreover, admitted the truth of Wakley's account, merely saying that they had received their instructions upon two separate occasions from the Council of the College to expel Wakley; and they identified a person in court, who turned out to be Mr. Wilde, the solicitor to the College, as the individual who had told them that for whatever they did the authorities of the College would hold them indemnified.

As Sir Richard Birnie would not grant a warrant the matter ceased there as far as legal proceedings on Wakley's part were concerned. Some preliminary steps were taken to bring Ledbitter to justice in another way, but Wakley was not truly desirous of prosecuting the man and did not persevere in the face of tedious formality. If he could have prosecuted the Council of the College for the assault he would have done so ; this he said repeatedly, and no one can doubt that he meant what he said, but he was advised that his chance of making out a legal case against them was slender. A moral case, however, was easily to be established against them, and Wakley's pen was not idle. It is characteristic of him that after one powerful outburst of rage, his allusions to the personal indignity that he had undergone became infrequent and dispassionate. The fact that the Council had expelled him by violence and with the assistance of Bow Street officers from the theatre of the College added no bitterness whatever to his strictures. In fact, after the first natural feeling of wrath and insult had subsided, he was not ungrateful to his enemies for providing him with so graphic a proof of his contention that they were autocratic, careless of the rights of their commonalty, and unscrupulous in their methods of preserving their own position as irresponsible rulers. These three propositions he demonstrated week after week ceaselessly and remorselessly, and concluded by recommending the London students not to affiliate themselves to the College of Surgeons at all but to be content with the licence of the Apothecaries' Hall, which Company charged less in fees and did more to protect its general body. His argument in support of this advice to students was ingenious. It was based on the working of the Apothecaries Act of 1815, which had been unduly pressed by the Apothecaries' Hall against the College of Surgeons, properly qualified surgeons having been prosecuted by the Hall for dispensing medicines. The Hall, in fact, took active and selfish steps in defence of those possessing its licence, and Wakley, whilst reprobating the institution of prosecutions against the members of the College of Surgeons, advised the coming men to join the Hall. This advice may or may not have stung the Council of the College into reprisals ; it was calculated to damage the corporate purse, which Wakley said was the tenderest spot in the corporation, but certainly their next move was a strong and almost unwarrantable one. It was no less than a motion for a rule in the court of King's Bench calling upon Thomas Wakley, Thomas King, George Walker, and George Darby Dermott (whose name had not previously been conspicuous in the proceedings of the reformers) to show cause why a criminal information' should not be filed against them for certain misdemeanours committed in the theatre of the Royal College of Surgeons of England on the occasion of the riotous proceedings at the College in protest against the exclusion of the naval surgeons from the King's levées. The motion was heard by Lord Tenterden who made the rule absolute against Wakley and King, and discharged it against the other defendants, stating in his remarks from the bench that it was illegal for the members to discuss in the theatre of the College any subject not connected with the acknowledged duties of the corporation.

Wakley undismayed responded with an entire elaborate

and cut-and-dried scheme for a new corporation of surgeons to be entitled the London College of Medicine, to have a Royal Charter and to do everything as properly as the existing College did everything improperly. The London College of Medicine was really a socialistic dream. The idea of founding such an institution undoubtedly sprang up in Wakley's mind as the swiftest and most drastic method of punishing the College of Surgeons. When he formulated the scheme for it he was not in the mood to weigh matters as calmly and judiciously as was his wont, for undoubtedly a great sense of personal anger had been roused in him by the institution of criminal proceedings against himself and his colleagues. This bent his judgment, which had not been warped in the least by the violent physical treatment that he had received. He over-estimated—and for the first time—the power of his pen. As a destructive weapon it had proved terrific ; he now proposed to employ it in construction. The London College of Medicine, "founded upon the most enlarged and liberal principles, in which all legally qualified practitioners, whether physicians, surgeons, or apothecaries," were to be "associated upon equal terms" and to be "recognised by the same title," was obviously fore-doomed to failure. Below is an abridgment of its prospectus, by which it will be seen that its constitution was really an attack on the College of Surgeons. The new College proposed to do for the public and the profession everything that the old one did not do, and for the neglect of which the more advanced reformers found such bitter fault with it. After a preliminary clause stating that all persons in the United Kingdom at present holding a medical or surgical degree or diploma were eligible to be chosen as Fellows without examination, it proceeded as follows :—

"The possessors of the diploma of the London College of Medicine are denominated Fellows, and will enjoy, both in and out of the College, the title of Doctor.

"The London College of Medicine will be under the government of a Chancellor, Vice-Chancellor, and Senate.

" The Senate will consist of not less than thirty-six Fellows elected by ballot, annually, by the Fellows in general convocation.

" The Chancellor, Vice-Chancellor, and Scrutators are elected by the Senate ; a majority of the Senate to be present, or the election void ; the elections to be conducted by ballot, and the decision of the majority, final.

" On each examination of candidates for the diploma, seven of the Senate constitute a medical jury ; the Scrutators are ineligible to the office of jurymen.

" On each examination the votes of a majority of the jury to decide the candidate's admission or rejection.

" The examination of candidates will be conducted in public by the Chancellor or Vice-Chancellor, the Scrutators, and the medical jury.

"Candidates are not required to produce any certificates whatsoever; the capability of undergoing a fair and searching professional examination being considered the only professional qualification necessary for obtaining the diploma.

" The fee demanded for the diploma of the College is three guineas from gentlemen engaged in practice, and five guineas from students. No candidate after a second rejection to be eligible for re-examination until twelve months shall have elapsed."

Wakley went to a personal friend, who was to be in the immediate future his political god-father, joseph Hume, for assistance in the matter, and Hume consented to take the chair at the preliminary meetings, which were enthusiastic entirely because Wakley's strictures against the College of Surgeons were so forcible and so amusing. Hume had once been a medical man, but his whole career was now political, and he really did not understand the nature of the departure he was being made to join. If Wakley had submitted his scheme to any man of Hume's talent but who was in touch with the needs of the profession, a lecturer or a man with experience on a hospital staff, he would have received criticism and guidance that would have prevented him from pursuing with so much energy such a will-o'-the-wisp as the scheme for founding the London College of Medicine was bound to prove. But Hume, a reformer and great politician, almost a statesman, was ignorant of the true needs of the medical man or the extent to which the College of Surgeons had abused its position. He was informed by Wakley, who was too angry at the time to be able to inform him quite impartially, and so when things were referred to his judgment he could only frame an answer in accordance with one-sided information.

But in the absence of competent advice Wakley, with immense perseverance, wrote up the cause of the London College of Medicine, where the ruling body was to be elected by universal suffrage ; where there were to be no grades of rank or distinctions in title ; where no monopoly in the teaching or the granting of certificates to the taught was to be countenanced ; where the fees were to be low and only the standard of courtesy between examiners and examined high. But write as he would he could not galvanise this stillborn scheme into life. It was without the elements of existence. To begin with, unless the Government granted the promoters a charter their association among themselves was no use. Unless the State recognised the diplomas of the new college there would be no inducements to candidates to present themselves to obtain them. Now it was not for a moment probable that Government would have anything to do with the new scheme. A Royal Charter had been granted to the College of Surgeons together with much money. Against this Charter a petition had been presented to Parliament which had so little to recommend it to the notice of the House that after a perfunctory order to the impeached corporation to present certain accounts the matter dropped out of notice. The House would certainly consider the new scheme the outcome of private ill-will against the officers of the older body, who had already been recognised by the Crown and were in receipt of public money. To support a rival body designed in every way to ruin that corporation would be to stultify the action of the Crown in granting the Charter and to waste the money already granted with no niggard hand. So that if Wakley had been supported by the mass of the College in the way that he confidently expected he had nothing to hope for from Government. But as a matter of fact for the first time the better sort of his own particular followers and readers were not wholly with him. They admitted the perfect unselfishness of his project, but they did not want it. They had no real hate of their College or its authorities. They desired it to be reformed and they thought that Wakley might reform it. But they did not want it destroyed and a new institution with no history and no prestige substituted for it; so that the London College of Medicine died of inanition before anyone save its inventor and a few ardent and not wholly disinterested colleagues would allow that it had ever been born. The criminal proceedings against Wakley and King also came to a speedy termination. Though supported by Lord Tenterden's rule and dared by Wakley to proceed, the Council decided to let the matter drop. So that the outcome of the great and stormy meeting of February 14th, 1831, was nothing at all save that the naval surgeons were readmitted to the King's levées, to agitate for which was the reason that Wakley summoned the members together. Wakley was advised that he could not prosecute the Council, and he did not desire to prosecute Ledbitter. The Council having been successful in their initiatory steps against Wakley decided that it would be impolitic to proceed further. The London College of Medicine, instituted to meet the wants of the rank and file of the profession and to take the place of the College of Surgeons, whose behaviour towards its members was so ruthless, came to an early and inglorious end.

During the next three years Wakley's intentions to carry on his agitation against the College of Surgeons were not altered, but he decided to change his methods. He had done as much as was possible in his private capacity and as a journalist. It remained now for Government to carry on the work that he had commenced, and to carry it on with a far larger scope. The Royal College of Surgeons of England was not the only medical corporation in the kingdom that did not do its duty by its commonalty, and the behaviour of the hospital officials of the metropolis was not the only feature in medical education that needed improvement in the interests of the students. A thorough scheme of reform devised for the good of the public as well as of the profession —in short, a new Medical Act—was wanted, and this could only be carried through with the aid of a party in Parliament. The failure of the London College of Medicine showed Wakley that he must not expect much from any co-operation of the profession, and he resolved to transfer the scene of his struggles from Lincoln's Inn Fields and the columns of the " Lancet " to Westminster.

CHAPTER XXV

[1823–1834]

The First Ten Years of the "Lancet": A Recapitulation—The Early Staff of the Paper—The Mills Family—A few Details of Private Life—The Kindness of Mr. Goodchild—The Move to Bedford Square—Wakley resolves to Contest the Borough of Finsbury.

A PERIOD has now been reached when Wakley began to lead three careers, any one of which would have sufficed to satisfy the appetite of most men for hard work. While remaining a journalist he desired to represent a London constituency in Parliament, and to be also coroner for one of the divisions of Middlesex. In a short time he achieved each aspiration, being elected Member·for Finsbury in 1835 and Coroner for West Middlesex in 1839. For purposes of clearness his life will be told in two divisions from this point, otherwise the constant change of scene and breaks in narrative would make the story impossible to follow. It is proposed to treat his parliamentary career first, because his parliamentary work was in very direct continuance with his struggles in the cause of medical reform, and a brief reconsideration of what he had already effected will show that before he turned his thoughts towards Parliament he had advanced his projects by seven-leagued strides.

The "Lancet" was started in the interests of the profession at large inclusive of the students, and was designed to show that the great hospitals of the metropolis were managed to the advantage of a few rather than of the community, and that medical men as a body were wronged by their leaders. The establishment by the action at law with Abernethy of the right of the "Lancet" to publish the lectures delivered to hospital classes was much more than the solution of an undecided question in copyright. The privileges of copyright would have prevented, and actually did prevent, Wakley from printing the lectures. But when he proved the lectures to have been delivered in a public capacity he gained his point, and in doing so damaged the unearned fame of many eminent teachers and got his journalistic foot for the first time into those fastnesses of privacy—the metropolitan hospitals. The articles against malpraxis among hospital surgeons immediately followed, and reached their climax in the sensational case of Bransby Cooper v. Wakley. They did good and harm. They roused a wholesome distrust in the minds of the profession of the system under which such mishaps were possible. They sounded a revolt against a nepotism that nowadays seems too monstrous to have existed, but which appeared seventy years ago to be natural and void of reproach. They stirred up in the minds of the profession at large a determination to be better treated and only to be ruled by those who were worthy to rule them. All this was effected by Wakley, and almost immediately a purer and better state of things was brought about within our hospital walls. The harm that these articles did was much less than the good, but must not be overlooked. The public dissemination in the "Lancet" of such bitter criticism on lecturers, surgeons, and administrators in the well-known hospitals of London brought the profession of medicine into public and unequivocal disrepute. The "Lancet" speedily became a purely medical journal, but others besides medical men read it, and learned with some shattering of their idols that the great Abernethy more than once attempted to give his students unfair measure in return for their fees, that the great Cooper considered the indispensable qualification for an appointment at Guy's Hospital to be relationship or apprenticeship to himself, and, finally, that medical staffs selected in accordance with these principles, not only at Guy's Hospital, but at all the metropolitan hospitals, more than occasionally failed to attain to the high standard of skill and knowledge that was to be expected of them and with which they were generally credited. A second disadvantage to the profession that followed on Wakley's revelation of hospital mismanagement was the stirring up of bad blood. Some men were for Wakley and some were against, but his excessively plain speaking and downright methods of conducting a dispute made it imperative that those who were on his side should quarrel outright with those who were not.

From reviewing and criticising the administration of the hospitals Wakley passed naturally to the consideration of the corporation which granted the diploma most sought after by the students. This, the Royal College of Surgeons of England, was officered by the very hospital surgeons whose scientific methods left in Wakley's opinion so much to seek. The Council of the College were hospital surgeons wholly or in large majority. They were chosen for life and nominated their own successors. They selected examiners from among themselves and took no certificates save from hospital surgeons. Here the "Lancet" did good from the first days of its existence. By his outspoken denunciations in the columns of his paper Wakley roused a wide-spread feeling among the members against their Council. He then exposed the unsoundness of the constitution of the College; he criticised certain of the by-laws in such a way as to ensure their repeal; he summoned the first public meetings ever held by the members, and dominated those meetings; he placed the College on its defence, and elicited from the Council a poor refutation of the charges brought against them; he organised a petition to Parliament for State assistance in his schemes for reform; and he came into personal conflict with the Council in an attempt to assert on behalf of the members a right to meet in the theatre of their College to discuss matters of professional interest. All these things he had accomplished before he decided that only in Parliament could he carry the work on further.

A few words should be said of Wakley's staff during the first ten years of the "Lancet," for had he not been loyally supported by his assistants he never could have accomplished what he did during the period, or have laid the foundation for his great success in the future. From the beginning he was helped by Cobbett and Wardrop, but on the paper being transferred to the offices of Messrs. Mills, Jowett & Mills he was introduced to a family with whom he was to remain for many years in close contact, and whose assistance to the "Lancet" can be over-estimated with difficulty. Mr. Mills, senior, had four sons, Samuel, George Ireland, James Basnett, and Alexander Dickson. Samuel was in his father's firm, and became head-printer to the "Lancet," while the three younger sons joined the staff in different capacities. George Ireland Mills succeeded to much of Lambert's editorial work when that gentleman retired from the staff after the Bransby Cooper case. He later became Wakley's private secretary, and was for some time his deputy-coroner. James Basnett Mills was a very fine young scholar. He frequently acted as Wakley's amanuensis. He eventually took orders, and was classical coach to no less a person than Benjamin Jowett, the famous Master of Balliol, who was a son of the partner in the firm of Mills, Jowett & Mills; while his next pupil was Wakley's eldest son. Alexander was a proof-reader in the establishment when the printing of the "Lancet" was removed to Bolt Court. He was the first sub-editor of the paper, and combined the duties with those of publisher. Alexander Mills's room formed the business office of the "Lancet" and here the meetings of the staff took place on Friday nights. Friday was the only day upon which Wakley went regularly to the office of his paper, it being his habit to do most of his editorial work at home. But on Friday evening he would go to the office to supervise the "make-up" and arrange with his staff for the next issue. These meetings were of a very jovial description, the usual attendants being Keen, a barrister and the legal adviser to the "Lancet"; John Yonge Akerman, the numismatist, at this time William Cobbett's secretary, and later, secretary to the Society of Antiquaries; Henry Smith, the "maker-up" of the paper, a practical printer as well as a journalist, and afterwards editor of the "Cambridge Chronicle"; G. F. Knox, the dentist to the Westminster Hospital; James Wardrop, and William Lawrence. Cobbett would generally join the party, punch was brought, the battles of the past week were re-contested, and the attacks of the next week planned. Wakley was most ably and enthusiastically helped by his small staff. He took his own line always, he wrote the greater part of his leading articles, and he dictated the whole of the policy of his paper; but he was fortunate beyond measure in obtaining allies of such worth. And there was much for them to do. The pages of the "Lancet" were not filled, as might be supposed from the frequent allusions to them, with abuse of hospital officials and criticism of the Royal College of Surgeons of England. To depict Wakley justly it has been necessary to show how his paper had its origin in a desire to remedy the flagrant abuses that called for a new Medical Act, and how his resolve to sit in Parliament sprang from intention to complete there what the "Lancet" had begun. But the staff of the "Lancet" had much to occupy them outside these matters—reports of meetings, reviews of books, and attacks on quackery for example, while Wakley was not monomaniacal on medical reform.

Wakley's public career has bulked so largely that almost nothing has been said of his private life. Nor is there very much to say. The rise of the "Lancet" from a young man's journalistic venture to an assured and serious success was accompanied by a commensurate rise in the private fortunes of the editor. These, when they were last the subject of mention, were, it may be remembered, at a low ebb. The disastrous fire had consumed his goods, which were not insured to their full worth, and the Hope Fire Assurance Company, by resisting his claim for compensation, had kept him out of his money until his practice was ruined. The fire cost him £1600 and a practice of £700 per annum for which a large sum in ready money had been paid. He received in compensation all that he could legally claim—

viz., £1200, and was unable to make up his mind how to use this sum to the best advantage. His father-in-law looked askance upon him, not desiring to support his daughter's husband, yet thinking that the possibility of his having to do so was far from remote. The ready-money practice that he purchased in Norfolk Street, Strand did not give him congenial occupation, and, much as his wife loved her husband, she did not conceal from him that she had a cordial dislike of his profession. She was also aware that her wealthy parents desired for her and the two children then born a fitter environment than Norfolk Street.

This was the state of Wakley's domestic affairs when the " Lancet " was first published. The paper proved almost immediately a pecuniary success. The circulation was shown in one of the earlier libel actions to be large, and it was considerably increased by the editor's attitude towards the College of Surgeons. From a journalistic point of view his resolute stand against corruption in that body was his greatest coup, as it was among the most important achievements of his life. The other successes of the "Lancet" were smaller and more personal. However earnestly Wakley might plead that his actions and counter-actions at law had all been undertaken in defence of the broad principles of reform, a certain proportion of his readers would be unable to see how their interests were advanced by his pugnacious tactics. They might hope that he would win in the magnanimous way that outsiders generally desire victory to go to a gallant fighter against odds, but it was more or less as outsiders that they watched the contests. The attack on the College of Surgeons, on the other hand, was so clearly made in the interests of the profession at large that the feeling of being merely interested as spectators disappeared from the mind of his readers and was replaced by a very definite and properly selfish partisanship. In his crusade against the College Wakley was obviously fighting the battle of all the medical men in the kingdom save a few privileged persons, and his list of subscribers at once increased rapidly, while his own position rose from that of a journalist who

catered capably to the wants of his public, and now and
again furnished them with a thoroughly enjoyable sensation,
to that of a leader of a liberal movement attended from the
first with success and promising greater things in the future.
Upon the more general recognition of Wakley as a single-
minded reformer followed a vast improvement in the position
of his paper.   It gained in power and importance, its opinion
had to be reckoned with, while its intolerance and scurrility
—the occasional presence of which cannot be denied—were
seen not to be its essentialities.

One of the first persons to recognise the great position
that Wakley was securing for himself and his paper was
Mr. Goodchild, his father-in-law.   The very business
qualities in that gentleman which had led him to bitterly
resent the failure that had attended Wakley's fortunes consequent on the Argyll Street outrages made him prompt to
recognise the quick passage of his son-in-law from unmerited
discredit to a position of influence and responsibility that
was rapidly passing to one of power.   The instinct of the
successful commercial man warned him that in the "Lancet"
Wakley had a great property, and that the shrewdness,
humour, and force that were displayed in the editing must
secure him a prominent public career.   He was, moreover,
casting about for a fitting opportunity to come to the succour of his daughter, and the rising position of the "Lancet,"
together with the storminess of its career, afforded him an
excellent one.   It would be generous to help and it would
not be foolish, so he approached his son-in-law and offered
to assist him in his literary venture.   This timely aid
completely turned the scale of fortune in Wakley's favour.
As soon as circumstances warranted his doing so he gave
up the house in Norfolk Street and took one in the
pleasanter neighbourhood of Thistle Grove, which had
the attraction for himself, his wife, and children of possessing a large garden.   Thistle Grove was then almost a
country lane, but now it is a street called Drayton Gardens,
in the heart of that thickly populated part of Brompton
and Chelsea that delights to disguise itself under the name

of South Kensington. The street still preserves many of the features of suburban villadom. Here his two younger children—Henry and james—were born, and here he stayed until 1828, when he moved into No. 35, Bedford Square, the house which is associated with all his public life as Member of Parliament for Finsbury and Coroner for Middlesex.

The neighbourhood of his new address was chosen for a very definite purpose, and one which was approved of by Mr. Goodchild in a practical manner—which means to say that he helped Wakley to find the necessary money to make so important an alteration in his domestic affairs. Wakley's intention now was to offer himself as political candidate for the borough of Finsbury, and Bedford Square was fortunately situated for the purpose, being near the office of the "Lancet," and also on the edge of the enormous parliamentary district which he aspired to represent. Immediately upon his establishment in his house he set about using it in accordance with his designs. An open-handed, cheery, and humorous man he delighted in good company, and it must not be supposed that all the profuse hospitality which at once became the rule in the domestic management of 35, Bedford Square, was the outcome of a design upon the minds of his possible electors. But while he revelled in the entertainment of his friends he was assiduous in the reception of his political allies, medical and lay. At his fortnightly gatherings for whist or chess he collected round him a large number of staunch friends who were attracted by his eloquence, his audacious defence of popular rights, his determination, self-confidence, and kindliness of manner. And most of his guests believed in him and prophesied for him a speedy success in the political world, thereby confirming him in his intention and endorsing the opinion of his once angry father-in-law.

CHAPTER XXVI

[1832–1834]

Wakley's Aim in entering Parliament—The Amendments to the Apothecaries Act—A "Member for Medicine"—The Borough of Finsbury—Parochial Work—Wakley's Local and General Claims as a Parliamentary Candidate—The Support of Hume and Cobbett —The Invitation of his Constituents.

WAKLEY'S aim in entering Parliament was very definite. At a time when all around was reforming itself or being reformed, when the word " Radical " was for the first time attached collectively to the more progressive groups of English politicians because of their constant and common demand for radical reform in one direction or another, Wakley desired to represent the interests of his profession in Parliament and to press there for reform in medical politics. Over and over again in his war against the constituted authorities of the professional world, in his conflicts with the College of Surgeons, and in his attempts to break down the barriers of secrecy erected by the administrators of the hospitals to screen their work, he had felt the need for a strong friend within the walls of Parliament House. The great English corporations had many such friends. Sir Henry Halford and Sir Astley Cooper were powers in the social world whose influence could always be brought to bear upon political questions and whose persons were familiar to many legislators. When the members of the College of Surgeons presented their petition to the House of Commons it was received without enthusiasm, almost without comment, and no attempt was ever made to inquire into the justice of their demands. This apathy on the part of the House Wakley considered to have been directly due to the private representations of the impeached corporation. He believed that the College of Surgeons had been able to catch the ears of individual members of the Government, and his grounds for the belief were very sound. He desired, therefore, that someone with real knowledge of the needs of the medical profession should be in Parliament to prevent such petitions being brushed aside contemptuously. Rating the influence of a private member very high, he thought that if a well-informed man could give the legislature the benefit of his experience on medical topics from the advantageous standpoint of being himself a legislator the assistance would receive respectful attention, while a few well-timed words from such a man would show up manœuvres similar to those by which the cause of medical reform had been recently strangled. Wakley perceived that it was imminent that other medical questions would find their way into the House. Reform was the order of the day all round, and the constitutional agitation that was spreading far and wide in opposition to authorities or privileges having no better reason for their existence than an ancient history was certain not to stop at one petition against the ruling body of one corporation. He felt that the movement represented by that petition was gaining in strength, and inasmuch as the possessors of power do not usually resign their positions upon moral conviction, but generally await the legal curtailment of their privileges—this being the first thing, as a rule, to bring moral conviction into play—he foresaw that the House of Commons must be the ultimate scene of the adjustment of many disputes involving the rights of the medical man.

The Apothecaries Act of 1815, for example, was to be amended, greatly to the disgust of the Master and Wardens of the Worshipful Company, who were straining every nerve to resist projects of reform which would interfere with their valuable warrant to dispense medicines and to prevent other persons from doing so. The rights and wrongs of the questions here raised must have been absolutely unintelligible to the lay member of Parliament. The Apothecaries Act of 1815 created a large class of general practitioners in England who had a monopoly of dispensing and could if they chose enforce their privileges against duly qualified practitioners not belonging to their Society. Yet many of the Licentiates of the Society desired the Act to be amended, and one of the reasons given by them for this was that under an amended Act the status of the English general practitioners would be raised and they would thus be better able to resist the very general invasion of the country by graduates of the Scotch Universities. On the other hand, a large number of the Licentiates joined the officers of the Society in protesting against the abolition of their privileges, and one of the reasons which they gave for desiring to remain in their present estate was that the Society by exercising a monopoly in England and Wales of the right to carry on the business of apothecaries, was able to fine and otherwise harry the Scotch interloper back to his country. And this view at first sight seemed to be sound because the Scotch medical corporations petitioned Government urgently in favour of the amending of the Apothecaries Act, clearly believing that their country had more to gain under the new proposals than under the old charter. Here was a coil! In the matter of an ancient City Company persons who were not within the fold asked for its reform, while persons who were within the fold could not agree among themselves whether it ought to be reformed or no, the two parties differing entirely as to what they wanted while both used the same argument to enforce their views. Wakley had the whole matter at his fingers' ends and only desired to expound it to the legislature, his feeling being that the country as well as the House ought to be properly informed on such points—or injustice would be done. Questions arising out of the existing Poor-law, out of the State regulation of the study of anatomy, and out of the acknowledged abuses existent in the administration of the law in coroners' courts were also engaging the attention of Parliament at the time, and in every case the editor of the

" Lancet" felt that the medical profession needed a voice within the House to make medical matters, often of a severely technical kind, distinct to the comprehension of the legislators.

That was his single aim in desiring to enter the House— to further the cause of medical reform, to be an expert witness ready to hand whenever a point arose in the deliberations of the House where the views of one thoroughly experienced in medical matters might be valuable. He was not without the exaltation that every man must feel within his breast on attaining a position entitling him to hope for a voice in the government of his country. Wakley was, on the contrary, an ambitious man, and to sit in the mother of Parliaments had for him, being young and the architect of his own fortunes, a promise of pleasure that it would not have had either for one grown grey beneath the worries of public life or for one born in a social sphere where a seat in the House of Commons was but a due appanage to hereditary position. But the cause of medical reform was the cause that he intended to advocate there if he could obtain the suffrages of his fellow citizens.

It is not sufficient, however, for a young man to have a call to politics, as a revivalist preacher has a call to a pulpit, to justify him in attempting to obtain a seat in the House of Commons, and had Wakley offered himself as a political candidate for Finsbury solely on the ground that he felt within himself the capability of being useful to his generation because of his professional knowledge he would have been wrong and also unsuccessful. If he had acted upon his own initiative his opponents would have been able to say : "Granted that the House is sorely in want of a 'Member for Medicine,' a member who shall at all times and seasons be watchful over the best interests of the profession, a member who shall keep the House in touch with the true trend of feeling in the profession and help it to discriminate between the real hardship and the hardship that only looks real in a petition—granted all that, but who says that you are the man for the post ? Who says that you are right in claiming for yourself this proud and representative position?" And had Wakley come forward and invited suffrages as the "Member for Medicine" such questions would have been very hard for him to answer. Clearly he could not claim to represent the whole profession when he was at personal war with many of the leaders and untiring in his criticisms of the Charters by which the different corporations were ruled. He would have had to explain that the powerful individuals and wealthy societies on whose methods or morals he had felt it his duty to comment severely were already represented in Parliament, being in a position to make their views known to members of the House, while it was the interests of the profession at large that required protection, which interests he desired to represent. It would have been a fair answer, but not a very conclusive one, so that it is fortunate that Wakley never placed himself in a position where he would have been compelled to make it by claiming to be the "Member for Medicine." It was his aim to promote medical reform in Parliament and it was on account of the work in that direction that he had already done and that he proposed to do, that he felt his political aspirations to be reasonable; but he saw from the beginning that no such simple electoral cry as "justice for Doctors" would secure him a seat. There was no constituency in England then, and there is not one now, where the personalities of the medical men or the importance of the medical interests are so predominant as to warrant a candidate asking for a seat to represent them. Wakley stood for Finsbury at the first election after the great Reform Bill as an advocate of advanced reform principles, as the supporter of all schemes for the amelioration of the condition of the people, and as the avowed enemy of all monopolies, religious disabilities, and protectionist tariffs on the nation's daily food—a comprehensive, if somewhat vague, programme.

The newly-constituted borough of Finsbury comprised the whole of the thickly-populated district extending from Seven Dials in the south-west to Stoke Newington in the north-east. It included nearly all the parish of St. James's, Clerkenwell, the parishes of Stoke Newington, Islington, St. Luke, St. George-the-Martyr, St. Giles-in-the-Fields, and St. George's, Bloomsbury; the liberties of Saffron Hill, Hatton Garden, Ely Rents, the Rolls, and the Charterhouse; Lincoln's Inn, Gray's Inn, and those parts of the parishes of St. Sepulchre and St. Andrew's, Holborn, and of Furnival's Inn and Staple Inn respectively which were without the liberty of the City of London. The approximate population of this, one of the largest of the boroughs called into existence by the Reform Bill, was 330,000, and it was regarded as among the most important of the metropolitan seats. To this enormous constituency Wakley had become favourably known during his four years' residence in Bedford Square. Shortly after he became a parishioner of St. Giles-in-the-Fields and St. George's, Bloomsbury, he subscribed to a fund opened by a Mr. George Rogers, a prominent local tradesman, for remedying the many parochial abuses flourishing under the patronage of the select vestry of the combined parishes. The rents in Bloomsbury were high, but the rates levied were out of all proportion enormous, and Wakley was solicited to take the chair at a public meeting of the ratepayers convened to protest against the burdens under which they lay. He consented and filled the post so satisfactorily that his intercourse with his future constituents daily increased and the feeling of interest created in his favour acquired fervency. He was elected a churchwarden in the popular cause, and was commissioned to defend the ratepayers when a Select Committee of the House of Commons had the doings of the vestry under consideration. Here he afforded such further proofs of energy and capacity that he was recognised by his neighbours for a man who would be an ideal representative of local interests in Parliament. In addition to his special claims he had the general claim of his record. His work in the " Lancet" as a medical reformer had attracted the attention of all classes. He was a man who had fought the monopolists of his own profession with unflinching courage and great success. He had established a reputation as a public speaker not only at the meetings held in advocacy of the cause of medical reform, but at the poll for the office of coroner for Middlesex, a post for which he was a candidate in 1830 under circumstances that will be described later. Here he became known to the general public for the first time as an orator, as one who possessed the magic power of holding a large audience, of carrying it with him in his sentiments and of playing with its finer feelings while dominating its coarser. Finally Wakley was selected by Joseph Hume and William Cobbett as a proper person to fill a seat in the first Reform Parliament, and each had a right to speak on the subject with authority. Hume, the member for Middlesex, had been a consistent Liberal and exponent of reform principles for fifteen years in the House and was regarded by the public as a parliamentary leader in the fight for an extended and purified franchise that had just been won. Cobbett was general of the popular forces without the walls of Westminster, his vigorous, clear, un-scrupulous pen having contributed more to the bloodless revolution of 1831 than any one man's individual efforts. He popularised each step, making it comprehensible by the clarity of his language and reasonable by the convincing strength of his arguments, and sent to the poll voters by the thousand educated to understand their new privilege.

It was natural that Cobbett, who on the passing of the Reform Bill became a political power, should think of Wakley as a man for whom a seat must be found in Parlia-ment. He had known him intimately for ten years. He had assisted him in the publication and editing of the " Lancet," and having lent him the benefit of his stormy experiences in the battles against the College of Surgeons, it is not surprising that he considered him to have fought those battles upon proper lines. In approving of Wakley and commending him to Finsbury as a reform candidate, Cobbett was promoting the election of a man to whom he had taught the game of constitutional agitation. Hume's connexion with Wakley was later, dating only from the presentation of the petition of the members of the College of Surgeons to the House of Commons. Hume, in the character of a retired medical man, had been present at the meetings of the members which had their outcome in the petition, and, being on those occasions brought into close contact with Wakley, had been very much impressed with his powers as a speaker and as an organiser, and with the obvious enthusiasm and sincerity of his actions.

Consequently, when, at the end of 1831, Earl Grey came into power pledged to pass the great Reform Bill, Hume and Cobbett recommended Wakley to the voters of Finsbury, but only at the last moment, and when there were already four candidates in the field—a Whig, the Right Honourable Robert Grant, afterwards governor of Bombay ; Mr. Serjeant Spankie, a Conservative barrister ; and two Liberals, Mr. Christopher Temple, also a barrister, and Mr. Charles Babbage, the inventor of the calculating machine. The Liberal candidates were not prepared to go the lengths necessary to commend them to Hume and Cobbett, who therefore fell back on Wakley. Then it was that Wakley's local work bore fruit. Immediately upon his name being mentioned a large and influential body of ratepayers, six hundred in number, with Rogers at their head, organised themselves into an election committee and sent him the following letter of invitation :—

"We, the undersigned, electors of the Borough of Finsbury, being anxious that our newly-attained franchise should be used as a means of promoting the interests of the great body of the people, and believing that your political opinions are in unison with our own, respectfully request you to state whether you are willing to become our representative in Parliament provided you are elected in a constitutional manner.

"We on our part pledge ourselves to the endeavour to impress upon our fellow electors the propriety of protecting our representatives from electioneering expenses of every description : and we will ourselves promote that object to the utmost of our power, knowing as we do that in asking you to devote your time and unceasing attention to our interests in Parliament we require of you as great a sacrifice as an honest man can or ought to make.

"We invite a public reply to this requisition, and in that reply we

Q

invite you to declare your opinions on the great political questions which are at this moment so important to all—namely, the extension of the suffrage, the duration of Parliament, the abolition of all property qualifications either for electors or elected, the repeal of the law of primogeniture, the continuance of tithes, corn laws, trade monopolies, stamps on newspapers, and the system of slavery.

" We are also anxious to learn your sentiments on the propriety of a complete revisal of the laws, civil, criminal, and parochial, with a view to simplify and condense their enactments and thereby to relieve the community from the enormous expense at present invariably incurred in every attempt to obtain justice.

" We shall also be glad to learn from you how far, in your opinion, a representative ought to be governed by the opinions of a majority of his constituents, when made known to him through a public meeting convened for that purpose, and how far he is in honour bound at their request to resign his trust into their hands.

" Should your opinions on the above subjects accord with our own, we pledge ourselves to nominate and support you at the ensuing election, and from our knowledge of the opinions and wishes of our fellow-electors we confidently anticipate that our exertions will lead to a successful and triumphant termination."

Wakley, on receiving this flattering invitation, at once made up his mind to accept it. He knew the strength of the forces that would be arrayed against him, but none the less he desired to put his fortune to the trial.

CHAPTER XXVII

[1832–1834]

Wakley's First Contest for the Borough of Finsbury—The Economy of his Candidature—The Second Contest—The famous Tom Duncombe—The Third Contest—The Interposition of Mr. Hobhouse—The Fairness of Wakley's Tactics—His Success—Enthusiasm in the Borough.

WAKLEY replied to the questions of the electors of Finsbury in a manner satisfactory to them and in so doing committed himself to a parliamentary programme from which he never swerved. He declared himself to be in favour of an extension of the suffrage, of triennial elections to Parliament, of the removal of property qualifications from candidates, of the repeal of the Corn Laws, of the abolition of slavery, and of the suspension of the Newspaper Stamp Act. He held that as to broad lines of conduct the electors had a right to control the elected and to compel him to ratify pledges given when they entrusted him with their suffrages, for which reason he objected to the Septennial Act and would have parliamentary elections made for shorter periods. He expressed himself strongly, though in general terms, upon the necessity that existed for a thorough overhauling of much of the legal procedure of the country with a view of affording the poor litigant a better chance against a wealthy adversary.

He then put the words of the electors promising to protect their candidate from electioneering expenses of every description to a practical test by refusing to take any part in the business of the election. He did not personally canvass a single voter, he entered but one of his committee-rooms during the whole contest, and then simply in the desire to remove a wrong impression that he was careless of the issue and blind to the exertions of his committee. He addressed a few meetings of the electors in various parts of his large constituency, but so short an interval—less than a fortnight—remained between his acceptation of the invitation to contest the borough and the day of nomination that he had not time to cover all the ground.

The nomination took place at Islington Green on Saturday, December 8th, 1832. The candidates were the Right Honourable Robert Grant, Lord Glenelg's brother, and a Privy Councillor; Serjeant Spankie; Temple, a wealthy barrister of good family; Babbage and Wakley; and at the show of hands the returning officer declared that the choice of the electors had fallen upon the first and last named. The others demanding a poll, the polling was commenced on the following Monday, and two days later the number of recorded votes for the respective candidates was announced as follows :—

Grant	4278
Spankie	2848
Babbage	2311
Wakley	2151
Temple	787

It should be mentioned in reference to the general position occupied in the first poll of Finsbury by the Radicals that Mr. Grant was an especially strong candidate and received much support from both sides. Although a Whig in politics he was the champion of the movement for the abolition of the civil disabilities of the Jews, a movement which formed a specific part of the Radical programme, and received the support of Macaulay, Hume, and O'Connell. He was a famous scholar, with an almost unprecedented record at Cambridge, had held many legal appointments, and had sat in Parliament for fourteen years; but these things did not avail him in his candidature of Finsbury so much as his untiring support of the jewish cause, with its implied hostility to narrow clericalism. The election was conducted in a peaceful and orderly manner, the respective candidates being exceedingly courteous in their demeanour towards each other and evidently friendly in their rivalry. Mr. Spankie in particular went out of his way to refer to the consideration he had received at the hands of Wakley and Wakley's committee.

Mr. George Rogers, the chairman of this committee, immediately after the contest gave a touch of his quality as the organiser of a real reform campaign, one where the people's minds and not their self-interests dictated their choice. He took complete charge of the pecuniary business connected with Wakley's candidature with such economical effect that the whole expenses of the election in this enormous constituency—including printing, the sums paid to poll-clerks and check-clerks, and the sum paid as a fifth share of the expenses incurred for the erection of five polling-booths—scarcely exceeded £150. In a letter to Wakley he stated that the expenses of the successful candidates amounted to "thousands," which is a vague figure supplied by a biassed witness. But the Reform Bill and speeches during its passage through the House had directed so much attention to the enormous expenses that were incurred of necessity by parliamentary candidates that the fact that Wakley's candidature had cost anything like so small a sum led to much discussion and correspondence. Letters poured in upon Wakley and his committee to know how it was possible, the writers not perceiving the difference between the position of the man who approaches his constituency because he wants to go into Parliament and the position of the man whom his constituency approaches because they desire him to be their representative. As a result Rogers, not without pardonable pride in his own economy and the excellence of his management—who does not know that honest conceit of the organiser ?—wrote to the "Lancet" to show how it was done, and Wakley in publishing the letter headed it "Exposures at the Finsbury

Election," a title which was apt enough on the face of it, but which, having regard to the contents, was bound to irritate the returning officer. Rogers allowed, roughly speaking, £100 for individual expenses, of which he gave no account, feeling probably that it was little enough to spend on advertisement of a candidate's virtues in such an enormous borough as one numbering a population of 330,000 and some 16,000 electors. But Wakley also had to pay, like the other four candidates, one-fifth of the expenses of erecting poll-booths and hustings, of securing the attendance of poll-clerks, of painting and fixing of notice-boards and printing voting-papers and of sundry other trifling things necessary to the business of the election. The bill for these as rendered in the lump was £463, making Wakley's share £92. Rogers returned it to Mr. Satchell, the returning officer, saying that he could not pay it as many of the charges were illegal. Satchell amended his charges and sent in an account for £286, Wakley's share being £57. Rogers said that this second sum was nearly double as much as Satchell was entitled to charge, and personally tendered £37 12s. in full discharge of all Wakley's separate liability. This sum Satchell accepted under protest, saying that it was not the sum that was due, but that he would take it so as to bring to an immediate close any relations with Rogers. To which Wakley and Rogers retorted that, as the money was not theirs to spend, but belonged to a committee to whom an account of their stewardship would have to be rendered, it was impossible that more than the legal sum should be paid.

So Wakley's first attempt at entering Parliament stamped him as a man of his word and a very good pupil of Hume. He adopted a broad liberal policy and placed economy in the front of it, and the result could hardly be other than gratifying to him. In the short space of a fortnight he so cordially recommended himself to the electorate that he polled over 2000 votes, 1400 of which were plumpers. The absence of Mr. Temple from the poll might and probably would have seen Wakley member for Finsbury at his first attempt.

His second opportunity followed very soon, and being accepted by him with eagerness again led to failure. But as in the first instance the circumstances under which failure came raised the candidate still higher in the estimation of his committee and of the whole electorate as a patriotic and determined man. Robert Grant was appointed in the spring of 1834 to the office of Governor of Bombay, and Wakley was again called upon by his committee to present himself on the hustings to put forward his and their opinions and solicit suffrages upon them. In a characteristic open letter to the medical profession he begged the medical electors of Finsbury to continue their labours in his behalf, clearly implying that he was especially desirous of being elected as a medical reformer, although he had identified himself of necessity as well as through conviction with the general progressive cause. Unexpectedly, however, a complication again occurred in his candidature. Until the day for nomination was very near at hand there had been only three candidates for Grant's seat—Mr. Pownall, an influential Middlesex magistrate; Babbage, standing as a Whig; and Wakley as a Radical. Suddenly there appeared on the scene Mr. Thomas Slingsby Duncombe, a Radical also, and a man of no small importance. A beau, a wit, and a trifler, yet an industrious man of affairs; an aristocrat, owing all his pleasures in life to the privileges of his birth and position, and a Chartist in politics before the just and unjust discontents of the nation had crystallised into the famous demand for a Charter; a puritan in public business and the intimate associate of Lords Alvanley, Deerhurst, and the leaders in the social excesses of the Regency; careful of the people's welfare and hopelessly prodigal of his own goods, 'Tom Duncombe was the very man to commend himself to the enormous constituency of Finsbury—the very man to turn the hearts of a mixed electorate from a Conservative predilection to an ardent affection for the Radicalism of which he was the humorous and fascinating prophet. There was no central organisation in those days to prevent a multiplicity of candidates presenting themselves on the same ticket (to use an Americanism), and it was left to such superabundant wooers of the constituency to arrange among themselves how best the common enemy should be defeated. Duncombe and Wakley came to an arrangement immediately. They mutually agreed that whoever should poll the larger number of votes on the first day should publicly release his pledged supporters from the onus of plumping, and, further, should warn them that the primary object was to defeat Pownall, the secondary to return their particular favourite of two persons pledged in large matters to vote in the same way. Nothing could have been more graceful than Wakley's manner of falling in with this arrangement. It must have been a great disappointment to him to have had his pre-emption contested, yet he had the admirable sense to see that for a candidate who had openly claimed for the people their right to be served by whomsoever they pleased it would be illogical to object to their exercise of choice. Babbage was always out of the running, his scientific attainments forming no recommendation of him to the constituency, while his politics were not sufficiently progressive to render him a true ally of the Radicals. He stood in the Liberal interest, but he was a transcendental mathematician and not the stuff of which popular legislators are made. Duncombe was different. If a group of Finsbury electors, uncertain of Wakley's complete fitness, liked to invite Duncombe to come to assist them in breaking down the Tory power and replacing the scholarly and aristocratic Grant by a thorough-going Radical, Wakley perceived that he must allow their right to do so. His clear duty was to enter into a compact with Duncombe by which it should be ensured that the better man of the two should also be too good for Pownall. Duncombe's immediate followers were perhaps more numerous. They were certainly earlier in the field than Wakley's, and on the second day Wakley withdrew from the contest. The electors in the reform interest, unpledged to either candidate, had only been waiting to learn for whom to vote in their solidity. They at once flocked to the poll and returned

Duncombe at the head with 2514 votes. The figures were as follows :—

Duncombe	2514
Pownall	1915
Wakley	695
Babbage	379

Wakley's figures represented the votes that he received on the first morning only.

His conciliatory conduct had its very prompt reward. In January, 1835, less than seven months after his second unsuccessful candidature, the country was involved in the second general election after the great Reform Bill. The two sitting members, Mr. Serjeant Spankie, Conservative, and Mr. Duncombe, Radical, presented themselves for re-election, and Wakley offered himself in opposition to the former ; but neither Pownall nor Babbage essayed his fortune again. The reform party for the third time was not unanimous in its choice. Mr. Henry Hobhouse, the brother of Sir John Cam Hobhouse, came forward in answer, as he said, to an invitation from the Radical interest so general that he could not help securing the seat for the reform party if the promises made to him were kept. Wakley's faithful committee regarded Hobhouse as a Whig, and therefore a covert foe to reform more to be dreaded than any reactionary Tory, and strongly objected to his being, as they considered it, foisted on the borough. So Wakley was again placed, by want of proper organisation in the Liberal party, in the disagreeable situation of not being perfectly certain whether the electors in general would consider his candidature as tending to the interests of the party or no. Warmly supported by a large body of followers as he was, the violent language of the more immediate *entourage* of Cobbett and his school, and Wakley's own uncompromising speeches, no less than the sample of his actions supplied by his proceedings in opposition to the College of Surgeons, had scared off many of the voters who were willing to espouse the cause of Lord Melbourne generally and Tom Duncombe in particular. They wanted a Radical, but not an iconoclast, and they were not quite certain where Wakley might stop. Moreover, Wakley's fearless method of conducting the "Lancet" had raised up for him many bitter personal enemies, who, without any patriotic or political object, would still consider it right to oppose such a man in every way and almost excusable to misrepresent him grossly if occasion should offer itself.

The split began to look serious, as neither Wakley nor Hobhouse considered it his duty to withdraw. Rogers took the first step. A meeting of the electors of Finsbury was convened by advertisement in the daily papers, at which upwards of 2000 persons attended, when it was resolved without a dissentient voice that Duncombe and Wakley should be supported " as the only candidates entitled to receive the votes of the electors at the poll in the reform interest." Hobhouse, however, persisted, refusing to recognise the meeting as a representative one and relying on the promises of what must have been a really substantial proportion of the electors, and these were loud in urging that Wakley should again retire rather than split the Radical vote and so allow Mr. Serjeant Spankie to keep his seat. Even so good a friend to Wakley personally and to the causes in behalf of which he stood as joseph Hume, seems to have taken this view, as the following private letter from him to Wakley shows :—

' As the time approaches," wrote Hume, " the conversation I had with you respecting Spankie comes more and more home, and my object is to keep Spankie out at all hazards. I want very much to see you and any two or three of your powerful friends, in order to see whether any arrangement can be made amongst the Reformers to compromise the differences and get in two reformers. The continued differences between Hobhouse and you must let Spankie in, which would be the greatest misfortune possible at this crisis, when all good men must join in keeping down the Tories. Let me hear from you soon for the good of the cause you and I so much advocate—good government."

Wakley had, however, issued an election address in which he had promised his supporters to abide by the result of the

general meeting of electors. This meeting had confirmed
him in his intention to stand, and he notified to Hume that
he considered it as much his duty as his pleasure to proceed
with the candidature. He published a manifesto declaring
that he was not guilty of the folly or wickedness of hazard-
ing the success of the cause by producing dissensions in the
ranks—clearly implying that such folly and wickedness might
be attributed to Hobhouse—and recalling to mind his position at the poll on the first occasion, when, coming late into
the field and with four opponents, he received over 2000
votes, 1400 of which were plumpers. Having done nothing
to forfeit the esteem of the constituency since, and much to
gain its increased regard, he declared himself determined on
this occasion to proceed to the poll, convinced that on the
last day of the election he should have the honour of addressing his friends in the proud position of their representative
in Parliament.

With notable generosity under the circumstances and in
proof of his real desire that the men should be returned
whom the constituency wished to have as their burgesses he
offered to make the same arrangement with his rivals in the
Radical interest as had been made at the preceding election.
He promised to retire from his candidature on the second
day of the poll if he were the last man of the three, and to
throw all his influence into their scale if such an arrangement were made reciprocal. Duncombe, who favoured
Wakley's candidature, at once fell in with the proposal, but
Hobhouse refused, and, although he was at the bottom of
the poll on the first day, continued to stand and thereby to
split the votes in the Radical interest until noon of the second
day, when he finally withdrew.

The result of the poll fully justified Wakley in persevering,
for the figures were as follows :—

Duncombe	.	.	.	.	.	.	4497
Wakley .	.	.	.	.	.	.	3359
Spankie .	.	.	.	.	.	.	2332
Hobhouse	.	.	.	.	.	.	1817

Wakley's return was received by his supporters in the borough with extraordinary enthusiasm. Duncombe, the Yorkshire squire and cosmopolitan man of fashion, was a highly creditable representative and a vastly popular man, and was carried on the strength of these undefined qualities to the head of the poll ; but Wakley was the people's choice. He lived among them. He had been churchwarden of two large parishes and assiduous in the discharge of his parochial duties. He was personally known to hundreds of the electors as a man who desired to see the people well fed, well housed, prosperous in their health, and cared for in their sickness. He was a speaker after their hearts. His deliberate choice of Saxon English and simple similes, no less than his somewhat unbridled exercise of talents for mimicry and invective, enthralled his poorer constituents, while the more substantial voters recognised, in addition to his eloquence, his dauntless courage, his tenacity of purpose, and his chivalry towards friend and foe in all these contests. On the result of the poll becoming known Wakley's horses were taken from his carriage on Islington Green and he was dragged home in triumph. Arrived there the crowd insisted upon hearing him over and over again from the balcony of his drawing-room. Some ten thousand persons assembled in the square, the railings of which were thrown down and considerable damage was done, the enthusiastic demonstration in his favour continuing till a very late hour at night.

CHAPTER XXVIII

[1835]

A Bird's-eye View of General Politics—National Poverty and Hunger—The Reform Bill and the Rise of Chartism—The Poor-law Amendment Act and its Influence on the Repeal of the Corn Laws— The Irish Question in 1835—Wakley's Attitude towards the Three Agitations—The Spirit of the Times.

IT is not within the scope of this book to enter into constitutional history, save where constitutional history and the history of medical reform are identical, but a few words on the political state of the country at the time of Wakley's election to Parliament, on the aims of political leaders and on the general feeling of the people, are necessary to the complete understanding of Wakley's career. These words will form only the briefest summary of their subjects and may be open to the reproach that it is impertinent to the reader's intelligence to recall such elementary historical facts. That, however, is a risk which must be run with the object of telling a clear story.

At the close of the war with Napoleon, as marked by the Battle of Waterloo, Great Britain was weighed down by taxation enforced to meet the colossal expenses which she had incurred in behalf of the peace of Europe. In that very year—the year, by-the-by, when Wakley came to London— the land-owners, from which class both temporal estates of Parliament were drawn, passed an Act having for its object the aggrandisement of their own pecuniary position. The high price of corn, which was one of the direct consequences of the war, pleased their pockets. With a perfectly honest as well as traditional belief that the benefits derived from

the soil of the country should be confined by State interference to the possessors of that soil, there being no just
necessity that the other fifteen-sixteenths of the population
should take aught from the land which did not belong to
them, the landlords of Great Britain secured the passage of
a measure prohibiting the introduction into the land of
foreign corn until wheat had reached the astounding price
of eighty shillings a quarter. Speaking sweepingly, but not
at random, this meant that the poor were kept permanently
hungry. Hence, when other circumstances—wars and
rumours of wars, bad harvests, fiscal blunders, and blunders
in colonial policy—combined to make the whole nation feel
the stress of living beyond its income, the poor became
particularly hungry. The results of these exacerbations of
their misery were such explosions as culminated in the
Peterloo " massacre " and the Cato Street " conspiracy," to
take two examples of wide-spread and serious disaffection.
This background of poverty, of real and abiding misery,
must not be overlooked, for all the political events of the
reigns of George IV. and William IV. take their tint to some
extent from it.

Wakley arrived in Parliament at the time of the great
bloodless revolution, at the time which the most powerful
and popular Conservative leader of the century denominated the collapse of Dukism. The iniquitous corn-tax
remained, although its oppressiveness had been recognised
and attempts made to relieve it by a little botching and
tinkering with sliding scales. But the franchise had been
liberally lowered by the Reform Bill, and with the representation of the people more fairly distributed towns like
Manchester, Leeds, and Birmingham, having immense
esteem for the commercial position of the country and no
particular respect for the peer or the land-owner, had a
voice in the government. Surely, thought the poor, something will be done for us now. Yet within a year it became
only too clear that this great measure had not satisfied
the people. They might have seen that the repeal of the
Corn Laws would almost certainly follow, but they did not

desire to wait, and they wanted other things, the hungry
stomach not generally accompanying either the far-seeing
eye or the patient spirit.   In truth, the great Reform Bill
at the moment of becoming law pleased few people.   It
was a curtailment of the privileges of the land-owners that
they could not be expected to welcome in their hearts, even
though a land-owning legislature had approved it, and Lord
Grey was looked upon by many of his order—the politicians
of the Carlton, Brookes's and Boodles's—as little better than
a traitor.   On the other hand, the measure was not sweeping
enough to benefit the working-man directly.   In the form in
which it finally received the sanction of the Crown it admitted
the middle and lower middle classes to the suffrage, but so
far from conferring the same upon the working-man it
actually deprived certain tillers of the soil, already enjoying
a vote under the peculiar circumstances of some of the
ancient boroughs, of their time-honoured and illogical privileges.   Out of this natural and widespread discontent arose
the movement known as Chartism, a movement which
aimed at the following radical changes in the Constitution :—
(1) universal suffrage ; (2) annual Parliaments ; (3) payment
of members ; (4) abolition of property qualification for parliamentary candidates ; and (5) vote by ballot.   To three of
these innovations Wakley was already to a certain extent
pledged by his answers to his constituents when he entered
the House, although Chartism did not exist as an entity with
a formulated programme, a policy, and an accepted appella-
tive until two years later.   With regard to payment of
members Wakley never expressed any definite opinion ; he
disapproved of anything that was likely to interfere with the
independence of a member's vote, but he strongly objected
also to poverty forming an invincible barrier between an
able man and parliamentary service.   He was, as a matter
of fact, content that members should not be paid under an
invariable rule, seeing that in those exceptional cases where
a large number of his fellow-citizens desired a man to represent them in Parliament they generally combined to secure
their candidate against grave pecuniary loss.   Wakley firmly

believed in the ballot and supported its introduction into parliamentary elections at all times and with unbounded enthusiasm. His constituents at Finsbury did not make this a test question when bargaining with him for their suffrages ; he voluntarily added it to his programme.

Chartism formed only one of the three great agitations which were imminent in 1835, and the attendant storms of which convulsed the unrestful times in which Wakley's political career was run. The other two were the agitation for the establishment of Free Trade, and that for the Repeal of the Act of Union in Ireland ; but it was the permanent misery of the people and their bitter disappointment at the result of the Reform Bill which made all three movements so notorious for the spirit of open rebellion with which they were conducted. Dissatisfaction was not, it must be remembered, confined to the agricultural labourer. Many manufacturing firms were discharging large numbers of their hands. Improvements in machinery assisted them in their economy, while stagnation in the markets prevented them from quickly disposing of their goods and justified them in a course of retrenchment. So that the distress in the rural districts owing to the price of corn and the pitiful wages current became shared in the manufacturing districts, and the factory hand "out at play," as he euphemistically termed both going on strike and being without a job, was a much nastier and more dangerous person to deal with than his bucolic fellow-sufferer.

A union between the ill-treated agricultural labourer and his better educated and worse mannered companion in misery, the factory hand, was brought about undesignedly by the new Poor-law Amendment Act. Previously to the passing of this Act in 1834 the management of the pauper was vested entirely in the hands of the local vestry, each parish looking after the poor in its own district. The result of this arrangement was that in-door relief was hopelessly mismanaged, scattered rural districts being unable to support the poor in an adequate workhouse. Out-door relief, on the other hand, was more spontaneous and better directed, the recipients of assistance being personally known to the distributor of the charity, very generally the squire or the rector. But it was to be urged against this that able-bodied men out of work got relief without doing anything in return for it, while loafers multiplied in many districts, and rural immorality became a serious national trouble. In 1832 it was thought necessary to appoint a Royal Commission to look into the matter and advise a remedy. The outcome of this Commission was the Act of 1834, which was framed with philanthropic intent, but which was too much directed towards relieving the owners of land and houses of the burden of their responsibility to be fair or satisfactory to the community. Before the passage of the Act of 1834 it was possible for a pauper to become entitled to relief simply by being hired or employed in a parish, or by renting a tenement therein, or by apprenticeship, as well as by birth. The amended law laid down that birth should be the *only* means of obtaining settlement for purposes of relief, unless other means were agreed to by the guardians under the Act in any particular case. This rule bore exceedingly hardly upon the labouring classes. In certain districts where the landlords were selfish or recklessly cruel the cottages on their estates were destroyed in order that the territorial magnates might become exempt from the maintenance of the population. Such was the extreme value of the land that was under tillage that in many places the owners could afford to allow large tracts to go out of cultivation, and they preferred to do this rather than make themselves responsible for the relief of the peasants who should have been resident on the soil and employed in its cultivation. We can imagine the plight of these poor labourers. Their claim to relief from starvation was only to be made good by journeying back from the place to which starvation had already driven them, to a place where there was no roof to shelter them, no work to sustain them, and where the rulers of the district would consider their reappearance an intolerable intrusion. Wherever they went all who availed themselves of their labour were solicitous that they should not become dwellers on the soil, and con-

R

sequently the filthiest corners in the cities became their necessary refuge. Here they foregathered with their companions in misfortune, the superseded manufacturing hands, as well as with the frankly vagrant and criminal classes, and out of this ill-omened amalgamation was formed a body of desperate men who were at once the objects of the fear and the hate of the legislative classes of all creeds. The selfish and the ignorant saw in these unfortunate people only impudent rebels trying to emulate in their occasional outbursts of riot and incendiarism the excesses of the followers of Robespierre. The kindly-hearted and the well-informed saw in them the main obstacle to the practical treatment of all the great questions in philanthropy and economics, inasmuch as every movement for the popular good was certain to receive their baneful support and so to be at once unfairly discredited by its involuntary association with them. The Chartists failed to secure any of their objects at the time of demanding them only because of the unbridled violence of the rabble hanging on to the fringe of the movement. And the repeal of the Corn Laws, which proved an immediate relief of the pitiful condition of things that has been briefly sketched above, would not have been secured without even fiercer fighting had it not been that the leaders were determined and patient men, men strong to resist the forcing of their hands by turbulent supporters.

The Irish Question in 1835 was almost at its acutest stage. The Catholic Emancipation Act of 1829 had been granted grudgingly—many thought in fear—and the value of the concession had been ruined because of the widespread feeling that justice had only been done under compulsion. At the same time the mental descendants of Lord George Gordon found the Catholic Emancipation Act unpardonable and dangerous, and dangerous certainly it was in that it made of the Repeal demonstrations that are associated with O'Connell's name a hopeful effort. The Irish peasant knew that O'Connell had demanded Catholic Emancipation, and that having been refused at first, so far from being abashed, had said that he would compel the

English to grant the concession. In the end Emancipation was conceded, and when O'Connell promised later that he would compel the English to give him Repeal of the Union he was naturally and implicitly believed. Wakley could not do other than favour the Repeal party. It was in no way linked to the Liberal interests, O'Connell, as is well known, being equally ready to accept help from Sir Robert Peel as from Lord John Russell, from Lord Melbourne as from the Duke of Wellington, but the election addresses of both Wakley and Duncombe had committed them to the support of the Liberator in his demands, as all genuine promoters of the Reform cause, afterwards named Chartists, were bound to do. The reformers, apart from refinements, really desired government for the people by the people. Their great idea was that the predominant will of the people should form the determining factor in making the laws of the country. This was O'Connell's own rough-and-ready argument for the Repeal of the Union. He had nothing to say against the Union as evidencing the wish of the majority at the time, although he had a great deal to say against the corrupt way in which the majority had been persuaded to wish for what was bad for them. His great point was that the generation which he represented had no part in what their fathers had done, and that the majority of them were distinctly in favour of Repeal. Such reasoning was convincing to Wakley, who entered Parliament ready to consider O'Connell, and, therefore, the more violent followers of O'Connell, his colleagues in thought.

Wakley's attitude towards the three great movements which were engaging the attention of Parliament at the time of his election, and which have been thus cursorily brought before the reader, was simple and consistent. Firstly, he was pledged to the main doctrines of Chartism before the Chartists had actually defined their demands. Secondly, he was strenuously in favour of Free Trade, as the misery that was entailed upon the poor, both agricultural and urban, by the high price of food was well known to him. His relations and the friends of his childhood kept him posted in the condition of the labourer on the land, and it chanced that the plight of the West-country labourers was especially cruel. His constituency of Finsbury comprised an enormous area of slums in addition to the wealthy and respectable vicinage of Bedford Square, and the appalling condition of want in which many of the dwellers in Seven Dials were forced to abide had roused in him a generous indignation. He was unable to look upon the question of feeding the poor as a party one, openly declaring in his election speeches that whichever leader would annul the working of the Corn Laws and make it possible for the poor to escape from compulsory starvation would be the proper leader for the reformers to place at their head. These tenets, it may here be said, roused the greatest indignation in the breast of Wakley's father, Mr. Henry Wakley of Membury. This gentleman was a Tory and a Protectionist as became a land-owner and a practical agriculturalist, and although proud of his son's success he made no secret that he considered his son's doctrines in the matter of Free Trade pernicious. Thirdly, Wakley supported O'Connell in his demands for revocation of the Irish Act of Union, both for party reasons and by conviction. He was not prepared to endorse O'Connell's violent denunciations of all opponents or to believe unhesitatingly in the impassioned scenes from Paradise which that masterly orator was wont to paint for the encouragement of his Celtic audiences ; but with the attempt to secure the repeal of an Act, the national majority in favour of which had been dishonestly secured, and the national majority against which was in the next generation overwhelmingly large, Wakley was in full accord.

One thing may be pleaded as an excuse for this obtrusion of a chapter upon elementary politics, and it is this : Party spirit ran so high in the thirties and forties that contemporary literature is more than occasionally an untrustworthy guide to the truth. The times were transitional— they were really times of revolution—and various classes of men were so straightly set against each other in politics that they had not time to consider each other's claims to a hearing. To an Irish Catholic whoever was not a Repealer was a traitor; to an Orangeman whoever was a Papist was a jesuit spy and a political intriguer; to a land-owner a Free-Trader appeared as a thief; to many Free-Traders a land-owner was the same; to the extreme Tories the " People " appeared as savage brutes intent on obtaining for themselves a universal and furious misrule; while to the extreme Radicals the Tory was not only a person by temperament opposed to every movement that should sweeten life for the poor, but he was a dark intriguer against the Crown, a person with a plot up his sleeve for the abduction of Princess Victoria of Kent or—to plumb the very depths of absurdity—for the establishment of the Duke of Wellington on the throne of England. The refuting of these ridiculous accusations and counter-accusations encroached so much on the leisure of the various party leaders that they often missed opportunities of comparing views and so ascertaining that in very truth they had many sentiments in common; while the air was rent with simultaneous shrill cries from such separate quarters that the political health of the country was made to appear pitiful and desperate, whereas it was in fact fairly good and improving by great strides.

CHAPTER XXIX

[1835]

Wakley's Opportunity in the House—The Case of the Dorsetshire Labourers—His Special Fitness to Plead their Cause—His First Great Speech.

WAKLEY was very literal as well as very honest in his interpretation of his parliamentary duties. He was at first an infrequent speaker, although an assiduous attendant at Westminster, but his taciturnity was dictated by the fact that the special causes which he had been instructed by his constituents to plead did not come before the House, nor did matters affecting the medical profession present themselves. He questioned Sir Robert Peel upon certain new regulations of the College of Physicians of London, and elicited an answer from the leader of the House, revealing that the proceedings of the corporation were quite incomprehensible to the great statesman, and he contributed a few practical words to several desultory discussions on Poor-law topics ; but otherwise he did not break silence for nearly half a year. His reticence was not dictated by any shyness or gaucherie, for all contemporary historians agree that he dropped readily into the forms of the House and its methods of procedure, but from an estimable intention to take part only in the debates where he could offer an original view or could confirm the opinions of others from his stock of personal knowledge. He had a mandate from his constituency, while he was pledged to the profession and the numerous readers of the "Lancet" to advance in all possible ways within the walls of Parliament the cause of medical reform. When it was his duty towards his constituency or towards his journalistic public to speak he would speak, but only then ; on other occasions he was content to vote with the advanced Reform party to which he had given his adherence.

Within six months, however, a great opportunity came for a display of his talents as a speaker, and he was not slow to seize it. The theme was one that raised within him honest indignation and deep pity, while it was also one which a member sworn to champion the rights of the people was bound to bring to the notice of the House. In 1833 England had been greatly stirred by the remarkable exemplification of the harshness of the law relating to conspiracy, as shown by what was known as the case of the Dorsetshire labourers. This case was as follows. Six men—agricultural labourers in a little Dorsetshire village— were arrested and tried for the crime of " unlawfully administering a secret oath." Encouraged by the example of the London labourers and of the factory hands of both Birmingham and Manchester, who had formed unions and paraded the streets with impunity, certain luckless hinds of Tolpuddle, or Tolpiddle, a hamlet near Dorchester, number- ing at that time a little over three hundred souls, combined to resist the reduction of their wages from seven shillings a week to six. And certainly with wheat at eighty shillings a quarter the weekly wage of six shillings was not much for a man to live on, and to the most optimistic land-owner must have seemed a slender pittance on which to support a wife and family. However, their action was treated by the law as a serious one, having almost a political bearing, and to the astonishment of the whole of the country they were sentenced by Mr. Baron Williams to seven years' trans- portation. The general stupefaction at the rigour of this sentence had developed during the next two years into a movement not only in the West of England but in many agricultural constituencies all over the kingdom for the free pardon of the misguided men. Wakley was at once seen by the organisers of the movement to be the best possible mouth-piece for a vigorous protest in the House against the sentences.   He had a reputation among the people as an orator ; he was known to be fearless in his demands for the cessation or remedy of abuse ; he was a new man, uncommitted to any clique or party faction, around whose words the special interest of curiosity would cling ; lastly, he was a West-country man, and could be entrusted, therefore, with particular fitness to plead the cause of the Dorsetshire labourers.   On March 27th, 1835, Wakley presented no less than sixteen petitions, representing over 13,000 persons, for the reprieve of these poor fellows.   He urged their cause in a brief speech, revealing the fact that the wives of these men, who, poor wretches, had been reduced to the direst straits of poverty by the transportation of their husbands, had been roughly refused relief on applying to the parish authorities, and finally gave notice that he would move a resolution on that day three months that their sentences should be commuted.

On that day (june 25th, 1835) Lord john Russell, the Home Secretary, requested Wakley to postpone the motion he had on the paper on the ground that Government had already recommended a partial remission of the sentences, and the member for the Eastern Division of Dorsetshire spoke to the same effect.   But Wakley refused to do this. Sir Robert Peel had gone out of office in the spring of 1835 and Lord Melbourne had just begun his second and prolonged premiership.   As far as Wakley owned allegiance to a party, that party was in power, and ready to listen to a man in whom they had been informed that they would find a valuable recruit.   He rose in a crowded House to make his first serious oratorical effort, and the result was of such vital importance to his parliamentary career that the following transcript of his words from Hansard, though lengthy, is not too long :—

" He began by expressing his astonishment that the foreman of the Grand Jury should endeavour, even before the case was heard there, to interpose between the sufferers and the seat of mercy, and he hoped that if any other hon. member was connected with the prosecution he would at least hear the discussion.   The member for Dorsetshire was himself the foreman of the Grand Jury, and he, upon an *ex-parte* statement, having found a true bill against the unfortunate men, came forward in the House and, before he had made his statement, repeated the evidence given in a Court of Justice. Now, under what circumstances were those men prosecuted? He begged the attention of the House, for if he should fail in his object he could only say that the people of England would hereafter look in vain for justice at the hands of that assembly. He believed that every one in the House well knew that the Trades' Unions were instituted in London in July, 1833. When was the union of Tolpuddle instituted? In the November of that year, after the Trades' Union had been established in London for four months. Hundreds of men belonged to them, and Government permitted—at least had not interfered with—them. No party was prosecuted and thus, by acquiescence at least, Government gave their sanction to those Unions. It could be proved that in numberless instances police officers in plain clothes belonged to them, and if any one would read the evidence given before a committee of that House it would be at once inferred that the information of those police officers was regularly transmitted to the Home Office. The Dorsetshire labourers having received notice (pray let gentlemen mark this) that their wages were to be reduced from 7s. a week to 6s. a week, they having wives and families, they wrote to their brothers in London and communicated to them their distressed condition. What was the reply? 'We have established the unions for our protection here; we are given to understand that they are strictly legal; we walk in procession in this metropolis and neither police magistrates, nor the ministers, nor the judges of the land interfere with our operations. We recommend you to do the same.' The men of Dorset, seeing that there was a protecting power in those Unions in the metropolis, immediately set to work to establish one there, and it was not established in those distant villages until such Unions had existed for four months in London unmolested. He asked the House whether it was possible for them to believe that those men imagined they were committing any offence against the law in establishing such an union? A member had stated that a placard containing extracts from certain Acts of Parliament relating to Unions was found in the pocket of one of the men. That was true: but when did the poor man obtain possession of it? Why on the Sunday previous to the day of his being taken into custody—the individual obtaining cognisance of the nature of his offence (if he had committed any) only after the offence had been perpetrated. These men were actually going to break up their Union in consequence of seeing that paper, but they had not time to accomplish its dissolution. A prosecution was determined on by the magistrates of Dorset, and one afternoon a constable called at the cottages of the men telling them there was a criminal charge against them. So great was their conviction of their innocence that they went with only one officer all the way to Dorchester under the impression that they were to return the next day. On their arrival they were examined by the magistrates and remanded to the gaol. The next morning the magistrates actually, instead of bringing them into open court, visited them in the gaol, took the remainder of their depositions in private, and made out their commitment in the gaol. Even the witnesses were committed to gaol in order that they might be compelled to give the required evidence at the trial of the accused. And who was the chief witness whom it was necessary to imprison in order to secure his testimony ? Why, the son of the gardener who was in the employment of that very magistrate who caused the labourers to be apprehended—in fact the whole matter looked like a conspiracy to entrap the accused. He admitted that societies bound together by secret oaths ought not to be tolerated, but no objection to them in point of law in the case could exist, as combinations for the protection of wages were strictly legal. Besides, he contended that men should not be punished for alleged offences, the law against which had not been clearly defined and settled. The proceedings connected with their commitment and trial were equally unfair. On the Sunday before the trial an officer connected with the County Court visited Tolpuddle and other neighbouring villages in order to make inquiries relative to the characters of the individuals who were to be summoned as jurors on the trial of the labourers, and the neighbours were asked who would be safe persons to put into the jury box on that occasion. In pursuance of the objects sought to be obtained by this unjust inquisition a tradesman of the name of Bridle, a linendraper at Bere Regis, was challenged by the Crown and turned out of the jury box, his disqualifying offences being that he was not a farmer and that he had occasionally heard one of the Lovelesses, two of whom were among the six convicted men, preach in the Methodist Chapel of Bere Regis. Now, seeing such a determination on the part of the magistrates and the prosecutors, was it likely that the men would have a fair and impartial trial ? The House would imagine what were the feelings of the judge and jury when they heard the charge which was delivered by the former to the grand jury of the county :—

" ' Gentlemen,' said Mr. Baron Williams, ' there is only one other subject on which I shall presume to give you information : it is the case at the conclusion of your calendar—the charge of administering secret or as they are called, and properly called, secret and unlawful oaths. Gentlemen, you are probably aware that the Act 37 George III., c. 123, *seems* to allude particularly to seditious societies and confederacies ; but though it does *not*, it has been decided that the combination or confederacy, be it which it may, need not be for a seditious purpose, but that other unlawful purposes of combination are embraced in the Act of Parliament. If, therefore, you should have evidence that a person or persons had administered an oath to bind to secrecy, though there should be no evidence to satisfy you that it was connected with mutinous and seditious purposes, yet there can be no doubt that it would come within the meaning of the Act. Gentlemen, having had my attention called to it I cannot refrain from making some observations on the nature and quality of these offences. In the first place, it is no light matter to receive an oath in the secret manner alluded to, especially if it should appear to be for illegal purposes, as it is disparaging and bringing into discredit the administration of oaths altogether, thereby affecting that which is essential to the purity of judicial oaths, upon the obligation of which the administration of justice depends. It has been observed by moralists (among whom I may mention Dr. Paley) that a frequent and familiar administration of an oath, even for purposes of justice, is much to be regretted, and, if there be any truth in such an observation, how much more applicable is it where the administration of an oath places the party in so doubtful a state of morality, that a casuist would be puzzled to decide what course the party ought to pursue? Certainly, in courts of law we could not allow of his acting under that obligation, but how far it would be incumbent on him to disclose anything against his oath is a question of doubtful morality and is one of the baneful effects resulting from the administration of an oath, which puts the party in such a predicament; openness and publicity of conduct have hitherto been considered the criterion of honesty; and I fear it would be an evil day for this country if the disposition of such openness should fail; all secret societies which are self-constituted, self-elected, are calculated to shake the foundations of society and bring the country into extremely perilous circumstances; the misery of these particular cases is this—that men subject themselves for the irresponsible conduct of others who have no regard for the individuals over whom they exercise this authority; the unhappy men who have been thus misled are in a state of the most wretched subjection and debasement. Of all the persons affected by it, not even excepting the public, the unfortunate persons themselves who are brought into the trammels of these bonds and have had an oath of this kind administered to them are affected the worst. Sure I am that in my own experience I have known that they have been compelled by forced oaths to make out of their scanty means contributions to so large an amount as would not be endured if demanded by Government for the service of their country. The arbitrary demands made on them have, in many instances, exceeded anything before known in this or in any other country; nor does the evil rest here, for when men unite themselves to such societies the common right of labouring for whom they please is taken from them; this is undoubtedly a very serious subject, and as far as your influence extends, I doubt not that every means will be used on your parts for the prevention of this great, and I fear prevalent mischief.'

" Such was Mr. Baron Williams's charge to the jury selected to try these men. Thus the jury was led to infer that all secret societies are illegal. Now, after such a charge as that, coming from such high authority, it was impossible to expect that the men should have a fair trial, the impression made upon the jury by such language as that, would be that the parties had committed a very heinous offence. Now, what was the evidence to make it appear to the jury that the combination was illegal ? The rules of the Society were laid before them, and there was not one rule among. them which he (Wakley) considered illegal. Yet the illegality of the association was the foundation, in all the counts of the indictment, for sustaining the allegations with regard to the illegality of the oath. Had the indictment been framed in accordance with the spirit and the letter of an Act passed in the 39th of George III.—avowedly framed for the purpose of putting down all secret associations, with the exception of the society of Freemasons and two or three other societies therein specifically named —then, indeed, doubts might justly have been entertained whether these men had not offended against the conditions of that Statute, notwithstanding the repeal of the combination laws.

" But there was a motive for not prosecuting them under that statute. The poor fellows might then have been proceeded against summarily before the magistrate and been committed to prison for three months for taking an oath not required or authorised by law, whereas under the 37th George III. the judge, upon the conviction of the accused, had the power of transporting them for the term of seven years—a power which he could not exceed, and which, in the discharge of his duty, he exercised to the very utmost. It was true that the society was proved to be secret, but he (Wakley) denied that it was an illegal combination. He called the attention of the House to the Act of 1826, an extract from which he would read to the House, which provided that workmen of the country might legally combine to any extent or in any form they pleased with respect to the trades in which they were engaged without subjecting themselves to any legal condemnation, and if he should succeed in proving that, he thought no gentleman would say that the merely administering the oath made them illegal. The Act to which he referred was the Sec. 4 George IV. c. 129; it said : ' Provided always that nothing in this Act shall subject any persons to punishment, which shall meet together for the purpose of consulting upon the rate of wages, or the prices which the persons present at such meeting shall demand, or upon the time for which the said persons should work, at any manufacture, trade or business.' Now the combination of those men was to protect themselves ; they had notice of a diminution of their wages from 7s. to 6s. and they followed the example set them in London to protect themselves and their families from a diminution in their scanty earnings, which was to them nothing less than starvation. He would refer to a case in 1816, when the Unions did not create such agitation and excited no such morbid feeling, and he thought from the language then used by Mr. Justice Holroyd, that all parties must admit that he considered the 37th of George III. did not apply to those societies, unless their object was strictly illegal. The combination in that case was one of poachers who went out at night with blackened faces to kill game. He would quote the charge from Carrington's and Paine's reports—the case was tried at Gloucester Spring Assizes, April 11th, 1816; the indictment was against sixteen persons for administering unlawful oaths; the judge summed up as follows. 'If the oath administered by the prisoner to the poachers was intended to make them believe themselves under an engagement it is clearly within the clause, whether the book was the Testament or not. As to the assembly itself, it is impossible that the meeting to go out with faces disguised can be other than an unlawful assembly, and therefore the oath to keep it secret is clearly an oath prohibited by this Act.' That in his opinion decided the question as to the oaths which could only be considered illegal if the society were illegal, but the union of the labourers was legal and the Act under which they were punished did not apply to their case. Under these circumstances was it possible that the country could be justified in demanding the infliction of the sentence upon the men? He (Wakley) had asked almost one-half of the barristers in the House, and none could tell him under what precise Act those men were condemned or that their conviction had been legal. He therefore appealed to justice for a remission of the sentence imposed on the unfortunate men.

" He would now throw aside the question of law and go to the question of facts—to the character and conduct of the men. Was it proved in the court that any of the men had been guilty of threatening their fellow-labourers or in any degree given offence to their neighbours? He had evidence, on the contrary, that six better labourers and more honest men did not exist in the kingdom. Two of them—men who had never been anything in their lives but common labourers—had, by dint of study and application, become so qualified in mental capacity as to be enabled to give lectures in the neighbourhood to their fellow labourers, and had been received into the Wesleyan Conference as preachers. He (Wakley) feared very much that that was their great offence. He feared there was something behind the scenes which would not, but which ought, to come out. The two men had large congregations attending them, and he much feared there was something in their treatment to which he would not then further advert. George Loveless, at the age of twenty-eight, with a salary of 7s. a week, had

succeeded in purchasing a small theological library and had studied
with so much assiduity that there was no man in the neighbourhood
who could compete with him in point of theological knowledge, but he
(Wakley) could prove that in political discussions he had taken no part.
With the exception of one individual who had been charged when a
boy twelve years of age with taking a piece of old iron from a farmyard
valued at 4d., not one of the individuals was even accused of the
slightest breach of the law. It was admitted, in fact, by all persons
acquainted with the characters that six more honest, peaceable, and
industrious men were not to be found in the county of Dorset. Four
of them were relations, the sister of the two Lovelesses having married
Thomas Standfield. Their employers at Tolpuddle bore one and all
the highest testimony to their good conduct. He had received a note
from a lady who had employed four of the men for several years.
That lady said, 'George Loveless, James Loveless, Thomas Standfield,
and John Standfield were agricultural labourers of mine for many years.
I most willingly comply with your request, and now state that they
were all honest and industrious men.' Under date April 28th, 1835.
The lady's name was Northover. Who, then, could describe the
cruelty of the sentence passed on these meritorious men? He blushed
for the character of his country while he related the particulars of such
a barbarous transaction. To show the stamp of mind and the estimable
character of George Loveless, he would read an extract from a letter
written by him from on board the hulk in which he was confined
immediately after his conviction and previous to leaving this country.
The letter was addressed to his wife in all the confidence of matrimonial
attachment and unrestrained domestic intercourse, never expecting
that it would be seen by any individual except the object of his anxious
solicitude at home—least of all did he ever expect that any portion of
his letter would ever be read in the British House of Commons. He
might observe that when he asked Loveless's wife whether she had
received any letter from her husband that would enable to judge of his
character by the tone and temper of his language she handed to him
this letter and it had been in his possession within a few days of twelve
months. Never should he forget with what trembling hands she gave
him those documents, her countenance denoting almost insupportable
agony, scarcely mitigated by an unceasing flow of tears, and her little
children witnessing and partaking of the sorrows of the scene. The
letter was dated from Spithead, May 28th, 1834, and was remarkable
as containing not one word expressive of indignation or complaint
against his prosecutors. It was as follows: 'I thank you, my dear
wife, for the kind attention you have ever paid me, and you may safely
rely upon it that as long as I live it will be my constant endeavour to
return that kindness in every possible way, and hope to send to you as
soon as we reach our place of destiny, and that I shall never forget the

promise made at the altar; and though we may part awhile I shall consider myself under the same obligations as though living in your immediate presence.'

" What member of the House could have expressed himself to the object of his affections in more delicate or refined terms? How undying and unalterable was the force of his attachment to a deeply affectionate wife. In a portion of another letter which he would read; this virtuous man—stigmatised as a common criminal—was anxious that the moral and spiritual education of his children should not be neglected during his absence. Really, to see such a man as this torn from his wife and infant offspring, dragged from his friends and country on grounds so slight, doubtful, and suspicious, was enough to drive the working millions of this country into madness and revenge. In the letter to which he had referred Loveless says: ' Be satisfied, my dear Betsy, on my account. Depend upon it, it will work together for good, and we shall yet rejoice together. I hope you will pay particular attention to the morals and spiritual interests of the children. Don't send me any money to distress yourself; I shall do well, for He who is Lord of the winds and waves will be my support in life and death.' Poor fellow, he needed the support of the Lord who ruled over the winds and the waves, for he had found only cruelty and persecution in the decrees of the great men of the earth. Was it fitting, was it just, that such a man as this, for a doubtful offence, should be torn from his loved family and expatriated for the lengthened period of seven years? This excellent man and his brother were the two selected to be left in New South Wales, while the sentence of the others had been shortened. (This was the remission of punishment already alluded to as having been pleaded by Lord John Russell as a reason why Wakley should defer his motion.) There had not been a just consideration shown in this case—no adequate discussion and examination into its merits—no ordinary adherence to the dictates of justice. The prosecution was one uniform and unmitigated act of tyranny. The husband was torn from his wife and the son from his mother, and no distinction whatever was made between the case of a man who had reached the age of fifty-seven years and a boy of twenty. The two Standfields were father and son—the one a man, the other almost a child. 'And hear it,' said the hon. member, apostrophising the House, ' Ye Gentlemen of England who are husbands, fathers, and brothers—who have wives and children of your own. One woman —ah ! poor creature, how painfully is she figured in my mind at this moment—having a husband and six children had taken from her her two brothers, her husband, and her eldest son all at one fell swoop; and this, my lord (addressing Lord John Russell), is your boasted England ! This is your country of equal laws and justice. I do appeal to your lordship——' (The Speaker : Order, order !) ' I am aware that I am out of order in addressing the noble lord personally, yet I trust he will receive the appeal personally, for personal it is intended to be.' The cause of the sufferers, continued Wakley, came not within the limits of any ordinary rules, and the pain which it excited was calculated to lead to a divergence from ordinary arrangements. He called upon the noble lord to extend justice—mercy—to those individuals, and if they were allowed to return home he would himself give personal or pecuniary security for the good behaviour of the two Lovelesses. He implored the House, he entreated the noble lord, to take this fitting opportunity of extending mercy to the men, thereby gratifying thousands of the labouring classes who had appeared before the House as petitioners. Enough had already been done to deter others from following their example, and there was no longer reason why mercy should not be extended to these poor men. He lamented that the labouring classes had no representatives in the House. He had no desire to press the motion to a division; he hoped the noble lord would see the propriety of bringing the men back to their country. As to remaining in the colony, the hand of persecution had reached the poor men even there. Would the House believe that the two brothers had been separated, that George Loveless was in a hut 250 miles from the sea-shore, and James was in a part of the country in which the men were actually dying of famine and in want of work ? As long as George and James Loveless were in New South Wales and were confined there against their will they would be neither more nor less than transported men, suffering all the miseries concomitant to a forced separation from the persons whom they dearly loved and whose happiness constituted a part of their existence. The noble lord shall judge whether George and James Loveless would feel their continuance in New South Wales under any circumstances to be less than a forced transportation by an extract which he would read from a letter that within the last fortnight had been received from George Loveless: ' From what I can observe,' he says, ' of this country, it is not such a paradise as is generally supposed by the people of England. Bread is uncommonly dear, more than double the price of bread in England, and other provisions in proportion. Clothing is dearer than provisions ; thousands of persons are actually starving in this country, as many cannot get employment and many are too idle to work. As yet I see nothing to attract my attention, to make me stop in the country one day after I obtain my liberty and have the means to return ; in fact at present I despair of ever getting money to go to England, and yet nothing would yield me so much satisfaction—nay, nothing in this world will satisfy me until I return to you and the children.'

" What mitigation of punishment would that be which was attended with such reservation as a five years' domiciliation in such a country under such afflicting circumstances? His prayer to the House was for the restoration of all the prisoners to their families. He beseeched them to concede the favour, to gratify the humane wishes of the working people of England, who had implored the House for mercy to their fellow-labourers. The people of England, he could assure the House, felt deeply on the subject. To the working classes especially it was a constant subject of agitation, and unless the men were restored that agitation would continually increase. The society was legal with the single exception of the oath; and when the object was legal the oath alone could not make the society illegal. He hoped the House would interpose its authority. It was nothing to say there was no precedent; let them make one as soon as they could, for it was well said yesterday night they did not need one to do right. He had no object in bringing forward the motion but the interests of the working classes. He trusted there would be no misinterpretation of his motives; he had entered the motion two months ago, in hopes that the men would be restored without his bringing it forward—that the entering the motion on the books would lead to investigation and that investigation would lead to a conviction that the men had committed no offence whatever in a moral point of view. The laws had been vindicated by the transportation, the power of law had been displayed, it had been made evident that the unions would be repudiated and condemned, and he was convinced that no evil would arise from the restoration of those individuals to their native country."

CHAPTER XXX

[1835]

*Effect of Wakley's Speech—Release of the Dorsetshire Labourers—
The County Coroners Bill—Mr. Warburton's Parliamentary
Committee in 1834—Mr. Guthrie's Evidence before this Committee
—The Rejection of Mr. Cripps's County Coroners Bill—Wakley
Encouraged to Persevere.*

WAKLEY'S speech in behalf of the Dorsetshire labourers
occupied two and a half hours in its delivery, and throughout the whole time he held the closest attention of the House.
At no moment did his words provoke any manifestation of
dissent, while loud support was frequent and forthcoming
from either side of the chamber. When he resumed his
seat the general applause was so hearty and unrestrained
that he could not but feel that he had achieved a real
oratorical triumph and in the most critical assembly in
Europe.

The motion was seconded by Joseph Hume, who expressed
the feelings of the House by his highly complimentary
references to Wakley's opening. Lord John Russell
supported the action of the Crown in refusing clemency,
a view that was also taken by Sir Robert Peel, the
leader of the Opposition, and Mr. Serjeant Wilde (afterwards Lord Chancellor Truro). Daniel O'Connell made a
characteristic speech. Out of his numberless experiences
of similar victories he foresaw that the approval of the
House was entirely an academic recognition of Wakley's
oratorical powers, and would have no practical result when
it came to the telling of votes. He therefore urged Wakley,
as a majority could not be hoped for, to withdraw his

motion and get up petitions out of doors and thus bring the matter to the earnest attention of Government. Wakley in a brief reply said that he felt it his duty to press his motion "for an Address to the King, praying that His Majesty would be pleased to grant a pardon to, and direct the recall of, the six labourers convicted at Dorchester in the spring of 1833" to a division. Hume was his co-teller, and O'Connell's prophecy was verified, for only eighty-four members voted with Wakley, and three hundred and ten against.

It has not been without design that a verbatim transcript from Hansard of Wakley's first great effort in the House has been given. That such a speech loses much of its effectiveness when reduced to writing need not be insisted upon. It was essentially an impassioned appeal for speedy justice, and without the ring of the orator's voice, without the stir of his gestures and the play of his countenance such performances must lose actuality and be lacking in conviction. At the same time there can be read in his words enough to make us comprehend why the delivery of this speech settled at once and for ever his position in the House, and established his reputation as a speaker. For two and a half hours he kept the attention of a willing House fixed upon the plight of those poor Dorsetshire labourers. When he commenced to speak the Tories desired to hear nothing of them, for the feelings of the land-owners were utterly averse from the extension of mercy to any agitators against the low rate of agricultural wages; while the Liberals, his own party, were still more anxious that neither the House nor the country should spend time in discussing a miscarriage of justice which had occurred in their previous régime. Lord John Russell, again, was a new Minister and ambitious of becoming, or rather remaining, a popular legislator, therefore he objected to Wakley's estimating the remission of the sentences already proposed by Government as inadequate, and demanding of the House a larger measure of clemency. In addition to these elements of hostility to the speaker on party grounds Wakley had another ordeal before him, and one of which he was fully aware. He was not an unknown man in the House. His reputation as a speaker had preceded him, and the House was prepared with some little malice to hear the crude and robustious declamations of a demagogue and to class him with Henry Hunt and one or two other mob-orators as a noisy failure. Those who only knew of him as the man of many libel actions, and the leader of a revolt in the medical profession against properly constituted authority, had thoroughly made up their minds as to the fare that such a person would present to their palates. The case of the Dorsetshire labourers was an easy one for tub oratory, and to tub oratory they composed themselves to listen with what patience they might. What did they hear? No rush of garish sentiment, no thump of unrestrained gesture, and not a single ill-chosen word. A simple but learned summary of the legal aspects of the case of the Dorsetshire labourers, followed by a determined but temperate demand for justice and a sober appeal for mercy. And all this couched in the clearest possible phraseology, informed with good taste, not without humour, tinged with passion, and most unmistakably from the heart. Wakley rose to make his first great speech a comparatively unknown man, with a record not calculated to win him the good graces of an assembly ever jealous of the manners of its members. He sat down with an undisputed claim to first-class oratorical powers, and with a recognised position in the House as a fit and proper person for its counsels.

Although Wakley lost his motion and in a very decisive manner, his efforts eventually prevailed. The agitation for the release of the Dorsetshire labourers was not allowed to flag because of the temporary check which it had received at St. Stephen's. Hume and Wakley, profiting by O'Connell's advice, solicited subscriptions from the people at large and were soon able to convince the Government that the popular sentiment was also the humane one. On March 19th, 1836, within nine months of his great speech, Wakley elicited from Lord John Russell a reply to a question in the House to the effect that all the six Dorsetshire labourers had received a free pardon and were to be instantly brought back to their native village at the Government's expense. This result was hailed by the extreme Reform party as a signal triumph—a proof, as Wakley called it, of the sovereignty of the people. On April 25th, 1836, a public dinner was held under the presidency of Wakley at White Conduit House to celebrate the remission of the sentences. Nearly 500 persons attended, and both O'Connell and Wakley met with an enthusiastic reception.

The next occasion that Wakley played an important part in Parliament was during the debates upon Mr. Cripps's County Coroners Bill. This Bill would have certainly passed the House as drafted by Mr. Cripps, the member for Cirencester, had it not been for Wakley's earnest opposition. He had criticised many of its clauses in the columns of the "Lancet" when it was first presented to Parliament two years before his election for Finsbury, and he may be said to have been waiting to spring on it should it ever emerge again from obscurity. It did peep forth and received the reward of its temerity, being rejected by a House much better instructed in its meaning and in medical politics as a whole than the assembly to whose notice it had been originally introduced. This enlightenment was due in some measure directly to Wakley's speeches and writings, but in a larger degree to the report of Mr. Warburton's Parliamentary Committee on Medical Education, which had been presented to the House in the interval between the introduction of Mr. Cripps's measure and the postponed discussion thereon.

Warburton's Committee was the outcome of a joint endeavour on the part of himself and Wakley to find a constitutional remedy for the many undoubted abuses that were rife in the medical profession. At the date that Warburton moved for the appointment of such a Committee of Inquiry—viz., February, 1834—Wakley was not in the House, but without his aid the unanimous agreement of Parliament would not have been obtained for the departure.

It was Wakley's ever-recurring revelations of the extraordinary anomalies present in the system of medical education that, being persisted in for over a decade and being uncontroverted and practically uncontrovertible, finally bore splendid fruit. In fact, Warburton's Committee was the result of Wakley's successful agitation. The dull, feeble exclusiveness of the Royal College of Physicians of London, the tyranny and ineptitude of the Royal College of Surgeons, the pettifogging malice of the Society of Apothecaries—these were his weekly themes, and not bad samples of his weekly phraseology; and so pungently did he treat them and with such perfect disregard for the private position or importance of the figure-heads in the various corporations that everyone read the articles. They possessed the piquancy of their unstudied insolence and compelled attention from those quite innocent of any desire to see justice done to the rank and file of the medical profession. So that when Warburton asked the House to appoint the Committee he appealed to an alert assembly wherein there was already a general feeling that some such inquiry ought to be made. He obtained what he wanted immediately. In a second way Wakley was largely responsible for Warburton's Committee, inasmuch as it was he who showed Warburton how to secure the evidence, and what evidence to look for. Wakley had dissected the Charters of all three of the London corporations, and he knew what each body could do by law, and what each body could not do by law, as well as what each body had taken upon itself to do by custom. He knew where the law had been evaded, where it had been broken, and where it had been stretched, and in all these practices he knew when the result bore hardly upon the student and the workings of medical education. All this knowledge he placed unreservedly at Warburton's disposal, and its possession enabled that gentleman to act with confidence and to steer his Committee with discretion.

On Tuesday, February 11th, 1834, Warburton moved for his Parliamentary Committee of Inquiry into the state of the medical profession. Joseph Hume supported him, holding up to ridicule the anomalies of the Apothecaries Act that have been already detailed, as affording proof of the necessity for some one to be present in Parliament to interpret medical matters to the legislature. The motion was agreed to without a division and an exceptionally strong Committee was appointed. Warburton was chairman, and was supported by, among others, Lord Howick (the late Earl Grey, eldest son of Earl Grey, the Prime Minister at that date and the introducer of the great Reform Bill), Mr. J. Abercromby (elected Speaker of the House of Commons in the following year), Mr. Halford (son of Sir Henry Halford, the all-powerful President of the Royal College of Physicians of London), Daniel O'Connell, Mr. Spring Rice (afterwards Chancellor of the Exchequer and raised to the peerage as Lord Monteagle), Joseph Hume, Lord Oxmantown (afterwards Earl of Rosse, F.R.S., of telescope fame), and Sir Robert Peel.

The Committee was appointed to take evidence on the following important and diverse subjects :—Treatment of parochial poor ; farming of sick poor ; treatment in institutions supported by voluntary, life, and annual subscriptions ; mode of appointing officers of such ; appointments to gaols, asylums, and similar institutions ; regulations of private lunatic asylums ; the proper qualifications for masters in lunacy ; the state of medical practice generally and its supposed effect on the public health ; the practices of unqualified persons and quacks as regards public health and reputation of the profession ; the public sale of secret remedies ; the revenues of endowed institutions and the numbers of patients treated in them and the state of those patients ; the mode of appointment of Army and Navy medical officers ; the number of students attached to " chartered " hospitals and fees paid by them ; the qualifications and legal rights of Fellows and Licentiates of the Royal College of Physicians, of Members of the Royal College of Surgeons and of Licentiates of the Apothecaries' Company ; the fees charged at the foregoing institutions and the manner in which such

funds are appropriated ; the system of medical apprenticeship ; the status of chemists in regard to dispensing ; the
actual amount of wealth in possession of each of the
chartered medical institutions ; and the appointment of
medical professors and courts of examiners at both the
corporations and the universities.

The following were among some of the witnesses called :—
Mr. Cæsar Hawkins, Sir Henry Halford, Sir George Tuthill,
Dr. Hume, Dr. Copland, Dr. Elliotson, Dr. Farre, Dr.
Birkbeck, Dr. James Johnson, Mr. Cooper and Mr. Morson
(chemists), Mr. Guthrie, Sir Astley Cooper, Mr. Charles Bell,
Mr. James Wardrop, Mr. Benjamin Travers, Mr. Brodie,
Mr. Richard Grainger, Mr. Carpue, Mr. William Lawrence,
Sir Anthony Carlisle, Mr. Joseph Henry Green, and Dr.
Somerville. The Apothecaries' Company sent six special
witnesses, and most of the private teachers, as well as Carpue
and Grainger, had an opportunity of addressing the Com-
mittee. Professor Macartney came from Dublin, Mr. Hey
and Mr. Crosse represented provincial surgery worthily ;
Professors Christison, Allison, Abercromby, Poole, Thom-
son, and Maclagan were present from Edinburgh. Glasgow,
Aberdeen, and St. Andrews also sent witnesses.

All the evidence of these gentlemen was printed by Wakley
in the " Lancet " and copiously annotated, so that both the
House and the medical profession had a chance of learning
the real need that existed for reform, not only from persons
interested in altering the existent and corrupt state of affairs,
but out of the mouths of those very heads of the profession
whose rule had been so bitterly attacked by the " Lancet,"
and whose rejoinder had been an invariable and stiff-necked
assertion that things were very well as they were, and that
the disaffected persons were either malicious malcontents
striving to be important or their silly hoodwinked followers.
Wakley for ten years had made certain statements in the
" Lancet." Now was the hour of his triumph, for witness
after witness willingly or unwillingly confirmed these statements and made it clear to the country that medical reform
was really required upon the very lines indicated by the

journal which was by solemn agreement on the part of the London surgeons and teachers condemned as hopelessly wrong-headed and prejudiced. The country during the sitting of this Committee was no longer listening to Wakley, but to all sorts and conditions of expert testimony to the accuracy of his words.

Mr. Guthrie, for example, speaking in behalf of the College of Surgeons, of which body he had been elected President in 1833, gave it in evidence that he considered that the process by which the twenty existing members of the Council, or governing body, elected the twenty-first man to their body was an absurd plan, and that any other would be most acceptable. Immediately afterwards he added that no other plan would be as satisfactory. He thought that surgeons should not dispense their medicines or practise midwifery, as anyone who gave time to such trivialities would have none left for the acquisition of the principles of pure surgery; but he admitted that if only the non-dispensers could be chosen on the Council the power would be absolutely in the hands of two hundred pure surgeons to govern eight thousand persons presumably as well educated as themselves—viz., the members. He defended the system by which the ten senior men of the twenty-one Councillors were examiners, in spite of the fact that Councillors were chosen for life and that some of the senior men would therefore presumably be past their work. And he spoke well of the high rate of fees exacted from the London student. His evidence was printed at length in the "Lancet," much to his disgust, and proved in the clearest possible way that Wakley had not been exaggerating during the past ten years when he described the Council of the College as "a self-perpetuating junto" and its educational scheme as useless, giving as his reasons, firstly, that pharmacy and midwifery were not included in it, and, secondly, that the examiners were not fit and proper persons. If these facts had been elicited before the Committee from Scotch or Irish teachers jealous of certain of the advantages enjoyed by the London corporations, or if they had been insinuated by Grainger or Carpue,

sore at the greedy opposition offered by the College professors to all private tutorial enterprise, or if they had been
advanced by Wakley himself—a known foe to the College of
Surgeons—the public might have looked with suspicion on
the evidence as tainted.   But Guthrie was speaking for the
College—as the President of the College in fact—in favour
of keeping things as they were, and he satisfactorily convinced the Committee of the urgent need of reform.

It was in a House in full possession of such evidence as
this taken before a Parliamentary Committee that Wakley
criticised Mr. Cripps's County Coroners Bill from a medical
aspect.   The House was prepared to believe that in matters
of medical reform the honourable member knew what he
was talking about.   He was listened to with attention and
was able to secure the approval of the members for several
amendments, chief among which was that the medical
witness should be treated as an expert and should be paid at
inquests one guinea for his attendance and another for
making a post-mortem examination if directed to do so by
the Court.   The Bill was afterwards rejected as a whole, but
Wakley's prompt and successful employment of the first
opportunity that had presented itself to him to watch over
the interests of the medical profession in Parliament did not
go without recognition at the time, while it led to practical
results in the immediate future.   He was publicly thanked by
several medical associations.   He was also begged to renew
his endeavours in the next session of Parliament to obtain
adequate remuneration for medical witnesses in the coroners'
courts.

CHAPTER XXXI

[1836]

The Medical Witnesses Bill—Petitions in its Favour—Daniel Whittle Harvey—Wakley's Speech in Support of his Motion—Hearty Co-operation of Prominent Lawyers—Permission given to Introduce the Measure into the House—Its rapid Transformation into Law.

THE flattering manner in which Wakley's amendments to Mr. Cripps's defunct County Coroners' Bill, securing for the medical witness adequate remuneration for his services, had been received by the House and the press, as well as the numerous petitions that had reached him on the subject from his professional brethren, decided him to ask leave to bring in a measure dealing exclusively with the subject.

It should here be said that Wakley's views on the coroner's office were very well known indeed to the metropolis, and, for that matter, to the general public. They had become familiar to the House during the debates on Mr. Cripps's Bill, and had been received with respect there, as has been said ; but very little that fell from his lips in St. Stephen's had not been already asserted to the readers of the "Lancet" and to the free voters of Middlesex in the year 1830, when he offered himself for the post of coroner for Middlesex. On that occasion he made a series of most important speeches on the duty of the coroner, all tending to show that the office ought to be held by a medical man. The arguments that he employed then will be fully stated in dealing with his career as coroner for Middlesex, to which post he was ultimately elected in the year 1839. Their connexion with his views on the position of the medical man as an expert witness is not very close, but the memory of Wakley is so closely bound up with his tenure of the coroner's bench that to dismiss his views on the scope and privileges of the office in any summary manner, when an opportunity might seem to be present for dilating upon them, would come as a surprise unless it were explained. More, then, is not said here because so much more will have to be said very shortly.

Wakley's motion that leave be given to bring in a Bill to provide for proper payment to medical witnesses at inquests was set down for March 8th, 1836. Before he began to speak to it several petitions were presented in support of his contention. Mr. Wilkes, the member for Boston, told the story of an incident which had occurred in the practice of one medical man, but it was of so typical a nature that it had been put into the form of a petition in favour of Wakley's measure and presented to the House as such. The petitioner had been requested by the coroner of his district to undertake the post-mortem examination of the body of a person who had died under circumstances warranting the supposition that he had been murdered. The petitioner found that to make his evidence worth anything the contents of the stomach must be analysed. As a result of this necessity the inquest was adjourned two or three times for several days, a good many hours of which were employed in carrying out the coroner's instructions. When the petitioner subsequently gave his evidence the coroner and jury unanimously expressed their sense of its extreme value and their approbation of the talent that he had shown in his scientific examination of the viscera. Further, they recommended to the parochial authorities that he should be paid ten guineas for his services. In accordance with this recommendation the medical man approached the parochial authorities, only applying, however, for three guineas, the scale of payment being made on the scale of one of Wakley's recently successful amendments to Mr. Cripps's Bill—viz., one guinea for the evidence and two guineas for the necropsy. The answer of the parochial authorities was the one that they felt themselves regretfully constrained to render. They said that they had no power whatever to make the medical man compensation out of any fund under their control. This case was felt by the House to put the matter in a very small compass. Here was a man who, by the expenditure of much time, during which he was employing hardly-won learning and experience, had been enabled to help the cause of justice materially. He had, in fact, filled with success the part now played by the scientific analysts attached to the Home Office. His work was acknowledged by the court and the jury as having materially assisted them in the discharge of their duties. They desired, therefore, to reward him, but found themselves unable to do so.

Immediately after this petition was laid on the table another was presented from a group of Surrey medical men, begging the House to take into consideration the difficulties with which medical men had to contest as witnesses at coroners' inquests. Sir John Reid, the member for one of the divisions of the county, who had charge of the petition, added that for his part he considered that no individuals in the social scheme of the day were so badly paid for their labours as the gentlemen of the medical profession—an expression of opinion that was received by the House with cheers.

Several other members presented petitions of the same tenor, among which was one signed by eight hundred and twenty-six gentlemen "distinguished for their professional eminence in London," not including "sixty-five professional gentlemen resident in the Borough of Southwark." Among the signatories of this petition, the title of which shows that eminence was rather a usual quality with the metropolitan medical man of the day, may be mentioned Sir Astley Cooper and Sir Anthony Carlisle. It was presented by Daniel Whittle Harvey, and it is probable that the personal influence of this gentleman had something to do with the inclusion of names in its endorsement whose owners would have been unwilling on private grounds to subscribe themselves as supporters of any movement inaugurated by

Wakley. But Daniel Whittle Harvey was in a sort of way a political power, being a speaker of real eloquence as well as unparalleled fluency, and a great favourite with popular audiences. He had started in life as a solicitor, but was removed from the rolls at his own request on determining to join the Bar. The Benchers of the Inner Temple, however, refused to call him for reasons which a Parliamentary Committee afterwards found wholly groundless, and the publicity given to the injustice that he had received increased his popularity. He stood for Colchester in 1818 in the Radical interest, and continued to represent that town until the passing of the Reform Bill, when he was elected for Southwark. He was at this time editor of the " Weekly True Sun " and was one of Wakley's most intimate associates in the House, being always ready to place at the disposal of his brother journalist the fruits of his long parliamentary experience. Some three years later Harvey was appointed Commissioner of the Metropolitan Police, when he was compelled by the regulations of his office to retire from the House, but during his political career he was one of the most prominent personalities in the Reform party, and a few words recalling him to the reader's mind are not out of place.

Wakley, in rising to bring forward his motion, said that from the very favourable manner in which the House had received the petitions just presented he thought he should not have to occupy the attention of the House for very long. When the County Coroners Bill was brought before the House last year members would recollect that it contained a clause professing to provide for the remuneration of medical witnesses at inquests, which clause, however, shared the fate of the whole Bill, the Bill being rejected by the House, and very properly so, being perfectly unsuited to the object which it should have sought to attain. He was ready to admit that in some respects medical men might not be more useful, when they attended as witnesses, than other men, but he urged that it should be borne in mind that medical men attended inquests in their professional capacity—they did not attend as casual observers of the event which might have occasioned the inquest, but as professional men, who alone could give information essential both to the ends of justice and as the basis of a true verdict. The duties of medical men were exceedingly important and were very difficult of accomplishment and very frequently attended even with danger to life. A post-mortem examination was not to be conducted in haste or without knowledge or trouble. Many instances within the speaker's knowledge had arisen where such an examination had necessarily been protracted through a period of eight or ten hours, and yet where the medical witnesses who conducted it obtained no kind of remuneration, the coroner having no power to award them the slightest compensation. He went on to assure the House that such a state of things was not so injurious to the medical profession as to the public at large, in that it defeated the whole object which the public had in view in holding a coroner's inquest. The coroner's office was one of the most important offices in England, and was almost the only office to which the people still had the power to elect their own judge. Yet unless this judge was empowered to give compensation to medical witnesses the court had a tendency to become almost useless. When a coroner called a medical witness before him he had not the power to require the witness to make a post-mortem examination, although the result of such examination might be the only means of enabling the jury to return a correct and faithful verdict. Quackery was at the moment producing more victims than it had ever done at any former period. It was fearful to observe the consequences which flowed from the quack advertisements with which the newspapers teemed, and he for one would be glad indeed if His Majesty's Government would resolve on the removal of these disgraceful outrages on society by preventing quack medicines from going forth under the authority of Government stamps. He then alluded to an inquest held a few days previously at Woolwich Barracks on the body of a marine who had died after being flogged.

Several medical men had attended, all of them without obtaining any compensation, and had given evidence which had produced in the minds of many of the jury the impression that a most terrible outrage had been committed. Had these gentlemen been selfish or mercenary enough to refuse to attend, or had they withheld their evidence as professional men the cause of justice would have been improperly represented. And how frequently did similar instances occur. Taking into consideration these points, and observing the anxiety of the people to have faithful verdicts recorded, he trusted that the House would not refuse to grant that compensation to medical witnesses which would be ensured by the passing of this Bill. He was sure from what he had observed that the principle of the Bill would be sanctioned by the House, and he did not propose at this stage to enter into details, but merely with these observations to move that leave be given to introduce a measure to provide for the payment of medical men who might attend as witnesses at coroners' inquests.

The Attorney-General (Sir John Campbell, afterwards Lord Chancellor) "ventured to believe" that such a Bill would be exceedingly useful. He confirmed Wakley's statement that in many cases justice had been obstructed in consequence of competent medical evidence not having been given before the coroner's court, while the niggardly manner in which medical men were treated made the absence of their evidence no just matter for surprise. Juries were either without medical evidence altogether, or, when it was obtained, the injustice of refusing to award a fair and honourable remuneration was committed. He would only advise the mover in framing the Bill that he must be careful lest it should be so worded as to be made the means of a job on the part of the coroners themselves. With this caution he certainly thought that when medical men were called in to assist they ought to be properly compensated.

Mr. Warburton, in seconding the motion, said that of course the mover would take care in his Bill that medical

witnesses should be paid for their attendance, but he should
think that in cases where persons of superior information
were called and where their apparatus for analysis was
costly the remuneration would fall short of what it ought
to be unless account were taken of the heavy expenses
involved in the education of such a person. He alluded to
the story told by the member for Boston, and considered
that in that case the petitioner ought to have applied to the
Home Office for payment, lest the ends of justice should be
defeated.

The Bill was also supported by the Solicitor-General
(Sir R. Rolfe), among others, only one objection being
expressed to the measure by Mr. Jervis, Q.C., the member for
Chester. Mr. Jervis did not object to the Bill, but observed
with regard to the existing law that a coroner, if he desired
the presence of a medical witness, could issue a warrant to
the parochial officers ordering them to send one ; in such a
case he contended that the medical man would undoubtedly
have a claim upon the officers which he could enforce.

Wakley rose to answer the objection of Mr. Jervis.
He thought that that gentleman was not quite correct in
his statement. True, the coroner might order the overseers
to obtain the medical witness, but it was equally true that
the witness might, if he pleased, refuse to give evidence.
He might say, "I will not open the body ; I will give no
testimony respecting a post-mortem examination," and the
coroner had no power whatever to compel him to give his
opinion as to the cause of death or to commit him for
contempt of court. He (Wakley) desired to give the
coroner more power, but as a set-off against that power he
desired to give the medical man due compensation. He
would, he assured the House, take the greatest care to so
frame the provisions of the Bill as to make jobbing impossible. In Ireland much jobbing had taken place under
the Coroners Act, but with that example before his eyes
he would take care that nothing of the kind should happen
here.

Leave was given to bring in the Bill amid the cheers of

the House.   Its after-history was short and uneventful and
its details need not be mentioned.   It provided for the payment to all medical witnesses at coroners' inquests of one
guinea for their evidence and one guinea for post-mortem
examinations, including any scientific analyses that might
be deemed necessary by the court.   It became law in
upwards of three months, not the least discussion on its
clauses ever occurring, so entirely was it both in spirit and
detail to the mind of the House.   The only alteration made
to it in Committee was verbal.   From beginning to end
Wakley's conduct of his measure was marked by tact and
thoroughness.   He knew exactly what was wanted and was
able to explain satisfactorily the meaning of his provisions.
A large sum of money was thus annually secured to the
medical profession for professional services, while the public
received an additional security against the risks of murder
the importance of which cannot easily be exaggerated.

CHAPTER XXXII

[1836]

The Newspaper Stamp Duties—Wakley's Views on a Free Press— Edward Lytton Bulwer's Attitude towards the Question—The Debate in the House—Wakley defers his Motion for Repeal at the Request of the Chancellor of the Exchequer—The Proposals of the Government—Criticisms by the Press of Wakley's Conduct—The Approval of Leading Liberals.

" MR. WAKLEY gave notice that on March the 8th he would move for leave to bring in a Bill to allow Medical Witnesses their expenses for attending Coroners' inquests ; on March the 15th he would move for the total repeal of the Stamp duty on Newspapers ; on March the 20th he would move for the repeal of the Septennial Act."

This short item of parliamentary news, extracted from " Bell's Weekly Messenger " for 1836, shows that Wakley took his position as a reformer very seriously, and that he had no intention of allowing his activity and promises without the House to be followed by idleness and non-performance within its walls. Having safely piloted the Medical Witnesses Bill to harbour he immediately turned his attention to the Newspaper Stamp Act.

The taxation of newspapers, an impost that was first levied at the beginning of the eighteenth century, had grown gradually heavier and heavier, until in 1830, when Wakley's interest in politics first became serious and definite, it really amounted to what he and Hume invariably termed it, namely, a tax on knowledge. The first tax on newspapers was imposed in 1712, when it was enacted that all papers containing public news or intelligence were to be taxed at the rate of a halfpenny if printed on half a sheet of paper and a penny if on a whole sheet. The same Act imposed a tax of a shilling on any advertisement that appeared in a paper published weekly or more often. In 1776 the newspaper stamp duty was three-halfpence and in 1789 it had risen to twopence. The advertisement duty of a shilling was doubled in 1757, and in 1789 Pitt increased it by sixpence, making the duty half-a-crown on each advertisement. Again, in 1804 the newspaper stamp duty was raised to threepence-half-penny, and the duty on advertisements to three shillings and sixpence. In 1815 the newspaper stamp duty had become fourpence the advertisement duty remaining unabated, while the duty on paper, before printed, varied from three-halfpence to threepence per pound. In 1833, in consequence of agitation within and without Parliament, the advertisement duty was reduced to eighteenpence. Three years later a new and highly successful agitation against the impost was carried on, and with the story of this movement Wakley's name is closely associated. What he and others did at this juncture will now be told : the results of their labours, as seen in the reforms of the next twenty-five years, can be set out in a few words. These results were that on September 15th, 1836, the newspaper stamp duty was reduced to a penny on papers containing 1530 square inches, three-halfpence if above that and under 2295 square inches, and twopence if of the latter size or above. Again in 1853 the stamp duty was reduced to a penny for every sheet under 2295 square inches ; while the advertisement duty was entirely abolished by an Act passed August 4th, 1853. In 1855 the newspaper stamp duty was entirely abolished, and on October 1st, 1861, the paper duty was done away with, thus leaving newspapers free.

In this story of increasing taxation and gradual remission by far the most important episodes were the two in which Wakley was actively concerned—viz., the agitation of 1833, which produced the reduction in the tax upon adver-tisements, and that of 1836, which resulted in an important and substantial remission of the stamp duty. The taxation had all been on the ascending scale before, but these two occasions marked the feeling of the country that a highly-taxed press was not creditable to a free nation ; and on both occasions, within and without the House, Wakley was earnest in his endeavours to obtain remission of the burden upon the purveyors of news and knowledge.

His views on the subject were first communicated to the country at large in a speech to his constituents made in the Hall of Science, City Road, one week previous to the date on which he was announced to bring forward his motion in Parliament. The ostensible purpose of the assembly over which Wakley then presided was to organise a petition to Parliament for the total repeal of the stamp duties on newspapers, but the real object that he had in convening the meeting was to make clear to the country the views on the subject of taxation of the press held by the man who was about to move the total repeal of the tax. The question was one that had a certain familiarity for his hearers, because on each of the occasions that the tax had been made heavier the more enlightened of both parties in the country had clamoured against the impost and brought forward arguments to show that it was not the fiscal benefit that the various Governments sought for the country in thus taxing the diffusion of knowledge, but really the muzzling a too critical press, a press that was too prone to teach the people things which it was better for an unreformed Parliament that they should not know. Since the passing of the Reform Bill the question of the newspaper stamp duties had been twice before the House. Once it had been brought forward by Joseph Hume, and on the second occasion, which was only a few months previous to Wakley's motion, by Edward Lytton Bulwer, the novelist. Hume's motion was for the repeal of what was known as the "Trash Act," a piece of legislation designed by Castlereagh to check the licence of political pamphleteers, and in moving the repeal of that obnoxious Act, Hume's argument for a free press included a demand for the abolition of the newspaper stamp duties. Bulwer's motion was for a Committee to inquire whether the newspaper stamp duties could not be advantageously reduced from fourpence to a penny, and his conduct in bringing forward the motion was severely criticised by the Radical press, whose party had entrusted him with a commission to move the total repeal of the tax. Bulwer did not, however, believe that such a motion had any chance of success, and desired to propose a compromise. This not being agreeable to his party he made his motion for a Committee of Inquiry, to the disgust of the more ardent spirits. "Wakley will not play fast and loose with this subject," said Daniel Whittle Harvey's paper, "as did that sublime humbug, Mr. E. L. Bulwer. This latter gentleman did grossly disappoint and deceive us. Having declared in the House that he would not be a party to any compromise ; that he would hear nothing about reduction, but have the total repeal or none at all—he had gained our implicit confidence. The friends of unstamped knowledge, beguiled by his pompous declamations, abandoned the question to his guardianship in the perfect assurance that he would either see the matter finally set at rest—in the only way it can— by a total repeal or else compel the recreant Whigs to incur eternal disgrace by opposing the motion in the teeth of all their past professions. How different the farce he enacted. Well, indeed, may the Whig-Radicals blush for their champion. After all his solemn *fanfaronnade*—after all his high-coloured pictures of the vices of ignorance and the benefits of knowledge—after his magniloquent boasts that he would not even consent to a penny postage—the fire of his eloquence ends in the smoke of a hypocritical motion for a Committee to inquire whether it was possible to reduce the tax to one penny without injury to the revenue. Such was the sublime Bulwer's *finale*—just as though the affirmative of the inquiry had not been proved a thousand times over, and as though (were it even not proved) a question of such moment—one involving the intellectual emancipation of millions—ought to be treated as a paltry measure of finance." These were hard sayings, but men did not mince their words in those days. Bulwer's motion was withdrawn and no harm was done to the cause.

It was, therefore, a threadbare topic to which Wakley addressed himself, but it was also a topic upon which the more thoughtful of the community had pondered much. His speech was devoted chiefly to showing very clearly that the reformers, in delegating to him this important motion, would not find in him a second Bulwer. He dwelt strongly on the fact that the fiscal side of the question was simply not worth considering compared with the immense moral benefits that would accrue from the repeal of the taxes on knowledge. If the people were resolved to do away with the taxes by standing on their undoubted right to receive without undue expenditure information upon the laws of the land by which they were judged and condemned, Wakley was certain that sooner or later—and probably sooner—the taxes would be remitted. The taxes brought the Government £450,000, and he begged his audience to consider, firstly, how paltry a sum this was to urge as a reason for the necessity of maintaining a tax upon the knowledge of the people, and secondly how self-confessedly feeble must that Chancellor of the Exchequer be who could not see any way of substituting for an odious tax some fairer impost that would bring to the revenue the small sum over which there was so much disposition to haggle. Next, Wakley warned his hearers against listening to any proposal for half-measures. He inveighed against the substitution of a lighter tax and against any measures proposing to include the postage rate in the duty on the paper or on its advertisements. Such projects he considered obscured the question at issue, which was—Ought the people to get their information wholly and entirely free ? and tended to split up the supporters of the general principle into the factious partisans of this or that view. He concluded by warning his hearers against open violation of the law. He deplored the fact that unstamped newspapers had received popular support, saying that if the same measure of support had been given to the legitimate agitation as to the illegal dissemination of unstamped sheets the hands of the reformers would have been immensely strengthened in Parliament and it was possible that the people already would have obtained what they wanted.

With his closing sentences his audience did not seem disposed to agree. Three men were at this time in prison for the publication of unstamped newspapers. They were Henry Hetherington, the publisher of the "Poor Man's Guardian," a paper whose title-page bore the legend, "Published in Defiance of the Law to try the power of Right against Might"; John Cleave, the editor of the "Weekly Police Gazette" and the "Penny Gazette of Varieties"; and James Watson, an intimate associate of the latter. In the eyes of the people these men had suffered for doing what the constitutional agitators had openly approved. Such men as Grote—the historian of Greece—and his friends Sir William Molesworth and Charles Buller, James Silk Buckingham—whose pockets had suffered severely from the suppression for political reasons of the "Calcutta Journal,"—Joseph Hume, Edward Lytton Bulwer, Daniel O'Connell, Daniel Whittle Harvey, and Wakley, were known to hold this taxation of newspapers in abhorrence. How, then, could it be wrong for Hetherington, Cleave, and Watson openly to revolt by deed as well as word? Wakley thereupon treated his electors to a few wise words upon the difference between lawless rebellion and constitutional agitation, not the least practical of his assertions being that the latter generally obtained its just demands, while the former must stir up enmity to the best of causes among good citizens.

Wakley's declaration for a total repeal of the duties—to be obtained, however, by the employment of constitutional agitation only—was hailed with very general satisfaction. The press of the country were satisfied to leave this matter in his hands, and even the most extreme Radical wing of the party, for whom the enterprising editor of the "Weekly Police Gazette" had an heroic appearance as long as he was serving the cause in durance, were content to wait calmly for the issue of Wakley's motion. His reputation for unflinching resolve as well as the public record of his career secured him from any imputation of weakness or half-heartedness, though he might deprecate for politic or moral reasons open defiance of the existing law. With what was admitted on all sides to be a good cause, with a thorough knowledge of all the arguments that might be employed against him as well as of those that he might successfully advance, and with promises of substantial support within the House, Wakley confidently expected success for his motion, and this fortunate issue was anticipated by all his friends and co-workers. But the events of March 15th, 1836, did not fulfil these happy hopes. Wakley and Daniel Whittle Harvey having presented numerous petitions on behalf of the repeal of the newspaper stamp duties, chiefly from the metropolitan constituencies, the Chancellor of the Exchequer, Thomas Spring Rice, suggested that Wakley should consent to allow him to state what were the intentions of the Government in the matter and should defer the discussion on his own motion till such a time as the subject of the stamp duties on newspapers was before the House in the financial statement for the year. Wakley consented to adopt this course, and the House having resolved itself into Committee, the Chancellor of the Exchequer proceeded to explain the views of himself and his colleagues on the Treasury Bench. He said that it was his intention to propose the consolidation into one Act of all the Acts imposing stamp duties of any description, at that time distributed over one hundred and fifty statutes, some relating to England, some to Scotland, and some to Ireland, without order or method, and exhibiting a farrago of legislation by which the most subtle lawyer frequently found himself bewildered. He could not hold out to the honourable member for Finsbury, for whom he entertained feelings of the greatest respect, a promise to come forward with any proposition for a total repeal of the newspaper stamp duty. Such a reform was not in accord with his own feelings and the public service would not be promoted by it. The State undertook the duty of conveying newspapers free of postage to all parts of the country, therefore a certain proportion of the stamp

duty should be regarded as payment for services rendered
rather than as a tax.   Again, he considered free newspapers
would work unfairly towards the dweller in the country who
would have to pay carriage-rates to obtain his information,
while the urban dweller would be equally posted in the
march of events with nothing to pay for the privilege.   He
intended, therefore, to propose that there should be a stamp
duty of one penny on a newspaper instead of fourpence.
He promised that he would listen to all arguments from the
junior member for Finsbury and would make the best case
that he could against the extreme step of a total repeal of
the taxes, if the House on their side would go with him to
the extent that he had already indicated in an attempt to
deal with what he confessed to be a crying evil.   He concluded by congratulating Wakley on his recent public
utterances warning his followers against breaches of the
existing law.   Duncombe and Wakley both said a few
words pledging themselves to continue their efforts for total
repeal, while Hume congratulated the Chancellor of the
Exchequer on his proposals " as far as they went." Bulwer
seized the opportunity to point out to the House that they
were now agreeing with great unanimity to the very reform
which he himself had previously advocated, when his action
had drawn down upon him continued and bitter attacks
for his love of compromise.   He had been told that his
suggestion constituted a breach of faith with those who had
committed their interests to him, and he could not refrain
from pointing out that in the hands of the honourable
member for Finsbury the proposal for total repeal of the
duties had only resulted in obtaining the same concession
that he (Bulwer) had asked for.

Wakley's conduct was subjected to a very mixed reception
by the press.   He had pointed out to his constituents and
to the public that he would not submit to any compromise.
They had entrusted him with a mission—namely, to move
for the total abolition of newspaper stamp duties.   This
mission he intended to carry out.   Neither any offer of
reducing the duty nor any plan whereby part of the duty

should be regarded as a carriage-rate would be accepted favourably by him. The various journals written in support of the Reform party, as well as those representing advanced Radicalism, and what is now termed Socialism, had all combined to rely on the firmness of his attitude. They rejoiced with acclamation over the fact that Wakley, the straightforward democrat, had the matter in his charge instead of "the sublime" Bulwer—novelist, dandy, playwright, and aristocrat. And lo! the result of Wakley's parliamentary manœuvres was the securing of an offer from Government containing the identical two measures of compromise which Wakley had declared that he would on no account agree to. The fourpenny tax was to be reduced to a penny, and the penny was to be regarded not as a tax but as payment for the carriage of the paper. Moreover, the suggestions of the Government were identically those of the maligned Bulwer, who had not omitted to point this out with some asperity in the House. The "Times" was immediately up in arms against Wakley, calling him the puppet of Spring Rice and sneering at him as cajoled into accepting a compromise in spite of his professions. The "Dispatch" owned itself puzzled. "judge our surprise," runs its comment, "when, instead of moving (what appeared on the list of notices) for a total repeal of the stamp duties on newspapers, Mr. Wakley moved the order of the day, 'That the House resolve itself into committee on the Stamp Acts.' Gods! we exclaimed, the man has surely been bamboozled by the Chancellor of the Exchequer." For a few hours it was rife in Tory and Radical circles that Wakley, the incorruptible member for Finsbury, had shaken hands with Spring Rice, a stiff-necked Whig, over a question involving a tax upon the knowledge of the people. On the other hand, the papers which really understood what had happened —those whose editors were behind the scenes and in touch with the leaders in the movement—were unanimous in praise of Wakley's conduct in acceding to the request of the Chancellor of the Exchequer to defer his motion. Hume wrote to the press to explain that the course which Wakley

had taken was the right one under the circumstances. The
"Political Examiner" spoke strongly in favour of his conduct, denouncing the short sight of the "Times" and of
those who detected in a necessary piece of diplomacy a
useless piece of treachery. Cleave, the irresponsible editor
of the "Weekly Police Gazette," whose opinions might be
taken to represent the sentiments of the more violent and
socialistic section of the Radical party, was equally satisfied
with the course pursued. Cleave was one of the very
persons whose conduct in issuing unstamped papers in
defiance of the law Wakley had specifically condemned, but
Cleave had sufficient insight into character and motive to
understand that Wakley was the last man in the world to
play fast and loose with pledges. Public opinion, in fact,
was about evenly balanced. Wakley, however, was not a
man to allow himself or his actions to be misunderstood for
any length of time. Throughout his life he was frank with
his pen, and he immediately wrote a circular letter to all the
journals of importance in the metropolis and provinces in
which he explained his reasons for the course he had adopted.
When the Chancellor of the Exchequer asked him to defer
his motion, because Government had a suggestion to make,
said the letter, the Reform party in Parliament at once saw
that by allowing Mr. Spring Rice to have his way the issue
would be considerably narrowed. The Reformers would
obtain what the right honourable gentleman promised and
still be free to agitate later for a total repeal. Had the total
repeal been the motion before the House it might have been
lost and nothing have been passed, whereas total repeal
could now be moved as an amendment to Mr. Spring Rice's
measure of compromise ; and should it not be carried, at
any rate the reduction of the duty from fourpence to a penny
was secure. Wakley concluded his letter by pressing upon
the people at large to sign petitions in every locality in favour
of total repeal.

Wakley's management of the whole matter gained him the
approval of the House for its moderation and wisdom. It .
was distinctly to his personal advantage to be brought into

contact with such people as Bulwer, Grote, Buller, and Molesworth, and that in the honourable position of leader. These men recognised that Wakley's prudence and pliability had advanced the cause a distinct stage. They knew of his promise to the Finsbury electors that he would have no compromise but that he would divide the House on the question of total repeal or nothing. And they appreciated how much more palatable to a man of his disposition it would have been to keep literal faith with his constituents and to have made a stirring appeal to the House for the freedom of the press, even though he should actually retard that freedom by so doing. Appreciating these things they gave to Wakley a generous meed of approbation. They saw that he was not afraid to take the risk of temporary mis-apprehension to gain the end that they all had in view, and they regarded his attitude as entirely consistent and under the circumstances the only one that was likely to be successful. No one doubted that he would seize the first opportunity to defy the Government and to declaim his unappeasable hatred of compromise and his intention to be faithful to the very letter of his pledges to his constituents, but in the meantime such action would have retarded the progress of the very movement at the head of which the Reformers had placed him.

CHAPTER XXXIII

[1836-1837]

Wakley's Position in the House—The Lord's Day Observance Bill —Flogging in the Army—The Publication of Lectures Bill—The Poor-law Amendment Act—Other Reform Measures—An Indefatigable Member of the Legislature.

THE fulness with which Wakley's connexion has been described with these three prominent movements during his first period as representative of Finsbury in Parliament need not be repeated in recording his subsequent parliamentary career. But his methods in the House of treating these three widely different affairs have been dealt with at length because they were both characteristic and successful, raising him in a few months from comparative political obscurity to a position of influence and popularity. The affair of the Dorsetshire labourers stamped him as an orator ; his conduct of the motion for abolition of the newspaper stamp duties proved him a sound tactician ; while his management of the legislation for the remuneration of medical witnesses showed him to be specially mindful of the needs of his profession, upon which needs he had based his principal right to a seat in the House. In all the other measures before the House Wakley voted as a consistent Radical, thorough-going and passionate enough to co-operate with Daniel O'Connell, yet sufficiently aware of the needs for compromise and of the advantages of circumspection and of taking advice to be admitted by the philosophical Radicals, of whom Grote was the most typical leader, into their intimate counsels. No attempt will therefore be made to register all that was said and done by him in general politics. His frequent speeches as reported in Hansard were always vigorous, pithy, and humorous ; and their tenour can be deduced readily from the fact that he was a broad-minded and consistent Reformer, insisting largely on the rights of the people, and especially anxious that the people should have, as far as possible, equal chances with the governing classes of getting wholesome food, healthy houses, and adequate education.

In some minor measures he took a more individual part. His motion in favour of the repeal of the Septennial Act came to nothing. It was a subject upon which he felt strongly, and in all his addresses at Finsbury he said plainly that he thought members of Parliament should come before their constituencies more frequently to render an account of their doings and to be judged by them. He was not disposed to support the foolish demand of the Chartists for annual elections, an innovation which would have made the life of public men an unendurable nuisance, and would have destroyed all chances of individual action ; but he considered that triennial parliaments constituted the logical mean between the existing system and the demand soon to be formulated in the Charter. His motion to this effect never came on for debate in the House, being shelved, in spite of his protests, to make room for more urgent and pressing matters, but he had the courage of his convictions, for he persistently volunteered to offer himself every three years, or every session if they liked, to the electors of Finsbury, that they might ratify their choice or change their minds.

Wakley's avowed disrespect for one element of the British Constitution—viz., the House of Lords—and for such venerable institutions as the medical corporations, together with his close association in the work of reform with a great number of earnest Dissenters, had given rise to a popular belief that he desired the disestablishment of the national Church and even that he was a freethinker and an atheist. Undoubtedly he was a man with many enemies, for the fact that such was his reputation could only have been due to gross and purposed misrepresentation of facts. He was a regular churchgoer and had been brought up in strict observance of the ordinances of the Protestant faith. There was not in his life, public or private, one single thing that could have given even colour to the rumour that he was lax in his religious opinions save his attitude towards the Lord's Day Observance Bill. He objected to the entire closing of shops of all kinds on Sunday, and when the question was before the House in june, 1836, during a debate on Sir Andrew Agnew's Bill, prohibiting all open labour on Sunday except works of mercy or necessity, he contended that such universal and compulsory closing of shops was unfair to working men, who, being employed during the whole week, and in those days up till a late hour on Saturday night, were often unable to do their shopping on pay-nights. The public-houses were open, but at no other mart could a workman spend his money save over the publican's bar. It may with truth be claimed for Wakley that in some degree he was a pioneer in the movement which has been recently brought to a successful issue for opening museums and picture galleries on Sundays for the benefit of those who have no chance of seeing the nation's treasures at other times. Over sixty years ago Wakley inveighed against the narrow Sabbatarianism that thought it wicked to delight the eye and instruct the mind on the seventh day as "only another of the hydra heads of cant, sham, hypocrisy, privilege, and monopoly." He advocated in the House that the British Museum should be open on the days that work-men could visit it, such as holidays and Sundays, and objected to the monopoly of the Fellows of the Zoological Society or the proprietors of the Zoological Gardens, who enjoyed, as they still enjoy, the privilege of a Sunday ticket, while the working man was excluded on the only day when he could be present. It is difficult to believe that views so reasonable, even then so widely held and now so remark-ably endorsed, could ever have been tortured into dis-respect towards the Established Church, but they seem to be the only opinions that he ever held to which an honest section of the Church of England could have objected.

In the same year—viz., 1836—the attention of Parliament
was drawn to the barbarous practices attendant upon
flogging in the army. Wakley was fully conversant with the
subject, as the "Lancet" had several times related the
horrors which accompanied this form of military punishment.
Daniel O'Connell, in the course of a debate upon what was
known as the Mutiny Bill, pleaded for the entire abolition
of flogging. In this view the majority of military men and
the parliamentary representatives of garrison towns agreed
with him. Wakley protested indignantly against the practice. Was it intended, he asked, to punish insubordination
by death ? Surely not. Yet there were numerous cases of
men being flogged to death. In short, capital punishment
was of frequent occurrence for mere offences against discipline. He challenged any members in favour of this
degrading practice to avow their opinions on the subject
from the hustings and find out in that practical manner
what their constituents felt on the subject. He further
commented on the varying severity of the punishment. It
was not, he said, necessarily the number of strokes inflicted
which regulated the severity of the pain, but also the time
occupied in administering a flogging. He quoted the
terrible case of William Saundry, who had recently died
after being flogged at Woolwich, and demanded that the
House should be furnished with an official report of the
inquest in this and similar cases. He also used the significant words, "Ah, had there been a medical coroner !"—
significant because ten years later it was his duty as a
coroner to conduct an inquiry into a case where death had
followed upon military flogging, and he performed this duty
with such determination, eloquence, and furious anger that
he roused in the whole nation a feeling that the monstrous
custom must no longer exist under civilised laws. The
story of the death of Frederick White at Hounslow, as
revealed before Wakley the coroner, did what no efforts of
his or of O'Connell in the House of Commons could effect,
and it may truly be said that it gave Wakley an opportunity
for which he had long been waiting.

U

A Bill providing for the publication of lectures passed the House of Lords, also in 1836, without attracting much notice, but Wakley had more than one opportunity in the lower chamber of expressing his opinions upon it. It is certain that no member had a greater right to hold opinions and to express them in the matter, seeing that it was at his action in publishing Abernethy's lectures in the early numbers of the " Lancet " that the Bill was aimed. Wakley said that if the Bill was intended to apply generally to England unless proper amendments were introduced he should divide the House against the motion, for it seemed to him that it was intended, not only to prevent the publication of lectures, but of criticisms on lectures. Again, if it was intended to apply only to private lectures it would be a proper protection, but if it was intended to shield public as well as private lectures he should consider that it ought not to receive the sanction of the House. In the present state of the law no such protection was needed, for it had been laid down by Lord Eldon that private lectures could be protected if it were proved that there was a breach of implied contract between the lecturer and his individual hearers. In the case of Abernethy v. Hutchinson an injunction was granted to restrain the publication of lectures without any means of discovering whether the lectures in question were original or not—whether they were, in fact, fit subjects for copyright protection. Subsequently, however, it was proved in Chancery that Abernethy's lectures were public, being delivered on a public occasion and in a public capacity, the consequence of which was to deprive Abernethy of the protection and remedy he asked for. Wakley considered it absurd that such a Bill should pass the Lords without a word of discussion, and unless the Lord Advocate, who had charge of the measure in the Commons, assured him that public lecturers were not to be shielded from public notice he should divide the House against the Bill. Although Wakley was speaking here in defence of the principle which had dictated his own actions of thirteen years previously he was not really any longer concerned in a practical manner with the fate of the Bill, for the position of the "Lancet" had now much altered, and so far from hospital surgeons and lecturers issuing injunctions to restrain Wakley from publishing their words his reporters were given every facility, and in most cases the original MSS. were sent to the office before the delivery of the lectures. In fact, after the final decision of the protracted case of Abernethy v. Hutchinson, the heads of the medical profession decided to follow the lead originally given by Sir Astley Cooper and to admit the right of the medical public to hear their words. Wakley's protest in the House was made to defend his past conduct, not his present interests. It received no real support, only a few among his immediate colleagues promising to vote with him in favour of an amendment condemning the extension of copyright privileges to public lecturers. Seeing how much the feeling of the House was against his amendment Wakley did not press the matter to a division, but in committee he again uttered his protest. It was, however, without avail and the Bill was passed, on the motion of Lord John Russell, by twenty votes.

In August, 1836, we find Wakley supporting a motion brought forward by Mr. John Walter, the proprietor and manager of the "Times," and son of the founder of the paper, to inquire into the working of certain clauses in the Poor-law Amendment Act. . Wakley and Walter were friends, and although the "Times" occasionally commented very severely on the acts and sentiments of the member for Finsbury, we find the proprietor of the paper addressing Wakley in a letter as "Dear Friend," and asking him to call at Printing House Square on days that suit him "between four and nine in the evening—tea always at half-past eight." In his speech in support of Walter's motion Wakley quoted instances that had become known to him through the "Lancet" of insanitary workhouses, where the food was bad and the ventilation deficient, and said that the Poor-law Commissioners seemed to him—speaking not without knowledge of the subject—to desire to treat poverty as crime, and the pauper as a fit subject for penal environment. On

February 20th, 1837, he seconded Mr. Fielding's motion for the entire repeal of the Act. On this occasion he called attention to the fact that the new law had been put in practice in rural districts where the poor were ignorant and unorganised, but that in large towns its introduction had been delayed. As an example he mentioned the town of Nottingham, where in the preceding winter, according to one of the newspapers of the town, one-fifteenth of the population were on the parish, and £5000 had been raised by subscription to maintain the principle that no out-door relief should be given. Wakley spoke on other occasions against the working of the Act, his special charges against it being that the abolition of out-door relief was brutal to the rural poor, and that the workhouses into which they were driven were ill-constructed and ill-managed. But though he protested much from his place in the House against the Act, his best work in relation to Poor Law was done from the editorial chair. All the arguments that he used in Parliament were used again in the articles which culminated in the establishment of the "Lancet" Commission to inquire into the state of the sick poor in workhouses.

Wakley spoke at length in support of a resolution brought forward by Sir William Molesworth in the spring of 1837 to abolish the property qualification of members of Parliament, and he supported Daniel O'Connell on several occasions in his claim for Ireland of the right to, govern herself, notably during the debate on the Municipal Corporations (Ireland) Reform Bill.

In July, 1837, there was a general election, and Wakley was able to go to his constituents conscious of having justified their choice and of having established a right to ask for a continuance of their suffrages. For over and above the merits of his individual performances he had worked loyally for the cause of Reform in the most practical manner possible. During the last year, according to a useful little publication entitled "The Parliamentary Vote-Book or Election Guide," there had been sixty-nine principal questions before the House of Commons, " beginning with the election of the Speaker and ending with the Lords Amendments on the Municipal Corporation Reform Bill." On these sixty-nine questions Sir Robert Peel gave in all but twenty votes, Silk Buckingham gave thirty-two, O'Connell thirty-three, Hume thirty-five, Warburton forty-five, and Wakley fifty-one, the highest number in the book.

CHAPTER XXXIV

[1837-1841]

*Wakley Heads the Poll at his Second Election—Amendment to
Queen Victoria's First Speech from the Throne—His Attitude
towards Chartism—His Friendship with the Leading Chartists—
The Case of the Glasgow Cotton-spinners—Sir James Graham's
Vaccination Bill—Extra-mural Burial—Infanticide and Illegiti-
macy—General Radical Views—Wakley's Hatred of Lawyers.*

IN July, 1837, Wakley came before the electors of Finsbury
for the second time, a new Parliament having been summoned on the occasion of the death of King William IV.,
which took place at Windsor on june 20th. His election
address was very brief, consisting only of two or three .
sentences in which he avowed his intention of steering clear
of all profuse expenditure and electioneering intrigue, and
protested that he filled the part of member for Finsbury with
the keenest pleasure to himself, and not, he hoped, without
profit to his constituents. He concluded by referring to the
cordial assurances of support that he had received from all
parts of the borough.

Opposition, however, came from a place where it was
least expected. Mr. George Rogers, who had been the
chairman of Wakley's committee in all his previous contests,
successful and unsuccessful, for the representation of the
borough, and whose efforts in Wakley's behalf had been
sincere and exceedingly useful, suddenly announced his
absolute hostility to his quondam friend's re-election. The
exact cause of this defection does not appear, but that
Rogers was in a furious state of anger and jealousy there is
no doubt. He had counted for so much in the original

winning of the seat for Wakley that Wakley's progress in the House unsupported by him seemed to him to constitute profound ingratitude. He had meant to lead the member for Finsbury on a string, and he found that Wakley never responded to his little jerks. Rogers's opposition took the form of a pamphlet, in which he reviled Wakley as a breaker of pledges and a time-server. He wanted to hear the rant and fustian which he loved, and which Wakley had occasionally talked to mass meetings, shouted out in the House of Commons, and he saw in Wakley's attitude of moderation and observance of courtesy only sheer sycophancy. Before Wakley entered Parliament, complained Rogers, he had said that " he would glory in standing up alone in the House challenging corruption on its high altar and exposing it to the detestation of the country. . . . ." He had said that " his voice was too powerful to be put down by the 'ya, ya's' of puny beings whose brains were so pappy as to be unfit for the purposes even of dissection." But when he got into Parliament, so far from " challenging corruption on its high altar," he became " a member of the Reform Club and an associate of corruptionists." Poor Rogers did not effect much by his splenetic circular. He may possibly have caused Wakley a few qualms of regret for some of the more unbridled expressions that had been used by him on former occasions, but that he did not turn the hearts of many voters from their former allegiance was shown by the following result at the poll :—

Wakley	4957
Duncombe	4895
Perceval	2470

Wakley thus headed the poll, obtaining a majority of 2487 votes over his Tory opponent, who was Mr. Dudley Perceval nephew of Spencer Perceval, Bellingham's victim. This was the largest majority obtained by any candidate at this general election.

In the first Parliament of our reigning Sovereign Wakley's

earliest act was almost revolutionary. Never a Chartist either at heart or in profession he moved an amendment to the first speech of Queen Victoria from the Throne the tendency of which was very similar to that of much of the Chartist literature to appear a little later. His amendment was a resolution in favour of the ballot and of shorter duration of parliaments, but only twenty members voted with him. Wakley complained that the Ministry (Lord Melbourne's) had forgotten the fact that it had many Radical supporters, and spoke in favour of the ballot as giving working men a fair opportunity of choosing their own members and so of assuring themselves that their interests would be properly guarded. He described himself as a representative of labour having no connexion with any political circle or monopoly, and he called upon all other members who had secured a seven years' lease of the House through the popular vote to support his amendment. But Lord John Russell, the leader of the Liberal party in the Lower House, declared that he could not countenance any such attempts to re-open the questions that had been settled by the Reform Bill. Wakley was his own teller, and among the twenty who voted with him were Hume, Grote, Sir William Molesworth, and Duncombe.

Lord John Russell's declaration was received by many outside the walls of Parliament with open displeasure, for, especially in the manufacturing quarters, the people had been led to believe that the Reform Bill was only the pre-liminary step to further changes to be effected in the im-mediate future. That Lord John Russell was right from a party point of view is very probable, but his speech on this occasion led to developments that Liberal and Conservative leaders alike were soon to find very impatient of manage-ment. A conference was held almost immediately between certain Liberal members of Parliament and the heads of such organisations as were possessed by the working men. At this conference the claims of the working men were formulated, the following five things being demanded : (1) universal suffrage, (2) annual Parliaments, (3) payment of members, (4) abolition of property qualification for Parliamentary candidates, and (5) vote by ballot. O'Connell is said to have had the fortunate inspiration of giving this programme the name of "The Charter," and at once the movement was launched that was to lead to ten years of trouble. Wakley's connexion with the Chartists was never close. He was one of the Liberal members present at the meeting when the people's demands were first defined. This was only to be expected, as it was his speech that had led up to the meeting and he was avowedly in sympathy with all popular aspirations towards self-government ; but there his relations with this luckless movement ceased. He acknowledged the right of the people to be discontented, and was ready to be their mouth-piece in giving vigorous expression to the bitter suffering that was rife among artisan and labouring folk alike, but with the methods of the Chartists he could not go. He did not believe that their agitation would come to any practical ends. He thought that the leaders had begun wrongly in stirring up an agitation outside Parliament. His panacea for wide-spread political and social wrongs was proper representation of the people within the House, and he considered that triennial parliaments would secure this. By meeting their representatives more frequently and having more opportunities of ratifying their choice the people could ensure having their interests attended to. When a parliament had been chosen in which a majority of honest men was really pledged to the cause of the people the essential demands of the Charter would follow as a matter of course. Wakley considered that the programme of Chartism was overloaded and unpractical. He foresaw the enrolment under its flag of all sorts and conditions of malcontents, and he absolutely refused to take any personal part in the proceedings. No effort was spared by Mr. George Attwood, who presented the petition of the Chartists to the House, and Feargus O'Connor, editor of the "Northern Star" and the most eloquent and hot-headed of the leaders, to secure his presence at some of their meetings, but he was resolute in keeping aloof. He was certain that

the Chartists, by asking too much and in an unwisely dicta-
torial manner, would prevent the true sufferers from obtaining
their just demands while effecting nothing themselves. At
the same time his sympathies were in favour of a constitutional
agitation for several of the demands of the Chartists.

When Attwood presented to the House the great petition
of the Chartists begging for the appointment of a commission
to inquire into the Charter Wakley spoke eloquently in its
favour. This petition bore more than a million and a
quarter signatures, and although drawn up on narrow strips
of parchment and tightly rolled is described as having been
as big as a large coach wheel. The ponderous document
was rolled up the floor of the House by two officials and lay
between the benches while Attwood explained its tenor in
politic phrases. He toned down the vehement pleadings
and party cries, deprecated the use of force among his
followers, and disclaimed all illicit armament, incendiarism,
and violence. Lord John Russell, representing the Government, moved the rejection of Attwood's motion and attempted
with more or less success to show that the grievances of
the masses were overstated. In so doing he referred to
the condition of the agricultural labourers of Devonshire,
and declared his disbelief in the pictures that had been
drawn of their plight, " for he himself was concerned in the
affairs of that county." Wakley at once gave some terrible
details of privation and suffering drawn from his personal
knowledge as the son of a Devonshire farmer. His picture
of the lives of some of these field-slaves, who toiled from
sunrise to sunset in all weathers for a paltry wage of seven
shillings a week, and after long hours of effort under a
scorching sun or in a bleak easterly drizzle slept in sheds,
barns, and outhouses in the garments they had worn throughout the day, bore the stamp upon it of terrible truth.
Disraeli, then sitting in his first Parliament as member for
Maidstone, and Daniel O'Connell both voted in support of
some parts of the petition, but the motion was defeated by a
crushing majority.

For those leaders among the Chartists whose irregular

advocacy of what they believed to be the just cause of the people brought them within the grip of legal punishment Wakley had a very soft spot in his heart. Their fate was only what he had predicted for them, and their combination against the law had been broken down exactly as he had foreseen that it would be, but he never forgot that many of their tenets were his tenets. When Feargus O'Connor was incarcerated in York Castle on the charge of seditious libel he turned to Wakley for help in his trouble. He was from his own point of view treated with unnecessary severity—in fact, the conditions of his imprisonment seem to have been open to quite as much question as were the conditions of the Kilmainham prisoners in more modern times. Wakley responded at once and proceeded to heckle the Government persistently on the subject, making Mr. Fox Maule (afterwards Earl of Dalhousie), the Under Secretary of State for the Home Department, and a personal as well as political friend of his own, his special victim.. He displayed similar zeal in behalf of Henry Vincent, who was confined in Millbank, and Collins and Levett, who were imprisoned at Warwick. The severity meted out to the latter pair caused the two members for Finsbury to move and second a motion asking for a full and particular inquiry into their cases. Duncombe, who proposed the motion, made in his speech a masterly arraignment of the policy of coercion. Wakley's speech was rather fervid than argumentative, and Disraeli supported the motion, but the result of the division was that only 29 voted for the motion and 117 against it. So much for Wakley's connexion with the Chartists. He was sympathetic, and that was all. He considered their methods wrong and foolish, and refused to allow his judgment to be warped by his sympathy.

On February 12th, 1838, Wakley spoke on a breach of privilege motion, because the daily papers, in reporting certain petitions before the House, omitted to mention the petition presented by him having reference to certain Glasgow cotton-spinners, a combination of whom having been found guilty of intent to murder in some trades' union disputes had been sentenced to seven years' penal servitude. On the following day Wakley made a vigorous speech in behalf of these men. From the character of the evidence brought forward against them he said that a full inquiry into the nature and doings of the Cotton-spinners' Association must be held. He had given notice of two resolutions which he desired to bring forward ; he would, however, only ask the House to consider one of them— one pleading for delay. To this step he was prompted by mere prudence. He urged the Government not to transport these men until the whole affair had been thoroughly investigated. He expressed an opinion that any high-handedness or severity on the part of the authorities would be taken by the working classes at large as an evidence of hostility and would be fraught with the gravest danger to the institutions of the country. His intercession at the time led to nothing, but it made him for the next two years the channel for the transmission to the House of numerous petitions in favour of leniency towards the convicts, who were ultimately reprieved in July, 1840. The remission of their sentences was probably due to the uncertainty of the law in respect of trade combination, for however provoked these men may have been by the hard terms of their masters, however inflamed by incendiary speeches, and however innocent of wicked intent, the fact remains that they were found guilty of molesting certain fellow workmen who had accepted terms in opposition to the dictates of the union, one of whom died from his injuries. The crime was not a light one, and the House, well aware of the terrible catastrophes that had occurred in many manufacturing districts, in Birmingham notably, on account of collision between the workmen, the masters, and what are now termed the blacklegs, could hardly have been expected to release the convicts immediately. To many it will seem that the seven years' transportation originally allotted to them was not an excessive penalty, and no one will consider the two years that they actually experienced to have been other than their desert.

During the next three years until the beginning of 1841 purely medical matters were not much before the House, whose attention, it may be readily understood, was sufficiently engrossed by the reactionary wave following the Reform Bill, by the turbulence of the Chartists following that reactionary wave, by the ever-green troubles of Ireland, and by the anti-Corn Law agitation now beginning to assume serious proportions. In June, 1840, Sir James Graham's Vaccination Bill came on for discussion. Speaking on this Bill, Wakley stated that in its existing form the poorer classes had a great objection to such a piece of legislation. They did not approve of the working of the Bill being put into the hands of the Poor-law Commissioners. As the Bill at that time ran, the persons appointed to vaccinate were the Poor-law medical officers and these only. Wakley argued that each person ought to be allowed to employ his own medical man if he so desired ; otherwise this Bill gave too much power to the Poor-law officer. He moved an amendment to this effect, but the division did not altogether encourage him, 39 only voting for the amendment and 56 for the Bill as it stood. Undismayed, however, he maintained, when the next clause came up for discussion, that the Bill tended to pauperise the working classes, and this time he contrived to get the words " with medical officers appointed by the boards of guardians or with any other legally qualified medical practitioner or practitioners" inserted. He thus effectually vindicated the right of ordinary practitioners to become vaccinators under the Act. Wakley also secured the necessary support for an amendment making it a penal offence to inoculate with small-pox, or to expose persons intentionally to infection. This amendment was accepted without opposition.

Early in 1841 several matters of medical interest were before the House, and in each debate Wakley took a prominent part, being by this time a person to whose views official position lent much weight. Earlier in his parliamentary career, although his tact and unexpected moderation of language, as well as his obvious belief in the views to which he gave expression, had ensured for him respectful attention, he could only quote experience as the editor of a new and very revolutionary journal. He now spoke in the position of Coroner for Middlesex, to which post he had been elected in 1839, and of editor of a journal that was becoming accepted week by week with increasing uniformity as the organ of the profession at large. Consequently on measures concerning the relations of the medical profession to the public, whenever such relations were under discussion, he could talk with the double authority of a practical man and a man who was in a famous position for theorising.

A measure aimed against the burying of the dead in the overcrowded churchyards of the cities was brought forward at this time. In some of the most densely packed districts of London this was still the custom, while a strong prejudice existed against distant graveyards and suburban cemeteries. The popular sentiment that a man should be buried where he had lived, worked, and died is a feeling that is not extinguished, and one against which the utilitarian will probably war for some time in vain, but Wakley spoke relentlessly against it. His medical knowledge and special information as coroner gave a point to his speeches, and he treated the House to some plain speaking against the prolongation of a system by which the dead poisoned the living.

Another subject with which his position as coroner gave him a special right to deal in the House was infanticide in its relation to illegitimacy. Illegitimacy was on the increase in the early forties to an alarming extent. This, he said, was the direct consequence of the misery and distress prevalent among the labouring classes. The peasant or artisan who could look forward with any certainty to secure wages, and wages high enough to enable him to support a wife and family, was, he contended, an unknown person in Great Britain. The consequence of this inability to contract regular unions with any ordinary prudence was necessarily an increase of illegitimacy, and this increase of illegitimacy coincided, as it always must, with an increase of infanticide.

This sequence brought Wakley round to his favourite stand-point—that laws against consequences must be useless, and must serve only as an irritant of the conditions they would remove. Causes, primal causes, must always be attacked by the thorough-going legislator. General legislation for the working classes, improvement in their wages, the cheapening of their food, and the provision of a sanitary environment in their homes were the only possible means that any rational man would attempt to provide for the prevention of the increase of such a crime as infanticide and such moral delinquency as the illicit propagation of the species.

Of the numerous topics during these three years on which Wakley spoke as a consistent supporter of a general progressive programme only the briefest mention need be made. He was a Reformer as he understood the word, and when the topics are mentioned the direction of his vote and the tenor of his speeches may be at once guessed. It is needless to say that he spoke in favour of the equalisation of taxation of property of all kinds and against all sinecures and hereditary pensions. Where such opinions brought the position of the House of Lords or certain members of that House into discussion his remarks on that institution were not laudatory. He does not appear to have held definite views with regard to any reform that he desired to see in the Upper House, but he did not desire its abolition. Indeed, he spoke on one occasion against this radical suggestion, evidently believing that a revising chamber of some sort was necessary to the Constitution, although he did not approve of the one that was set over the deliberations in which he was taking part. He objected to the hasty adjournment of the House over long holidays at Easter and Whitsuntide when public business was in arrears. He inveighed against the way in which political prisoners were treated, considering as political offenders the leaders of the Chartists and Irish Repeal movements. He displayed great activity on Supply, examining and criticising the votes on Royal Palaces with a fervour learned from Hume, and with a detail which might even now be commended to the attention of the senior member for Northampton. He bitterly compared the reckless expenditure on plumbing at Buckingham Palace with the niggardly way in which the Government considered the wide-spread distress among the labouring poor.

Many of Wakley's speeches during this period present one curious feature which should be noticed. They abound with derogatory allusions to lawyers and the legal profession. On July 26th, 1839, shortly after he had been elected coroner, a measure was before the House with regard to the appointment of Metropolitan Police Magistrates. A clause requiring these officials to be " barristers of seven years' high standing" attracted Wakley's attention. " Why," he asked, "should lawyers be of necessity the persons whose duty it should be to inquire into matters of common sense and justice ? There are no men to be met with in society so utterly destitute of common sense as lawyers." A barrister took up the cudgels for his profession and accounted for Wakley's dislike of lawyers by the fact that he was a non-legal coroner and feared that he might be ousted to make room for a lawyer. He also criticised Wakley's attitude towards Lord Chief Justice Best after judgment had been given against him upon the plaint of Mr. Tyrrell* as unbecoming. But this did not deter Wakley from continuing to allude to lawyers in a persistently uncomplimentary strain. In 1840, on the debate with regard to the salary of an Admiralty judge to be appointed to deal especially with Admiralty cases, the Bill (a Government one) fixed the salary for this official at £4000. Joseph Hume (then no longer member for Middlesex, but the representative of Kilkenny, to which seat he had been elected on the recommendation of Daniel O'Connell) moved that the sum be reduced by £1000. In this economical resolve he was supported by Wakley, whose arguments against the proposed salary were not economic, albeit he described the emolument as " disgracefully lavish," but were based on an assumption of the general incompetency of the legal profession. " Whatever the skill of the

* See Chapter XIII.

man may be," he said, " no lawyer is, or in my opinion ever will be, worth more than £3000 a year." On April 29th, 1840, we find him speaking in the same vein. He strongly objected to the Juvenile Offenders Bill in the form that it was then offered for the consideration of the House. The Bill provided power of summary jurisdiction for three magistrates ostensibly to save the juvenile offender from the contamination of evil communications when awaiting trial. Wakley did not deem such summary jurisdiction necessary, for he held that a boy of fourteen was entitled to be tried by a jury, " who would be more likely to look upon his case from a humane view than a magistrate." In summing up the character of the country justices of the peace on this occasion Wakley employed terms as sweeping as unjust : " A more incompetent body of men can nowhere be found. . . . . A body of men more characterised by ill-temper, faction, and the most besotted ignorance cannot be found than the magistrates of this country." In the same year he made an important speech in qualified support of the County Coroners Bill, now in charge of Mr. Somerset Pakington, when he protested against the power given to magistrates ; and his numerous speeches during this and the following years with relation to the powers and doings of the Poor-law Commissioners had almost entirely the same bearing. His criticisms were directed against the giving of too much power to these Commissioners and to magistrates.

Wakley had been on the whole successful in his legal struggles, and was himself learned in the law, so that his dislike of a lawyer must be regarded as unreasonable though it was none the less strong and sincere.

CHAPTER XXXV

[1841-1845]

Wakley's Third Election—Re-elected for Finsbury Unopposed—His Consistently Liberal Views—The Debate on Lord Mahon's Copyright Bill—Wakley ridicules the Claims of Authors—Wakley's Personal Appearance at this Time—" Punch " and its Criticisms of Wakley—Tom Hood speaks for Authors—Death of Mr. Henry Wakley of Membury—The Game Laws—A Fracas in the House—Mr. Wodehouse apologises—The great· Courtesy of Sir Robert Peel.

IN 1841 the long Melbourne Ministry came to an end—an ignominious end, for a direct vote of want of confidence was carried against the Government.   Wakley submitted himself for re-election to the borough of Finsbury, and was returned unopposed.   He neither canvassed nor issued any lists of his supporters, nor did he, either directly or indirectly, countenance the solicitation of votes for him by others.   He signified to his constituency through a small committee of local men his willingness to serve the borough again in Parliament if his services in the past were considered to justify his re-election.   Upon being nominated he addressed the constituency in three or four different localities, once in each locality.   In the course of these speeches he first pledged himself to be invariably true to the general Radical progressive programme as his constituents had formulated it in their original letter inviting him to become their member.   He then pointed out the view that such a general programme would compel him to take of the more important matters impending in public affairs and in the cause of medical reform.   Lastly, he recalled to the electors the fact that he was in Parliament to serve them more especially, though in general politics he was pledged to a general attitude, and he desired to know what their views were, firstly, on such matters as concerned all men, secondly, on such particular matters as concerned the denizens of Finsbury. This confidence in his electorate proved admirable policy, as his seat was never challenged from 1837 until his resignation in 1852, a fact which was most remarkable in 1841, when the muddling and shilly-shallying of Lord Melbourne's Government led to a notable victory for the Tories under Sir Robert Peel. Neither the Tory reaction nor the fact that Wakley had allowed himself to criticise his leaders jeopardised his position with his supporters.

During the next ten years, that is, from 1841 until the commencement of 1852, Wakley's attendance at the House was assiduous, while he served on a large number of important committees. He was, however, no longer so frequent a speaker. This was not because he was less ardent in his championship of the causes that he had taken under his particular care, but because the Tory Government of Sir Robert Peel and its successor, the Opportunist Government of Lord John Russell, offended his particular susceptibilities —doubtless now grown a little blunter—less than the Whig Government of Lord Melbourne had done. Many of the topics, to which allusion has already been made as engaging the attention of Parliament between 1837 and 1841, remained in an unsettled condition during the next decade, and deferred Bills or amended Bills dealing with them came before the House with regularity. On various public health matters, such as the establishment of public municipal abattoirs and the prevention of intra-mural burials, Wakley was several times heard. The Chartist agitation was alive, and where the demands of its promoters could be met by constitutional means in the House Wakley's voice was ever ready. He presented numerously signed petitions complaining of the treatment to which the political prisoners, as he insisted upon regarding them, were subjected in provincial gaols, and on one occasion, when supporting Duncombe in a motion for a committee to inquire into the condition of convicts, he inveighed against the persecution of political malcontents. But he remained as resolute as heretofore not to be dragged into any position that could be interpreted as unconstitutional opposition to the laws of his country. He had on more than one occasion to speak in favour of the ballot, and whenever he did so his remarks were worth listening to, for his belief that open voting often resulted in the return of the weaker candidate was very implicit and generally found vent in amusing terms. His dislike to the legal profession was exhibited in such various forms as a speech against the granting of pensions to Lord Chancellors, a disagreement with Lord Ashley (the philanthropic Earl of Shaftesbury) whose championship of the rights of children he strenuously backed, on the question of the appointment of legal Lunacy Commissioners, and numerous speeches against the acts and methods of the Poor-law commissioners. On one occasion he stigmatised the average unpaid provincial magistrate as "an incompetent oaf," and at all times and in all places he displayed towards the legal profession the curious intolerance already alluded to.

In April, 1842, what is known as Lord Mahon's Copyright Bill came on for discussion in the House. Without mentioning various small Acts dealing with replicas of sculpture, with dramatic rights, and with the publication of engravings, the copyright law of the kingdom was at that time administered under an Act passed at the end of the reign of George III. (1814, 54 Geo. III. c. 156). This Act gave copyright in books for a term of twenty-eight years certain and the residue of the life of the author. Lord Mahon's Bill provided for the extension of the term of copyright to forty-two years certain, and proposed, also, to extend it beyond the life of the author should he be living at the end of that term. The measure was substantially the same as Serjeant Talfourd's Bill, which had been introduced into Parliament in 1836 by the learned and eloquent author of " Ion," and had for its worthy object the consolidation or amendment of the law relating to literary and artistic property of all sorts, the extension of the term of copyright in such property, and the provision of penal clauses in protection of the privileges of the legal owners of the same. Serjeant Talfourd's Bill had been shelved, one of the most relentless of its critics having been Wakley, who held that the attempt to protect the author would militate against the interests of the printer, the publisher, and the people without doing the protected producer any good whatever. When Lord Mahon (afterwards Earl Stanhope) Under Secretary of State for Foreign Affairs undertook the conduct of Serjeant Talfourd's Bill he found in Wakley the same bitter opponent. The Bill came on for second reading on April 6th, 1842, and a protracted debate ensued. The proposer of the motion was followed by Macaulay, who in no very enthusiastic way enforced the claims of authors. Wakley, in the course of a long speech designed to bring the claims of authors into ridicule, recited Wordsworth's most namby-pamby poems, " I met Louisa in the Shade," and the same poet's " Address to a Butterfly." " Give a poet an evening sky, dew, withering leaves, and a rivulet and he would make a very respectable poem always," said Wakley. This remark was greeted with much laughter. " Why, anybody might do it ! " (Laughter and cries of " Try it.") " Try it ! Why, he had tried it (great laughter), and there (pointing to Monckton-Milnes) is an honourable gentleman who has also tried it and is a poet of the first water," and he continued by challenging the first Lord Houghton to disagree with his estimate of much that was written. " I myself could string such compositions together by the bushel. I could write them by the mile." Wakley's speech was really more a running stream of badinage than the unfolding of a serious argument. His general thesis was that authors got quite enough already, but he did not bring forward much logic to prove it. He questioned the worth of the labours of an author compared with those of a scientific man. Yet the latter's work was unprotected and freely accrued to the public good. He declared that Milton, Bacon, and Shakespeare had worked and made their greatest efforts more for honour than gain. " Cannot authors of the present day," he concluded by asking, " be stimulated to such exertions as had been made by these men without being allowed to thrust their hands into the pockets of the people ? "

Monckton-Milnes, in spite of the flattering allusion to himself, severely blamed the manner in which Wakley had treated the subject in selecting for quotation as samples the weakest works of so admirable a poet as Wordsworth. He considered the tone and manner in which the member for Finsbury had held up Wordsworth to the ridicule of the House in bad taste. Some curious divisions on different amendments then followed, more than one being carried against Lord Mahon. One of the essential principles of the Bill was attacked in an attempt made to amend out of it the principle that copyright should run under certain circumstances after the author's death for the good of his surviving family. Lord Mahon, defeated on one such provision, proposed the insertion of a clause providing for the sanctity of copyright for seven years after the death of the author, should this make up a longer period than forty-two years. The possessor of the copyright was to have protection for forty-two years certain or for life and seven years more, whichever was the longer term. This was opposed by Macaulay, but carried by Lord Mahon by 91 votes against 23. Wakley was, of course, in the " No " lobby. Macaulay himself, however, proposed that the extended term should be " forty-two years certain." This was opposed by Wakley and Villiers, among others, but was carried by 96 to 17. In no less than three of the divisions on this stage of the Bill, Wakley acted as teller, while Gladstone and Disraeli both spoke. Macaulay virtually moulded the Bill.

Wakley's view of the copyright question was certainly inspired by his close acquaintance with one side of it only. He had been bitterly attacked for infringing Abernethy's copyright by the publication of the surgical lectures in the " Lancet." He had defended his action, successfully as it happened, on the grounds that lectures spoken in public capacity ought to be printed for the public good. He now tried to bring this principle home to all literary and artistic productions, dividing the output of the author and the artist into two classes—the bad, which could not be reasonably protected, and the good, which reflected such honour upon, and perhaps brought such profit to, its creator that it would be ridiculous to give him a long monopoly in its sale or to bring any hereditary principles to bear upon it, lest either process of protection should debar the public from profit.

It can be readily believed that many authors did not approve of the way in which their claims were thus coolly set aside, and the press was very unanimous in finding Wakley's arguments faulty and his attack upon Wordsworth a grave error in manners. "Punch' made immense capital of so inviting a theme. The great satirical journal was founded on July 17th, 1841, and seems to have seen at once in Wakley an excellent object for attack. The reason for this is obvious. Wakley was well-known throughout England by name, but in London, where the "London Charivari" expected to obtain its principal circulation, he was by this time an exceedingly familiar personality. As editor, coroner, political reformer, and energetic vestryman he was known by hearsay to the whole metropolis and by sight to a very large number of persons—to more persons, in fact, than other men of equal distinction in public affairs—for he was not a man who could be passed in the street unnoticed. All who saw Thomas Wakley striding along in the streets in his attempt to keep pace with his over-numerous engagements asked who he was, and once seen his was a figure and face not easily to be forgotten. Tall, erect, square-shouldered, and perfectly proportioned—a man of bulk, but yet of lightness—his frame bore the proofs of his great muscular strength and of his incessantly active life. His clean-shaven, florid face was replete with expression, the mouth always critical, whether smiling approval or sternly set in anger or concentrated thought, and the resolute blue eye was alive to all that was presented to its gaze. His golden hair, worn in natural and lengthy clusters nearly down to his coat

collar, was fine and waved in the little breeze that his
energetic and springy gait stirred up around him. To this
sketch the detail must be added that he was always
elaborately dressed in the fashion of the day, which fashion
allowed of some personal splendour. The long surtout
with its rolled velvet collar, the low-cut flowered waistcoat,
revealing the spotless frills of a shirt got up in the days of
country bleaching grounds and manual wringing, the lofty-
crowned beaver and the nankeen trousers of a gentleman of
the " forties " presented a gorgeous picture which the gentleman of these more restrained days cannot aspire to emulate.
Wakley was undoubtedly in 1841 one of the most widely
known men in London, so that in satirising him " Punch "
had an easy task, for everyone knew whom the joke was aimed
at. Yet it was a tribute to his importance that " Punch " in
an initial volume should have chosen him for an object of
satire.

Save in one instance—the instance of Wakley's views on
copyright—" Punch " was not very happy in setting any
mark of ridicule upon Wakley. In 1841 Wakley was
suspected of leaning towards the Conservatives and especially
towards Sir Robert Peel. This was because, as has been
seen, in the matter of reform he did not consider that Lord
John Russell was prepared to go far enough or Lord
Melbourne to move quick enough, while he held that the
Chartists desired to go a great deal too far and too quick.
This critical attitude offended certain members of each
section of the Radical party, who, in hunting about for some
stick to throw at the object of their temporary dislike, hit
upon a droll accusation that Peel had been approached by
Wakley with a view to office. This was the point of
" Punch's " joke against Wakley—that, being a well-known
Radical, he was at heart a Tory, or prepared from motives
of self-interest to become one. Hence we find Wakley
described as out of place and inserting an advertisement
for any light job in the hope that it may catch the eye of Sir
Robert Peel or Lord Stanley. Again, we see him depicted
as the seducer of Norma and her fellow-vestal in Bellini's

Engraved by W. H. Egleton, from a painting by K. Meadows, Esq.

Thomas Wakley

opera of that name, which had but recently been heard for the first time in London. Lord Melbourne is the deserted Norma and Sir Robert Peel the newer love. These jokes, though neatly made, were unfair, because they grossly misinterpreted Wakley's political attitude, holding up his very sensible moderation as cynical self-seeking.

But Wakley's speech on the copyright question furnished " Punch " with a better opportunity. Here Wakley had evidently blundered. He had dismissed the claims of . authors cavalierly and on insufficient grounds, he had spoken contemptuously of Wordsworth whose years if not his fame should have protected him from such treatment, and, of course in joke, he had suggested that he could write bushels and miles of such stuff himself. " Punch" fastened on the assertion and announced the appearance of " Wakley's Warbler, being Finsbury Fragments by a Coroner," and gave as an imaginary specimen of Wakley's muse the following lines :—

"TO MY LOVE.

" The sun upgetting, The dews at setting,
The leafy treeses, The murmuring breezes,
The kisses glowing, The glances knowing,
The girls all crying, The men all lying ;
They move the heart so That I can't part so ;
And ere I know it I shine a poet.
O Amaryllis, Or Rose or Phillis,
Or as it may be My Poll or Phœbe,
Don't be so cruel, My darling jewel,
Come on not slackly, * * * * *
—Madam, your servant to command,

J. (*sic*) WAKLEY."

Tom Hood among authors stood up for his order in one of the latest essays that came from his pen. His kindly reproof of Wakley will be found in a volume entitled "Whimsicalities" which appeared two years before his death. Hood alludes thus to Wakley's facetious claim that he could write such stuff by the mile and string it together by the bushel :—

" Hark thee, Thomas. . . . . It must often have puzzled editors to account for the deluge of poetry, so-called, which of late years has poured into the Balaam-boxes of the periodicals. Indeed, there is no magazine or literary journal but from time to time has had to announce the utter impossibility of returning such contributions to the authors— just such an impossibility as beset Mrs. Partington when she attempted to send back the Atlantic. For our own part the phenomenon has been a standing wonder, as month after month [Hood speaks as editor of the " New Monthly Magazine "] we found our library table covered with fresh verse-rhyme enough to fill whole magazines. *Where* could it all come from? What sort of laborious creatures could thus keep spin, spin, spinning on, without profit and without encouragement, for not a hundredth—no, not a thousandth part obtained insertion. The mystery, however, is solved. The deluge of bad poetry, the rush of rhyme is accounted for, and editors in future will be able to attribute any extraordinary high tide of sing-song to its true source. Astounding as it may seem, considering his multifarious occupations as Member of Parliament, Coroner, and Editor of a medical work, yet by his own confession, during the debate on the Copyright Bill, Mr. Wakley, besides spouting, sitting on bodies, and ' Lancet '-guiding, has actually been composing poetry—not by the page or sheet, but by the standard mile and imperial bushel. It would of course be impossible to trace all the effusions of such a very prolific versifier; but personally we are convinced that we have been favoured with at least a few pecks, and rods, poles or perches of the manufacture of this new Thomas the Rhymer. All the anonymous pieces were his, of course, as well as those signed T. or W., and we venture to attribute to the same hand, on internal evidence, a few furlongs of poetry that have been sent under other initials."

The following are a few examples of the wide range of subjects on which Wakley considered that he had a mandate to speak in this Parliament, because anyone who aspired to be a typical exponent of progressive Radicalism must have an opinion on each and all of the points involved. On the question of enclosing common lands, which was under debate in April, 1842, he was naturally one of those who insisted on the right to enquire into the titles by which many of the territorial class possessed land enclosed by them but really dedicated to the public in former centuries by use and custom. It was a question with the details of which he was familiar, owing to the fact that his father, Mr. Henry Wakley of Membury, had been a Com-

missioner under the Act and a very prompt and thorough-
going official. Mr. Wakley, senior, was at this date still alive
and, although he had reached the great age of ninety-two,
was in full possession of his faculties and able to render
practical assistance to his son out of his reminiscences. It
may be mentioned here that he died after a very short
illness on August 26th of this year.

On certain points arising out of the by-laws existent at the
Customs Offices Wakley spoke in 1842. He was always
anxious that the food of the people should be as lightly
taxed as possible, and above all fairly taxed, for it was one
of his standing arguments that material happiness led to
moral rectitude as surely as moral rectitude led to the keeping of the law. He pointed out with a precision of detail
unfamiliar to those who had not enjoyed the advantage of
being born in a cider county that the dues on apples should
not be entirely assessed by bulk. Unripe crab-apples could
hardly be considered as equal in value to the same bulk of
ribston-pippins, and he thought the House should attend
to these matters, which were not such trifles to the poor
consumer as they might seem.

In 1844 he is found vigorously supporting Duncombe,
who presented a petition from Joseph Mazzini protesting
against the action of Sir James Graham in opening letters
addressed to Mazzini and his friends. The contents of these
letters were alleged to have been communicated to Austria
and so to have led to the death of certain of Mazzini's
fellow-conspirators abroad, and it was felt by many, without
need for expression of any opinion upon Mazzini's aspirations or tactics, that the proceeding complained of was an
unworthy one.

On the question of the Game Laws Wakley felt strongly,
and in 1845 he spoke in favour of John Bright's motion for
the appointment of a Commission to enquire into their
working. He presented numerous petitions on the subject,
and took part in several rather heated debates, for the landlords were resentful of any attempt to enquire into their
privileges or into the scale of punishment meted out to

those who infringed those privileges. All his life long
Wakley had been an ardent sportsman. He was the son of
sportsmen. He had shot much as a boy, and the very first
use he had made of his prosperity was to purchase a property which allowed him to practise his favourite form of
sport. At the time of John Bright's motion Wakley was the
possessor of a fine sporting estate at Harefield Park in the
county of Middlesex on the banks of the River Colne, and
four miles from Uxbridge, where he was in the habit of
spending every minute that he could spare from his
numerous parliamentary, official, and editorial duties, and
where he was a strict preserver of game. In supporting
John Bright in his attempts to obtain the remission of
penalties for poaching Wakley had some difficulty, therefore, in showing that his attitude was consistent. He was
twitted in the House by Lord Robert Grosvenor (afterwards
Lord Ebury) with being himself an ardent votary of the
sport, which could not be supported without the rigid
enforcement of the very laws an inquiry into the working of
which he was prepared to demand. Wakley replied by
admitting to the House that he was a preserver of game, but
gave at the same time an example of his treatment of
poachers. He said that he would not allow anyone to
steal his pheasants, but that he would always feed a hungry
man, and that the peasantry around Harefield were aware of
this and preferred to go up to the house and ask for food to
committing a felony. As a matter of fact, though Wakley
modestly did not take the House into his confidence, it was
quite well known throughout the country-side that he prosecuted poachers rigidly, but that, also, he invariably supported the wife and family of the married delinquent
until that person, having paid the legal penalty, was free
to look after his family himself. Nobody is strictly logical,
and Wakley's conduct in these matters would certainly not
have stood the test of a rational scrutiny ; but at any rate he
showed himself to be no hypocrite of Butler's sort, for if he
compounded with the sin of game-preserving he damned it
at the same time.

For an aggressive man, which he undoubtedly was, Wakley's demeanour in the House was singularly ingratiating. It is easy for a man of colourless views or lymphatic temperament so to order his words and actions that they shall never give personal offence, and it is doubly easy for one who is lukewarm in his convictions. But Wakley was an ardent and thorough politician holding views on many points that were black in hue to the Tory glance, and gloriously rosy to his own; consequently he was not without his moments of extreme provocation. But he always kept his temper perfectly under control, and in the only fracas with which he was associated in Parliament he was the justly offended party.

In July, 1844, during one of the ever recurring debates on the Poor-law Amendment Act the subject of rural incendiarism in the eastern counties came under discussion. Wakley tried to point out that these offences usually occurred in parts of the country where the educational standard was low and where squiredom was supreme. He referred especially to Norfolk. Mr. Edmond Wodehouse, a Norfolk man and one of the members for that county, hotly protested against this attack on landlords and said that there were other places where incendiarism was not unknown, as the hon. member for Finsbury could tell them himself. Wakley rose and said: "I have been a member of this House for nine years, and during that time I do not recollect that any hon. member has had occasion to complain of any personal remarks made by me upon him. My object has always been to confine myself to the question before the House and never to utter a single word that should give any individual offence. I cannot say that the same conduct has always been extended to me. But when hon. gentlemen permit themselves to descend in the course of discussions on public affairs to refer to the private life of other hon. members and to cast imputations upon them in those relations, that is a course so contrary to the honour and dignity of the House that, being pursued, it becomes the duty of the member so referred to to require an explanation in the presence of the House. It has occurred to me in the course of the discussion in Committee on this Bill to make some observations on the state of education in Norfolk and Suffolk—did I not also (added Wakley stopping and turning to the member sitting on the bench beside him) allude to Middlesex ? For I had no intention to make any invidious distinctions in the matter ; I had no intention in the remarks I made to suggest any reflection upon any individual whatever. Sir, I have had during my life some difficulties to contend with. I came to this town unknowing and unknown. I fought my own battle, not always an easy one, and I have a family of children— sons. The remarks which the hon. member for Norfolk used at the conclusion of his speech were these—I am certain of them, for I took them down at the time—' No one is more capable of giving an opinion on the subject of incendiarism than the hon. member for Finsbury himself.' Now it seems too horrible to suppose such a thing as that the hon. member intended these words to apply personally to me ; that any hon. member in the House, without being provoked by any remark of mine, should apply such remarks to me. I know that every man who has been engaged in the work of Reform as I have been must be prepared for attacks on his public character ; but I was not prepared for an unfair attack on my private character in this House. I never fought a battle unfairly in my life. There is not an act of my life from the first moment of my existence that I would not court inquiry into. And if any gentleman wishes to go into such an inquiry I will give him every facility in my power for pursuing the inquiry in the most minute details. Sir, these observations were applied to me publicly in this House ; and if I did not dare to ask for an explanation of their meaning and to court investigation of their truth I should not dare to enter these walls again. I could not again presume to face this body of honourable gentlemen. I am therefore quite ready to go into an inquiry into the matter to which it is possible the words of the honourable member may refer. I have nothing to fear from inquiry ; but I have everything to fear from insinuation when insinuation is made the vehicle of the foulest calumny that was ever cast upon the character of any man. At all events, there is but one proper mode in which I should deal with this matter. I do not intend to make this matter the subject for private quarrel or dispute with the hon. member, for I have nothing to fear from publicity. I think I have the right to ask the hon. member what meaning he attached to the words I have read to the House, as applied to me ; and before I call upon him to do so I will state to the House the circumstances to which I believe they were intended to refer. Sir, it happened that I had the misfortune once to have my house burned. I brought an action against the insurance company in which I was insured for the loss. They resisted that action, it went for trial, and the result of that trial was that every farthing which I went against the company for was given me by the jury. The present Lord Denman was my counsel ; Lord Tenterden was the judge who tried the case ; and after the trial one of the jurymen, who was himself a proprietor in the office, joined with some of my friends who had taken up the matter, and they subscribed the money to pay my expenses as between attorney and client. Sir, these are facts recorded in the papers of the day. I suffered very much then, and I have since suffered from aspersions which have been cast upon me in reference to this case. I have been most shamefully and cruelly used, and I trust that the House will not think that under the circumstances I have unnecessarily trespassed upon its time in calling its attention to this matter. I have made this appeal with the greatest possible pain, with the greatest possible reluctance, as you may readily suppose. I believe I mentioned that every farthing was recovered from the office and was paid. I throw myself, therefore, not on the humane consideration of the House, but upon its sense of justice, and I ask the hon. member to state the meaning of the words he used, and which he applied to me ; and I call upon him further, for my sake, if he knows anything of a reproachful nature against my character—if from any source or channel whatever he has heard anything injurious to me—I call upon him not to shrink from declaring it, but, on the contrary, to state it to the House without reservation."

Mr. Wodehouse replied that he was glad to have afforded the hon. member an opportunity of giving a distinct explanation upon the matter he had alluded to—*a subject which had already remained too long in doubt.* After that explanation he felt it his duty to tender an apology. He desired to say .... that the hon. gentleman and his associates were too lavish in accusing landlords of selfishness. He trusted that the House was satisfied with his apology.

A dead silence prevailed when the member for Norfolk resumed his seat, and after a momentary interval the Speaker put the question, "That this House resolve into the said Committee (a Committee of the whole House on the Poor-law Amendment Act) on Monday next at 12 o'clock." This being agreed to, the House adjourned.

The event occurred on Saturday. On the following Monday Mr. Wodehouse rose and said : " Perhaps the House will allow me to say a few words upon a matter of personal interest to myself. It has been intimated to me that the explanation which I gave the hon. member for Finsbury on Saturday was not as satisfactory as that hon. gentleman had a right to demand. I have no hesitation in saying that I then acted under an erroneous impression with respect to the trial to which I referred. The hon. member for Finsbury appears to me, by the explanation which he has since given, to have had a verdict distinctly in his favour. I therefore feel that as I may have been the instrument of injury to the hon. gentleman, it is now my bounden duty to do my best to be the instrument of reparation. It is a duty which I owe not only to himself in the first instance, but in the next place to all those who are connected with him by relationship, and lastly to all who are connected with him by public representation, to make the explanation which I now make. And I hope the matter will not be permitted to go further, for I tender the explanation as due from one gentleman to another, and am obliged to the House for the opportunity it has afforded me of making this further explanation."

Sir Robert Peel said : "The explicit declaration which has now been made must have convinced everyone that the hon. member for Finsbury is an honourable and innocent man, and I think that hon. gentleman may retire from the House to-night with a full understanding that he has had complete reparation made to his injured feelings."

Mr. Wakley then said : "I cannot refrain from expressing my gratitude to the hon. member for Norfolk for the kind explanation which he has given and offering my grateful acknowledgments to the House for the handsome manner in which they have treated me on this painful occasion. At the same time I beg to say that I receive the acknowledgment of the hon. gentleman with the spirit of frankness with which it has been made, and I feel convinced that he cast an imputation on me which he has not felt himself justified in doing under the circumstances which have since come to his knowledge. In saying this I am bound to state that I consider this acknowledgment will be most satisfactory to every member of my family."

This incident furnished Sir Robert Peel with an opportunity for the performance of a very graceful act. Estimating rightly the great pain that this sudden and wanton resuscitation of a gross imputation upon their father's character would give to Wakley's sons he addressed a long and eloquent letter to the eldest of the three, then a young man of twenty-three, in which he testified to the complete esteem in which Wakley was held by the whole House. The letter was an eloquent eulogy on Wakley as reformer, orator, and parliamentarian, and, coming from the most powerful and prominent statesman in the kingdom and a nominal political foe, formed a remarkable testimonial to Wakley's public merits.

CHAPTER XXXVI

[1846–1852]

Wakley's Fourth Election for Finsbury—The Brief Opposition of Samuel Warren—Wakley's Medical Registration Bill—Its Tenor and Provisions — Referred to a Select Committee — Graham, Macaulay, and Sir Robert Inglis—Mr. Rutherfurd's Medical Registration Bill—Its Fate and the Reason—The English Homœopathic Association—The Ecclesiastical Titles Bill—Wakley withdraws from the Representation of Finsbury—An Estimate of his Parliamentary Position.

THERE seemed every probability of a contest for Finsbury at the general election of July, 1846, consequent upon the fall of the Peel Government. Peel, having carried the Free Trade measure through the House, had raised up to himself a large number of bitter enemies—the Protectionists, with Lord George Bentinck and Disraeli at their head. They nominally belonged to Peel's party, but were now determined to get rid of him. An Irish Coercion Bill gave them the opportunity, for the followers of O'Connell, who had supported Peel in the abolition of the Corn Laws, of course voted against him when such a measure was under debate. Lord John Russell formed a Liberal Ministry and Wakley and Duncombe again offered themselves to their faithful electors of Finsbury. Samuel Warren, author of "The Diary of a Late Physician" and "Ten Thousand a Year," suddenly announced his intention of coming forward. The joint committee of Wakley and Duncombe went to considerable expense in the dissemination of election literature, with the result that Warren as suddenly withdrew from his candidature on the ground that owing to the season of the year most of his very influential supporters would be out of town or abroad. Wakley, in addressing his constituents from the hustings, spoke on behalf of "our friend Tommy," as he affectionately termed Duncombe, as well as for himself, and attributed Warren's attempt to give trouble to personal motives. He said that Warren had a spite against himself. It is clear that both the old members looked upon any attempt to unseat them as unwarrantable impudence, and that Wakley intended from the first to show the intruder that he would meet with so vigorous an opposition that if he had any private animosity to gratify he would be wiser to find some easier and cheaper design. Warren, of course, came in for general abuse as a member of the legal profession, too many of whom, in Wakley's opinion, already occupied the benches of St. Stephen's. But it was as an author that Wakley poured contempt upon him. He had at that time produced the two books, by which he is still known, and Wakley roundly stigmatised the lurid inaccuracy of the one and the sensationalism and forced humour of the other. He disposed of Warren's hint that he had the support of the aristocratic residents of Finsbury, who were naturally holiday-making in July, by saying that if that gentleman had any influential friends abroad they were probably at Botany Bay. This sally was received with unbounded delight and disposed of Warren's pretensions entirely. No one else being hardy enough to oppose such keen fighters as Wakley and Duncombe, they were duly declared re-elected without opposition. As a little matter of curiosity, Wakley was the first man returned to this Parliament in the kingdom.

In the same year he obtained leave to bring in a measure entitled A Bill for the Registration of Qualified Medical Practitioners and for Amending the Law relating to the Practice of Medicine in Great Britain and Ireland. This was his greatest parliamentary work, and its indirect results to the medical profession were of incalculable good. Direct results it had not, for it never became law, but it led to the appointment of a Select Committee of sound, shrewd, important men, whose deliberations resulted in the Medical Act of 1858.

Wakley's Bill was short and exceedingly clear, and the gist of it was to ensure that there should be accurate registration of the whole profession, with strong penal powers capable of being set in motion against pretenders. It was, in fact, a Bill against quacks. It provided for the appointment of a Registrar for each of the three divisions of the United Kingdom. It specified that his duties were to make within thirty days of the passing of the Act a list of all the members of the profession properly qualified in his division of the United Kingdom, whether by degree, diploma, certificate, or licence. To this list were to be added as fit subjects for registration all persons who had been in actual practice as apothecaries since 1815, and all surgeons and assistant-surgeons of the Army, Navy, or Honourable East India Company. In accordance with such official lists, which were to be entitled the Medical Registers for England, Scotland, and Ireland respectively, certificates were to be issued annually to all the names included at a fee of five shillings. Every person thus registered was to be entitled to practise in that division of the United Kingdom where his certificate was issued and to charge for visits and attendance and to recover such charges, as far as they were reasonable, in any court of law, with full cost of suit. He was to be exempt from serving on juries. None but registered persons were to be thus privileged, and clauses were provided for the summary punishment of unregistered practitioners, whether detected practising without a qualification or with a qualification obtained by irregular means, while it was also made penal to falsely pretend to possess a qualification. The recovery of the penalties was simple and swift. The purification of the register—that is to say, the honour of the profession—was to be left in the hands of the various universities or corporations whose graduates or diplomates composed the profession. The three Registrars were merely officers bound to register persons who possessed certain qualifications and who complied with the regulations of the office by proving their ownership of the same and paying their fees. A name once on the register could only be removed by the authorisation of the body from which its owner derived his qualification. The professional crimes which, if proved, warranted such authorisation were specified as "conduct calculated to bring scandal and odium on the profession by publishing indecent advertisements or pamphlets or immoral or obscene prints or books .... or any other disgraceful and unprofessional behaviour." The names of convicted criminals could be erased by the Registrars.

With regard to medical education Wakley saw that a Bill which proposed to "distinguish between legally qualified physicians, surgeons, and apothecaries and mere pretenders to a knowledge of medicine and surgery"—as his preamble bluntly put it—must enact that proper tests should be applied to the candidates for a position on the register, lest the distinction between those included in and those excluded from the official lists should be one without a difference. After repealing the enactment requiring five years' apprenticeship to an apothecary (55 Geo. III., cap. 194, s. 15), Wakley's Bill enacted a scheme of uniformity of education, qualification, and fees throughout the kingdom. No details were suggested, the proposer knowing that the various views of the numerous bodies granting medical qualifications would have to be heard on the subject; but the principle of one portal to the medical profession, by which all practitioners were placed upon one level at the commencement of their careers, was strongly insisted upon. The duty of keeping the various bodies up to the proper educational standard by inspection and supervision of the examinations was to be confided to one of the State departments.

Petitions flowed in at once both for and against the Bill, the majority being in its favour. The better class of the general practitioners saw in the measure an immense raising of their standard, for, should it become law, unfair competition between the men who had properly qualified and

those who had not would cease, many quacks would find
their proceedings illegal, while the proposal to make the
examinations of similar stringency at all the different
examining boards would do away at once with a source of
frequent heart-burning within the ranks of the profession.
In spite, however, of the popularity of the measure with the
class whom it was designed to benefit, Wakley found that
he was not able to get his Bill adopted by the Government,
he therefore acquiesced in the suggestion that a Select Committee of the House should inquire into the subject.   This
may not seem a very great advance on the road towards
medical reform.   Twelve years ago, as we have seen, Warburton had secured the appointment of a Select Committee
with a somewhat similar reference, but no legislation had
followed upon the recommendations of that deliberative
body.   It is true that Sir James Graham had taken charge of
a Medical Bill framed to some extent in accordance with
those recommendations, but he had been compelled to
abandon it, finding it impossible within the scope of one
measure to please all the governing bodies of the various
institutions concerned as well as all their commonalties,
whose interests, unfortunately, were too often not identical
with those of their rulers.   Still Warburton's Committee had
done good work, and had let a flood of light in upon many
dark corners, thereby facilitating future reform in every
direction.   Wakley, ever sanguine and ever practical, refused
to look upon the check as in any way a defeat, but wrote
hopefully in the " Lancet " that the Select Committee would
do their best to arrive quickly at certain unanimous recommendations such as could be transformed into law without
debate or alteration.

The Committee consisted of twelve persons, among whom
the most important, both from their weight in the House
and their knowledge of the subject, were Sir James Graham,
Macaulay, Wakley, and Sir Robert Inglis.   Graham had all
the evidence of the last Committee at his fingers' tips ;
Macaulay was the ablest committee-man of his time, absolutely untiring and resolutely critical ; and Wakley was a

model expert upon the subject, for inasmuch as every movement towards medical reform had been engineered in his paper while a large proportion of them owed their origin to his brain, he knew exactly which were the true and which were the spurious grievances, which were the concessions that the governing bodies or the commonalties ought to make, and which were the principles that they must be allowed to maintain. Sir Robert Inglis was the steady, consistent, and recognised champion of the Church of England. His presence on the Committee greatly strengthened it in popular esteem.

The Committee commenced their sittings on June 4th, 1847, with Macaulay as chairman, by taking the evidence of Dr. John Ayrton Paris, the President of the Royal College of Physicians of London, and sat from that date with the greatest regularity until February, 1848, when a new Committee was formed, which included Wakley and Inglis, but not Macaulay. This body sat until July 4th, 1848, under the chairmanship of Mr. Rutherfurd, the Lord Advocate of Scotland. During this time representative members of all qualifying bodies were examined at length, as well as known advocates for reform in these bodies, and those who are curious to read the evidence will find it reported at great length in the "Lancet." The thoroughness of the cross-examination to which many of the witnesses were subjected is extraordinary, and of all the questioners none was so close as Wakley. Years of writing on the subject from every conceivable point of view had caused him to be conversant with all the doubtful points that might arise in any man's evidence as soon as the explanation of the witness's position made it clear why he had been summoned, and in most cases Wakley knew the true answer to his queries and was, therefore, not to be put off with anything less. He seems at the same time to have been very generous where matters of opinion and not matters of fact were at issue.

All the proceedings of this Committee were a personal triumph for himself, and he knew how to behave well in the hour of victory. Had his Bill eventually become law he would have hardly secured so much prestige in the medical profession as he did by the course which events took. Had his Bill been discussed in the House he would have made certain speeches to defend its principles and many of its details that were sure of attack, but he would have been dealing with laymen. The medical profession, recalling that his attitude towards the heads of the corporations had been antagonistic without variation, would have always desired to know what the other side had to say. Before the Select Committee the other side attended and said what they could, almost every word justifying Wakley's strictures. It has not been given to many agitators to enjoy the supreme pleasure of a triumph like Wakley's, when it became his duty to his Queen and country to cross-examine the Presidents of the London corporations concerning their methods. Twenty-one years previously—only twenty-one years—Wakley had formulated certain complaints against the College of Surgeons. He had addressed meetings and had ensured the passing of resolutions, but no concessions from the Council to the members had followed. The invariable line of the authorities towards the leader of the movement for reform was one of concentrated contempt. He was expelled from hospitals and spoken of as a self-seeking and libellous adventurer. Sixteen years before—only sixteen years—he had been violently assaulted in the theatre of the College in an attempt by Bow Street runners to throw him into the road. His offence was that he desired to know what, if anything, those authorities were going to do to remove a certain slur upon the reputation of one branch of their members. Now he sat to hear what they had to say in response to a movement for reform in medical education and in the methods taken to protect the material and social interests of the profession. These matters had been left to their care; and their evidence, while given for the instruction and assistance of the Select Committee, was virtually an account of their stewardship. Wakley could, indeed, afford to couch his questions in an amiable tone, for every sitting that he attended must have reminded him of his rapid passage from the contempt of these witnesses to their hatred, from their hatred to their fear, from their fear to their respect, and from their respect in many cases to their friendship.

The outcome of this Committee was like that of the previous one in direct legislation. On Friday, May 4th, 1849, the Lord Advocate stated in the House that a measure with reference to the registration of duly qualified practitioners in medicine and surgery was in preparation and that he hoped to lay it upon the table in eight or ten days. But the Lord Advocate had awkward people to deal with, as poor Sir James Graham had previously found. The corporations and certain bodies leagued together to bring about what each considered to be the one necessary reform, or series of reforms, could not be got to agree, and without some general gratification of the medical profession a Bill having for its object the welfare of the profession was destined to fail. It should here be brought to memory that some six years previously—namely, on September 14th, 1843—the College of Surgeons had been granted a new Charter, the Charter under which it now exists. This Charter was to many mouths which had opened their lips for bread a veritable stone. The demand for reform had only produced the creation of a superior class within the commonalty of the College—the Fellows, to whom alone, instead of to the members at large, was granted the privilege of choosing the Council or ruling body. The Council could, it is true, be no longer called a self-electing junto, and to this extent the new Charter was an improvement upon that granted forty years previously, but the mass of the College were as far off as ever from having a voice in their own government. This had caused great dissension, greater indeed than ever, because disappointment was now added to a sense of wrong, and a large number of members joined a body called the National Institute of Medicine, which promised with some pomp "to embrace all persons possessed of any recognised qualification or licence," and proposed later to afford medical education and to examine and grant diplomas. This body, badly managed, with no sufficient reason for its existence, no enlightened leaders, no definite programme, and no scrupulous morality in tactics, objected to Wakley's Bill, which did not provide for the incorporation of its associates, and later objected to the Lord Advocate's Bill for the same reason. The Society of Apothecaries wanted no legislation that deprived them of their monopolies. The Royal College of Physicians of London desired no change at all, its only movement being one of jealousy towards the University of London, whose medical faculty was rapidly becoming important. The College of Surgeons mainly stood out against the foolish pretensions of the National.. Institute. With such a set to please it can hardly be wondered at that the Lord Advocate should abandon his Bill. Nor can it be wondered at that ten years elapsed before any real reform took place. When that reform came it came in the shape of the Medical Act of 1858. This Act adopted Wakley's registration clauses almost entirely, and got over the inherent difficulties of pleasing all the views of all the bodies by the creation of a General Council of Medical Education and Registration whereon each body should be represented. Its penal clauses, however, were not so simply and directly stated as in Wakley's Bill—indeed, at the present moment few men can say for certain what are the disciplinary powers of the General Medical Council—while its aim was more altruistic and broader. Wakley's was primarily a Bill against quackery and for the general practitioner. The Act of 1858 was designed to define and consolidate the interests of the medical profession, and its attitude towards quackery was less an integral part of its claim for attention than were its educational promises and its provision for official and administrative routine.

Wakley's career in Parliament was now nearly at a close. He spoke in favour of Lord Harry Vane's Coroners Bill in 1851, the main provision of which was that coroners should be paid by fixed salaries instead of by fees. He also defended his son, Mr. Henry Membury Wakley, the deputy-coroner for Middlesex, from an attack made upon him by Lord Robert Grosvenor at the instigation of a body known as the

English Homœopathic Association, of which his lordship was the president. Lord Robert Grosvenor wanted the discretion of the coroner to appoint a deputy to be taken from him, because, he alleged, this deputy was incompetent. Wakley hit his old foe without the gloves, denouncing the Association as "an audacious set of quacks" who had only brought forward this trumpery accusation that they might advertise themselves in the House, and as "noodles and knaves, the noodles forming the majority and the knaves using them as tools." He then read a declaration signed by twelve of the jury to the effect that Mr. Henry Membury Wakley had performed his duty on the particular occasion complained of in an able and impartial manner. Hume called attention to the fact that the appointment of Mr. Henry Membury Wakley as deputy-coroner had been duly confirmed by the Lord Chancellor, and the matter was allowed to drop.

In the game of political manœuvring played round the question of ecclesiastical titles in the latter part of 1850 and during the whole of 1851 Wakley did not take a prominent part. He followed Lord Stanley as far as Lord Stanley took a lead, but he was not the sort of man to be whirled off his balance by shouts of "No Popery," any more than he was the sort of man to condone in the Pope or any other foreign ruler, temporal or so-called spiritual, acts of aggression that could not be laughed at as meaningless pretence. Lord John Russell treated the appointment by the Pope of Cardinal Wiseman to the Roman Catholic See of Westminster as a serious menace to the British Constitution and sorely tried his followers by so doing. His language inflamed the people and gave them a right to expect an immediate measure forbidding the practice of naming Roman Catholic Sees with English names, while his party position in the House did not allow him to feel sure of being able to pass any measure of practical use that would prevent the Roman Catholics from doing as they liked. The day of religious persecution was gone by, and, just as all thinking people had recognised the fact, Lord John Russell, with the authority lent him by his premiership, introduced an Ecclesiastical Titles Bill which looked like a piece of contemptible persecution. Wakley followed in the lead of Tories and Peelites alike and denounced the measure as idle and out of date. One of the loudest voices on the same side was that of John Sadleir, who, by virtue of his unrestrained and furious denunciation of the anti-Catholic party, earned for himself the unthinking confidence of a section of his countrymen. This confidence he utterly betrayed, and sought death at his own hand rather than face those whom he had defrauded and ruined. At the inquest Wakley as coroner was confronted with the body of his old political foe and there and then formally recognised it as the corpse of John Sadleir, about which primary point there was some uncertainty.

The Ecclesiastical Titles Bill was the last question of prime importance in the political world upon which Wakley spoke in Parliament. Lord John Russell, after being defeated in the House, returned to office because no one else was in a position to form a Government; but during that uncomfortable twelve months of sufferance Wakley only said a few words on general Reform topics. In 1852 Lord John Russell resigned and Lord Stanley, now Earl Derby by the death of his father, was sent for by the Queen. Wakley refused to stand for Finsbury again. He never gave any reason to his constituents save that his time was too much occupied to allow him to have the honour to represent them ; but he had a very good one. The terribly laborious life that he led as coroner for Middlesex, as regular attendant at the House of Commons, and as editor of the " Lancet " was telling seriously upon his health. For fifteen years he had worked with relentless energy. He had spoken and written volumes, he had driven literally thousands of miles to hold courts. His family and his friends alike pointed out to him that it was impossible for him to continue such a career of persistent over-pressure without incurring a risk that amounted well-nigh to a certainty of break-down. He was reluctant to listen to their suggestions for his retirement, which in the first instance was only designed to be temporary, but a serious collapse awoke him to a sense of the value of the advice that had been given him, and he issued a short farewell letter to his constituents, begging them to return another Radical in his place, and thanking them for their loyal support during eighteen years of political life. His announcement was received with loud regret by his constituents, and by the general Reform party whose policy he had so emphatically and unswervingly supported and not infrequently helped to dictate, while by many political foes his retirement from parliamentary life was alluded to on the hustings as a distinct loss to public affairs and to the domestic life of the House of Commons.

Wakley's career in Parliament was an unmitigated success. It was never crowned by office, but this he never expected, having openly declared that he would serve no party, but only his conscience and the constituents who had chosen him to represent them. This sort of independent member rarely turns out worthy even of comment. He is almost invariably a political crank, an unmanageable and difficult man, one who, in his anxiety to escape being an accessory to the selfishness of party, erects into a fetich, with much more exclusive selfishness, every little idea of his own. Wakley had nothing in common with such aggressive nuisances. He was the most adaptable and obliging private member that it is possible to imagine about all small things. In large things he followed a very clear and well-defined policy of the Radical sort, moulding his actions upon the notions of useful reform that had been developed in him by his early intolerance of the hapless condition of the medical profession when he first joined it. As then all his plans and movements were designed to help the rank and file against the oppression of their rulers, so later in Parliament every public act or word of his had for its object the betterment of all classes who were unable to better themselves. Grievance-hunter he might be called, agitator he certainly was, but in general and medical politics alike he was always on the side of those whom he conceived to be oppressed, while his methods for their relief at the same time displayed enthusiasm and sincerity, tempered with good sense, knowledge of the world, and general sympathy. If the story of his parliamentary career has been rightly told it should need no summary to help in its comprehension. Wakley can be absolutely judged by his words and deeds. But the evidence of an eye-witness and contemporary thinker may be with advantage added, that the reader may learn what was the opinion of thoughtful men of Wakley as an orator and a democratic force, and may decide how far the tale as it is here told bears out the estimate formed fifty years before.

" Mr. Wakley as a speaker in the House of Commons is more distinguished for shrewdness and common-sense than for any of the higher accomplishments of the orator. A plain, simple, blunt, downright style disarms suspicion and bespeaks confidence, even at the outset of his address. A manly frankness both in his bearing and delivery, precludes the idea of any preparation or of any design to entrap by means of the ordinary tricks and contrivances of the practised debater. He has a brief, conversational manner, as though his thoughts were quite spontaneous and not the result of preparation. He seems to be thinking what he shall say next, as if the subject came quite fresh to his mind and he were, by a sort of compulsion, drawing as much truth out of it as he could. This gives both freshness and vigour to his speeches. By his singular shrewdness and common-sense, his perfect command of temper, his good-humoured irony, his store of information, available at the moment on almost all subjects, he has acquired an amount of influence in the House disproportioned to the demands of his position. He has inspired much confidence in his judgment, and by an original, because an unfettered, turn of thinking he contrives to strike out new views of the subject before the House and to supply materials for thinking or debating out of what seem to be threadbare themes. This is the consequence of the original turn of his mind and the independence of his position.

" He has no party ties ; he has received no training ; he has no class prejudices such as obtain influence in the House of Commons; but has been a shrewd and constant observer of human nature in all grades and is not burdened with an overpowering sense of immaculate purity of public men. Still, you never hear from him those coarse charges of personal corruption against individuals which will often fall from Mr. Duncombe, notwithstanding his gentlemanly manners and superficial refinement. Broad as his insinuations sometimes are, there is a degree of delicacy in the phraseology in which they are clothed ; and though he often indulges in a sarcastic humour it seldom or never carries a venomous sting. Although a very harsh and un-compromising popular advocate, determined in his exposure of public abuses and still more in his championship of the neglected poor, he shows a gentlemanly respect for the forms and restraints which experience has rendered necessary in debate and a forbearance to press charges to useless extremities of personality. If he has not quite conquered the prejudices entertained towards Ultra-Radical intruders by men of birth and station he has at least made them feel his intellectual power and acknowledge his moral equality. In this respect he has done more to advance the interests of the millions by making their advocacy respectable than have many more flashy and showy popular leaders. His style of speaking is the most simple and unaffected. He has been too busily engaged in the hard work of life to have had much time to bestow on oratory. The structure of his speeches is quite inartificial, and the language usually the most simple and colloquial of every-day life. It is plain, even homely, without being inelegant; a manliness of sentiment and a quiet self-possession in the speaker imparts a kind of dignity to the most ordinary expressions. There is breadth and force in his argument and declamation; and a rough pathos in his descriptions of pauper suffering which is often far more stirring and affecting than the most accomplished eloquence of more finished speakers. Mr. Wakley does not so much make speeches, as deliver the thoughts which burden his mind on any given subject with frankness and sincerity. Even hard words do not come offensively from him, such is his good humour and the amenity of his disposition. He constantly displays great shrewdness of perception, unmasking the motives of opponents with a masterly power and, at the same time, with an avoidance of coarse imputation. Yet he can be sarcastic when he chooses; but his sarcasm is more in the hint conveyed and in the knowing look of face and tone of voice than in any positively cutting expressions. He handles the scalpel with delicacy and skill, never cutting deeper than is absolutely necessary. Some of his points have, from time to time, told remarkably well; such, for instance, as that in which he described the Whig Ministry as being made of 'squeezable' materials. That one expression contributed considerably towards gaining for him the position he holds in the estimation of the House of Commons.

"Mr. Wakley has extraordinary energy both physical and mental. To see him bringing up his portly, bulky frame along the floor of the House of Commons, with swinging arms, and rolling, almost rollicking gait—his broad fair face inspired with good humour, and his massive forehead set off by light, almost flaxen hair, flowing in wavy freedom backwards around his head, and the careless ease of his manly yet half-boyish air, as though he had no thought or care beyond the impression or impulse of the moment; to watch the frank, hearty

goodwill with which he greets his personal friends as he throws himself heedlessly into his seat, and interchanges a joke or an anecdote,
or perhaps some stern remark on the passing scene, with those around;
then, in a few minutes afterwards, rising to make, perhaps, some
important motion, laying bare some gross case of pauper oppression,
or taking up the cause of the medical practitioners with all the zeal of
one still of the craft; to witness the freshness and vigour with which
he throws himself into the business before him, you would little guess
the amount of wearying labour and excitement he has already gone
through during the day; yet he has perhaps been afoot from the
earliest hour, has perchance presided at more than one inquest during
the morning, listening with a conscientious patience to the evidence,
or taking part with an earnest partisanship in the case; then off as
fast as horses could carry him down to the committee-rooms of the
House of Commons, there to exhibit the same restless activity of mind,
the same persevering acuteness, the same zeal and energy; and after
hours, perhaps, spent in this laborious duty, rendered still more
irksome by a heated atmosphere and the intrigues of baffling opponents,
returning home to accumulate the facts necessary for the exposure of
some glaring abuse in the Post-office or the Poor-law Commission, or
to manage the multifarious correspondence which his manifold public
duties compel him to embark in. Yet such is often the daily life of
this hard-working man: he is absolutely indefatigable; nothing daunts
him, nothing seems to tire him."

This description of Wakley in the House of Commons
from the pen of Mr. G. H. Francis appeared in "Fraser's
Magazine," and was afterwards published with similar essays
in a volume entitled "Orators of the Age." It is an outspoken appreciation which, if not entirely complimentary, is
still one which any man might be proud to have earned and
which bears the imprint of truth on every line.

CHAPTER XXXVII

[1827–1831]

The Coroner's Inquest Seventy Years ago—The " Lancet" and Medical Coroners—Examples of Foolish Verdicts—Wakley stands for the Coronership of East Middlesex—A General Meeting of the Freeholders—John St. John Long—The Terrible Case of Catherine Cashin—Wakley as Prosecutor before the Coroner—The Praise of Dr. Roderick Macleod—Wakley Defeated at the Poll—Trial of Long for Manslaughter—Conviction and Acquittal—The Testimonial of Dr. Ramadge—Ramadge v. Wakley—Verdict for Dr. Ramadge, Damages One Farthing.

WAKLEY the coroner is better known to memory than Wakley the Radical politician or Wakley the medical reformer. His parliamentary course came to a close when he was in his fifty-seventh year, but he retained the coronership until his death ten years later, while in his earliest efforts towards a public career it was to the coroner's bench that he aspired and not to a seat in the House of Commons. To begin at the beginning it is necessary to retrace our steps some twenty-four years, and take up the tale of Wakley's life in 1827.

One of the earliest regular tenets which the readers of the " Lancet" were expected by Wakley to hold was that the office of coroner should be vested in a medical man. Almost from the commencement of his editorship, certainly as soon as he felt that he had a following willing to be educated to his ideas, he commenced to familiarise the notion, then quite novel, that the coronership was a medical post. He considered the coroner's inquest to be a most valuable institution, and if properly conducted a safeguard

z

to the public second to none ever devised by a civilised legislature. But its utility he held to be greatly limited, and in many instances entirely defeated, by the inefficiency of the individuals who at that time—it was about the year 1827 that he began writing voluminously in this strain—filled the office, and by the sordid environment of the court. The taint of the tavern-parlour vitiated the evidence, ruined the discretion of the jurors, and detracted from the dignity of the coroner. The solemnity of the occasion was too generally lightened by alcohol or entirely nullified by the incompetency of the judge. In short, the tribunal designed by Edward I. to be one of the most important in his kingdom, whose presidency was to be held by a knight "of the most meet and most lawful men of the county," had been universally degraded to a dreary farce, stage-managed by a foolish beadle, where the legal administration was ignominiously known as "crowner's quest law"—a thing proverbially to be laughed at, and where the majesty of death evaporated with the fumes from the gin of the jury. The harmonic meeting-room of the Sol's Arms was no exaggeration, and Dickens probably drew little Swills from life.

Wakley perceived at once that half the evidence given at these courts was unnecessary, and that on numerous occasions testimony most vital to a thorough inquiry into the cause of death was not forthcoming, and that both the superfluity and the scarcity were due, as a rule, less to the legal incompetency of the coroner than to his ignorance of the elements of medicine. Leaving entirely out of his argument the discretionary powers vested in a coroner, in the exercise of which every whit as much as in his exercise of his judicial functions it was necessary for him to be guided by medical knowledge, Wakley commenced a series of articles deeply regretting that so important an institution as a court of first instance appointed to inquire solemnly into the cause of all doubtful or unexplained deaths should be so constituted that no cause ever was explained from a medical point of view, except where it explained itself publicly. The procedures of the court, also, had fallen into universal and well-merited contempt. For both these regrettable conditions he saw one remedy—the appointment of medical coroners. To the medical coroner the viewing of the body was not a repulsive piece of pretence, for to him the appearance of a corpse might tell much in support or contradiction of the statements shortly to be affirmed on oath before him. To the medical coroner the evidence of friends, physicians, nurses, and eye-witnesses as to injuries or previous illnesses had a very real meaning, and in addition its relation to any undisputed facts before the court must be clear to him in a way that it could not be clear to persons ignorant of medicine. The medical man alone could know the dose of a given drug that must be held a poison, the extent to which an indulged habit became a risk, or what depth of wound in a certain place would or would not account for a fatal issue. Against the advantages of having an expert in the judge's seat were to be set the apparent disadvantage that the training of the medical man, being what it was, unfitted him for a post where evidence had not only to be received, but sifted and weighed. Here, it was claimed, the medical man gave way to the lawyer. Wakley never conceded this point, asserting roundly that any man could learn in two hours all the law that it was necessary to know to be a competent coroner, while the appreciation of evidence at its proper value was a task that every uneducated juror was invited by the British Constitution to undertake, and that there was nothing in the medical curriculum to unfit a man for the task. "The statute of the 4th Edward I., which comprehends nearly all the law relating to the office of coroner," wrote Wakley in 1828, "is a short Act of Parliament, which any man who runs may read and understand. Any man of ordinary understanding who has read this statute and who has served occasionally as juryman or witnessed a few trials so as to acquire some general information as to the common rules of evidence is competent, as far as legal qualifications are concerned, to discharge the duties of the office of coroner. But the medical qualifications which would enable a coroner to discharge with efficiency the duties of his office are of a far higher order, and can hardly be expected to be possessed by any man not a member of the medical profession."

From the time of the appearance of the article containing these words until his election as coroner for Middlesex in 1839 the "Lancet" was full of proofs of the accuracy of his words. Cases were collected regularly where the coroner could not possibly do his duty as a judge of a court held to inquire into the cause of a death on account of his fundamental ignorance of the sort of things that would cause death. Medical evidence could be given at an inquest in the same way that it could be given in a high court, but the coroner was placed at a disadvantage by comparison with a learned judge. In other courts the cause of death was but one issue of a suit. If it were by chance the vital issue thorough medical evidence was at once forthcoming and counsel specially instructed attended for the purpose of weighing and sifting that evidence. If it were not the most vital issue, the judge, taking a broad view, relegated the question to its proper sphere of importance. But in the coroner's court the cause of death was not merely the most vital issue—it was the *only* issue; while the coroner had no power to remunerate special medical evidence and neither he nor his jury derived the benefit of lucid explanations. Post-mortem examinations were but infrequently ordered, so that many of the verdicts arrived at were necessarily the result of haphazard and ignorant guidance.

Some of the examples that were printed in the "Lancet" during 1828, 1829, and 1830, in illustration of the view that an inquest confided to the supervision of a non-medical coroner presented so many obvious opportunities of error that it ceased to be a public safeguard, are undoubtedly very remarkable. To mention a few, there is the story of a case of poisoning by prussic acid in which the jury were clearly misdirected. They brought in a verdict of "Suicide during temporary derangement." There was not only no evidence pointing towards suicide or insanity, but the probability of an accident having occurred, and the possibility that the accident was due to the carelessness of some person other than the deceased, would have occurred to anyone who knew, as the coroner apparently did not know, what was the poisonous dose of prussic acid and what the therapeutic use of this deadly remedy. Again, an inquest is discussed at some length where a verdict of manslaughter was given against an operating surgeon whose procedure had been perfectly correct, while the fatal injuries he was supposed to have caused might have been the natural—that is, pathological—lesions due to the patient's condition, or might, at any rate, have been the natural sequels of such lesions. Only a medical man, Wakley insisted, could have interpreted the medical evidence to the jury in such a way as to ensure justice being done. In a third case a jury brought in a verdict of—"Died by the visitation of God and not in consequence of the neglect of any person or persons," where it was perfectly clear to any medical man reading the evidence that the luckless baby, whose death was the subject of the inquiry, had been poisoned by overdosing with mercury and had been, in addition, neglected by the medical attendant. The coroner knew nothing of mercurial salivation, the only medical evidence forthcoming was interested, and as a result a miscarriage of justice occurred that would have been impossible if a medical coroner had presided. Another case, where the pious but meaningless verdict of " Death by the visitation of God " was given by the jury at the express direction of the coroner, and where all the evidence pointed to the most human agency in the matter, was a wholesale catastrophe due to arsenic poisoning. A family circle having partaken of a particular pie, two died at once, a third some twenty-four hours later, and a fourth was exceedingly sick. The remnants of the pie were thrown into the yard, and some fowls who ate it died there and then. The bearing of all this totally escaped the coroner, who obtained from his jury the verdict that he desired. Wakley used this case more than once as a most striking example of the necessity for medical coroners. The bodies were afterwards exhumed and the cause of death was then found to be arsenic poisoning.

At the time that Wakley began printing these lapses on the part of legal coroners he had no other object than the disinterested one of securing to the medical profession a popular right of entry to compete for the honourable post of coroner, with its responsibilities, position, and emoluments. He was convinced absolutely that only a medical man could make a good coroner, and he desired to benefit the public as much as the profession by getting medical men to come forward as candidates. But in August, 1830, the death occurred of Mr. Unwin, the coroner of East Middlesex. Wakley lost no time in urging upon the profession to select a medical man and to combine in persuading the freeholders of the county, to whose hands at that time the appointment was confided, to vote for their candidate. The fact was immediately pointed out to him, though he can hardly have needed the information, that he was the member of the profession most fitted to take the field, seeing that he was well versed in the arguments proving that the coronership should be a medical appointment, that he had as a newspaper proprietor unrivalled opportunities of appealing widely to the profession and the electors, and that, lastly, he was not hampered by the ties of private practice. To this Wakley responded by offering himself as a candidate for the vacant post.

On August 24th, 1830, a meeting of the freeholders was held at the Crown and Anchor Tavern, Strand, to consider the claims of the first medical candidate for the coronership of East Middlesex. Some four hundred voters were present and the proceedings were enthusiastic. Not all the speeches betrayed the knowledge of the subject which might have been expected from such convinced partisans ; but in truth the cry against the monopoly of the coronership by attorneys, which in Wakley's numerous articles had only formed a minor point, found such enthusiastic echo in the breast of the medical profession that the earlier speeches to the meeting were rather of the nature of tirades. One gentleman could not have done Wakley's cause much good by his violence, but a sentence from his arraignment of the legal profession deserves quotation. He is not meaning to abuse lawyers, or, rather, he is not meaning to assert their unfitness to be coroners. On the contrary, he is pointing out the necessity that the coroner should have legal knowledge. He is imagining the wicked counsel pleading before a coroner who, having no legal knowledge (query, because a lawyer) and a heart fraternally inclined towards his brother in corruption, listens, acquiesces, and misdirects :—

'For, suppose that some lawyer, a bad man, a Satan of his species, with a seared, cold, blighted heart, who had spent the whole course of his life in defamation, in one continuous struggle, to crush truth, to beard honest men, to blast with faint praise, or sickly innuendoes, the evidence of every worthy witness, and this to screen the murderer, to pander to the adulterer, to assist the secret poisoner, in order that he might sop his crust in the dripping-pan greased by their unhallowed gains, in order that he might clutch at a livelihood which all honest men had denied him,—suppose such a man were to be employed by one of his patrons to go to an inquest, to beard and dictate to the coroner, to be insolent to the jury, to tell them they were fools, to twist and contort evidence so as to confuse the reporters, to tear the consolation of public respect from the fretted bosom of the relations, by allusions which had no reference to the case; suppose, I say, such a man were being successful in all, or even in one of these base and accursed objects, is it not desirable that the coroner should possess legal information sufficient to know how to put down the impudent effrontery of such a wretch as this? sufficient knowledge of human nature to know that this man would himself be the first to snap the cord of all principle, to undermine the foundations of all society, to use poison, or treachery (that mental poison), or anything to gain his end, and, therefore, to defend the jury from fearing him, to point out the odious and too evident nature of his mission?"

Such rhodomontade as this did not advance Wakley's candidature, the marvel being that it was received with applause and not with open ridicule, but fortunately speakers with more command over their adjectives followed. By these Wakley's great interest in all questions of medical jurisprudence was insisted upon, as well as the fearlessness and freedom from prejudice that were revealed by the attitude that he had adopted towards the Council of the College of Surgeons and the authorities of the metropolitan hospitals. With reference to any doubts whether the discharge of the coroner's duties in Wakley's hands while gaining in medical efficiency might lose in legal, one speaker summed up amidst loud cheering the claims of the candidate to a sufficient knowledge of the law. Referring to the sensational case of Bransby Cooper *v.* Wakley, he said :— " I ask the freeholders of Middlesex, Do they want a man learned in the law ? If so, much as I may pity their want of judgment and taste, I can supply them to their heart's content, for the man who could defeat Sir James Scarlett in his own court and browbeat the lawyers must surely have law enough to satisfy the blindest lover of perplexities and forms."

The result of the meeting was very satisfactory to Wakley. He received numerous pledges of support, while his theory that, apart from his own personal claims, the office of coroner should be held by a medical man received considerable endorsement from the press. The " Morning Herald," the " Examiner," the " Spectator," the " Morning Advertiser," and " Bell's Life in London " supported the man or the theory, or both, and so numerous were the personal pledges received that Wakley, who had at first not seriously believed that his chances were good, began to look forward with confidence to the outcome of what promised to be a close struggle.

That confidence was not lessened by the events arising out of a terrible tragedy which occurred in London at this very juncture. For it was in the month of August, 1830, and in the same week that Wakley made public his intention of seeking the suffrages of the freeholders for the vacant coronership of East Middlesex, that John St. John Long, one of the most notorious charlatans of this century, was found guilty of manslaughter by a coroner's jury, and it was by Wakley's personal exertions that the righteous verdict was secured.

John St. John Long was an extraordinary man. Born in an Irish village and of humble extraction—his father was a

basket-maker and he himself was apprenticed to the trade—
he became "a pupil," probably the sort of pupil that cleans
out the studio and washes the palettes, of a certain Daniel
Richardson, a Dublin painter. He started on his own account
as a portrait-painter in the year 1821, for the following
advertisement appeared in a Limerick paper, published on
February 10th of that year. It spoke more for the enterprise
than the culture of its author :—

"Mr. John Saint John Long," it ran, "Historical and Portrait
Painter, the only pupil of Daniel Richardson, Esq., late of Dublin,
proposes during his stay in Limerick to take portraits from Italian
Head and whole length; and parson desirous of getting theirs done in
historical, hunting, shooting, fishing, or any other character; or their
family, grouped in one or two paintings from life-size to minature, so
as to make an historical subject, choseing one from history."*

He met with some success among his easy-going com-
patriots and then turned to London as a larger field for his
talent and ingenuity. Here he obtained work from certain
of the anatomical lecturers, whose scarcity of human subjects
whereon to instruct their pupils by actual dissection compelled them to fall back upon coloured charts. Long picked
up the rudiments of medical science by preparing these
drawings and copying the letterpress, and then, with the
audacity of his class, started as a physical saviour of mankind, his stock-in-trade being a liniment, an ointment, and a
few scraps of topographical anatomy. No quack ever had
quite such brilliant success, but to no quack, perhaps, ever
came quite such a brilliant idea. Long's liniment was not
only curative but preventive and diagnostic. Placed upon
the skin over a healthy organ no reaction occurred, but
placed upon the skin over a tuberculous lung or a podagric
joint rapid ulceration followed. This ulceration was, so he
alleged, nature's process: it represented the healthy rejection
by a tissue that desired to be sound of the mischievous
elements previously present in its meshes. Long claimed

"A Book about Doctors," by J. Cordy Jeaffreson.

an infallible eye for incipient phthisis and suppressed gout. He cultivated society assiduously, as became a man of good birth—for as such he was received in London drawing-rooms !—good presence, artistic talent, and unrivalled scientific prescience. In society he met his earliest and most faithful dupes. He did not wait for his patients to come to him. His method was simpler. He prophesied approaching death for apparently healthy persons within hearing of the relations or friends of those persons. The terrible rumour went round the *salon,* and on the following day the victim would arrive at 41, Harley Street, Long's house, and demand an explanation of the grim vaticinations. Then Long produced a bottle and applied to the foot or the shoulder or the breast of the doomed person a few drops of its blistering contents, and, lo ! ulceration appeared. " You were sicken-ing for this or that," cried Long, " but you have taken it in time." The sore was then kept open by an irritating oint-ment for such period as the patience of the victims or their purse warranted, and was finally allowed to heal. The sums that were made by Long surpass belief. A writer in the " Gentleman's Magazine " mentions that from July, 1829, to July, 1830, this surprising adventurer's pass-book displayed a series of credit payments due to a single year's operation amounting to no less than £13,400. This year marked his zenith, for at the end of it came his great rebuff. Hitherto his method had proved infallible. It was the regular quack method, only dignified by the good manners, plausibility, and real talent of an utterly unscrupulous man. Very bad cases were refused because the malady was too far advanced. The remedy, although styled absolutely infallible, was only, it appeared, for those in whom disease had not committed serious ravages. In cases that were treated with no satis-factory results the failure was attributed to the fact that the patient had not employed the treatment with sufficient per-severance. This was a most usual occurrence, seeing that lavation and inunction with vitriolic preparations have no inherent enticements of their own, and that the patient who found no commensurate improvement was apt to weary of the recurring agony. Friends doubted, the regular medical practitioner was called in, and Long washed his hands of a person of little faith. Cases that started in health returned after a time to health, having enjoyed the privilege of some weeks', or it might be months', torture at a price which made even the most stoical of these imaginary invalids wince.

But in the summer of 1830 a catastrophe occurred in the practice of John St. John Long which aroused an uproar throughout the kingdom. Two Irish girls, Cashin by name, called upon him, the younger being in delicate health and seeking advice. Long pursued his usual tactics, the crafty tricks that had brought so many to his net. For the sick girl he prescribed a harmless inhalation, but seeing in the healthy girl an opportunity for a brilliant cure he prophesied to a third person, the girl's own mother, that unless she underwent treatment by the application of his fluid she would infallibly fall into a rapid consumption. The rest is sheer horror. The luckless girl submitted her perfectly healthy body to the manipulation of this callous brute. This was on August 3rd, 1830. For the next ten days she suffered agony. On August 14th she was in a condition of extreme pain and exhaustion. An enormous and unhealthy ulcer had been created upon her back, and she was perilously ill and vomiting continually. On the following day Long saw her, and relying presumably upon her stamina, assured her that in a short time she would be in better health than she had ever been in her life. On the next day, August 16th, her friends sent for Sir Benjamin Brodie. But it was too late. Mortification had set in, and on August 17th Catherine Cashin died at the age of twenty-four, having passed from perfect health through unspeakable torture to the grave in exactly one fortnight.

The "Lancet" having enlightened such of the public as would consent to being enlightened, a loud uproar arose throughout England. An inquest was held, which Wakley attended at the request of the relatives of the deceased. Wakley was at first unwilling to appear personally, urging that as a candidate for the vacant coronership of Middlesex his interference might be deemed to be due to a desire to advertise his claims for the post, and that having denounced Long as a quack in the columns of the "Lancet" his opinion might be considered biassed and his advocacy do more harm than good. The Cashin family would, however, take no denial. They were friendless in London and knew of Long's immense influence with his fashionable clients. Unless Wakley would espouse their cause they believed that the murderer of their lost relative would escape the hands of justice. Wakley appeared before the coroner as the representative of the Cashins, and Mr. Adolphus, Q.C., represented Long. Undoubtedly, Long would have got off scot-free had it not been for Wakley's interference. All sorts of excuses were made for him, and influential persons of every degree strained their power in this direction and that to accomplish his acquittal. Wakley, however, having undertaken the prosecution, went through with the task in characteristic manner. He brushed aside the sophistries of Mr. Adolphus, who would have persuaded the jury that all the medical profession was jealous of Long, and that the error of diet committed by the unfortunate victim in assuaging her feverish thirst with plums was responsible for her inability to resist Long's healing treatment and so for her sudden decease ! Wakley pointed out to the jury that the facts before them did not allow of any interpretation but one, and that one was that Long had killed Catherine Cashin by rubbing her back with corrosive substances. A verdict of manslaughter against Long was obtained, but the issue of the warrant for his apprehension was scandalously delayed, and had it not been for Wakley's persistency it is probable that the wretched pretender would have escaped punishment after all.

By his conduct of this matter Wakley was seen to possess in a remarkable manner the qualities that fitted him for the coronership. The people and the press applauded the verdict against Long, and attributed that verdict to Wakley. His old opponent, Dr. James Johnson, said in the hostile columns of the "Medico-Chirurgical Review" that Wakley had "acquitted himself both ably and judiciously. True, he had justice, popularity, and some of the best feelings of our nature on his side; but then he was opposed to a lawyer whose practice at the Old Bailey and engagement in cases declined by the respectable members of the Bar rendered him capable of using all kinds of mean artifices and personal insults for the purpose of browbeating his antagonist. Yet Mr. Wakley set him down repeatedly, and that by coolness of temper and strength of argument. Galled and foiled and irritated to fury by a medical man uneducated to the Bar, and whom he hoped to crush by his Newgate ribaldry, he at length appealed to the coroner to prevent Mr. Wakley from opposing him at all. These attempts showed the extremities to which he was driven, and the sentiments of the jury as well as of the spectators were often and unequivocally evinced in favour of his antagonist." Other papers followed in the same enthusiastic strain, and Wakley's chances of obtaining the coronership became very good indeed. Enormous meetings were held in his favour in Islington and Clerkenwell, and the candidate's personal speeches were received everywhere with enthusiastic applause. A universal suffrage would have given him the appointment, but the final issue showed that whatever the people might think the freeholders were not sufficiently familiar with the new idea that it was possible for the coroner to be a medical man. Mr. Baker, a solicitor, who, by the way, was earlier in the field than Wakley, obtained a larger number of votes, but the contest was very severe, Wakley being in a minority of only 136 on a poll of 7204. As in his first attempt to enter Parliament, so in his first attempt to obtain a coronership Wakley was beaten, but on each occasion the defeat was so narrow as to form certain promise of future victory.

It will be well here to finish the story of John St. John Long, as Wakley's hostility to the quack involved him in a libel action with a member of the medical profession. Long, pursued relentlessly by Wakley's pen, was placed in the dock of the Old Bailey on October 30th, 1830, charged with the manslaughter of Catherine Cashin. Counsel for the prosecution took the same line that Wakley had done before the coroner. They demonstrated to the satisfaction of the jury that Catherine Cashin had died from injuries due to certain applications sold to her by John St. John Long, a person practising as a medical man but possessing no degree or diploma, and they warned the jury against having their attention diverted from this the real question into considering whether Long's remedies had ever done anyone else any good on other occasions. Long's counsel put a marquis, a marchioness and her daughters, and the heir to one of the oldest earldoms in the kingdom into the box. These persons—one of whom during the course of the trial sat by the judge's side and chatted with him—testified to their belief in Long's treatment and his humanity, but did not persuade the jury to think highly of their own wisdom. The jury found Long guilty, and Mr. Justice Parke fined him £250, which sum the convict extracted from his pocket and paid there and then. Scarcely had the loud outcry at the disgraceful leniency of this sentence died away than a second of Long's victims perished, and a second coroner's jury brought in a verdict of manslaughter against him. He was again placed in the dock at the Old Bailey, and the facts revealed a denser ignorance and a more atrocious insensibility to suffering than in the case of Catherine Cashin, but the medical evidence was so shaky that the judge gave the prisoner the benefit of the doubt.

It will be thought that by this time Long was sufficiently discredited. A few might still be his dupes at heart, and a few more might pretend to continue in their belief rather than publicly write themselves down as credulous asses, but Long could not have expected at this season many complimentary letters upon his skill in diagnosis or his ingenuity in treatment. Yet precisely now—that is to say, in March, 1831—he received such a testimonial, a lengthy one, one indited apparently out of the fulness of the writer's heart, and actually signed by a medical man, a Doctor of Medicine

of Oxford University and a Fellow of the Royal College of
Physicians. It was a certain Dr. Francis H. Ramadge who
thus leapt to fame in the columns of the "Sunday Times,"
where Long published the effusion. In his letter, which Dr.
Ramadge alleged had not been written with a view to
publication, Long's treatment of the two murdered women
was commended, while he was commiserated with on the
unfortunate issue of his therapy and the unmerited obloquy
that he had incurred. Sir Benjamin Brodie and a medical
man named Vance, who had given halting evidence against
Long in the course of the two trials, were severely handled,
and Long was consoled for any ignorance he might have of
anatomy by the information that, at any rate, he knew more
than many hospital officials. Wakley published this extraordinary letter in the " Lancet," and said that if Dr. Ramadge
wrote it he must be considered to have placed himself at
once outside the pale, and he recommended him forthwith
to abandon the ranks of a profession which he had disgraced. Dr. Ramadge replied to the " Lancet," acknow-
ledging the letter as emanating from himself, and maintained
that he had a right to his private opinion. The Medical
Society of London expelled Dr. Ramadge from their body
on the ground that by writing such a letter he had
improperly and shamefully advocated empirical practice and
cast unjust aspersions upon his medical brethren. As a
result of this position of affairs a medical man some few
weeks later refused to meet Dr. Ramadge at a patient's
bedside, alleging that his conduct had been found to be
such that no medical man of respectability ought to consult
with him. The patient's friends sided with the second
medical man, whose treatment, as it turned out, did more
for the patient than Dr. Ramadge's methods. An account
of this case, which certainly placed Dr. Ramadge in the
doubly unenviable light of a disreputable man and also an
ignorant man, appeared in the " Lancet." Dr. Ramadge
brought an action for libel. Wakley defended his conduct
in person, and commented with much severity on the
plaintiff's want of medical skill and unjustifiable advocacy

of John St. John Long, who was in the court and had the
pleasure of hearing himself alluded to casually as a quack
and a felon.   He maintained that to hold Dr. Ramadge up
to contempt was justifiable, and indeed the only course open
to an honest medical journalist. After a few minutes'
consultation by the jury a verdict was given for the ·plaintiff
for one farthing.

CHAPTER XXXVIII

[1831–1839]

More Cases of Ill-considered Verdicts—Wakley's Claims on the Coronership—A Vacancy for West Middlesex—Wakley's Precarious Pecuniary Position — He resolves to Compete — The Boundaries of the West Middlesex District—The Opposition of the Middlesex Magistrates — A Hollow Victory for the Medical Candidate.

DURING the next ten years Wakley kept his contention that the peculiar fitness of medical men for the post of coroner must end in the medical coroner being a very usual officer in every county persistently present in the minds of his readers. A large quantity of correspondence detailing instances in which coroners' verdicts had been improperly returned through failure to provide adequate medical testimony or failure to appreciate such testimony when offered was inserted in the "Lancet," and each communication of this nature received caustic comments from the editorial pen. "Incapacity of an attorney," "Gross case of misdirection to a jury," and "Verdict in the absence of medical testimony" were frequent headings to notes and even leading articles, and this is not surprising when some of the examples of the verdicts returned at inquests are examined. In an inquest, for example, held on the body of a woman who had died from *cholera*, the jury, under the direction of the coroner, returned a verdict of *manslaughter*. The testimony of four medical men who had examined the body availed nothing against that of three children, one of whom stated that the deceased was "knocked over" an iron railing, while a second asserted that she was "pushed against"

2 A

an iron railing, and a third, omitting the railing, swore that the victim was simply knocked about. Again, a youth fifteen years of age had been " knocked against a wall, struck very violently right and left on the head, then dashed upon the pavement, and kicked by his assailant, an active, strong man, several times. On struggling to his feet he was again knocked down." The after-history of the case was very clearly given on sworn evidence. The lad went home, vomited blood, and during the next week complained of pain in the head and stomach. He continued to vomit frequently for the next month, and four weeks and five days after the assault died under the care of the parish medical officer. The necropsy revealed considerable laceration of brain substance and the commencing formation of an abscess in the left ventricle. The jury after hearing the evidence were anxious to bring in a verdict of manslaughter. They were over-ruled by the coroner, who informed them that if they did the parish would be put to an expense of £100 to £150, and probably the man would be acquitted after all. A verdict therefore was returned of " Died from extravasated blood in the brain, but the jury are not satisfied that it arose from natural causes." Again, a woman who was known to have fractured her second and third cervical vertebræ was said by the coroner's jury, unassisted by any medical evidence, to have died from apoplexy. Any one of these cases would have gone far to prove that Wakley was right in talking of the coroner's inquest as held by too many coroners as a meagre, miserable, and worthless institution. He was known to be hunting for such cases ; but discounting all his weighty bias in the matter, their very existence proved that the coroner's inquest was not the safeguard that it should be. That Wakley collected his examples of malpraxis was quite well recognised, and that they formed but a fraction of the inquests which were properly conducted and which, after due deliberation, ended in the return of a correct verdict was known to all, but the fact that one such case of gross error could occur proved the coroner's inquest to be no very real security to the public.

In Middlesex, at any rate, Wakley made certain of the popular vote for any future occasion by the publication of these cases, generally with full names and dates.

In other directions his claims to the next vacant coronership, if he cared to apply for the post, grew very manifest. He had fought a gallant fight in his attempt to obtain the coronership of East Middlesex. He had resisted on his election to Parliament several obnoxious measures dealing with the privileges of the coroner, and in 1836 he had framed and carried the Medical Witnesses Remuneration Bill. Until the passage of this measure it had been open to disputants of his theory that the medical man made the best coroner to retaliate that medical men often might attend inquests and throw valuable light on the cause of death and thus strengthen the hand of the non-medical coroner, but that they wriggled out of these duties because there was no provision made for their remuneration. This could not be contradicted because the "Lancet" contained records of cases where the coroner had been unable to charge his jury properly since he could not find anyone to make a necropsy for him. In country districts where the medical man and the coroner were well known to each other it was deemed by many coroners not only to be no slight but a piece of kindly consideration not to summon a medical witness. He could not be paid, therefore why trouble him? Wakley's Act removed the difficulty under which both coroner and medical man laboured. The coroner would no longer have any scruple about summoning a medical witness, and the medical man would receive some return for his services to the court. According, then, to persons of the opposite way of thinking to Wakley, matters after 1836 should have gone perfectly smoothly. Wakley's own Act should have nullified the necessity for medical coroners by providing an adequate supply of paid medical witnesses. But nothing of the sort occurred. Wakley's Act put large sums of money into the pocket of the medical profession, but it did not save the non-medical coroner from his blunders. Cases where no medical men were called as witnesses were just as numerous as before, but whereas the previous absence of medical evidence may have been partly due to voluntary abstention of the medical profession, it was now due to economy on the part of the coroner. The county authorities when auditing the county accounts were apt to refer very strongly to the payments made to medical witnesses, saying with the positiveness that goes hand in hand with ignorance that when the cause of death was very evident it was absurd to put the public to expense in ascertaining the cause from a medical man. Many lay coroners listened to these grumblings with too open ears and preferred to risk misdirecting a jury to submitting themselves to the blame of the county authorities, and as a result some of the cases which occurred in the courts of lay coroners, after Parliament had made provision for proper expert evidence, were as flagrant as those that had been the frequent cause of previous scandal. And nothing, Wakley urged, would ever stop these cases save the appointment of medical coroners who would summon medical evidence where it was required with a practical knowledge of the occasion and uninfluenced by motives of parsimony or politeness.

His second opportunity to try his chances with the freeholders of Middlesex did not come until January, 1839, when the death of Mr. Stirling on the 17th of that month caused a vacancy in the coronership of West Middlesex. Wakley was at once urgently desired by a great number of the electors from all parts of the county to become a candidate for the vacant office, and with apparent alacrity he accepted their invitation. It may be thought strange that he required to be invited before coming forward. Since his near defeat ten years previously he had resolutely stood his ground, pleaded the cause of the medical coroner, and refuted or flouted the arguments of all who were opposed to him. In his attitude during this decade he appeared to be waiting for a chance to pounce on the next vacant coronership. But in truth this was not so, and when the chance came again it found him at first doubtful of his course. His hesitation was entirely due to his pecuniary position.

Money was at this time a serious question with Wakley. His conduct with regard to financial matters had always been supremely careless. Receiving money with one hand he threw it away with the other. Ever since the "Lancet" had proved a success he had received large sums and spent larger. Always in difficulties, he was always hopeful and always lavish. But at this particular time—that is during the years of 1837 and 1838—he was seriously embarrassed by the frequent and heavy calls upon his purse.

The contest for the office of coroner was an exceedingly expensive affair. The times were corrupt and election work was conducted throughout by agents, of whom there were a large number employed on both sides and to whom money was given by the principals without question, only the position in the final poll being regarded. His first contest for the coronership had cost Wakley a very large, nay, an enormous sum of money. He really never knew the exact figure, but the total he believed to be over £7000. This sum had been raised through the good nature of his friends and relations in part, in part by pawning the profits of the "Lancet" to certain persons who had nearly from its commencement been associated with him in its conduct and were therefore cognisant of its large and increasing circulation and its substantiality as a source of revenue, and in part from the trustees of his marriage settlement. He proved unsuccessful, and all the money appeared to have been thrown away, leaving him with a burden of debt that would have frightened a man more concerned about his pecuniary position from day to day and less obstinately reliant on his own abilities and fortunate stars. He had resolutely set to work to wipe off the debt and had in part succeeded when his three attempts to represent the borough of Finsbury in Parliament interfered with his projects of economy and raised his liabilities again to the point which they had reached in 1830. Then came success in Parliament, and hand in hand with this success came increase of income through the ever improving circulation of his journal and increase of expenditure through the purchase of the lease of Harefield Park, the more important and luxurious style of living in Bedford Square, and the support and education of a family. His father-in-law often assisted generously, particularly in discharging any liens upon the " Lancet," as he foresaw that it would be a terrible day for Wakley when the control of that property which he had created, and which his individuality and prowess had made valuable, should pass from him. His father-in-law had also helped Wakley in his parliamentary campaign. He gave him the land which allowed him to satisfy the law with regard to property qualification before offering himself to the borough electors, and he subsequently lent him or gave him considerable sums. But Wakley could not go for ever to him, so that it can be understood that he had to give the matter some little thought before accepting the invitation of certain of the free voters to be their candidate again for the vacant coronership. On the one hand, he desired the position, while the annual income, never less than £1500 or £1800, was a strong inducement to him to compete. On the other hand, a large sum of ready money had to be found immediately, while a failure to attain his object for a second time would plunge him into embarrassment that would seriously jeopardise the " Lancet " and his position in Parliament. The fortune that had been spent in the previous contest, however, decided Wakley's friends again to help him. That money was irretrievably wasted if Wakley did not come forward again, whereas if he did come forward and win, it could be regarded as having conduced to his success. It was made easy for him to mortgage his wife's income for £2000, which he did. He stood for the coronership and was overwhelmingly successful.

There were about 9000 freeholders in the county of Middlesex, not including the cities of London and Westminster. The western division of the county contained more than half of these—*i.e.*, 5000 odd; but all the freeholders had the right to vote for both divisions, a curious and anomalous state of affairs which met with Wakley's approval. The division between eastern and western Middlesex, speaking roughly, was the Great North Road. West Middlesex, for which Wakley now became coroner, was bounded on the west by Buckinghamshire, the following places on the border marking the extreme points of his jurisdiction : Harefield Park (his own country residence) ; Uxbridge, four miles south of this ; West Drayton, Colnbrook, and Staines. On the eastern boundary, which was not a very direct straight line, were situated Barnet, Hornsey, Highgate, and the commencement of the Great North Road where it joined the City Road. On the north lay Hertfordshire, the bounding localities being Rickmansworth, Pinner, Stanmore, Elstree, and Mill Hill. The southern boundary was formed by the north bank of the River Thames from Staines to the precincts of the City of Westminster, the places on that bank being Shepperton, Sunbury, Hampton, Teddington, Twickenham, Isleworth, Brentford, Hammersmith, and Fulham. The division between West Middlesex and Westminster followed roughly the course of Piccadilly, the northern side being Middlesex and the southern Westminster. The division between West Middlesex and the City followed the line of the Farringdon Road.

Anyone who will allow his mind to dwell on the size of this vast constituency—it comprised over three hundred square miles and contained 200,000 more persons at that time than the eastern division of the county—and will at the same time imagine it scoured from end to end by competing agents during a poll that lasted a week will understand that the contest was one from which an impecunious man might well shrink. Wakley, however, having accepted the invitation of the freeholders, dashed for victory with characteristic ardour. He had better cards in his hand than on the previous occasion, not the least telling being his unlooked-for success in Parliament. Also, since 1829 many medical coroners—upwards of twenty—had been actually appointed in various parts of the kingdom entirely owing to his writings, and their successful administration compared favourably with some of the lapses reported in the "Lancet" as occurring in the courts of their lay brethren. Before the polling began Wakley said that he was absolutely certain of success, and by February 7th the Middlesex magistrates, the county authorities to whom the coroner would look for payment of his fees, appear to have thought so also. For they made an attempt to diminish the value of the prize now within Wakley's grasp that was as bold in its conception as it was ludicrous in its failure. They suddenly represented to the Lord Chancellor, at the request of fifteen freeholders, that the duties of the coronership for the county of Middlesex were so overwhelmingly arduous that two men should not be asked to undertake them. The magistrates therefore prayed the Lord Chancellor to supersede the writ that he had issued for the election on February 18th and to appoint that two coroners should be elected to fill the vacancy in the coronership of one division of Middlesex. The action of the magistrates was not creditable to their sagacity. Tories to a man, they dreaded the employment of a Radical, and in particular of a Radical who had spoken evilly of the unpaid justiciary. Wakley's only serious opponent, a solicitor named Adey, was much more after their heart. When it was seen that Mr. Adey was certain to be worsted the magistrates hoped to secure his return for half the district if they could persuade the Lord Chancellor, Lord Cottenham, to appoint two coroners. But the personal and political prejudices leading to their action were recognised by the press, and the move was stigmatised by, among others, the "Globe," the "Examiner," the "Morning Chronicle," and the "Lancet" as unworthy and disingenuous. The latter it certainly was, for the work had previously been done to the apparent satisfaction of the magistrates by Mr. Stirling single-handed, and Mr. Stirling was a practising solicitor, clerk to these very magistrates, and *ninety-four* years of age ! The Lord Chancellor curtly answered the memorialists that he saw no reason for acceding to their request.

On February 18th polling began, and by the evening of the

same day Wakley had polled 1824 votes, against 471 given for his opponent. On Wednesday Adey had still not registered much more than a quarter of the number of the votes that had been given for Wakley, and on the evening of that day he retired. Strong pressure had been put upon him by Wakley's personal and political foes to contest the election to the end of the seventh day, which would have meant an enormously increased expense to Wakley, but he had the sense to refuse to accede to such malicious advice, which, moreover, would not have had the desired effect of depleting Wakley's purse, as the freeholders themselves formed a committee to defray all Wakley's future charges by subscription. The " Morning Chronicle " said in recommending such a fund to the public : " This is not the battle-ground of Reformer and Tory, and we should deprecate its being made so. The man best able to discharge the duties of coroner is the man who ought to be elected. The freeholders of the county are manifestly in favour of Mr. Wakley ; and his opponents say by their thus vexatiously carrying on the contest, ' If we cannot beat him by votes we will ruin him by expense.' " Other papers wrote in a similar strain concerning any prolongation of opposition to Wakley's election, and a fund was rapidly raised large enough to make Adey's supporters decide to abandon further resistance. The final result of the poll was—Wakley, 2015 ; Adey, 582 ; and on February 25th, 1839, Wakley became coroner of West Middlesex.

CHAPTER XXXIX

[1839]

Wakley's Reforms as Coroner — Their Cold Reception — His Instructions to the Constabulary of Middlesex — Accusation of holding too frequent Inquests — Abuse in the Political Journals — The Case of Thomas Austin — The Censure of the Middlesex Magistrates — The Report of their Committee appointed to Inquire into the Proceedings of the Two Coroners — Complete Exoneration of Wakley — The Meaning of certain of his Instructions to the Constabulary.

WAKLEY immediately began his work as coroner upon the lines that he had, with a reiteration that would have been wearisome had it not been so necessary, declared to be the only proper ones. Every death the reason of which was not apparent upon the face of its circumstances was made the subject of an inquiry, and in every inquiry where the facts demanded medical elucidation or where the court required medical advice a qualified practitioner was summoned, and if necessary a post-mortem examination was made. The juries that were provided by the energy of the beadle did not escape scrutiny, with the result that Wakley's first move was to supersede that functionary altogether and employ a servant of his own—a sort of informal coroner's officer— upon the difficult and unpleasant task of collecting from twelve to twenty-three capable citizens to act as jurors. The beadle was too prone to look complacently upon the defection of such of the persons whom he summoned as were able to reward him for his amiable disposition, with the result that his juries had not as a rule a high tone, nor could they be said to be largely composed of responsible or well-educated citizens. Wakley declared that he would not have his court made a mockery by the quality of his juries, and his officer was instructed to summon fit and proper persons and to take no denial. Again, he was determined that all inquests conducted by himself should have the dignity, or at any rate the decency, due to the importance of the tribunal and the solemnity of the occasions upon which its deliberations were held. He was resolute that no trace of the ribaldry or tipsy familiarity that had disfigured proceedings at inquests all over the kingdom should appear in his district of West Middlesex. He insisted upon a sober jury as well as a respectable one, and he was no less determined to have orderly proceedings. Counsel, solicitors, and witnesses— ordinary and expert, medical and lay—were made to understand that contempt of court was as serious a crime before a coroner as before a judge or even a chancellor.

Reasonable as all these innovations were, they did not meet with the approbation of everybody. There were beadles and jurymen who were insulted and who were not slow to bare the wounds in their self-esteem to the sympathetic gaze of Wakley's enemies, never weak either in numbers or quality. Solicitors, naturally sore at the violent language that Wakley invariably used both in Parliament and in the " Lancet " to describe their professional methods, were prompt to prophesy the impossibility that so prejudiced a man should become an unprejudiced judge. Here and there an inquest was held which seemed to the relatives of the deceased to be unnecessary, and which, they were informed, would never have been held in the days of that regretted nonagenarian, Mr. Stirling. These families naturally felt very much aggrieved. The authorities at hospitals, lunatic asylums, and poor-houses were also opposed to the new coroner. Wakley had been unsparing in his criticisms of the administration of these places, and it was confidently supposed that he would take the opportunity of revenge offered whenever an unfortunate inmate died, and would hold an inquest at which he would act rather as public prosecutor than judge, hale those responsible for the management of the institution before him, and direct the jury to find them guilty of having caused, or at least contributed towards, the fate of the deceased. Such was the ridiculous view that people, who ought to have known better, took of Wakley's honest efforts towards reform. And all this simmering discontent found its way to the ears of the Middlesex magistrates, whose hostile attitude towards Wakley's pretensions to the coronership had not abated a whit on seeing these pretensions remarkably ratified by the freeholders, and who would seem to have been waiting for an opportunity to censure an officer whose general politics they detested and whose particular merits they were blind to.

Wakley soon gave them the very opportunity that they desired. In September, 1839, he issued certain instructions to the constabulary of West Middlesex which roused excitement throughout the county and led to a special meeting of the Middlesex magistrates and later to a parliamentary inquiry. These instructions, which were issued above his signature, were as follows :—

" I have to request that after the 29th day of the present month of September, 1839, all applications relative to the holding of inquests may be made to me at 35, Bedford Square, London.

" QUESTIONS TO BE ANSWERED WHEN APPLYING FOR A WARRANT :—

" On applying for warrants for the taking of inquests in the Western Division of Middlesex the constable or beadle is desired to answer such of the following questions as may concern each particular death.

" 1. When did the death happen ?

" 2. When was the body found ?

" 3. Was the deceased a male or a female—an infant, a lunatic, or a pauper ?

" 4. What is thought to have been the cause of death ?

" 5. Is the body in a fresh state or a decomposed state ?

" 6. If it be supposed that poison was the cause of death, what was the poison ?

" 7. If any medical practitioner was in attendance before death, what is his name ?

" 8. If the death was sudden, was there any previous illness, and for what length of time ?

" 9. At what public-house or other place is the inquest to be held ?

" 10. How far is the body from that public-house or other place ?

"NOTICE IS TO BE GIVEN TO THE CORONER BY HEAD-
BOROUGHS, POLICE, PARISH CONSTABLES, AND
BEADLES IN ALL CASES:—

" 1. When persons die suddenly.

" 2. When persons are found dead.

" 3. When persons die from any acts of violence or any accident.

" 4. When women die during labour or a few hours after delivery.

" 5. When persons are supposed to have died from the effects of poisons or quack medicines.

" 6. When persons die who appear to have been neglected during sickness or extreme poverty.

" 7. When persons die in confinement, as in prisons, police offices, or station houses.

" 8. When lunatics or paupers die in confinement, whether in public or in private asylums."

Now certainly these instructions do not in themselves read as very inflammatory. Firstly, they were not, it will be seen, to be applied rigidly in every case. The officials had discretion in following them. Secondly, they were designed to facilitate the coroner's work by preventing unnecessary inquests ; for if the coroner received a full and satisfactory report from the constable, one which tallied with a common-sense view of the case as well as with the view of an official investigator who was also a medical expert, no inquest would be held, to the economy of the public funds and of the investigator's time. In the third place, the universal rule that all deaths in gaols, lunatic asylums, and places where the proper working of the Poor-law might have obviated the catastrophe should be made the subject of inquiry formed an excellent guarantee to the public that the public departments were managed with due care and efficiency. Lastly, the provision to inquire into deaths where, on the face of it, unqualified medical practice seemed to count for something in the unfortunate issue was intended to protect the public against the dangers of quackery.

Of course, Wakley had gone too fast, particularly in this last direction ; but it is astonishing, reading them now, to understand the excitement which these instructions, having for their object reform in the procedure of his own coroner's court, created in the public mind.   To begin with, it was assumed by the public that it was Wakley's object to hold as many inquests as he could, quite regardless whether the public weal demanded such multiplications of scrutiny.   It is difficult to say who started this rumour, but it received at once very wide credence.   It had a certain air of probability about it and was industriously spread by Wakley's enemies, and indeed, by all those whose comfort was likely to be interfered with under the new regulations.   Whoever could foresee trouble for himself in the future made haste to discount it by imputing to the new coroner's energy the vulgar motive of fee-grabbing.   The political newspapers— such as the " Times," the " Morning Advertiser," the " Morning Herald," and the " Observer "—wrote leading articles in opposition to Wakley's new regulations, entirely based on the supposition that it was his intention to increase the number of inquests immoderately and autocratically. Politics soon began to play a part in the frequent denun- ciations of the unfortunate coroner.   When Wakley saw the storm that was gathering around him he addressed one of his juries in defence of his new regulations.   He pointed out that the coroner was the *people's* judge, the only judge whom the *people* had the power to appoint, while the office had been specially instituted for the protection of the *people*, and declared his belief that all the baiting to which he was now being vexatiously subjected came from " certain persons in authority who had been, and wished to continue to be, free from observation and control," and who were now " becoming apprehensive of the prospect of having the atten- tion of the public directed to their conduct."   He referred, of course, by these expressions to the Government officials in charge of gaols and of the administration of the Poor- law, and to the owners and managers of lunatic asylums. A correspondent in the " Morning Herald " commented gracefully on Wakley's address to the jury by saying that he had " obviously resolved to combine his electioneering with his official labours and had converted, in fact, the coroner's court. into a district committee *pro tem.* . . . . This is the secret of all Mr. Wakley's palaver. It all tends to the hustings. This villainous iteration about *the people, the people, the people,* has very little to do with the crowner's quest, but it has a vast deal to do with the next election for Finsbury." Hospital officials followed the suit of Government employés and political foes, declaring that Wakley's new regulations contained a deliberate insult to the medical profession. Inquests were to be held, forsooth, on all persons who had died during labour or a few hours after delivery ! What meant this intolerable intrusion upon a mourning household except that Wakley desired to sit in judgment on his brother medical men, protected by his position in the coroner's chair ? The profession was warned through the medium of that section of the medical press whose interests were opposed to Wakley's that the coroner's inquest under the new rules would certainly be used as an instrument of terror over them exactly as the "Lancet" had attempted to terrorise those in charge of hospitals by gross abuse of all concerned in the administration. And just as the excitement was at its highest occurred a case which gave colour to much that Wakley's enemies were saying and writing, though that coincidence did not deter him from doing exactly what he conceived to be his duty in the teeth of all opposition.

On September 30th, 1839, exactly twenty-four hours after the new regulations came into force, there died in the Hendon Union a pauper aged seventy-nine years named Thomas Austin. The immediate cause of death was not in dispute : he fell into a copper in the laundry and perished of the scalding that he received. No notice was given to the coroner and Austin's body was duly buried in Hendon churchyard by order of the guardians. Wakley heard of the accident and its fatal result, and attended at the union to hold an inquest. He there learned that the body of the man had been interred. He immediately sent a requisition to the vicar and churchwardens demanding the exhumation of the body. His request was refused peremptorily by a churchwarden, whom Wakley declared to have been guilty of a gross piece of contempt of court for which he could be summarily punished. Ultimately the opposition gave way and the inquest was held, a verdict of accidental death being returned with a rider to the effect that there had been contributory neglect on the part of the workhouse authorities in not placing a railing round the copper. The master of the workhouse, resenting this and hoping to embarrass the coroner, exclaimed with triumph when the verdict was given: "The jury have found a verdict, but have not identified the body." Wakley, however, had the last word, and blandly inquired: "If this is not the body of the man who was killed in your vat, pray, Sir, how many paupers have you boiled?"

The case offered an excellent opportunity to Wakley's enemies to take serious steps—more serious than the strongly worded attacks which they had inspired in the daily press. A meeting was held at the Clerkenwell Sessions House on October 10th, 1839, at which the Rev. Theodore Williams, the vicar of Hendon, who was a magistrate, attended and formally complained of Wakley's conduct in no measured terms. He even went so far as to suggest that not only should Wakley's fees be refused, but that a requisition should be made by the bench to the Lord Chancellor to remove him from his position of coroner. A long discussion ensued, in which Wakley did not find one supporter among the magistrates so completely did prejudice occupy their minds. Without going to quite the lengths to which the vicar of Hendon desired to commit them they gave proof of the bent of their minds by their unjust action with regard to the coroner's fees. The accounts for August had been audited and passed by the finance committee, but notwithstanding that circumstance a motion was made to refer back those accounts to that committee on the ground that they were not accompanied by the required vouchers. That motion, conveying as it did a severe censure on the coroner in the form of an imputation on his honesty, was carried

without one dissentient voice, while at the same time another
motion was adopted for the appointment of a committee
of magistrates "to inquire into the cause of the increase of
inquests since the enactment of the 1st and 2nd Vict., c. 68
(Wakley's Act securing remuneration to medical witnesses),
and to reconsider the schedule of fees now paid under that
statute and to report generally."

Great was the jubilation among Wakley's enemies when
the result of this sitting of the Middlesex magistrates became
public. The anonymous venom of private and political
opponents had received the official endorsement of a bench
of magistrates, affixed presumably after due deliberation,
and not only had Wakley been found guilty of having held
unnecessary inquests, but so certain were the bench of this
that they had taken the extreme step of withholding his fees.
The "Morning Herald" led the way in showering abuse
upon Wakley, but was pulled up sharp when at a full and
congenial gallop of vituperation by a threat of legal proceedings, Wakley having discovered that a very fine example
of "an inquest . . . . got up for the sake of securing a
fee" (to quote the words of the libel), which had been
published in the columns of that paper under the heading,
in large capitals, "Mr. Wakley's Coronership," had occurred
under the coronership of the late Mr. Stirling *exactly ten
months before Wakley's election to office!* This little slip gave
pause to the "Morning Herald," but other journals kept up
the cry, and so persistently that for the honour of journalism
it must be believed that in popular opinion Wakley was
really guilty. He was known to be a man with great expenses. He had openly allowed that his income was a small
one compared with these expenses. What more likely than
that he did hold unnecessary inquests, seeing that the more
inquests he held the more money he would receive ? And
what more likely than that he had designed his new regulations with the express intent of enabling him to hold an
increased number of inquests ? The cynical and probable
answer to these questions, the only answer that would
satisfy the public mind, into which suspicion had been

thoroughly instilled, was—Nothing could be more likely. Wakley, in fact, stood convicted of having prostituted his public calling to his private needs unless he could actually show that the assumption made throughout against him was a false one, and that the number of inquests during his term of office had not increased and was not likely to increase. The public, reading the new instructions, had taken it for granted that inquests would be much more frequent, for they looked at Wakley's regulations only to discover the openings therein indicated for the holding of a coroner's inquiry. They entirely omitted to grasp how many situations which under a less orderly and well-informed coroner would have led to an inquest, would by the aid of Wakley's regulations be revealed as perfectly natural. The public had followed the lead of the press and the magistrates had followed the lead of the press and public. It would have been in vain for Wakley to explain his new regulations further. Nothing would clear him immediately save a flat contradiction of the statement that the number of inquests had increased.

Within three weeks this contradiction was forthcoming, and it was furnished by the report of that very committee of magistrates which had been appointed to inquire and report generally upon the subject at the meeting held on October 10th, when Wakley's accounts were insultingly referred back to the finance committee. On October 22nd Wakley received a letter inviting his attendance at the Sessions House to give an explanation as to the necessity of holding inquests in certain cases, a list of which was sent to him. Wakley waited upon the magistrates because, as he explained to them, he was willing cheerfully to give all explanation of his conduct and courted a complete examination of his procedure as coroner, but inasmuch as the magistrates had no legal right whatever to summon him before them he handed in a formal protest against the proceedings, with a request that it should be attached to the minutes of the meeting. Mr. Baker, the coroner for East Middlesex, had also been summoned, as had Mr. Bell, Wakley's official clerk, who had for fifteen years acted in the same capacity for Mr. Stirling, and whose clerical efficiency was now in question, seeing that he was responsible for the accounts which the magistrates had refused to settle. The magistrates made a thorough but very courteous inquiry, and the three officials answered with fulness and readiness. As a consequence of this unexpected cordiality—for Wakley made no secret of his own belief that he would not obtain fair treatment—the report was ready for the magistrates on the last day of the month, or just three weeks from the appointment of the committee. To say that it was received with astonishment by the public hardly expresses the feeling created. The findings of the committee were briefly as follows, as far as Wakley was concerned :—(1) Wakley had held a *less* average number of inquests than his predecessor, Mr. Stirling; (2) a *less* sum of money had been paid for the attendance of medical witnesses; (3) a *less* sum of money had been paid for post-mortem examinations; and (4) Wakley's disbursements for the expenses of inquests were considerably *lower* than those of Mr. Baker in the adjoining division, being, in fact, £1 0s. 3d. for each inquest against £1 11s. 2¼d. (The figures did not include the coroner's fee of £1 1s.) There had been an increase in the number of inquests held in some directions, but a great decrease in others, and Mr. Bell testified to the numerous occasions on which Wakley had refused to issue warrants, being satisfied by the answers to the preliminary inquiries that the death in question was perfectly natural. Mr. Bell also testified that the accounts which had been repudiated as irregular had been rendered in exactly the same shape and style as the late Mr. Stirling's, whose demands had always been satisfactorily settled. The committee read and approved Wakley's famous instructions, merely saying that he was not justified by law in holding inquests on every case of sudden death, as thus deaths from " fever or other apparent visitations of God" would become the subject of the coroner's inquest, which had clearly not been intended by the statute of 4th Edward I.

The whole report was a complete triumph for Wakley, whose sole fault was found to be that he differed from the views of the first Edward upon Providential design. And the debate which followed upon it confirmed the good impression that had been made, for the magistrates found that Wakley's conduct in the Hendon episode was right and according to law, and that the Rev. Theodore Williams's view was entirely wrong. It was now seen that the instructions to constables and others had a very real meaning and that they acted in the direction of checking unnecessary inquests. The public also perceived that Wakley's declared intention of holding inquests upon all those who died in prisons, asylums, or poorhouses was dictated by a proper and humane desire to make the coroner's court a protection for the people. Gross cruelties were undoubtedly perpetrated in these institutions, and it was his intention to prevent them at any rate in West Middlesex. On less obvious points in the meaning of his regulations Wakley explained himself now that the great reaction in his favour gave him an audience who would, for the first time, listen to an explanation. He pointed out that he had not declared an intention of holding an inquest upon every sudden death, but had only desired that notice should be given to him of all such deaths, when he would decide by the answers obtained to his preliminary inquiries whether the event had been natural or not. This, as a medical man, he could do and feel certain that his judgment was right. With regard to the regulation that the coroner should receive notice of all cases where women had died during labour or within a few hours of delivery it has been said that Wakley went a little too fast here. He certainly should have made his meaning more clear, as he ran a great risk of estranging the sympathies of the medical profession, in whose particular interest he had been acting throughout, as was very apparent by the allusion to quack medicines. The suggestion that he desired to sit in judgment on his brother practitioners was a subtle and plausible one and in certain quarters received credence. His real object was to stop unqualified practice in the interests both of the public and the medical profession. He was aware that it was the habit of many medical men to keep assistants to attend their obstetric cases for them, and he knew that the majority of these assistants were unqualified and that some were undoubtedly ignorant. He was far-seeing enough to detect the mischief that such "covering" would work in the profession twenty years before the General Medical Council existed and fifty years before it acted; and he intended in all cases where a woman had died in childbirth under circumstances that pointed to neglect or ignorance on the part of an unqualified man to fix some responsibility for the death upon the shoulders of both employer and assistant. It was notorious, also, that it was the habit of dirty, stupid women to attend upon their pregnant sisters unsupervised by medical men, and that their ministrations resulted too often in unspeakable misery to the patients and sometimes in a terrible spread of disease. The suppression of this practice as well as the termination of the scandals arising out of the employment of incompetent assistants had been aimed at by Wakley in the best abused of his instructions to the constabulary of Middlesex. To protect the public against unqualified practice and the medical profession against unfair competition was, in short, his double and doubly praiseworthy object in framing the regulation on account of which he was denounced as a callous violator of all decency, a person in whose estimation the sanctity of grief weighed nothing in comparison with a coroner's fee.

CHAPTER XL

[1840–1846]

Wakley accused of usurping Magisterial Functions—Indignation of the Middlesex Magistrates—The Appointment of a Parliamentary Committee to Inquire into the Middlesex Coronerships — The Evidence of Baker, Wakley, and other Witnesses—The Findings of the Committee—Wakley's Prolonged Struggle with the Magistrates —The " Ingoldsby Legends " and Wakley—The Composite District of West Middlesex—Three Specimen Medical Inquests—The Hounslow Flogging Case.

THIS triumphant issue of Wakley's first serious encounter with the magistrates of Middlesex did not at once establish amicable relations between him and that body. Almost immediately an attempt was made to discredit his authority and judgment by an indignant criticism of certain proceedings which had occurred at one of his inquests, strong expressions of censure being made use of regarding his conduct. These should never have been employed by the. magistrates, who held a commission to administer the law and should have remembered that Wakley's position in the public eye was more important than their own even when considered legally. The inquest itself was not especially interesting either from a medical or a forensic point of view. A fish-hawker of Uxbridge had been stabbed in the abdomen by a lad aged fifteen years under circumstances which led to a verdict from the coroner's jury of "Wilful Murder." Wakley instructed the constable in charge of the case to take the lad direct to Newgate upon a warrant made out by himself. The case had been previously before the Middlesex magistrates, who had adjourned their inquiry until the completion of the coroner's inquest. The result of Wakley's action was that when the magistrates again met there was no prisoner before them. They were excessively annoyed at being placed in a position in which they conceived that Wakley had exceeded his powers at the expense of their dignity. They rebuked the constable for carrying out Wakley's orders and gave an impetuous freedom to their speech in registering their opinions of the coroner's behaviour in taking an important duty out of their hands. They conceived that Wakley had committed the boy solely out of an idea that by so doing he would make them look ridiculous. It was as much as to say, "You excellent gentlemen can deliberate over the boy's case if you like, but any opinion you arrive at will be only interesting to yourselves and not of any practical value to the public, for I have committed him to Newgate, whence he will be taken before your superiors." As a matter of fact Wakley had been actuated by no such stupid and vulgar motive, but only by what he conceived to be prudence and a regard for the public time. A similar case had occurred in a neighbouring jurisdiction and Wakley, feeling that his brother coroner had been right on that occasion, followed the precedent. The magistrates, however, believed that they were a deeply insulted body, and a movement was set on foot for the appointment of a Select Committee of the House of Commons to inquire into the whole question of the Middlesex coronerships. Other factors soon took their part in keeping the movement going. The vicar of Hendon, in the suddenly assumed character of an energetic magistrate, had not forgotten the official snub that he had received as the result of interfering with the exhumation of the body of Thomas Austin, and was glad to learn that a further opportunity would be given to discuss that case before a new tribunal. The magistrates as a body had another grievance against Wakley. During the winter he had held an unusually large number of inquests by deputy, and they were uneasy as to the legality of his action in so doing. Three sets of charges were thus formulated against Wakley :—

(1) that he had overstepped the jurisdiction of his office and trespassed upon that of the magistrates by committing the Uxbridge prisoner to Newgate; (2) that he had held unnecessary inquests, notably in the case of Thomas Austin; and (3) that he had allowed an unusually large number of inquiries to be conducted by deputy. On these grounds the appointment of a Parliamentary Committee was sought. Wakley, true to his previously expressed desire that his public duties should always be subject to the scrutiny of the public, so far from offering any opposition to its appointment, spoke in its favour, and on March 17th, 1840, certain members of Parliament were commissioned to report upon the whole matter. Their reference was "to inquire into any measures which have been adopted for carrying into effect in the county of Middlesex the provisions of the Act 1 Victoria, c. 68, and also into any proceedings of the Justices of the Peace in relation to the office of coroner in the said county." The Committee was a strong one and consisted of these fifteen persons, : Lord Teignmouth (chairman), Colonel Thomas Wood, Mr. William Williams, Mr. Mackinnon, the Solicitor-General for Ireland, Mr. Cripps, Mr. Thomas Duncombe, Sir James Duke, Lord Eliot, Mr. Aglionby, Sir Thomas Freemantle, Sir Benjamin Hall, Mr. Gally Knight, Sir George Strickland, and Wakley himself. Of these, five were to form a quorum.

After a preliminary discussion upon their mode of proceeding the first meeting for hearing evidence was held on May 29th, 1840, Lord Teignmouth being in the chair, and the first witness called was Mr. William Baker, who for nine years and eight months had been the coroner for the eastern division of the county. Mr. Baker, in the course of his evidence, expressed his opinion that the scale of payment to witnesses, both medical and others, under the Act was fair, but thought there should be some fee to the jurymen—an opinion that is now gaining ground rapidly. On the question of deputy coroners he said that Wakley's predecessor frequently held inquests by deputy, as also did his own predecessor, Mr. Unwin, although he had never done

duty by deputy himself.   This evidence was very valuable
to Wakley, as showing that the qualms of conscience which
had ·overtaken the Middlesex magistrates in the matter of
deputy coroners were of recent origin, being, in fact, con-
temporaneous with his election to office.   Mr. C. Wright,
clerk to the committees of the Middlesex magistrates, was
examined next, particularly on the question of the holding of
too frequent inquests.   He stated that forty-eight inquests
had been held in the county the expenses of which were dis-
allowed by the magistrates ; of these, thirty were in Wakley's
district ; and subsequently the expenses in forty-seven of
the cases were allowed, those in one only being refused.
The deputy clerk was examined next upon the incidental
expenses of the two coronerships of Middlesex, using the
figures which had already been prepared for the committee
of Middlesex magistrates.   He deposed that between
August 14th and September 14th, 1839, forty-seven inquests
were held by Wakley, who paid out of pocket £49 9s. 6d.—
a fraction over £1 for each inquest.   During the same
period Mr. Baker held thirty-nine inquests and paid expenses
out of pocket £60 1s.—a fraction over £1 10s. for each
inquest.   Mr. Thomas Bell, clerk to Wakley, deposed that
he was for fifteen years clerk to Wakley's predecessor, Mr.
Stirling, during which time the accounts were made up in
the same way as they were at present.   In Mr. Stirling's case
there had been no obstacle or objection to the payment of
such accounts, although there had been several since Wakley's
appointment to the office.   Mr. Bell had never heard of any
objection being made by magistrates to the employment
of deputy coroners till Wakley was appointed to the office.
Sir Peter Lawrie, one of the Middlesex magistrates, was
examined next, and from him it was elicited that one of the
magistrates who greatly objected to the payment of the
present coroner's accounts was the implacable vicar of
Hendon.   Sir Peter Lawrie said that his attention had
never been drawn either to the coroner's accounts or to the
practice of holding inquests by deputy before Wakley's
appointment ; and he also added that previously to the

fracas arising out of the disinterment of the body of Thomas Austin, the vicar of Hendon had not as a justice of the peace given any special attention to the county finances, but that on the morning of the next quarter sessions he had told Sir Peter Lawrie he was "going to attend for the express purpose of objecting to the coroner's accounts." On June 30th Wakley's examination commenced, for in the proceedings of this Parliamentary Committee to inquire into his own behaviour he occupied the Gilbertian position of criminal as well as judge. His examination turned chiefly on the alleged want of accord between the local justices and the coroner. He was questioned closely upon the case where he had himself made out a warrant for the committal of a prisoner to Newgate on the charge of murder. The constable, Wakley admitted, said that he had been directed to take the prisoner back to Uxbridge, so that he might go before the magistrates, but he (Wakley) insisted on his being at once removed to Newgate, a coroner's verdict *in esse* being of more importance in his eyes than a magisterial decision *in posse*. Subsequently the magistrates met to investigate the case, and he knew that there was no prisoner forthcoming. But he learned also that his proceedings were made the subject of severe censure, and that the unfortunate constable, who only acted under his orders, was also severely rebuked. With regard to the Hendon case Wakley related the whole story over again, pointing out that it was his undoubted duty to hold the inquest, and that he was therefore compelled to ask the vicar and churchwardens of Hendon to disinter the body. They had refused to pay any attention to his warrant, and he had consequently been compelled to hire labourers to perform the task and to pay them himself. Wakley was followed by Mr. Serjeant Adams, who was examined on July 3rd with respect to the same case. He remembered a complaint being made at the Quarter Sessions held the previous October of indelicacy on the part of the coroner for the western division of the county in having the body of a pauper raised and exhibited to view whilst the vicar was performing the funeral service over another body in the churchyard—"but no one doubted Mr. Wakley's right to disinter the body." Much of the learned serjeant's evidence was in the form of a discussion as to whether the phrase "duly held," as applied to an inquest, signified that the inquest had been *necessary*, but he was unable to help the Committee to any definite conclusions.

The Committee reported on July 27th, 1840, and agreed to eleven resolutions, of which the seventh, eighth, and ninth had reference to Wakley personally, namely :—7. That the magistrates in disallowing the fees for inquests held by deputy acted in conformity to the law, but that Mr. Wakley, in appointing a deputy during his temporary illness, followed the practice of his predecessors, and that by 6 and 7 Will. IV., c. 105, coroners in case of illness or unavoidable absence were empowered to appoint their own deputy officers. 8. That with reference to an inquest held at Hayes the proceeding of the magistrates in committing an individual to Newgate on a charge of manslaughter after the jury had found a verdict of wilful murder was strictly legal. (This was the case upon which Wakley had relied as a precedent for his conduct in the matter of the Uxbridge lad, but the Committee did not take the same view. They considered that at any rate the magistrates were within their rights in committing the prisoner in what terms they pleased and in disregarding the coroner's jury, who had taken a more serious view. 9. That in reference to another inquest, the coroner having committed an individual to Newgate, and it being alleged that the magistrates had censured the coroner and rebuked the constable, the Committee having no distinct proof of the terms or form of such censure abstain from expressing any opinion thereon. 10. The tenth resolution was to- the effect that any interference of individual magistrates with the coroner for Middlesex had been overruled by the general court, and that the magistrates as a body showed a disposition to uphold the authority of the coroners and to work well with them.

The result of the Parliamentary Committee was satisfactory

to Wakley, but not quite so satisfactory to Mr. Baker. Mr. Baker was an admirable official, as good a living argument for the legal coroner as Wakley was for the medical. The magistrates designed to do him honour at the expense of his colleague by inquiring into the conduct of the coronerships, and they succeeded in effecting the reverse. That he did not appreciate their attentions may be read in the following passage from his book on Coroners' Law, which was published in 1851, and remained the best text-book on the subject as long as the law continued unaltered :—

"Considering the useful and important functions which justices of the peace and coroners are reciprocally called upon to perform in penitentiaries, gaols, unions, workhouses, lunatic asylums, and other places," wrote Mr. Baker, "it seems quite clear that such public officers should stand with regard to the exercise of their duties in a perfect state of independence relative to one another, more especially as by the Poor-law Act all justices of the district in which a union is established are ex-officio guardians of the poor; and that in calling into action the judicial functions of the coroner that officer ought not to be fettered by the apprehension of a personal or vexatious exercise of authority by individuals on whose conduct he may be called upon to adjudicate. . . . . It is much to be regretted that a disposition on the part of the magistrates of some counties prevails to exercise too rigid an economy with regard to the payment of fees and expenses of inquests out of the county rates; and by laying impediments in the way of the coroner, and imposing restrictions upon him which the law never contemplated, they indirectly attack the efficiency of the office."*

From this time forward, although the relations between himself and the Middlesex magistrates did not at once become smooth, no more trouble was experienced by Wakley about his conduct of inquests. He had proved to the public, to the magistrates, and to the House of Commons that none of the charges against him would bear even the flimsiest investigation ; while he had demonstrated in addition to the magistrates a fact that other opponents had found out

* "A Practical Compendium of the Recent Statute Cases and Decisions Affecting the Office of Coroner." By William Baker, one of the Coroners for Middlesex. 1851.

before—namely, that he was an awkward man to attempt to confine or coerce. He was quite ready to meet the views of persons able to express them in a reasonable manner, but he was not to be browbeaten. Moreover, he was an old hand at a newspaper war and entered into the spirit of it, so that the unfair and even libellous criticisms upon him instead of making him amenable only made him more determined to conduct matters in his own way. For several years the Middlesex magistrates put him to great trouble concerning his fees, which does not appear as a very dignified or worthy attempt at reprisal. His disbursements were often very heavy in the aggregate, even though the individual inquests were economically conducted, for his district was so enormous. The county consequently would frequently owe him large sums of money, which it would have been exceedingly agreeable to him, living in the expensive style that he did, to obtain quickly, but which he never could extract from them without delays and formalities which, under the circumstances, were almost impertinent. The chief items in his claims against the county were for "mileage"—that is, for money allowed to the coroner for expenses and calculated at so much a mile, a shilling being the usual figure, from his residence to the place of the inquest. The magistrates complained that by taking up his abode at Harefield Park, on the extreme confines of his district, he had made the mileage expenses as heavy as possible. Now, to begin with, this contention was beside the point. Having no legal force it could only have been employed vexatiously. There was no dispute that Harefield Park was within the district, and as the law said nothing of any necessity that the coroner should live in the centre of his district this objection to payment of Wakley's claims was quite untenable. Wakley's reply, however, took no legal grounds. He simply said that he had resided at Harefield some years before he was elected coroner, and that in a district so large if he lived in the centre of it he would almost invariably have a long way to drive to each inquest, whereas by residing half at Harefield Park and half at Bedford Square he gave the county a double chance that he would be near the scene of action. In calling attention to the fact that his claim for mileage must of necessity be high because of the number of inquests that it was his duty to hold, he was always able to refer to the admittedly arduous nature of his work, so arduous that the magistrates themselves had petitioned the Lord Chancellor to appoint two people to do it. After a time this bickering over accounts ceased, and the magistrates were content to put up with a man who would not acknowledge their authority, yet whose duties towards the county which they and he served were always rigidly, and even enthusiastically, discharged.

But although peace was ultimately made Wakley never forgave the bench for their bitter and sustained opposition to him at the beginning of his official relations with them. He resented the attempts to personally humiliate him, which were marked, and openly declared that their original design had been to drive him from the coronership. But more than his personal grievances he deplored the publicity that his quarrels with the magistrates received, because of the harm that he feared might thus be done to the future chances of medical men becoming coroners. He thought that the relations between himself and the Middlesex magistrates might be taken by the people as typical of those that would result from the choice of medical men, whereas the opposition to him had been in the first instance wholly political and unconnected with his profession. Whether future elections of medical coroners were endangered or not there are no means of judging, but certainly these two years of quarrelling earned Wakley an unfair public reputation as a difficult man. His high opinion of the dignity and utility of his office which led him to assume an antagonistic demeanour towards all who attempted to lower the one or lessen the other was very generally treated by the press as a manifestation of fussiness, until time proved Wakley right in his views, and a much suaver man than his early actions promised. The following lines from the " Ingoldsby Legends " reflect the erroneous estimate of him very distinctly, and probably were written with the identical Uxbridge case as a text, although they did not appear till some years later—not indeed until Barham was dead and public opinion of Wakley as a coroner had completely veered round :—

> " They sent for the May'r and the Doctor, a pair
> Of grave men, who began to discuss the affair,
> When in bounced the Coroner, foaming with fury,
> ' Because,' as he said, ' 'twas pooh-pooh ! ing his jury.'

> " Then commenced a dispute, and so hot they went to't,
> That things seemed to threaten a serious *émeute*,
> When, just in the midst of the uproar and racket,
> Who should walk in but St. Thomas à Becket.

> " Quoth his saintship, ' How now ?   Here's a fine coil, I trow !
> I should like to know, gentlemen, what's all this row ?
> Mr. Wickliffe—or Wackliffe—whatever your name is—
> And you, Mr. May'r, don't you know, sirs, what shame is ? ' " *

The records in the coroner's court of such a jurisdiction as that over which Wakley held sway would make curious and interesting reading.   His inquests averaged fifteen per week, and the cases which came before him presented a variety that must have been almost peculiar to his district.   A large metropolitan area supplied catastrophes of all the usual and unusual urban varieties, and questions of the liability of employers, the adequacy of hospital administration, the management of reformatories, and the sanitation of house property among others were offered to well-selected juries for their consideration.   A large country area, on the other hand, brought its tale of rural woe.   There were spots on the Hertfordshire and Buckinghamshire borders whose primeval ignorance and deep poverty seemed incredible recalling that the inhabitants were within a day's walk of the largest city in the world.   Here the death of the miserably paid, under-fed labourer in his dirty hut, of the wayside tramp in the ditch, of the gamekeeper and the poacher, provoked investigation into the Corn Laws, the

* " The Brothers of Birchington, a Lay of St. Thomas à Becket." The Ingoldsby Legends.   Third Series.   1847.

Poor-law Amendment Act, and the Game Laws; while occasionally some bucolic crime, terrible with the blind savagery of the primitive man, would come before a jury so primitive themselves that the particular note of horror would fall upon deaf ears. On one occasion it was found that the jury who had been summoned to an inquest to be held in a hamlet near Harrow had divided among themselves the raiment of the body, contributing their rejected rags to protect it from nakedness!

Many of the inquests held by Wakley were reported in the "Lancet," but only when there was a strong medical interest attached to some of the evidence. Wakley was before all things a medical coroner, and firmly convinced that a good coroner without medical knowledge could not be. Whenever he had a case before him where scientific knowledge came into play he gave that case full publicity, that it might form an argument for the future election of medical coroners. The early reports were written by George Ireland Mills, afterwards deputy-coroner for West Middlesex, the second of the Mills brothers whose early and intimate friendship with Wakley has already been recorded. Many of the cases so reported are also to be found in the "Annual Register," a publication which has always given a generous proportion of its space to the chronicles of horror and crime, and among them a few cases may be mentioned which in particular during the first seven years of Wakley's coronership drew attention to the utility that a medical coroner might be to the community. A deaf lad who had gone to a certain Dr. Turnbull of Russell Square, an oculist and aurist of note about the beginning of the present reign, died in the medical man's consulting-room during an operation. The evidence showed that the deceased had received from Dr. Turnbull or his assistant some sort of bellows, with directions how to use them. He died whilst forcing air up his nose. Turnbull was an able, inventive man and properly qualified, but his methods were reprehensible. He boldly held out hopes of cure to the incurable, magnified small mishaps into constitutional conditions requiring his exceptional skill for their remedy, was heroic in the application of treatment, and, generally speaking, played a part towards the public which a self-respecting practitioner would not have done. His practice was so enormous that on more than one occasion his neighbours in the quiet square had complained to the police of the obstruction to the traffic on the pavement caused by Turnbull's gratuitous patients assembling without his house at certain hours, and once at least this fortunate man had to appear in a police-court to be fined for his popularity. The irregularities in Turnbull's methods, despite this great public favour, were well known to Wakley, who saw in the death of the lad their possible result. It chanced also that a fatality had occurred but a few days before in Mr. Baker's jurisdiction, sudden death having followed the use of these same bellows for deafness. Wakley, therefore, ordered a post-mortem examination to be made, when certain appearances were described to the jury which Mr. Savage, the lecturer on anatomy at Westminster Hospital, attributed to the injection of cold air into the Eustachian tubes; while Liston, the great surgeon, ascribed the boy's death to shock following on the same treatment, although he was not so positive in his evidence that the physical signs discovered post mortem had the significance that Mr. Savage gave them. Wakley expounded this evidence to the jury, with the result that Turnbull was cautioned, by a rider to the verdict, never again to trust his instrument in unprofessional hands. Another case which caused much popular sensation was that of a cabman who had been plied with raw spirits by one of his fares with a view of ascertaining how much alcohol the poor wretch could carry. The cabman collapsed and died, and Wakley had considerable difficulty in persuading the jury that the cause of death had been the imbibition of spirits, for they one and all refused to believe that raw spirit of potable description was a virulent and rapid poison if taken in sufficiently large doses. Wakley's little lecture on physiology enlightened the public. Another case which occurred in Wakley's district was remarkable, firstly, by its medical bearings, and, secondly, because of the extraordinary coincidence that it formed. A well-known member of the Bar, a serjeant-at-law and leader on the Midland Circuit, was found in his study deluged with blood, the belief of those who found him being that he had cut his throat. No medical evidence being offered, Wakley ordered an adjournment to allow of a post-mortem examination being made, when it was discovered that the hæmorrhage had proceeded from the lungs, and not from any external wound, self-inflicted or other. The coincidence lay in the fact that several years before the case occurred Wakley had given as an example of the necessity for medical knowledge in the coroner the supposititious instance of a death from pulmonary hæmorrhage being mistaken for cut-throat. He pointed out that many people believed it to be wrong, dangerous, and impedimental to the course of the law to touch a corpse until after the inquest ; that, consequently, such a case unless medical evidence was provided might be reported to the jury as a suicide upon unchallenged testimony and a verdict obtained in accordance. The supposititious case as put by Wakley was considered exceedingly far-fetched, so that it was extraordinary that a very similar one should have occurred in real life in his own experience within a few years.

The publication of these and other cases served to impress on the public mind the feeling that with a medical coroner the inquest was a safeguard that it never could be where the coroner was a lawyer. And that some such general impression was created is shown by the extraordinary outburst of public sympathy that greeted the action of the coroner of West Middlesex in the most sensational inquiry that it was ever his duty to hold. When in August, 1846, in accordance with Wakley's direction, a jury found that Private White, of the Seventh Hussars, had died from the effects of a flogging administered according to the ordinary regulations then existing in the Army, the anger of many worthy and influential people as well as of military martinets would have seriously jeopardised Wakley's position had it not been for the strong public credit which he enjoyed by that time as a fair judge, a shrewd man, and a logical interpreter of medical evidence. There was judgment as well as humanity behind the endorsement that Wakley's conduct then received, and the popular confidence which he enjoyed enabled him to carry through a bitter struggle with constituted authority before which a weaker man or a man less reinforced by public opinion would have almost certainly succumbed. A righteous cause has strength, but the solid front of a great public department does not collapse before mere righteousness.

CHAPTER XLI

[1846]

The Death of Frederick John White—The Report to Sir James M'Grigor—The Action of the Vicar of Heston—Wakley holds an Inquest—Adjournment for Assistance of Mr. Day—Second Adjournment for Assistance of Erasmus Wilson—The Evidence —The Verdict—Public Opinion and the Disputes that arose —Wakley's Attitude criticised — The Fortunate Result of the Inquest.

ON June 15th, 1846, at the Cavalry Barracks, Hounslow Heath, a private of the Seventh Hussars named Frederick John White received one hundred and fifty lashes with the cat-o'-nine tails, administered by two regimental farriers in pursuance of a sentence pronounced by a district court-martial held to inquire into a sudden assault made by him upon his sergeant. White took his flogging manfully in the presence of his colonel and Dr. Warren, the surgeon of the regiment, and walked to the station hospital, of which he continued an inmate until July 11th, the day of his death. During the weeks that elapsed between his entry into the hospital and his end he was at one time apparently convalescent, the external wounds on the back having healed. Suddenly he manifested serious symptoms of cardiac and pulmonary mischief. Pleurisy and pneumonia developed, followed by complete exhaustion and paralysis. On the occurrence of these symptoms a communication was made by Colonel Whyte, the colonel of the regiment, and Dr. Warren to Sir James M'Grigor, the Director-General of the Army Medical Department, for the scandal that would ensue if Private White died in the hospital, where he had been sent to recover from the effects of a military flogging, was clearly foreseen. Sir James M'Grigor instructed Dr. John Hall, a first class staff-surgeon, to proceed to Hounslow and to report to headquarters upon the condition of Private White and the circumstances of his illness. Dr. Hall arrived in time to see White die. He reported to the Director-General that on July 6th, the very day upon which it had been intended to discharge White from the hospital as convalescent, he began to complain of pain in the region of the heart ; that from that day he went downhill rapidly, and that it would be difficult to ascertain the cause of death without making a careful post-mortem examination. On July 13th a post-mortem examination was accordingly made by Dr. Hall, Dr. Warren, and an assistant staff-surgeon, Dr. Reid. The result of this examination, as reported to Sir James M'Grigor, was briefly as follows :— That the parts upon which the punishment had been inflicted had healed and that the discoloration to be seen on the back of the corpse was due to the gravitation of the blood to the parts, White having been strictly confined to his bed for the last days of his life. A portion of the integument from between the shoulder-blades, over the part where the punishment had been most severe, having been removed, was found to be natural and, with the exception of the discoloration already noted, quite healthy. There were signs of old pulmonary and cardiac mischief and of recent pneumonia, pleurisy, and endocarditis, and the liver was found to be considerably enlarged. The certificate of the cause of death, " drawn up for the satisfaction of the officer commanding the Seventh Hussars," to use the signatories' own phrase, ran as follows :—

" Having made a careful post-mortem examination of Private Frederick White of the Seventh Hussars, we are of opinion that he died from inflammation of the pleura and of the lining membrane of the heart ; and we are further of opinion that the cause of death was in nowise connected with the corporal punishment he received on the 15th of June last.

(Signed)   " JOHN HALL, M.D., *Staff Surgeon First Class.*
J. L. WARREN, M.D., *Surgeon Seventh Hussars.*
F. REID, M.D., *Assistant Staff Surgeon.*"

The death was registered at Isleworth on Dr. Warren's certificate as having occurred from inflammation of the heart, and on the same day the regimental sergeant-major informed the Rev. H. S. Trimmer, the vicar of Heston, in which parish the Hounslow Cavalry Barracks were situated, of the intention of the authorities to bury the deceased on the following day, and further added that the death was the result of " liver complaint." The discrepancy between the reason assigned by the surgeon to the regiment and that assigned by the sergeant-major for the death of White led to inquiries, in answer to which the latter frankly stated that the deceased private had been flogged in military fashion *five* weeks before his death. The vicar said that under those circumstances he should require to have the authority of the coroner before permitting the funeral to take place, and communicated with Wakley, who issued the usual warrant for an inquest to be held on July 15th.

Accordingly, on July 15th an inquest was held at the barracks. After the coroner and the jury had examined the body the three surgeons who had made the post-mortem examination for the information of the Director-General and the satisfaction of the colonel of the regiment presented themselves to give evidence. It became known, however, that their report to Sir James M'Grigor and to Colonel Whyte had been made without any examination of more than a portion of the skin of the back. They had not looked at the spine or the muscles covering it or even beneath the skin. This was the more extraordinary because the man had been paralysed in his lower extremities for two days before his death and had lost control over his bladder. The significance of the omission was pointed out by Wakley to the jury, and on his advice they nominated a surgeon unconnected with the persons interested in the case to complete the examination of the body. Mr. Horatio Grosvenor Day, a surgeon residing at Isleworth, was nominated by the jury to make an independent examination, and Wakley having made out the requisite order for this gentleman adjourned the inquest until the 20th of the month. But at the adjourned inquest it was elicited that Mr. Day also had not considered it necessary to make any examination at all of the back and spine of the deceased, having clearly mistaken the object for which he had been asked to give his assistance. Wakley considered the omission very unfortunate, as the inquiry could not proceed until a fresh necropsy had been made with special reference to the matters upon which information was required by the court. The jury requested that before Wakley adjourned the inquiry again he would appoint some London surgeon unconnected in the remotest way with the circumstances of the case and of undeniable position in his profession to make a thorough examination of the body and give the court and jury the benefit of his views. The coroner appointed Mr. (afterwards Sir) Erasmus Wilson and issued a warrant for the disinterment of the body, adjourning the inquest for the second time until July 27th. On this day, and also on August 3rd—for the length of the proceedings compelled a third adjournment— the medical evidence was at last given completely.

It now appeared that the unfortunate White had received no food for seventeen hours before his punishment, and that after he had been flogged and had walked over to the hospital he had requested the sergeant to give him a basin of tea as he felt very faint, which request the sergeant had refused. From the notes in the hospital ward-book and from the medical register, which were both produced, and from statements in the course of Dr. Warren's evidence, it seemed that the patient when he entered the station hospital immediately after the flogging had been inflicted was medically examined, and his back was found to be lacerated and covered with blood, while between the shoulder-blades there was a wound about six inches long and four or five inches wide. He was said to be " severely punished from the neck to the loins." Fomentations of lukewarm water were employed until June 22nd, and from that date until June 25th the dressing was a cetaceous lead ointment. On June 25th a number of small boils appeared on the patient's back. Dr. Warren said that the poultices were ordered to be applied immediately, but in the ward-book dated June 28th it was stated that the poultices were ordered for another patient. At any rate, White did not get them on the 25th. On the 28th the medical register said that the boils were discharging but much inflamed. After this some little discrepancy was revealed between the register for which the medical officer was responsible and the ward-book kept by the hospital orderly. On July 1st the register reported that the back was nearly well, "only for the small boils that have not cicatrised over," but the hospital orderly's report showed that the poultices were still being applied to cover four or five boils. From July 1st to July 4th the medical register was silent, but the ward-book told of purges and poultices. On the latter date the patient was much better, volunteered to clean an outhouse, and actually did half an hour's work. But on July 5th he complained of pain in the right side, and on the 6th the medical register spoke of a pain that was located in the region of the heart and aggravated by inspiration. On the 7th he was obviously in pain and ill. On the 8th the symptoms of pleurisy and pneumonia were marked, and this condition was treated by purgatives and the abstraction of thirty-two ounces of blood. On the 9th a note recorded the great relief which had followed the bleeding. On the 10th he was removed from the surgical to the medical wards as paralysis was found to have supervened in the lower extremities. On the 11th the register recorded the patient's death. He had totally lost motion and sensation in the lower limbs and control over the bladder. He had a rapid, irregular pulse, a cold skin, and was throughout the day in a condition of stupor or collapse. He died in the evening, three-quarters of an hour after Dr. Hall's arrival. Such was the general gist of the examination of Dr. Warren as medical officer of the regiment, of hospital orderlies, sergeants, and certain other patients in the hospital.

Dr. Warren, who was not sworn, gave more particular medical evidence. He deposed that he had examined Private White most carefully to ascertain if he was fit to undergo corporal punishment or imprisonment and had certified in the affirmative. He stated that the injured back was nearly well at the end of a fortnight, and that he had intended to discharge the patient from hospital on July 6th, and had told him so on the previous day. When for the first time the patient complained of internal pains he was examined with the stethoscope, and from that time until his death he was treated for inflammation of the heart and pleura. Dr. Hall, who was sworn, described the results of the post-mortem examination made by him in company with Dr. Warren and Dr. Reid, his presence being due to the command of Sir James M'Grigor. These were in accordance with the view, already expressed in the joint certificate, that the deceased had died from inflammation of the pleura, the lung, and the lining membrane of the heart. Dr. Hall had made no examination of the muscles of the back or of the parts below the skin, a piece of skin which had been dissected from the back having been examined and found healthy. He did not believe that the condition of the internal organs had any connexion with the injuries received during the flogging. Dr. Reid gave evidence to the same effect, merely explaining at length what were the exact post-mortem appearances of the heart. Mr. Horatio Grosvenor Day then deposed that he first examined the body of the deceased on July 16th at Hounslow Barracks by the order of the coroner. He then came to the conclusion that death had been produced by pleurisy and pneumonia. He had been hampered in his examination by the fact that the body had previously been examined by the three military surgeons, so that many of the viscera were out of place and the contents of the chest much decomposed. He made no examination of the muscles of the back or of the spinal cord. He was present at such an examination made on July 22nd by Erasmus Wilson in Heston churchyard, the body having been exhumed by the coroner's order, and had signed with that gentleman a statement of the appearances that were then present in the tissues of the back. Erasmus Wilson, consulting surgeon to the St. Pancras Infirmary, lecturer on anatomy and physiology at the Middlesex Hospital Medical School, and author of works on those two subjects and on cutaneous diseases, gave evidence next. He said he had examined the back of the deceased on July 22nd by order of the coroner. He had examined the back only, the other parts of the body not being in a state to be further scrutinised. Upon raising the muscles over the region of the ribs and spinal column he had found the deepest layer in a state of disorganisation. Between the sixth and seventh ribs the muscles were in a pulpy state, and in the groove between the ribs and spine they were in a similar condition. The contents of the spinal canal were in a state of decomposition. Erasmus Wilson considered that two questions arose out of the foregoing facts : (1) How did the pulpy disorganisation of the muscles originate ? and (2) Could their state have influenced the organs of the chest ? He considered, firstly, that the pulpy softening of the muscles was due to their excessive contraction during the agony of punishment which had produced laceration and inflammation of the substance. Regarding the second question, he had no doubt that these causes were responsible directly or indirectly for the inflammation of the contents of the chest. Cold and moral depression might have had their influence, but the influence of laceration and decomposition of muscles closely adjacent to the lining membrane of the thorax would certainly have produced the same effect. In this case he pointed out that the morbid changes in the pleura took place on the same side as the disorganisation of the muscles. It was his opinion that Frederick John White would be living had not the punishment been inflicted. He had no doubt whatever on the point.

On August 3rd the medical witnesses made additional statements. Dr. Warren and Dr. Reid, having heard the depositions of all the medical witnesses, said that they did not believe the death to have been in any way due to the punishment inflicted. Mr. Day, who had assisted Erasmus Wilson to make the post-mortem examination upon which that gentleman had based his opinions, considered the cause of the change in the muscles a matter of conjecture. That they were changed was certain, but the curious appearances might have been due to putrefaction. The flogging might have indirectly caused the disorganisation. A paper signed by him and by Erasmus Wilson was put in proving that, whatever the pathology or causes of the development of this pulpy disorganisation of the muscles of the back might be, the condition had actually existed and was witnessed by both experts. Mr. Day added that the softening of the muscular fibres had been noticed in the external intercostal muscles but not in the internal intercostal muscles, and could not, therefore, be in close proximity to the pleura, so as to account for a spread of mischief to that membrane.

Erasmus Wilson having heard the additional statements in court, as well as the depositions of all the witnesses, gave it as his opinion that death had been due to the flogging and its effects. The painful laceration of the skin had, he argued, affected the internal organs, and in support of this he quoted the well-known connexion between superficial burns and visceral lesions. He pointed out as an anatomical fact that there are no internal intercostal muscles in the particular region in question, so that Mr. Day's remark must count for nothing. If one layer of muscles was affected in that situation it must have been in contact with the pleura.

The coroner having summed up the evidence the jury returned the following voluminous verdict :—

"That on July 11th, 1846, the deceased, Frederick John White, died from the mortal effects of a severe and cruel flogging of one hundred and fifty lashes which he received with certain whips on the 15th day of June, 1846, at the Cavalry Barracks on Hounslow Heath, at Heston ; and that the said flogging was inflicted upon him under a sentence passed by a district court-martial composed of officers of the Seventh regiment of Hussars duly constituted for his trial. That the said court-martial was authorised by law to pass the said severe and cruel sentence ; and that the said flogging was inflicted upon the back and neck of the said Frederick John White by two farriers in the presence of John James Whyte, the Lieutenant-Colonel, and James Low Warren, the surgeon, of the said regiment ; and that so and by means of the said flogging the death of the said Frederick John White was caused."

In returning their verdict the jury made use of the strongest language in an appended rider, wherein they expressed their horror and disgust that the law of the land provided that the revolting punishment of flogging should be permitted upon British soldiers; and they implored "every man in the kingdom to join hand and heart in forwarding petitions to the legislature praying in the most urgent terms for the abolition of every law and order and regulation which permits the disgraceful practice of flogging to remain one moment longer a slur upon the humanity and fair name of the people of this country."

Upon the announcement of this verdict the great excitement which the proceedings had caused in the public mind became evident. The newspapers teemed with allusions to the inquest, generally of an uncomplimentary nature towards the Service. This was due not so much to the merits of the humane side of the question as to the curious blundering of the military authorities. Such minor points as the fact that the first necropsy had been made, not for the satisfaction of justice, but "for the satisfaction of the Colonel of the Seventh Hussars"; that the sergeant-major had reported the case to Mr. Trimmer as one of liver complaint, and had exaggerated the interval between the flogging and the death; and that the patient a few hours before his death had been moved from his ward to give an appearance of a break in the continuity of his disease, gave colour to the popular view that attempts had been made to baulk honest inquiry. The inhumanity of flogging the man after a seventeen hours' fast, and refusing him a cup of tea after he had paid the penalty of his insubordination, also prejudiced the popular opinion profoundly against White's judges. The subject was incidentally noticed in the House of Commons, when Wakley was found to be prepared to combat the statements of his critics, for the political journals had warned him of the tone which the comments upon his behaviour as coroner would take. He knew that he would be accused of partiality, for in 1836, in the debate upon the Mutiny Bill, he had, as has been recorded, protested strongly against the flogging of insubordinate soldiers, and had stated that the brutal punishment had been followed by death. Feeling certain that he would be reminded that he could not have been free from prejudice while conducting the inquiry, he had provided himself with three letters—one from the solicitor who had watched the case on behalf of the officers of the Seventh Hussars ; one from Mr. Trimmer, the vicar of Heston and a Middlesex magistrate, whose public spirit and acumen had led to the inquiry being made ; and one from an independent spectator, a barrister and retired Indian judge. The third letter was an enthusiastic encomium of Wakley's behaviour ; but the other two, which were couched in soberer terms, declared that his conduct of the inquest had been fair and impartial, and that in his summing-up the coroner had laid no special stress on the arguments of either side. The first two of these Wakley read aloud to the House, in answer to a formal question, and from that moment routed any plans on the part of his political foes to make insulting reflections.

Some quarrelling, however, over the verdict was inevitable. The country was so strongly in favour of the humane rider appended by the jury that all who took the other side, whether from honest conviction or from reasons of convenience, were stung into justification of their attitude. A triple course was then open to them—they could abuse the judge as biassed, the expert witness for the other side as ignorant, or the jury as foolish. The jury were let alone. They were drawn from the people, and their verdict was popular, and to say that they had been unable to follow the reasoning of the case would have been exceedingly bad policy. In political circles Wakley had taken care of himself by reading to the House remarkable testimony to his impartiality, while he was always an awkward subject for abuse, as he had an inconvenient habit, when he seemed most careless, of turning suddenly and rending his abusers. There remained Erasmus Wilson, at this time only thirty-seven years of age and by no means the important figure in medical science or politics that he was twenty-five years later. He was simply a rising young man. Wilson had against his views the views of Mr. Day and of the three military surgeons. The evidence of the latter was considered by the public to be tainted. No doubt they had earnestly desired, for the sake of their department and their duties in that department, that the death of White should be found to be unconnected with the punishment he had received. But there was no reason to suppose that they did not speak with perfectly honest conviction, and on reading their evidence after the lapse of fifty years it can be well understood that many should have been of their way of thinking and that they themselves should have been entirely certain that Erasmus Wilson and the jury had erred. That White died from pneumonia, pleurisy, and endocarditis there was no doubt. That the punishment he had received might *directly* cause these terrible sequelæ was just conceivable. The probability of the conception was increased when the subject, from constitution, from previous damage to structure, or from ill-regulated habits of life, had a predisposition to readily break down, and all these factors were present in White's case. So that in arguing that the flogging had no connexion whatever with the death the military surgeons had a very difficult task when the *indirect* effects of such treatment were taken into account. The punishment that White had undergone would certainly lower his whole vitality and leave him more susceptible of any malign influence either existing in himself or present in his environment. It was allowed by all that the connexion between flogging and pleurisy with pneumonia and endocarditis was difficult to trace, while the connexion of two at any rate of these pathological conditions with cold was obvious. But how far the effects of cold would be rendered additionally mischievous where the resistance of the subject had been already annulled by physical torture was another matter. The military surgeons had been in fault in giving their definite opinion that flogging could have had nothing to do with White's death before making a thorough post-mortem examination, and without remembering how difficult it would be to prove that no *indirect* injury had accrued to White from so serious a punishment.

Mr. Day's evidence was perfectly honest and straightforward, but it really amounted to nothing at all. His first necropsy was admittedly made upon the parts of the body that had already been examined by three other medical men, under circumstances that precluded him from forming any judgment, and his further examination of the body consisted in looking on while Erasmus Wilson discovered the pulpy condition of the muscles of the back. The position of Erasmus Wilson was not an easy one. He found a pathological state for which he could give no very definite reason, and one which, indeed, was unknown to science. That he found the condition admits of no doubt, firstly, because, like others, he had no object in giving evidence except that of establishing the truth ; and, secondly, because Mr. Day, who did not agree with the general view of the case, also recognised the pulpy state of the muscles, and explained it by saying that the changes were possibly putrefactive. With this condition of the muscles, for which he admitted he could find no scientific precedent, Erasmus Wilson tried to connect the michief in the pleura, lungs, and heart—a direct sequence of pathological events ending in death. But the reasoning was not cogent. The analogy drawn from the fact that large surface burns are frequently followed by visceral lesions possessed some point, but was only an analogy. The assertion that the changes could not be putrefactive because they had taken place in the deep structures while the more superficial planes of the body remained unaltered was only an assertion of a probability. All these arguments were thrashed out in the "Lancet," to which Erasmus Wilson contributed several earnest and elaborate papers in explanation of his evidence, but it is doubtful if either side ever convinced the other. What, however, is not doubtful is this—that the public entirely repudiated scientific evidence in the matter. It was not Erasmus Wilson's able scientific arguments which accounted for the verdict of the jury with its pathetic rider. It was his broad and comprehensive assertion that, whatever might be the pathological details, had it not been for the flogging the

man Frederick White would be alive, which obtained from
a jury of Frederick White's countrymen a verdict affixing
the stain of blood-guiltiness upon the regulations of Her
Majesty's Army. The jury felt that they represented the
feelings of Great Britain. Flogging in the Army must be
abolished, and they were doing their best towards that end.
Here they had a case in which directly or indirectly a man's
death was due to the horrible practice. Let others settle
the possibility of the directness, or the measure of the in-
directness, the verdict must be one of manslaughter against
the regulations.

Such is the story of the famous Hounslow inquest, which
not only aroused more public interest, probably, than any
inquiry ever held in a coroner's court, but certainly placed a
national veto upon the inhuman practice of flogging in the
Army. Great modifications were almost immediately introduced into this method of punishment, so great that when
in 1881 the Army Act formally abolished the practice few
knew that it was still sanctioned by the law of the land.

CHAPTER XLII

[1846–1861]

The " Medical Times " and the Hounslow Inquest—Three Success-
ful Libel Actions against Healey and others—Peace on the Coroner's
Bench—Some Inquests between 1846 and 1861—The Case of John
Sadleir—Charles Dickens as Juryman—His Testimony to Wakley's
Humanity.

ONE dissentient voice alone was found amid the public con-
gratulation that was evoked by the verdict in the Hounslow
flogging case. The " Medical Times," a paper started in
1839 in opposition to the "Lancet," could find no words
too hard for Wakley, and could frame no accusations
against him sufficiently enormous or unlikely. He had
been an advocate and not a judge. He had adjourned the
case when he saw it going against his wishes and had " used
the interval in instructing his friend Wilson, a man formerly
his own servant, to get up his set-off testimony to the
marplot truths of regular and well-informed science. . . . .
The judge took refuge in a hireling witness and a hugger-
mugger autopsy. . . . . There was something absolutely
execrable in the coroner's farcical impersonation of judge-
ship. . . . . Coroner Wakley seemed like a man compro-
mised to infamy or worse—personal unhappiness—if it
should be proved that White died without murderous guilt
in some survivor. . . . . He suggests, insinuates, applauds,
encourages, assails, twists, twirls, and manœuvres in every
shape, form, and direction to conjure up against an honest
practitioner a fictitious semblance of murder ! . . . . Why
this needless display of ingenuity to get up against Dr.
Warren, or, failing him, Colonel Whyte, or, failing him, the

2 D

farrier, a colourable semblance of murder? There is, of course, but one reply—Wakley wants a public sensation to help his fortunes in a forthcoming election." And so on, and so on. Some of these libels were published while the jury were still sitting. Wakley at once moved in the Court of Queen's Bench for a criminal information against the proprietors of the paper, a certain Healey, who was also editor, and a man named Cooke. A *rule nisi* was obtained, but was subsequently discharged by the Court, for reasons which it is difficult for the lay mind to appreciate, seeing the coarse and evident nature of the libels. Wakley had defended himself against Healey's slander in a speech made at Exeter Hall and had then used retaliatory terms which the Court considered to justify the refusal to him of the exceptional assistance of a criminal information. Healey cherished a deep hatred for the editor of the "Lancet." As early as 1843 the "Medical Times," with this man as editor, had begun to libel Wakley in a particularly offensive and audacious manner. Healey made no statements, but he was prolific of the darkest insinuations against Wakley's private morality and political honesty. For the most part what he said was so obviously ridiculous and inspired by personal spite that Wakley was content to let the public judge between his slanderer and himself. When Healey termed Erasmus Wilson "a man formerly Wakley's servant" because Wakley's son had been Wilson's pupil and later his demonstrator of anatomy, the extent to which he was prepared to distort the truth placed him without the range of respectable controversy. Wakley's words in the "Lancet" addressed to the profession on the subject were: "We have sometimes been asked why we omit to notice the libels against the private character of the editor of this work, which we were informed often appeared in the leading articles of the 'Medical Times.' Our answer always has been that we did not believe that such a trashy production was read by the members of the profession; and, secondly, that the motives of the slanderer were so palpably obvious and his stupidity so thoroughly apparent that if the rogue

were allowed rope enough he was sure to cheat the execu-
tioner at the Old Bailey." To this policy of silent contempt
Wakley rigidly adhered for two years, but in February,
1845, at the instance of his Finsbury constituents, he
suddenly turned round upon the foe and instituted civil
proceedings against the proprietors of the publication, one
of whom was Healey, the editor, and the other, at that time,
a man named Weathers. Healey and Weathers allowed
judgment to go by default and were fined £150 damages
and the costs of the action, their conduct being made the
subject of severe stricture by Chief Baron Pollock. The
printers of the "Medical Times," Messrs. Kelly and Co.,
called on Wakley, apologised for the attacks that had been
made upon him, and stated that they had refused to publish
the "Medical Times" for the future.

Healey, however, persisted in his course ; indeed, the
unlucky man made it the object of his life for many years to
injure Wakley. He continued to publish the libellous statements and added a reflection upon the Chief Baron's judicial
integrity implying that Sir Frederick Pollock had leant
towards Wakley's side because "he had been a fellow
member of Parliament." He called for public subscriptions
to pay his damages and help him to persevere in his great
work of exposing the medical member for Finsbury. Wakley
brought a second action against Healey, with whom in this
instance was associated Cooke as publisher. On this
occasion the jury found for Wakley with damages £175 and
costs of the suit. The defendants then issued a writ of error,
and at this time occurred the Hounslow inquest. So that
at the time when the violent onslaughts upon Wakley as
coroner were made, both Healey and Cooke had been found
guilty of libelling him, the former having had double
experience of the inconvenience of his conduct. Wakley's
failure to obtain a rule for criminal information caused
delay in the proceedings of the third suit against Healey,
the writ in which was issued immediately upon the refusal of
the rule. The case was not heard until November 13th,
1849. In the meantime the writ of error in the second suit,

which was to have been argued in the Exchequer Chamber, collapsed. No counsel appeared for the defendants, and judgment was given for the plaintiff, the costs and damages of this suit amounting in all to £362. The third action against Healey was tried before Chief Baron Pollock and a special jury, and a verdict was returned for Wakley with damages £350. Against this verdict the defendants Healey and Cooke appealed alleging misdirection and excessive damages. A court consisting of the Chief Baron and three other judges found that there had been no misdirection and that considering the nature of the libels the jury might undoubtedly have awarded a much larger sum. The small sum had been fixed because it had been stated that Healey was not in a position to pay more, which was possible, for he never paid even that.

When the stormy developments which ensued upon the Hounslow inquest finally were set at rest Wakley had peace in his coroner's seat. Many of the Middlesex magistrates had on this occasion supported his authority and borne evidence to his impartiality, and thus an understanding between him and the bench was at last established, which, although it never amounted to cordiality, remained the respectful neutrality of persons who have no reason to think lightly one of another. Attempts were made both within and without the House to prove that Wakley had prostituted the office of coroner to his desire to achieve popularity among his constituents, but the thorough manner in which his duties were discharged and the great practical utility of many of his suggestions were easier of appreciation by the people than were the underhand schemes which were credited to him by his detractors. As a consequence the general feeling was, firstly, disbelief in the everlasting stories of his manœuvring; and, secondly, indifference to the question. Wakley was a good coroner—that could not be gainsaid; and whether his virtues in office had their origin in a moral desire to do right or a political desire to get on did not concern the community. His right to employ a deputy had been legally recognised, and the charges made against him of excessive expenditure had ended in his complete vindication. With regard to his enthusiasm for his work there had never been any question. All had allowed that he was remarkably energetic ; and now his critics, who had hitherto pointed out that his energy was misdirected and due to improper motives, were reduced to silence, convinced either that they had been in error or that it was dangerous to record further slanders.

Among the inquests held by Wakley between the year 1846 and the year 1861, when his health compelled him to leave England, many, as might be expected, presented points of medico-legal interest. In such cases a synopsis of the evidence and the result of the necropsy were frequently inserted in the " Lancet." Wakley's deliverances from the bench in these cases were often well worth hearing. They were intended to form a regular vindication of the right of a medical man to the coroner's position, and to prove to demonstration that a medical coroner alone could be capable of interpreting the value of medical evidence to a jury. On such points, therefore, as the extent to which homœopathic treatment could be held accountable for an untoward result ; as the proper interpretation of the physical signs of death or of separate existence ; as the quantity of prussic acid contained in apparently innocuous solutions like almond water and the poisonous doses of prussic acid and other deadly drugs ; as the workings of the Poor-law Acts ; and as the value of immediate medical assistance in cases of emergency —on all these and numerous cognate subjects his words attracted attention for they were instinct with good sense. Now and again his medical views, based on the knowledge of his day, would hardly meet with acceptance at this end of the century. The, spirit which Wakley inculcated was, for example, right when he reproached a well-known physician in uncompromising terms for bleeding and not cupping an apoplectic patient, ridiculing the excuse that he "had not his cupper with him" as a reason for inactivity. The overweening sense of personal importance which placed the health of the patient lower in the scale than the dignity of the physician was deserving of rebuke ; but we know now that cupping is practically useless in such cases, whereas the bleeding which had been performed by the physician might in some cases, if heroic in quantity, have proved salutary.

Wakley was particularly watchful over children, and several of his inquests were held because there had been a reasonable impression abroad that the treatment of the parents had contributed to the death of the child. One such case occurred in the neighbourhood of his own house, namely, in Prince's Street, Fitzroy Square, the inquest being held on November 28th, 1848. A child aged fourteen and a half years had been tied up to a bedpost by her mother and the room locked, while the mother went out for the day. On the mother's return the child was found to be dead, having apparently been strangled in an effort to sit down, whereas the rope had been so adjusted that she was unable to ease her irksome position. Wakley told the woman to consider herself in custody and administered the usual caution before taking her evidence. He then committed her for manslaughter, of which crime she was afterwards found guilty by a jury ; but an amiable judge considering that she had acted more through ignorance than from premeditated cruelty sentenced her to one year of hard labour only.

Before bringing the account of Wakley's coronership to a close, mention must be made of two more inquests, one because of the temporary importance of the victim and the extremely sensational nature of the episode, and the other because Wakley's conduct during the inquiry has been handed down to eternal fame. These are large words, but accurate in this connexion, for Charles Dickens chanced to be on the jury and wrote his recollections of the circumstances. The first was the case of John Sadleir, to which allusion has already been made. John Sadleir was member of Parliament for Sligo county and had held the post of Junior Lord of the Treasury in Lord Aberdeen's short-lived coalition Ministry, when Gladstone was Chancellor of the Exchequer and Palmerston Home Secretary. Sadleir had sprung into prominence among his Irish countrymen as a violent opponent of that anti-Catholic movement which was brought to a crisis by the Ecclesiastical Titles Bill and Lord John Russell's indiscreet behaviour. A body was found behind Jack Straw's Castle on Hampstead Heath under circumstances that pointed to suicide distinctly but not quite conclusively. The clothes were undisturbed, but a hat was found at some distance from the body. By the side of the body was a bottle labelled " Essential Oil of Almonds " ; a silver cream-jug was discovered also close at hand, which had evidently been the receptacle of the poison, for it still smelt strongly of the essence. A case of razors lay near. At the inquest a surgeon deposed that he had found a considerable quantity of oil of almonds as well as some opium in the stomach of the deceased. Wakley himself identified the body for the information of the jury as that of John Sadleir, M.P., who had been well known to him in the House of Commons. From the evidence of Sadleir's butler it appeared that the deceased had told a servant to procure some essential oil of bitter almonds the evening before the discovery of the body. At this point the coroner seemed disposed to close the inquiry, when it was given in evidence that the deceased had left three letters in the hall of his house in Portland Place. These letters proved to be of a highly sensational character, revealing the story of enormous frauds. Sadleir's countrymen had trusted him, not only with their suffrages but with their money, and he had been entirely unworthy of the confidence bestowed on him, being simply a cruel audacious swindler. In these letters he accused himself of "most infamous villainy," and mentioned that " no torture could be too much for such crimes. But," he said, " I cannot live to *see* the tortures I have inflicted on others." He spoke in a similarly repentant strain in a letter to a fellow Irish member. The letters and all the facts pointed to determination on the part of Sadleir to kill himself, and the jury omitted the usual formula and agreed that the deceased had clearly known the meaning of the action when he killed

himself, and was not suffering from temporary derangement. It was an important circumstance that Wakley
should have been able personally to identify the body as
that of Sadleir, for no sooner did the news of the death
reach the public than an astounding rumour was spread
and gained wide support that Sadleir was still alive and had
escaped to the Continent. The rumour gave details. A
pauper's body had been bought by Sadleir, who saw that
the day when he must fly with his ill-gotten wealth had
arrived. This body he had exposed on Hampstead Heath
attired in his own clothes and under circumstances that
should leave no doubt that it was himself who had perished.
The servant who swore that the body was his master's, and
who volunteered the information concerning the purchase
of the poison, was said to be Sadleir's accomplice. Had
Wakley not been able from personal knowledge to assure
himself and others that the body on which the inquest had
been held was undoubtedly that of Sadleir an exhumation
might have been necessary, so firm a hold on the popular
imagination had the story of the substituted corpse taken.
In fact, in spite of the coroner's additional testimony, many
people persisted in believing that Sadleir had escaped with
his booty, £200,000 being the sum he was reputed to have
secured. Twelve years later Miss Braddon used the
rumours concerning Sadleir in the plot of one of her
earliest sensational stories, entitled " The Trail of the
Serpent "; and only recently a London newspaper revived
the *canard* and treated it seriously.

The inquest which Dickens has immortalised occurred
much earlier in Wakley's career. The subject of inquiry
was the death of an unfortunate infant, whose mother had
committed either murder or the minor offence of concealment of birth. It was to decide this point that a jury was
empanneled, and how Dickens came to be of that jury he
tells in his own inimitable manner, smartly hitting off at the
commencement an abuse which altogether disappeared in
Wakley's court when the beadle was dispensed with and a
special coroner's officer employed to summon the jury.

"The beadle," says Dickens, "did what melancholy did to the youth in Gray's Elegy—he marked me for his own. And the way in which the beadle did it was this: he summoned me as a juryman on coroner's inquests. In my first feverish alarm I repaired 'for safety and for succour'—like those sagacious Northern shepherds who, having had no previous reason whatever to believe in young Norval, very prudently did not originate the hazardous idea of believing in him—to a deep householder. This profound man informed me that the beadle counted on my buying him off, on my bribing him not to summon me, and that if I would attend an inquest with a cheerful countenance and profess alacrity in that branch of my country's service the beadle would be disheartened and would give up the game. I roused my energies, and the next time the wily beadle summoned me I went. The beadle was the blankest beadle I ever looked on when I answered to my name, and his discomfiture gave me courage to go through with it."

The inquest came off in the parish workhouse, and Dickens, who was already famous to the world as the author of "Sketches by Boz," "Pickwick," and "Oliver Twist," notes his impression that he was unanimously received by his brother jurymen "as a brother of the utmost conceivable insignificance." He proved himself by his own confession to be no fit occupant of the jury-box, being crammed with prejudice in favour of the humaner verdict. From the moment that he gathered the outlines of the story he set himself to work to get the poor girl acquitted. His great opponent was, he says, "a broker who had lately cheated me fearfully in the matter of a pair of card-tables and was for the utmost rigour of the law." The evidence showed that the miserable girl, who was present during the proceedings seated on a chair and looking very weak and ill, had given birth to a child but a few days before, and had cleaned her mistress's doorstep immediately afterwards. Dickens recalls the lack of sympathy of the workhouse nurse, who stood beside her, the brutality of the mistress, and the utter solitary misery of this orphan maid-of-all-work. He proceeded to cross-examine the mistress in the interest of the girl.

"I took heart," he says, "to ask this witness a question or two which hopefully admitted of an answer which might give a favourable turn to the case. She made the turn as little favourable as it could be, but it did some good, and the coroner, who was nobly patient and humane (he was the late Mr. Wakley), cast a look of strong encouragement in my direction. . . . . I tried again and the coroner backed me again, for which I ever afterwards felt grateful to him, as I do now to his memory,* and we got another favourable turn out of some other witness, some member of the family with a strong prepossession against the sinner. I think we had the doctor back again, and I know that the coroner summed up for our side and that I and my British brothers turned round to discuss our verdict and get ourselves into great difficulties with our large chairs and the broker. At that stage of the case I tried hard again, being convinced that I had cause for it, and at last we found for the minor offence of only concealing the birth."

Dickens did not abandon his advocacy of the poor girl when he had got the kinder verdict of concealment of birth registered, but with characteristic thoroughness ensured that she should have certain comforts in prison and retained at his own expense counsel for her defence, the result of which powerful advocacy was that the poor girl met with lenient treatment for her weakness. "I regard this," said Dickens, in conclusion, "as a very notable uncommercial experience, because this good came of a beadle. And to the best of my knowledge, information, and belief it is the only good that ever did come of a beadle since the first beadle put on his cocked hat."

With Dickens's estimate of Wakley as a coroner this section of his life is fitly closed. Wakley himself would

---

* The inquest took place in 1841, when Dickens was living in Devonshire Terrace, Regent's Park, but the account did not appear until more than twenty years later, just after Wakley's death. Dickens has one other allusion by name to Wakley as a coroner. It occurs in a whimsical letter written in 1840 to Mr. Thomas J. Thompson, the father of Lady Butler, the artist. Dickens describes himself as "raving with love for the Queen," then a bride, and expresses a wish that in the event of his early death, he should be "embalmed and kept (if practicable) on the top of the Triumphal Arch at Buckingham Palace, when she is in town, and on the north-east turrets of the Round Tower, when she is at Windsor." He signs himself Mr. Thompson's "distracted and blighted friend," and begs him in a postscript not to "show this to Mr. Wakley, the coroner, if it ever comes to that."

have desired no other critic, and having earned Dickens's
praise would have considered that no higher eulogy could
possibly be bestowed upon him. And, indeed, that the man
to whom officials of all sorts were hateful, from Mr. Bumble
to Lord Decimus Tite Barnacle, from the Worshipful
Mr. Nupkins to Mr. Justice Stareleigh, should praise the
official in Wakley, and that the most powerful friend that
the poor and suffering have ever known should praise the
patience and humanity in him, constitute a tribute to his
memory transcending in force and conviction any words
from other lips. Dickens as a judge of practical politics or
polite manners might not be considered in the place most
fitted for him ; exception might be taken to his opinions.
But Dickens as a judge of how the official should behave to
the poor, and of how a popular court should be conducted,
is ideally situated ; and the man whom he has commended
in such relations need not fear the judgment of posterity.

CHAPTER XLIII

Two Sections of Wakley's Life Completed—Further Notice of Wakley as Journalist—The Growth of the " Lancet "—Wakley s Personal Influence ever Present—His Views on Educational Developments and their Foresight—The Charter of the College of Surgeons in 1844—The Medical Act of 1858—The Study of Anatomy at the Beginning of the Century—Burke and Hare—Bishop and Williams , —The Anatomy Acts—A Brief Summary of Forty Years of Reform.

THE career of Thomas Wakley has now been nearly told. His rise from the position of youngest son of a gentleman farmer to that of senior parliamentary representative of the largest borough constituency in the kingdom and coroner for Middlesex has been traced step by step. The influence that he exercised upon the administration of law and justice in the coroner's court still abides. His work in Parliament has been chronicled with such fulness as the scheme of this biography allowed, and if a disproportionate amount of space appears to have been allotted to minor measures or matters of no distinct public importance, it is because the intent has been to write the life of Thomas Wakley and not an account of the first twenty-five years of her present Majesty's reign or the reigns of her two predecessors—a task which the chronicler hastens to add he would be quite unfit to undertake. Where Wakley was the moving spirit or leader the circumstances which led up to his acts and their outcome have been given in full. Where he simply followed others it has been considered sufficient to mention the fact, assuming that the parts played by such men as Peel, Cobden, the fourteenth Earl of Derby, Brougham, Melbourne, Macaulay, Joseph Hume, Gladstone, Bulwer Lytton, Benjamin D'Israeli, and many others whose names have been scattered up and down these pages, are familiar to the reader, forming as they do the national history of the first half of the nineteenth century. To avoid continual breaks in different parts of Wakley's career, whereby great difficulty would have been caused to the reader or many cross-references necessitated, this life has been written in separate sections. Firstly, Wakley's journalistic career has been described; secondly, his parliamentary career; and thirdly, his career as coroner. The latter two sections are now complete; to the first we must return, merely premising that the real Wakley is seen in a consideration of all three sections, blended as his triplicate work was in one inextricable, often incoherent, but always resolute and passionate, struggle to attain the objects of general and medical reform as he understood them.

The detailed story of the "Lancet," its work and its aims, was broken off in the year 1834 (when it became necessary to describe the editor's parliamentary career) with a summary of the work of the paper during its first decade, showing how it passed, in the opinion of the profession, through every phase of appreciation from contempt to repute. Until 1836 it continued to be published in Bolt Court. But in this year the business department of the paper had so much increased in importance that Wakley took new premises in Essex Street, Strand, and for six years was his own publisher—in reality, if not in name. Difficulties, however, arose which Wakley had not contemplated, and for the next five years Mr. John Churchill, the founder of the well-known firm of medical publishers, undertook the responsibility from his place of business in Prince's Street, Leicester Square. In 1847 Wakley again resolved to be his own publisher, and the present offices of the "Lancet" were taken. From this time until Wakley's death in 1862 the future of the paper justified his fondest hopes. He treated it as an inexhaustible gold mine and more than once seriously jeopardised its material prospects thereby; but if the paper was true to his implicit belief in its prospects he also was true to his ideal of what the paper should be. Conducted strictly on the lines laid down by an

inexperienced and hot-headed youth, it established for itself
a secure and enormous success. And from those lines the
"Lancet" has never deviated. Alterations in circumstances
caused it to expand considerably in most directions, to
contract in a few, and to be modified in many. But the
various departments of the paper at the present day were all
inaugurated by him or were the natural outgrowth of his
parental scheme, while the death of the abuses on which he
had so much to say was the natural outcome of his words.
After 1833 the "Lancet" was no longer a weekly diary of
its editor's hopes of, and aims towards, medical reform.
For the first ten years of its existence the paper was Wakley's
life, and every word of it must be considered by anyone
who would tell the story of that life. The leading articles
were his personal impressions on medical politics ; he
inspired the reviews and made the jokes. Hospital reports
were obtained by him, and from their consideration he proved
to the hilt the accuracy of many of the numerous allegations
which he made against the medical charities of the
metropolis. Legal proceedings decorated the pages of the
paper frequently, and in a large proportion of these trials
Wakley was either plaintiff or defendant. But as his life
broadened a medical paper could no longer form even an
expanded diary of his doings ; while as the "Lancet" grew
and waxed strong the necessity for constant justification of
its words and sentiments went. Success justified both it and
its founder, and the extremely personal nature of much of
the earlier writing became uncalled for. The "Lancet" no
longer required to be an apology for the life of Wakley. It
became more entirely a fulfilment of the promise conveyed
in its later sub-title, "A Journal of British and Foreign
Medicine, Physiology, Surgery, Chemistry, Criticism, Literature, and News." In it were to be found, as would be
expected from this title, the lectures, official and otherwise,
delivered by the great masters of the sciences, and reviews
of all important books falling under its comprehensive
heading. The best teachers at the schools sent contributions ; the articles on professional politics were written by

men within the ruling circles of the different bodies ; and the news was contributed from numerous centres by persons pecuniarily interested in making it copious and up to date. Wakley's spirit, however, presided over all. His views were prominently put forward in the leading articles and his plans for reform continued to be as religiously carried on in his large and successful journal as ever they were in the bygone days of persistent struggle. The subjects on which he continued to write himself were medical education, medical politics, the canker of quackery, and the professional welfare of the medical man. Most of the outspoken leading articles upon these topics which appeared in the " Lancet " between the years 1834 and 1850 were from his pen, and they display not only courage and sincerity, but a really remarkable prescience. For example, in 1843 a concession was made by the Royal College of Surgeons of England to public opinion and a new Charter was applied for and obtained under which the Council should no longer consist of twenty-one persons perpetually entitled to elect their successors and endowed with absolute power over the commonalty. Under the new Charter the Fellows of the College were created and electoral and political privileges confided to them—a body practically unlimited in numbers. Wakley detected at once that the reform did not go far enough in one direction and that in others it was no reform at all. The Charter abolished the inherent right of the members of being appointed to the governing body and by implication to the office of President, while it set up an invidious class distinction within the ranks of the profession which was certain sooner or later to breed trouble. That trouble is with us now—fifty years later. The language of modern contention is moderate, but no one can mistake the fact that beneath the civilly worded resolutions of the different associations for collegiate reform there lie a very real sense of injustice and a lively determination to obtain redress. The arguments that are being used now are Wakley's arguments of fifty years ago. Again, in 1858 came the great Medical Act under which the General Council of Medical

Education and Registration of the United Kingdom was constituted. The Act was a reform, but in so far as it represented the practical outcome of the patient and strenuous efforts of Wakley, Warburton, Hume, and one or two others it was not a complete success. "After a struggle of thirty years," wrote Wakley, "it is something to have advanced a single step in the right direction ; it is an important one, and only the first. As a beginning, however, we hail it as a great boon ; but we only regard it as the commencement of a series of important changes." He then proceeded to point out the viciousness of the principles upon which the members of the Council were chosen in terms which nowadays would all be covered by the phrase that he demanded a more direct representation of the body of the profession. The method in which such representation could be made more direct he indicated by reference to the representative of the College of Surgeons upon the General Medical Council, saying that if this gentleman is chosen by a council—that of the College of Surgeons—not itself elected by the members, he is no representative of the members. This very argument was used in the campaign of one of the candidates for a seat upon the General Medical Council at the election in 1896, and will be so used again.

The establishment of the General Medical Council was a triumph for Wakley, in that some such council had been urged ceaselessly upon the country by him as a means of protecting the public from quacks, and of regulating the education of the profession. The measure of security enjoyed by the public under its auspices, and the high level of medical education now maintained, are the outcome of those struggles against abuses in which Wakley played the foremost part. Similarly the new Charter of the College of Surgeons was an answer to Wakley's untiring abuse of the system by which a score of gentlemen governed the College autocratically, chose the lecturers, appointed the examiners, selected their successors and, for the most part, neglected their duties. But neither reform satisfied him, for neither went to the root of the evil. The General Medical Council was not representative of the profession ; and the invention of a higher diploma was no reply to the appeal of the commonalty of the College of Surgeons for justice. When Wakley said these things half-a-century ago, they attracted but little attention ; if any one thought about them he would have regarded them as an ungracious inspection of gift-horses. Now all are aware that the General Medical Council has not the confidence of the whole profession, and that the members of the Royal College of Surgeons of England are not enamoured of their Charter.

Wakley was as fortunate in his prognostication of good as of ill, as is shown by the part that he played in the passage of the Anatomy Acts. Allusion has been made to the position of hospital students in Wakley's day as regards anatomy and the difficulty of obtaining bodies for dissection. This difficulty and the institution of the vile trade of the resurrectionist which followed as a natural consequence upon the scarcity of subjects were recognised on all hands as matters requiring amendment. The large sums paid by students to obtain materials wherefrom to learn practical anatomy, and the poor substitutes of plates and diagrams with which they had too often to be contented, were grave blots on a system of medical education to the darkness of which the horrors of rifled churchyards added in no small degree. Suddenly a tremendous element of terror was introduced into the situation by the tragedies in Edinburgh with which the names of Burke and Hare are for ever associated in infamy. The facts of the tragedies are too well known to call for a detailed description. Suffice it to say that these two men, frequently with the assistance of a woman named MacDougal, were during the years 1827 and 1828 engaged in carrying on a ghastly traffic in human bodies. Their plan was to induce strangers, preferably lads or women, to accept the shelter of their roof. The victims, having been stupefied by drink, were deliberately smothered and their bodies sold to certain Edinburgh surgeons for dissection. Hare gave evidence for the Crown and admitted having been implicated in a series of these frightful crimes, and his evidence so incriminated Burke as to lead to a sentence of death being passed on that monster. Burke afterwards made a confession admitting his guilty knowledge of murders extending over quite a long period. The result of the excitement caused by these revelations effected what no amount of sober representation on the part of the managers of anatomical schools had been able to obtain. A Parliamentary Committee was appointed to inquire into the study of anatomy as practised in the United Kingdom and into the best method of obtaining bodies for the purpose.

Mr. Henry Warburton, whose name has often been mentioned as a practical champion of the true interests of the medical profession in Parliament, was appointed chairman, and the sittings began on April 28th, 1828. The first witness was Sir Astley Cooper, who, after pointing out the necessity of practical anatomy for the proper education of a surgeon, went on to say that teachers of anatomy were completely "at the feet of the resurrection men." Subjects for dissection were obtained almost exclusively by exhumation, with the exception of the negligible quantity which were handed over by executioners in pursuance of the sentence of a criminal court. It was the fact that the bodies of executed murderers were the only legal subjects of dissection in the kingdom that caused such difficulty in obtaining corpses for the medical schools; the relatives of the dead would not allow the bodies of their friends to be treated in a manner that was by law reserved for the utterly criminal and disgraced. As to the question of price, Sir Astley Cooper said that in his student days subjects cost two guineas, but that now ten guineas were not uncommonly given. When asked how the price was kept up he said that one resurrection man would spoil bodies he did not want so that a rival body-snatcher should not get them and thus glut the market. He said that sextons were nearly always in the pay of resurrectionists, who were often "persons of property." Among the other witnesses were Brodie, Abernethy, and Joshua Brookes. These all gave evidence as to the necessity of dissection, and the last named, whose school in Blenheim Street was one of the largest in London, deposed that he was so much at the mercy of resurrection-men that he had recently been subjected to outrage for not giving a douceur of £5 to certain of them at the beginning of each session. The ruffians had obtained several highly decomposed bodies and had laid them or strewed parts of them in the streets adjacent to his dissecting-room so as to enrage the populace against him. In his student days Joshua Brookes added that he had given two guineas per body, but recently he had had to pay as much as £16.

Wakley was called as a witness in recognition of the powerful articles in the early numbers of the " Lancet " dealing with the inadequacy of the medical education of the day. After the usual evidence as to the necessity for dissection he said that in 1815 and thenceforward until 1822 bodies had been sufficiently plentiful for the wants of London students. But in 1823 the College of Surgeons drew up a by-law under which the Council declared that they would not accept certificates of dissection except for work that had been performed in the winter season. The obvious effect of this was to increase the demand at that season and to raise the price. Wakley considered the dissecting-rooms during the winter to be much overcrowded with students and under-supplied with bodies. He laid the whole blame on the objectionable by-law of the College of Surgeons, which limited the number of recognised institutions and ruined the private schools. He said that the increased influx of pupils brought about by these by-laws had been the cause of the suddenly increased demand for subjects and consequent running-up of the prices. He went on to show that seven hundred bodies per annum would be ample to supply the wants of London, and that more than one thousand unclaimed bodies were buried by parish authorities in the metropolis yearly.

During the next year Warburton introduced his Bill, the gist of which was " that men and women, males and females, who died in workhouses or who had the misfortune to die in hospitals without being claimed within a certain time of death should be sold for dissection." This Bill was not clear about licensing anatomy schools, nor did it provide for the Christian burial of the remains after dissection. With slight modifications it passed the Commons, but when Lord Calthorpe introduced it in the spring of 1829 into the Upper House it was opposed by a group of peers headed by the Archbishop of Canterbury and withdrawn. Soon after the withdrawal of the Bill a new tragedy—this time in London—called attention to the absolute necessity for the legal regulation of the study of anatomy. An Italian boy, aged about fourteen, who made his living by exhibiting tame mice in the streets, was enticed by two ruffians—Bishop and Williams—to their den in Bethnal Green one autumn night in the year 1831, where he was murdered by being thrust head foremost into a shallow well. When his struggles ceased his teeth were extracted, and the two murderers, with an accomplice named May, set out to dispose of the body. Some suspicious circumstances, however, attracted the attention of Mr. Partridge, the demonstrator of anatomy at King's College, to whom the body was offered, and the murder came to light, both men being convicted and executed.

As the result of the popular sensation Warburton thought the time had arrived to introduce a second Anatomy Bill. This, although it met with some opposition in the Commons, passed both Houses without much alteration and became law in 1832. In the debates the same arguments were used as had been previously employed. They were founded on the medical evidence of Astley Cooper, Wakley, and others, and on the revelations of the Edinburgh and London tragedies, and amounted to an assertion, which was not contradicted, that if bodies were not forthcoming by legal methods murder would ensue. The following is briefly an account of the provisions :—

" An Act for regulating Schools of Anatomy, by which (after abolish-ing the former practice of the dissection of criminals after their execu-tion) it is provided that the executor or other person having lawful possession of the body of a deceased person, and not being entrusted with it for interment only, may permit the body of such person to undergo anatomical examination, unless in his lifetime the deceased shall have expressed, in such manner as in the Act specified, a wish to the contrary; or unless the surviving husband, or wife, or known relation of the deceased shall object; and further that the Secretary of State for the Home Department may grant licences to practise anatomy to any Members of the Royal College of Physicians or Surgeons, or to any graduates or licentiates in medicine, or to any professor of anatomy, medicine, or surgery, or to any student attending any school of anatomy, the application for such licence being countersigned by two justices of the peace; and persons so licensed may receive or possess for anatomical examination, or examine anatomically under such licence and with such permission as aforesaid any dead body; but no anatomical examination is to be conducted save at some place of which the Secretary of State has had a week's notice, and the Secretary of State may appoint inspectors for all such places, who are to make quarterly returns as to the dead bodies carried in for examination there."

To the value of this Act Wakley often bore testimony in the "Lancet," but at the same time he saw blemishes in its working to which he alluded in terms that might almost have led his readers to suppose that he considered the defects to overshadow the advantages. Wakley found fault with Warburton's Act because it put no restraint on the parochial authorities with regard to the unclaimed dead, but left them free either to dispose of the bodies to their own advantage or to bury them as they pleased. He desired to compel the parochial authorities and the superintendents of hospitals and asylums to forward notice to the Inspector of Anatomy whenever a dead body should be in their possession under the circumstances described in the Act, and he further desired that the Inspector should distribute such bodies not only to the schools recognised by law but to those schools in proportion to the number of students. He did this to defeat the manœuvring of the big hospitals against the smaller ones and against the private schools. The wealth of the big institutions enabled them to obtain bodies to the exclusion of rivals who frequently offered better tuition at lower fees, and as an indication of the fact that Wakley was right may be quoted the conduct of the treasurer of Guy's Hospital three years after the passage of Warburton's Act. This gentleman undertook that his institution should receive all the sick paupers of the Southwark Union and all incurables without the usual weekly subsidy from the guardians on condition that every body available should be sent to his school and no other !

Wakley's general praise of this Act was as well bestowed as his general blame of the Charter of the College of Surgeons granted in 1844, or of the Medical Act of 1858. The latter Acts he foresaw had not settled the points they purported to deal with, so that future controversy was inevitable. The former he believed to have virtually abolished terrible dangers to the community—the danger of uneducated surgeons and the danger of stealthy assassination. The faults which he found in the Anatomy Act have since been removed, some by time and some by legal amendment. It is open to an institution to make a private bargain to ensure to itself a supply of bodies, but all such bargains are known to the Inspector of Anatomy, who distributes the subjects strictly in proportion to the number of students. If an institution has a private supply of its own, so many the fewer subjects does it require, and does it obtain, from the public supply. The Act has provided, as Wakley said that it would, an adequate number of bodies for the teaching òf anatomy in the medical schools, and has abolished the trade of the resurrectionist, with its daily routine of impiety and its occasional divagations into murder.

There now only remain to be considered a few scattered passages in Wakley's life, such, for example, as his attitude towards quacks, towards the Poor-law, and towards adulteration of food. But before passing to these subjects it is right to look back and recall what was accomplished mainly by him during his career as a medical reformer. This can be summarised in a few words. In 1823, when the "Lancet" was founded, there was no Medical Act either protecting the public or regulating the medical profession ;

nepotism was the one prevailing force at the metropolitan hospitals ; favouritism determined all official appointments and elections ; the horrible trade of the resurrectionist was thriving ; and the provisions for medical education were disgraceful. Within forty years the hospitals of London had resolved that the first qualification that a member of their staffs must have was merit ; the Anatomy Act had abolished the resurrectionist ; the Medical Act had met many of the crying grievances of the profession ; and the London medical student was receiving a magnificent education. To obtain this education he had no longer to pay exorbitant fees ; and to become in turn a teacher and a hospital official himself he had to buy out no predecessor. In the fight for all these reforms Wakley led the way .

CHAPTER XLIV

*Wakley's Attitude towards Quacks—Chabert, the " Fire King "—
Wakley's Public Exposure of him—Dr. Elliotson—His Experiments in Animal Magnetism at University College Hospital—Knave
or Dupe ?—The Exposure of the O'Keys by Wakley—Elliotson's
Resignation of his Posts.*

THE pages of the "Lancet" offer numberless examples of Wakley's "shortest way with dissenters" from orthodox medical faith. He had a genuine horror of quacks and was keenly alive to the wrongs which the medical profession suffered then, as it suffers now, from the lying statements and impudent pretensions of charlatans. The avowed quack, possessing no medical qualifications and glorying in, or affecting to glory in, their absence, who promises the public all sorts of cures for all sorts of diseases upon methods unknown to that hide-bound victim of formulæ, the educated practitioner, found in Wakley a relentless foe. He never tired of ridiculing the claims of such persons, and had an inexhaustible vocabulary of contempt wherewith to describe their methods and their drugs. With the more insidious quack—he who works from within the ranks of the profession and employs illicit means of treatment apparently for the benefit of his patients, but really for the gratification of his own vanity or greed—Wakley was equally severe, pointing out that whether honest or no in his departure from accepted medical tracks the result would be the same. He would fill his pockets at the expense either of foolish dupes who are ever seeking some new thing or of despairing sick groping blindly for the remedy which honest men have told them does not exist at the present time for their hopeless plight. Against these two unamiable classes Wakley was always ready to fight to the end. He examined their systems, analysed their nostrums, and roundly abused the public for their credulity and the State for its apathetic attitude towards mischievous or criminal persons. As good examples of his methods the exposures of Chabert the "Fire King" and the O'Keys, Dr. Elliotson's mesmeric mediums, may be mentioned. Chabert was a blatant quack, a fire-eater, a prussic acid swallower, and an obviously vulgar impostor, whose rightful sphere in life was the booth of a country fair. Dr. Elliotson was one of the most distinguished physicians of his time, a man generally accepted, not only in his profession, but among the public at large, as an acute and profound thinker. But to both Wakley meted out the identical treatment of complete exposure as soon as their methods appeared to him to endanger the reputation of medicine, or the health of the suffering public. Chabert he ridiculed as a common cheat, while Dr. Elliotson received always the respect due to a man of great performance in his profession. But this distinction was not carried further. In each case Wakley, having discovered trickery, warned the public that they had been gulled.

M. Chabert flourished in London at the end of 1829. He was said to be a discharged *chef de cuisine*, and he appeared nightly at the Argyll Rooms in the character of a "Fire King," when he went through some sort of a performance in support of his professions of ability to endure enormous heat. He swore that he could withstand the temperature of an oven at cooking power and that he could drink with impunity and even relish oil raised to 350° F., boiling water, and molten lead. Nor was this the limit of his talents. Not only did he claim for his corporeal system a remarkable security from the attacks of heat, but he also pretended that he was organically protected from the action of certain poisons—for example, prussic acid, arsenic, and phosphorus—which lethal substances he pretended to swallow in the presence of his dupes. He asserted that he had an antidote to their actions. Such rudimentary trickery would not in our days be considered worthy of the notice of a

serious scientific paper—though whether this silent contempt
for chicanery is not giving the charlatan an unfair chance
at the expense of the public is an arguable point—but sixty-
five years ago the level of general knowledge was lower and
Chabert's assumptions were accepted with equanimity by
responsible persons. Among them, surprising to say, were
to be found several members of the medical profession.
Wakley, therefore, announced his intention of exposing the
" Fudge King," as he called him. He challenged him to
drink boiling water in public concerning the temperature of
which a proper jury of spectators was satisfied. With
regard to Chabert's ability to swallow prussic acid Wakley
said that he would attend the wizard's performances and
would invite him to administer his prussic acid, with or
without the antidotes, to certain dogs, the insinuation being
clear that it was not prussic acid at all that the " Fire King "
was in the habit of swallowing publicly, but some innocuous
fluid. Chabert ignored this challenge save by a ridiculous
offer to accompany Wakley into an oven at a temperature of
600° F. or join him in quaffing oil at 350° F. Wakley, not,
as he said, feeling disposed for public immolation, and
having put forward no claims to a knowledge of the trick,
simply reiterated his request that Chabert would allow him
to attend a public performance with two dogs and a small
supply of prussic acid of whose purity he was himself convinced. Chabert and one of the dogs were to drink a portion of the prussic acid in view of the public, and then
receive the benefits of the antidote, when, according to
Chabert's professions, they should feel no ill-effects. The
other portion of the prussic acid was to be given to the
second dog, which not being treated with the antidote would
die, as a visible proof to the audience of the genuineness of
the poison which Chabert had swallowed. In pursuance of
his design Wakley made a grim application to the magistrates of Bow Street to inquire into his own position
supposing he should induce Chabert to drink a genuine
prussic acid, " which," said Wakley, " will infallibly kill him
at once." The magistrates, in answer to this startling

question, said that although they felt it right that Chabert's pretensions should be stringently tested in the interests of the public, Wakley must beware of urging the man towards self-murder. They considered that the responsibility of any untoward accident would fall upon Wakley's shoulders. Wakley pointed out that he was not going to administer the prussic acid himself, but should simply take care that real prussic acid was forthcoming. Then if Chabert persisted in his claim either to immunity from the effects of that poison or to the possession of an antidote he would ask that the experiments should be performed with a substance of undoubted virulence. It would be Chabert's own act if harm accrued to him. Accordingly on Saturday, February 4th, 1830, the Argyll Rooms were crowded from floor to ceiling, a large number of scientific and medical men being present in addition to the usual crowd, in the expectation of seeing Chabert respond to Wakley's challenge. Chabert opened the ceremony by a quaint speech in broken English, in which he tried to shuffle out of the consequence of his stupid boasts. He asserted that he had never said that *he* would swallow prussic acid himself, but that he would give it to dogs and then cure them with his antidote. On this so prolonged were the shouts of ridicule from the spectators that Chabert's manager had to come to his assistance by supporting his statement. This was a foolish proceeding, as the printed bills actually outside the Argyll Rooms at the time flatly contradicted both the wizard and his manager. In answer to loud calls from the audience Wakley then rose to speak. He denounced the subterfuges of Chabert, and produced a small vial of prussic acid from his pocket which he proceeded to offer to the " Fire King," assuring him at the same time that he knew it to be out of the question that any antidote could save him if he drank it. " You will give one gasp and be dead in ten seconds," said Wakley, tendering the vial with a smile. The poor charlatan tried in vain to interrupt Wakley's relentless words and, while refusing the poison, to get a hearing from his excited audience. But in vain. The general feeling was wholly against him, and at last he fairly fled from the platform shouting promises to give passes to the audience entitling them to be present at an uninterrupted *séance* at a future date. In the front of the hall, however, he was caught by the crowd and roughly handled, and finally fled in a dishevelled condition to the friendly shelter of a neighbouring coal-cellar.

The other person whose detection in quackery forms an excellent example of Wakley's methods of dealing with imposture was Dr. Elliotson, the popular member of scientific and literary society, whom Thackeray depicted under the name of Dr. Goodenough, and to whom he dedicated "Pendennis." Elliotson was the senior physician on the staff of University College Hospital, a staff second to none in Europe for brilliancy, comprising as it did Samuel Cooper, of the Surgical Dictionary; Liston, the most marvellous operator of his day, certainly the boldest and probably the most successful surgeon London has ever seen; Richard Quain, the author of " The Anatomy of the Arteries"; Anthony Todd Thompson, author of "The Dispensatory" and a mine of pharmacological lore; and Robert Carswell, the most learned pathologist in England. He was co-professor at the medical school of University College with these, with Robert Grant, the zoologist, author of "Outlines of Comparative Anatomy" and Huxley's predecessor as Fullerian Professor at the Royal Institution; and with Sharpey, the profound physiologist, and the autocrat of the elections of the Royal Society. In this splendid company Elliotson more than held his own. A comprehensive lecturer in the class-room, a most acute physician in the wards, and an original, unconventional thinker in every capacity of life, he was respected and admired by his colleagues, much consulted by the public, and immensely popular with the students. Being such a man as he was, the story of his connexion with animal magnetism and of his experiments in a kind of black art conducted at University College Hospital, forms one of the most extraordinary pages in the medical history of the century. And at the outset of the story it should be said that Elliotson was believed by all who knew him to have acted in perfect good faith—to have been, in fact, a dupe and not a rogue. He was a great experimenter and prided himself on his receptivity and readiness to learn. He had made many valuable observations in the uses of drugs, and he was wont to stimulate his classes by pointing out that in the domain of therapeutics the student had open before him a virgin country waiting the explorer. Anatomy and surgery as then taught appeared more or less finite subjects. The enormous developments that physiology and pathology would experience as a result of the study of micro-organisms were not foreseen, and Elliotson, a sanguine, imaginative man, looked about him in vain for some outlet for his inventive mind. As bad fortune would have it he came across at this juncture a certain Baron Dupotet, who had experimented in Paris with mesmerism. He obtained for Dupotet permission to make a trial of his methods of healing in the wards of University College Hospital. Elliotson's own association with these experiments was at first that of an interested spectator. Avowedly on the look-out for departures in therapeutics, Baron Dupotet's claim to relieve, and in some cases cure, epilepsy by the production of the mesmeric slumber seemed to him to fall within the range of legitimate inquiry. Had he stopped here all would have been well. Had he been content with a simple attempt to benefit the sick, of whose desire to recover there could be no doubt, and whose only collusion would have consisted in a reasonable endeavour to play into the hands of the physician by faithful obedience to orders, no one would have objected—at any rate, no one would have had a good case on which to found their objections. But, unfortunately for Elliotson, he was led to employ mediums of whose good faith he had no proper guarantee, and by their pretended powers and revelations to see in mesmerism a new force for good or ill in the world. Everything that is or has been meant by the terms hypnotism and hypnotic suggestion, Perkinism and animal magnetism, transferred vision, exoneurism, and telepathy, seems to have been put in practice by Elliotson in conjunction with his two mediums, Elizabeth and Jane O'Key, while his initial intention to use the new force, whatever it might be, as a therapeutic measure was entirely lost sight of. These two hysterical girls being thrown into slumber were invited to tell the time by watches applied to their elbows or navels; were asked questions as to the proper medical treatment of themselves and other patients; and were apparently twisted into convulsions by passes made at them from a distance by Elliotson or by contact with certain fluids or metals which had been previously charged with "magnetism" by being held in Elliotson's hand. The performance was mystical and inconclusive, for no certain results were ever obtained. It, moreover, showed a tendency to degenerate into indecency, while the only therapeutic innovations that resulted from it would have given effect to the dangerous precedent of allowing patients to prescribe for themselves and even to interfere with the prescriptions of their fellow-sufferers less marvellously gifted. It was no wonder that the hospital authorities were much exercised in their minds at Elliotson's behaviour. Two camps were quickly formed. The governors were opposed to the continuance of performances which were gaining the institution much unfavourable notoriety and cheap ridicule. Certain of the students, headed by Liston, supported the governors' view. On the other hand, Elliotson had a grand argument and a great following. The argument was, of course, that all innovators are deemed mad or dishonest by their slower-witted coævals and that the wild impossibility of to-day becomes the trite routine of to-morrow. The following consisted of the majority of the students, who were personally attached to Elliotson, who could bear witness to his wisdom and sincerity in other things, who were content to believe what he believed, and who were, moreover, fascinated by the atmosphere of occultism. The "hospital of all the talents," as it was called in recognition of the all-round scientific excellence of its staff at the time, was thrown into absolute disorder.

The attention of Wakley was naturally directed to the situation, and he immediately wrote in the "Lancet" that the solution to the trouble lay entirely in the answer to the question whether the O'Keys were or were not honest and trustworthy. If they were trustworthy—and in no walk in life would the words of hysterical epileptic young women placed suddenly and by accident in a position of enormous public notoriety be considered worth any attention at all— then Elliotson, Dupotet, and their disciples had made a discovery. But if the O'Keys were impostors, what were Dupotet and Elliotson? Clearly dupes or rogues. From this inference articles in the "Lancet" allowed no escape. Elliotson accepted the challenge with a willingness and alacrity that certainly vouched for his good faith. He offered to bring his mediums to Wakley's house in Bedford Square and there exhibit their powers of prophecy, transferred vision and clairvoyance, and extraordinary susceptibility to certain metals and fluids. Accordingly on August 16, 1838, a performance—for no other name describes the proceedings—was given in the drawing-room of 35, Bedford Square, for the benefit of ten persons, five chosen by Wakley and five invited by Elliotson. Among those invited by Elliotson to be present was Mr. J. Fernandez Clarke, at that time and for many years a member of the staff of the "Lancet" and the author of some interesting autobiographical recollections of the medical profession. Mr. Clarke was regarded by both sides as a friend, and although he was present by Elliotson's request was willing to further Wakley's intent to arrive at the truth. Accordingly, at a particular experiment an arrangement was made between them to test the honesty of one of the mediums, Elizabeth O'Key. Of this girl it was alleged by Elliotson that she would fall into convulsions upon being touched by a piece of nickel, but would remain placid under contact with lead. Discs of these two metals were then given by Elliotson "charged with magnetism" to Wakley, who was seated in front of the girl, a screen of pasteboard being set between them. Wakley immediately gave the nickel, unperceived by

Elliotson, to Clarke, who put it in his pocket and walked to the other end of the room, where he remained during the experiment. Wakley now having nothing but the lead in his possession, to which metal the medium was supposed not to react, bent forward and touched the girl's right hand. As he did so a bystander by arrangement whispered audibly : " Take care that you do not apply the nickel too strongly ! " Immediately the medium fell into strong convulsions, much to the gratification of Elliotson, who said that "no metal but nickel had ever produced these effects " and that " they presented a beautiful series of phenomena." Wakley at once pointed out that no nickel had been used, and upon Dr. Elliotson's indignant protest Clarke came forward and explained the trick that had been played, producing the nickel from his own waistcoat pocket. Wakley now said that his point was made and that the girl was proved an impostor, but Elliotson was persistent that some error had occurred. He considered it possible that in some unexplained way " the power of nickel had been present." The experiments were consequently persevered in both on that day and on the following day, with the result that the behaviour of the muddled mediums became entirely at variance with that which was expected of them. Not only did they fall into convulsions on contact with the unexciting lead, but they remained impassive when rubbed with the influential nickel. They drank water which had been " mesmerised "—this was Elliotson's word, and the process consisted in the owner of the master mind placing his finger in the fluid for a few minutes—without a spasm, when it should have rendered them rigid ; while water straight from the pump produced opisthotonos ! " Mesmerised " gold from Elliotson's hands had no ill-effect on them, while sovereigns non-impregnated with the magnetic fluid and emanating from the trouser-pockets of sceptics produced neurotic results of a marked character.

Wakley denounced the whole thing in the " Lancet " as a pitiable delusion. He made no reflections upon Elliotson, who was a personal friend of his own, and had been a writer in the " Lancet" from the inception of the paper, but he told the whole story of the experiments to the public, and no one who read the account could fail to see that Elliotson had omitted proper precautions, that his so-called scientific experiments were parlour jugglery indifferently stage-managed, and that he himself had imported into the question a degree of personal interest which had unbalanced him and unfitted him for the responsible posts of senior physician to the University College Hospital and professor of medicine in the medical school. In December of the same year the Council of University College passed a resolution to the effect that the hospital committee were to hold themselves instructed to take such steps as they should deem advisable to prevent the practice of mesmerism or animal magnetism in future within the hospital. Dr. Elliotson considered this resolution personally offensive to himself and at once lodged his resignation of the posts of physician to the hospital and lecturer to the medical school with the Council of University College, at the same time making an appeal to the students to demonstrate in his favour against the limitation which had been put by the Council upon the range of legitimate scientific inquiry. The students at an exciting meeting, and by a slender majority, ratified the action of the Council, resolving that they " sincerely regretted the circumstances which had *necessarily* led to Dr. Elliotson's resignation." On the same day Dr. Elliotson's resignation was accepted by the Council.

CHAPTER XLV

The Position of the Medical Referee Fifty Years ago—Wakley takes up the Cudgels for the Medical Profession—Good Companies Mend their Ways—The Establishment of the New Equitable Life Assurance Company—Its Immediate Success—The Outcome to the Medical Profession.

AT the present time, if a man desires to insure his life the assurance office which he may happen to select for the purpose will almost certainly instruct him to be examined by its salaried medical officer, and in many cases the salary is by no means a bad one. In addition to this the office will want a report from the applicant's own medical man, in which case it will pay a fee for the service rendered to it. In good companies this fee is from one to two guineas. There are provident and semi-charitable institutions which afford livelihood for an executive staff, but which do not find themselves able to pay the medical man from whom they seek valuable assistance more than half a guinea, but these institutions are on a different footing. All medical men know that they will obtain fair treatment from first-class life assurance offices.   But this was not always the case.   Fifty years ago the medical man derived nothing from the life assurance companies at all, save from two or three honourable and exceptional institutions.   The applicant for a policy was told by the office that before he could be insured he must get his medical man to report upon his life. The name of the medical man being given to the office an application was sent to him to answer certain questions. In careful offices the questions were numerous and searching.   Sometimes to answer them honestly a physical examination of their subject was necessary. But if this was not required, at all events the medical man who had a proper sense of his responsibility in the matter was compelled to render a careful written report of the state of the health of his patient, to compile which he had to consult case-books as well as to rely upon dearly bought knowledge and experience. For this he was not paid by anyone. The office declared that it was no business of its. It would not accept the life without the report, but at the same time it was the applicant's duty to furnish it. The applicant said that he did not want the report, but that the office insisted upon his having it. He would not pay for it and he did not desire the medical man to do more than write him a general kind of testimonial for which there would, of course, be no charge. If the medical man wanted a recommendation of any kind from one of his patients he would not expect to pay for it. To pay would be to make of an ordinary courtesy a venal transaction, and the offer of a fee would be an insult. Similarly the public considered that the medical man who had attended them knew the state of their health and that he ought, therefore, to be so obliging as to say to the office what this state of health was. If the medical man was paid for such information his good faith in the matter became at once a subject of doubt, but if his report was spontaneously made its honesty would not be called in question. Some saw a little difference between "mutual" offices, meaning offices where all profits were divided annually among the insured in the office, and "proprietary" offices, meaning offices where all profits were divided among shareholders not necessarily policy-holders also. In the first case they considered that the medical man should be paid by the assurance office to send reports, for the office represented the assured *en masse*, and it would save trouble if all the payments were made by the assured collectively, as represented by the office, instead of by each policy-holder individually. In the second case they considered that the applicants for assurance should pay for the report of the medical officer, inasmuch as it was they who desired the benefits of assurance. The profits belonged to the shareholders and could not be squandered on medical fees.

This was the state of affairs in 1840, when Wakley first took up in the " Lancet " the question of the attitude of the life assurance companies towards the medical man. He attacked the grievance with all the vigour and ardour that distinguished his earlier efforts in behalf of the medical profession, those made, for example, to obtain remuneration for medical witnesses and an independent medical press. Article after article flowed from his pen, outspoken, to the point, and occasionally abusive. The policy of the companies in withholding from medical men the remuneration to which their services clearly entitled them was denounced as suicidal and also mean. The finest safeguard that an office could have against the risk of accepting a bad life at first-class prices must be the honest opinion of the applicant's private medical man. The officer of the company would see the applicant for a policy but once. He necessarily must make his examination upon a stereotyped plan, for in a good office he could not otherwise get through the work ; but it would often occur that his plan, while working well to meet the necessities of rapid summary judgments would not provide for the detection of less obvious features in the physical condition of his subject, such, for example, as the sequelæ of old disease, or the weaknesses due to hereditary predisposition. Upon such matters the only proper person to advise the company was the applicant's family attendant. Why should such advice be rendered gratuitously ? Further, seeing that candour to the company might in conceivable instances cause the medical man to lose his patient, how could the companies always expect from a class whom they treated with meanness and contempt voluntary and valuable assistance ? And if they did expect it, said Wakley, let them expect it in vain : withstand all temptation to be obliging and the victory must come to the medical man. The medical man was not paid, or very grudgingly paid, by the applicant for the policy simply because the companies by hook or crook had been able to obtain as much assistance as they wanted without putting their hands into their well-replenished coffers, yet not enough assistance to enable them to carry on their business with proper absence of risk. But only let the medical man make it clear that he would not answer the questions of a life assurance office unless he was properly paid by that office for his trouble, and the companies would, sooner or later, and probably sooner, make advances towards him. Following this advice many medical men refused to give the assistance demanded of them by the companies, a proceeding which was denounced by a section of the papers of the day, medical and lay, as an illicit combination of the profession against the public, but which was commended by other journals as a reasonable measure of self-protection. In five years—that is to say, by the year 1850—Wakley was able to report considerable progress in the movement. All over the United Kingdom he had stirred up medical men to demand payment from the life assurance offices before rendering assistance, with the result that out of a list of one hundred and two companies given in the Post Office Directory for that year, forty-eight, and these of the highest standing, had given in to the demands of the profession—or, in Wakley's words, " had come over to the side of honesty and liberality."

But Wakley desired to go quicker than this, and while doubling the force and frequency of his contemptuous allusions to the policy pursued by those companies which still maintained their parsimonious attitude, he began to foreshadow an ideal office worked by medical men for medical men, where the general practitioner should take the place of the solicitor as agent and referee. An ever-green subject with him was the profuseness with which the public seemed ready to reward the solicitor as compared to the medical man, and when he was able to treat the question of the relations of the life assurance offices with the medical profession from that point of view he was on familiar and favourite ground.

"We have before us," he said in one article, "the receipt for the annual policy on a life insured in a proprietary office some years since, at the age of thirty-four, for £1000. The annual premium is £26 10s. This office is one that refuses to pay medical fees, but pays the ordinary commission to solicitors and agents. On this policy 10 per cent. on the premium was paid to the solicitor through whom the assurance was effected for the first year, and 5 per cent. for every succeeding year. The probable mean duration of a healthy life at thirty-four years of age, according to the calculation of Mr. Farr, is thirty-one years. Supposing the assurer to live the average time of a person in health the solicitor will have received no less a sum than £42 8s., besides interest, while the paltry single payment of £1 1s. to the medical referee was refused. The medical referee wrote a responsible report. Positively the only trouble incurred by the solicitor was in writing a letter to the secretary to inform him that the party in question was about to insure in the —— office. Is this justice ? "

This question Wakley proceeded to answer by asserting that justice would not be done until medical men were able to enter into negotiation with a company that would not only recognise the justice of their claim to some remuneration, and that at a fair scale, but would also make of medical men the agents of the company and, in short, treat them in the same way that solicitors were treated by the offices. Accordingly, in February, 1851, the New Equitable Life Assurance Company was started, the main reason of its existence being the intention on the part of Wakley and a few enthusiastic friends to show that an office where the medical profession obtained their rights would be more prosperous than those offices which withheld from the profession their rightful fees.

"The directors of the New Equitable," said the first prospectus, " have determined that all medical questions shall emanate from, and the answers be directed to their own medical examiners, by which course of proceeding should any proposed assurance be declined, no statement of particulars will be necessarily made to the board, the replies being deemed strictly professional and confidential. After duly considering the important position of medical practitioners with respect to life assurance, the trouble imposed on them, and the valuable nature of the information which it is in their power alone to supply, the directors of the New Equitable have resolved to award a payment of two guineas to every legally qualified medical practitioner for every official report rendered by him to the medical examiner of the company. . . . . The directors will invariably recognise every qualified member of the profession whom they may consult not only as the referee of the party whose life is proposed for assurance, but as their own medical adviser in the case, on whose written and well-digested report they must mainly rely in forming their decision. . . . . It has long been the practice for several of the most respectable of the assurance offices to allow to solicitors and attorneys a commission of 10 per cent. on the first year's premiums paid by parties introduced by them, and 5 per cent. annually afterwards so long as the policies remain in force. The directors of the New Equitable have resolved to allow commissions of equal amount, under similar circumstances, to members of the medical profession."

The company got to business without delay and met with success from the first. The medical profession gave the scheme hearty and spontaneous support, and letters arrived daily at the office containing offers of assistance in making known the value of the new scheme, applications for agencies and shares, and proposals for life assurance. A firmly established conviction of the soundness of the under-taking, as well as a strong feeling of indignation against the offices which had previously denied to the medical practi-tioner his just rights, commended the New Equitable to all the readers of the " Lancet," and once more Wakley was to see a departure planned by him sail straight into popularity. The first annual report showed that the infant institution had made wonderful headway in so short a period as one year, and was already able to court comparison with the most successful life assurance óffices in the kingdom. The directors had issued during the first year of the company's existence 355 policies covering insurances to the extent of £168,765, the annual income of these policies amounting to over £6000—figures which meant a remarkable success forty-five years ago. Indeed, the published accounts of several of the oldest and best companies in the kingdom showed that the prestige and the wide advertisement due to an ancient history had not enabled them to transact so much business during the year 1851–52 as had been trans-acted by the New Equitable Company. The pleasure of this success was enhanced for Wakley, who was one of the directors, by the knowledge that the principle put forward by the New Equitable as the sole reason of its existence— namely, the recognition of the services of the medical referee—must now be adopted by all the companies that desired to hold their own against the sturdy growth of the infant office. In particular he rejoiced over the fact that the wealthy company in which so many medical men held policies, the Clerical, Medical, and General Life Assurance Company, had fallen in with his views after an obstinate rejection of them for very many years, for in January, 1852, the directors of this company promised a fee of one guinea to the medical attendants of persons proposing to assure in all cases in which the board had sought from them advice or information. The second annual report showed a continuance of the public favour. From one client alone the office accepted a proposal to assure for £50,000, and this client was introduced by a medical·man. The sum was re-assured in other offices by the directors of the New Equitable, who considered their company too young to run such risks, and who were thus enabled to approach their oldest and strongest rivals in the character of patrons. The entire number of proposals received from the date of the first policy in February, 1851, to December 31st, 1852, was 834 for assuring £349,122. The number of policies actually issued was 677 for assuring the sum of £278,855, and the income derivable from these policies in premiums amounted on the whole to £10,652, the average amount of each policy being £411. These figures showed substantial patronage, while others in the report showed able and watchful management. For instance, the expenses incurred during 1852 by the New Equitable Company were but £3700, although £882 had been paid as fees to medical referees. Other companies not doing so large a business or receiving the same amount in premiums had returned their expenditure for the year at £7000, although they had in many cases been unable to afford to pay for medical advice concerning the risks that they had accepted. The moral drawn by the directors of the New Equitable, who had only been called upon to satisfy one claim during the first twenty-three months of the existence of their company, was that the unbiassed reports of medical referees obtained by just payment formed the greatest safeguard that an assurance office could have. An office that was protected by such information took no risks, and could, therefore, afford to be generous. As a consequence of these figures, and of the strict confirmation of Wakley's assertions thus furnished by the directors of the New Equitable Company, thirty-eight more companies joined the forty-two who were on the side of justice, eighty offices in all beginning in 1853 to advertise their willingness to pay medical men for their valuable services and to show respect where they had formerly inflicted insult. The report of the work done by the company during 1853 showed further progress. During the year 463 proposals to insure the sum of £182,770 had been received. Out of these proposals 348 policies had been issued, assuring the sum of £134,930. The annual premiums payable on these new policies amounted to £5227. The fourth annual report continued the satisfactory tale. It showed that the total number of policies issued by the office up to the end of 1854 had increased from 1025 to 1282, and that the premiums payable on them amounted to an annual income of £18,750. The next annual report, that for 1855, stated that the number of policies issued had reached 1604, the annual premiums due thereon making in the aggregate a sum of £22,733.

So far the records of the company showed uninterrupted progress. But in 1856 the directorate decided to make a great departure. A proposal for amalgamation was entered into with the Medical, Legal, and General Life Office, the board falling in with the proposal by the narrow majority of one. The unanimous consent of the shareholders of both companies given at meetings specially convened for the purpose seemed to justify the course that had been taken, and a Bill for the complete unification of the two concerns obtained parliamentary consent during the year, while as a tribute to the fortunate career of the younger venture it was agreed to call the joint company the " New Equitable." Wakley, although he remained on the directorate, did not approve of the amalgamation of the New Equitable office with the Medical, Legal, and General office. The New Equitable had been started in defence of a principle, that principle being the due recognition of the services that medical men were able to render to life assurance offices. By amalgamation with the Medical, Legal, and General this principle was lost sight of. The joint company trading under the title of the "New Equitable" became directly comparable in scheme to other offices. It proposed to pay its medical referees—an innovation which all respectably conducted companies had by this time begun to sanction—but its special connexion with the medical profession was gone. Wakley recognised that the amalgamation had been made in response to a forward movement, and that the figures went to prove that double the amount of business would be done at less than double the expense, but he saw that the individuality of the original company would be lost. Remarkable success had attended its early career, and Wakley attributed this success to the idiosyncrasy of its constitution as a life assurance company to be managed by doctors for doctors. Events not long after Wakley's death proved him to have been right in his surmises, for the New Equitable fell upon evil days. As far, however, as Wakley's personal share in it went it was a success. Until the amalgamation with the Medical, Legal, and General its position was an honourable one and a remarkable one considering its youth and the fact that it had been started in opposition to traditional wisdom. Its prosperity did not wane until its peculiar character was gone, while its institution established the unquestioned right of medical men to be properly paid by life assurance companies for their services and the extreme value of those services.

What the aggregate sum paid in the United Kingdom at the present moment to medical men as referees in life assurance matters may be it would be idle to guess ; it is doubtful whether there is sufficient evidence before the public to enable an expert statistician to hazard a reasonable estimate. But two things are certain : firstly, that the sum is very large and not decreasing ; and, secondly, that it is to the establishment of the New Equitable Life Assurance Company in 1851 that the receipt of this sum by medical men of the present day is due.

CHAPTER XLVI

The "Lancet" Analytical Sanitary Commission—The Editorial Definition of its Scope—The Inquiry into the Adulteration of Coffee.

IN 1851 Wakley commenced in the columns of the " Lancet" the most useful agitation in favour of legislative reform that ever engaged his attention, alert as he had shown himself during twenty-five years of public life to learn where the popular wrong lay and to propose a practical and effective remedy for it. It was in this year that he decided to issue the results of microscopical and chemical analyses of the food-stuffs, solid and fluid, in general consumption by the nation. The idea was not a new one—in fact, it had been present in his mind ever since his first election to Parliament —but the gigantic labour of such an inquiry, if worked with proper thoroughness and security from error, had hitherto prevented him from embarking upon it : he knew the grave responsibilities that it would involve. " We have undertaken," he said at the commencement of the inquiry, " a task large enough to engage the attention of the Government of this country. With the exception of officers to observe and report upon diseased meat or fish, the public authorities take no cognisance of the adulteration and poisoning by the slower but equally sure mode of adulteration of food and drinks. We will bring the microscope and the test-tube to bear with unerring truth upon things hidden and secret enough to the unaided senses . . . . . for the protection of the public, the advantage of the fair trader, and the ultimate exposure and punishment of the fraudulent one."

This sentence formed a general introduction to the new inquiry. The special introduction to the series of articles which were issued under the generic title of "The 'Lancet' Analytical Sanitary Commission" defined the scope of the proposed inquiry, which was to form nothing less than an attack upon prevalent methods of adulteration and sophistication of food so thorough and uncompromising that it would on the one hand frighten individual evil-doers into better behaviour and on the other open the eyes of Parliament to the absolute necessity for State interference.

The special introduction ran as follows :—

"THE ANALYTICAL SANITARY COMMISSION.

"RECORDS OF THE RESULTS OF MICROSCOPICAL AND CHEMICAL ANALYSES OF THE SOLIDS AND FLUIDS CONSUMED BY ALL CLASSES OF THE PUBLIC.

"'Forewarned, Forearmed.'

" Uncontaminated air and pure water are now universally regarded as necessary to the maintenance of healthy existence, and to obtain them we have appointed ' Boards of Health' and 'Commissions of Sewers.' That unadulterated Food, the bone and muscle of the body, is not less requisite, will be readily allowed, and it will appear on reflection as somewhat remarkable that the interests of the public in these important particulars should not hitherto have been watched over and protected by any authorised body or commission.

" That the various articles of consumption differ greatly in quality and are subject to numerous adulterations must be evident to all from the slightest consideration and examination of the subject; and if any general proof were required to establish the truth of this position it would be found in the low and unremunerative prices at which many commodities to be genuine are now commonly sold. That, therefore, there is much relating to our food and drink requiring exposure and remedy cannot be doubted.

" We propose, then, for the public benefit to institute an extensive and somewhat vigorous series of investigations into the present condition of the various articles of diet supplied to the inhabitants of this great metropolis and its vicinity, and probably the inquiries will be extended to some of our distant cities and towns.

" One especial feature of these inquiries will be that they are all based upon actual observation and experiment; the microscope and test-tube throughout these investigations will be our constant companions. We shall borrow but little from the writings of others, preferring to labour and think for ourselves and to work out our own conclusions in an independent manner.

"A second feature will consist in the introduction of faithful engravings illustrating all the more important points and particulars of each article.

"A third and highly important feature will be the *publication* of the *names* and *addresses* of the parties from whom the different articles, the analyses of which will be detailed, were purchased ; the advantages of such a course of proceeding require no explanation.

"Experience has shown that any merely general exposure of the nature of the adulterations practised on the public through their food is not sufficient to deter from a repetition of them, and that the only way in which it can be hoped that such fraudulent practices can be stayed and the public protected is by such proceedings as will entail personal discredit and probable loss.

"Now although we are fully and firmly determined to protect the interests of the public, we at the same time do not desire to inflict injury on any one, as a proof of which we shall refrain from giving the names of adulterators for the space of three months from this date, and shall at present, in connexion with the analyses, merely indicate the street or place in which each vitiated commodity subjected to examination was purchased.

"Notwithstanding that we should be perfectly justified in at once making known the name of the tradesman and merchant who is dis-honest enough to adulterate the article which he vends, and although to such a proceeding he could raise no sufficient objection, nor hope for the sympathy of the public, yet desiring to avoid all appearance of harshness, we shall refrain, as we have stated, from doing so at present, but give him the benefit of this distinct warning.

"That the public at large will be greatly benefited by these inquiries is obvious, and many of our colonists (at least such as import any article of food into this country). That the revenue itself will be largely the gainers, might be very easily and satisfactorily proved.

"The honest tradesman or merchant will also be benefited ; he has nothing to fear but, on the contrary, much to gain, for while he will be able to secure fair prices for a genuine commodity, his name also will be made known to the public, and he will be upheld in his true light and character as an upright and honourable tradesman.

"Who, then, will fear the disclosures it will be our duty to make ? Fraudulent dealers—whether they be wholesale merchants, knavish manufacturers, dishonest brewers, or adulterating retailers—they alone will have cause to fear, but none whatever rightfully and legally to complain of the consequences of their own unprincipled proceedings.

"The urchin who filches a bun, a penny-piece, or the value of one, breaks the law and is liable to punishment, and even imprisonment—is it to be supposed, therefore, that the cunning and systematic adulterator of our food and drink, who robs us not only of our money, but sometimes even of our health and strength, is less guilty? that he is to be allowed to violate the law with impunity in his daily dealings and not only to go unpunished, but to carry about with him, as at present he commonly does, in his intercourse with his fellows, the undeserved reputation of an honest man? That the law, while it rigorously punishes the trivial offender, should allow the greater criminal to go at large unscathed is an insult to common sense.

"But the question is not merely one of honesty and dishonesty, of profit and loss, it is also sanitary, one of health, and even in some cases of life itself, of which many proofs might be readily adduced.

"Thus the physician, having carefully planned the diet of his patient, too often finds his well-grounded hopes frustrated through the nefarious practice of adulteration.

"In one case he orders arrowroot and isinglass—the first is very commonly adulterated with potato or some other farina, whilst for the second is substituted some ill-prepared form of gelatine.

"In another case he prescribes strong coffee or tea, it may be to counteract the effect of some narcotic poison. The one is adulterated with a large quantity of chicory, and the other consists of exhausted tea-leaves re-dried.

"Examples like these, affecting strength, health, and sometimes life, might be multiplied to almost any extent; but these few observations are sufficient to show the vast interests involved in the consideration of the subject of the adulteration of the food and drink consumed by the public.

"In treating the several subjects which will come under our notice we do not intend to confine ourselves to any very strict order of arrangement, but shall probably from time to time turn aside from our regular course to take into consideration such subjects as may happen to be possessed of peculiar or temporary public or professional interest."

In accordance with this introduction the following articles of food were then made the subjects of microscopical and chemical examination : coffee, sugar, arrowroot, London water, chicory, mustard, bread, cocoa, farinaceous foods, oatmeal, tea, milk, isinglass, vinegar, spices, curry, bottled fruits and vegetables, anchovies and potted meats, sauces, jellies, and jams, lard and butter. Two substances not food-stuffs, but counting for much in the comfort of humanity—tobacco and opium—were added to the list.

The method of treating the first article—coffee—was the plan followed in all the subsequent inquiries and will be detailed for that reason. It formed a good example of thoroughness; it left no loophole for offenders and allowed no possible cavil on the ground of any doubtful honesty of purpose. There was, in fact, no shrinking on the part either of the editor or of the expert Commissioner, who was, as is now well known, the late Dr. Arthur Hill Hassall. The scheme upon which the examinations were made was due to the joint invention of Wakley, Sir William Brooke O'Shaughnessy, a very old and regular contributor to the "Lancet," and Dr. Hassall. The first article appeared on january 4th, 1851, and commenced by boldly stating it to be a fact that coffee was largely adulterated. To obviate all possibilities of contradiction it was pointed out that, whereas between certain dates the population of Great Britain had increased and the greater use of the commodity was vaunted by dealers and by the promoters of the temperance cause, the amount imported under the name of coffee had decreased. In 1849 the amount derived by the Exchequer from the coffee duties was said to be £709,632 3s. 11d., and in 1850 it amounted to only £642,519 10s. 9d. One of two things had happened : either an increased demand for coffee was being fraudulently met, or the people, having discovered the beverage as supplied to them by sophisticating dealers to be nasty and non-nutritious, were deserting it. Another significant fact was that chicory was being cultivated in large quantities in this country, and yet little or none of it was retailed to the public under its own name.

Next careful descriptions with illustrations were given of the microscopic appearances of a section of the unroasted coffee berry, of the roasted berry, and of the investing membrane of the berry. These appearances were contrasted with illustrations of roasted chicory root ; while the minute structures of the farinæ of various grains and fruits were pointed out, the differences between corn-flour, potato-flour, and bean-flour on the one hand and ground coffee on the other being elaborately distinguished. The ground being thus cleared the Commissioner went promptly to the root of his work. He gave the results of the microscopic examination of thirty-four different coffees of all qualities and prices which were being sold under such attractive titles as, to mention a few, "Fine Old Turkey Coffee," "Fine Jamaica Coffee," "Finest Berbice Coffee," "Finest Java Coffee," "Delicious Family Coffee," and "Delicious Drinking Coffee." The result of this examination was little short of sensational. It justified every word that Wakley had predicted when he promised to publish investigations into the food of the people in his columns and virtually made an alteration in the law necessary. The thirty-four coffees were with three exceptions adulterated, and the three exceptions all occurred in samples of coffee retailed at a high price. The cheap and popular beverages were uniformly impure. Chicory was present in thirty-one instances, roasted corn in twelve, and bean-flour and potato-flour in one case each. In sixteen cases the adulteration consisted of the substitution of chicory for coffee only, in the other fifteen the coffee had undergone additional treatment with bean-flour, potato-flour, or roasted corn. In many instances the quantity of coffee present was very small, actually more than four-fifths of the bulk of some of the samples being formed by alien substances. The gross aggregate of the adulterations detected amounted to more than one-third of the entire bulk of the quantities purchased, from which the startling calculation was drawn, that the revenue had been defrauded during the year 1849 of no less a sum than £300,000, the figures for that year being used as a basis of calculation.

The results of a second or confirmatory examination were then appended. Here twenty samples of various coffees had been purchased at the establishments of different metropolitan grocers and tea and coffee merchants, and in every single case the coffee was found to be adulterated, in sixteen the tampering being of the grossest character. To defend the honest trader from his fraudulent competitors the names and addresses of the two dealers from whom the three pure samples had been purchased were printed at full, and the names of the adulterators were promised at a later date unless subsequent examination of their wares showed them to have profited by the warning.

2 G

The results of the first Analytical Sanitary Commission published by the "Lancet" created the excitement that its editor expected. The daily press reprinted large portions of the article and was outspoken in praise of the enterprise of those who had undertaken it and the admirable work that was foreshadowed by it, declaring it to be the duty of the legis‐ lature immediately to adopt effective measures to secure the public against such frauds. Accordingly, the Chancellor of the Exchequer (Sir Charles Wood), in the Budget which he presented to the House in the early spring of 1851, made a statement upon the subject; but it did not tend to allay the widespread feeling of distrust and indignation of the public, and produced much dissatisfaction among the owners of coffee estates and respectable wholesale dealers. Sir Charles Wood justified the mixing of chicory with coffee—a pro‐ ceeding which, it should be clearly understood, had been legalised by a Treasury minute—on the ground that the former was a cheap and nutritious root, the addition of which to the expensive berry resulted in a fragrant blend which could be sold at a price within the reach of the purse of the poor. To this Wakley replied that, firstly, chicory should not be sold as coffee; if the poor desired to buy chicory they should at least know that when they asked for coffee a mixture containing chicory is what they would obtain, in varying proportions, but seldom or never under 25 per cent. Secondly, he pointed to the gross injustice that was being done to colonial importers. These were at that date protected to a certain extent, the duty on colonial coffee being 4d. a pound and that on French coffee 6d.; but they derived no benefit from the protection, for they could not compete against home-made messes compounded of potato-flour and colouring matters; while a proposal to do away with this measure of protection was among the sug‐ gestions of the Chancellor of the Exchequer. Thirdly, he pleaded the cause of the honest traders. If adulteration by chicory was made illegal—i.e., if the offending Treasury minute was expunged—he believed that the poor would be properly catered for and a pure beverage provided for them at moderate prices, and that the straightforward dealer who scorned to sell sophisticated goods under lying titles would have an equal chance with his less scrupulous rivals.

On March 15th, 1851, Dr. Hassall immensely strengthened the position taken up by the " Lancet" with regard to coffee by making an analytical examination of chicory which disposed of the pretension possessed by the now notorious shrub to valuable dietetic qualities. Dr. Hassall found it neither wholesome nor nutritious, and not a particularly easy substance to obtain pure or cheap. Of thirty-four samples of chicory purchased at the establishments of different metropolitan grocers, or supplied as samples from wholesale dealers, fifteen were found to be adulterated, the substituted matters being roasted corn or acorns, while the price of undoubtedly pure chicory was so comparatively high as to make it unlikely that this form of adulteration alone would be employed by unscrupulous traders.

On April 26th, 1851, a second report was made by Dr. Hassall upon coffee and its adulteration, and on this occasion the expressed determination of publishing names of adulterators was carried out, for the full addresses of all the persons from whom the samples had been purchased were appended to the results of the analysis. "We are fully aware," ran the opening sentences of this report, "that in following this course we incur immense responsibility. . . . . We know that we expose ourselves to abuse, threats, legal proceedings, and to misconstruction and misrepresentation of our motives and intentions ; but strong in our cause we will not allow these considerations to deter us from fearlessly pursuing the course we deem necessary to effect our objects." Forty-two samples of coffee were purchased at different metropolitan establishments for the purposes of the second examination. In spite of the publicity that had been given to the ways of the adulterator, thirty-one samples were even now found to be adulterated with chicory. In two cases only was any other adulteration than that with chicory observed ; in one the added substance was presumed to be horse-chestnuts, while in the other it appeared to be some amorphous colouring matter, in all probability a constituent of bad chicory and not owing its presence to any special malignity of the shopman towards his customers. Some of these adulterated samples were purchased under assurance that the coffee in question contained no chicory, while many of them were described by their retailers as coffee of unprecedented strength and fragrance. The chief deduction to be drawn from this second inquiry was that the diminished ratio of adulterators to honest tradesmen showed that some retailers, in consequence of the exposures made, or threatened to be made, had abandoned the use of chicory entirely. Others, who had adopted a middle course and who were selling the genuine coffee and the legally adulterated coffee as separate articles, were commended for their frankness save where no care had been taken in the purchase of the chicory ; but as it was now an open secret that chicory was itself an article, subject to adulteration of crude and pernicious sort the Commissioner did not hold a trader quit of corrupt practices if he added what he had bought elsewhere as chicory without taking proper precautions against the substitution of acorns or horse-chestnuts. If the retail grocer was satisfied to buy any powder that was offered to him as chicory he would certainly purchase pulverised rubbish specially prepared to meet the willingness of the English poor to purchase a coffee that was not genuine.

A third inquiry was held later in the same year into the sophistication of the coffee of commerce, and on this occasion the subject of Dr. Hassall's investigation was canister coffee. This coffee, it had been asserted by the "Lancet" at the commencement of the inquiry, was more generally adulterated than loose coffee, and the result proved the accuracy of the statement. Of twenty-nine packages, canisters, and bottles of coffee submitted to analysis, twenty-eight were adulterated, the adulteration in every case consisting of chicory, to which in five instances other substances such as roasted wheat farina and powder resembling crushed mangel-wurzel and pounded acorns had been added.

CHAPTER XLVII

The " Lancet " Analytical Sanitary Commission (continued) : An Inquiry into various Food-stuffs—Mr. Scholefield's Act and Subsequent Legislation.

THE method employed in dealing with the analysis of coffee was followed in the analyses of other substances which appeared in the columns of the " Lancet " during the next ten years, so that it will be sufficient to illustrate the task that Wakley set himself if not much more than the bare results of the different investigations are related.

The second substance dealt with by the Analytical Sanitary Commission was sugar. Having described the macroscopic and microscopic appearances of sugar, both cane and grape, and detailed the foreign bodies—such as lime, lead, sawdust, starch, and acari—commonly found in impure specimens, the Commissioner gave the results of the examination of thirty-six brown sugars of different qualities and prices. Acari were present in thirty-five of the samples. Grape-sugar was detected in every sample, usually a proof of sophistication, for most of these sugars purported to be the much more powerful sweetening agent, cane-sugar. Stony particles or grits were observed in eleven samples, and woody fragments in thirteen. In four samples a variable quantity of flour had been introduced, evidently for the purpose of adulteration. Fifteen samples of lump sugar were then examined, and the results were found to compare very favourably with the results of the examination of moist sugar, for there were no acari, no grape-sugar, and no grits. Samples of moist sugar were then purchased in different parts of the metropolis, and every single one contained deleterious material, while two had been adulterated with flour.

The next article which fell under the Commission was arrowroot. The name "arrowroot" had been made, by dealers in the first place and in the second place by the general public, to cover almost every fecula bearing any resemblance to the true Maranta arundinacea, no matter how dissimilar the original plant might be. As a result there were several powdered substances in the market varying in price from a few pence to two or three shillings per pound, none of which were Maranta, but all of which had the valid claim of custom to the appellation "arrowroot." The Commissioner decided to get over this confusion by stating in his analyses the name of the plant from which the arrowroot was derived, to which end he examined specimens under the following names—Maranta arrowroot; Manihot arrowroot, or tapioca; Tacca arrowroot, a pulped tuber from Otaheite; Curcuma arrowroot; Arum arrowroot, the tubers of cuckoo-pint; and British or potato arrowroot, which was, frankly, potato-meal. The adulterations to which arrowroot was found to be commonly subjected were (1) the mixing of other tubers in varying proportions with true Maranta, (2) the substitution of an inferior for a superior root, or (3) the addition to one of these genuine "arrowroots" of some fecula not generally recognised as arrowroot at all. The most common sophistication in the trade was the addition to the genuine Jamaica arrowroot or Maranta root of potato-flour or tapioca in varying proportions. A second form of adulteration was the substitution of sago or potato-meal for Maranta. A third was the addition of potato-flour to an inferior root such as tapioca. The net result of the examination of fifty samples differing in quality, price, and appearance was instructive. Of the first seventeen samples, all highly priced arrowroots varying from 1s. 8d. to 3s. 6d. per pound, ten were found to be unadulterated and seven adulterated, four to an extreme extent. Of the next twenty-eight samples of lowly priced arrowroots varying from 1s. to 1s. 6d. per pound, seventeen were found to be unadulterated and eleven adulterated, five of the latter very grossly. In one of these adulterated specimens a few grains of genuine Maranta arrowroot were detected by the microscope, but three samples consisted of a mixture of potato-meal and sago-flour, while a fourth proved to be potato-meal only. The last five samples were articles sold in canisters which bore the dealers' warranty setting forth the very superior and unusual quality of the article and challenging observation and scrutiny. Of these one was marked "Superfine West India Arrowroot Warranted Genuine"; this was heavily charged with potato-flour. A second was "Recommended by the Faculty" as the most nourishing of all foods for children and invalids ; this was entirely tapioca save a few grains of Maranta arrowroot. A third was "Warranted Free from Adulteration" and was merely potato-fiour. The fourth and fifth were labelled "Arrowroot" and consisted of nothing but potato-flour.

Pepper next engaged the Commissioner's attention, with the result that he discovered that more than half the pepper purchased previously to certain convictions secured by the Excise officers was adulterated, but that subsequent to the enforcement of the law by the Excise authorities with regard to this particular condiment adulteration in an extensive form had ceased, forming a remarkable example of the practical effect of a little of the legislative interference which it had been Wakley's chief aim to make general by the institution of the Analytical Sanitary Commission.

The next inquiry was larger in scope and of a different character. Its subject was the water-supply of London, and it was dealt with in a fearless and uncompromising manner. The nature of the various impurities of water was first explained, and the action of the reservoir or cistern in favouring such impurities was discussed. A number of experiments were recorded dealing with the action of water on lead and iron, and the sources of the London water-supply at that date were investigated. The summary of the investigation ran as follows :—

"The waters at present in use in this metropolis are all hard, and have all the disadvantages of hard waters; they are, moreover, river waters, and for the most part contaminated to a great extent with organic matter, dead and living; add to these points their further deterioration by contact with lead in cisterns and by the accumulation and growth of animal and vegetable productions which take place in those receptacles, and the case is proved against the whole of the present supplies of the metropolis."

From big to little—the next investigation concerned mustard. Here the Commissioner succeeded in demonstrating that genuine mustard, whatever the price paid, apparently was not to be obtained in the year 1851. Of forty-two samples submitted to examination every one was adulterated, and in every case the adulteration was the same in kind, varying only in degree, and consisted of the admixture of wheat-flour and turmeric as a colouring agent.

Bread came next and formed the subject of a thorough investigation. The first report dealt merely with the chief constituents of bread as made from wheat, barley, oat, rye, rice, or Indian corn-flour. The diseases of cereal grasses were detailed and the microscopic appearances of ergot and the different smuts, rusts, and mildews were described. Next the results of the chemical and microscopical examination of forty-four samples of wheat-flour purchased from different corn-chandlers and bakers residing in the metropolis were given, to show that in no instance was there any other farina than wheat observed. This satisfactory result was attributed to the repeal of the Corn Laws, but it also pointed to the fact that the millers and corn-dealers were honest folk and that the bakers must be considered to bear the responsibility for anything other than wheat-flour found in bread. Twenty-four samples of bread having been purchased at random at the establishments of bakers in the metropolis, the result of examination was that every sample was found to be adulterated with alum.

Cocoa was analysed on precisely similar lines to those employed when dealing with coffee, and the result was that of fifty-six samples examined, many of which were warranted pure and possessing all sorts and kinds of charming qualities, eight only were found to be genuine. Sugar was present in forty-three samples, its amount varying from 5 almost to 50 per cent., and starch was found in forty-six samples, its amount varying also from 5 to 50 per cent. The starch was derived from wheat-flour, potato-flour, sago-flour, or a mixture of these in varying proportions.

Passing over the inquiries made into the purity of opium, tobacco, and certain invalid foods as being hardly germane to an inquisition held upon the food-stuffs of the people, we come to tea. Tea formed the subject of a very lengthy and exhaustive examination. The leaves of the common willow, oak, sloe, hawthorn, elder, beech, elm, and an inferior sort of camellia were depicted side by side with illustrations of the genuine leaf of the tea-plant. Thirty-five samples of black tea bought at random in London shops were then analysed. Out of this ordeal the popular beverage emerged satisfactorily by comparison with the results found in the cases of coffee, arrowroot, and cocoa. In all thirty-five samples no other leaves but those of genuine tea were found. Twenty-three only, however, were perfectly pure, twelve having been treated with blacklead, indigo, turmeric, and mica, these last iridescent particles being added to give a sort of glaze to the leaves. No grosser adulterations were detected, but lest these reassuring results should blind the public to the possibility of the same being practised an account was added of the trial, instigated by the Excise, of a man and his wife for the manufacture of spurious tea. In this case the inspector under the Excise Act found the prisoners on premises at Clerkenwell busily engaged in their nefarious trade. There was an extensive furnace in one of the rooms, before which was suspended an iron pan containing sloe leaves and "spent" tea leaves which had been purchased from coffee-shop keepers. On searching the place an immense quantity of these spent tea leaves and bay leaves were found, as well as every description of ingredient likely to be employed for the purpose of illicit manufacturing of tea—such, for example, as gum, copperas, and black-lead. There was a very large quantity of spurious tea in the room of the exact appearance of genuine tea, and in another room were nearly 100 lb. of re-dried tea leaves, bay leaves, and sloe leaves spread out to dry. The practices revealed in this case were commoner, Wakley considered, than would appear probable by the results of the analyses of the Commission. He believed that such wicked fabrication was very extensively practised, old leaves purchased from coffee-houses and restaurants being the chief stock-in-trade. These leaves were treated with gum and mica to give richness and bloom to the appearance of the mess and sulphate of iron was added to make the decoction astringent. Chestnut leaves and sloe and bay leaves were occasionally used to give bulk. In the course of this investigation, it may be added, twenty specimens of green tea were examined, when it was found that the whole of them were artificially coloured.

In twenty-six samples of milk fourteen were adulterated, the addition being simply water. It was not found that any more complicated form of adulteration was practised, such as the simulation of creaminess by the addition of sheep's brains or flour. Isinglass and gelatin were examined, with the result that each was found to be sold to the public for the other, in spite of the fact that they possess different qualities and that as a rule isinglass is better than gelatin. Thirty-three samples of vinegar were examined and the amount of acetic acid contained in them was found only in twenty-three cases to reach the standard laid down by the " Lancet " as necessary to constitute a good vinegar. The addition of 1 part in 1000 of sulphuric acid was permitted by law, but many of the specimens exceeded the legal limit in this direction.

Spices next engaged the attention of the Commissioner, and out of twenty-one samples of ground ginger fifteen were found to be adulterated, the substances detected being sago-flour, potato-starch, wheat-flour, ground-rice, cayenne pepper, mustard husks, turmeric, or any combination of these. In whole cinnamon of twelve samples seven were found genuine, while the other five were examples, not of adulteration, but of calm substitution, for in each case the thing sold as cinnamon proved to be the vastly cheaper cassia.   In powdered cinnamon of twenty samples six were genuine; three consisted entirely of cassia and ten were adulterated with baked wheat-flour, sago-flour, and arrow-root.   It is significant to note from Maculloch's Commercial Dictionary that the heavy duty on cinnamon caused the consumption of cassia in the United Kingdom to rise to treble its former amount between the years 1820 and 1840. Examination of eighteen samples of nutmegs, despite fables of Yankee astuteness in manufacture, showed them all to be genuine.   Mace, cloves, and allspice came out of the ordeal in a similarly handsome manner.   Of twenty-one curry powders nineteen contained ground-rice, flour, salt, and colouring matter—red lead, for example—in varying propor-tions.   Thirty-four samples of bottled fruits and vegetables were all artificially coloured with copper.   Of twenty-eight samples of anchovies seven were not anchovies at all, two contained some genuine among the spurious fish, while the brine of twenty-three samples was charged with Armenian bole or Venetian red.   Various potted meats and fish and sauces were examined and in many of them colouring matter was found to have been introduced.   Of thirty-five samples of preserves and jellies thirty-three were found to contain copper, but it was suggested that the copper saucepans in which they were prepared were responsible for this.

Many of these examinations—for example, those on such important commodities as coffee and bread—were repeated from time to time, and their results as given showed that matters greatly improved in London after the revelations of the "Lancet" Commission.   In 1857 the investigation was carried into certain provincial towns.   Among others, Birmingham, Manchester, Liverpool, and Leeds were visited, and the results of investigations in these cities led to the conclusion that London was worse supplied with the neces-sities of life than the large provincial towns; but in 1858 adulteration did not exist to more than one-tenth the extent that it had done at the opening of the Commission. Despite the success of his undertaking, however, Wakley declared that he had no intention of abandoning the subject until effective legislation had been secured.

He had not long to wait, and the "Lancet" Commission was a prelude to all our present laws in respect to the adulteration of food. The popular excitement created by the revelations of the Commission transcended even Wakley's enthusiastic expectations and made legislation against such abuses a matter of immediate importance. A Select Parliamentary Committee was appointed and entered upon its labours in 1855. It examined as far as possible all those likely to have any special knowledge of the known adulterations, the methods necessary to detect them, their injury to the public health, and their effect on the national revenue. The evidence given before this Select Committee confirmed the researches of the "Lancet" Commission, not only in spirit, but in detail, and as a result the first general Adulteration Act was drafted and became law in 1860. This is known as Mr. Scholefield's Act. Its first section enacted that every person knowingly selling food or drink mixed with any ingredients injurious to health, and every person selling as pure any article of food or drink which is adulterated, should for every such offence on summary conviction pay a penalty not exceeding £5 with costs. Wakley was but moderately satisfied with this Act. The measure dealt with adulteration in but one of its aspects—namely, as it affected health; it did not touch upon the broader question of fraud. Wakley doubted if the small pecuniary penalties proposed to be inflicted by the Act would be deterrent, and pointed out that the appointment of analysts was left by the Act entirely optional. As the district boards and town councils empowered to make the appointments were largely composed of the very class of tradesmen who were the chief gainers from the practice of adulteration, he thought it probable the power would not be used. Future legislation, he said, was imperative, and his words were confirmed some ten years after his death. A second Act was passed in 1872. A second Select Committee sat in 1874 to inquire into the working of the two Acts, Mr. Schole-field's and that of 1872, under which many technical difficulties had arisen, and the result of this second Committee was the Sale of Food and Drugs Acts of 1875 and 1879. All this train of legislation was the direct outcome of Wakley's Analytical Sanitary Commission.

CHAPTER XLVIII

The Poor-law Amendment Act of 1834—Wakley's Hatred of it, and the Reasons—The Treatment of the Sick Poor in Workhouses—Wakley threatens an Immediate Inquiry—The "Lancet" Enquiry undertaken Three Years after Wakley's Death.

IN dealing with Wakley's parliamentary career his extreme dislike of the "New Poor-law" or the Poor-law Amendment Act of 1834 was noticed, but to make plain his real attitude in the matter it is necessary to state briefly the provisions of the Act. Until the year 1834 the Poor-laws of England had been mainly framed against vagrancy, "sturdy" mendicancy, and "valiant" pauperism. The first variation from these generally repressive measures is to be found in a compulsory levy in support of the sick and aged made in different parishes early in Queen Elizabeth's reign, the compulsion, partly legal and partly spiritual, being supplied by the bishops and the justices of the peace. Later in the reign of the same monarch came a celebrated statute (43 Eliz., c. 2) taxing every parish for the support of its poor in a defined manner and with drastic authority for giving effect to the provisions. To all intents and purposes this was the law to the amendment of which Wakley so strongly objected, for the system inaugurated by Queen Elizabeth's Act remained in operation for two hundred and thirty-three years—or between 1601 and 1834—without material modification. But a laxity towards the able-bodied loafer gradually crept in. As a result the condition of the pauper became in many places so comfortable and so superior to that of the self-supporting labourer that a large proportion of the inhabitants of a village would demand State aid. The evidences of serious moral deterioration of the lower orders soon became clear, and in 1832 a Commission of Inquiry was appointed to report upon the whole subject. The great source of abuse was then found to be the out-door relief afforded to the able-bodied poor or their families and given in kind or money. This form of charity was made the subject of all sorts of fraudulent claims. In some villages the eleemosynary assistance took the form of money in aid of wages, and in some the pauper obtained his house rent, or part of it, free, and those who were not ashamed to become pauper members of the community enjoyed a prosperity that was denied to their independent fellows. The in-door relief as furnished by the workhouse of the time was also found by the Commission of Inquiry to be badly administered and expensive. Upon such a report legislative interference was clearly bound to follow, yet the opposition to amendment was very strong—strong on the part of the pauper, with whom the world went very well under a system by which his scanty wages were supplemented by comparatively large and unearned additions, strong on the part of the employers of pauper labour, and strong on the part of the numerous owners of cottages or apartments inhabited by the poor, the rents being paid by the community. But the Commission of Inquiry had done more than expose a bad state of affairs. It had proved that progress from year to year was taking place towards a worse state. It had proved that a pauperised peasantry meant a vicious peasantry, and fear prevailed where reason had not been so effective and procured the passage of the Act of 1834 (41 s., Will. IV., c. 78). The main directions in which this Act altered the existing state of affairs in England—the only division of the kingdom contemplated in the Act—were two. Firstly, out-door relief except as medical attendance was abolished. All relief for the future was to be given in the workhouse. Secondly, a uniform method of administration was established for all England, so that there should be no inducement for paupers to wander from rigorous to more kindly districts. To this end a central board was appointed to regulate the working of the Act, to make it symmetrical, and decide in what districts and at what time out-door relief was to cease. Permanent officials were appointed to work under this board, this being the only way of securing good administration, for the framers of the Act clearly saw that many things would have to be done by the officials that would be so unpopular in the different localities that the tenure of their appointments must not be determined by annual election or popular vote. The central board was empowered to cause any number of parishes which they might think convenient to be incorporated for the purpose of workhouse management. Such "unions," as they were and are termed, swept away numberless old landmarks in the country, but were necessary to the proper administration of the Act. In fact, within the four years succeeding 1834 three hundred and twenty-eight unions had workhouses complete, each provided with auditor, chaplain, medical officer, relieving officer, master and matron of the workhouse, schoolmaster, schoolmistress, and porter. The Act met with the greatest possible practical success. An enormous number of paupers became self-respecting and self-supporting labourers, many parishes were relieved of ruinous rates, and for numerous though round-about reasons public morality improved. What, then, had Wakley to object to ? For that he did object to the new law most vigorously both the leading articles in the " Lancet " and his speeches in Parliament go to prove.

The whole of Wakley's attitude on the Poor-law question shows remarkable intuition and good fortune. The intuition was displayed in his immediate appreciation of the fact that numberless persons would be tried very severely by the working of the Act, in spite of the great success with which its operations were attended at the outset. His good fortune was that while his early estimate of the new piece of legislation was sentimental and inspired by bad information, he later found cause for most serious criticism and was able to remain a consistent foe to certain portions of the Act while acquiescing in the benevolence of other portions. There is no doubt that many poor of many districts found the working of the Poor-law Amendment Act harsh. The law of settlement was particularly severe in its working towards people who had been accustomed to regard residence and employment and not only birth as constituting claims upon the local rates. The workhouse test of poverty, again, was very drastic. The new poorhouses were often far from the parish where the pauper lived, although built as much as possible in the centre of the union. To people accustomed to unlimited assistance from wealthy neighbours while living in a rate-paid tenement among their friends it was intolerable that before they could obtain charity they should be forced to go afield at all. They considered that to do so was to surrender their whole independence, and submit to a discipline and rigour that savoured of prison routine. At first Wakley took entirely and uncompromisingly the part of the outraged poor, as he conceived them to be. He attacked the Act on every conceivable point and spoke of it with a scorn and fury that had no bounds. Workhouse relief was always represented as a particularly cruel form of imprisonment; to deny the poor indiscriminate alms at their own homes was represented not as a simple method of protecting the industrious from the lazy and the community from *chantage* but as a deliberate persecution of the poor by the rich; the necessary appointment of a central board of administration became "the payment of a pack of lazy, underworked, overfed officials, from the public purse"; there was nothing whatever about the Act that was not horrible, vicious, inept, and malignant. Much of this rather loose and badly distributed abuse arose from two causes. The first was Wakley's real sympathy with the oppressed, and he conceived, as Dickens did, that the poor were oppressed under the new Act. Dickens was never able to get the idea out of his head, for exactly thirty years after the Act came into force he wrote as follows* :—

"My Lords, gentlemen, and honourable boards, when you in the course of your dust-shovelling and cinder-raking have piled up a mountain of pretentious failure you must off with your honourable

* "Our Mutual Friend," Book iii., Chapter viii.

2 H

coats for the removal of it. . . . . For when we have got things to the pass that with an enormous treasure at our disposal to relieve the poor the best of the poor detest our mercies, hide their heads from us, and shame us by starving to death in the midst of us, it is a pass impossible of prosperity, impossible of continuance. . . . . This boastful handiwork of ours which fails in its terrors for the professional pauper, the sturdy breaker of windows, and the rampant tearer of clothes, strikes with a cruel and a wicked stab at the stricken sufferer, and is a horror to the deserving and unfortunate."

This apostrophe of the Poor-law Commissioners upon the death of Betty Higden depicts precisely Wakley's original views of the Poor-law Amendment Act. They did honour to his heart rather than to his head, and were due, as has been said, to two causes. The first was sentiment, the second was his impression that the Act proposed to deal unfairly with the medical profession. Believing this, he could find no stick too heavy with which to beat it, and his desire to champion the cause of the poor was eternally kept alive by the feeling that all opposition to the Act meant assertion of the rights of the medical man. Here Wakley, with his unrivalled knowledge of the ins-and-outs of the medical profession gathered from ten years' editorship of the "Lancet," was able to put his finger at once upon a blemish in the Act. There was no proper provision for the medical attendance that was so freely promised by the Act. The Act was one of economy. It was one designed to make the able-bodied work, to make those in full wages save against a rainy day, and to make the well-paid of a family help the ill-paid. In no case were those in good health to be assisted by the State save as a last resort. As a result the medical man became a very important factor in the working of the Act. It rested upon his decision whether an individual should be helped or should not, and although the Act was one of economy the medical man must be paid properly. But this was not generally done. The care of the sick pauper was thrown upon him in many places in return for a pittance. When this became known to Wakley, as it did very soon from his editorial letter-bag, his indignation at the regulations concerning the medical care of the

sick poor spread to the whole Act, and his early denunciations of its working must be taken to represent his particular resentment of the sweating of medical men as much
as his general sympathy with the poor and down-trodden.

When Wakley began to concentrate his attention upon
the treatment meted out to the Poor-law medical officer he
was close on the heels of the great reproach under which
the working of the new Act lay—namely, that its provision
for the sick poor was totally inadequate and conceived in
an ignorant and barbarous spirit. By 1840 his ideas had
become a little less sweeping. The humanitarianism of his
views was not quite so wholesale, and the existence of a real
scandal in the working of the Act was thereby made
apparent. This scandal was the fact that the workhouses
were badly built, badly administered, death-traps to those
admitted, and foci of disease to those without.

"We know of no fact in statistical science," wrote Wakley in April,
1841, "so firmly established as that of the excessive mortality in the
present workhouses. The Poor-law Commissioners themselves will
admit that a *primâ-facie* case has been made out. According to the
returns of their own officers it appears that out of 12,313 poor people
in workhouses *two thousand five hundred and fifty-two* perished in one
year! . . . . It is not, however, our duty, or the duty of those who
support the system of out-door relief, to prove that the workhouses
increase the mortality of the poor. The *onus probandi* lies with the
apostles of the new system. They are bound to prove that the workhouses do *not* increase the mortality and sufferings of the destitute.
But this they have never attempted. The Commissioners have, on the
contrary, circumspectly withheld the most decisive information and
have kept the Government, the House of Commons, and the public in
the dark. They have never even stated in their reports the number of
deaths in the workhouses under their administration. . . . . The
question is simply this: If the feelings of the poor were consulted, and
they received an equal amount of relief at their own homes, would as
many die as now perish in the workhouses? Do 2552 in 12,313
paupers perish annually out of doors? The Poor-law Commissioners
might have furnished *data* for a direct answer to the question. They
are fond of experiments. Why did they not give out-door relief
exclusively in a certain number of unions and count the number of
deaths among the recipients? There would have been nothing in-
humane or revolting in *this* experiment. In the absence of the direct

observations which should have been furnished to the Secretary of State and to Parliament we submit the following facts to public attention:—In 1837 2552 paupers *died* out of 12,313 in workhouses; 382 persons *died* out of 12,313 persons in the district of St. Giles's, London. How is this enormous difference to be accounted for? The *age* of the inmates will account for a part of the difference. The proportion of *old persons* is greater in the workhouses than in the unhealthy district of the metropolis. But the mortality of persons in England above the age of sixty is 7½ per cent., according to Mr. Edmonds, and if none of the 12,313 inmates of workhouses had been under sixty years of age the deaths should not have exceeded 936 ! . . . .

" Are the paupers sick at the time of their admission into the destructive workhouses? A certain number are admitted in a state of sickness, but the proportion is not much greater than in the general population. About 6 in 100 are constantly sick in St. Giles's district, and we have deduced the following results from a table published by the Poor-law Commissioners in their last report (p. 10), professing to show the number of paupers relieved in 178 unions during the quarters ending Christmas, 1838, and Christmas, 1839. According to this table, of 67,497 persons who received in-door relief 4117 persons were relieved ' *on account of sickness or accident.*' Only 6 in 100 received into the workhouses were relieved ' on account of sickness or accident.' The diseases which prove so fatal, therefore, assail the poor after their entrance into these ANTE-CHAMBERS OF THE GRAVE.

" The number constantly sick *in the 110 workhouses* was 1407 in 12,713, or nearly 11 per cent.; the number stated to be *infirm* was 36 per cent.; but this evidently included the infirm from *age* as well as the infirm from lameness, blindness, and chronic diseases of various kinds. The mortality among the infirm pensioners on the list of the East India Company's labourers in London was 16 per cent., annually (Maculloch's Statistics of the British Empire, art.: Vital Statistics); it is at least as high among infirm out-door paupers in the metropolis. But the mortality of young able-bodied adults and the aged or infirm taken together was 29 per cent. in the ten metropolitan workhouses ! "

As will be gathered from these quoted words, Wakley did not abandon his early position. He only modified it. He ceased to seek arguments in favour of out-door relief, though he continued to regard the workhouse test of poverty as cruel and faulty. But he reserved his chief energies for denunciation of the workhouse treatment of the sick. To this subject during the last fifteen years of his life he constantly recurred. He did not lose sight of other points in Poor-law administration that fell within the scope of his work as member of Parliament, coroner, or editor. On the contrary, he spoke several times in the House on the causes of excessive mortality in rural districts, on the treatment of the insane pauper by the State, and on the scanty remuneration of the Poor-law medical officer; while he proposed a scheme for pensioning that officer upon his superannuation not unlike the one that has come into force under the Act of last year. But in the front of all his interest in Poor-law matters he ever placed the urgent necessity that existed for improving the accommodation of the sick in workhouses, asserting and re-asserting that here at any rate existed a blot upon the Act which its most ardent admirers could not conceal, and which the most ingenious economists could not excuse. He never, however, took any more practical steps towards exposing the evils of whose existence he was so certain. He threatened more than once, as in the words just quoted, to make the matter one for immediate inquiry; but the opportunity never arrived. Probably he trusted a little too much to the power of his pen and hoped for a bloodless revolution—a reform that should follow upon denunciation. But three years after his death his words bore splendid fruit. His successor as director of the fortunes of the "Lancet," Dr. james Wakley, had always considered that to make a complete investigation into the treatment of the sick poor in workhouses had been confided to him as an editorial legacy from his father. When, therefore, two tragedies in rapid succession—one occurring in December, 1864, and the other early in 1865—called the attention of the public to this very topic in an urgent and even heartrending manner, Dr. james Wakley seized on the psychological moment and instituted an inquiry. He appointed as Commissioners the late Dr. Francis Edmund Anstie, afterwards editor of the "Practitioner," the late Dr. Carr of Greenwich, and Mr. Ernest Hart, and published in the "Lancet" the results of their investigations. Dr. Anstie took the largest part in examining the London infirmaries, and to his able pen was due the general summary of results and recommendations which prefaced the reports of the particular inquiries of the Commission. To tell what followed would be to go distinctly beyond the scope of this biography, but it is in no way far-fetched to claim for Wakley the credit of having thoroughly prepared both the public and the medical profession for terrible revelations. He had promised that the " Lancet " would make these revelations, and the son who succeeded him kept the father's word.

CHAPTER XLIX

A Few Family Details—Hospitality at Harefield Park and Bedford Square—The Pressure of Work between 1839 and 1852: a Day's Routine—Letter to Douglas Jerrold—The Breakdown at last—The Progress of Disease—A Sojourn at Madeira—Death.

WAKLEY as a family man has not made any appearance in these pages, the reason being that although he possessed pronounced family instincts he was never sufficiently at leisure to do them justice, so that his attentions to his immediate domestic circle were necessarily fitful and capricious. Throughout his married life he was engaged in the arduous struggle of working out his public career, and his home life had been merely a quiet background for the incidents that have been chronicled. His wife was an affectionate, retiring woman unfitted to be the mate of a public man to this extent that she had the strongest possible dislike to the causes which dragged her husband from her side to play his ever busy part in the world. She deeply regretted his entry upon a parliamentary career—so deeply that the sentiment of sorrow quite overshadowed that of legitimate pride in the success that had attended his several electioneering campaigns. Over and above the certainty that she felt that in the turmoil of public life there would be but little respect for family ties, she knew the grave expenses in which such a life would involve a man of Wakley's disposition. The heavy drain upon his purse contingent on his position as editor of the " Lancet" ought, considered his wife, to have been sufficient responsibility even for so sanguine a man as he; while surely the quarrels that arose from his journalistic enterprise should have sufficed to keep him from seeking another arena for disputes. The

"Lancet" had received in her eyes a very valuable stamp of approval in that her father had seen in it a road to success for her husband at a time when his fortunes were at their lowest, and had persuaded and encouraged him to persevere in his literary venture, not only by words of approval, but by loosening his purse-strings. The editorship having become in itself a career, was it necessary to imperil the profits accruing therefrom by ventures in the stormy waters of general politics ? Mrs. Wakley held very strongly that it was not and took no active part in her husband's public life, which she considered to have divided him from her. A kindly, generous gentlewoman, she did not share his ambitions ; while she had for him what he never had for himself —a fear of the future. Mrs. Wakley died at Brighton in 1857 after a long illness.

Wakley's family consisted of three sons and one daughter. The daughter died when a child, but of the three sons the two elder are alive at the present time, Mr. Thomas Henry Wakley, the senior proprietor of the " Lancet," and Mr. Henry Membury Wakley, a barrister and at one time deputy coroner for West Middlesex under his father. Towards his sons Wakley was an indulgent parent. He was ambitious for them, but he was not at all the kind of martinet in the family circle that might have been expected, seeing how masterful a person he was in public life. Anyone who has gathered a rightful idea of Wakley's work during the period corresponding to the passage of his three sons from babyhood to manhood—that is from 1823 to 1852—will understand that he had but little time to devote to them personally; but they were very much in his thoughts. He trusted them largely and made them handsome allowances and always spoke of the " Lancet " as having been created by him with a view to forming a property for their future support. This was not strictly accurate, for the " Lancet " owed its origin to Wakley's determination to organise plans for the reform of the medical profession ; but the fortunes of the paper grew step by step with his children, and he came to regard its pecuniary future and theirs as inextricably bound

up. His schemes for his sons' careers were not exactly fulfilled, for he originally destined his eldest for the Church,
while the second was to succeed him as coroner, and the
third was to edit the " Lancet." The eldest who found that
life in conservative Oxford was not without its drawbacks to
the son of a prominent Reformer, was withdrawn from
Wadham and the classics in favour of London University,
and natural science. The second made no serious attempt
to sit on the coroner's bench. Dr. James Goodchild
Wakley, the youngest son, succeeded his father as editor of
the " Lancet," a post which he filled for more than a quarter
of a century until his death in 1886, his eldest brother being
associated with him in the management. On the death of
Dr. Wakley, Mr. Thomas Henry Wakley and his son Mr.
Thomas Wakley, junior, became the editors, a third generation being thus introduced.

If Wakley's absence of leisure caused him to be but little
with his family it did not prevent him from being an excellent and generous host both in Bedford Square and at
Harefield Park. He and his three sons were great sportsmen, being in particular devoted to shooting, and Harefield
Park, where game was plentiful and strictly preserved—as
was laughingly pointed out in the House of Commons—was
the scene of many merry *réunions*. Catholic in his tastes,
popular in many walks of life, and contemptuous of class
distinctions, Wakley was able to collect round him at Harefield Park and equally at Bedford Square men of the most
varied grades of social standing and shades of political
opinion. Eminent colleagues in the House of Commons
and aristocratic Whigs from the Reform Club foregathered
round his table with the humbler members of the Liberal
party and with its supporters in the Borough of Finsbury,
with the staff of the " Lancet," with the county neighbourhood from Harefield, and with numerous well-known and
more or less distinguished personages in the literary and
artistic worlds. Count D'Orsay and Baron Liebig, Charles
Dickens and Professor Broussais, Douglas Jerrold and
Robert Liston, Duncombe, Attwood and Francis Place the

tailor, Feargus O'Connor and Erasmus Wilson, Brougham, Joseph Hume, and Daniel O'Connell are a few names that can be recalled of men who must, in many instances, have been surprised at finding themselves beneath the same roof.

It was at the busiest period of his life that his hospitality was most profuse and that his table became a meeting-place for persons of such widely different social standing and moral aim. For between the years 1839 and 1852—the twelve years when he was editor, coroner, and member of Parliament at the same time—he was daily brought into contact with all sorts and conditions of men, and whenever he desired to see more of anyone he straightway asked him to dinner. He was so over-occupied that in no other way could he cultivate the acquaintances towards which he felt drawn or devise plans for future development of work. Conversation at the dinner-table was possible. Conversation whilst presiding at an inquest, sitting upon a Parliamentary Committee, or writing leading articles against time was not. For during these twelve years his toil was incessant and gigantic. Under each separate division of his life he has appeared in these pages as a busy man, but what the aggregate amount of labour he demanded of himself amounted to is difficult of conjecture. As editor his management of the "Lancet" was not nominal, but very real. Until the last two years of his life he was the absolute dictator of the policy of the paper and the most powerful and impressive leader-writer on the staff. He spared no pains in amassing his material or verifying his details. The invariably contentious nature of his articles made it necessary for him to be careful that they should be accurate, while it was not in him to speak half-heartedly upon any of the numerous subjects in which his personal feelings were deeply involved. Consequently he was as a journalist exceedingly unsparing of himself, writing with facility, it is true, but writing after the utmost trouble had been taken to obtain facts correctly and with a pen surcharged with conviction. As a member of Parliament he displayed the same tireless activity and the same remarkable combination of industry and passion. An adaptable and accessible man his time was constantly at the disposal of other members of the House or of his constituents, while his open-mindedness and business capacity made his a welcome voice at the deliberations of all sorts of Parliamentary Committees. The invitation to sit upon a Parliamentary Committee, whatever its object or reference, he considered to be a highly honourable compliment and he was most particular in the punctuality of his attendance. In short, he took his parliamentary career very seriously. He was not only a robust and fervent pleader for the causes in which he was personally interested, but he was a senator who was unfailingly mindful of the grave business responsibilities that he had accepted. With him the initials " M.P." were not the mere hall-mark of the approbation and trust of a few of his fellow citizens. They were his brevet to help in the government of his country for the good of his countrymen. As coroner he was again conspicuous, not only for the zeal with which he discharged his duties, but for the keen sense which he always displayed of the importance of those duties. While engaged upon them they engrossed him. He made strenuous efforts that his charges to the juries should contain everything that could help the right, and a miscarriage of justice in one of his courts would have inflicted upon him, to his own thinking, a stigma of personal shame.

It is desired to show by this recapitulation of what has already been told that Wakley's work was arduous from every aspect of consideration—physical, mental, and moral. Neither his limbs nor his feelings escaped racking. The following is a programme of the day's work during these twelve years. It does not describe the routine of an extraordinary day, but of every day throughout the period. At eight in the morning Wakley would arrive at the " Lancet" office, breakfast, and go through his letters. Soon after the parish clerks and coroner's officers would arrive and the list of inquests for the day would be made out. Then the editorial work for the day was arranged, concerning which Wakley was most precise in his directions, allotting it with every

precaution to secure the most useful material and the most
trustworthy results for his readers. By nine his carriage,
with fast trotters, always especially selected for their severe
work, would come to the door, and he would start on his
round of inquests. He rarely returned before six, and
usually took his luncheon in his carriage, where he had
elaborate arrangements both for feeding and writing, re-
cesses containing the necessaries for a picnic, and a flap
writing-table that could be let down from the front of the
brougham over his knees. On completing his round he
would, if necessary, attend any Committee of the House
to which he belonged, arriving back at the office by six
o'clock. He would then sleep for an hour or so. On
waking he would put in order what he had written while
driving from one court to another, would look through the
" copy " which had been sent in by the staff during the day,
and finally interview the printer. Then he would go to the
Reform Club or to Bedford Square for dinner, and thence
to the House of Commons. On returning from the House,
possibly at a late hour, he would finish dealing with the
voluminous correspondence of the day, answering such communications as must necessarily be replied to under his own
hand regardless of the flight of time, and making notes concerning other answers to be dictated in the morning. And
so to bed, having during his fifteen or sixteen hours of work
driven sixty or seventy miles, held a dozen inquiries under all
sorts of uncomfortable and depressing surroundings into the
causes of various terrible tragedies, having had but one comfortable meal, having sat on, perhaps, more than one Parliamentary Committee, and having certainly voted and probably
spoken upon all measures where he considered his speech or
his vote due to his constituents or to the causes whose
advocacy he had espoused. And this routine of physical
work, enough in itself to ensure breakdown if persisted in,
Wakley conducted with an enthusiasm that reduplicated the
necessary wear and tear. He was not content with overwork. All his overwork must be done with zeal and enthusiasm as though he were determined to wear out his

heart and his nerves as much as his muscles. And this continued for twelve years.

In 1850 he seems to have felt the first warnings that he
was over-taxing his strength, and he made a few attempts
at relaxation. Until that time he had relied on his splendid
physique and abstemious habits to carry him through. But
in this year he wrote the following letter to Douglas Jerrold,
which clearly shows that he felt the terrible monotony of
his life of perpetual toil and that he was longing for a
break :—

"MY DEAR OLD JERROLD,—Though, by-the-bye, I adhere to your
declaration that nobody that chooses is ever more than six-and-twenty
years of age.

"I sha'n't see you again—God bless your witty old brain—for a long
time, as I am going to make the tour of England, starting to-day. I
want to thoroughly renovate my health, which is already by rest very
greatly mended, and travelling about and change from London will
complete the renovation better than any other thing. I cannot be idle
during the journeyings, so as I stroll or railway from town to town and
hamlet to hamlet I shall occupy the intellectual portion of me—the
which *unoccupied* is miserable and unhealthy—with writing a history of
the present state and condition of the medical profession in England.
So for a couple of months or so you should clap your hands on the
'Lancet,' or ask George Churchill to give you one; whenever any
such papers appear, look at them. In some respects I promise the
profession a few very curious and interesting 'whats-a-names.' One,
if not two, of the papers shall expand the domain of medicine by
means of some marvellous facts, gathered collaterally with the statistics.
I am going first to Bristol, Gloucester, Worcester, Birmingham, M.,
L., and so on.

"God preserve you, Jerrold. You are one of the bright lights of the
day ! . . . .

"T. W."*

M. and L. signified Manchester and Leeds or Liverpool,
but he never found any opportunity of making the tour he
proposed to himself. His idea of a holiday was certainly
grotesque. It was simply that he should be relieved of
arduous duties in London so that he might be free to undertake arduous duties in the country, but the point of intro-

* The original of this letter was kindly lent to the author by Mr.
Alexander Dickson Mills.

ducing the letter here is that it shows that he was not unaware that he had given too liberal drafts upon his constitution.

In the winter of 1851 came the serious breakdown of which mention has already been made and the onset of which he certainly feared. One night he was found by a policeman unconscious outside the door of the "Lancet" office. He had that day started at sunrise from Harefield, had held seven inquests in different parts of his great district, and had been unable to snatch more than a hurried mouthful of food. On arriving at length in London urgent business claimed him at the House of Commons and he had barely time to eat a hurried meal before driving on to Westminster. It was past midnight when he left the House and even then he was not free to go to bed. He was at that time occupying chambers in Pall Mall, but it was his intention to attend to his correspondence at the "Lancet" office before retiring. The spirit was willing, but the flesh revolted on the doorstep, and the policeman found him lying on the pavement in a dead faint.

This occurrence put him seriously on his guard and gave his wife and family a right to insist that he should not continue in his suicidal policy of persistent toil. Not without reluctance he consented to curtail his duties by resigning his seat in Parliament, and in 1852 he did not offer himself for re-election. Upon the death of Mrs. Wakley five years later he made a further concession to increasing weakness by permitting his eldest and youngest sons, who through a pecuniary arrangement between themselves and their father had now become part proprietors of the "Lancet," to have a share in the management of the paper. In the winter of 1860 he began to be troubled with a persistent and severe cough, attended by occasional attacks of hæmoptysis. It was soon perceived by his medical advisers that he was seriously ill and losing flesh steadily though slowly. His desire to keep at work was unabated, as was his keen interest in the conduct of the "Lancet" and in the various events of the numerous social questions whose solution he had at heart ; but these only made more pathetic the obvious fact that ,he had no longer the physical force necessary to keep pace with his immense mental activity. This, of course, is a common story—common to the evening of most big and busy lives ; but in Wakley the position was more than usually sad because of the notable energy and vitality which had inspired all his work. In January, 1861, marked debility awoke him too late to a sense of the urgency of his symptoms. He repaired to Brighton and placed himself under the care of Dr. Alfred Hall, the physician who had the last charge of his deceased wife, and who still resides at Brighton and remembers his patient vividly. Brighton and Dr. Hall's treatment suited him admirably, and for some time he made steady progress towards recovery of health and strength, but, as so frequently happens in cases of chronic phthisis, every forward step was succeeded by a little slip back due to onsets of hæmoptysis. The attacks were trifling in themselves, but were nevertheless mischievous because of their possibilities. They kept the recollection of his condition before the patient and prevented the restfulness so necessary to his condition. In the spring of 1861 he returned to London and was then decidedly in better health. He resumed his coroner's duties until july, when; he went to Scarborough. Here the fact that he was not improving—that, indeed, the sub-acute phthisical condition was more pronounced—became manifest. He returned to London in September, and, on the advice of Dr. C. J. B. Williams and Dr. Alfred Hall among others, sailed for Madeira in October. The outward voyage, notwithstanding the inconvenience of ocean travelling thirty-five years ago, proved beneficial. He sailed upon a small Union Line steamer of 600 tons called the " Dane," and the voyage, which occupied nine days, was a very pleasant one. There happened to be on board Dr. Grabham,* the son of

* Dr. Grabham was making his first voyage out as a qualified man in 1861. He settled some few years later in Madeira, and practises there still. He has kindly furnished much of the information in this chapter.

an old fellow student, and one or two others of congenial spirit, and he obtained the rest and relief from care that he had not previously enjoyed while sojourning in English watering-places within easy communication with his work. His spirits rose with the reinforcement of his hopes of recovery. In Madeira he hired a small house with large balconies, standing in a grove of trees, and settled down for the winter to live a life as far as possible out of doors in the balmy atmosphere ten degrees north of the Tropic of Cancer. The hilly nature of the country precluded him from walking, but he manifested his originality by refusing to be carried in a slung hammock in accordance with the custom of the island. This mode of locomotion he considered effeminate, and accordingly set to work to devise a chair which could be carried on the shoulders of bearers, the invalid remaining in a sitting posture. His brief sojourn at Madeira was happy. He made many friends. The English colony, who knew their visitor by name as a terrible Radical and unconscionable fighter, were surprised and relieved to find him a simple, unostentatious, pleasant man, full of reminiscences, but not in the least egotistical, an expert whist and chess player, and in particular one whose interest in life had not decreased with his frailer hold upon it. He was untiring in his inquiries into the social history of the island, and scathing in his contempt for the dirty ways of the native Portuguese. He investigated the pomology of the island, which resulted in his arranging for fruit-trees to be sent to England, and he promised that one of his first actions on his return would be to expose the fraudulent shipments of pseudo-Madeira wine then taking place regularly. For a time he seemed to be gaining strength. His appetite returned, his weight increased, and his own expectations were exhibited in a letter which appeared in the " Lancet " of April 19th, 1862, in which he said that his restoration to health was sufficient to warrant him in hoping that he would be able in a very few weeks to return home and resume his official duties as coroner. Acting upon this, a house was taken for him at Hillingdon and put in order to receive him, and he made arrangements to return to England in the "Comet" leaving Madeira on May 24th. But on May 11th, when landing from a small boat in which he had been sailing round the coast, he slipped and fell on the beach. The fall brought on a severe hæmorrhage from the lungs from which he never rallied. All that could be done for him was done by Dr. Lund and Dr. Grabham, but their efforts proved of no avail. He died peacefully and painlessly five days later. His body was embalmed in accordance with his expressed wishes in the event of death overtaking him while abroad and was brought to England in the cabin which he had previously taken for his return passage.

He was buried on June 14th, 1862, with his wife and daughter at Kensal Green Cemetery, his funeral being at his own desire very simple and the attendance strictly confined to members of his family.

CHAPTER L

In Conclusion

" HANG your reform!" said Mr. Chichely. "There's no greater humbug in the world. . . . . I hope you are not one of the 'Lancet's'
men, Mr. Lydgate——"
    " I disapprove of Wakley," interposed Dr. Sprague; "no man more:
he is an ill-intentioned fellow. . . . . But Wakley is right sometimes,"
the doctor added, judicially; " I could mention one or two points in
which Wakley is in the right."—Middlemarch, Book II. Chapter 16.

The difficulty of arriving at a definite opinion concerning
Wakley under which poor Dr. Sprague—a physician distinguished, we are told, for "weight" rather than for "penetra-
tion "—laboured was one in which many of Wakley's contemporaries were involved. Dr. Sprague, while disapproving
of Wakley, was forced to admit that there were points
concerning which he was right. Dr. Sprague, as became a
respectable and respected member of one of the London
Colleges, wished to wholly condemn the great agitator
against the methods of those Colleges, but he felt that to
do so would be unjust because of the manifest good sense
which had inspired other of Wakley's work—for instance, his
crusade against badly conducted inquests. George Eliot
was accurate, as only she could be, in thus describing Dr.
Sprague as muddled and uncertain in his estimate. She has
in so doing exactly recorded the way in which many worthy
members of the profession regarded Wakley while his
general work of reform was in its fierce inception. The
reason for this is now manifest. These men lived in Wakley's
own time and could not appreciate how much in advance of
that time he was. It is impossible to correctly interpret the

work of a reformer from hour to hour. When a man spends his days in battle against wrongs and abuses it is, and must ever be, his fate to be compelled to wait for years without recognition of the value of his work—if value there be—by persons whose good opinion is alone worth having. The reason of this is that the honest reformer and the irresponsible crank make appeals to the public judgment so similar in appearance that only the very discriminating can detect which is the man of barren promise and which the man of fruitful performance. Without allowing a not inconsiderable space of time to expire before giving an account of Wakley's full and energetic life no adequate and impartial view of him could be obtained. A mountain cannot be seen from its side or even from its base, some little peak, some unimportant excrescence of the outline, obscures the whole view. We must get to a distance. Just so with these big and busy careers. They cannot be judged during their course, and they cannot be summed up at their immediate close ; distance—a long distance—of time must be allowed to elapse before the manner of life that has been led and the amount of good or, it may be, ill that the world has reaped can be estimated.

In the case of Thomas Wakley this is very well seen in the way that contemporary historians have been unable to make up their minds whether to approve of him or to disapprove of him most. They never seem to have been sure whether it was the real Wakley upon whom they were pronouncing an estimate or only one of the many sides of his character. William Nassau Molesworth, an accurate and laborious historian, dismisses him with a few words as a Radical. "The History of Our Own Times" depicts him only as a Radical. From these it might have been expected that at any rate his radicalism would be undisputed. But it was not so. "Punch," at the time when Wakley was most persistently before the public as a Reformer, devoted many pages of pictures and many columns of print to the attempt to show that he was less than half-hearted as a Radical and really by conviction a Tory. Dickens discusses Wakley's qualities as a coroner at length, but does not allude at all to his work as a medical reformer or as a politician. Now Dickens was a personal friend and was not only familiar with Wakley's political work but shared many of his views— for example, his belief in the right thinking of the masses and his hatred of the Poor-law Amendment Act and red-tapeism. From the greatest English romancer to a purveyor of curbstone doggrel is a far cry, but James Catnach's publications represented general opinion in a wonderfully accurate manner. They reflected the views of the man in the street, and, at the same time, coloured those views. In Catnach's " Political Alphabet for the Rise and Instruction of Juvenile Politicians " the rhymer picked out what he considered to be the salient points in the chief public characters of the date— 1842 or thereabouts. Wakley represents the W's in this medley—the obviously greatest man for the initial, the Duke of Wellington being alluded to with affectionate familiarity as Arthur and Nosey. It is as a sworn foe to the Corn Laws that Catnach presents Wakley in the following stanza :—

> " **W**. is Wakley a Doctor so bold,
> Who declares on the Corn Bill an Inquest he'll hold ;
> When the jury he'll charge, and England shall see
> A verdict returned of *Felo-de-se*."

Wakley's association with Cobden over-topped in the mind of the popular ballad-monger all his other work, even his championship of the liberty of the press. Barham was also a popular ballad-monger, though he rightly earned his position as a brilliant humorist, and his description of Wakley makes him a prick-eared public official. In Saunders's " Eminent Political Reformers," edited by William Howitt and published in 1840, the chief characteristics of Wakley's public career are said to be his enmity to the Poor-law Amendment Act and his disapproval of the severity and inexpediency of the treatment of Canada by Sir Robert Peel. Hansard, on the other hand, reports Wakley's contributions to debates on these two subjects with comparative curtness as a rule, while his speeches upon such topics as an unstamped cheap press, flogging in the Army, the protection of women and children in factories, medical evidence in coroners' courts, the Sunday opening of museums, the property qualification of members of Parliament, the Chartist agitation, copyright, and motions for reform in the medical profession are given at length.

But all this discrepancy of opinion concerning Wakley's work did not arise from the fact that the work was too recent to be correctly appraised. There was another thing which tended to interfere with just judgment—namely, that enthusiasm of his to which allusion has so frequently been made in the course of this biography. It was his habit to write, to speak, and to act as if nothing on earth mattered to him save the question under discussion, and more, as if the man to whom any other question might appear as of even comparative importance was convicted of foolishness. This coercive method had a double effect. It drove into fierce opposition men of an argumentative turn of mind, while it compelled the adherence of the large class which desires to have its opinions selected for it before it can display the courage of the same. Consequently Wakley's audience was never neutral, but always for him or against him, and his name was always associated by friend or foe with the particular subject his treatment of which had either compelled admiration or provoked animosity.

It was with a view of enabling a right estimate of Thomas Wakley to be formed that this biography has been written. With the facts of his busy life before us it is possible to take an all-round survey before summing up, while time has cooled the hot personal feelings that prevented Wakley's contemporaries from delivering an unimpassioned verdict upon his merits. The following words of the late Sir John Eric Erichsen will be found in a letter addressed by him to the editors of the " Lancet" and published on December 28th, 1895, in the columns of that paper :—

" The present generation of medical men," wrote Sir John Eric Erichsen, " know little of him (Wakley) and are for the most part ignorant how much they owe to him for exposing and fearlessly attacking the manifold abuses that existed in every department of the profession in the colleges, hospitals and medical schools in the first third of this century.   Corruption, jobbery, nepotism, promotion by purchase were rife in the colleges and hospitals and medical education was at a low ebb when Wakley entered on his career as a journalist.   By his outspoken and fearless denunciations of these abuses he brought about their reform and so cleared the road to fame and fortune for those members of the profession who had to rely solely on their own ability and power of work.   It was, in fact, Mr. Wakley who made a William Jenner or an Andrew Clark possible."

Surely this high estimate of the value of Wakley's work was just ?

INDEX

Printed by BALLANTYNE, HANSON & Co.
London & Edinburgh

A Classified Catalogue

OF WORKS IN

GENERAL LITERATURE

PUBLISHED BY

LONGMANS, GREEN, & CO.

39 PATERNOSTER ROW, LONDON, E.C.

91 AND 93 FIFTH AVENUE, NEW YORK, AND 32 HORNBY ROAD, BOMBA

CONTENTS.

INDEX OF AUTHORS AND EDITORS.

History, Politics, Polity, Political Memoirs, &c.

Abbott.—*A History of Greece*
By Evelyn Abbott, M.A., LL.D.
Part I.—From the Earliest Times to the Ionian Revolt. Crown 8vo., 10s. 6d.
Part II.—500-445 B.O. Crown 8vo., 10s. 6d.

Acland and Ransome.—*A Hand-*
book in Outline of the Political His-
tory of England to 1894. Chronologically Arranged. By A. H. Dyke Acland, M.P., and Cyril Ransome, M.A. Crown 8vo., 6s.

ANNUAL REGISTER (THE). A Review of Public Events at Home and Abroad, for the year 1895. 8vo., 18s.
Volumes of the *Annual Register* for the years 1863-1894 can still be had. 18s. each.

Arnold (Thomas, [D.D.), formerly Head Master of Rugby School.

Introductory Lectures on Mod-
ern History. 8vo., 7s. 6d.

Miscellaneous Works. 8vo., 7s. 6d.

Baden-Powell. — *The Indian*
Village Community. Examined with Reference to the Physical, Ethnographic, and Historical Conditions of the Provinces; chiefly on the Basis of the Revenue-Settlement Records and District Manuals. By B. H. Baden-Powell, M.A., C.I.E. With Map. 8vo., 16s.

Bagwell.—*Ireland under the*
Tudors. By Richard Bagwell, LL.D. (3 vols.) Vols. I. and II. From the first invasion of the Northmen to the year 1578. 8vo., 32s. Vol. III. 1578-1603. 8vo. 18s.

Ball.—*Historical Review of the*
Legislative Systems Operative in Ire-
land, from the Invasion of Henry the Second to the Union (1172-1800). By the Rt. Hon. J. T. Ball. 8vo., 6s.

Besant.—*The History of London.*
By Sir Walter Besant. With 74 Illustrations. Crown 8vo., 1s. 9d. Or bound as a School Prize Book, 2s. 6d.

Brassey (Lord).—Papers and Addresses.

Naval and Maritime. 1872-1893.
2 vols. Crown 8vo., 10s.

Brassey (Lord) Papers and A
dresses—*continued.*

Mercantile Marine and Navi
tion, from 1871-1894. Crown 8vo., 5

Imperial Federation and Col
isation from 1880 to 1894. Cr. 8vo.,

Political and Miscellaneo
1861-1894. Crown 8vo 5s.

Bright.—*A History of Engla*
By the Rev. J. Franck Bright, D.D.

Period I. *Mediæval Monarchy*: 449 to 1485. Crown 8vo., 4s. 6d.

Period II. *Personal Monarchy.* 148 to 1688. Crown 8vo., 5s.

Period III. *Constitutional Monarc* 1689 to 1837. Crown 8vo., 7s. 6d.

Period IV. *The Growth of Democra* 1837 to 1880 Crown 8vo., 6s.

Buckle.—*History of Civilisati*
in England and France, Spain a
Scotland. By Henry Thomas Buck 3 vols. Crown 8vo., 24s.

Burke.—*A History of Spain* fr
the Earliest Times to the Death of Ferdin the Catholic. By Ulick Ralph Bur M.A. 2 vols. 8vo., 32s.

Chesney.—*Indian Polity*: a View the System of Administration in India. General Sir George Chesney, K.C. With Map showing all the Administra Divisions of British India. 8vo., 21s.

Creighton. — *A History of* 7
Papacy from the Great Schism to 1
Sack of Rome. By M. Creighton, D. Lord Bishop of London. 6 vols. Cro 8vo., 6s. each.

Cuningham. — *A Scheme for .*
perial Federation: a Senate for Empire. By Granville C. Cuningh of Montreal, Canada. Crown 8vo., 3s.

Curzon.—*Persia and the Pers*
Question. By the Right Hon. Geo N. Curzon, M.P. With 9 Maps, 96 Ill trations, Appendices, and an Index. vols. 8vo., 42s.

De Tocqueville.—*Democracy*
America. By Alexis de Tocquevil 2 vols. Crown 8vo., 16s.

History, Politics, Polity, Political Memoirs, &c.—*continue*

Dickinson.—*The Development of Parliament during the Nineteenth Century.* By G. Lowes Dickinson, M.A. 8vo, 7s. 6d.

Ewald.—*The History of Israel.* By Heinrich Ewald. 8 vols., 8vo, £5 18s.

Follett.—*The Speaker of the House of Representatives.* By M. P. Follett. With an Introduction by Albert Bushnell Hart, Ph.D., of Harvard University. Crown 8vo, 6s.

Froude (James A.).

The History of England, from the Fall of Wolsey to the Defeat of the Spanish Armada.

Popular Edition. 12 vols. Crown 8vo. 3s. 6d. each.

'Silver Library' Edition. 12 vols. Crown 8vo., 3s. 6d. each.

The Divorce of Catherine of Aragon. Crown 8vo., 3s. 6d.

The Spanish Story of the Armada, and other Essays. Cr. 8vo., 3s. 6d.

The English in Ireland in the Eighteenth Century.

Cabinet Edition. 3 vols. Cr. 8vo., 18s.

'Silver Library' Edition. 3 vols. Cr. 8vo., 10s. 6d.

English Seamen in the Sixteenth Century. Cr. 8vo., 6s.

The Council of Trent. Crown 8vo., 6s.

Short Studies on Great Subjects. 4 vols. Cr. 8vo., 3s. 6d. each.

Cæsar : a Sketch. Cr. 8vo, 3s. 6d.

Gardiner (Samuel Rawson, D.C.L., LL.D.).

History of England, from the Accession of James I. to the Outbreak of the Civil War, 1603-1642. 10 vols. Crown 8vo., 6s. each.

A History of the Great Civil War, 1642-1649. 4 vols. Cr. 8vo., 6s. each.

A History of the Commonwealth and the Protectorate. 1649-1660. Vol. I. 1649-1651. With 14 Maps. 8vo., 21s.

Gardiner (Samuel Rawson, D.C.L. LL.D.)—*continued.*

The Student's History of England. With 378 Illustrations. Crown 8vo., 12s.

Also in Three Volumes, price 4s. each.

Vol. I. B.C. 55—A.D. 1509. 173 Illustrations.

Vol. II. 1509-1689. 96 Illustrations.

Vol. III. 1689-1885. 109 Illustrations.

Greville.—*A Journal of the Reign of King George IV., King William IV and Queen Victoria.* By Charles C. Greville, formerly Clerk of the Council.

Cabinet Edition. 8 Vols. Crown 8vo., 6 each.

'Silver Library' Edition. 8 vols. Crown 8vo., 3s 6d. each.

HARVARD HISTORICAL STUDIE

The Suppression of the African Slave Trade to the United States o America, 1638-1870. By W. E. B. D Bois, Ph.D. 8vo., 7s. 6d.

The Contest over the Ratificato of the Federal Constitution in Mass chusetts. By S. B. Harding, A. 8vo., 6s.

A Critical Study of Nullificatio in South Carolina. By D. F. Housto A.M. 8vo., 6s.

*** *Other Volumes are in preparation.*

Hearn.—*The Government of En land*: its Structure and its Developmer By W. Edward Hearn. 8vo., 16s.

Historic Towns.—Edited by E. Freeman, D.C.L., and Rev. William Hun M.A. With Maps and Plans. Crown 8v 3s. 6d. each.

Bristol. By Rev. W. Hunt. | Oxford. By Rev. C.
Carlisle. By Mandell | Boase.
Creighton, D.D. | Winchester. By G.
Cinque Ports. By Mon- | Kitchin, D.D.
tague Burrows. | York. By Rev. Jam
Colchester. By Rev. E. L. | Raine.
Cutts. | New York. By Theod
Exeter. By E. A. Freeman. | Roosevelt.
London. By Rev. W. J. | Boston (U.S.) By Hen
Loftie. | Cabot Lodge.

Joyce.—*A Short History of Ir land*, from the Earliest Times to 1608. P. W. Joyce, LL.D. Crown 8vo., 10s. 6

History, Politics, Polity, Political Memoirs, &c.—*contini*

Kaye and Malleson.—*HISTORY OF THE INDIAN MUTINY*, 1857-1858. By Sir JOHN W. KAYE and Colonel G. B. MALLESON. With Analytical Index and Maps and Plans. Cabinet Edition. 6 vols. Crown 8vo., 6s. each.

Knight.—*MADAGASCAR IN WAR TIME: THE EXPERIENCES OF* 'THE TIMES' *SPECIAL CORRESPONDENT WITH THE HOVAS DURING THE FRENCH INVASION OF* 1895. By E. F. KNIGHT. With 16 Illustrations and a Map. 8vo., 12s. 6d.

Lang (ANDREW).

PICKLE THE SPY: or, The Incognito of Prince Charles. With 6 Portraits. 8vo., 18s.

ST. ANDREWS. With 8 Plates and 24 Illustrations in the Text by T. HODGE. 8vo., 15s. net.

Laurie. — *HISTORICAL SURVEY OF PRE-CHRISTIAN EDUCATION.* By S. S. LAURIE, A.M., LL.D. Crown 8vo., 12s.

Lecky (WILLIAM EDWARD HARTPOLE).
HISTORY OF ENGLAND IN THE EIGHTEENTH CENTURY.
Library Edition. 8 vols. 8vo., £7 4s.
Cabinet Edition. ENGLAND. 7 vols. Crown 8vo., 6s. each. IRELAND. 5 vols. Crown 8vo., 6s. each.

HISTORY OF EUROPEAN MORALS FROM AUGUSTUS TO CHARLEMAGNE. 2 vols. Crown 8vo., 16s.

HISTORY OF THE RISE AND INFLUENCE OF THE SPIRIT OF RATIONALISM IN EUROPE. 2 vols. Crown 8vo., 16s.

DEMOCRACY AND LIBERTY. 2 vols. 8vo., 36s.

THE EMPIRE: its value and its Growth. An Inaugural Address delivered at the Imperial Institute, November 20, 1893. Cr. 8vo., 1s. 6d.

Lowell. — *GOVERNMENTS AND PARTIES IN CONTINENTAL EUROPE.* By A. LAWRENCE LOWELL. 2 vols. 8vo., 21s.

Macaulay (LORD).

THE LIFE AND WORKS OF L MACAULAY. 'Edinburgh' Edition. vols. 8vo., 6s. each.
Vols. I.-IV. *HISTORY OF ENGLAND.*
Vols. V.-VII. *ESSAYS; BIOGRAPH INDIAN PENAL CODE; CONTRIBU7 TO KNIGHT'S 'QUARTERLY MAGAZ.*
Vol. VIII. *SPEECHES; LAYS OF ANC ROME; MISCELLANEOUS POEMS.*
Vols. IX. and X. *THE LIFE AND LET OF LORD MACAULAY.* By the l Hon. Sir G. O. TREVELYAN, Bart.,

This Edition is a cheaper reprint of the Li Edition of LORD MACAULAY'S *Life and W*

COMPLETE WORKS.
Cabinet Edition. 16 vols. Post £4 16s.
Library Edition. 8 vols. 8vo., £.
'Edinburgh' Edition. 8 vols. 8vo each.

HISTORY OF ENGLAND FROM ACCESSION OF JAMES THE SECOND.
Popular Edition. 2 vols. Cr. 8vo.,
Student's Edition. 2 vols. Cr. 8vo.,
People's Edition. 4 vols. Cr. 8vo., 1
Cabinet Edition. 8 vols. Post 8vo.,
'Edinburgh' Edition. 4 vols. 8vo each.
Library Edition. 5 vols. 8vo., £4.

CRITICAL AND HISTORICAL ESS. WITH LAYS OF ANCIENT ROME, volume.
Popular Edition. Crown 8vo., 2s. 6
Authorised Edition. Crown 8vo., 2s or 3s. 6d., gilt edges.
Silver Library Edition. Cr. 8vo., 3s.

CRITICAL AND HISTORICAL ESS Student's Edition. 1 vol. Cr. 8vo., 6
People's Edition. 2 vols. Cr. 8vo., l
'Trevelyan' Edition. 2 vols. Cr. 8vo
Cabinet Edition. 4 vols. Post 8vo., 2
'Edinburgh' Edition. 4 vols. 8vo each.
Library Edition. 3 vols. 8vo., 36s.

ESSAYS which may be had separa price 6d. each sewed, 1s. each cloth.

Addison and Walpole.	Ranke and Gladston
Croker's Boswell's Johnson.	Milton and Machiav
Hallam's Constitutional History.	Lord Byron.
Warren Hastings.	Lord Clive.
The Earl of Chatham (Two Essays).	Lord Byron, and Comic Dramatis the Restoration.
Frederick the Great.	

MISCELLANEOUS WRITINGS
People's Edition. 1 vol. Cr. 8vo., 4s.
Library Edition. 2 vols. 8vo., 21s.

Macaulay (LORD)—*continued*.

MISCELLANEOUS WRITINGS AND SPEECHES.

Popular Edition. Crown 8vo., 2s. 6d.

Cabinet Edition. Including Indian Penal Code, Lays of Ancient Rome, and Miscellaneous Poems. 4 vols. Post 8vo., 24s.

SELECTIONS FROM THE WRITINGS OF LORD MACAULAY. Edited, with Occasional Notes, by the Right Hon. Sir G. O. Trevelyan, Bart. Crown 8vo., 6s.

MacColl.—THE SULTAN AND THE POWERS. By the Rev. MALCOLM MACCOLL, M.A., Canon of Ripon. 8vo., 10s. 6d.

Mackinnon.—THE UNION OF ENGLAND AND SCOTLAND: A STUDY OF INTERNATIONAL HISTORY. By JAMES MACKINNON, Ph.D. Examiner in History to the University of Edinburgh. 8vo., 16s.

May.—THE CONSTITUTIONAL HISTORY OF ENGLAND since the Accession of George III. 1760-1870. By Sir THOMAS ERSKINE MAY, K.C.B. (Lord Farnborough). 3 vols. Cr. 8vo., 18s.

Merivale (THE LATE DEAN).

HISTORY OF THE ROMANS UNDER THE EMPIRE. 8 vols. Crown 8vo., 3s. 6d. each

THE FALL OF THE ROMAN REPUBLIC: à Short History of the Last Century of the Commonwealth. 12mo., 7s. 6d.

Montague.—THE ELEMENTS OF ENGLISH CONSTITUTIONAL HISTORY. By F. C. MONTAGUE, M.A. Crown 8vo., 3s. 6d.

O'Brien.—IRISH IDEAS. REPRINTED ADDRESSES. By WILLIAM O'BRIEN. Cr. 8vo. 2s. 6d.

Richman.—APPENZELL: PURE DEMOCRACY AND PASTORAL LIFE IN INNER-RHODEN. A Swiss Study. By IRVING B. RICHMAN, Consul-General of the United States to Switzerland. With Maps. Crown 8vo., 5s.

Seebohm (FREDERIC).

THE ENGLISH VILLAGE COMMUNITY Examined in its Relations to the Manorial and Tribal Systems, &c. With 13 Maps and Plates. 8vo., 16s.

THE TRIBAL SYSTEM IN WALES: Being Part of an Inquiry into the Structure and Methods of Tribal Society. With 3 Maps. 8vo., 12s.

Sharpe.—LONDON AND THE KINGDOM: a History derived mainly from the Archives at Guildhall in the custody of the Corporation of the City of London. By REGINALD R. SHARPE, D.C.L., Records Clerk in the Office of the Town Clerk of the City of London. 3 vols. 8vo. 10s. 6d. each.

Sheppard. — MEMORIALS OF JAMES'S PALACE. By the Rev. EDG SHEPPARD, M.A., Sub-Dean of H. Chapels Royal. With 41 Full-page Plates Photo-Intaglio) and 32 Illustrations in Text. 2 vols. 8vo., 36s. net.

Smith.—CARTHAGE AND THE CART AGINIANS. By R. BOSWORTH SMITH, M. With Maps, Plans, &c. Cr. 8vo., 3s. 6d

Stephens. — A HISTORY OF T FRENCH REVOLUTION. By H. MOR STEPHENS. 3 vols. 8vo. Vols. I. and 18s. each.

Stubbs.—HISTORY OF THE UNIVE SITY OF DUBLIN, from its Foundation the End of the Eighteenth Century. By W. STUBBS. 8vo., 12s. 6d.

Sutherland.—THE HISTORY OF A TRALIA AND NEW ZEALAND, from 1606 1890. By ALEXANDER SUTHERLAND, M. and GEORGE SUTHERLAND, M.A. Cro 8vo., 2s. 6d.

Taylor.—A STUDENT'S MANUAL THE HISTORY OF INDIA. By Colonel M DOWS TAYLOR, C.S.I., &c. Cr. 8vo., 7s.

Todd. — PARLIAMENTARY GOVER MENT IN THE BRITISH COLONIES. ALPHEUS TODD, LL.D. 8vo., 30s. net.

Wakeman and Hassall.—ESSA INTRODUCTORY TO THE STUDY OF ENGLI CONSTITUTIONAL HISTORY. By Resid Members of the University of Oxfo Edited by HENRY OFFLEY WAKEM M.A., and ARTHUR HASSALL, M.A Cro 8vo., 6s.

Walpole.—HISTORY OF ENGLA FROM THE CONCLUSION OF THE GRE WAR IN 1815 TO 1858. By SPENC WALPOLE. 6 vols. Crown 8vo., 6s. ea

Wolff. — ODD BITS OF HISTOR being Short Chapters intended to Fill So Blanks. By HENRY W. WOLFF. 8vo., 8s.

Wood-Martin.—PAGAN IRELAN AN ARCHÆOLOGICAL SKETCH. A Handbo of Irish Pre-Christian Antiquities. By G. WOOD-MARTIN, M.R.I.A. With Illustrations. Crown 8vo., 15s.

Wylie. — HISTORY OF ENGLA UNDER HENRY IV. By JAMES HAMILT WYLIE, M.A., one of H. M. Inspectors Schools. 3 vols. Crown 8vo. Vol. I., 13 1404, 10s. 6d. Vol. II., 15s. Vol. III., 1
[Vol. IV. *In the pre*

Biography, Personal Memoirs, &c.

Armstrong.—*THE LIFE AND LETTERS OF EDMUND J. ARMSTRONG.* Edited by G. F. ARMSTRONG. Fcp. 8vo., 7s. 6d.

Bacon.—*THE LETTERS AND LIFE OF FRANCIS BACON, INCLUDING ALL HIS OCCASIONAL WORKS.* Edited by JAMES SPEDDING. 7 vols. 8vo., £4 4s.

Bagehot.—*BIOGRAPHICAL STUDIES.* By WALTER BAGEHOT. Crown 8vo., 3s. 6d.

Blackwell. — *PIONEER WORK IN OPENING THE MEDICAL PROFESSION TO WOMEN:* Autobiographical Sketches. By Dr. ELIZABETH BLACKWELL. Cr. 8vo., 6s.

Boyd (A. K. H.) ('A.K.H.B.').

TWENTY-FIVE YEARS OF ST. ANDREWS. 1865-1890. 2 vols. 8vo. Vol. I. 12s. Vol. II. 15s.

ST. ANDREWS AND ELSEWHERE: Glimpses of Some Gone and of Things Left. 8vo., 15s.

THE LAST YEARS OF ST. ANDREWS: SEPTEMBER 1890 TO SEPTEMBER 1895. 8vo., 15s.

Brown.—*FORD MADOX BROWN:* A Record of his Life and Works. By FORD M. HUEFFER. With 45 Full-page Plates (22 Autotypes) and 7 Illustrations in the Text. 8vo., 42s.

Buss.—*FRANCES MARY BUSS AND HER WORK FOR EDUCATION.* By ANNIE E. RIDLEY. With 5 Portraits and 4 Illustrations. Crown 8vo, 7s. 6d.

Carlyle.—*THOMAS CARLYLE:* A History of his Life. By JAMES ANTHONY FROUDE.

1795-1835. 2 vols. Crown 8vo., 7s.
1834-1881. 2 vols. Crown 8vo., 7s.

Digby.—*THE LIFE OF SIR KENELM DIGBY,* by one of his Descendants, the Author of 'The Life of a Conspirator,' 'A Life of Archbishop Laud,' etc. With 7 Illustrations. 8vo., 16s.

Erasmus.—*LIFE AND LETTERS OF ERASMUS.* By JAMES ANTHONY FROUDE. Crown 8vo.

Fox. — *THE EARLY HISTORY OF CHARLES JAMES FOX.* By the Right Hon. Sir G. O. TREVELYAN, Bart.

Library Edition. 8vo., 18s.
Cabinet Edition. Crown 8vo., 6s.

Halford.—*THE LIFE OF SIR HE HALFORD, BART., G.C.H., M.D., F..* By WILLIAM MUNK, M.D., F.S.A. 12s. 6d.

Hamilton.—*LIFE OF SIR WILL HAMILTON.* By R. P. GRAVES. 8vo. 3 15s. each. ADDENDUM. 8vo., 6d. sew

Harper. — *A MEMOIR OF H DANIEL HARPER, D.D.,* late Princip Jesus College, Oxford, and for many Head Master of Sherborne School. E V. LESTER, M.A. Crown 8vo., 5s.

Havelock.—*MEMOIRS OF SIR HE HAVELOCK, K.C.B.* By JOHN C MARSHMAN. Crown 8vo., 3s. 6d.

Haweis.—*MY MUSICAL LIFE.* the Rev. H. R. HAWEIS. With Portra Richard Wagner and 3 Illustrations. C 8vo., 7s. 6d.

Holroyd.—*THE GIRLHOOD OF M, JOSEPHA HOLROYD (Lady Stanle, Alderley).* Recorded in Letters of a dred Years Ago, from 1776 to 1796. E by J. H. ADEANE. With 6 Port: 8vo., 18s.

Lejeune.—*MEMOIRS OF BARON JEUNE,* Aide-de-Camp to Marshals Ber Davout, and Oudinot. Translated Edited from the Original French by ARTHUR BELL (N. D'ANVERS). W Preface by Major-General MAURICE, 2 vols. 8vo., 24s.

Luther. — *LIFE OF LUTHER.* JULIUS KÖSTLIN. With Illustrations Authentic Sources. Translated from German. Crown 8vo., 7s. 6d.

Macaulay.—*THE LIFE AND LET1 OF LORD MACAULAY.* By the Right : Sir G. O. TREVELYAN, Bart., M.P.
Popular Edition. 1 vol. Cr. 8vo., 2.
Student's Edition. 1 vol. Cr. 8vo.,
Cabinet Edition. 2 vols. Post 8vo.
Library Edition. 2 vols. 8vo., 36s.
'Edinburgh' Edition. 2 vols. 8vo each.

Marbot. — *THE MEMOIRS OF BARON DE MARBOT.* Translated from French. Crown 8vo., 7s. 6d.

Nansen.—*FRIDTIOF NANSEN, 1: 1893.* By W. C. BRÖGGER and NORI ROLFSEN. Translated by WILLIAM ARC With 8 Plates, 48 Illustrations in the and 3 Maps. 8vo., 12s. 6d.

Biography, Personal Memoirs, &c.—*continued*.

Romanes.—*THE LIFE AND LETTERS OF GEORGE JOHN ROMANES, M.A., LL.D., F.R.S.* Written and Edited by his WIFE. With Portrait and 2 Illustrations. Crown 8vo., 6s.

Seebohm.—*THE OXFORD REFORMERS —JOHN COLET, ERASMUS AND THOMAS MORE:* a History of their Fellow-Work. By FREDERIC SEEBOHM. 8vo., 14s.

Shakespeare. — *OUTLINES OF THE LIFE OF SHAKESPEARE.* By J. O. HALLI-WELL-PHILLIPPS. With Illustrations and Fac-similes. 2 vols. Royal 8vo., £1 1s.

Shakespeare's *TRUE LIFE.* By JAMES WALTER. With 500 Illustrations by GERALD E. MOIRA. Imp. 8vo., 21s.

Stephen.—*ESSAYS IN ECCLESIASTI-CAL BIOGRAPHY.* By Sir JAMES STEPHEN. Crown 8vo., 7s. 6d.

Turgot.—*THE LIFE AND WRITING. OF TURGOT,* Comptroller-General of France 1774-1776. Edited for English Readers by W. WALKER STEPHENS. 8vo., 12s. 6d.

Verney. —*MEMOIRS OF THE VERNE) FAMILY.*

Vols. I. & II., *DURING THE CIVIL WAR* By FRANCES PARTHENOPE VERNEY. With 38 Portraits, Woodcuts and Fac-simile Royal 8vo., 42s.

Vol. III., *DURING THE COMMONWEALTH* 1650-1660. By MARGARET M. VERNEY With 10 Portraits, &c. Royal 8vo., 21s.

Wellington.—*LIFE OF THE DUKE OF WELLINGTON.* By the Rev. G. R GLEIG, M.A. Crown 8vo., 3s. 6d.

Wolf.—*THE LIFE OF JOSEPH WOLF. ANIMAL PAINTER.* By A. H. PALMER. With 53 Plates and 14 Illustrations in the Text. 8vo., 21s.

Travel and Adventure, the Colonies, &c.

Arnold (SIR EDWIN).

SEAS AND LANDS. With 71 Illus-trations. Cr. 8vo., 3s. 6d.

WANDERING WORDS. With 45 Illustrations. 8vo., 18s.

EAST AND WEST: With 14 Illus-trations by R. T. PRITCHETT. 8vo., 18s.

AUSTRALIA AS IT IS, or Facts and Features, Sketches, and Incidents of Australia and Australian Life with Notices of New Zealand. By A CLERGYMAN, thirteen years resident in the interior of New South Wales. Crown 8vo., 5s.

Baker (SIR S. W.).

EIGHT YEARS IN CEYLON. With 6 Illustrations. Crown 8vo., 3s. 6d.

THE RIFLE AND THE HOUND IN CEYLON. With 6 Illustrations. Crown 8vo., 3s. 6d.

Bent (J. THEODORE).

THE RUINED CITIES OF MASHONA-LAND: being a Record of Excavation and Exploration in 1891. With 117 Illustrations. Crown 8vo., 3s. 6d.

Bent (J. THEODORE)—*continued*.

THE SACRED CITY OF THE ETHIO-PIANS: being a Record of Travel and Research in Abyssinia in 1893. With 8 Plates and 65 Illustrations in the Text. 8vo., 10s. 6d.

Bicknell.—*TRAVEL AND ADVENTURE IN NORTHERN QUEENSLAND.* By ARTHUR C. BICKNELL. With 24 Plates and 22 Illus-trations in the Text. 8vo., 15s.

Brassey.—*VOYAGES AND TRAVELS OF LORD BRASSEY, K.C.B., D.C.L.,* 1862-1894. Arranged and Edited by Captain S. EARDLEY-WILMOT. 2 vols. Cr. 8vo., 10s.

Brassey (THE LATE LADY).

A VOYAGE IN THE ' SUNBEAM;' OUR HOME ON THE OCEAN FOR ELEVEN MONTHS.

Library Edition. With 8 Maps and Charts, and 118 Illustrations. 8vo. 21s

Cabinet Edition. With Map and 66 Illustrations. Crown 8vo., 7s. 6d.

Silver Library Edition. With 66 Illustra-tions. Crown 8vo., 3s. 6d.

Popular Edition. With 60 Illustrations 4to., 6d. sewed, 1s. cloth.

School Edition. With 37 Illustrations. Fcp., 2s. cloth, or 3s. white parchment

Travel and Adventure, the Colonies, &c.—*continued.*

Brassey (THE LATE LADY)—*continued.*

SUNSHINE AND STORM IN THE EAST.
Library Edition. With 2 Maps and 141 Illustrations. 8vo., 21s.
Cabinet Edition. With 2 Maps and 114 Illustrations. Crown 8vo., 7s. 6d.
Popular Edition. With 103 Illustrations. 4to., 6d. sewed, 1s. cloth.

IN THE TRADES, THE TROPICS, AND THE 'ROARING FORTIES.'
Cabinet Edition. With Map and 220 Illustrations. Crown 8vo., 7s. 6d.
Popular Edition. With 183 Illustrations. 4to., 6d. sewed, 1s. cloth.

THREE VOYAGES IN THE 'SUNBEAM'.
Popular Ed. With 346 Illust. 4to., 2s. 6d.

Browning.—*A GIRL'S WANDERINGS IN HUNGARY.* By H. ELLEN BROWNING. With Map and 20 Illustrations. Crown 8vo., 7s. 6d.

Froude (JAMES A.).

OCEANA: or England and her Colonies. With 9 Illustrations. Crown 8vo., 2s. boards, 2s. 6d. cloth.

THE ENGLISH IN THE WEST INDIES: or, the Bow of Ulysses. With 9 Illustrations. Crown 8vo., 2s. boards, 2s. 6d. cloth.

Howitt.—*VISITS TO REMARKABLE PLACES.* Old Halls, Battle-Fields, Scenes, illustrative of Striking Passages in English History and Poetry. By WILLIAM HOWITT. With 80 Illustrations. Crown 8vo., 3s. 6d.

Knight (E. F.).

THE CRUISE OF THE 'ALERTE': the Narrative of a Search for Treasure on the Desert Island of Trinidad. With 2 Maps and 23 Illustrations. Crown 8vo., 3s. 6d.

WHERE THREE EMPIRES MEET: a Narrative of Recent Travel in Kashmir, Western Tibet, Baltistan, Ladak, Gilgit, and the adjoining Countries. With a Map and 54 Illustrations. Cr. 8vo., 3s. 6d.

THE 'FALCON' ON THE BALTIC: a Voyage from London to Copenhagen in a Three-Tonner. With 10 Full-page Illustrations. Crown 8vo., 3s. 6d.

Lees and Clutterbuck.—B.C. 1887: *A RAMBLE IN BRITISH COLUMBIA.* By J. A. LEES and W. J. CLUTTERBUCK. With Map and 75 Illustrations. Crown 8vo., 3s. 6d.

Max Müller.—*LETTERS FROM (* STANTINOPLE.* By Mrs. MAX MÜL With 12 Views of Constantinople and neighbourhood. Crown 8vo., 6s.

Nansen (FRIDTJOF).

THE FIRST CROSSING OF GRE LAND. With numerous Illustration a Map. Crown 8vo., 3s. 6d.

ESKIMO LIFE. With 31 Illustrati 8vo., 16s.

Oliver.—*CRAGS AND CRAT* Rambles in the Island of Réunion. WILLIAM DUDLEY OLIVER, M.A. 27 Illustrations and a Map. Cr. 8vo.,

Peary. — *MY ARCTIC JOURNAL* year among Ice-Fields and Eskimos. JOSEPHINE DIEBITSCH-PEARY. Wit Plates, 3 Sketch Maps, and 44 Illustra in the Text. 8vo., 12s.

Quillinan.—*JOURNAL OF A * MONTHS' RESIDENCE IN PORTUGAL, Glimpses of the South of Spain. By QUILLINAN (Dora Wordsworth). Edition. Edited, with Memoir, by EDI LEE, Author of 'Dorothy Wordsworth Crown 8vo., 6s.

Smith.—*CLIMBING IN THE BRI ISLES.* By W. P. HASKETT SMITH. Illustrations by ELLIS CARR, and Num Plans.
Part I. *ENGLAND.* 16mo., 3s. 6d.
Part II. *WALES AND IRELAND.* 1 3s. 6d.
Part III. *SCOTLAND.* [*In prepar*

Stephen. — *THE PLAY-GROUNL EUROPE.* By LESLIE STEPHEN. Edition, with Additions and 4 Illustra Crown 8vo., 6s. net.

THREE IN NORWAY. By of Them. With a Map and 59 Illustra Crown 8vo., 2s. boards, 2s. 6d. cloth.

Tyndall.—*THE GLACIERS OF ALPS*: being a Narrative of Excur and Ascents. An Account of the and Phenomena of Glaciers, and an position of the Physical Principles to they are related. By JOHN TYN F.R.S. With numerous Illustrations. 8vo., 6s. 6d. net.

Whishaw.—*THE ROMANCE OF WOODS*: Reprinted Articles and Ske By FRED. J. WHISHAW. Crown 8vo.,

Veterinary Medicine, &c.

Steel (JOHN HENRY).

A TREATISE ON THE DISEASES OF THE DOG. With 88 Illustrations. 8vo., 10s. 6d.

A TREATISE ON THE DISEASES OF THE OX. With 119 Illustrations. 8vo., 15s.

A TREATISE ON THE DISEASES OF THE SHEEP. With 100 Illustrations. 8vo., 12s.

OUTLINES OF EQUINE ANATOMY : a Manual for the use of Veterinary Students in the Dissecting Room. Cr. 8vo., 7s. 6d.

Fitzwygram. — *HORSES AN. STABLES.* By Major-General Sir F. FITZ WYGRAM, Bart. With 56 pages of Illustra tions. 8vo., 2s. 6d. net.

'Stonehenge.' — *THE DOG I. HEALTH AND DISEASE.* By 'STONE HENGE'. With 78 Wood Engravings 8vo., 7s. 6d.

Youatt (WILLIAM).

THE HORSE. Revised and Enlarge by W. WATSON, M.R.C.V.S. With 5 Wood Engravings. 8vo., 7s. 6d.

THE DOG. Revised and Enlarged With 33 Wood Engravings. 8vo., 6s.

Sport and Pastime.

THE BADMINTON LIBRARY.

Edited by HIS GRACE THE DUKE OF BEAUFORT, K.G.; Assisted by ALFRED E T. WATSON.

Complete in 28 Volumes.   Crown 8vo., Price 10s. 6d. each Volume, Cloth.

*** *The Volumes are also issued half-bound in Leather, with gilt top.   The price can be ha from all Booksellers.*

ARCHERY. By C. J. LONGMAN and Col. H. WALROND. With Contributions by Miss LEGH, Viscount DILLON, Major C. HAWKINS FISHER, &c. With 2 Maps, 23 Plates and 172 Illustrations in the Text. Crown 8vo., 10s. 6d.

ATHLETICS AND FOOTBALL. By MONTAGUE SHEARMAN. With 6 Plates and 52 Illustrations in the Text. Crown 8vo., 10s. 6d.

BIG GAME SHOOTING. By CLIVE PHILLIPPS-WOLLEY.

Vol. I. AFRICA AND AMERICA. With Contributions by Sir SAMUEL W. BAKER, W. C. OSWELL, F. J. JACKSON, WARBURTON PIKE, and F. C. SELOUS. With 20 Plates and 57 Illustrations in the Text. Crown 8vo., 10s. 6d.

Vol. II. EUROPE, ASIA, AND THE ARCTIC REGIONS. With Contribu tions by Lieut.-Colonel R. HEBER PERCY, ARNOLD PIKE, Major ALGERNON C. HEBER PERCY, &c. With 17 Plates and 56 Illustrations in the Text. Crown 8vo., 10s. 6d.

BILLIARDS. By Major W. BROAD FOOT, R.E. With Contributions by A. H BOYD, SYDENHAM DIXON, W. J. FORD DUDLEY D. PONTIFEX, &c. With 11 Plates 19 Illustrations in the Text, and numerou Diagrams and Figures. Crown 8vo., 10s. 6d

BOATING. By W. B. WOODGATE With 10 Plates, 39 Illustrations in the Text and from Instantaneous Photographs, an 4 Maps of the Rowing Courses at Oxford Cambridge, Henley, and Putney.   Crow 8vo., 10s. 6d.

COURSING AND FALCONRY By HARDING COX and the Hon. GERALI LASCELLES. With 20 Plates and 56 Illus trations in the Text. Crown 8vo., 10s. 6d.

CRICKET. By A. G. STEEL an the Hon. R. H. LYTTELTON. With Con tributions by ANDREW LANG, W. G. GRACE F. GALE, &c. With 12 Plates and 52 Illus trations in the Text. Crown 8vo., 10s. 6d.

Sport and Pastime—*continued.*

THE BADMINTON LIBRARY—*continued.*

CYCLING. By the EARL OF ALBE-MARLE and G. LACY HILLIER. With 19 Plates and 44 Illustrations in the Text. Crown 8vo., 10s. 6d.

DANCING. By Mrs. LILLY GROVE, F.R.G.S. With Contributions by Miss MIDDLETON, The Hon. Mrs. ARMYTAGE, &c. With Musical Examples, and 38 Full-page Plates and 93 Illustrations in the Text. Crown 8vo., 10s. 6d.

DRIVING. By His Grace the DUKE of BEAUFORT, K.G. With Contributions by other Authorities. With Photogravure Intaglio Portrait of His Grace the DUKE OF BEAUFORT, and 11 Plates and 54 Illustrations in the Text. Crown 8vo., 10s. 6d.

FENCING,   BOXING,   AND WRESTLING. By WALTER H. POLLOCK, F. C. GROVE, C. PREVOST, E. B. MITCHELL, and WALTER ARMSTRONG. With 18 Intaglio Plates and 24 Illustrations in the Text. Crown 8vo., 10s. 6d.

FISHING. By H. CHOLMONDELEY-PENNELL, Late Her Majesty's Inspector of Sea Fisheries.

Vol. I. SALMON AND TROUT. With Contributions by H. R. FRANCIS, Major JOHN P. TRAHERNE, &c. With Frontispiece, 8 Full-page Illustrations of Fishing Subjects, and numerous Illustrations of Tackle, &c. Crown 8vo., 10s. 6d.

Vol. II. PIKE AND OTHER COARSE FISH. With Contributions by the MARQUIS OF EXETER, WILLIAM SENIOR, G. CHRISTOPHER DAVIS, &c. With Frontispiece, 6 Full-page Illustrations of Fishing Subjects, and numerous Illustrations of Tackle, &c. Crown 8vo., 10s. 6d.

GOLF. By HORACE G. HUTCHINSON. With Contributions by the Rt. Hon. A. J. BALFOUR, M.P., Sir WALTER SIMPSON, Bart., ANDREW LANG, &c. With 25 Plates and 65 Illustrations in the Text. Crown 8vo., 10s. 6d.

HUNTING. By His Grace the DUKE OF BEAUFORT, K.G., and MOWBRAY MORRIS. With Contributions by the EARL OF SUFFOLK AND BERKSHIRE, Rev. E. W. L. DAVIES, J. S. GIBBONS, G. H. LONGMAN, &c. With 5 Plates and 54 Illustrations in the Text. Crown 8vo., 10s. 6d.

MOUNTAINEERING. By C DENT. With Contributions by Sir W CONWAY, D. W. FRESHFIELD, C. MATTHEWS, &c. With 13 Plates an Illustrations in the Text. Cr. 8vo., 10s

POETRY OF SPORT (THE Selected by HEDLEY PEEK. Wit Chapter on Classical Allusions to Spo ANDREW LANG, and a Special Prefa the Badminton Library by A. E. T. WA With 32 Plates and 74 Illustrations ir Text. Crown 8vo., 10s. 6d.

RACING AND STEEPLE-CH ING. By the EARL OF SUFFOLK BERKSHIRE, W. G. CRAVEN, the Ho LAWLEY, ARTHUR COVENTRY, and AL E. T. WATSON. With Coloured Fr piece and 56 Illustrations in the Crown 8vo., 10s. 6d.

RIDING AND POLO.

RIDING. By Captain ROBERT V the DUKE OF BEAUFORT, the EAR SUFFOLK AND BERKSHIRE, the EAR ONSLOW, J. MURRAY BROWN, &c. 18 Plates and 41 Illustrations in the Crown 8vo., 10s. 6d.

SEA FISHING. By JOHN BIC DYKE, Sir H. W. GORE-BOOTH, AL C. HARMSWORTH, and W. SENIOR. 22 Full-page Plates and 175 Illustratio the Text. Crown 8vo., 10s. 6d.

SHOOTING.

Vol. I. FIELD AND COVERT. By WALSINGHAM and Sir RALPH PA GALLWEY, Bart. With Contributio the Hon. GERALD LASCELLES and STUART-WORTLEY. With 11 Full Illustrations and 94 Illustrations ir Text. Crown 8vo., 10s. 6d.

Vol. II. MOOR AND MARSH. LORD WALSINGHAM and Sir RALPH PA GALLWEY, Bart. With Contributio LORD LOVAT and Lord CHARLES LE KERR. With 8 Full-page Illustra and 57 Illustrations in the Text. C 8vo., 10s. 6d.

Sport and Pastime—*continued*.

THE BADMINTON LIBRARY—*continued*.

SKATING, CURLING, TOBOG-GANING. By J. M. HEATHCOTE, C. G. TEBBUTT, T. MAXWELL WITHAM, Rev. JOHN KERR, ORMOND HAKE, HENRY A. BUCK, &c. With 12 Plates and 272 Illustrations and Diagrams in the Text. Crown 8vo., 10s. 6d.

SWIMMING. By ARCHIBALD SINCLAIR and WILLIAM HENRY, Hon. Secs. of the Life-Saving Society. With 13 Plates and 106 Illustrations in the Text. Crown 8vo., 10s. 6d.

TENNIS, LAWN TENNIS, RACKETS AND FIVES. By J. M. and C. G. HEATHCOTE, E. O. PLEYDELL-BOUVERIE, and A. C. AINGER. With Contributions by the Hon. A. LYTTELTON, W. C. MARSHALL, Miss L. DOD, &c. With 12 Plates and 67 Illustrations in the Text. Crown 8vo., 10s. 6d.

YACHTING.

Vol. I. CRUISING, CONSTRUCTION OF YACHTS, YACHT RACING RULES, FITTING-OUT, &c. By Sir EDWARD SULLIVAN, Bart., THE EARL OF PEMBROKE, LORD BRASSEY, K.C.B., C. E. SETH-SMITH, C.B., G. L. WATSON, R. T. PRITCHETT, E. F. KNIGHT, &c. With 21 Plates and 93 Illustrations in the Text and from Photographs. Crown 8vo., 10s. 6d.

Vol. II. YACHT CLUBS, YACHTING IN AMERICA AND THE COLONIES, YACHT RACING, &c. By R. T. PRITCHETT, THE MARQUIS OF DUFFERIN AND AVA, K.P., THE EARL OF ONSLOW, JAMES McFERRAN, &c. With 35 Plates and 160 Illustrations in the Text. Crown 8vo., 10s. 6d.

FUR AND FEATHER SERIES.

Edited by A. E. T. WATSON.

Crown 8vo., price 5s. each Volume, cloth.

*** *The Volumes are also issued half-bound in Leather, with gilt top. The price can be had from all Booksellers.*

THE PARTRIDGE. Natural History by the Rev. H. A. MACPHERSON; Shooting, by A. J. STUART-WORTLEY; Cookery, by GEORGE SAINTSBURY. With 11 Illustrations and various Diagrams in the Text. Crown 8vo., 5s.

THE GROUSE. Natural History by the Rev. H. A. MACPHERSON; Shooting, by A. J. STUART-WORTLEY; Cookery, by GEORGE SAINTSBURY. With 13 Illustrations and various Diagrams in the Text. Crown 8vo., 5s.

THE PHEASANT. Natural History by the Rev. H. A. MACPHERSON; Shooting, by A. J. STUART-WORTLEY; Cookery, by ALEXANDER INNES SHAND. With 10 Illustrations and various Diagrams. Crown 8vo., 5s.

THE HARE. Natural. History by the Rev. H. A. MACPHERSON; Shooting, by the Hon. GERALD LASCELLES; Coursing, by CHARLES RICHARDSON; Hunting, by J. S. GIBBONS and G. H. LONGMAN; Cookery, by Col. KENNEY HERBERT. With 9 Illustrations. Crown 8vo, 5s.

RED DEER.—Natural History. By the Rev. H. A. MACPHERSON. Deer Stalking. By CAMERON OF LOCHIEL.—Stag Hunting. By Viscount EBRINGTON.—Cookery. By ALEXANDER INNES SHAND. With 10 Illustrations by J. CHARLTON and A. THORBURN. Crown 8vo., 5s.

*** *Other Volumes are in preparation.*

BADMINTON MAGAZINE (THE) OF SPORTS AND PASTIMES. Edited by ALFRED E. T. WATSON ("Rapier"). With numerous Illustrations. Price 1s. monthly.

Vols. I.-III. 6s. each.

Bickerdyke.—*DAYS OF MY LIFE ON WATERS FRESH AND SALT*; and other Papers. By JOHN BICKERDYKE. With Photo-Etched Frontispiece and 8 Full-page Illustrations. Crown 8vo., 6s.

Sport and Pastime—*continued.*

DEAD SHOT (*THE*): or, Sportsman's Complete Guide. Being a Treatise on the Use of the Gun, with Rudimentary and Finishing Lessons in the Art of Shooting Game of all kinds. Also Game-driving, Wildfowl and Pigeon-shooting, Dog-breaking, etc. By MARKSMAN. Seventh edition, with numerous Illustrations. Crown 8vo., 10s. 6d.

Ellis.—*CHESS SPARKS ;* or, Short and Bright Games of Chess. Collected and Arranged by J. H. ELLIS, M.A. 8vo., 4s. 6d.

Falkener.—*GAMES, ANCIENT AND ORIENTAL, AND HOW TO PLAY THEM.* By EDWARD FALKENER. With numerous Photographs, Diagrams, &c. 8vo., 21s.

Folkard.—*THE WILD-FOWLER :* A Treatise on Fowling, Ancient and Modern, descriptive also of Decoys and Flight-ponds, Wild-fowl Shooting, Gunning-punts, Shooting-yachts, &c. Also Fowling in the Fens and in Foreign Countries, Rock-fowling, &c., &c., by H. C. FOLKARD. *Fourth edition.* With 13 highly-finished Engravings on Steel, and several Woodcuts. 8vo., 12s. 6d.

Ford.—*THE THEORY AND PRACTICE OF ARCHERY.* By HORACE FORD. New Edition, thoroughly Revised and Re-written by W. BUTT, M.A. With a Preface by C. J. LONGMAN, M.A. 8vo., 14s.

Francis.—*A BOOK ON ANGLING :* or, Treatise on the Art of Fishing in every Branch ; including full Illustrated List of Salmon Flies. By FRANCIS FRANCIS. With Portrait and Coloured Plates. Crown 8vo., 15s.

Gibson.—*TOBOGGANING ON CROOKED RUNS.* By the Hon. HARRY GIBSON. With Contributions by F. DE B. STRICKLAND and 'LADY-TOBOGANNER'. With 40 Illustrations. Crown 8vo., 6s.

Graham.—*COUNTRY PASTIMES FOR BOYS.* By P. ANDERSON GRAHAM. With 252 Illustrations from Drawings and Photographs. Crown 8vo. 6s.

Lang.—*ANGLING SKETCHES.* By ANDREW LANG. With 20 Illustrations. Crown 8vo., 3s. 6d.

Longman.—*CHESS OPENINGS.* By FREDERICK W. LONGMAN. Fcp. 8vo., 2s. 6d.

Maskelyne.—*SHARPS AND FLATS :* a Complete Revelation of the Secrets of Cheating at Games of Chance and Skill. By JOHN NEVIL MASKELYNE, of the Egyptian Hall. With 62 Illustrations. Crown 8vo., 6s.

Park.—*THE GAME OF GOLF.* WILLIAM PARK, Jun., Champion 1887-89. With 17 Plates and 26 I tions in the Text. Crown 8vo., 7s. (

Payne-Gallwey (SIR RALPH, .

LETTERS TO YOUNG SHOOTERS Series). On the Choice and use of With 41 Illustrations. Crown 8vo.

LETTERS TO YOUNG SHOOTERS (S Series). On the Production, Prese and Killing of Game. With Di in Shooting Wood-Pigeons and Br in Retrievers. With Portrait a Illustrations. Crown 8vo., 12s. 6d

LETTERS TO YOUNG SHO (Third Series.) Comprising a Natural History of the Wildfov are Rare or Common to the Islands, with complete directi Shooting Wildfowl on the Coa Inland. With 200 Illustrations. 8vo., 18s.

Pole (WILLIAM).

THE THEORY OF THE MODERN TIFIC GAME OF WHIST. Fcp. 8vo.

THE EVOLUTION OF WHIST: a St the Progressive Changes which th has undergone. Cr. 8vo., 2s. 6d.

Proctor.—*HOW TO PLAY W* WITH THE LAWS AND ETIQUE1 *WHIST.* By RICHARD A. PROCTOR. 8vo., 3s. 6d.

Ronalds.—*THE FLY-FISHER'S .* MOLOGY. By ALFRED RONALDS. V coloured Plates. 8vo., 14s.

Thompson and Cannan. *.* IN-HAND FIGURE SKATING. By NOR G. THOMPSON and F. LAURA C Members of the Skating Club. V Introduction by Captain J. H. Th R.A. With Illustrations. 16mo., 6

Wilcocks.—*THE SEA FISHEI* Comprising the Chief Methods of Ho Line Fishing in the British and othe and Remarks on Nets, Boats, and B By J. C. WILCOCKS. Illustrated. Cr. 8

Mental, Moral, and Political Philosophy.

LOGIC, RHETORIC, PSYCHOLOGY, &C.

Abbott.—*THE ELEMENTS OF LOGIC.* By T. K. ABBOTT, B.D. 12mo., 3s.

Aristotle.

THE POLITICS: G. Bekker's Greek Text of Books I., III., IV. (VII.), with an English Translation by W. E. BOLLAND, M.A.; and short Introductory Essays by A. LANG, M.A. Crown 8vo., 7s. 6d.

THE POLITICS: Introductory Essays. By ANDREW LANG (from Bolland and Lang's 'Politics'). Crown 8vo., 2s. 6d.

THE ETHICS: Greek Text, Illustrated with Essay and Notes. By Sir ALEXANDER GRANT, Bart. 2 vols. 8vo., 32s.

AN INTRODUCTION TO ARISTOTLE'S ETHICS. Books I.-IV. (Book X. c. vi.-ix. in an Appendix). With a continuous Analysis and Notes. By the Rev. EDWARD MOORE, D.D., Cr. 8vo. 10s. 6d.

Bacon (FRANCIS).

COMPLETE WORKS. Edited by R. L. ELLIS, JAMES SPEDDING and D. D. HEATH. 7 vols. 8vo., £3 13s. 6d.

LETTERS AND LIFE, including all his occasional Works. Edited by JAMES SPEDDING. 7 vols. 8vo., £4 4s.

THE ESSAYS: with Annotations. By RICHARD WHATELY, D.D. 8vo., 10s. 6d.

THE ESSAYS. Edited, with Notes, by F. STORR and C. H. GIBSON. Crown 8vo, 3s. 6d.

THE ESSAYS: with Introduction, Notes, and Index. By E. A. ABBOTT, D.D. 2 Vols. Fcp. 8vo., 6s. The Text and Index only, without Introduction and Notes, in One Volume. Fcp. 8vo., 2s. 6d.

Bain (ALEXANDER).

MENTAL SCIENCE. Cr. 8vo., 6s. 6d.

MORAL SCIENCE. Cr. 8vo., 4s. 6d.

The two works as above can be had in one volume, price 10s. 6d.

SENSES AND THE INTELLECT. 8vo., 15s.

EMOTIONS AND THE WILL. 8vo., 15s.

Bain (ALEXANDER)—*continued.*

LOGIC, DEDUCTIVE AND INDUCTIVE. Part I. 4s. Part II. 6s. 6d.

PRACTICAL ESSAYS. Cr. 8vo., 2s.

Bray (CHARLES).

THE PHILOSOPHY OF NECESSITY: or, Law in Mind as in Matter. Cr. 8vo., 5s.

THE EDUCATION OF THE FEELINGS: a Moral System for Schools. Cr. 8vo., 2s. 6d.

Bray.—*ELEMENTS OF MORALITY,* in Easy Lessons for Home and School Teaching. By Mrs. CHARLES BRAY. Crown 8vo., 1s. 6d.

Davidson.—*THE LOGIC OF DEFINITION,* Explained and Applied. By WILLIAM L. DAVIDSON, M.A. Crown 8vo., 6s.

Green (THOMAS HILL).—THE WORKS OF. Edited by R. L. NETTLESHIP.
Vols. I. and II. Philosophical Works. 8vo., 16s. each.
Vol. III. Miscellanies. With Index to the three Volumes, and Memoir. 8vo., 21s.

LECTURES ON THE PRINCIPLES OF POLITICAL OBLIGATION. With Preface by BERNARD BOSANQUET. 8vo., 5s.

Hodgson (SHADWORTH H.).

TIME AND SPACE: A Metaphysical Essay. 8vo., 16s.

THE THEORY OF PRACTICE: an Ethical Inquiry. 2 vols. 8vo., 24s.

THE PHILOSOPHY OF REFLECTION. 2 vols. 8vo., 21s.

Hume.—*THE PHILOSOPHICAL WORKS OF DAVID HUME.* Edited by T. H. GREEN and T. H. GROSE. 4 vols. 8vo., 56s. Or separately, Essays. 2 vols. 28s. Treatise of Human Nature. 2 vols. 28s.

Justinian.—*THE INSTITUTES OF JUSTINIAN:* Latin Text, chiefly that of Huschke, with English Introduction, Translation, Notes, and Summary. By THOMAS C. SANDARS, M.A. 8vo., 18s.

Kant (IMMANUEL).

CRITIQUE OF PRACTICAL REASON, AND OTHER WORKS ON THE THEORY OF ETHICS.. Translated by T. K. ABBOTT, B.D. With Memoir. 8vo., 12s. 6d.

Mental, Moral and Political Philosophy—*continued.*

Kant (IMMANUEL)—*continued.*

FUNDAMENTAL PRINCIPLES OF THE METAPHYSIC OF ETHICS. Translated by T. K. ABBOTT, B.D. (Extracted from 'Kant's Critique of Practical Reason and other Works on the Theory of Ethics.') Crown 8vo, 3s.

INTRODUCTION TO LOGIC, AND HIS ESSAY ON THE MISTAKEN SUBTILTY OF THE FOUR FIGURES.. Translated by T. K. ABBOTT. 8vo., 6s.

Killick.—*HANDBOOK TO MILL'S SYSTEM OF LOGIC.* By Rev. A. H. KILLICK, M.A. Crown 8vo., 3s. 6d.

Ladd (GEORGE TRUMBULL).

PHILOSOPHY OF MIND : An Essay on the Metaphysics of Psychology. 8vo., 16s.

ELEMENTS OF PHYSIOLOGICAL PSYCHOLOGY. 8vo., 21s.

OUTLINES OF PHYSIOLOGICAL PSYCHOLOGY. A Text-book of Mental Science for Academies and Colleges. 8vo., 12s.

PSYCHOLOGY, DESCRIPTIVE AND EXPLANATORY ; a Treatise of the Phenomena, Laws, and Development of Human Mental Life. 8vo., 21s.

PRIMER OF PSYCHOLOGY. Cr. 8vo., 5s, 6d.

Lewes.—*THE HISTORY OF PHILOSOPHY,* from Thales to Comte. By GEORGE HENRY LEWES. 2 vols. 8vo., 32s.

Max Müller (F.).

THE SCIENCE OF THOUGHT. 8vo., 21s.

THREE INTRODUCTORY LECTURES ON THE SCIENCE OF THOUGHT. 8vo., 2s. 6d.

Mill.—*ANALYSIS OF THE PHENOMENA* OF THE HUMAN MIND. By JAMES MILL. 2 vols. 8vo., 28s.

Mill (JOHN STUART).

A SYSTEM OF LOGIC. Cr. 8vo., 3s. 6d.

ON LIBERTY. Crown 8vo., 1s. 4d.

ON REPRESENTATIVE GOVERNMENT. Crown 8vo., 2s.

UTILITARIANISM. 8vo., 2s. 6d.

EXAMINATION OF SIR WILLIAM HAMILTON'S PHILOSOPHY. 8vo., 16s.

NATURE, THE UTILITY OF RELIGION, AND THEISM. Three Essays. 8vo., 5s.

Mosso.—*FEAR.* By ANGELO MOSSO. Translated from the Italian by E. LOUGH and F. KIESOW. With 8 Illustrations. Cr. 8vo., 7s. 6d.

Romanes.—*MIND AND MOTION A MONISM.* By GEORGE JOHN ROMANE LL.D., F.R.S. Cr. 8vo., 4s. 6d.

Stock.—*DEDUCTIVE LOGIC.* By S GEORGE STOCK. Fcp. 8vo., 3s. 6d.

Sully (JAMES).

THE HUMAN MIND : a Text-book Psychology. 2 vols. 8vo., 21s.

OUTLINES OF PSYCHOLOGY. 8vo., 9

THE TEACHER'S HANDBOOK OF PS CHOLOGY. Crown 8vo., 5s.

STUDIES OF CHILDHOOD. 8v 10s. 6d.

Swinburne. — *PICTURE LOGIC :* Attempt to Popularise the Science Reasoning. By ALFRED JAMES SWINBURN M.A. With 23 Woodcuts. Crown 8vo.,

Weber.—*HISTORY OF PHILOSOPH* By ALFRED WEBER, Professor in the U versity of Strasburg. Translated by FRA THILLY, Ph.D. 8vo., 16s.

Whately (ARCHBISHOP).

BACON'S ESSAYS. With Annotation 8vo., 10s. 6d.

ELEMENTS OF LOGIC. Cr. 8vo., 4s. 6

ELEMENTS OF RHETORIC. Cr. 8v 4s. 6d.

LESSONS ON REASONING. Fcp. 8v 1s. 6d.

Zeller (Dr. EDWARD, Professor in t University of Berlin).

THE STOICS, EPICUREANS, A SCEPTICS. Translated by the Rev. O. REICHEL, M.A. Crown 8vo., 15s.

OUTLINES OF THE HISTORY GREEK PHILOSOPHY. Translated SARAH F. ALLEYNE and EVEL ABBOTT. Crown 8vo., 10s. 6d.

PLATO AND THE OLDER ACADEM Translated by SARAH F. ALLEYNE a ALFRED GOODWIN, B.A. Crown 8v 18s.

SOCRATES AND THE SOCRAT SCHOOLS. Translated by the Rev. J. REICHEL, M.A. Crown 8vo., 10s.

ARISTOTLE AND THE EARLIER PE PATETICS. Translated by B. F. C. C TELLOE, M.A., and J. H. MUIRHE, M.A. 2 vols. Crown 8vo., 24s.

Mental, Moral, and Political Philosophy—*continued.*
MANUALS OF CATHOLIC PHILOSOPHY.
(Stonyhurst Series).

A MANUAL OF POLITICAL ECONOMY. By C. S. DEVAS, M.A. Crown 8vo., 6s. 6d.

FIRST PRINCIPLES OF KNOWLEDGE. By JOHN RICKABY, S.J. Crown 8vo., 5s.

GENERAL METAPHYSICS. By JOHN RICKABY, S.J. Crown 8vo., 5s.

LOGIC. By RICHARD F. CLARKE, S.J. Crown 8vo., 5s.

MORAL PHILOSOPHY (ETHICS A NATURAL LAW). By JOSEPH RICKABY, Crown 8vo., 5s.

NATURAL THEOLOGY. By BERNA BOEDDER, S.J. Crown 8vo., 6s. 6d.

PSYCHOLOGY. By MICHAEL MAH S.J. Crown 8vo., 6s. 6d.

History and Science of Language, &c.

Davidson.—LEADING AND IMPORT-ANT ENGLISH WORDS: Explained and Ex-exmplified. By WILLIAM L. DAVIDSON, M.A. Fcp. 8vo., 3s. 6d.

Farrar.—LANGUAGE AND LANGUAGES: By F. W. FARRAR, D.D., F.R.S. Crown 8vo., 6s.

Graham. — ENGLISH SYNONYMS, Classified and Explained: with Practical Exercises. By G. F. GRAHAM. Fcp. 8vo., 6s.

Max Müller (F.).

THE SCIENCE OF LANGUAGE.—Found-ed on Lectures delivered at the Royal In-stitution in 1861 and 1863. 2 vols. Crown 8vo., 21s.

Max Müller (F.)—*continued.*

BIOGRAPHIES OF WORDS, AND T HOME OF THE ARYAS. Crown 8vo., 7s.

THREE LECTURES ON THE SCIE OF LANGUAGE, AND ITS PLACE. GENERAL EDUCATION, delivered at ford, 1889. Crown 8vo., 3s.

Roget.—THESAURUS OF ENGLI WORDS AND PHRASES. Classified Arranged so as to Facilitate the Express of Ideas and assist in Literary Composit By PETER MARK ROGET, M.D., F.R Recomposed throughout, enlarged and proved, partly from the Author's Notes, : with a full Index, by the Author's S JOHN LEWIS ROGET. Crown 8vo. 10s. 6

Whately.—ENGLISH SYNONYMS. E. JANE WHATELY. Fcp. 8vo., 3s.

Political Economy and Economics.

Ashley.—ENGLISH ECONOMIC HIS-TORY AND THEORY. By W. J. ASHLEY, M.A. Crown 8vo., Part I., 5s. Part II. 10s. 6d.

Bagehot.—ECONOMIC STUDIES. By WALTER BAGEHOT. Crown 8vo., 3s. 6d.

Barnett.—PRACTICABLE SOCIALISM. Essays on Social Reform. By the Rev. S. A. and Mrs. BARNETT. Crown 8vo., 6s.

Brassey.—PAPERS AND ADDRESSES ON WORK AND WAGES. By Lord BRASSEY. Edited by J. POTTER, and with Introduction by GEORGE HOWELL, M.P. Crown 8vo., 5s.

Devas.—A MANUAL OF POLITICAL ECONOMY. By C. S. DEVAS, M.A. Cr. 8vo., 6s. 6d. (*Manuals of Catholic Philosophy.*)

Dowell.—A HISTORY OF TAXATION AND TAXES IN ENGLAND, from the Earliest Times to the Year 1885. By STEPHEN DOWELL, (4 vols. 8vo). Vols. I. and II. The History of Taxation, 21s. Vols. III. and IV. The History of Taxes, 21s.

Jordan.—THE STANDARD OF VAL By WILLIAM LEIGHTON JORDAN, Fell of the Royal Statistical Society, &c. Cro 8vo., 6s.

Macleod (HENRY DUNNING).

BIMETALISM. 8vo., 5s. net.

THE ELEMENTS OF BANKING. 8vo., 3s. 6d.

THE THEORY AND PRACTICE BANKING. Vol. I. 8vo., 12s. Vol. II. 1

THE THEORY OF CREDIT. 8 Vol. I., 10s. net. Vol. II., Part I., 10s. 1 Vol. II., Part II., 10s. 6d.

A DIGEST OF THE LAW OF BIL OF EXCHANGE, BANK-NOTES, &c.
[In the pr

Mill.—POLITICAL ECONOMY. JOHN STUART MILL.
Popular Edition. Crown 8vo., 3s. 6d.
Library Edition. 2 vols. 8vo., 30s.

Political Economy and Economics—*continued*.

Mulhall.—*INDUSTRIES AND WEALTH OF NATIONS.* By MICHAEL G. MULHALL, F.S.S. With 32 full-page Diagrams. Crown 8vo., 8s. 6d.

Soderini.—*SOCIALISM AND CATHOLICISM.* From the Italian of Count EDWARD SODERINI. By RICHARD JENERY-SHEE. With a Preface by Cardinal VAUGHAN. Crown 8vo., 6s.

Symes.—*POLITICAL ECONOMY:* a Short Text-book of Political Economy. With Problems for Solution, and Hints for Supplementary Reading; also a Supplementary Chapter on Socialism. By Professor J. E. SYMES, M.A., of University College, Nottingham. Crown 8vo., 2s. 6d.

Toynbee.—*LECTURES ON THE INDUSTRIAL REVOLUTION OF THE 18TH CENTURY IN ENGLAND:* Popular Addresses, Notes and other Fragments. By ARNOLD TOYNBEE. With a Memoir of the Author by BENJAMIN JOWETT, D.D. 8vo., 10s. 6d.

Vincent.—*THE LAND QUESTION IN NORTH WALES:* being a Brief Survey of the History, Origin, and Character of the Agrarian Agitation, and of the Nature and Effect of the Proceedings of the Welsh Land Commission. By J. E. VINCENT. 8vo., 5s.

Webb.—*THE HISTORY OF TRADE UNIONISM.* By SIDNEY and BEATRICE WEBB. With Map and full Bibliography of the Subject. 8vo., 18s.

STUDIES IN ECONOMICS AND POLITICAL SCIENCE.

Issued under the auspices of the London School of Economics and Political Science.

THE HISTORY OF LOCAL RATES IN ENGLAND: Five Lectures. By EDWIN CANNAN, M.A. Crown 8vo., 2s. 6d.

GERMAN SOCIAL DEMOCRACY. By BERTRAND RUSSELL, B.A. With an Appendix on Social Democracy and the Woman Question in Germany by ALYS RUSSELL, B.A. Crown 8vo., 3s. 6d.

SELECT DOCUMENTS ILLUSTRATING THE HISTORY OF TRADE UNIONISM.
  1. The Tailoring Trade. Edited by W. F. GALTON. With a Preface by SIDNEY WEBB, LL.B. Crown 8vo., 5s.

DEPLOIGE'S REFERENDUM EN SUISSE. Translated, with Introduction and Notes, by C. P. TREVELYAN, M.A. [*In preparation.*

SELECT DOCUMENTS ILLUSTRATING THE STATE REGULATION OF WAGES. Edited, with Introduction and Notes, by W. A. S. HEWINS, M.A. [*In preparation.*

HUNGARIAN GILD RECORDS. Edited by Dr. JULIUS MANDELLO, of Budapest. [*In preparation.*

THE RELATIONS BETWEEN ENGLAND AND THE HANSEATIC LEAGUE. By Miss E. A. MACARTHUR. [*In preparation.*

Evolution, Anthropology, &c.

Babington. — *FALLACIES OF RACE THEORIES AS APPLIED TO NATIONAL CHARACTERISTICS.* Essays by WILLIAM DALTON BABINGTON, M.A. Crown 8vo., 6s.

Clodd (EDWARD).

THE STORY OF CREATION: a Plain Account of Evolution. With 77 Illustrations. Crown 8vo., 3s. 6d.

A PRIMER OF EVOLUTION: being a Popular Abridged Edition of 'The Story of Creation'. With Illustrations. Fcp. 8vo., 1s. 6d.

Lang.—*CUSTOM AND MYTH:* Studies of Early Usage and Belief. By ANDREW LANG. With 15 Illustrations. Crown 8vo., 3s. 6d.

Lubbock.—*THE ORIGIN OF CIVILISATION,* and the Primitive Condition of Man. By Sir J. LUBBOCK, Bart., M.P. With 5 Plates and 20 Illustrations in the Text. 8vo., 18s.

Romanes (GEORGE JOHN).

DARWIN, AND AFTER DARWIN: an Exposition of the Darwinian Theory, and a Discussion on Post-Darwinian Questions.
  Part I. THE DARWINIAN THEORY. With Portrait of Darwin and 125 Illustrations. Crown 8vo., 10s. 6d.
  Part II. POST-DARWINIAN QUESTIONS: Heredity and Utility. With Portrait of the Author and 5 Illustrations. Cr. 8vo., 10s. 6d.

AN EXAMINATION OF WEISMANNISM. Crown 8vo., 6s.

ESSAYS. Edited by C. LLOYD MORGAN, Principal of University College, Bristol. Crown 8vo., 6s.

Classical Literature, Translations, &c.

Abbott.—*HELLENICA.* A Collection of Essays on Greek Poetry, Philosophy, History, and Religion. Edited by EVELYN ABBOTT, M.A., LL.D. 8vo., 16s.

Æschylus.—*EUMENIDES OF ÆSCHYLUS.* With Metrical English Translation. By J. F. DAVIES. 8vo., 7s.

Aristophanes. — *THE ACHARNIANS OF ARISTOPHANES*, translated into English Verse. By R. Y. TYRRELL. Crown 8vo., 1s.

Aristotle.— *YOUTH AND OLD AGE, LIFE AND DEATH, AND RESPIRATION.* Translated, with Introduction and Notes, by W. OGLE, M.A., M.D., F.R.C.P., sometime Fellow of Corpus Christi College, Oxford. 8vo., 7s. 6d.

Becker (PROFESSOR).

GALLUS : or, Roman Scenes in the Time of Augustus. Illustrated. Post 8vo., 3s. 6d.

CHARICLES : or, Illustrations of the Private Life of the Ancient Greeks. Illustrated. Post 8vo., 3s. 6d.

Cicero.—*CICERO'S CORRESPONDENCE.* By R. Y. TYRRELL. Vols. I., II., III., 8vo., each 12s. Vol. IV., 15s.

Egbert.—*INTRODUCTION TO THE STUDY OF LATIN INSCRIPTIONS.* By JAMES C. EGBERT, Junr., Ph.D. With numerous Illustrations and Facsimiles. Square crown 8vo., 16s.

Farnell.—*GREEK LYRIC POETRY:* a Complete Collection of the Surviving Passages from the Greek Song-Writing. Arranged with Prefatory Articles, Introductory Matter and Commentary. By GEORGE S. FARNELL, M.A. With 5 Plates. 8vo., 16s.

Lang.—*HOMER AND THE EPIC.* By ANDREW LANG. Crown 8vo., 9s. net.

Lucan.—*THE PHARSALIA OF LUC* Translated into Blank Verse. By EDW RIDLEY, Q.C. 8vo., 14s.

Mackail.—*SELECT EPIGRAMS FR THE GREEK ANTHOLOGY.* By J. W. M KAIL. Edited with a Revised Text, In duction, Translation, and Notes. 8vo., 1

Rich.—*A DICTIONARY OF ROMAN A GREEK ANTIQUITIES.* By A. RICH, E With 2000 Woodcuts. Crown 8vo., 7s.

Sophocles.—Translated into Engli Verse. By ROBERT WHITELAW, M. Assistant Master in Rugby School. Cr. 8 8s. 6d.

Tacitus. — *THE HISTORY OF CORNELIUS TACITUS.* Translated i English, with an Introduction and No Critical and Explanatory, by ALB WILLIAM QUILL, M.A., T.C.D. 2 v Vol. I. 8vo., 7s. 6d. Vol. II. 8vo., 12s. 6

Tyrrell.—*TRANSLATIONS INTO GRE AND LATIN VERSE.* Edited by R. TYRRELL. 8vo., 6s.

Virgil.

THE ÆNEID OF VIRGIL. Transla into English Verse by JOHN CONINGT Crown 8vo., 6s.

THE POEMS OF VIRGIL. Transla into English Prose by JOHN CONINGT Crown 8vo., 6s.

THE ÆNEID OF VIRGIL, freely tra lated into English Blank Verse. W. J. THORNHILL. Crown 8vo., 7s.

THE ÆNEID OF VIRGIL. Transla into English Verse by JAMES RHOADE Books I.-VI. Crown 8vo., 5s. Books VII.-XII. Crown 8vo., 5s.

Poetry and the Drama.

Acworth.—*BALLADS OF THE MARATHAS.* Rendered into English Verse from the Marathi Originals. By HARRY ARBUTHNOT ACWORTH. 8vo., 5s.

Allingham (WILLIAM).

IRISH SONGS AND POEMS. With Frontispiece of the Waterfall of Asaroe. Fcp. 8vo., 6s.

LAURENCE BLOOMFIELD. With Portrait of the Author. Fcp. 8vo., 3s. 6d.

FLOWER PIECES; DAY AND NIGHT SONGS; BALLADS. With 2 Designs by D. G. ROSSETTI. Fcp. 8vo., 6s. large paper edition, 12s.

Allingham (WILLIAM)—*continued.*

LIFE AND PHANTASY : with Front piece by Sir J. E. MILLAIS, Bart., Design by ARTHUR HUGHES. Fcp. 8 6s.; large paper edition, 12s.

THOUGHT AND WORD, AND ASH MANOR: a Play. Fcp. 8vo., 6s.; 1 paper edition, 12s.

BLACKBERRIES. Imperial 16mo.,

Sets of the above 6 vols. may be had in form Half-parchment binding, price 30s.

Poetry and the Drama—*continued*.

Armstrong (G. F. Savage).

Poems: Lyrical and Dramatic. Fcp. 8vo., 6s.

King Saul. (The Tragedy of Israel, Part I.) Fcp. 8vo., 5s.

King David. (The Tragedy of Israel, Part II.) Fcp. 8vo., 6s.

King Solomon. (The Tragedy of Israel, Part III.) Fcp. 8vo., 6s.

Ugone: a Tragedy. Fcp. 8vo., 6s.

A Garland from Greece: Poems. Fcp. 8vo., 7s. 6d.

Stories of Wicklow: Poems. Fcp. 8vo., 7s. 6d.

Mephistopheles in Broadcloth: a Satire. Fcp. 8vo., 4s.

One in the Infinite: a Poem. Crown 8vo., 7s. 6d.

Armstrong.—*The Poetical Works of Edmund J. Armstrong*. Fcp. 8vo., 5s.

Arnold (Sir Edwin).

The Light of the World: or the Great Consummation. With 14 Illustrations after Holman Hunt. Cr. 8vo., 6s.

Potiphar's Wife, and other Poems. Crown 8vo., 5s. net.

Adzuma: or the Japanese Wife. A Play. Crown 8vo., 6s. 6d. net.

The Tenth Muse, and other Poems. Crown 8vo., 5s. net.

Beesly (A. H.).

Ballads and other Verse. Fcp. 8vo., 5s.

Danton, and other Verse. Fcp. 8vo., 4s. 6d.

Bell (Mrs. Hugh).

Chamber Comedies: a Collection of Plays and Monologues for the Drawing Room. Crown 8vo., 6s.

Fairy Tale Plays, and How to Act Them. With 91 Diagrams and 52 Illustrations. Crown 8vo., 6s.

Carmichael.—*Poems*. By Jennings Carmichael (Mrs. Francis Mullis). Crown 8vo, 6s. net.

Christie.—*Lays and Verses*. By Nimmo Christie. Crown 8vo., 3s. 6d.

Cochrane (Alfred).

The Kestrel's Nest, and oth Verses. Fcp. 8vo., 3s. 6d.

Leviore Plectro: Occasion Verses. Fcap. 8vo., 3s. 6d.

Florian's Fables.—*The Fables* Florian. Done into English Verse by Philip Perring, Bart. Cr. 8vo., 3s. 6d

Goethe.

Faust, Part I., the German Te with Introduction and Notes. By Albe M. Selss, Ph.D., M.A. Crown 8vo.,

Faust. Translated, with Note By T. E. Webb. 8vo., 12s. 6d.

Gurney.—*Day-Dreams*: Poem By Rev. Alfred Gurney, M.A. Cro 8vo., 3s. 6d.

Ingelow (Jean).

Poetical Works. 2 vols. Fc 8vo., 12s.

Lyrical and other Poems. Sele ted from the Writings of Jean Ingelo Fcp. 8vo., 2s. 6d. cloth plain, 3s. cloth g

Lang (Andrew).

Ban and Arrière Ban: a Rally Fugitive Rhymes. Fcp. 8vo., 5s. net.

Grass of Parnassus. Fcp. 8v 2s. 6d. net.

Ballads of Books. Edited ANDREW LANG. Fcp. 8vo., 6s.

The Blue Poetry Book. Edit by Andrew Lang. With 100 Illustratio Crown 8vo., 6s.

Lecky.—*Poems*. By W. E. Lecky. Fcp. 8vo., 5s.

Lindsay.—*The Flower Selle* and other Poems. By Lady Linds Crown 8vo., 5s.

Lytton (The Earl of), (Ow Meredith).

Marah. Fcp. 8vo., 6s. 6d.

King Poppy: a Fantasia. With Plate and Design on Title-Page by Burne-Jones, A.R.A. Cr. 8vo., 10s.

The Wanderer. Cr. 8vo., 10s. 6

Lucile. Crown 8vo., 10s. 6d.

Selected Poems. Cr. 8vo., 10s.

Poetry and the Drama—*continued.*

Macaulay.—*LAYS OF ANCIENT ROME, &c.* By Lord MACAULAY.
Illustrated by G. SCHARF. Fcp. 4to., 10s. 6d.
——————————————— Bijou Edition.
18mo., 2s. 6d. gilt top.
——————————————— Popular Edition.
Fcp. 4to., 6d. sewed, 1s. cloth.
Illustrated by J. R. WEGUELIN. Crown 8vo., 3s. 6d.
Annotated Edition. Fcp. 8vo., 1s. sewed, 1s. 6d. cloth.

Macdonald (GEORGE, LL.D.).
A BOOK OF STRIFE, IN THE FORM OF THE DIARY OF AN OLD SOUL: Poems. 18mo., 6s.
RAMPOLLO; GROWTHS FROM AN OLD ROOT; containing a Book of Translations, old and new; also a Year's Diary of an Old Soul. Crown 8vo., 6s.

Morris (WILLIAM).
POETICAL WORKS—LIBRARY EDITION. Complete in Ten Volumes. Crown 8vo., price 6s. each.
THE EARTHLY PARADISE. 4 vols. 6s. each.
THE LIFE AND DEATH OF JASON. 6s.
THE DEFENCE OF GUENEVERE, and other Poems. 6s.
THE STORY OF SIGURD THE VOLSUNG, AND THE FALL OF THE NIBLUNGS. 6s.
LOVE IS ENOUGH; or, the Freeing of Pharamond: A Morality; and *POEMS BY THE WAY.* 6s.
THE ODYSSEY OF HOMER. Done into English Verse. 6s.
THE ÆNEIDS OF VIRGIL. Done into English Verse. 6s.
———————
Certain of the POETICAL WORKS may also be had in the following Editions:—
THE EARTHLY PARADISE.
Popular Edition. 5 vols. 12mo., 25s.; or 5s. each, sold separately.
The same in Ten Parts, 25s.; or 2s. 6d. each, sold separately.
Cheap Edition, in 1 vol. Crown 8vo., 7s. 6d.
LOVE IS ENOUGH; or, the Freeing of Pharamond: A Morality. Square crown 8vo., 7s. 6d.
POEMS BY THE WAY. Square crown 8vo., 6s.
⁎⁎ For Mr. William Morris's Prose Works, see pp. 22 and 31.

Murray (ROBERT F.).—Author of 'The Scarlet Gown'. His Poems, with a Memoir by ANDREW LANG. Fcp. 8vo., 5s. net.

Nesbit.—*LAYS AND LEGENDS.* By E. NESBIT (Mrs. HUBERT BLAND). First Series. Crown 8vo., 3s. 6d. Second Series. With Portrait. Crown 8vo., 5s.

Peek (HEDLEY) (FRANK LEYTON).
SKELETON LEAVES: Poems. With a Dedicatory Poem to the late Hon. Roden Noel. Fcp. 8vo., 2s. 6d. net.
THE SHADOWS OF THE LAKE, and other Poems. Fcp. 8vo., 2s. 6d. net.

Piatt (SARAH).
AN ENCHANTED CASTLE, AND OTHER POEMS: Pictures, Portraits, and People in Ireland. Crown 8vo., 3s. 6d.
POEMS: With Portrait of the Author. 2 vols. Crown 8vo., 10s.

Piatt (JOHN JAMES).
IDYLS AND LYRICS OF THE OHIO VALLEY. Crown 8vo., 5s.
LITTLE NEW WORLD IDYLS. Cr. 8vo., 5s.

Rhoades.—*TERESA AND OTHER POEMS.* By JAMES RHOADES. Crown 8vo., 3s. 6d.

Riley (JAMES WHITCOMB).
OLD FASHIONED ROSES: Poems. 12mo., 5s.
POEMS: Here at Home. Fcp. 8vo 6s. net.
A CHILD-WORLD: POEMS. Fcp. 8vo., 5s.

Romanes.—*A SELECTION FROM THE POEMS OF GEORGE JOHN ROMANES, M.A., LL.D., F.R.S.* With an Introduction by T. HERBERT WARREN, President of Magdalen College, Oxford. Crown 8vo., 4s. 6d.

Shakespeare.—*BOWDLER'S FAMILY SHAKESPEARE.* With 36 Woodcuts. 1 vol. 8vo., 14s. Or in 6 vols. Fcp. 8vo., 21s.
THE SHAKESPEARE BIRTHDAY BOOK. By MARY F. DUNBAR. 32mo., 1s. 6d.

Sturgis.—*A BOOK OF SONG.* By JULIAN STURGIS. 16mo. 5s.

Works of Fiction, Humour, &c.

Alden.—*AMONG THE FREAKS.* By W. L. ALDEN. With 55 Illustrations by J. F. SULLIVAN and FLORENCE K. UPTON. Crown 8vo., 3s. 6d.

Anstey (F., Author of 'Vice Versâ').

VOCES POPULI. Reprinted from 'Punch'. First Series. With 20 Illustrations by J. BERNARD PARTRIDGE. Crown 8vo., 3s. 6d.

THE MAN FROM BLANKLEY'S: a Story in Scenes, and other Sketches. With 24 Illustrations by J. BERNARD PARTRIDGE. Post 4to., 6s.

Astor.—*A JOURNEY IN OTHER WORLDS:* a Romance of the Future. By JOHN JACOB ASTOR. With 10 Illustrations. Cr. 8vo., 6s.

Baker.—*BY THE WESTERN SEA.* By JAMES BAKER, Author of 'John Westacott'. Crown 8vo., 3s. 6d.

Beaconsfield (THE EARL OF).

NOVELS AND TALES. Complete in 11 vols. Crown 8vo., 1s. 6d. each.

Vivian Grey.	Sybil.
The Young Duke, &c.	Henrietta Temple.
Alroy, Ixion, &c.	Venetia.
Contarini Fleming, &c.	Coningsby.
	Lothair.
Tancred.	Endymion.

NOVELS AND TALES. The Hughenden Edition. With 2 Portraits and 11 Vignettes. 11 vols. Crown 8vo., 42s.

Black.—*THE PRINCESS DÉSIRÉE.* By CLEMENTINA BLACK. With 8 Illustrations by JOHN WILLIAMSON. Cr. 8vo., 6s.

Crump.—*WIDE ASUNDER AS THE POLES.* By ARTHUR CRUMP. Cr. 8vo., 6s.

Dougall (L.).

BEGGARS ALL. Cr. 8vo., 3s. 6d.

WHAT NECESSITY KNOWS. Crown 8vo., 6s.

Doyle (A. CONAN).

MICAH CLARKE: A Tale of Monmouth's Rebellion. With 10 Illustrations. Cr. 8vo., 3s. 6d.

THE CAPTAIN OF THE POLESTAR, and other Tales. Cr. 8vo., 3s. 6d.

THE REFUGEES: A Tale of Two Continents. With 25 Illustrations. Cr. 8vo., 3s. 6d.

THE STARK MUNRO LETTERS. Cr. 8vo, 6s.

Farrar (F. W., DEAN OF CANTERBURY).

DARKNESS AND DAWN: or, Scenes in the Days of Nero. An Historic Tale. Cr. 8vo., 7s. 6d.

GATHERING CLOUDS: a Tale of the Days of St. Chrysostom. Cr. 8vo., 7s. 6d.

Fowler.—*THE YOUNG PRETENDERS.* A Story of Child Life. By EDITH H. FOWLER. With 12 Illustrations by PHILIP BURNE-JONES. Crown 8vo., 6s.

Froude.—*THE TWO CHIEFS OF DUNBOY:* an Irish Romance of the Last Century. By JAMES A. FROUDE. Cr. 8vo., 3s. 6d.

Graham.—*THE RED SCAUR:* A Novel of Manners. By P. ANDERSON GRAHAM. Crown 8vo., 6s.

Haggard (H. RIDER).

HEART OF THE WORLD. With 15 Illustrations. Crown 8vo., 6s.

JOAN HASTE. With 20 Illustrations. Crown 8vo., 6s.

THE PEOPLE OF THE MIST. With 16 Illustrations. Crown 8vo., 3s. 6d.

MONTEZUMA'S DAUGHTER. With 24 Illustrations. Crown 8vo., 3s. 6d.

SHE. With 32 Illustrations. Crown 8vo., 3s. 6d.

ALLAN QUATERMAIN. With 31 Illustrations. Crown 8vo., 3s. 6d.

MAIWA'S REVENGE: Cr. 8vo., 1s. 6d.

COLONEL QUARITCH, V.C. Cr. 8vo. 3s. 6d.

CLEOPATRA. With 29 Illustrations. Crown 8vo., 3s. 6d.

Works of Fiction, Humour, &c.—*continued.*

Haggard (H. RIDER)—*continued.*

BEATRICE. Cr. 8vo., 3*s.* 6*d.*

ERIC BRIGHTEYES. With 51 Illustrations. Crown 8vo., 3*s.* 6*d.*

NADA THE LILY. With 23 Illustrations. Crown 8vo., 3*s.* 6*d.*

ALLAN'S WIFE. With 34 Illustrations. Crown 8vo., 3*s.* 6*d.*

THE WITCH'S HEAD. With 16 Illustrations. Crown 8vo., 3*s.* 6*d.*

MR. MEESON'S WILL. With 16 Illustrations. Crown 8vo., 3*s.* 6*d.*

DAWN. With 16 Illustrations. Cr. 8vo., 3*s.* 6*d.*

Haggard and Lang.—*THE WORLD'S DESIRE.* By H. RIDER HAGGARD and ANDREW LANG. With 27 Illustrations. Crown 8vo., 3*s.* 6*d.*

Harte.—*IN THE CARQUINEZ WOODS* and other stories. By BRET HARTE. Cr. 8vo., 3*s.* 6*d.*

Hope.—*THE HEART OF PRINCESS OSRA.* By ANTHONY HOPE. With 9 Illustrations by JOHN WILLIAMSON. Crown 8vo., 6*s.*

Hornung.—*THE UNBIDDEN GUEST.* By E. W. HORNUNG. Crown 8vo., 3*s.* 6*d.*

Lang.—*A MONK OF FIFE;* being the Chronicle written by NÒRMAN LESLIE of Pitcullo, concerning Marvellous Deeds that befel in the Realm of France, 1429-31. By ANDREW LANG. With 13 Illustrations by SELWYN IMAGE. Cr. 8vo., 6*s.*

Lyall (EDNA).

THE AUTOBIOGRAPHY OF A SLANDER. Fcp. 8vo., 1*s.*, sewed.

Presentation Edition. With 20 Illustrations by LANCELOT SPEED. Crown 8vo., 2*s.* 6*d.* net.

THE AUTOBIOGRAPHY OF A TRUTH. Fcp. 8vo., 1*s.*, sewed; 1*s.* 6*d.*, cloth.

DOREEN. The Story of a Singer. Crown 8vo., 6*s.*

Magruder.—*THE VIOLET.* By JULIA MAGRUDER. With 11 Illustrations by C. D. GIBSON. Crown 8vo., 6*s.*

Matthews.—*HIS FATHER'S SON:* a Novel of the New York Stock Exchange. By BRANDER MATTHEWS. With 13 Illustrations. Cr. 8vo., 6*s.*

Melville (G. J. WHYTE).

The Gladiators.	Holmby House.
The Interpreter.	Kate Coventry.
Good for Nothing.	Digby Grand.
The Queen's Maries.	General Bounce.

Crown 8vo., 1*s.* 6*d.* each.

Merriman.—*FLOTSAM:* The Study of a Life. By HENRY SETON MERRIMAN, With Frontispiece and Vignette by H. G. MASSEY, A.R.E. Crown 8vo., 6*s.*

Morris (WILLIAM).

THE WELL AT THE WORLD'S END. 2 vols. 8vo., 28*s.*

THE STORY OF THE GLITTERING PLAIN, which has been also called The Land of the Living Men, or The Acre of the Undying. Square post 8vo., 5*s.* net.

THE ROOTS OF THE MOUNTAINS, wherein is told somewhat of the Lives of the Men of Burgdale, their Friends, their Neighbours, their Foemen, and their Fellows-in-Arms. Written in Prose and Verse. Square crown 8vo., 8*s.*

A TALE OF THE HOUSE OF THE WOLFINGS, and all the Kindreds of the Mark. Written in Prose and Verse. Second Edition. Square crown 8vo., 6*s.*

A DREAM OF JOHN BALL, AND A KING'S LESSON. 12mo., 1*s.* 6*d.*

NEWS FROM NOWHERE; or, An Epoch of Rest. Being some Chapters from an Utopian Romance. Post 8vo., 1*s.* 6*d.*

*** For Mr. William Morris's Poetical Works, see p. 20.

Newman (CARDINAL).

LOSS AND GAIN: The Story of a Convert. Crown 8vo. Cabinet Edition, 6*s.*; Popular Edition, 3*s.* 6*d.*

CALLISTA: A Tale of the Third Century. Crown 8vo. Cabinet Edition, 6*s.*; Popular Edition, 3*s.* 6*d.*

Oliphant.—*OLD MR. TREDGOLD.* By Mrs. OLIPHANT. Crown 8vo., 6*s.*

Phillipps-Wolley.—*SNAP:* a Legend of the Lone Mountain. By C. PHILLIPPS-WOLLEY. With 13 Illustrations. Crown 8vo., 3*s.* 6*d.*

Quintana.—*THE CID CAMPEADOR:* an Historical Romance. By D. ANTONIO DE TRUEBA Y LA QUINTANA. Translated from the Spanish by HENRY J. GILL, M.A., T.C.D. Crown 8vo., 6*s.*

Works of Fiction, Humour, &c.—*continued.*

Rhoscomyl (OWEN).

THE JEWEL OF YNYS GALON: being a hitherto unprinted Chapter in the History of the Sea Rovers. With 12 Illustrations by LANCELOT SPEED. Cr. 8vo., 3s. 6d.

BATTLEMENT AND TOWER: a Romance. With Frontispiece by R. CATON WOODVILLE. Crown 8vo., 6s.

FOR THE WHITE ROSE OF ARNO: a Story of the Jacobite Rising of 1745. Crown 8vo., 6s.

Rokeby.—*DORCAS HOBDAY.* By CHARLES ROKEBY. Crown 8vo., 6s.

Sewell (ELIZABETH M.).

A Glimpse of the World.	Amy Herbert.
Laneton Parsonage.	Cleve Hall.
Margaret Percival.	Gertrude.
Katharine Ashton.	Home Life.
The Earl's Daughter.	After Life.
The Experience of Life.	Ursula. Ivors.

Cr. 8vo., 1s. 6d. each cloth plain. 2s. 6d each cloth extra, gilt edges.

Stevenson (ROBERT LOUIS).

THE STRANGE CASE OF DR. JEKYLL AND MR. HYDE. Fcp. 8vo., 1s. sewed. 1s. 6d. cloth.

THE STRANGE CASE OF DR. JEKYLL AND MR. HYDE; WITH OTHER FABLES. Crown 8vo., 3s. 6d.

MORE NEW ARABIAN NIGHTS—THE DYNAMITER. By ROBERT LOUIS STEVENSON and FANNY VAN DE GRIFT STEVENSON. Crown 8vo., 3s. 6d.

THE WRONG BOX. By ROBERT LOUIS STEVENSON and LLOYD OSBOURNE. Crown 8vo., 3s. 6d.

Suttner.—*LAY DOWN YOUR ARMS* (*Die Waffen Nieder*): The Autobiography of Martha Tilling. By BERTHA VON SUTTNER. Translated by T. HOLMES. Cr. 8vo., 1s. 6d.

Trollope (ANTHONY).

THE WARDEN. Cr. 8vo., 1s. 6d.

BARCHESTER TOWERS. Cr. 8vo., 1s. 6d.

TRUE (A) RELATION OF THE TRAVELS AND PERILOUS ADVENTURES OF MATHEW DUDGEON, GENTLEMAN: Wherein is truly set down the Manner of his Taking, the Long Time of his Slavery in Algiers, and Means of his Delivery. Written by Himself, and now for the first time printed. Cr. 8vo., 5s.

Walford (L. B.).

MR. SMITH: a Part of his Life. Crown 8vo., 2s. 6d.

THE BABY'S GRANDMOTHER. Cr. 8vo., 2s. 6d.

COUSINS. Crown 8vo., 2s. 6d.

TROUBLESOME DAUGHTERS. Cr. 8vo., 2s. 6d.

PAULINE. Crown. 8vo., 2s. 6d.

DICK NETHERBY. Cr. 8vo., 2s. 6d.

THE HISTORY OF A WEEK. Cr. 8vo. 2s. 6d.

A STIFF-NECKED GENERATION. Cr. 8vo. 2s. 6d.

NAN, and other Stories. Cr. 8vo., 2s. 6d.

THE MISCHIEF OF MONICA. Cr. 8vo., 2s. 6d.

THE ONE GOOD GUEST. Cr. 8vo. 2s. 6d.

'PLOUGHED,' and other Stories. Crown 8vo., 2s. 6d.

THE MATCHMAKER. Cr. 8vo., 2s. 6d.

West (B. B.).

HALF-HOURS WITH THE MILLIONAIRES: Showing how much harder it is to spend a million than to make it. Cr. 8vo., 6s.

SIR SIMON VANDERPETTER, and *MINDING HIS ANCESTORS.* Cr. 8vo., 5s.

A FINANCIAL ATONEMENT. Cr. 8vo., 6s.

Weyman (STANLEY).

THE HOUSE OF THE WOLF. Cr. 8vo., 3s. 6d.

A GENTLEMAN OF FRANCE. Cr. 8vo., 6s.

THE RED COCKADE. Cr. 8vo., 6s.

Whishaw.—*A BOYAR OF THE TERRIBLE:* a Romance of the Court of Ivan the Cruel, First Tzar of Russia. By FRED. WHISHAW. With 12 Illustrations by H. G. MASSEY, A.R.E. Crown 8vo., 6s.

Popular Science (Natural History, &c.).

Butler.—*OUR HOUSEHOLD INSECTS.* An Account of the Insect-Pests found in Dwelling-Houses. By EDWARD A. BUTLER, B.A., B.Sc. (Lond.). With 113 Illustrations. Crown 8vo., 3s. 6d.

Furneaux (W.).

THE OUTDOOR WORLD; or The Young Collector's Handbook. With 18 Plates 16 of which are coloured, and 549 Illustrations in the Text. Crown 8vo., 7s. 6d.

BUTTERFLIES AND MOTHS (British). With 12 coloured Plates and 241 Illustrations in the Text. Crown 8vo., 12s. 6d.

LIFE IN PONDS AND STREAMS. With 8 coloured Plates and 331 Illustrations in the Text. Crown 8vo., 12s. 6d.

Hartwig (Dr. George).

THE SEA AND ITS LIVING WONDERS. With 12 Plates and 303 Woodcuts. 8vo., 7s. net.

THE TROPICAL WORLD. With 8 Plates and 172 Woodcuts. 8vo., 7s. net.

THE POLAR WORLD. With 3 Maps, 8 Plates and 85 Woodcuts. 8vo., 7s. net.

THE SUBTERRANEAN WORLD. With 3 Maps and 80 Woodcuts. 8vo., 7s. net.

THE AERIAL WORLD. With Map, 8 Plates and 60 Woodcuts. 8vo., 7s. net.

HEROES OF THE POLAR WORLD. 19 Illustrations. Cr. 8vo., 2s.

WONDERS OF THE TROPICAL FORESTS. 40 Illustrations. Cr. 8vo., 2s.

WORKERS UNDER THE GROUND. 29 Illustrations. Cr. 8vo., 2s.

MARVELS OVER OUR HEADS. 29 Illustrations. Cr. 8vo., 2s.

SEA MONSTERS AND SEA BIRDS. 75 Illustrations. Cr. 8vo., 2s. 6d.

DENIZENS OF THE DEEP. 117 Illustrations. Cr. 8vo., 2s. 6d.

Hartwig (Dr. George)—*continued.*

VOLCANOES AND EARTHQUAKES. 30 Illustrations. Cr. 8vo., 2s. 6d.

WILD ANIMALS OF THE TROPICS. 66 Illustrations. Cr. 8vo., 3s. 6d.

Hayward.—*BIRD NOTES.* By the late JANE MARY HAYWARD. Edited by EMMA HUBBARD. With Frontispiece and 15 Illustrations by G. E. LODGE. Cr. 8vo., 6s.

Helmholtz.—*POPULAR LECTURES ON SCIENTIFIC SUBJECTS.* By HERMANN VON HELMHOLTZ. With 68 Woodcuts. 2 vols. Cr. 8vo., 3s. 6d. each.

Hudson.—*BRITISH BIRDS.* By W. H. HUDSON, C.M.Z.S. With a Chapter on Structure and Classification by FRANK E, BEDDARD, F.R.S. With 16 Plates (8 of which are Coloured), and over 100 Illustrations in the Text. Crown 8vo., 12s. 6d.

Proctor (Richard A.).

LIGHT SCIENCE FOR LEISURE HOURS. Familiar Essays on Scientific Subjects. 3 vols. Cr. 8vo., 5s. each.

ROUGH WAYS MADE SMOOTH. Familiar Essays on Scientific Subjects. Crown 8vo., 3s. 6d.

PLEASANT WAYS IN SCIENCE. Crown 8vo., 3s. 6d.

NATURE STUDIES. By R. A. PROCTOR, GRANT ALLEN, A. WILSON, T. FOSTER and E. CLODD. Crown 8vo., 3s. 6d.

LEISURE READINGS. By R. A. PROCTOR, E. CLODD, A. WILSON, T. FOSTER and A. C. RANYARD. Cr. 8vo., 3s. 6d.

*** *For Mr. Proctor's other books see Messrs. Longmans & Co.'s Catalogue of Scientific Works.*

Stanley.—*A FAMILIAR HISTORY OF BIRDS.* By E. STANLEY, D.D., formerly Bishop of Norwich. With Illustrations. Cr. 8vo., 3s. 6d.

Popular Science (Natural History, &c.)—*continued.*

Wood (REV. J. G.).

HOMES WITHOUT HANDS: A Description of the Habitation of Animals, classed according to the Principle of Construction. With 140 Illustrations. 8vo., 7s., net.

INSECTS AT HOME: A Popular Account of British Insects, their Structure, Habits and Transformations. With 700 Illustrations. 8vo., 7s. net.

INSECTS ABROAD: a Popular Account of Foreign Insects, their Structure, Habits and Transformations. With 600 Illustrations. 8vo., 7s. net.

BIBLE ANIMALS: a Description of every Living Creature mentioned in the Scriptures. With 112 Illustrations. 8vo., 7s. net.

PETLAND REVISITED. With 33 Illustrations. Cr. 8vo., 3s. 6d.

OUT OF DOORS; a Selection of Original Articles on Practical Natural History. With 11 Illustrations. Cr. 8vo., 3s. 6d.

Wood (REV. J. G.)—*continued.*

STRANGE DWELLINGS: a Description of the Habitations of Animals, abridged from 'Homes without Hands'. With 60 Illustrations. Cr. 8vo., 3s. 6d.

BIRD LIFE OF THE BIBLE. 32 Illustrations. Cr. 8vo., 3s. 6d.

WONDERFUL NESTS. 30 Illustrations. Cr. 8vo., 3s. 6d.

HOMES UNDER THE GROUND. 28 Illustrations. Cr. 8vo., 3s. 6d.

WILD ANIMALS OF THE BIBLE. 29 Illustrations. Cr. 8vo., 3s. 6d.

DOMESTIC ANIMALS OF THE BIBLE. 23 Illustrations. Cr. 8vo., 3s. 6d.

THE BRANCH BUILDERS. 28 Illustrations. Cr. 8vo., 2s. 6d.

SOCIAL HABITATIONS AND PARASITIC NESTS. 18 Illustrations. Cr. 8vo., 2s.

Works of Reference.

Longmans' *GAZETTEER OF THE WORLD.* Edited by GEORGE G. CHISHOLM, M.A., B.Sc. Imp. 8vo., £2 2s. cloth, £2 12s. 6d. half-morocco.

Maunder (Samuel).

BIOGRAPHICAL TREASURY. With Supplement brought down to 1889. By Rev. JAMES WOOD. Fcp. 8vo., 6s.

TREASURY OF NATURAL HISTORY: or, Popular Dictionary of Zoology. With 900 Woodcuts. Fcp. 8vo., 6s.

TREASURY OF GEOGRAPHY, Physical, Historical, Descriptive, and Political. With 7 Maps and 16 Plates. Fcp. 8vo., 6s.

THE TREASURY OF BIBLE KNOWLEDGE. By the Rev. J. AYRE, M.A. With 5 Maps, 15 Plates, and 300 Woodcuts. Fcp. 8vo., 6s.

TREASURY OF KNOWLEDGE AND LIBRARY OF REFERENCE. Fcp. 8vo., 6s.

Maunder (Samuel)—*continued.*

HISTORICAL TREASURY. Fcp. 8vo., 6s.

SCIENTIFIC AND LITERARY TREASURY. Fcp. 8vo., 6s.

THE TREASURY OF BOTANY. Edited by J. LINDLEY, F.R.S., and T. MOORE, F.L.S. With 274 Woodcuts and 20 Steel Plates. 2 vols. Fcp. 8vo., 12s.

Roget. — *THESAURUS OF ENGLISH WORDS AND PHRASES.* Classified and Arranged so as to Facilitate the Expression of Ideas and assist in Literary Composition. By PETER MARK ROGET, M.D., F.R.S. Recomposed throughout, enlarged and improved, partly from the Author's Notes, and with a full Index, by the Author's Son, JOHN LEWIS ROGET. Crown 8vo., 10s. 6d.

Willich.--*POPULAR TABLES* for giving information for ascertaining the value of Lifehold, Leasehold, and Church Property, the Public Funds, &c. By CHARLES M. WILLICH. Edited by H. BENCE JONES. Crown 8vo., 10s. 6d.

Children's Books.

Crake (REV. A. D.).

EDWY THE FAIR; or, The First Chronicle of Æscendune. Cr. 8vo., 2s. 6d.

ALFGAR THE DANE; or, The Second Chronicle of Æscendune. Cr. 8vo. 2s. 6d.

THE RIVAL HEIRS: being the Third and Last Chronicle of Æscendune. Cr. 8vo., 2s. 6d.

THE HOUSE OF WALDERNE. A Tale of the Cloister and the Forest in the Days of the Barons' Wars. Crown 8vo., 2s. 6d.

BRIAN FITZ-COUNT. A Story of Wallingford Castle and Dorchester Abbey. Cr. 8vo., 2s. 6d.

Lang (ANDREW).—EDITED BY.

THE BLUE FAIRY BOOK. With 138 Illustrations. Crown 8vo., 6s.

THE RED FAIRY BOOK. With 100 Illustrations. Crown 8vo., 6s.

THE GREEN FAIRY BOOK. With 99 Illustrations. Crown 8vo., 6s.

THE YELLOW FAIRY BOOK. With 104 Illustrations. Crown 8vo., 6s.

THE BLUE POETRY BOOK. With 100 Illustrations. Crown 8vo., 6s.

THE BLUE POETRY BOOK. School Edition, without Illustrations. Fcp. 8vo., 2s. 6d.

THE TRUE STORY BOOK. With 66 Illustrations. Crown 8vo., 6s.

THE RED TRUE STORY BOOK. With 100 Illustrations. Crown 8vo., 6s.

THE ANIMAL STORY BOOK. With 67 Illustrations. Crown 8vo., 6s.

Meade (L. T.).

DADDY'S BOY. With Illustrations. Crown 8vo., 3s. 6d.

DEB AND THE DUCHESS. With Illustrations. Crown 8vo., 3s. 6d.

THE BERESFORD PRIZE. With Illustrations. Crown 8vo., 3s. 6d.

THE HOUSE OF SURPRISES. With Illustrations. Crown 8vo. 3s. 6d.

Molesworth—*SILVERTHORNS.* By Mrs. MOLESWORTH. With Illustrations. Cr. 8vo., 5s.

Stevenson.—*A CHILD'S GARDEN OF VERSES.* By ROBERT LOUIS STEVENSON. Fcp. 8vo., 5s.

Upton (FLORENCE K. AND BERTHA).

THE ADVENTURES OF TWO DUTCH DOLLS AND A 'GOLLIWOGG'. Illustrated by FLORENCE K. UPTON, with Words by BERTHA UPTON. With 31 Coloured Plates and numerous Illustrations in the Text. Oblong 4to., 6s.

THE GOLLIWOGG'S BICYCLE CLUB. Illustrated by FLORENCE K. UPTON, with words by BERTHA UPTON. With 31 Coloured Plates and numerous Illustrations in the Text. Oblong 4to., 6s.

Wordsworth.—*THE SNOW GARDEN, AND OTHER FAIRY TALES FOR CHILDREN.* By ELIZABETH WORDSWORTH. With 10 Illustrations by TREVOR HADDON. Crown 8vo., 5s.

Longmans' Series of Books for Girls.

Price 2s. 6d. each.

ATELIER (THE) DU LYS: or, an Art Student in the Reign of Terror.

BY THE SAME AUTHOR.

MADEMOISELLE MORI: a Tale of Modern Rome.

IN THE OLDEN TIME: a Tale of the Peasant War in Germany.

THE YOUNGER SISTER.

THAT CHILD.

UNDER A CLOUD.

HESTER'S VENTURE

THE FIDDLER OF LUGAU.

A CHILD OF THE REVOLUTION.

ATHERSTONE PRIORY. By L. N. COMYN.

THE STORY OF A SPRING MORNING, etc. By Mrs. MOLESWORTH. Illustrated.

THE PALACE IN THE GARDEN. By Mrs. MOLESWORTH. Illustrated.

NEIGHBOURS. By Mrs. MOLESWORTH.

THE THIRD MISS ST. QUENTIN. By Mrs. MOLESWORTH.

VERY YOUNG; AND QUITE ANOTHER STORY. Two Stories. By JEAN INGELOW.

CAN THIS BE LOVE? By LOUISA PARR.

KEITH DERAMORE. By the Author of ' Miss Molly '.

SIDNEY. By MARGARET DELAND.

AN ARRANGED MARRIAGE. By DOROTHEA GERARD.

LAST WORDS TO GIRLS ON LIFE AT SCHOOL AND AFTER SCHOOL. By MARIA GREY.

STRAY THOUGHTS FOR GIRLS. By LUCY H. M. SOULSBY, Head Mistress of Oxford High School. 16mo., 1s. 6d. net.

The Silver Library.

CROWN 8VO. 3s. 6d. EACH VOLUME.

Arnold's (Sir Edwin) Seas and Lands. With 71 Illustrations. 3s. 6d.

Bagehot's (W.) Biographical Studies. 3s. 6d.

Bagehot's (W.) Economic Studies. 3s. 6d.

Bagehot's (W.) Literary Studies. With Portrait. 3 vols, 3s. 6d. each.

Baker's (Sir S. W.) Eight Years in Ceylon. With 6 Illustrations. 3s. 6d.

Baker's (Sir S. W.) Rifle and Hound in Ceylon. With 6 Illustrations. 3s. 6d.

Baring-Gould's (Rev. S.) Curious Myths of the Middle Ages. 3s. 6d.

Baring-Gould's (Rev. S.) Origin and Development of Religious Belief. 2 vols. 3s. 6d. each.

Becker's (Prof.) Gallus: or, Roman Scenes in the Time of Augustus. Illustrated. 3s. 6d.

Becker's (Prof.) Charicles: or, Illustrations of the Private Life of the Ancient Greeks. Illustrated. 3s. 6d.

Bent's (J. T.) The Ruined Cities of Mashonaland. With 117 Illustrations. 3s. 6d.

Brassey's (Lady) A Voyage in the 'Sunbeam'. With 66 Illustrations. 3s. 6d.

Butler's (Edward A.) Our Household Insects. With 7 Plates and 113 Illustrations in the Text. 3s. 6d.

Clodd's (E.) Story of Creation: a Plain Account of Evolution. With 77 Illustrations. 3s. 6d.

Conybeare (Rev. W. J.) and Howson's (Very Rev. J. S.) Life and Epistles of St. Paul. 46 Illustrations. 3s. 6d.

Dougall's (L.) Beggars All: a Novel. 3s. 6d.

Doyle's (A. Conan) Micah Clarke. A Tale of Monmouth's Rebellion. 10 Illusts. 3s. 6d.

Doyle's (A. Conan) The Captain of the Polestar, and other Tales. 3s. 6d.

Doyle's (A. Conan) The Refugees: A Tale of Two Continents. With 25 Illustrations. 3s 6d.

Froude's (J. A.) The History of England, from the Fall of Wolsey to the Defeat of the Spanish Armada. 12 vols. 3s. 6d. each.

Froude's (J. A.) The English in Ireland. 3 vols. 10s. 6d.

Froude's (J. A.) The Divorce of Catherine of Aragon. 3s. 6d.

Froude's (J. A.) The Spanish Story of the Armada, and other Essays. 3s. 6d.

Froude's (J. A.) Short Studies on Great Subjects. 4 vols. 3s. 6d. each.

Froude's (J. A.) Thomas Carlyle: a History of his Life.
1795-1835. 2 vols. 7s.
1834-1881. 2 vols. 7s.

Froude's (J. A.) Cæsar: a Sketch. 3s. 6d.

Froude's (J. A.) The Two Chiefs of Dunboy: an Irish Romance of the Last Century. 3s. 6d.

Gleig's (Rev. G. R.) Life of the Duke of Wellington. With Portrait. 3s. 6d.

Greville's (C. C. F.) Journal of the Reigns of King George IV., King William IV., and Queen Victoria. 8 vols., 3s. 6d. each.

Haggard's (H. R.) She: A History of Adventure. 32 Illustrations. 3s. 6d.

Haggard's (H. R.) Allan Quatermain. With 20 Illustrations. 3s. 6d.

Haggard's (H. R.) Colonel Quaritch, V.C.: a Tale of Country Life. 3s. 6d.

Haggard's (H. R.) Cleopatra. With 29 Illustrations. 3s. 6d.

Haggard's (H. R.) Eric Brighteyes. With 51 Illustrations. 3s. 6d.

Haggard's (H. R.) Beatrice. 3s. 6d.

Haggard's (H. R.) Allan's Wife. With 34 Illustrations. 3s. 6d.

Haggard's (H. R.) Montezuma's Daughter. With 25 Illustrations. 3s. 6d.

Haggard's (H. R.) The Witch's Head. With 16 Illustrations. 3s. 6d.

Haggard's (H. R.) Mr. Meeson's Will. With 16 Illustrations. 3s. 6d.

Haggard's (H. R.) Nada the Lily. With 23 Illustrations. 3s. 6d.

Haggard's (H. R.) Dawn. With 16 Illusts. 3s. 6d.

Haggard's (H. R.) The People of the Mist. With 16 Illustrations. 3s. 6d.

Haggard (H. R.) and Lang's (A.) The World's Desire. With 27 Illustrations. 3s. 6d.

Harte's (Bret) In the Carquinez Woods and other Stories. 3s. 6d.

Helmholtz's (Hermann von) Popular Lectures on Scientific Subjects. With 68 Illustrations. 2 vols. 3s. 6d. each.

Hornung's (E. W.) The Unbidden Guest. 3s. 6d.

Howitt's (W.) Visits to Remarkable Places. 80 Illustrations. 3s. 6d.

Jefferies' (R.) The Story of My Heart: My Autobiography. With Portrait. 3s. 6d.

Jefferies' (R.) Field and Hedgerow. With Portrait. 3s. 6d.

Jefferies' (R.) Red Deer. 17 Illustrations. 3s. 6d.

Jefferies' (R.) Wood Magic: a Fable. With Frontispiece and Vignette by E. V. B. 3s. 6d.

Jefferies (R.) The Toilers of the Field. With Portrait from the Bust in Salisbury Cathedral. 3s. 6d.

Knight's (E. F.) The Cruise of the 'Alerte': the Narrative of a Search for Treasure on the Desert Island of Trinidad. With 2 Maps and 23 Illustrations. 3s. 6d.

Knight's (E. F.) Where Three Empires Meet: a Narrative of Recent Travel in Kashmir, Western Tibet, Baltistan, Gilgit. With a Map and 54 Illustrations. 3s. 6d.

Knight's (E. F.) The 'Falcon' on the Baltic: a Coasting Voyage from Hammersmith to Copenhagen in a Three-Ton Yacht. With Map and 11 Illustrations. 3s. 6d.

Lang's (A.) Angling Sketches. 20 Illustrations. 3s. 6d.

Lang's (A.) Custom and Myth: Studies of Early Usage and Belief. 3s. 6d.

Lang's (Andrew) Cock Lane and Common-Sense. With a New Preface. 3s. 6d.

The Silver Library—*continued.*

Lees (J. A.) and Clutterbuck's (W. J.) B. C. 1887, A Ramble in British Columbia. With Maps and 75 Illustrations. 3*s.* 6*d.*

Macaulay's (Lord) Essays and Lays of Ancient Rome. With Portrait and Illustration. 3*s.* 6*d.*

Macleod's (H. D.) Elements of Banking. 3*s.* 6*d.*

Marshman's (J. C.) Memoirs of Sir Henry Havelock. 3*s.* 6*d.*

Max Müller's (F.) India, what can it teach us? 3*s.* 6*d.*

Max Müller's (F.) Introduction to the Science of Religion. 3*s.* 6*d.*

Merivale's (Dean) History of the Romans under the Empire. 8 vols. 3*s.* 6*d.* each.

Mill's (J. S.) Political Economy. 3*s.* 6*d.*

Mill's (J. S.) System of Logic. 3*s.* 6*d.*

Milner's (Geo.) Country Pleasures : the Chronicle of a Year chiefly in a Garden. 3*s.* 6*d.*

Nansen's (F.) The First Crossing of Greenland. With Illustrations and a Map. 3*s.* 6*d.*

Phillipps-Wolley's (C.) Snap : a Legend of the Lone Mountain. 13 Illustrations. 3*s.* 6*d.*

Proctor's (R. A.) The Orbs Around Us. 3*s.* 6*d.*

Proctor's (R. A.) The Expanse of Heaven. 3*s.* 6*d.*

Proctor's (R. A.) Other Worlds than Ours. 3*s.*6*d.*

Proctor's (R. A.) Our Place among Infinities : a Series of Essays contrasting our Little Abode in Space and Time with the Infinities around us. Crown 8vo., 3*s.* 6*d.*

Proctor's (R. A.) Other Suns than Ours. 3*s.* 6*d.*

Proctor's (R. A.) Rough Ways made Smooth. 3*s.* 6*d.*

Proctor's (R. A.) Pleasant Ways in Science. 3*s.* 6*d.*

Proctor's (R. A.) Myths and Marvels of Astronomy. 3*s.* 6*d.*

Proctor's (R. A.) Nature Studies. 3*s.* 6*d.*

Proctor's (R. A.) Leisure Readings. By R. A. PROCTOR, EDWARD CLODD, ANDREW WILSON, THOMAS FOSTER, and A. C. RANYARD. With Illustrations. 3*s.* 6*d.*

Rhoscomyl's (Owen) The Jewel of Ynys Galon. With 12 Illustrations. 3*s.* 6*d.*

Rossetti's (Maria F.) A Shadow of Dante. 3*s.* 6*d.*

Smith's (R. Bosworth) Carthage and the Carthaginians. With Maps, Plans, &c. 3*s.* 6*d.*

Stanley's (Bishop) Familiar History of Birds. 160 Illustrations. 3*s.* 6*d.*

Stevenson's (R. L.) The Strange Case of Dr. Jekyll and Mr. Hyde ; with other Fables. 3*s.* 6*d.*

Stevenson (R. L.) and Osbourne's (Ll.) The Wrong Box. 3*s.* 6*d.*

Stevenson (Robert Louis) and Stevenson's (Fanny van de Grift) More New Arabian Nights.—The Dynamiter. 3*s.* 6*d.*

Weyman's (Stanley J.) The House of the Wolf : a Romance. 3*s.* 6*d.*

Wood's (Rev. J. G.) Petland Revisited. With 33 Illustrations. 3*s.* 6*d.*

Wood's (Rev. J. G.) Strange Dwellings. With 60 Illustrations. 3*s.* 6*d.*

Wood's (Rev. J. G.) Out of Doors. With 11 Illustrations. 3*s.* 6*d.*

Cookery, Domestic Management, Gardening, &c.

Acton. — *MODERN COOKERY.* By ELIZA ACTON. With 150 Woodcuts. Fcp. 8vo., 4*s.* 6*d.*

Bull (THOMAS, M.D.).

HINTS TO MOTHERS ON THE MANAGEMENT OF THEIR HEALTH DURING THE PERIOD OF PREGNANCY. Fcp. 8vo., 1*s.* 6*d.*

THE MATERNAL MANAGEMENT OF CHILDREN IN HEALTH AND DISEASE. Fcp. 8vo., 1*s.* 6*d.*

De Salis (MRS.).

CAKES AND CONFECTIONS À LA MODE. Fcp. 8vo., 1*s.* 6*d.*

DOGS : A Manual for Amateurs. Fcp. 8vo., 1*s.* 6*d.*

DRESSED GAME AND POULTRY À LA MODE. Fcp. 8vo., 1*s.* 6*d.*

De Salis (MRS.).—*continued.*

DRESSED VEGETABLES À LA MODE. Fcp. 8vo., 1*s.* 6*d.*

DRINKS À LA MODE. Fcp. 8vo., 1*s.*6*d.*

ENTRÉES À LA MODE. Fcp. 8vo., 1*s.* 6*d.*

FLORAL DECORATIONS. Fcp. 8vo., 1*s.* 6*d.*

GARDENING À LA MODE. Fcp. 8vo. Part I., Vegetables, 1*s.* 6*d.* Part II., Fruits, 1*s.* 6*d.*

NATIONAL VIANDS À LA MODE. Fcp. 8vo., 1*s.* 6*d.*

NEW-LAID EGGS. Fcp. 8vo., 1*s.* 6*d.*

OYSTERS À LA MODE. Fcp. 8vo., 1*s.* 6*d.*

Cookery, Domestic Management, &c.—*continued*.

De Salis (MRS.).—*continued*.

PUDDINGS AND PASTRY À LA MODE. Fcp. 8vo., 1s. 6d.

SAVOURIES À LA MODE. Fcp. 8vo., 1s. 6d.

SOUPS AND DRESSED FISH À LA MODE. Fcp. 8vo., 1s. 6d.

SWEETS AND SUPPER DISHES À LA MODE. Fcp. 8vo., 1s. 6d.

TEMPTING DISHES FOR SMALL INCOMES. Fcp. 8vo., 1s. 6d.

WRINKLES AND NOTIONS FOR EVERY HOUSEHOLD. Crown 8vo., 1s. 6d.

Lear.—*MAIGRE COOKERY.* By H. L. SIDNEY LEAR. 16mo., 2s.

Poole.—*COOKERY FOR THE DIABETIC.* By W. H. and Mrs. POOLE. With Preface by Dr. PAVY. Fcp. 8vo., 2s. 6d.

Walker (JANE H.).

A BOOK FOR EVERY WOMAN. Part I., The Management of Children in Health and out of Health. Crown 8vo., 2s. 6d.
Part II. Woman in Health and out of Health. Crown 8vo., 2s. 6d.

A HANDBOOK FOR MOTHERS : being. being Simple Hints to Women on the Management of their Health during Pregnancy and Confinement, together with Plain Directions as to the Care of Infants. Crown 8vo., 2s. 6d.

Miscellaneous and Critical Works.

Allingham.—*VARIETIES IN PROSE.* By WILLIAM ALLINGHAM. 3 vols. Cr. 8vo., 18s. (Vols. 1 and 2, Rambles, by PATRICIUS WALKER. Vol. 3, Irish Sketches, etc.)

Armstrong.—*ESSAYS AND SKETCHES.* By EDMUND J. ARMSTRONG. Fcp. 8vo., 5s.

Bagehot.—*LITERARY STUDIES.* By WALTER BAGEHOT. With Portrait. 3 vols. Crown 8vo., 3s. 6d. each.

Baring-Gould.—*CURIOUS MYTHS OF THE MIDDLE AGES.* By Rev. S. BARING-GOULD. Crown 8vo., 3s. 6d.

Baynes. — *SHAKESPEARE STUDIES,* and other Essays. By the late THOMAS SPENCER BAYNES, LL.B., LL.D. With a Biographical Preface by Professor LEWIS CAMPBELL. Crown 8vo., 7s. 6d.

Boyd (A. K. H.) ('**A.K.H.B.**').

And see MISCELLANEOUS THEOLOGICAL WORKS, *p.* 32.

AUTUMN HOLIDAYS OF A COUNTRY PARSON. Crown 8vo., 3s. 6d.

COMMONPLACE PHILOSOPHER. Cr. 8vo., 3s. 6d.

CRITICAL ESSAYS OF A COUNTRY PARSON. Crown 8vo., 3s. 6d.

EAST COAST DAYS AND MEMORIES. Crown 8vo., 3s. 6d.

LANDSCAPES, CHURCHES, AND MORALITIES. Crown 8vo., 3s. 6d.

LEISURE HOURS IN TOWN. Crown 8vo., 3s. 6d.

Boyd (A. K. H.) ('**A.K.H.B.**').— *continued.*

LESSONS OF MIDDLE AGE. Crown 8vo., 3s. 6d.

OUR LITTLE LIFE. Two Series. Crown 8vo., 3s. 6d. each.

OUR HOMELY COMEDY : AND TRAGEDY. Crown 8vo., 3s. 6d.

RECREATIONS OF A COUNTRY PARSON. Three Series. Crown 8vo., 3s. 6d. each. Also First Series. Popular Edition. 8vo., 6d. Sewed.

Butler (SAMUEL).

EREWHON. Crown 8vo., 5s.

THE FAIR HAVEN. A Work in Defence of the Miraculous Element in our Lord's Ministry. Cr. 8vo., 7s. 6d.

LIFE AND HABIT. An Essay after a Completer View of Evolution. Cr. 8vo., 7s. 6d.

EVOLUTION, OLD AND NEW. Cr. 8vo., 10s. 6d.

ALPS AND SANCTUARIES OF PIEDMONT AND CANTON TICINO. Illustrated. Pott 4to., 10s. 6d.

LUCK, OR CUNNING, AS THE MAIN MEANS OF ORGANIC MODIFICATION? Cr. 8vo., 7s. 6d.

EX VOTO. An Account of the Sacro Monte or New Jerusalem at Varallo-Sesia. Crown 8vo., 10s. 6d.

Miscellaneous and Critical Works—*continued*.

CHARITIES REGISTER, THE ANNUAL, AND DIGEST: being a Classified Register of Charities in or available in the Metropolis, together with a Digest of Information respecting the Legal, Voluntary, and other Means for the Prevention and Relief of Distress, and the Improvement of the Condition of the Poor, and an Elaborate Index. With an Introduction by C. S. LOCH, Secretary to the Council of the Charity Organisation Society, London. 8vo., 4s.

Dreyfus.—LECTURES ON FRENCH LITERATURE. Delivered in Melbourne by IRMA DREYFUS. With Portrait of the Author. Large crown 8vo., 12s. 6d.

Gwilt.—AN ENCYCLOPÆDIA OF ARCHITECTURE. By JOSEPH GWILT, F.S.A. Illustrated with more than 1100 Engravings on Wood. Revised (1888), with Alterations and Considerable Additions by WYATT PAPWORTH. 8vo., £2 12s. 6d.

Hamlin.—A TEXT-BOOK OF THE HISTORY OF ARCHITECTURE. By A. D. F. HAMLIN, A.M., Adjunct-Professor of Architecture in the School of Mines, Columbia College. With 229 Illustrations. Crown 8vo., 7s. 6d.

Haweis.—MUSIC AND MORALS. By the Rev. H. R. HAWEIS. With Portrait of the Author, and numerous Illustrations, Facsimiles, and Diagrams. Crown 8vo., 7s. 6d.

Indian Ideals (No. 1).

NÂRADA SÛTRA: an Inquiry into Love (Bhakti-Jijnâsâ). Translated from the Sanskrit, with an Independendent Commentary, by E. T. STURDY. Crown 8vo., 2s. 6d. net.

Jefferies.—(RICHARD).

FIELD AND HEDGEROW: With Portrait. Crown 8vo., 3s. 6d.

THE STORY OF MY HEART: my Autobiography. With Portrait and New Preface by C. J. LONGMAN. Crown 8vo., 3s. 6d.

RED DEER. With 17 Illustrations by J. CHARLTON and H. TUNALY. Crown 8vo., 3s. 6d.

THE TOILERS OF THE FIELD. With Portrait from the Bust in Salisbury Cathedral. Crown 8vo., 3s. 6d.

WOOD MAGIC: a Fable. With Frontispiece and Vignette by E. V. B. Crown 8vo., 3s. 6d.

THOUGHTS FROM THE WRITINGS OF RICHARD JEFFERIES. Selected by H. S. HOOLE WAYLEN. 16mo., 3s. 6d.

Johnson.—THE PATENTEE'S UAL: a Treatise on the Law and Pra of Letters Patent. By J. & J. H. JOHN Patent Agents, &c. 8vo., 10s. 6d.

Lang (ANDREW).

LETTERS TO DEAD AUTHORS. 8vo., 2s. 6d. net.

BOOKS AND BOOKMEN. With Coloured Plates and 17 Illustrat Fcp. 8vo., 2s. 6d. net.

OLD FRIENDS. Fcp. 8vo., 2s. 6d.

LETTERS ON LITERATURE. 8vo., 2s. 6d. net.

COCK LANE AND COMMON SE Crown 8vo., 3s. 6d.

Macfarren. — LECTURES ON MONY. By Sir GEORGE A. MACFA 8vo., 12s.

Marquand and Frothingha A TEXT-BOOK OF THE HISTORY SCULPTURE. By ALLAN MARQUAND, P and ARTHUR L. FROTHINGHAM, J Ph.D., Professors of Archæology and History of Art in Princetown Univer With 113 Illustrations. Crown 8vo., 6

Max Müller (F).

INDIA: WHAT CAN IT TEACH Crown 8vo., 3s. 6d.

CHIPS FROM A GERMAN WORKS

Vol. I. Recent Essays and Addre Crown 8vo., 6s. 6d. net.

Vol. II. Biographical Essays. C1 8vo., 6s. 6d. net.

Vol. III. Essays on Language and Li ture. Crown 8vo., 6s. 6d. net.

Vol. IV. Essays on Mythology and Lore. Crown 8vo, 8s. 6d. net.

CONTRIBUTIONS TO THE SCIENC MYTHOLOGY. 2 vols. 8vo., 32s.

Milner.—COUNTRY PLEASURES: Chronicle of a Year chiefly in a Gar By GEORGE MILNER. Crown 8vo., 3s.

Miscellaneous and Critical Works—*continued.*

Morris (WILLIAM).

SIGNS OF CHANGE. Seven Lectures delivered on various Occasions. Post 8vo., 4s. 6d.

HOPES AND FEARS FOR ART. Five Lectures delivered in Birmingham, London, &c., in 1878-1881. Crown 8vo., 4s. 6d.

Orchard.—*THE ASTRONOMY OF 'MILTON'S PARADISE LOST'.* By THOMAS N. ORCHARD, M.D., Member of the British Astronomical Association. With 13 Illustrations. 8vo., 15s.

Poore.—*ESSAYS ON RURAL HYGIENE.* By GEORGE VIVIAN POORE, M.D., F.R.C.P. With 13 Illustrations. Crown 8vo., 6s. 6d.

Proctor.—*STRENGTH :* How to get Strong and keep Strong, with Chapters on Rowing and Swimming, Fat, Age, and the Waist. By R. A. PROCTOR. With 9 Illustrations. Crown 8vo., 2s.

Richardson.—*NATIONAL HEALTH.* A Review of the Works of Sir Edwin Chadwick, K.C.B. By Sir B. W. RICHARDSON, M.D. Crown 8vo., 4s. 6d.

Rossetti.—*A SHADOW OF DANTE :* being an Essay towards studying Himself, his World and his Pilgrimage. By MARIA FRANCESCA ROSSETTI. With Frontispiece by DANTE GABRIEL ROSSETTI. Crown 8vo., 3s. 6d.

Solovyoff.—*A MODERN PRIESTESS OF ISIS (MADAME BLAVATSKY).* Abridged and Translated on Behalf of the Society for Psychical Research from the Russian of VSEVOLOD SERGYEEVICH SOLOVYOFF. By WALTER LEAF, Litt. D. With Appendices. Crown 8vo., 6s.

Stevens.—*ON THE STOWAGE OF SHIPS AND THEIR CARGOES.* With Information regarding Freights, Charter-Parties, &c. By ROBERT WHITE STEVENS, Associate-Member of the Institute of Naval Architects. 8vo., 21s.

West.—*WILLS, AND HOW NOT TO MAKE THEM.* With a Selection of Leading Cases. By B. B. WEST, Author of "Half-Hours with the Millionaires". Fcp. 8vo., 2s. 6d.

Miscellaneous Theological Works.

** For Church of England and Roman Catholic Works see MESSRS. LONGMANS & Co.'s Special Catalogues.

Balfour. — *THE FOUNDATIONS OF BELIEF :* being Notes Introductory to the Study of Theology. By the Right Hon. ARTHUR J. BALFOUR, M.P. 8vo., 12s. 6d.

Bird (ROBERT).

A CHILD'S RELIGION. Cr. 8vo., 2s.

JOSEPH, THE DREAMER. Crown 8vo., 5s.

JESUS, THE CARPENTER OF NAZARETH. Crown 8vo., 5s.

To be had also in Two Parts, price 2s. 6d. each.

Part I. GALILEE AND THE LAKE OF GENNESARET.

Part II. JERUSALEM AND THE PERÆA.

Boyd (A. K. H.) ('A.K.H.B.').

OCCASIONAL AND IMMEMORIAL DAYS : Discourses. Crown 8vo., 7s. 6d.

COUNSEL AND COMFORT FROM A CITY PULPIT. Crown 8vo., 3s. 6d.

SUNDAY AFTERNOONS IN THE PARISH CHURCH OF A SCOTTISH UNIVERSITY CITY. Crown 8vo., 3s. 6d.

CHANGED ASPECTS OF UNCHANGED TRUTHS. Crown 8vo., 3s. 6d.

GRAVER THOUGHTS OF A COUNTRY PARSON. Three Series. Crown 8vo., 3s. 6d. each.

PRESENT DAY THOUGHTS. Crown 8vo., 3s. 6d.

SEASIDE MUSINGS. Cr. 8vo., 3s. 6d.

'TO MEET THE DAY' through the Christian Year : being a Text of Scripture, with an Original Meditation and a Short Selection in Verse for Every Day. Crown 8vo., 4s. 6d.

Miscellaneous Theological Works—*continued.*

De la Saussaye.—*A MANUAL OF THE SCIENCE OF RELIGION.* By Professor CHANTEPIE DE LA SAUSSAYE. Translated by Mrs. COLYER FERGUSSON (*née* MAX MÜLLER). Crown 8vo., 12s. 6d.

Gibson.—*THE ABBÉ DE LAMENNAIS. AND THE LIBERAL CATHOLIC MOVEMENT IN FRANCE.* By the Hon. W. GIBSON. With Portrait. 8vo., 12s. 6d.

Kalisch (M. M., Ph.D.).

BIBLE STUDIES. Part I. Prophecies of Balaam. 8vo., 10s. 6d. Part II. The Book of Jonah. 8vo., 10s. 6d.

COMMENTARY ON THE OLD TESTAMENT: with a New Translation. Vol. I. Genesis. 8vo., 18s. Or adapted for the General Reader. 12s. Vol. II. Exodus. 15s. Or adapted for the General Reader. 12s. Vol. III. Leviticus, Part I. 15s. Or adapted for the General Reader. 8s. Vol. IV. Leviticus, Part II. 15s. Or adapted for the General Reader. 8s.

Macdonald (GEORGE).

UNSPOKEN SERMONS. Three Series. Crown 8vo., 3s. 6d. each.

THE MIRACLES OF OUR LORD. Crown 8vo., 3s. 6d.

Martineau (JAMES).

HOURS OF THOUGHT ON SACRED THINGS: Sermons, 2 vols. Crown 8vo., 3s. 6d. each.

ENDEAVOURS AFTER THE CHRISTIAN LIFE. Discourses. Crown 8vo., 7s. 6d.

THE SEAT OF AUTHORITY IN RELIGION. 8vo., 14s.

ESSAYS, REVIEWS, AND ADDRESSES. 4 Vols. Crown 8vo., 7s. 6d. each.

I. Personal; Political. II. Ecclesiastical; Historical. III. Theological; Philosophical. IV. Academical; Religious.

HOME PRAYERS, with *TWO SERVICES* for Public Worship. Crown 8vo., 3s. 6d.

10,000/2/97.

Max Müller (F.).

HIBBERT LECTURES ON THE ORIG AND GROWTH OF RELIGION, as illustrat by the Religions of India. Cr. 8vo., 7s. (

INTRODUCTION TO THE SCIENCE RELIGION: Four Lectures delivered at t Royal Institution. Crown 8vo., 3s. 6d

NATURAL RELIGION. The Giffo Lectures, delivered before the Univers of Glasgow in 1888. Crown 8vo., 10s. 6

PHYSICAL RELIGION. The Giffo Lectures, delivered before the Univers of Glasgow in 1890. Crown 8vo., 10s. 6

ANTHROPOLOGICAL RELIGION. T Gifford Lectures, delivered before the U versity of Glasgow in 1891. Cr. 8vo., 10s. 6

THEOSOPHY, OR PSYCHOLOGICAL R LIGION. The Gifford Lectures, deliver before the University of Glasgow in 189 Crown 8vo., 10s. 6d.

THREE LECTURES ON THE VEDÂNT PHILOSOPHY, delivered at the Roy Institution in March, 1894. 8vo., 5s.

Phillips. — *THE TEACHING OF TH VEDAS.* What Light does it Throw on t Origin and Development of Religion? F MAURICE PHILLIPS, London Missio Madras. Crown 8vo., 6s.

Romanes.—*THOUGHTS ON RELIGIO* By GEORGE J. ROMANES, LL.D., F.R. Crown 8vo., 4s. 6d.

SUPERNATURAL RELIGIO an Inquiry into the Reality of Divine Revel tion. 3 vols. 8vo., 36s.

REPLY (A) TO DR. LIGHTFOOT ESSAYS. By the Author of ' Supernatur Religion '. 8vo., 6s.

THE GOSPEL ACCORDING TO S PETER: a Study. By the Author ' Supernatural Religion '. 8vo., 6s.

Vivekananda.—*YOGA PHILOSOPHY* Lectures delivered in New York, Winter 1895-96, by the Swami Vivekananda. c Raja Yoga ; or, Conquering the Intern Nature ; also Patanjali's Yoga Aphorism with Commentaries. Crown 8vo., 3s. 6d.

CPSIA information can be obtained
at www.ICGtesting.com
Printed in the USA
BVHW08*2328060818
523683BV00017B/1284/P